A Complete Manual for

CAMPUS PLACEMENTS

Quantitative Ability | Reasoning | Verbal Ability | Vocabulary

Includes

10 Mocks

HCL | HP | IBM | INFOSYS | WIPRO

CL MEDIA (P) LTD.

Edition : 2019

© PUBLISHER

No part of this book may be reproduced in a retrieval system or transmitted, in any form or by any means, electronics, mechanical, photocopying, recording, scanning and or without the written permission of the publisher.

ISBN   : **978-93-89310-09-2**

Typeset by   : *CL Media DTP Unit*

Administrative and Production Offices

Published by : **CL Media (P) Ltd.**

A-45, Mohan Cooperative Industrial Area, Near Mohan Estate Metro Station, New Delhi - 110044

Marketed by : **G.K. Publications (P) Ltd.**

A-45, Mohan Cooperative Industrial Area, Near Mohan Estate Metro Station, New Delhi - 110044

For product information :

Visit **www.gkpublications.com** or email to **gkp@gkpublications.com**

Preface

Dear Job aspirants,

This booklet is specially designed to help you master variety of questions. Each topic has an introduction that covers the underlying principles, followed by examples and an exhaustive exercise; explanations with answer keys are provided as a concluding section.

To understand these topics, you are advised to clear your concepts first with the help of solved examples and then solve the exercises. Finally, you must analyze your solutions with the given explanations and learn from the mistakes.

This is how, this book will prove to be a one stop solution for aspirants of **Campus Placement Exams** as it includes all the four sections viz. **Quantitaive Ability, Analytical Resonning, Grammar & Reading Comprehension and Vocabulary**.

In a nutshell, numerous examples and practice questions have been provided in the Quantitative Ability and Analytical Reasoning sections to help students master the fundamental concepts and advanced questions.

Furthermore as far as English Language is concerned, we all know the fact that it is certainly not the easiest of the nuts to crack and, therefore, selecting the right and precise content becomes inevitable in clearing any national level exam. Topics like, sentence correction and sentence completion form an essential part of all aptitude tests and thus we should be familiar with the nuances of grammar usage so that we can identify the errors and reach to the correct alternative.

It is against this backdrop that, special attention has been given in designing the English Language section of this book so that students can master their problem-solving skills rather than going through tedious grammar lessons. To sum up, we have made an attempt to make this book as interesting, amusing and interactive as possible.

Besides, there is a separate section of Vocabulary at the end which comprehensively covers sub-topics like Synonyms, Antonyms and other critical question types like one word substitutions, idioms etc. that will surely enhance your vocabulary.

Last but not the least, this book also contains 10 company specific mocks for students so that they can become familiarize with the pattern and identify their areas of improvements.

With that, we would like to wish you All the best !
Happy reading!

Career Launcher Team

To seek any clarification, please send your query at **www.careerlauncher.com/helpme.**

Contents

PART – 5 : COMPANY SPECIFIC MOCKS

PART - 1
QUANTITATIVE ABILITY

Number System and Algebra **1**

Introduction

Let us go back to our school days. This chapter is designed to give you a quick recap of what you had learnt during the school. A quick brush-up of the concepts shall help you in identifying and solving the problems at a greater pace.

Real Numbers

Numbers which can be commonly seen and identified and can be represented on a number line.

e.g.: -10, 2.77, 0, 1, 7

Number Line

It is a line on which all the positive and negative numbers can be marked in a sequence.

$$-\infty \longleftarrow\!\!+\!\!+\!\!+\!\!+\!\!+\!\!+\!\!+\!\!+\!\!+\!\!+\!\!+\longrightarrow +\infty$$
$$\quad\quad -3 \ -2 \ -1 \ \ 0 \ +1 \ +2 \ +3$$

Imaginary numbers

Those numbers that CANNOT be represented on a number line are imaginary numbers.

e.g.: $\sqrt{-1}$, $\sqrt{-5}$, etc.

* $\sqrt{-1}$ is represented by i.

Rational Numbers

All numbers that can be expressed in $\dfrac{p}{q}$ form, where p, q are integers and $q \neq 0$.

e.g.: $\dfrac{-5}{7}$, $1\dfrac{2}{3}$

Irrational Numbers

Those numbers that CANNOT be expressed in $\dfrac{p}{q}$ form.

e.g.: π, $\sqrt{2}$, $\sqrt{3}+1$

Fractions

All rational numbers which are in $\dfrac{p}{q}$ form, where p, q are integers and p is not a multiple of q.

p is called numerator whereas q is known as denominator.

Fractions are of the following types:

- **Proper:** $p < q$ e.g., $\dfrac{2}{7}$, $\dfrac{3}{8}$ etc.
- **Improper:** $p \geq q$ e.g., $\dfrac{6}{5}$, $\dfrac{5}{2}$ etc.
- **Mixed:** It is an integer plus a fraction

  e.g., $3\dfrac{1}{5}$, $7\dfrac{1}{3}$, etc.

Integers

All the rational numbers that do not have any decimal or fractional part.

$$-\infty, \ldots, -3, -2, -1, 0, +1, +2, +3, \ldots, +\infty$$

Whole Numbers

All non negative integers are whole numbers.
$W = \{0, 1, 2, 3, \ldots\}$.

Natural Numbers

Whole numbers, except zero, are called natural numbers.
$N = \{1, 2, 3, 4, \ldots\}$.

Odd Numbers

All natural numbers which are not divisible by 2 are odd numbers.
Such numbers are expressed as $2k \pm 1$ (k is any natural number). e.g.: 1, 3, 5, 7, ...

Even Numbers

All natural numbers that are divisible by 2 are called even numbers.
Such numbers are expressed as 2k (k is any natural number).
e.g.: 2, 4, 6, 8, ...

The box given below exhibits the types of numbers obtained while carrying out arithmetic operations between two type of numbers.

$$
\begin{array}{|l|}
\hline
\text{odd} \pm \text{odd} = \text{even} \\
\text{odd} \pm \text{even} = \text{odd} \\
\text{even} \pm \text{even} = \text{even} \\
\text{odd} \times \text{odd} = \text{odd} \\
\text{odd} \times \text{even} = \text{even} \\
\text{even} \times \text{even} = \text{even} \\
\hline
\end{array}
$$

Prime Numbers

All the natural numbers that are greater than 1, and are only divisible by 1 or the number itself, are called prime numbers.

The box given below depicts some of the characteristics of the prime numbers.

* There are 25 prime numbers upto 100

  2, 3, 5, 7, 11, 13, 17, 19, 23, 29, 31, 37, 41, 43,

  47, 53, 59, 61, 67, 71, 73, 79, 83, 89, 97.

* 2 is the only even prime number.

* 97 is the only prime number from 90 to 100.

* 91 is often mistaken as a prime,

  but it is not a prime

  $\because$ 91 = 7 × 13.

Co-primes:

Two numbers 'a' and 'b' are said to be co-prime if they don't have any common factor other than 1.

e.g.: (3, 5), (7, 12), etc.

Composite Numbers:

Numbers greater than 1 that are not prime are called composite numbers. e.g.: 4, 6, 8, 9, ...

*	1 is neither a prime number nor a composite number.
Reason:	A prime number has two factors, 1 and the number itself; whereas a composite number has more than two factors. Since, 1 has only one factor i.e., 1, hence it is neither a prime nor a composite numbers.

No.	Real	Imaginary	Rational	Irrational	Even	Odd	Prime	Composite	Whole	Natural	Integer	Fraction
3	Y	N	Y	N	N	Y	Y	N	Y	Y	Y	N
$\sqrt{3}$	Y	N	N	Y	N	N	N	N	N	N	N	N
$\frac{7}{2}$	Y	N	Y	N	N	N	N	N	N	N	N	Y
i	N	Y	N	N	N	N	N	N	N	N	N	N

Table 1: Classification of numbers

Perfect Numbers

A number 'a' is said to be perfect if the sum of its factors (excluding itself but including 1) is equal to 'a'.

e.g.: 6, 28, etc.

The perfect number 6 has 1, 2 and 3 as its factors, which sum up to 6.

Similarly, the perfect number 28 has 1, 2, 4, 7 and 14 as it's factors, which sum up to 28.

Try Yourself:

Classify the given numbers in all the types we just studied (real, integer, rational, prime, even, odd, natural, whole, etc).

$$23, \quad \frac{-7}{9}, \quad \sqrt{31}, \quad \sqrt{4}, \quad \frac{\sqrt{8}}{8},$$

$$11, \quad -7, \quad \frac{-7}{17}, \quad \frac{-7}{12}, \quad \frac{2}{8}$$

$$\frac{8}{2}, \quad 1, \quad 8, \quad 18, \quad 29, \quad \frac{31}{15},$$

$$\frac{15}{10}, \quad 2.76, \quad 3.33, \quad 10.82,$$

$$5, \quad 11, \quad 19, \quad 91, \quad 27, \quad -8,$$

$$-8.3, \quad \frac{-3}{6}, \quad \frac{-6}{3}, \quad 12.5$$

The Number Tree

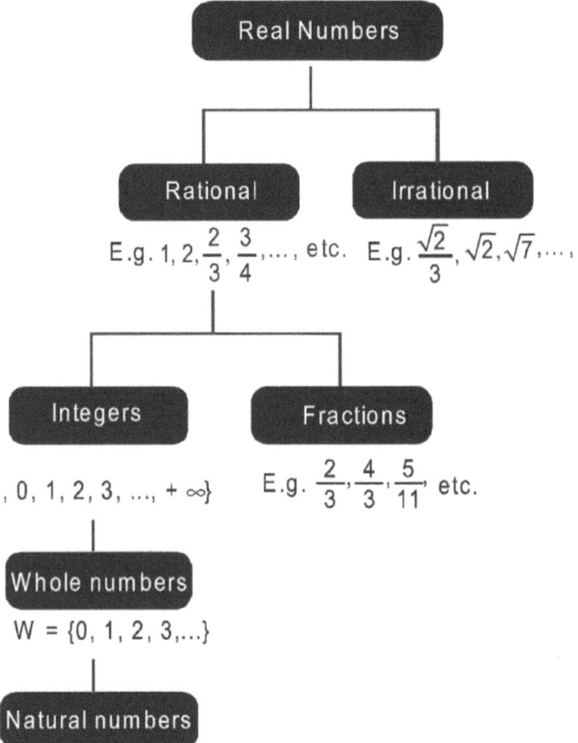

Conversion of recurring decimal into fractions

What is the $\dfrac{p}{q}$ form of 0.5555... (also represented as $0.\bar{5}$)?

Let, x = 0.55555...

$\Rightarrow 10x = 5.55555...$

$\therefore 9x = 10x - x = (5.5555...) - (0.55555...) = 5$

$\Rightarrow x = \dfrac{5}{9}$

If x = 0.232323...

$\Rightarrow 100x = 23.232323...$

$\therefore 99x = 100x - x = (23.232323...) - (0.232323...)$
$= 23$

$\Rightarrow x = \dfrac{23}{99}$

For a purely recurring number (all digits after decimal point recur) we can identify the procedure as:

The $\dfrac{p}{q}$ form of a purely recurring number

$= \dfrac{\text{The recurring part written once}}{\text{As many 9's as the number of digits in the recurring part}}$

In the number like 0.14333... i.e. $0.14\bar{3}$

Let x = 0.143333...

$\Rightarrow 100x = 14.3333...$

$\Rightarrow 1000x = 143.3333...$

$\Rightarrow 900x = 1000x - 100x$
$= (143.3333...) - (14.3333...) = 129$

$\Rightarrow x = \dfrac{129}{900}$

Thus for any recurring number we can identify the procedure as:

The $\dfrac{p}{q}$ form of any recurring number

$= \dfrac{\begin{array}{c}\text{(The non-recurring and recurring part written once)} - \\ \text{(the non-recurring part)}\end{array}}{\begin{array}{c}\text{As many 9's as the number of digits in the recurring part} \\ \text{followed by as many 0's as digits in non-recurring part.}\end{array}}$

Example 1:

Express $0.\overline{643}$ as a fraction.

Solution:

Let x = $0.\overline{643}$, then

$1000x = 643.\overline{643}$

$\therefore 1000x - x = 643.\overline{643} - 0.\overline{643}$

$\Rightarrow 999x = 643$

$\Rightarrow x = \dfrac{643}{999}$

Example 2:

Express $6.\overline{43}$ as a fraction.

Solution:

Let x = $6.\overline{43}$, then

$100x = 643.\overline{43}$

$\therefore 100x - x = 643.\overline{43} - 6.\overline{43}$

$\Rightarrow 99x = 637$

$\Rightarrow x = \dfrac{637}{99}$

Example 3:

Arrange the following rational numbers in ascending order:

$\dfrac{-7}{10}, \dfrac{5}{-8}, \dfrac{2}{-3}$

Solution:

$\dfrac{-7}{10} = -0.7, \dfrac{5}{-8} = -0.625$ and $\dfrac{2}{-3} = -0.666$

Clearly, $-0.7 < -0.666 < -0.625$.

So, $\dfrac{-7}{10} < \dfrac{2}{-3} < \dfrac{5}{-8}$

Example 4:

Arrange the following fractions in descending order

$\dfrac{31}{27}, \dfrac{43}{39}, \dfrac{57}{53}, \dfrac{27}{23}$ and $\dfrac{29}{25}$

Solution:

As the difference between the numerator and the denominator is same, the fraction with smallest denominator, i.e., $\dfrac{27}{23}$ is largest and $\dfrac{57}{53}$ is smallest.

Hence, the order is:

$\dfrac{27}{23} > \dfrac{29}{25} > \dfrac{31}{27} > \dfrac{43}{39} > \dfrac{57}{53}$

Example 5:

What is the divisor if dividend is 15968, quotient is 89 and the remainder is 37?

Solution:

$$\text{Divisor} = \left(\frac{\text{Dividend} - \text{Remainder}}{\text{Quotient}}\right)$$

$$= \left(\frac{15968 - 37}{89}\right) = 179$$

Divisibility Rules

(1) A number is divisible by 2 when its unit's digit is even or 0.

(2) A number is divisible by 3 when the sum of its digits is divisible by 3.

(3) A number is divisible by 4 when the number formed by the last two digits is divisible by 4 or the last two digits are 0.

(4) A number is divisible by 5 when its unit's digit is 5 or 0.

(5) A number is divisible by 6 when it is divisible by both 2 and 3.

(6) A number is divisible by 8 when the number formed by the last three right-hand digits is divisible by 8, or when the last three digits are 0.

(7) A number is divisible by 9 when the sum of its digits is divisible by 9.

(8) A number is divisible by 10 when its unit's digit is 0.

(9) A number is divisible by 11 when the difference between the sum of the digits in the odd and the even places is 0 or a multiple of 11. For example, if a number is abcd then $[(a + c) - (b + d)] = k$, where $k = 0$ or k is the multiple of 11.

(10) A number is divisible by 12 when it is divisible by both 3 and 4.

Example 6:

What least number must be subtracted from 2000 to get a number which is exactly divisible by 17?

Solution:

On dividing 2000 by 17, we get 11 as remainder.
∴ Required number to be subtracted = 11.

Example 7:

What least number must be added to 3000 to obtain a number exactly divisible by 19?

Solution:

On dividing 3000 by 19, we get 17 as remainder.
∴ Number to be added = (19 – 17) = 2.

Example 8:

Find the number which is nearest to 3105 and exactly divisible by 21.

Solution:

On dividing 3105 by 21, we get 18 as remainder.
∴ Number to be added to 3105 is (21 – 18) = 3.
∴ 3108 is the required number.

Example 9:

A number when divided by 342 gives a remainder 47. When the same number is divided by 19, what would be the remainder?

Solution:

On dividing the given number by 342, let k be the quotient and 47 the remainder.
Then, number = 342k + 47
= [(19 × 18k) + (19 × 2 + 9)] = [19 (18k + 2) + 9]
∴ The given number when divided by 19 gives (18k + 2) as quotient and 9 as remainder.

Alternate method:

342 is a multiple of 19, divide the remainder by the second dividend to get the remainder. 47 when divided by 19 gives 9 as remainder.

How to find whether a number is prime or not?

For small numbers, we could find by checking, if that number is divisible by any other prime number till that number itself.

But for the larger numbers like, say 631, there is an alternate method.

Step 1: Find the approximate square root of the given number, i.e. 25.

Step 2: Check if any prime number from 2 to 25 divides 631.

The prime numbers from 2 to 25 are 2, 3, 5, 7, 11, 13, 17, 19 and 23. Since none of these numbers divide 631 exactly, 631 must be a prime number.

Factorial

The continued product of first n natural number is called 'n factorial' and is denoted by n! or $\lfloor n$.

$$n! = 1 \times 2 \times 3 \times \ldots \times (n - 1) \times n$$

e.g.: $6! = 1 \times 2 \times 3 \times 4 \times 5 \times 6 = 720$
By definition $0! = 1$.

Highest Common Factor (HCF) and Lowest Common Multiple (LCM):

HCF and LCM are one of the basic concepts of mathematics which is having a variety of applications in our daily life.

To understand this topic let us first look at certain terms:

Factor:

Factors of a number are those numbers which when divide the original number, leave no remainder. When talking about the factor we consider only the positive integral factor.

For example,

Factors of 20 = 20, 10, 5, 2, 1

Factors of 100 = 100, 50, 25, 20, 10, 5, 2, 1

Factors of a number are always countable.

Multiple:

Multiples of a number are those numbers which when divided by the number leaves no remainder. When talking about the multiples we consider only the positive integral multiples.

For example,

    Multiples of 20 = 20, 40, 60, 80, etc.

    Multiples of 100 = 100, 200, 300, 400, etc.

Understanding HCF:

    Let us take two numbers 15 and 20

    Factors of 15 are = 15, 5, 3, 1

    Factors of 20 are = 20, 10, 5, 1

To find the HCF, check what is the highest factor common to both the numbers. We can find it as 5.

Understanding LCM:

    Let us take two numbers 15 and 20.

    Multiples of 15 = 15, 30, 45, 60, 75, 90, 105, 120, 135, etc.

    Multiples of 20 = 20, 40, 60, 80, 100, 120, 140, etc.

To find the LCM of these two numbers, check what is the lowest number common to the sets of multiples of both the numbers: We can find it as 60.

How to find HCF of two numbers?

There are two methods:

  a. Division method

  b. Prime factorisation method.

a.   **Division method:**

In this method divisor becomes dividend and remainder becomes divisor and this process continues till one can divide.

The last divisor is your answer.

Now, try to understand the following illustrative examples.

Example 10:

To find the HCF of 15 and 20.

```
15) 20 (1
    -15
    ────
    5) 15 (3
       -15
       ────
        0
```

So, HCF of 15 and 20 is 5.

Example 11:

To find the HCF of 20 and 28.

```
20) 28 (1
    -20
    ────
    8) 20 (2
      -16
      ────
      4) 8 (2
        -8
        ───
         0
```

So, the HCF of 20 and 28 is 4.

Example 12:

To find the HCF of 20, 28 and 45

We have seen that HCF of 20 and 28 is 4.

So, we will take HCF of 4 and 45.

```
4) 45 (11
   -44
   ────
   1) 4 (4
     -4
     ───
      0
```

So, HCF of 20, 28 and 45 is 1.

Note: The HCF of an odd number and an even number is always 1.

b.   **Prime factorization method:**

Write the number in terms of prime factors.

$20 = 2^2 \times 5^1$

$45 = 2^0 \times 3^2 \times 5^1$

For finding out their HCF, take the lowest power of all prime numbers. The HCF of 20 and 45 is $2^0 \times 3^0 \times 5^1$ i.e. 5.

How to find LCM of two or more numbers?

There are two methods
  i. **Division method**
  ii. **Prime factorisation method**

  i. **Division method:**
      LCM of 18, 27 and 30.

```
3 | 18,  27,  30
3 |  6,   9,  10
  |  2,   3,   5
```

      LCM = 3 × 3 × 3 × 2 × 5 = 270

  ii. **Prime factorisation method:**
      Take two numbers 20 and 45.
      Write the numbers in terms of prime factors.
      $20 = 2^2 \times 5^1$
      $45 = 2^0 \times 3^2 \times 5^1$

      For finding out their LCM, take the highest power
      of all prime numbers.
      The LCM of 20 and 45 is $2^2 \times 3^2 \times 5^1$ i.e. 180.

Example 13:
  Find the HCF of 24 and 72.

Solution:
  24 = 2 × 2 × 2 × 3
  72 = 2 × 2 × 2 × 3 × 3
  HCF = 2 × 2 × 2 × 3 = 24
  Similarly, you can find the HCF of sets containing
  more than 2 numbers.

Example 14:
  Find the largest number that can exactly divide
  513, 783 and 1107.

Solution:
  Required number = HCF of 513, 783 and 1107.
  Now, $513 = 3^3 \times 19$, $783 = 3^3 \times 29$, $1107 = 3^3 \times 41$
  $\therefore$ HCF $= 3^3 = 27$.
  Hence, the required number is 27.

Example 15:
  Find the least number exactly divisible by 12, 15,
  20 and 27.

Solution:
  Required number = LCM of 12, 15, 20, 27
  $\therefore$ LCM = 3 × 4 × 5 × 9 = 540

Example 16:
  Find the least number which when divided by 6, 7,
  8, 9 and 12 leaves the same remainder 1 in each
  case.

Solution:
  Required number = (LCM of 6, 7, 8, 9, 12) + 1
  $\therefore$ LCM = 3 × 2 × 2 × 7 × 2 × 3 = 504
  Hence, required number = (504 + 1) = 505

Example 17:
  The traffic lights at three different road-crossings,
  change after every 24 sec, 72 sec and 120 sec
  respectively. If they all change simultaneously at
  10 : 54 : 00 hr, then at what time will they change
  next simultaneously?

Solution:
  Interval of change = LCM of (24, 72, 120) sec
  = 360 sec.
  The lights will change simultaneously after every
  360s i.e., 6 min 00 sec.
  Next simultaneous change will take place at
  11 : 00 : 00 hr.

Example 18:
  How many three-digit numbers are divisible by 6?

Solution:
  There are 16 numbers before 100 which are
  divisible by 6.
  There are 166 numbers before 999 which are
  divisible by 6.
  Total three-digit numbers divisible by 6 are
  166 – 16 = 150.

Important results:

If 2 numbers a and b are given, and their LCM and HCF
are L and H respectively, then L × H = a × b.

LCM and HCF of fractions

$$\text{LCM of fractions} = \frac{\text{LCM of numerators}}{\text{HCF of denominators}}$$

$$\text{HCF of fractions} = \frac{\text{HCF of numerators}}{\text{LCM of denominators}}$$

e.g.: Find the LCM and HCF of $\dfrac{25}{12}$ and $\dfrac{35}{18}$.

$$\text{LCM} = \frac{\text{LCM of 25 and 35}}{\text{HCF of 12 and 18}} = \frac{175}{6}$$

$$\text{HCF} = \frac{\text{HCF of 25 and 35}}{\text{LCM of 12 and 18}} = \frac{5}{36}$$

Note: Do not directly apply the formula if the fractions are not in their simplest form.

Example 19:

The HCF of two numbers is 11 and their LCM is 693. If one of the numbers is 77, find the other.

Solution:

The other number = $\dfrac{11 \times 693}{77} = 99$

Decimal system:

A number 78324 can be represented as

$7 \times 10000 + 8 \times 1000 + 3 \times 100 + 2 \times 10 + 4 \times 1$

$= 78324$

So, what could be the place value of 8 in the above number?

Since, it is in the thousand's place it can be represented as

$8 \times 1000 = 8000$ which is the place value.

Note: A two-digit number xy can be represented as 10x + y and a three-digit number xyz can be represented as 100x + 10y + z.

Example 20:

The difference between a two-digit number and the number obtained by interchanging the digits is 81. What is the difference between the digits of the number?

Solution:

Let ten's digit be x and unit's digit be y.
Then $(10x + y) - (10y + x) = 27$
$\Rightarrow 9(x - y) = 81$
$\Rightarrow x - y = 9$

Unit's place digit of a number

The digit at the unit's place of any number is the remainder when the number is divided by 10.

For example, lets consider the number 364. The remainder when 364 is divided by 10 is 4. Hence '4' is the unit's digit of the number 364.

To find the unit's digit of a number which is the product of two or more numbers, multiply the unit's digit of the numbers and find the units digit of the resultant number. For example, 19 × 64, the product of the units digit of 19 and 64 is 36 and the unit's digit of 36 is 6, hence the unit's digit of 19 × 64 is 6.

Unit's digit of higher powers of any number:

$2^1 = 2$	$2^2 = 4$	$2^3 = 8$	$2^4 = 16$
$2^5 = 32$	$2^6 = 64$	$2^7 = 128$	$2^8 = 256$
$2^9 = 512$	$2^{10} = 1024$	$2^{11} = 2048$	$2^{12} = 4096$

We can see that the unit's digit of 2^1, 2^5, 2^9 is 2, units digit of 2^2, 2^6, 2^{10} is 4, units digit of 2^3, 2^7, 2^{11} is 8 and units digit of 2^4, 2^8, 2^{12} is 6.

Therefore after every four powers of 2, the units digit of the number starts repeating. Thus we say that cyclicity of unit's digit of higher powers of 2 is 4.

Similarly the digits whose cyclicity is 4 are 2, 3, 7 and 8. The digits whose cyclicity is 2 are 4 and 9.

Any power of numbers whose unit's digit 1, 5 or 6 always ends in 1, 5 and 6 respectively.

For example, $11^2 = 121$, $25^2 = 625$ and $16^2 = 256$.

Perfect square:

A number is said to be a perfect square if and only if the square root of that number is an integer.

Some important facts about perfect squares:

(1) The square of an even number is always even.
(2) The square of an odd number is always odd.
(3) Square of an integer cannot end in 2, 3, 7 or 8.
(4) The square of a real number (negative or positive) is always positive.

Some important formulae used in simplification:

(1) $(a + b)^2 = a^2 + b^2 + 2ab$
(2) $(a - b)^2 = a^2 + b^2 - 2ab$
(3) $(a + b)^2 = (a - b)^2 + 4ab$
(4) $a^2 - b^2 = (a - b)(a + b)$
(5) $a^3 + b^3 = (a + b)(a^2 - ab + b^2)$
(6) $a^3 - b^3 = (a - b)(a^2 + ab + b^2)$

Example 21:

Simplify $\dfrac{527 \times 527 \times 527 + 183 \times 183 \times 183}{527 \times 527 - 527 \times 183 + 183 \times 183}$

Solution:

The given expression is equivalent to

$$\dfrac{(527)^3 + (183)^3}{(527)^2 - 527 \times 183 + (183)^2}$$

We know that, $\dfrac{a^3 + b^3}{a^2 - ab + b^2} = a + b$

In the above example a = 527 and b = 183
$\therefore$ The expression is equal to $(527 + 183) = 710$

Example 22:

Simplify $\left(\dfrac{(614+168)^2 - (614-168)^2}{614 \times 168} \right)$

Solution:

Let a = 614 and b = 168, then the expression

becomes $\dfrac{(a+b)^2 - (a-b)^2}{ab} = \dfrac{4ab}{ab} = 4$

Example 23:

Find the square of 1605.

Solution:

$(1605)^2 = (1600 + 5)^2$

$= (1600)^2 + 2 \times 1600 \times 5 + (5)^2$

$= 2560000 + 16000 + 25 = 2576025$

Example 24:

Find the value of 896 × 896 – 204 × 204.

Solution:

$a^2 - b^2 = (a + b)(a - b)$

(where a = 896 and b = 204)

$= (896 + 204)(896 - 204) = 1100 \times 692 = 761200$

Example 25:

Evaluate: $(57)^2 + (43)^2 + 2 \times 57 \times 43$

Solution:

$a^2 + b^2 + 2ab = (a + b)^2 = (57 + 43)^2$
$= 100^2 = 10000$

Example 26:

Simplify $(81)^2 + (68)^2 - 2 \times 81 \times 68$

Solution:

$(81 - 68)^2 = 13^2 = 169$

Example 27:

Evaluate: $(313 \times 313 + 287 \times 287)$

Solution:

$a^2 + b^2 = \dfrac{1}{2}[(a+b)^2 + (a-b)^2]$

(where a = 313 and b = 287)

$= \dfrac{1}{2}[(313+287)^2 + (313-287)^2]$

$= \dfrac{1}{2}\left[(600)^2 + (26)^2 \right] = 180338$

Rules of counting numbers:

1. Sum of first n natural numbers = $\dfrac{n(n+1)}{2}$

2. Sum of first n odd numbers = n^2

3. Sum of first n even numbers = $n(n + 1)$

4. Sum of the squares of first n natural numbers

$= \dfrac{n(n+1)(2n+1)}{6}$

5. Sum of the cubes of first n natural numbers

$= \left[\dfrac{n(n+1)}{2} \right]^2$

Example 28:

If square root of 15 = 3.88, the value of square root of $\dfrac{5}{3}$ is

Solution:

$\sqrt{\dfrac{5}{3}} = \sqrt{\dfrac{5 \times 3}{3 \times 3}} = \dfrac{\sqrt{15}}{3} = \dfrac{3.88}{3} = 1.29$

Example 29:

A four-digit number divisible by 7 becomes divisible by 3, when 10 is added to it. Find the largest such number.

Solution:

Largest four-digit number is 9999.
On dividing 9999 by 7, we get 3 as remainder.
Largest four-digit number divisible by 7 is 9996.
Let 9996 – x + 10 be divisible by 3.
By trial and error, we find that x = 7
Required number = (9996 – 7) = 9989.

Example 30:

A three-digit number 4a3 is added to another three-digit number 984 to give the four-digit number 13b7 which is divisible by 11. Find the value of (a + b).

Solution:

```
    4 a 3
  + 9 8 4
  -------
  1 3 b 7
```

Here a + 8 = b, if 13b7 is divisible by 11 then (7 + 3) – (b + 1) = 0; b = 9 and a + 8 = b or a = 1. Hence, a + b = 9 + 1 = 10

Example 31:

Of the three numbers, the sum of the first two is 45; the sum of the second and the third is 55; and the sum of the third and thrice the first is 90. Find the third number.

Solution:

Let the numbers be x, y and z. Then, x + y = 45; y + z = 55 and 3x + z = 90.

y = 45 – x and z = 55 – y = 55 – (45 – x) = 10 + x

∴ 3x + 10 + x = 90 or x = 20

y = (45 – 20) = 25 and z = (10 + 20) = 30

∴ Third number = 30

Polynomials

The word 'poly' means **many** and the word 'nomial' means **terms.** So, polynomial is an algebraic expression which consists of many terms involving powers of the variable.

For example, $5x - 5$, $x^2 + 5x + 6$, $y^3 + y^2 + 2z$.

The general form of a polynomial is $a_0 + a_1x + a_2x^2 + a_3x^3 + \ldots + a_{n-1}x^{n-1} + a_nx^n$, where $a_0, a_1, a_2, \ldots, a_n$ are real numbers and n is a non-negative integer. Polynomial may be in more than one variable.

e.g., $x^2 + y^2 - 4$, $2x^2 + y^2 + z$.

Types of polynomials:

Polynomials can be classified as follows:

1. **By coefficients:** The basis of classification here is nature of the coefficients.
   a. In $5x^2 + 3x + 6$, the coefficients are 5, 3 and 6 and all are integers. So, this is called polynomial over the set of integers.
   b. In $\frac{2}{3}x^2 - \frac{4}{5}x + 2x - 3$, the coefficients are $\frac{2}{3}, -\frac{4}{5}, 2$ and -3, and all are rational numbers. So, this is called polynomial over the rational numbers.
   c. In $\sqrt{3}x^2 - 11x + \sqrt{3}$, the coefficients are real numbers. So, this is called polynomial over the real numbers.
2. **By the number of terms:** The basis of classification here is number of the coefficients.
   a. **Monomial:** consisting of a single term. For example, $\sqrt{5}x, -8y^2, 15mn^2$.
   b. **Binomials:** consisting of two terms. For example, $2n + 3y$, $n - 5$, $y^2 + 3y$

   c. **Trinomials:** consisting of three terms. For example, $5x^3 - 3x^2 + 2$, $x + y - 2$, $x^5 + x^4 + x^2$
   d. **Polynomials:** consisting of more than three terms.

      e.g., $x + y + z + m$, $x^5 + x^4 + x^3 + x^2$, $a + 2b + 2c + 3d + 4e$.
3. **By degree:** The highest exponent of any monomial of the given polynomial is called the degree of the polynomial; for example, $x^6 - 3x^4 + 12$. In this example, the highest exponent of a term is 6. So this polynomial is of degree 6.

   $5y^3$ is a monomial of degree 3.

   $4x^2 y^3 z^2$ is a monomial of degree $2 + 3 + 2 = 7$.

   $\sqrt{5} x^3 y^3$ is a monomial of degree $3 + 3 = 6$.

   5 is a monomial of degree 0 (because 5 can be written as $5x°$).

   $-\frac{4}{15} mn^3$ is a monomial of degree $3 + 1 = 4$.

   $y^7 - 5x^2 + 3y^2 = 8$ is a **polynomial** of degree 7.

Linear polynomial

A polynomial of degree one is called linear polynomial.

For example, $5x + 3y$, $5x - 4$, $\frac{1}{3}x$, $x + \frac{5}{2}$ are linear polynomials.

Linear equation

In the earlier topic we have learnt about linear polynomials. An equation consisting of only linear polynomials is called a linear equation.

For example, $3x - 2 = 7x$; $\frac{1}{2}y + 1 = 3y + \frac{2}{3}$ are linear equations in one variable, and $3x + 4y = 20$; $5x + 20 = 3y + 5$ are linear equations in two variables.

Solved Examples

Example 32:

Is the expression $5x^2 - 3\sqrt{x} + 10$ a polynomial?

Solution:

No, because for a polynomial the condition is that power of x or a variable must be a non-negative integer. Here in $3\sqrt{x}$, x has a power $\frac{1}{2}$ which is not an integer.

Example 33:

If $3x + 15 = 60$, find x.

Solution:

$$3x + 15 = 60$$
$$\Rightarrow 3x = 60 - 15 = 45$$
$$\Rightarrow x = \frac{45}{3} = 15$$

Example 34:

Six years ago the age of Ram was thrice the age of Shyam and after six years Ram will become twice the age of Shyam. Find the present age of Shyam.

Solution:

Let the present age of Ram be 'x' years, and the present age of Shyam be 'y' years.

Then $x - 6 = 3(y - 6)$

$\Rightarrow x - 6 = 3y - 18$

$\Rightarrow x - 3y = -12$ ... (i)

And $(x + 6) = 2(y + 6)$

$\Rightarrow x + 6 = 2y + 12$

$\Rightarrow x - 2y = 6$ ... (ii)

Subtracting (ii) from (i), we get

$$\begin{aligned}
x - 3y &= -12 \\
\underline{x - 2y} &= \underline{6} \\
-y &= -18
\end{aligned}$$

$\therefore y = 18$ and $x = 42$

So, Ram's present age is 42 years and Shyam's present age is 18 years.

Example 35:

The sum of a two-digit number and the number obtained by interchanging the digits of this number is 33. Find the number(s).

Solution:

Let unit's digit of the number be x and ten's digit be y. Then,

Number = $10y + x$

$\therefore 10y + x + 10x + y = 33$

$\Rightarrow 11x + 11y = 33$

$\Rightarrow x + y = 3$

$\therefore$ The value of x is either 1 or 2. Similarly, the value of y is either 2 or 1.

So, the possible numbers are 12 and 21.

Simultaneous equations

When there are two linear equations in two variables, it is called simultaneous linear equations in two variables.

For example, $2x + 3y = 12$ and $4x + 9y = 15$, $6x + 2y = 24$ and $10x + 13y = 53$ are simultaneous equations.

Format of simultaneous linear equations:

$a_1x + b_1y = c_1$ and $a_2x + b_2y = c_2$

Important rule:

Simultaneous equations may be consistent or inconsistent and may have no solution or unique solution or infinite solutions. The nature of these solutions can be determined by the following rules.

(i) If $\dfrac{a_1}{a_2} \neq \dfrac{b_1}{b_2}$, then the system (equations) is consistent and has unique solution.

(ii) If $\dfrac{a_1}{a_2} = \dfrac{b_1}{b_2} \neq \dfrac{c_1}{c_2}$, then the system (equations) is inconsistent and has no solution.

(iii) If $\dfrac{a_1}{a_2} = \dfrac{b_1}{b_2} = \dfrac{c_1}{c_2}$, then the system (equations) is consistent and has infinite number of solutions.

Solved Examples

Example 36:

If $2x + y = 35$ and $3x + 4y = 65$, find x and y.

Solution:

$2x + y = 35$ ... (i)

$3x + 4y = 65$ ... (ii)

Multiplying (i) by 4, we get

$8x + 4y = 140$ ... (iii)

Subtracting (ii) from (iii), we get

$$\begin{aligned}
8x + 4y &= 140 \\
\underline{3x \pm 4y} &= \underline{65} \\
5x &= 75
\end{aligned}$$

$\Rightarrow x = \dfrac{75}{5} = 15$.

Substituting the value of x in (i), we get $30 + y = 35$

$\Rightarrow y = 5$

Example 37:

Five years ago, A was thrice as old as B and 10 years hence A shall be twice as old as B. Find the present age of A.

Solution:

According to the given condition,

$A - 5 = 3(B - 5)$

$\Rightarrow A - 5 = 3B - 15$

$\Rightarrow A + 10 = 3B$ and $\dfrac{A + 10}{3} = B$

And $A + 10 = 2(B + 10)$

$\Rightarrow A + 10 = 2B + 20$

$\Rightarrow \dfrac{A - 10}{2} = B$

$\therefore \dfrac{A - 10}{2} = \dfrac{A + 10}{3}$

$\Rightarrow 3A - 30 = 2A + 20$

$\Rightarrow A = 30 + 20 = 50$

So, the present age of A is 50 years.

Example 38:

A person has only 25-paise and 50-paise coins. In total, he has 40 coins and their value is Rs. 12.50. Find the number of 50-paise coins.

Solution:

Suppose that he has x number of 25-paise coins and y number of 50-paise coins.

Then $x + y = 40$ ... (i)

and $\dfrac{1}{4}x + \dfrac{1}{2}y = 12.50$

$\Rightarrow x + 2y = 50$ ... (ii)

Subtracting (i) from (ii), we get

$$
\begin{array}{r}
x + 2y = 50 \\
\underline{-\ x +\ y = \_40} \\
y = 10
\end{array}
$$

So, he has 10 fifty-paise coins.

Exercise

Exercise – I

1. The LCM of two numbers is 5200 and their HCF is 40. If one of the numbers is 520, the other number is
   (1) 240 (2) 560
   (3) 400 (4) 320

2. The sum of the squares of first ten natural numbers is
   (1) 281 (2) 385 (3) 402 (4) 502

3. The sum of first ten odd numbers is
   (1) 105 (2) 100 (3) 110 (4) 120

4. HCF of $\dfrac{3}{5}$ and $\dfrac{12}{13}$ is

   (1) $\dfrac{3}{65}$ (2) $\dfrac{3}{130}$ (3) $\dfrac{3}{5}$ (4) $\dfrac{3}{13}$

5. Which of the following groups of numbers contain only irrational numbers?

   (1) $\sqrt{4}, 8$ (2) $\dfrac{3}{2}, \sqrt{4}, -7, -\dfrac{9}{8}$

   (3) $\pi, (\pi-1), (3+\sqrt{2}), -\sqrt{3}$ (4) $\dfrac{3}{2}, \sqrt{4}, -\dfrac{7}{\sqrt{2}}, -\dfrac{9}{8}$

6. Find the digit in the units place in the product 254 × 361 × 159 × 18.
   (1) 1 (2) 6
   (3) 4 (4) 8

7. The largest number among the following is

   (1) $(2 + 2 \times 2)^3$ (2) $\left[(2+2)^3\right]^{\frac{1}{2}}$

   (3) 2^5 (4) $(2 \times 2 - 2)^7$

8. The smallest number among the following is
   (1) $(7)^3$ (2) $(8.5)^3$

   (3) $(4)^4$ (4) $\left(6^5\right)^{\frac{3}{5}}$

9. Find the sum of the first 50 even numbers.
   (1) 1275 (2) 2650
   (3) 5100 (4) 2550

10. Find a if 7a4 is divisible by 9.
    (1) 6 (2) 5
    (3) 4 (4) 7

11. Find the value of 4056 ÷ 26 of 26 − $\sqrt[3]{216}$.
    (1) 6 (2) 0
    (3) 26 (4) 104

12. Evaluate: 18.18 ÷ 9 + 2.7 of 3
    (1) 101.2 (2) 27.32
    (3) 10.12 (4) 10.13

13. Evaluate: 8127 − 5422 + 1614 − 808
    (1) 3580 (2) 3058
    (3) 3503 (4) 3511

14. Evaluate: $11^2 + 11^4 \div 11^3 - 11 + (0.5)\,11^2$
    (1) 302.5 (2) 181.5
    (3) 484.0 (4) 121

15. Which one of the following is incorrect?
    (1) Square root of 5184 is 72.
    (2) Square root of 15625 is 125.
    (3) Square root of 1444 is 38.
    (4) Square root of 1296 is 34.

16. The unit's digit of the product (247 × 318 × 577 × 313) is
    (1) 2 (2) 1
    (3) 4 (4) 6

17. The sum of first 45 natural numbers is
    (1) 2070 (2) 1053
    (3) 1280 (4) 1035

18. What least value must be assigned to * so that the number 451*603 becomes exactly divisible by 9?
    (1) 2 (2) 7
    (3) 8 (4) 5

19. What least value must be assigned to * so that the number 63576 * 2 is divisible by 8?
    (1) 1 (2) 2
    (3) 3 (4) 4

20. If the HCF of two numbers is 3 and their LCM is 24, find the two numbers.
   (1) 24, 1
   (2) 3, 8
   (3) 3, 24
   (4) 6, 24

21. Evaluate: 1399×1399
   (1) 1687401
   (2) 1901541
   (3) 1943211
   (4) 1957201

22. Find the value of $397 \times 397 + 104 \times 104 + 2 \times 397 \times 104$.
   (1) 250001
   (2) 251001
   (3) 260101
   (4) 261001

23. The expression $\dfrac{1}{1.2} + \dfrac{1}{2.3} + \dfrac{1}{3.4} + \ldots + \dfrac{1}{n(n+1)}$ for any natural number n, is
   (1) always less than 1
   (2) always greater than 1
   (3) always equal to 1
   (4) None of these

24. LCM of $\dfrac{1}{4}$ and $\dfrac{1}{8}$ is
   (1) $\dfrac{1}{2}$
   (2) 1
   (3) $\dfrac{1}{4}$
   (4) $\dfrac{1}{8}$

25. The greatest fraction among $\dfrac{3}{7}, \dfrac{2}{5}, \dfrac{7}{13}, \dfrac{4}{7}$ and $\dfrac{4}{9}$ is
   (1) $\dfrac{4}{7}$
   (2) $\dfrac{4}{9}$
   (3) $\dfrac{2}{5}$
   (4) $\dfrac{7}{13}$

Exercise – 2

1. Two rational numbers lying between $\dfrac{4}{5}$ and $\dfrac{6}{7}$ are
   (1) $\dfrac{65}{84}, \dfrac{5}{6}$
   (2) $\dfrac{29}{35}, \dfrac{5}{6}$
   (3) $\dfrac{29}{35}, \dfrac{62}{70}$
   (4) $\dfrac{28}{34}, \dfrac{35}{39}$

2. The lowest four-digit number which is exactly divisible by 2, 3, 4, 5, 6 and 7 is
   (1) 1400
   (2) 1300
   (3) 1250
   (4) 1260

3. The least number which on division by 35 leaves the remainder 25 and on division by 45 leaves the remainder 35 and on division by 55 leaves the remainder 45 is
   (1) 2515
   (2) 3455
   (3) 2875
   (4) 2785

4. The sum of the two numbers is twice their difference. If their product is 27, the numbers are
   (1) 5, 15
   (2) 10, 30
   (3) 9, 6
   (4) 9, 3

5. A heap of coconuts is divided into groups of 2, 3 and 5, and each time one coconut is left out. The least number of coconuts in the heap is
   (1) 31
   (2) 41
   (3) 51
   (4) 61

6. The largest fraction among the following is
   (1) $\dfrac{17}{21}$
   (2) $\dfrac{11}{14}$
   (3) $\dfrac{12}{15}$
   (4) $\dfrac{5}{6}$

7. What is the remainder when 2^7 is divided by 7?
   (1) 2
   (2) 4
   (3) 1
   (4) None of these

8. If square root of 12 is x, find $\sqrt{\dfrac{4}{3}}$.
   (1) $\dfrac{x}{2}$
   (2) $\dfrac{x}{6}$
   (3) $x + 1$
   (4) $\dfrac{x}{3}$

9. If the product of three consecutive integers is 720, then their sum is
   (1) 54
   (2) 45
   (3) 18
   (4) 27

10. How many numbers between 200 and 600 are divisible by 4, 5 and 6?
   (1) 5
   (2) 6
   (3) 7
   (4) 8

11. Which of the following is exactly divisible by 99?
   (1) 114345
   (2) 135792
   (3) 3572404
   (4) 913464

12. The number $(10^n - 1)$ is divisible by 11 for
   (1) even values of n.
   (2) odd values of n.
   (3) all values of n.
   (4) n = multiples of 11.

13. Evaluate:

$$3 + \cfrac{3}{3 + \cfrac{1}{3 + \cfrac{1}{3}}}$$

(1) 1   (2) 3   (3) $\dfrac{43}{11}$ (4) $\dfrac{63}{19}$

14. The ratio between a two-digit number and the sum of the digits of that number is 4 : 1. If the digit in the unit place is 3 more than the digit in the ten's place, what is that number?
(1) 24   (2) 63   (3) 36   (4) 42

15. The difference between two numbers is 1365. When larger number is divided by the smaller one, the quotient is 6 and the remainder is 15. The smaller number is
(1) 270   (2) 360   (3) 240   (4) 295

16. 243 has been divided into three parts such that half of the first part, one-third of the second part and one-fourth of the third part are equal. The largest part is
(1) 108   (2) 86   (3) 92   (4) 74

17. The number which is formed by writing any digit 6 times (e.g. 111111, 444444, etc.) is always divisible by
(1) 7
(2) 11
(3) 13
(4) All of these

18. The number nearest to 99547 which is exactly divisible by 687 is
(1) 100166
(2) 99615
(3) 99579
(4) 98928

19. Which largest number of five digits is divisible by 99?
(1) 99999
(2) 99981
(3) 99909
(4) 99990

20. Which smallest number of six digits is divisible by 111?
(1) 111111
(2) 110011
(3) 100011
(4) 100001

21. If 'n' is positive integer, then $(3^{4n} - 4^{3n})$ is always divisible by
(1) 145
(2) 17
(3) 112
(4) 7

22. When 'n' is divided by 4, the remainder is 3. What is the remainder when '2n' is divided by 4?
(1) 1   (2) 6   (3) 3   (4) 2

23. 172172 is divisible by
(1) 7
(2) 11
(3) 13
(4) All of these

24. Six bells commence tolling together and toll at intervals of 3, 6, 9, 12, 15 and 18 seconds respectively. In 30 minutes, how many times do they toll together?
(1) 4   (2) 10   (3) 11   (4) 15

25. When 'n' is divided by 5 the remainder is 2. What is the remainder when n^2 is divided by 5?
(1) 2   (2) 1   (3) 3   (4) 4

Exercise – 3

1. In a school there are 850 students. If the number of girls is 56 less than the number of boys, what is the number of boys in the school?
(1) 451
(2) 450
(3) 453
(4) 620

2. Solve $\dfrac{2}{5x} - \dfrac{5}{2x} = \dfrac{1}{15}$

(1) $-\dfrac{61}{2}$ (2) $-\dfrac{63}{2}$

(3) $-\dfrac{2}{63}$ (4) $-\dfrac{2}{61}$

3. In a cricket match Sachin scored 15 runs more than Vinod. If together they had stored 245 runs, how many runs did each of them score?
(1) 115, 130
(2) 120, 125
(3) 110, 135
(4) 105, 140

4. The length of a rectangle exceeds its breadth by 7m. If the perimeter of the rectangle is 94m, what are the length and the breadth of the rectangle?
(1) 28 m, 22 m
(2) 25 m, 24 m
(3) 30 m, 15 m
(4) 27 m, 20 m

5. The ratio between the two complementary angles is 2 : 3. What is the value of each angle?
(1) 36°, 54°
(2) 18°, 27°
(3) 30°, 60°
(4) 14°, 76°

6. The sum of the digits of a two-digit number is 9. If the digits of the number are interchanged the number increases by 63, what is the original number?
(1) 18   (2) 36   (3) 72   (4) 27

7. For $\dfrac{3x+5}{3-2x} = \dfrac{5}{3}$ the value of x is:
(1) 1   (2) – 1   (3) 0   (4) – 2

8. If five times a number is subtracted from 20 the resultant is three times the same number added to 4, what is the number?
(1) 2   (2) 5   (3) 8   (4) 6

9. The length of a rectangular plot is $2\dfrac{1}{2}$ times its width. If the perimeter of the plot is 70 m. What is the length of plot ?
(1) 25 m   (2) 15 m
(3) 33 m   (4) 16 m

10. X has twice as much money as Y. Y has thrice as much money as Z. If X, Y and Z together have Rs. 1,000, what is the amount with X?
(1) Rs. 100   (2) Rs. 200
(3) Rs. 400   (4) Rs. 600

11. A man is 36 years old and his son is one-fourth as old as him. In how many years will the son be four-seventh as old as his father?
(1) 24 years   (2) 27 years
(3) 32 years   (4) 21 years

12. The difference between the ages of X and Y is 15 years. If X's age is four times the age of Y, what is X's age?
(1) 3 years   (2) 5 years
(3) 20 years   (4) 12 years

13. A number when divided by another number gives quotient as 6 and remainder as 1. If the first number is 36 more than the second number, what are the numbers?
(1) 40, 9   (2) 38, 2
(3) 43, 7   (4) 47, 11

14. In a rectangle, the length is thrice of its breadth. If the perimeter of the rectangle is 32cm, what is the length of the rectangle?
(1) 4 cm   (2) 9 cm
(3) 12 cm   (4) 16 cm

15. A father's age is 20 years more than that of his son. Five years later, the father's age will be thrice as that of his son. What is the present age of the father?
(1) 20 years   (2) 25 years
(3) 30 years   (4) 35 years

16. A two digit number has 3 in its units place and the sum of its digits is $\dfrac{1}{7}$ th of the number itself.
The number is:
(1) 33   (2) 43
(3) 53   (4) 63

17. If $x = \dfrac{a+2}{3}$, find the value of 'a' from the equation $3x - 2 = 2x + 4$.
(1) 14   (2) 15
(3) 16   (4) 17

18. An obtuse angle of a parallelogram is twice its acute angle. Find the measure of each angle of the parallelogram.
(1) 60°, 60°, 120°, 120°
(2) 55°, 55°, 110°, 110°
(3) 70°, 140°, 50°, 100°
(4) 65°, 130°, 60°, 120°

19. When 16 is subtracted from twice the number, the result is 20 less than thrice of the same number. What is the number?
(1) 1   (2) 2
(3) 3   (4) 4

20. Sum of two positive integers is 45. The greater number is twice the smaller number. What is the smaller integer?
(1) 20   (2) 15
(3) 30   (4) 18

21. If the sum of three consecutive whole numbers is 384, what are the numbers?
(1) 126, 127, 128   (2) 128, 129, 130
(3) 127, 128, 129   (4) None of these

22. Mr. Shah is 30 years older than his son who is 5 years old. After how many years would Mr. Shah become 3 times as old as his son then ?
(1) 7 years   (2) 7.5 years
(3) 10 years   (4) 8 years

23. Sum of two positive integers is 62 and their difference is 12. Find the integers.
    (1) 26, 36   (2) 25, 37
    (3) 47, 15   (4) 30, 32

24. When a number is added to its half, we get 117. Find the number.
    (1) 80   (2) 76
    (3) 78   (4) 82

25. Find the ratio between the two numbers whose sum and difference are 25 and 5, respectively.
    (1) 2 : 5   (2) 3 : 2
    (3) 1 : 3   (4) 2 : 1

Exercise – 4

1. A man is thrice as old as his son. After 14 years, the man will be twice as old as his son. Find their present ages.
   (1) 42 years, 14 years
   (2) 40 years, 13 years
   (3) 36 years, 12 years
   (4) 45 years, 15 years

2. Divide 300 into two parts so that half of one part may be less than the other by 48.
   (1) 164, 136
   (2) 106, 194
   (3) 168, 132
   (4) 186, 114

3. In an isosceles triangle, the equal sides are 2 more than twice of the third side. If the perimeter of the triangle is 19. The length of one of the equal sides is :
   (1) 3 cm   (2) 5 cm
   (3) 8 cm   (4) 6 cm

4. P has Rs. 570 and Q has Rs. 350 with them. How much money should Q receive from P so that Q has Rs.120 less than 3 times what is left with P?
   (1) Rs. 330
   (2) Rs. 320
   (3) Rs. 260
   (4) Rs. 310

5. The difference between a two digit number and the number obtained by interchanging its digits is 81. What is the difference between the digits of the number?
   (1) 7   (2) 8
   (3) 9   (4) 6

6. 2 mangoes and 5 oranges together cost Rs. 15 and 4 mangoes and 3 oranges together costs Rs. 23. Find the individual cost of a mango and an orange.
   (1) Rs. 4, Rs. 2
   (2) Rs. 3, Rs. 3
   (3) Rs. 5, Re. 1
   (4) Re. 1, Re. 1

7. The sum of numerator and denominator of a certain fraction is 11. If 1 is added to the numerator, the value of fraction becomes $\frac{1}{2}$, the fraction is:
   (1) $\frac{3}{8}$ (2) $\frac{2}{9}$
   (3) $\frac{1}{10}$ (4) $\frac{6}{5}$

8. A workman is paid Rs.15 for each day he is present and is fined Rs.3 for each day, he is absent. If he works for x days in a month and earns Rs.360. The value of x is:
   (1) 22   (2) 24
   (3) 25   (4) 21

9. The perimeter of an isosceles triangle is 23 cm. The length of its congruent sides is 1 cm less than twice the length of its base. The length of each side is:
   (1) 3 cm, 10 cm, 10 cm
   (2) 5 cm, 9 cm, 9 cm
   (3) 8 cm, 8 cm, 7 cm
   (4) 4 cm, 9 cm, 10 cm

10. The sum of two numbers is 2490. If 6.5% of one number is equal to 8.5% of other, then one of the numbers is:
    (1) 1008   (2) 1079
    (3) 1411   (4) 3718

11. At a fair, a "bull's eye" was rewarded 20 paise and a penalty of 8 paise imposed for missing the "bull's eye". A boy tried 50 shots and received only 48 paise. How many "bull's eye" did he hit ?
    (1) 15   (2) 17
    (3) 16   (4) 18

12. A father is 25 years older than his son. Five years before, he was six times his son's age at that time. How old is the son ?
    (1) 6 years   (2) 8 years
    (3) 10 years   (4) 12 years

13. A father gives his son Rs. 3,000 for a tour. If he extends his tour by five days, he has to cut down his daily expenses by Rs. 20. The tour will now last for:
(1) 25 days   (2) 30 days
(3) 20 days   (4) 36 days

14. The sum of three fractions is $2\dfrac{11}{24}$. When the largest fraction is divided by the smallest fraction, the fraction thus obtained is $\dfrac{7}{6}$ which is $\dfrac{1}{3}$ more than the middle fraction. The three fractions are:
(1) $\dfrac{1}{2}, \dfrac{2}{3}, \dfrac{3}{4}$ (2) $\dfrac{2}{3}, \dfrac{3}{4}, \dfrac{4}{5}$
(3) $\dfrac{3}{4}, \dfrac{4}{5}, \dfrac{5}{6}$ (4) $\dfrac{3}{4}, \dfrac{5}{6}, \dfrac{7}{8}$

15. If A was half as old as B ten years ago and he will be two thirds as old as B in eight years, what are the present ages of A and B?
(1) 28 years, 46 years
(2) 22 years, 40 years
(3) 24 years, 42 years
(4) 12 years, 30 years

16. A certain number of articles are purchased for Rs.1,200. If price per article is increased by Rs. 5, then 20 less articles can be purchased. What is the original number of articles?
(1) 60   (2) 80
(3) 50   (4) 90

17. A person purchased a certain number of eggs at four a rupee. He kept one fifth of them and sold the rest at three a rupee and in the process gained a rupee. How many eggs did the person buy ?
(1) 30   (2) 40
(3) 50   (4) 60

18. An elevator has a capacity of 12 adults or 20 children. How many adults can board the elevator with 15 children?
(1) 6   (2) 5
(3) 4   (4) 3

19. Two years ago, a father's age was three times the square of his son's age. In three years time, his age will be four times as that of his son's age. What are their present ages?
(1) 24 years, 6 years
(2) 27 years, 3 years
(3) 25 years, 7 years
(4) 29 years, 5 years

20. A sum of Rs. 10 is divided among a number of persons. If the number is increased by $\dfrac{1}{4}$th , each will receive 5 paise less. The number of persons is:
(1) 20   (2) 10
(3) 40   (4) 80

21. Tina's sister is younger to her by 3 years and her brother is elder to her by 4 years. The sum of the ages of Tina, her sister and her brother is 73 years. What is Tina's age ?
(1) 22 years   (2) 24 years
(3) 20 years   (4) 25 years

22. A half–ticket issued by railway costs half the full fare but the reservation charge is same on half–ticket as on full–ticket. One reserved first class ticket for a journey between two stations costs Rs. 362 and one full and one half–reserved first class ticket costs Rs.554. The reservation charge is:
(1) Rs. 18   (2) Rs. 22
(3) Rs. 38   (4) Rs. 46

23. A purse contains Rs.130 in equal denominations of 50 paise, 10 paise and 5 paise. How many coins of each type are there?
(1) 100   (2) 200
(3) 150   (4) 250

24. A father said to his son, "I was as old as you are at present, at the time of your birth." If the father's present age is 38 years, what was his son's age five years ago?
(1) 14 years old   (2) 19 years old
(3) 38 years old   (4) 33 years old

25. Ankita purchased a certain number of articles at a rate of 5 for 50 paise. If she had purchased them at a rate of 11 for one rupee, she would have spent 50 paise less. How many articles did Ankita purchase?
(1) 15   (2) 25
(3) 55   (4) 45

Ratio, Proportion and Averages $\quad$ **2**

Introduction

This is one of the most important topics in arithmetic from examination point of view. Ratio is an extension of the concept of fractions. These are fairly simple topics and will need a focussed approach to refresh these concepts that you learnt during your school days.

Ratio

The concept of ratios is used for comparing two or more quantities of a similar kind. The definition of ratio is given below:

The ratio of the quantity "A" to the quantity "B" is a relation that tells us what multiple or fraction the quantity "A" is of the quantity "B".

The ratio of quantity A to quantity B is denoted by A : B and it is measured by the fraction $\dfrac{A}{B}$. The quantities A and B are called the terms of the ratio. Also note that, as both the terms A and B of a ratio are of a similar kind, the resulting ratio A : B has no unit and hence it is purely a number.

Consider the two quantities A and B such that A : B = 2 : 3. In what ways can we interpret this relation? Read the following.

i. $\qquad$ The ratio B : A is 3 : 2.

ii. $\qquad$ A is $\dfrac{2}{3}$rd part of B.

iii. $\qquad$ B is 1.5 times that of A.
iv. $\qquad$ B is 50% more than A.
v. $\qquad$ A is 33.33% less than B.

If both the terms of a ratio are multiplied or divided by the same (non-zero) quantity, then the value of the ratio remains the same. In terms of notations:

$\dfrac{a}{b} = \dfrac{ka}{kb}$ (Here, k is any non-zero real number.)

Example 1:
Solve these problems
I. A and B got 175 and 225 marks respectively. What is the ratio of their marks?
II. X scored 105 marks out of 150 and Y scored 175 marks out of 200. What is the ratio of the percentage marks scored by each?

Solution:

I. $\quad A : B = \dfrac{175}{225} = \dfrac{7}{9} = 7 : 9$

II. $\quad X : Y = \dfrac{105}{150} \times \dfrac{200}{175} = 4 : 5$

Example 2:
5 kg of wheat flour is mixed with 500 gm of sugar extract. What is the ratio of sugar extract to the rest of the mixture after adding 1.5 kg of water?

Solution:
We first need to express all quantities in a single unit.
Wheat flour = 5 kg
Water = 1.5 kg
Sugar extract = 500 gm = 0.5 kg
Total weight of the mixture = 7 kg

Ratio of sugar extract to the rest of mixture = $\dfrac{0.5}{6.5}$

= 1 : 13

Example 3:
Divide Rs. 1000 between A and B in the ratio of 7 : 3.

Solution:
Let us assume that A gets Rs. 7x and B gets Rs. 3x as 7x + 3x = 1000

$\Rightarrow x = \dfrac{1000}{10} = 100$

$\Rightarrow$ A gets Rs. 700 and B gets Rs. 300

Example 4:
What must be subtracted from the numerator and the denominator of the fraction $\dfrac{6}{7}$ to give a fraction equal to $\dfrac{16}{21}$?

Solution:
Let the number subtracted be x.

$\Rightarrow \dfrac{6-x}{7-x} = \dfrac{16}{21}$

On solving, we get x = 2.8

Example 5:

Ram's father is thrice as old as Ram was, 2 years ago. Five years from now, his father's age will be 6 years more than twice the Ram's age. What is Ram's present age?

Solution:

Let Ram's present age be X and his father's present age be Y.
$Y = 3(X - 2)$ and $(Y + 5) - 6 = 2(X + 5)$. Solving, we get, X = 17 years and Y = 45 years.

Example 6:

A's income is $\dfrac{2}{3}$rd of B's income. B's income is 75% of C's income. What is the ratio of C's income to A's income?

Solution:

B's income = $\dfrac{3}{2}$ of A's income.

C's income = $\dfrac{4}{3}$ of B's income = $\dfrac{4}{3} \times \dfrac{3}{2}$ of A's income $\Rightarrow$ Required ratio = 2 : 1.

Example 7:

Let the ratio A:B is measured by the fraction $\dfrac{X}{Y}$.

If the quantities A and B are fractions then can X and Y be integers?

Solution:

Let A = $\dfrac{a}{b}$ and B = $\dfrac{c}{d}$

Now A : B = $\dfrac{X}{Y} = \dfrac{ad}{bc}$.

As each of a, b, c and d are integers, ad and bc are integers as well. So, X and Y are integers.

Example 8:

Let one or both of the two quantities P and Q $(P \neq Q)$ are surds.

If $\dfrac{P}{Q} = \dfrac{p}{q}$ then can p and q simultaneously be integers?

Solution:

If either or both of the quantities P and Q $(P \neq Q)$ are surds then there exist no two integers p and q which can exactly measure the ratio P: Q. In terms of the notations, if $\dfrac{P}{Q} = \dfrac{p}{q}$ then not both of p and q are integers. Choose arbitrary values for P and Q. Try to simplify the fraction $\dfrac{P}{Q}$ so that you can get both p and q as integers. You will never be successful!!

Comparison of Ratios

Question: Which of the following is/are correct?

(1) $\dfrac{113}{115} > \dfrac{13}{15}$ (2) $\dfrac{87}{85} < \dfrac{27}{25}$

(3) $-\dfrac{27}{17} > \dfrac{-13}{9}$ (4) $-\dfrac{15}{19} < -\dfrac{5}{9}$

Two compare two ratios $\dfrac{a}{b}$ and $\dfrac{c}{d}$, first make their denominators of the same sign. Now

I. If $(ad - bc) > 0$ then $\dfrac{a}{b} > \dfrac{c}{d}$

II. If $(ad - bc) < 0$ then $\dfrac{a}{b} < \dfrac{c}{d}$

III. If $(ad - bc) = 0$ then $\dfrac{a}{b} = \dfrac{c}{d}$

Apply the above concepts for each option. You will see that (a), (b) and (d) are correct and (c) is incorrect.
There are some other methods and shortcuts as well, to compare the ratios. Read the following concepts and understand the following examples carefully and make yourself comfortable with these methods as they are extremely helpful in Data Interpretation problems.

Now, we will discuss some important properties of the ratios. Let us assume a ratio $\dfrac{A}{B}$. What happens when we add or subtract the same quantity from both the numerator and the denominator?
The result, in fact, depends on whether

$\dfrac{A}{B} > 1$ or < 1? We have summarized the results for both the cases as under:

Case I:

If $\dfrac{A}{B} > 1$.

1. $\quad \dfrac{A+x}{B+x} < \dfrac{A}{B} \quad (x > 0)$

2. $\quad \dfrac{A-x}{B-x} > \dfrac{A}{B} \quad (x > 0)$

Case II:

If $\dfrac{A}{B} < 1$

3. $\quad \dfrac{A+x}{B+x} > \dfrac{A}{B} \quad (x > 0)$

4. $\quad \dfrac{A-x}{B-x} < \dfrac{A}{B} \quad (x > 0)$

You can verify the above results by choosing any arbitrary values for A, B and x. Try to memorize these results as these are extremely helpful in Data Interpretation problems.

Example 9:

Which one is the greatest of $\dfrac{13}{11}$, $\dfrac{15}{13}$, $\dfrac{11}{9}$ and $\dfrac{12}{10}$

Solution:

Difference in the numerator and denominator is 2 in each case. Also, the fractions are all more than

1. Therefore, greatest fraction is $\dfrac{11}{9}$.

[**Note:** Here, Case I – (2) is used]

Example 10:

Which of the following is the smallest:

$\dfrac{14}{25}$, $\dfrac{57}{100}$, $\dfrac{49}{86}$, $\dfrac{3}{5}$

Solution:

One way of solving such a problem is to convert each into decimals and then compare.

Another way is to equalize either numerator or denominator of every two fractions that are being compared.

Suppose, we have $\dfrac{a}{b}$ and $\dfrac{c}{d}$ to be compared.

If a = c, then the fraction with the higher value of denominator is smaller.

If b = d, then the fraction with the lower value of numerator is smaller.

Comparing $\dfrac{14}{25}$ with $\dfrac{57}{100}$, $\dfrac{14}{25} = \dfrac{56}{100} < \dfrac{57}{100}$.

So, $\dfrac{57}{100}$ is eliminated.

Now comparing $\dfrac{14}{25}$ with $\dfrac{49}{86}$, $\dfrac{14}{25}$

$= \dfrac{98}{175}$ & $\dfrac{49}{86} = \dfrac{98}{172}$. So, $\dfrac{49}{86}$ is eliminated

Comparing $\dfrac{14}{25}$ with $\dfrac{3}{5}$, $\dfrac{3}{5}$

$= \dfrac{15}{25} > \dfrac{14}{25}$. So $\dfrac{14}{25}$ is the smallest.

Example 11:

Pompo and Rompo are two countries engaged in a war. Pompo possesses 8 tanks and Rompo possesses 11 tanks. They get external support from neighbouring countries, of two tanks each. Which of the two countries is supposed to have a relatively greater increase in strength?

Solution:

For Pompo's = $\dfrac{\text{Final}}{\text{Initial}} = \dfrac{10}{8}$

For Rompos = $\dfrac{\text{Final}}{\text{Initial}} = \dfrac{13}{11}$

As $\dfrac{10}{8} > \dfrac{13}{11}$ Pompo had a relatively greater increase in strength.

Now, we will learn some very important properties of ratios by solving the following problems. These properties will be very useful in solving problems in Algebra. Understand each step thoroughly.

Example 12:

If $a : b = 2{:}5$, then find the ratio $2a - 3b : 5a + 7b$.

Solution:

$$a:b = \frac{2}{5} \Rightarrow \frac{2a-3b}{5a+7b}$$

$$= \frac{2\dfrac{a}{b}-3\dfrac{b}{b}}{5\dfrac{a}{b}+7\dfrac{b}{b}} = \frac{2\times\dfrac{2}{5}-3}{5\times\dfrac{2}{5}+7} = -\frac{11}{45}$$

▌Proportion

When two ratios are equal, the four quantities composing them are said to be *proportionals*. In terms of the notations, if $\dfrac{A}{B} = \dfrac{C}{D}$ then A, B, C and D are proportionals. We use the symbol ":: " to express it mathematically. So whenever we write A : B : : C : D, it is interpreted as A, B, C and D are proportionals. The terms A and D are called the *extremes* and the terms B and C are called the *means*. It is very easy to note that $A \times D = B \times C$ This result is more commonly expressed as:
"Product of the extremes = Product of the means".

Continued Proportion:

a, b, c, d, e, f...are said to be in continued proportion if

$$\frac{a}{b} = \frac{b}{c} = \frac{c}{d} = \frac{d}{e} = \frac{e}{f} = ...$$

When three quantities a, b and c are in continued proportion then b is called the *mean proportional* and c is called the *third proportional*.

$$\frac{a}{b} = \frac{b}{c} \Rightarrow b^2 = a \times c$$

When four quantities a, b, c and d are proportionals then d is called the *fourth proportional*.

Example 13:

As amount of Rs. 1,150 is to be divided among A, B and C such that the ratio of share of A to that of B is equal to 3 : 2 and share of B to share of C is equal to 3 : 4. Find their individual share.

Solution:

Here A : B = 3 : 2 = 9 : 6 and B : C = 3 : 4 = 6 : 8
Therefore, A : B : C = 9 : 6 : 8
Rs. 1150 can be divided between them as follows:

$$A's\ share = \frac{1150\times9}{23} = Rs.\ 450$$

$$B's\ share = \frac{1150\times6}{23} = Rs.\ 300$$

$$C's\ share = \frac{1150\times8}{23} = Rs.\ 400$$

Example 14:

In the year 1996, the monthly allowances given to A, B and C were in the ratio of 5 : 3 : 1. If C's monthly allowance was Rs. 1000 then what was total allowance received by A, in that year?

Solution:

C's share = Rs. 1,000
A's share : C's share = 5 : 1
Therefore, A's monthly share = Rs. 5,000
A's share for whole year = 5000 × 12 = Rs. 60,000

Example 15:

From a total of Rs. 159000, Rs. 5000 is to be divided between A and B in the ratio of 2 : 3. The rest of the money is to be divided among A, B and C in the ratio of 5 : 3 : 3. How much money did A and B get, respectively?

Solution:

Rs. 5,000 is to be divided between A and B in the ratio of 2 : 3.
A's share = Rs. 2,000; B's share = Rs. 3,000
Amount left is 1,54,000 and it is to be divided in the ratio of 5 : 3 : 3.
A's share = Rs. 70,000; B's share = Rs. 42,000
C's share = Rs. 42,000
A's total share = Rs. 72,000
B's total share = Rs. 45,000

Example 16:

Ratio of a : b is same as that of b : c, where a, b and c are positive numbers. If a = 10 and c = 40, find b.

Solution:

a : b = b : c
b × b = a × c
b × b = 400
$b = \sqrt{400}\ = \pm20$
So, b = 20.

Example 17:

Divide 156 in 4 parts such that they are in continued proportion and the sum of the first and third part is in a ratio of 1: 5 with the sum of the second and the fourth part.

Solution:

$$156 = a + b + c + d$$

$$\frac{a}{b} = \frac{b}{c} = \frac{c}{d} = k$$

$\Rightarrow b^2 = ac$ and $c^2 = bd$

$\Rightarrow a, b, c, d$ are in a G.P.

Let the common ratio of the G.P. be r. We have,

$$\frac{a+c}{b+d} = \frac{1}{5}$$

or $\dfrac{a+ar^2}{ar+ar^3} = \dfrac{1}{5} \Rightarrow \dfrac{1+r^2}{r+r^3} = \dfrac{1}{5} \Rightarrow r = 5$

$\Rightarrow a + 5a + 25a + 125a = 156$

$\Rightarrow a = 1, b = 5, c = 25$ and $d = 125$

Example18:

Find the third proportional to 3, 5.

Solution:

Let the third proportional be "x" then $3 : 5 :: 5 : x$

$$\frac{3}{5} = \frac{5}{x} \Rightarrow x = \frac{25}{3}.$$

Example 19:

Find the fourth proportional to 1, 2 and 3.

Solution:

Let the fourth proportional be "x" then $1 : 2 :: 3 : x$

$$\frac{1}{2} = \frac{3}{x} \Rightarrow x = 6.$$

Example 20:

Find the mean proportional to 27, 3.

Solution:

Let the mean proportional be "x".

$27 : x :: x : 3$

$$\frac{27}{x} = \frac{x}{3} \Rightarrow x^2 = 81 \Rightarrow x = \pm 9$$

As 27 and 3 are positive quantities, we will take x to be positive only. So, x = 9.

Operations on Ratios

Let $\dfrac{A}{B} = \dfrac{C}{D}$. Three very important results are derived from the following operations.

1. Componendo operation
2. Dividendo operation
3. Componendo and Dividendo operation

Componendo Operation:

As $\dfrac{A}{B} = \dfrac{C}{D}$

$$\frac{A}{B} + 1 = \frac{C}{D} + 1 \Rightarrow \frac{A+B}{B} = \frac{C+D}{D}$$

This operation is called componendo. We will make use of this important result while solving problems in a variety of topics.

Dividendo Operation:

As $\dfrac{A}{B} = \dfrac{C}{D}$

$$\frac{A}{B} - 1 = \frac{C}{D} - 1 \Rightarrow \frac{A-B}{B} = \frac{C-D}{D}$$

This operation is called dividendo. This is an equally important result.

Componendo and Dividendo Operation:

When we combine the results of componendo and dividendo operations, we get following important result.

If $\dfrac{A}{B} = \dfrac{C}{D}$ then $\dfrac{A+B}{A-B} = \dfrac{C+D}{C-D}$

We will solve a few examples using the above results.

Example 21:

If $p : q :: r : s$ then prove that

$$2p + 3q : 2p - 3q :: 2r + 3s : 2r - 3s$$

Solution:

We have $\dfrac{p}{q} = \dfrac{r}{s}$

Multiplying both the sides by $\dfrac{2}{3}$ we get

$$\frac{2}{3} \times \frac{p}{q} = \frac{2}{3} \times \frac{r}{s} \quad \text{Or} \quad \frac{2p}{3q} = \frac{2r}{3s}$$

Using the componendo and dividendo property we get

$$\frac{2p+3q}{2p-3q} = \frac{2r+3s}{2r-3s}$$

Example 22:

Solve for x, $\dfrac{\sqrt{1+x} + \sqrt{1-x}}{\sqrt{1+x} - \sqrt{1-x}} = 2$

Solution:

$$\frac{\sqrt{1+x} + \sqrt{1-x}}{\sqrt{1+x} - \sqrt{1-x}} = 2$$

Applying the Componendo and Dividendo:

$$\frac{(\sqrt{1+x} + \sqrt{1-x}) + (\sqrt{1+x} - \sqrt{1-x})}{(\sqrt{1+x} + \sqrt{1-x}) - (\sqrt{1+x} - \sqrt{1-x})} = \frac{2+1}{2-1}$$

Or $\dfrac{2\sqrt{1+x}}{2\sqrt{1-x}} = \dfrac{3}{1}$

Simplifying and then squaring on both sides, we get:

$$\frac{1+x}{1-x} = 9$$

You can proceed to get $1+x = 9 \times (1-x)$ and solve for x. Another way of proceeding from here is to apply componendo and dividendo, one more time. So that we get:

$\Rightarrow \dfrac{(1+x) + (1-x)}{(1+x) - (1-x)} = \dfrac{9+1}{9-1} = \dfrac{5}{4}$. This gives,

$$x = \frac{4}{5}.$$

Example 23:

If $\dfrac{a}{b} = \dfrac{c}{d}$ then prove that

a. $\dfrac{a \pm b}{b} = \dfrac{c \pm d}{d}$

b. $\dfrac{a+b}{a-b} = \dfrac{c+d}{c-d}$

c. $\dfrac{a+b}{a-b} = \dfrac{c+d}{c-d}$

Solution:

a. $\dfrac{a}{b} = \dfrac{c}{d} \Rightarrow \dfrac{a}{b} \pm 1 = \dfrac{c}{d} \pm 1$ Or $\dfrac{a \pm b}{b} = \dfrac{c \pm d}{d}$

b. $\dfrac{a}{b} = \dfrac{c}{d}$

$\dfrac{a+b}{b} = \dfrac{c+d}{d} = k \text{(say)}$

$\Rightarrow (a+b) = bk \text{ and } (c+d) = dk$

$\Rightarrow \dfrac{a+b}{c+d} = \dfrac{b}{d}$ ... (i)

Similarly,

$$\frac{a-b}{c-d} = \frac{b}{d} \qquad \text{... (ii)}$$

From (i) and (ii)

$$\frac{a+b}{a-b} = \frac{c+d}{c-d}$$

c. $\dfrac{a}{b} = \dfrac{c}{d} = k, \text{say}$

$\Rightarrow a = bk \text{ and } c = dk$

So that, $\dfrac{a \pm c}{b \pm d} = \dfrac{bk \pm ck}{b \pm d} = k = \dfrac{a}{b}$

Example 24:

If $\dfrac{a}{b} = \dfrac{c}{d} = \dfrac{e}{f} = K$, then prove that

a. $\dfrac{a+c+e}{b+d+f} = K$

b. $\dfrac{pa+qc+re}{pb+qd+rf} = K$

(p, q and r are not all zero)

c. $\left(\dfrac{pa^n + qc^n + re^n}{pb^n + qd^n + rf^n}\right)^{\frac{1}{n}} = K$

(p, q and r are not all zero)

Solution:

$\dfrac{a}{b} = \dfrac{c}{d} = \dfrac{e}{f} = K$, given

$\Rightarrow a = bK, c = dK \text{ and } e = fK$

Substituting, we get

a. $\dfrac{a+c+e}{b+d+f} = \dfrac{bK+dK+fK}{b+d+f} = K$, hence proved.

b. $= \dfrac{pbK + qdK + rfK}{pb+qd+rf} = K$, hence proved.

c. $\left(\dfrac{p(a)^n + q(c)^n + r(e)^n}{pb^n + qd^n + rf^n}\right)^{\frac{1}{n}}$

$= \left(\dfrac{p(bK)^n + q(dK)^n + r(fK)^n}{pb^n + qd^n + rf^n}\right)^{\frac{1}{n}} = (K^n)^{\frac{1}{n}} = K$

Direct Proportion and Inverse Proportion

Direct Proportion: Let there be two variables A and B. They are said to be in *direct proportion* if the ratio A : B is constant for all the possible values of A and (the corresponding values of) B. We can understand this in terms of percentages also:

Two quantities A and B are in *direct proportion* if change in the value of A, by a certain percentage, always corresponds to the same percentage change in the value of B. Direct Proportion is characterized by the following equation:

$$\Rightarrow \frac{A}{B} = K, \text{ a constant}$$

Can you think of some real life examples of the quantities A and B which are in direct proportion? Here are a few examples.

   i. "A" is Speed and "B" is Distance.
      (For a constant time).
   ii. "A" is radius of the circle and "B" is the Perimeter.

Note: That $\frac{B}{A} = \frac{1}{K}$, again a constant . So When A is in a direct proportion to B then B is in a direct proportion to A as well.

Inverse Proportion: Two variables A and B are said to be in *inverse proportion* if the product A×B is constant for all the possible values of A and (the corresponding values of) B. We can understand this in terms of percentages also:

Two quantities A and B are in *inverse proportion* if increase/decrease in the value of A, by a certain percentage, always corresponds to the same percentage decrease/increase in the value of B.

Inverse Proportion is characterized by the following equation:

A × B = K, a constant

Can you think of some real life examples of the quantities A and B which are in inverse proportion?

   i. "A" is Speed and "B" is Time. (for a fixed distance)
   ii. "A" is the number of people working on a given project and "B" is the time taken in the completion of the project.

Note: That when A is in inverse proportion to B then B is in inverse proportion to A as well.

Example 25:
Speed of car 'A' is twice that of truck 'B'. Both started from a point X and reached a point Y. If 'B' took 3 hours more than 'A', what is the time taken by the truck 'B'?

Solution:
Since distance is constant, speed & time are inversely proportional. Let v_A = speed of A, v_B = speed of B, t_A = time taken by A; t_B = time taken by B

or $\dfrac{v_A}{v_B} = \dfrac{2}{1} \Rightarrow \dfrac{t_A}{t_B} = \dfrac{1}{2}.$

If A takes x hrs.

then $\dfrac{x}{x+3} = \dfrac{1}{2} \Rightarrow x = 3$

$\Rightarrow$ B takes 6 hrs.

Averages

An average or an arithmetic mean is the sum of all observations divided by the total number of observations.

$$\text{Average} = \frac{\text{Sum of all observations}}{\text{Total number of observations}}$$

e.g., If the ages of five members of a club are 40 years, 45 years, 55 years, 60 years, and 40 years respectively, then their average age

$$= \frac{40+45+55+60+40}{5} = \frac{240}{5} = 48 \text{ years}$$

Weighted Average

Suppose in the above example, there are 2 members aged 40 years, 3 members aged 45 years, 4 members aged 50 years and 5 aged 55 years, then their average age is

$$\frac{\{(2\times40)+(3\times45)+(4\times50)+(5\times55)\}}{(2+3+4+5)} = \frac{690}{14} \text{ years}$$

Here, $\left(\dfrac{2}{14}\right)$, $\left(\dfrac{3}{14}\right)$, $\left(\dfrac{4}{14}\right)$ and $\left(\dfrac{5}{14}\right)$ are called the weights attached to each category of members.

This average is also called the **weighted average** of the age of the members of the club.

Example 26:
A school has only three classes comprised of 40, 50 and 60 students respectively. In these classes, 10%, 20% and 10% students respectively passed in the examination. The percentage of students passed in the examination from the entire school is:

Solution:

Total number of students = 40 + 50 + 60 = 150

Number of students passed

$$\left(\frac{10}{100}\times 40+\frac{20}{100}\times 50+\frac{10}{100}\times 60\right)$$

$$= (4 + 10 + 6) = 20$$

Percentage of students passed

$$= \frac{20}{(40+50+60)}\times 100 = 13\frac{1}{3}\% \;.$$

Central Value Meaning of Average

Average can also be seen as the central value of all the given values.

For example, what will be the average 214, 215, 219 and 224 ?

Let us assume the central value of all the given numbers = 215.

Now, find the deviations of all the numbers from 215.

214 215 219 224

When assumed central value is (214), the sum of the deviations = (–1) + (0) + (+4) + (9)

Now, finding the average of deviations given us

$$\frac{-1+0+4+9}{4}=\frac{12}{4}=3$$

So, average = assumed central value + average of deviations = 215 + 3 = 218

Thus, we can assume any value to be the assumed average and then find the average of all the deviations; and when we add all the numbers and divide it by number of numbers, 0 is assumed to be the central value.

Example 27:

The average score of Sachin after 25 innings is 46 runs per innings. If after the 26th innings, his average score increased by 2 runs, then what is his score in the 26th innings?

Solution:

Runs in 26th inning = Total runs after 26th innings – Total runs after 25th innings = 26 × 48 – 25 × 46 = 98

Alternatively, this question can be done by the above given central value meaning of average. Since the average increases by 2 runs per innings, we can assume that 2 runs have been added to his score in each of the first 25 innings. Now, the total runs added in these innings have been contributed by the scored in the 26th inning, which must be equal to 25 × 2 = 50 runs.

And after contributing 50 runs, his score in the 26th inning is 48 runs.

Hence, runs scored in the 26th inning = new average + old innings × change in average = 48 + 25 × 2 = 98.

Properties of Average

1. Average always lies in between the maximum and the minimum value. It can be equal to the maximum or minimum value if all the numbers are equal.
   For example– A1, A2, A3 and A4 are four numbers given where A1 > A2 > A3 > A4

2. Average is the resultant of net surplus and net deficit, as used in the central tendency method.

3. When weights of different quantities are same, then simple method is used to find the average. However, when different weights of different quantities are taken then it is known as weighted average. Here the method of weighted average is used to find the average.
   For example, assume per capita income of India is USD 500 and per capita income of US is USD 200. Now if we merge India and US into one country then it is observed that per capita income of this new country will not be equal to
   $$\frac{500+200}{2}=\text{USD }350$$

4. If the value of each quantity is increased or decreased by the same value S, then the average will also increase or decrease respectively by S.

5. If the value of each quantity is multiplied by the same value S, then the average will also be multiplied by S.

6. If the value of each quantity is divided by the same value S ($S \neq 0$) then the average will also be divided by S.

Example 28:

Lovely goes to Patna from New Delhi at a speed of 40 km/hr and returns with a speed of 60 km/hr. What is her average speed during the whole journey?

Solution:

Let the distance between Patna and New Delhi be 'd' kms.

Time taken from Patna to New Delhi $=\left(\dfrac{d}{40}\right)$ hours

Time taken from New Delhi to Patna $=\left(\dfrac{d}{60}\right)$ hours

$$\text{Average speed} = \frac{\text{Total distance travelled}}{\text{Total time consumed}}$$

$$= \frac{d+d}{\dfrac{d}{40}+\dfrac{d}{60}} = \frac{2\times40\times60}{40+60} = 48 \text{ km/hr}$$

Example 29:

A batsman makes a score of 87 runs in the 17th inning and thus increases his average by 3. Find his average after 17th inning.

Solution:

Let the average after 16 innings be 'A'. Then, average after 17 innings = A + 3
According to the question

$$\Rightarrow \left(\frac{16A+87}{17}\right) = (A+3) \Rightarrow A = 36$$

Average after 17 innings = A + 3 = 36 + 3 = 39

Mixture and Alligation

Suppose we have 5 L of water and 2.5 L of pure milk. Let us try to answer following questions.

Q 1. If they are mixed to give a 7.5 L solution then what is the ratio between the quantity of milk and water in it?

Q 2. If we want to make a solution which has only 80% milk then in what ratio should we mix the milk and water?

Alligation is an arithmetic method of solving similar problems. The concept of alligation can be used to solve similar problems in various other areas as well.

For example, problems involving

(i) Profit and Loss.

(ii) Time Speed and Distance.

Common problems based on alligation are related to mixtures and solutions, profit & loss, cost price, selling price etc.

We are giving a formula, specific to cost price and selling price problems. We will solve a problem based on the same and thoroughly understand how the formula is used to solve this problem.

Rule of Alligation

When we mix a cheaper (lesser cost price) sample and a dearer (more cost price) sample, the cost price of the mixture lies between the cost prices of the two. This cost price is called the mean price. All these quantities are related as in the following formula:-

$$\frac{\text{Quantity of Cheaper}}{\text{Quantity of Dearer}} = \frac{\text{C.P. of Dearer} - \text{Mean Price}}{\text{Mean price} - \text{C.P. of Cheaper}}$$

It can also be represented as:

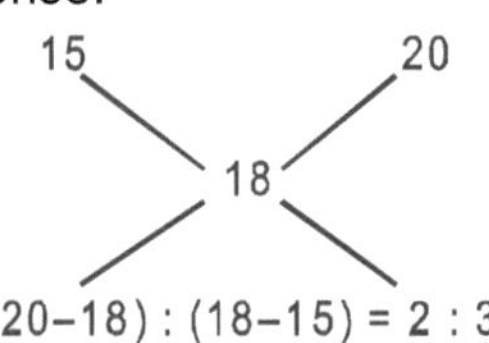

(Cheaper quantity) : (Dearer quantity)
= (b – x) : (x – a)

Make yourself comfortable with this visualisation. This is very helpful.

Example 30:

Anil buys two varieties of sugar costing Rs. 15 per kg and Rs. 20 per kg. He mixes these two varieties in a certain ratio that costs him Rs. 18 per kg. Find the ratio of the cheaper quantity to that of the dearer quantity.

Solution:

Using alligation, Rs. 18 per kg. is the mean cost price.

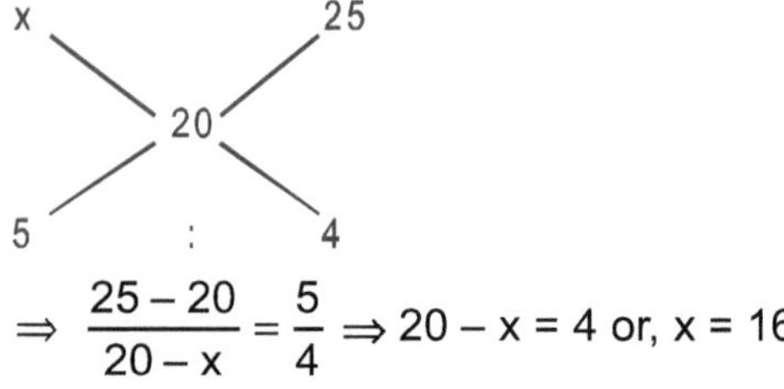

(20–18) : (18–15) = 2 : 3
Thus, ratio of cheaper quantity to dearer quantity is
= (20 – 18) : (18 – 15) = 2 : 3

Example 31:

Akash buys a certain variety of rice and mixes it with another variety of rice costing Rs. 25 per kg in the ratio of 5 : 4. If the mixture costs Rs. 20 per kg, what is the cost price of the other variety?

Solution:

Let the cost of the cheaper variety of rice be Rs. x per kg.
Using alligation:

$$\Rightarrow \frac{25-20}{20-x} = \frac{5}{4} \Rightarrow 20 - x = 4 \text{ or, } x = 16$$

∴ Cost price of cheaper variety of rice = Rs. 16 per kg.

Example 32:

A dealer buys 11 kg of wheat for Rs. 275 and mixes it with another quality of wheat in the ratio of 4 : 5. If the price of the resulting mixture is Rs. 30 per kg, what is the cost price of the other quality of wheat ?

Solution:

CP of 1 kg of wheat is $= \dfrac{275}{11} = \text{Rs. } 25 / kg$

Using Alligation:

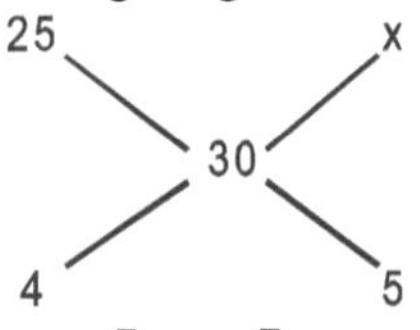

$$\therefore \dfrac{5}{x-30} = \dfrac{5}{4} \Rightarrow x = 34$$

$\therefore$ CP of the other quality of wheat is Rs. 34 per kg.

Example 33:

A trader mixes two varieties of apples, costing Rs. 24 per dozen and Rs. 36 per dozen and sells them at the rate of Rs. 33 per dozen, there by gaining 10% on the transaction. The ratio in which he mixes these varieties is:

Solution:

SP of the mixture = Rs. 33 per dozen

$\therefore$ CP of the mixture is

$$= 33 \times \dfrac{10}{11} = \text{Rs. } 30 \text{ per dozen}$$

($\because$ All the quantities must be in same unit)

Using alligation:

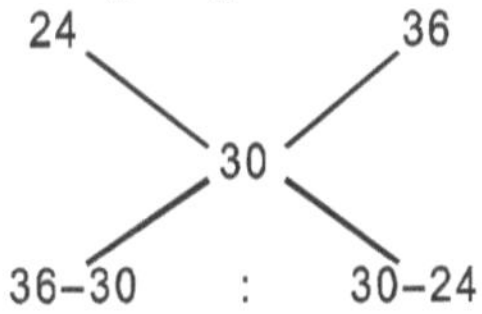

$$\Rightarrow \text{Ratio of the mixture} = \dfrac{36-30}{30-24} = 1 : 1$$

When we use alligation method to solve problems from other areas, we change the terms involved in the above formula accordingly. Let us solve some other similar problems.

Carefully note how and on which quantities, we are applying alligation rule.

Example 34:

The ratio in which 30% alcohol solution should be mixed with 50% solution in order to get a 42% solution is:

Solution:

Using alligation:

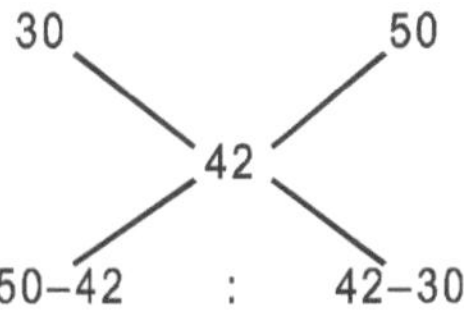

$$\Rightarrow \text{Required ratio} = \dfrac{50-42}{42-30} = 2 : 3.$$

Example 35:

11 L of water is mixed with a certain quantity of milk such that the mixture costs Rs. 1 per litre. If the cost of pure milk is 110 paise per litre, then the amount of milk in the mixture is:

Solution:

Let the quantity of the milk be 'x' L.

CP of water = 0

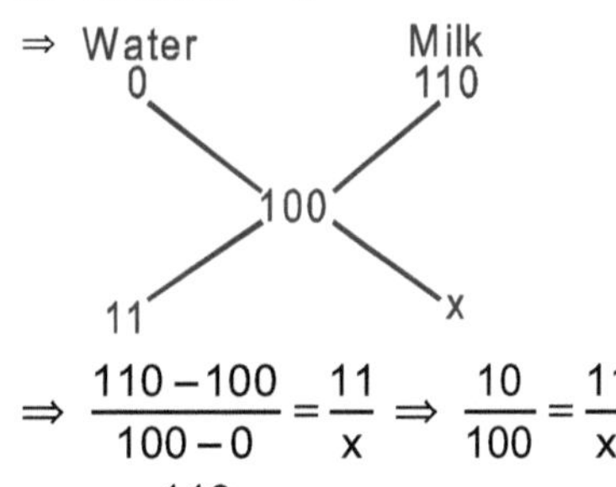

$$\Rightarrow \dfrac{110-100}{100-0} = \dfrac{11}{x} \Rightarrow \dfrac{10}{100} = \dfrac{11}{x}$$

$$\Rightarrow x = 110$$

thus quantity of milk in mixture = 110 L.

Example 36:

Sheetal removed a certain quantity from a solution of 70% milk and replaced it by pure water. The concentration of the resulting mixture is now 60%. What fraction of milk did Sheetal remove?

Solution:

Pure water is 0% milk solution:

$\therefore$ Using alligation

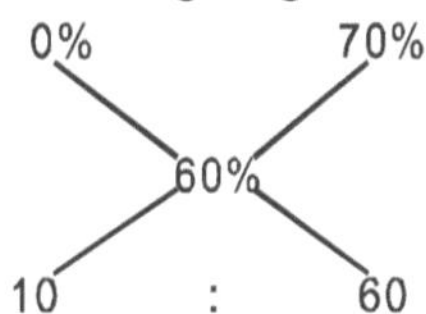

Thus, the ratio of water to that of original solution is = 1 : 6

Thus, fraction removed is $= \dfrac{1}{7}$

Example 37:

Rashmi has 40 cups. She sells some at a profit of 15% and the rest at a loss of 5%. She gains 10% on the entire transaction. What is the number of cups she sells at a profit of 15% ?

Solution:

Using alligation:

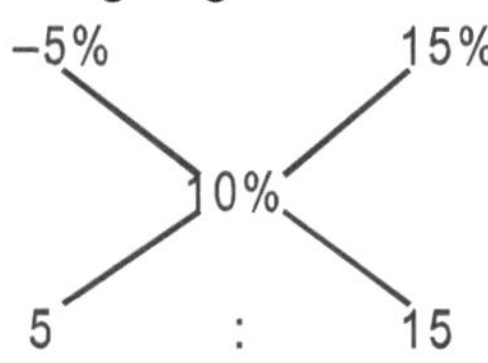

5% loss is represented as –5%

Ratio between the no. of cups sold at a loss to that sold at a profit = 5 : 15 = 1 : 3

$\therefore$ No. of cups sold at a profit = $\dfrac{3}{4} \times 40 = 30$ cups.

Example 38:

A man sells two cycles for Rs. 2100 and gains 5% in the transaction. He incurs a loss of 3% on one and a profit of 7% on the other. Find the cost of each cycle.

Solution:

Total CP of both the cycles is to be found out.

$$\dfrac{SP - CP}{CP} = \dfrac{5}{100} = \dfrac{1}{20} ;$$

$$SP = \left(\dfrac{1}{20} + 1\right) CP$$

or $CP = \dfrac{20}{21} \times 2100 = Rs. 2000$

Using alligation:

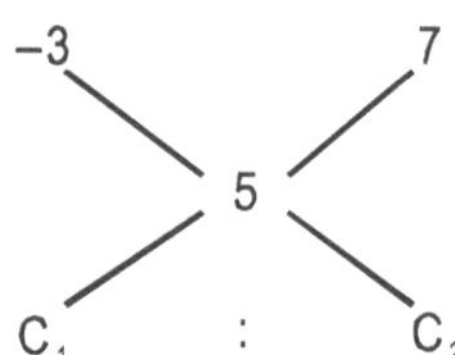

C_1 and C_2 are the cost prices of the cycles.

$$\therefore C_1 : C_2 = \dfrac{7 - 5}{5 + 3} = 1 : 4$$

$$\Rightarrow C_1 = \dfrac{1}{5} \times 2000 = Rs. 400$$

and $C_2 = \dfrac{4}{5} \times 2000 = Rs. 1600$

Example 39:

A property dealer purchases two flats for Rs. 60 lakhs. He sells one at a loss of 5% and the other at a gain 10%. He looses 10% in the entire transaction. What is the cost of each flat?

Solution:

Using alligation:

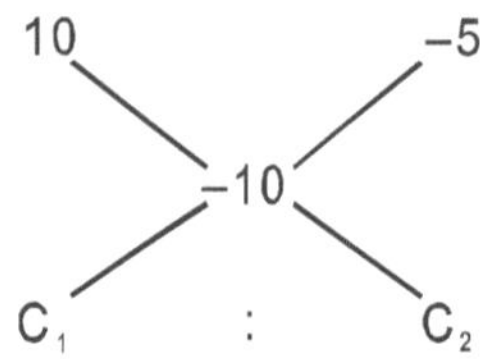

C_1 and C_2 are the cost of each flat.

$$\because \dfrac{C_1}{C_2} = \dfrac{-5 + 10}{10 + 10} = \dfrac{5}{20} = \dfrac{1}{4}$$

$$\Rightarrow C_1 = \dfrac{1}{5} \times 60,00,000$$

= Rs. 12 lakhs and C_2 = 48 lakhs.

Removal and Replacement by equal amounts

Consider a vessel that contains 100 L of milk and contains no other ingredient. Let us remove 5 L of the vessel's content and replace it by 5 L of water. After the operation, the total volume of the vessel's contents is still the same i.e. 100 L but the quantity of milk in the vessel is only 95 L. Let us replace 5 L of the vessel's contents by 5 L of water, one more time. When we remove 5 L content from the vessel this time, what quantity of milk do we remove? Is it still 5 L? No! In the solution, the ratio of milk was 19 : 20 (out of 100 L, 95 L was milk.).In every sample (5 L or 10 L or 20 L or 100 L) of this solution, milk will be in this ratio only. Hence, when we remove 5 L of this solution from the vessel, we effectively remove only 4.75 L of milk. After the second removal and replacement, the ratio of milk, in the 100 L solution, is 361 : 400.

Similar operations can be carried out, in succession. After every such operation, the ratio of milk, in the 100 L solution, will keep changing. Calculation of the ratio of milk at the end of 2 or 3 or 4 such operations, in succession, is not very difficult. To calculate the ratio of milk at the end of 100 or 1000 such operation, in succession, is not an easy job.

Fortunately, we have a general formula for this and the following table 'derives' the same. We can generalize,

Quantity of milk, after the nth operation $= \dfrac{(100 - 5)^n}{100^{n-1}}$

$$\Rightarrow \dfrac{\text{amount of milk left in the vessel}}{\text{original amount of milk in the vessel}}$$

$$= \dfrac{(100-5)^n}{100^n} = \left(\dfrac{100-5}{100}\right)^n$$

We can further generalize this result. Let the vessel initially contained x units of an ingredient X and let in n successive operations, y units of the vessel's contents are replaced by y units of some other ingredient, Y. Then,

Quantity of the ingredient X in the vessel, after the nth operation

$$= \dfrac{(x-y)^n}{x^{n-1}} \text{ And,}$$

$$\dfrac{\text{Quantity of ingredient X left in the vessel}}{\text{Original quantity of the ingrdient X in the vessel}}$$

$$= \dfrac{(x-y)^n}{x^n} = \left(\dfrac{x-y}{x}\right)^n$$

Example 40:

A container contains 100 kg of milk. From this container 10 kg of milk was taken out and replaced by water. This process was further repeated three times. How much milk does the container have now?

Solution:

Amount of liquid left after n operations, when the container originally contains 'a' units of liquid from which 'b' units are taken out each time and replaced

$$= a \times \left\{ \left(\dfrac{a-b}{a}\right)^n \right\} \text{ units} = 100\left(\dfrac{100-10}{100}\right)^4 \text{ kg}$$

$$= 100 \times \dfrac{9}{10} \times \dfrac{9}{10} \times \dfrac{9}{10} \times \dfrac{9}{10} = 65.61 \text{ kg}$$

Example 41:

A vessel contains 10 L of milk. First, 2L of the vessel's contents are removed and replaced by 2L of water. Subsequently, 4L of vessel's contents are removed and replaced by 4L of water. Finally, 6L of vessel's contents are removed and replaced by 6L of water. What is the amount of milk left in the vessel?

Solution:

The following table shows the quantities of milk and water:

	Milk (in L)	Water (in L)
Initial	10	0
After the first removal and replacement	(10 −2) = 8	2
After the second removal and replacement	$\left(8-\dfrac{4}{5}\times 4\right)=\dfrac{24}{5}$	$\left(2-\dfrac{1}{5}\times 4\right)+4=\dfrac{26}{5}$
After the third removal and replacement	$\left(\dfrac{24}{5}-\dfrac{12}{25}\times 6\right)=\dfrac{48}{25}$	$\left(\dfrac{26}{5}-\dfrac{13}{25}\times 6\right)+6=\dfrac{202}{25}$

As clear from the table, the amount of milk left in the vessel is $\dfrac{48}{25}=1.92$ L

Example 42:

A vessel contained a 10L mixture of milk and water. First, 1L of the vessel's contents are removed and replaced by 1L of water. Subsequently, 2L of vessel's contents are removed and replaced by 2L of water. Finally, 3L of vessel's contents are removed and replaced by 3L of water. If the ratio of milk and water in the final solution is 1 : 1, then what was the ratio of milk and water in the original solution?

Solution:

Let the initial amount of milk and water be 10x and (10 – 10x) respectively. The following table shows the quantities of milk and water:

	Milk (in liters)	Water (in liters)
Initial	10x	10 – 10x
After the first removal and replacement	10x – 1 × x = 9x	10 – 9x
After the second removal and replacement	$9x-2\times\dfrac{9}{10}x=\dfrac{36}{5}x$	$10-\dfrac{36}{5}x$
After the third removal and replacement	$\dfrac{36}{5}x-3\times\dfrac{18}{25}x=\dfrac{126}{25}x$	$10-\dfrac{126}{25}x$

As clear from the table, the ratio of milk and water in the final solution is $\dfrac{126x}{250-126x}=1$.

$$\Rightarrow x = \dfrac{125}{126}.$$

Exercise

Exercise – I

1. A : B = 3 : 7 and the sum of A and B is 45. Find the value of B.
    (1) 28   (2) 33.5
    (3) 31.5   (4) 36

2. A fraction bears the same ratio to $\dfrac{3}{7}$ as $\dfrac{1}{27}$ does to $\dfrac{1}{35}$. Find the fraction.

    (1) $\dfrac{4}{9}$ (2) $\dfrac{1}{3}$ (3) $\dfrac{3}{5}$ (4) $\dfrac{5}{9}$

3. Mean proportional between 8 and 72 is
    (1) 24   (2) 40
    (3) 16   (4) 32

4. Fourth proportional to 3, 15 and 27 is
    (1) 39   (2) 135
    (3) 81   (4) 45

5. Third proportional to 20 and 30 is
    (1) 40   (2) 55
    (3) 60   (4) 45

6. What must be added to each term of the fraction $\dfrac{4}{9}$, so that it becomes $\dfrac{2}{3}$?
    (1) 1   (2) 6
    (3) 11   (4) 16

7. The ratio of $4^{3.5} : 2^5$ is same as:
    (1) 2 : 1   (2) 4 : 1
    (3) 7 : 5   (4) 7 : 10

8. If X and Y shared in the ratio of 2 : 7, what is the ratio of X's share to the difference between Y's & X's shares?
    (1) 2 : 7   (2) 4 : 10
    (3) 2 : 5   (4) 2 : 9

9. What must be subtracted from each term of the ratio 68 : 49 so that it becomes 3 : 4?
    (1) –125   (2) 0
    (3) 5   (4) 125

10. Rs. 3,960 is divided among A, B and C such that half of A's part, one third of B's part and $\dfrac{1}{6}$ th s of C's part are equal. Then B's part is
    (1) Rs. 1,080   (2) Rs. 960
    (3) Rs. 1,720   (4) Rs. 1,540

11. In question number 10 above, what is the ratio of A's share to the difference of B and C?
    (1) 2 : 9   (2) 2 : 5
    (3) 4 : 5   (4) 2 : 3

12. Two numbers are in the ratio of 5 : 3. If 9 is subtracted from both of them, the ratio becomes 23 : 12. The first number is:
    (1) 52   (2) 53
    (3) 55   (4) 54

13. If 4x = 3y = 2z, then x : y : z is
    (1) 4 : 3 : 2   (2) 2 : 3 : 4
    (3) 3 : 4 : 2   (4) 3 : 4: 6

14. In a ratio equal to 4 : 9, the antecedent is 36, the consequent is:
    (1) 79   (2) 16
    (3) 72   (4) 81

15. In a mixture of 100 L, the ratio of milk and water is 3 : 1. If 200 L of water is added in the mixture, what will be the new ratio of milk and water?
    (1) 1 : 3   (2) 3 : 1
    (3) 2 : 5   (4) 5 : 2

16. If $\dfrac{a}{3} = \dfrac{b}{4} = \dfrac{c}{7}$ then, $\dfrac{(a+b+c)}{c}$ is:
    (1) 7   (2) 2
    (3) $\dfrac{1}{2}$ (4) $\dfrac{1}{7}$

17. Two whole numbers whose sum is 84 cannot be in the ratio of:
    (1) 9 : 3   (2) 3 : 5
    (3) 19 : 2   (4) 2 : 19

18. It is given that 0.35 part of a number is equal to 0.07 part of another number. The ratio of the two numbers is:
(1) 1 : 2
(2) 1 : 5
(3) 2 : 1
(4) 1 : 4

19. A box containing a dozen ceramic mugs is dropped. Some of the mugs broke. Which of the following cannot be the ratio of broken and unbroken mugs?
(1) 2 : 1
(2) 5 : 7
(3) 7 : 5
(4) 3 : 2

20. If $(a + b) : (b + c) : (c + a) = 6 : 7 : 8$ and $(a + b + c) = 14$, then the value of c is:
(1) 6
(2) 7
(3) 8
(4) 14

21. The ratio of third proportional to 12 and 30 and the mean proportional between 9 and 25 is:
(1) 2 : 1
(2) 5 : 1
(3) 7 : 15
(4) 9 : 14

22. The ratio of A's money to that of B's money is 4 : 5 and B's money to C's money is 2 : 3. If A has Rs. 800, then total amount of money among A, B and C is:
(1) Rs. 2,790
(2) Rs. 3,300
(3) Rs. 3,000
(4) Rs. 3,620

23. The number 68 is divided into two parts such that one-seventh part of the first is equal to one-tenth part of the second. Find the first part.
(1) 7
(2) 22
(3) 28
(4) 32

24. Rs. 9,700 has been divided among X, Y and Z such that if their shares are reduced respectively by Rs. 30, Rs. 20 and Rs. 50, the balances are in the ratio of 3 : 4 : 5. What is Y's share?
(1) Rs. 3,180
(2) Rs. 3,220
(3) Rs. 3,253.33
(4) Rs. 3,200

25. The sides of a triangle are in the ratio of $\frac{1}{2} : \frac{1}{3} : \frac{1}{4}$ and its perimeter is 104 cm. The length of the longest side is:
(1) 52 cm
(2) 48 cm
(3) 32 cm
(4) 26 cm

Exercise – 2

1. The sum of Rs. 530 is divided among A, B and C such that A gets Rs. 70 more than B and B gets Rs. 80 more than C. What is the ratio of the amount with A and C?
(1) 25 : 18
(2) 18 : 10
(3) 9 : 5
(4) 5 : 2

2. An amount of money is distributed amongst A, B and C such that A gets half that of B and B gets twice that of C. What is the ratio between the share of B to that of the sum of the shares of A and B ?
(1) 2 : 5
(2) 2 : 3
(3) 3 : 2
(4) 4 : 3

3. In a class of 500 students, the number of boys equals the number of girls. If $\frac{1}{5}$th of the girls left the class and 25 boys joined in, what is the ratio of the number of boys to the number of girls, now?
(1) 3 : 2
(2) 12 : 7
(3) 11 : 8
(4) 9 : 8

4. The present ages of a man and his son are in the ratio of 7 : 2. After 15 years, their ages would be in the ratio of 2 : 1. What was father's age when the son was born?
(1) 25
(2) 30
(3) 35
(4) 42

5. Four years ago, a man's age was 6 times that of his son. 12 yrs from now, his age will be twice that of the son. What is the ratio of their present ages?
(1) 6 : 1
(2) 7 : 1
(3) 8 : 2
(4) 7 : 2

6. The ages of A and B are in the ratio of 3 : 1. Fifteen years hence, the ratio will be 2 : 1. Their present ages are:
(1) 30 years, 10 years
(2) 45 years, 15 years
(3) 21 years, 7 years
(4) 60 years, 20 years

7. In 80 L mixture of milk and water, milk and water are in the ratio of 5 : 3. If 16 L of this mixture is replaced by 16 L of milk then the ratio of milk and water in the resulting mixture becomes:
(1) 2 : 1
(2) 6 : 3
(3) 7 : 3
(4) 8 : 3

8. Brass is an alloy of copper and zinc and has no other metal in it. In a sample of brass, copper and zinc are in the ratio of 13:7. How much copper will be there in a 500 kg sample of this alloy?
(1) 300 kg
(2) 325 kg
(3) 175 kg
(4) 150 kg

9. The numerator and the denominator of a rational number differ by 40 and its simplest form is $\frac{2}{7}$. What is the number?
(1) $\frac{8}{48}$
(2) $\frac{56}{16}$
(3) $\frac{20}{60}$
(4) $\frac{16}{56}$

10. A sum of money is divided among A, B and C in such a manner that for each one rupee that A gets, B gets 65 paise and C gets 35 paise. If C's share is Rs. 560, the sum is:
(1) Rs. 2,400
(2) Rs. 2,800
(3) Rs. 3,200
(4) Rs. 3,800

11. The manufacturing cost of a product involves only the expenses on Labour (L), the raw material costs (R), and the overheads cost (O). If L:R:O is equal to 5:7:3 and the product is sold at 20% profit then what is the ratio of the raw material costs to the profit?
(1) 5 : 2
(2) 10 : 3
(3) 3 : 5
(4) 7 : 3

12. The ratio of boys and girls in a class of 72 is 7 : 5. How many more girls should be admitted to make the number of boys and girl equal?
(1) 9
(2) 12
(3) 220
(4) 240

13. The income's of A and B are in the ratio of 3 : 2 and their expenses are in the ratio of 5 : 3. If each of them saves Rs. 3000, then B's income is:
(1) Rs. 10,000
(2) Rs. 6,000
(3) Rs. 9,000
(4) Rs. 12,000

14. What must be added to each term of 7 : 19 such that they are in the same ratio as 20 to 40?
(1) 5
(2) 7
(3) 11
(4) 12

15. In a school, 10% of total no. of boys are equal to $\frac{1}{4}$th of the girls. What is the ratio of boys to girls in that school?
(1) 3 : 2
(2) 5 : 2
(3) 2 : 1
(4) 4 : 3

16. If it is given that x varies inversely as the square of y and that y = 2 for x = 1, then the value of x for y = 6 will be:
(1) 3
(2) 9
(3) $\frac{1}{3}$
(4) $\frac{1}{9}$

17. The compounded ratios of (2 : 3), (6 : 11) and (11 : 2) is:
(1) 1 : 2
(2) 2 : 1
(3) 11 : 24
(4) 36 : 121

18. Ratio of the earnings of A and B is 4 : 7. If the earnings of A increases by 50% and those of B decrease by 25%, the new ratio of their earnings become 8 : 7. What is A's earning?
(1) Rs 21,000
(2) Rs 26,000
(3) Rs 28,000
(4) Data Inadequate

19. The average age of three boys is 25 years and their ages are in the proportion of 3 : 5 : 7. The age of the youngest boy is:
(1) 21 years
(2) 18 years
(3) 15 years
(4) 9 years

20. The value of a diamond varies directly as the square of its weight. If a diamond worth Rs. 10,000 is divided into 2 pieces having weight in the ratio of 4 : 6, what is the loss in value?
(1) 52%
(2) 48%
(3) 36%
(4) None of these.

21. A bag contains 50p, 25p and 10p coins in the ratio of 5 : 9 : 4, amounting to Rs 206. Find the number of 50p coins.
(1) 100
(2) 125
(3) 150
(4) 200

22. Find x : y : z, if 2x + y – 5z = 0 and 3x – 2y – 4z = 0
(1) 1 : 2 : 1
(2) 1 : 1 : 1
(3) 1 : 1 : 2
(4) 2 : 1 : 1

23. The volume of a sphere varies directly as the cube of its radius. If three cubes of radius 3cm, 4cm and 5cm are melted and recast into a solid sphere, then find the radius of the sphere.
(1) 5.5 cm
(2) 6 cm
(3) 7 cm
(4) 7.5 cm

24. The cost of digging a mine 'd' ft deep has two parts. One of the parts varies directly as d and other part varies directly as d^2. If the cost of digging two mines 10ft and 15ft deep are Rs 2,050 and Rs 4,575 respectively, then find the cost of digging a mine 20ft deep.
(1) Rs 5,800
(2) Rs 6,075
(3) Rs 8,100
(4) Rs 10,100

25. A writer gets a fixed amount for his book apart from the royalty that he gets per book sold. He gets Rs 30,000 and Rs 50,000 for 1000 and 2000 books sold respectively. What is his income per book, if 5000 books are sold?
(1) Rs 17
(2) Rs 20
(3) Rs 21
(4) Rs 22.

Exercise – 3

1. The average of first nine prime numbers is:
(1) 9
(2) 11
(3) $11\dfrac{1}{9}$
(4) $11\dfrac{2}{9}$

2. The average of 2, 7, 6 and x is 5 and the average of 18, 1, 6, x and y is 10. What is the value of y?
(1) 5
(2) 10
(3) 20
(4) 30

3. The average age of the boys in the class is 16 years and that of the girls is 15 years. The average age for the whole class is:
(1) 15 years
(2) 15.5 years
(3) 16 years
(4) Cannot be determined

4. The average score of a cricketer for ten matches is 38.9 runs. If the average score for the first six matches is 42 runs, then find the average for the last four matches.
(1) 33.25
(2) 33.5
(3) 34.25
(4) 35

5. The average of five numbers is 27. If one number is excluded, the average becomes 25. The excluded number is:
(1) 25
(2) 27
(3) 30
(4) 35

6. The average of 9 numbers is 20. If the average of first 5 numbers is 18 and that of last 5 numbers is 23, then the middle number is:
(1) 20
(2) 25
(3) 30
(4) Cannot be determined

7. The average of the two digit numbers, which remain the same when the digits interchange their positions is:
(1) 33
(2) 44
(3) 55
(4) 66

8. The average weight of 16 boys in a class is 50.25 kg and that of the remaining 8 boys is 45.15 kg. Find the average weight of all the boys in the class.
(1) 47.55 kg
(2) 48 kg
(3) 48.55 kg
(4) 49.25 kg

9. The average of four numbers is 60. If the first number is one-fourth of the sum of the last three numbers, then the first number is:
(1) 15
(2) 45
(3) 48
(4) 60.25

10. The average of ten numbers is 7. Each number is multiplied by 12, then 6 is added to each number. At last each number is divided by 15, then the average of new set of numbers is:
(1) 6
(2) 9
(3) 10
(4) 15

11. If the mean of a, b, c is M and ab + bc + ca = 0, then the mean of a^2, b^2, c^2 is:
(1) M^2
(2) $3M^2$
(3) $6M^2$
(4) $9M^2$

12. If the mean of 5 observations x, (x + 2), (x + 4), (x + 6) and (x + 8) is 11, then the mean of the last three observations is:
(1) 11
(2) 13
(3) 15
(4) 17

13. The average weight of A, B and C is 45 kg. If the average weight of A and B be 40 kg and that of B and C be 43 kg, then the weight of B is:
(1) 17 kg
(2) 20 kg
(3) 26 kg
(4) 31 kg

14. Three years ago, the average age of a family of 5 members was 17 years. A baby was born, but the average age of the family is still the same today. The present age of the baby is:

(1) 1 year
(2) $1\frac{1}{2}$ years
(3) 2 years
(4) 3 years

15. The average age of 8 men is increased by 2 years when two of them whose ages are 21 years and 23 years are replaced by two new men. The average age of the two new then is:
(1) 22 years
(2) 24 years
(3) 28 years
(4) 30 years

16. The average salary of all the workers in a workshop is Rs. 8000. The average salary of 7 technicians is Rs. 12000 and the average salary of the rest is Rs. 6000. The total number of workers in the workshop is:
(1) 20
(2) 21
(3) 22
(4) 23

17. The average weight of a class of 24 students is 35 kg. If the weight of the teacher be included, the average rises by 400 g. The weight of the teacher is:
(1) 45 kg
(2) 50 kg
(3) 53 kg
(4) 55 kg

18. A pupil's marks were wrongly entered as 83 instead of 63. Due to that the average marks for the class got increased by half. The number of pupils in the class is:
(1) 10
(2) 20
(3) 40
(4) 73

19. Average of ten positive numbers is $\overline{x}$. If each number is increased by 15% , then $\overline{x}$:
(1) remains unchanged
(2) decreases
(3) increases by 10%
(4) increases by 15%

20. Of the three numbers, the first is twice the second and the second is twice the third. The average of the reciprocal of the numbers is $\frac{7}{72}$. The numbers are:
(1) 16, 8, 4
(2) 20, 10, 5
(3) 24, 12, 6
(4) 36, 18, 9

Exercise – 4

1. In two different alloys containing copper and iron, the ratios of copper and iron are 5 : 8 and 5 : 3. Equal quantities of the two alloys are melted to form a third alloy. What is the ratio of copper and iron in the third alloy?
(1) 103 : 105
(2) 15 : 24
(3) 3 : 8
(4) 105 : 103

2. A dealer mixes three varieties of rice costing Rs. 20 per kg, Rs. 26 per kg and Rs. 30 per kg such that the mean price of the mixture is Rs. 25 per kg. If the mixture contains 2 kg of the third variety and 3 kg of the first variety, how much quantity of the second variety does it contain?
(1) 2 kg
(2) 5 kg
(3) 3 kg
(4) 10 kg

3. A trader mixes three qualities of sugar costing Rs. 15 per kg, Rs 18 per kg and Rs 22 per kg and sells it at a price of Rs 22 per kg making a profit of 10%. If the mixture contains 4 kgs of the first quality of sugar, then find the difference between the amount of second quality of sugar and the third quality of sugar in the mixture.
(1) 20 kg
(2) 10 kg
(3) 3 kg
(4) 4 kg

4. Ayan mixes three varieties of salts costing Rs. 15 per kg, Rs 18 per kg and Rs 20 per kg and sells the mixture at Rs 8 per kg and there by incurring a loss of 50%. If the mixture contains 6 kg of the first variety, then find the quantity of second and third variety of salt in the mixture, if both of them are integral multiple of a kg.
(1) 1 kg, 1 kg
(2) 1 kg, 2 kg
(3) 2 kg, 1 kg
(4) 2 kg, 3 kg

5. Ayan mixes three varieties of tea costing Rs. 20 per kg, Rs 30 per kg and Rs 24 per kg and sells it at Rs 30 per kg making a profit of 20%. If the mixture contains 1 kg of the first variety, then the quantity of the second and third variety can never be
(1) 2 kg, 5 kg
(2) 4 kg, 15 kg
(3) 6 kg, 25 kg
(4) 7 kg, 30 kg

6. Three mixtures containing water and alcohol in the ratio of 5 : 2, 6 : 1 and 4 : 3 are mixed in equal quantities. The ratio of water to alcohol in the resulting mixture is:
(1) 5 : 2
(2) 7 : 3
(3) 6 : 4
(4) 7 : 4

7. Three mixtures containing milk and water in the ratio of 5 : 1, 2 : 1 and 3 : 1 are mixed in the ratio of 1 : 2 : 3. The ratio of milk to water in the resulting mixture is:
(1) 3 : 1
(2) 2 : 1
(3) 4 : 3
(4) None of these

8. Two alloys containing copper and nickel in the ratio of 2 : 3 and 7 : 3 are melted and mixed in the ratio of 2 : 1 to get a new alloy. Find the ratio of copper to nickel in the new alloy.
(1) 1 : 2
(2) 1 : 1
(3) 3 : 2
(4) 2 : 5

9. Sugar at the rate of Rs 15 per kg is mixed with sugar at the rate of Rs 20 per kg in the ratio of 2 : 3. Find the price per kg of the mixture.
(1) Rs 18
(2) Rs 16
(3) Rs 17
(4) Rs 19

10. A man has whisky worth Rs 22 per L and another lot worth Rs 18 per L. Equal quantities of these are mixed with water to obtain a mixture of 50 L worth Rs 16 a litre. Find how much water the mixture contains.
(1) 5 L
(2) 10 L
(3) 15 L
(4) 20 L

11. A mixture of a certain quantity of wine with 20 L of water is worth Rs 90 per litre. If pure wine be worth Rs 108 per litres, how much wine is there in the mixture?
(1) 120 L
(2) 75 L
(3) 50 L
(4) 100 L

12. In what proportion must water be mixed with spirit to gain $16\frac{2}{3}\%$ by selling it at cost price?
(1) 1 : 7
(2) 1 : 6
(3) 1 : 5
(4) None of these.

13. A person has a chemical worth Rs 25 per litre. In what ratio should water be mixed with that chemical so that after selling the mixture at Rs 20 per litre he may get a profit of 25%.
(1) 1:4
(2) 4:1
(3) 16:9
(4) 9:16

14. There are 65 students in a class, Rs. 39 are distributed among them in such a manner that each boy gets 80 paise and each girl gets 30 paise. Find the number of boys in that class.
(1) 26
(2) 39
(3) 40
(4) 25

15. A trader has 50 kg of pulses, part of which he sells at 8% profit and the rest at 18% profit. He gains 14% on the whole. What is the quantity sold at 18% profit ?
(1) 20 kg
(2) 30 kg
(3) 40 kg
(4) 10 kg

16. There/were some rabbits and pigeons in a zoo. The number of heads and legs, when counted/were zoo and 580 respectively. How many pigeons were there?
(1) 110
(2) 90
(3) 80
(4) 70

17. A jar contains a mixture of two liquids A and B in the ratio of 4 : 1. When 10 L of the mixture is replaced with equal amount of liquid B the ratio becomes 2 : 3. How many litres of liquid A was contained in the jar?
(1) 12 L
(2) 20 L
(3) 16 L
(4) Data Insufficient

18. Weights of two friends Ram and Shyam are in the ratio of 4 : 5. Ram's weight increases by 10% and the total weight of Ram and Shyam together becomes 82.8 kg, with an increase of 15%. By what percent did the weight of Shyam increase ?
(1) 12%
(2) 16%
(3) 20%
(4) 19%

19. How much water must be added to a cask which contains 40 L of milk at the rate of Rs. 3.5 per L so that the cost of milk reduces to Rs 2 per L?
(1) 25 L
(2) 30 L
(3) 35 L
(4) None of these.

20. Parul purchased 150 kg of wheat at the rate of Rs 7 per kg. She sold 50 kg at a profit of 10%. At what rate should she sell the remaining wheat to get a profit of 20% on the total deal ?
(1) Rs 7.50
(2) Rs 7.70
(3) Rs 8.75
(4) Rs 8.50

Percentages

Percentages is one of the most commonly used mathematical concepts in real life. This is a simple concept with various applications. Hence, you are expected to be absolutely comfortable with this concept. In order to increase your comfort levels, you will do well to keep calculating percentages mentally, whenever you get an opportunity to do so in real life.

Percent of a number

Percent mean, per 100. Here "cent" stands for 100.
To find the percent of a number, convert the percent into fraction and multiply the resulting fraction with the number,

e.g. 60% of $500 = \dfrac{60}{100} \times 500 = 300$

Example 1:
Express 30 as a percent of 45.

Solution:

$$\left(\dfrac{30}{45}\right) \times 100 = 66.67\%$$

Example 2:
Find 40% of 3340.

Solution:

$$\left(\dfrac{40}{100}\right) \times 3340 = 1336$$

Conversion of a fraction or a decimal into a percent

A fraction or a decimal can be converted into a percentage by simply multiplying it by 100.

So, the fraction $\dfrac{1}{5}$ expressed as a percentage is

$\dfrac{1}{5} \times 100 = 20\%$
And the decimal 0.05 expressed as a percentage is 0.05 × 100 = 5%

Converting a percentage into a fraction

A percentage when divided by 100 is converted into a fraction. So, 20% as a fraction is $\dfrac{20}{100} = \dfrac{1}{5}$.

The % sign is dropped when we divide the percentage by 100.

Example 3:
Express 40% in decimal terms.

Solution:

$$40\% = \dfrac{40}{100} = 0.4$$

Fraction of a number

To determine the fraction of a number we multiply the fraction and the number. Therefore,

$\dfrac{1}{4}$ th of 20 is $\dfrac{1}{4} \times 20 = 5$; $\dfrac{1}{3}$ rd of 33 is $\dfrac{1}{3} \times 33 = 11$, etc.

Fraction of a fraction and Relative Percentage

To find the fraction of a fraction we multiply both the fractions.

For example $\dfrac{1}{4}$ th of $\dfrac{1}{5}$ th is nothing but

$\dfrac{1}{4} \times \dfrac{1}{5} = \dfrac{1}{20}$ and $\dfrac{1}{3}$ rd of $\dfrac{3}{5}$ th is $\dfrac{1}{5}$ etc.

Similarly, 25% of 20% is $\dfrac{25}{100} \times 20\% = 5\%$

which is equivalent to 20% of 25%,

i.e. $\dfrac{20}{100} \times 25\% = 5\%$

Reciprocal Percentage Equivalent:

Tables can take care of multiplications encountered. But if one has to develop speed in division, where the real tediousness lies, reciprocal percentage equivalent are an absolute must. The following may help you in memorizing the reciprocal equivalents.

If reciprocal of 2 is 50%, that of 4 will be half of 50% i.e. 25%. Similarly, reciprocal of 8 be half of 25% i.e. 12.5% and that of 16 will be 6.25%.

Reciprocal of 3 is 33.33%. Thus reciprocal of 6 and 9 will 16.66% and 11.11% respectively.

Reciprocal of 9 is 11.11 and reciprocal of 11 is 09.090909. Reciprocal of 9 is composed of 11s and reciprocal of 11 is composed of 09s.

Reciprocal of 20 is 5%. Reciprocal of 21 is 4.75% and of 19 is 5.25%. Thus we can easily remember reciprocals of 19, 20, 21 as 5.25%, 5, 4.75% i.e. 0.25% more and less than 5%

Similarly, reciprocal of 25 is 4%. Reciprocal of 24 is 4.16% and of 26 is 3.84%. Thus we can easily remember reciprocals of 24, 25, 26 as 4.15%, 4, 3.85% i.e. 0.15% more and less than 4%

Reciprocal of 29 is 3.45% (i.e. 345 in order) and reciprocal of 23 is 4.35% (same digits but order is different)

Reciprocal of 22 is half of 09.0909% i.e 4.545454% i.e consists of 45s

Reciprocal of 18 is half of 11.1111% i.e. 5.55555% i.e. consists of only 5s

Thus the work may seem to be a huge task, but if one uses a smart approach, it is hardly anything.

If any calculation has 9 in the denominator, the decimal part will be only 0909.. or 1818… or 2727… or 3636…e.g.

$\dfrac{84}{9}$ will be 9.272727 can be found out in a jiffy

One can also calculate any fraction of the type $\dfrac{(n-1)}{n}$ $(n \le 30)$ within a second if one knows the reciprocal percentage equivalent. E.g. $\dfrac{11}{12}$ will be nothing but $1 - \dfrac{1}{12}$ i.e. the complement of 0.08333 which is 0.91666. Similarly if I know $\dfrac{1}{23}$ is 0.0435, $\dfrac{22}{23}$ will be 0.9565.

Other Fraction Percentage Equivalents:

Knowing the reciprocal percentage equivalents is just a qualifying criteria. To gain a competitive advantage one needs to go beyond. One also needs to remember tables of $\dfrac{1}{8}$ (or of 12.5) and $\dfrac{1}{12}$ (or of 8.33).

$\dfrac{1}{8}$ is 12.5%, $\dfrac{2}{8}$ is 25%, $\dfrac{3}{8}$ is 37.5%, ….. $\dfrac{5}{8}$ is 62.5%… $\dfrac{7}{8}$ is 87.5%

Lets say one has to find 37.5% of 128. This will be nothing but $\dfrac{3}{8}$ * 128 which is 48. And percentages like 37.5% and 62.5% are used very regularly.

Also tables of $\dfrac{1}{12}$ will help one find percentages like 83.33%, which is nothing but $\dfrac{5}{6}$ th.

Example 4:

A's income is 70% of B's income. B's income is 50% of C's income. If C's income is Rs. 1,00,000, what is A's income?

Solution:

$$\text{B's income} = \left(\dfrac{50}{100}\right) \times \text{Rs.100000} = \text{Rs. 50,000}$$

$$\text{A's income} = \left(\dfrac{70}{100}\right) \times \text{Rs. 50000} = \text{Rs. 35,000}$$

Alternative Method:

$$\text{B's income} = \dfrac{50}{100} \text{ of C's income}$$

$$\text{A's income} = \dfrac{70}{100} \text{ of B's income}$$

$$= \dfrac{70}{100} \times \dfrac{50}{100} \text{ of C's income}$$

$$\text{A's income} = \dfrac{35}{100} \times 100000 = \text{Rs.}\,35,000 \,.$$

Successive Percentage Changes

If a number is changed (increase/decrease) by a% and in the second step, this changed number is again changed(increase/decrease) by b%, then

$$\text{Net percent change} = \left[a + b + \dfrac{a \times b}{100} \right]\%$$

If a or b or both show decrease, then put a (–ve) sign before a and b, otherwise (+ ve) sign will remain.

Example 5:

If the price of an item is increased by 20% and then a discount of 10% is given on the increased price, what will be the effect on sale?

Solution:

$$\text{Using percent change} = \left[a + b + \dfrac{a \times b}{100} \right]\%$$

$$= 20 - 10 - \dfrac{20 \times 10}{100} = 8\% \text{ (increase)}$$

Example 6:

The number of seats in an auditorium is increased by 25%. The price on a ticket is also increased by 12%. What is the effect on the revenue collected?

Solution:

Let the initial number of seats be 100 and price per ticket be Re. 1

Then, Revenue = number of seats × price per ticket

Increased number of seats = $\dfrac{125}{100} \times 100 = 125$

Increased price of a ticket = $\dfrac{112}{100} \times 1 = $ Rs. 1.12

Increased revenue = 125 × 1.12 = Rs. 140

Percentage increase in revenue

$$= \left(\dfrac{140 - 100}{100}\right) \times 100 = 40\%$$

Short cut:

Using % increase $= a + b + \dfrac{a \times b}{100}$

∴ Percentage increase in revenue

$$= 25 + 12 + \dfrac{25 \times 12}{100} = 25 + 12 + 3 = 40\%.$$

Example 7:

The length of a rectangle is increased by 10%. What will be the percentage decrease in its breadth so as to have the same area?

Solution:

Let length and breadth of the rectangle be l and b respectively.

Area = lb

Increased length and breadth = l' and b'; Area = l'b'

$$l' = \dfrac{110}{100} l = \dfrac{11}{10} l \;\Rightarrow\; \dfrac{11}{10} lb' = lb \;\Rightarrow\; b' = \dfrac{10}{11} b$$

decrease in breadth = $b - b' = b - \dfrac{10}{11}b = \dfrac{1}{11}b$

Percentage decrease in breadth

$$= \dfrac{b}{11b} \times 100 = \dfrac{100}{11} = 9\dfrac{1}{11}\%$$

Short cut:

Applying percent change $= a + b + \dfrac{ab}{100}$

Let decrease in breadth be x%, then

$$0 = 10 - x - \dfrac{10 \times x}{100} \;\Rightarrow\; \dfrac{11x}{10} = 10$$

$$\Rightarrow\; x = \dfrac{100}{11} = 9\dfrac{1}{11}\%$$

Example 8:

If the side of a square is increased by 25%, then its area is increased by what percent?

Solution:

Let the side be 10 cm. Then the area will be 100 cm².

New side = 125% of 10 = 12.5 cm;

Area = $(12.5)^2$ = 156. 25

∴ Percentage increase in area = 56.25%

Short cut :

If x is the percentage increase in the side of a square, then increase in area is given by

$$x + x + \dfrac{x \times x}{100} = 2x + \dfrac{x^2}{100}$$

$$= 25 + 25 + \dfrac{25 \times 25}{100} = 56.25\%$$

Example 9:

Express 50 g as a percentage of 4 kg.

Solution:

$$\dfrac{50 \text{ gm}}{4 \text{ kg}} \times 100 = \left(\dfrac{50 \text{ gm}}{4000 \text{ gm}}\right) \times 100 = 1.25\%$$

Example 10:

X's income is 50% more than Y's. By how much percent is Y's income less than X's?

Solution:

Using formula, m = 50

$$= 33.33\%$$

Example 11:

In a market survey, 20% opted for product B. The remaining individuals were uncertain. If the difference between those who opted for product B and those who were uncertain was 720, then how many individuals were covered in the survey?

Solution:

Clearly, 80% were uncertain.

80% of x – 20% of x = 720

Or 60% of x = 720 or $\dfrac{60}{100} x = 720$ or x

$$= \dfrac{720 \times 100}{60} = 1200$$

You may encounter the following types of questions in the examination

Types of questions	Examples	Approach to the question
1. Convert x percentage into fraction.	Express 12% as a fraction.	$x\% = \dfrac{x}{100} = \dfrac{12}{100} = \dfrac{3}{25}$
2. Convert fraction or decimal into percentage.	Express $\dfrac{5}{11}$ as percentage.	Multiply the fraction by 100. $= \dfrac{5}{11} \times 100 = 45.45\%$
3. If A's income is x% of B's income and B's income is given, then find A's income.	A's income is 40% of B's income. If B's income is Rs. 10,000, what is A's income?	$A = \dfrac{x}{100} \times P$ $\dfrac{40}{100} \times 10000 = $ Rs. 4,000
4. If A's income is r% more than B's income, then by how much % is B's income less than A's income?	X's income is 25% more than Y's. By how much % is Y's income less than X's income?	Difference $= \dfrac{r}{100+r} \times 100$ $= \dfrac{25}{125} \times 100 = 20\%$
5. If A's income is r% less than B's income, then by how much % is B's income more than A's income?	X's income is 40% less than Y's. By how much % is Y's income more than X's income?	Difference $= \dfrac{r}{100-r} \times 100$ $= \dfrac{40}{60} \times 100 = 66.67\%$
6. If the price of a commodity increases by r%, find the % decrease in the consumption given that expenditure remains same.	If the price of potato is increased by 20%, by how much should the consumption be decreased so as to maintain the same expenditure?	Expenditure = Price × Consumption Decrease $= \dfrac{r}{100+r} \times 100$ $= \dfrac{20}{120} \times 100 = \dfrac{50}{3} = 16.67\%$
7. If price of one unit changes by a % and the number of units consumed changes by b%, then what is the % change in expenditure	If the price of potato is increased by 20% and consumption decreased by 10%, what will be the percentage change in expenditure?	Net change $= a + b + \dfrac{ab}{100}$ $= 20 - 10 - \dfrac{20 \times 10}{100} = 8\%$
8. If the population of a country increases in the first year and decrease next year.	The population of a town is 18000. It increases by 10% during first year and by 20% during the second year. The population after 2 years will be	$N_F = N \times \dfrac{100+x}{100} \times \dfrac{100+y}{100}$ $= 18000 \times \dfrac{110}{100} \times \dfrac{120}{100}$ $= 23760$ **Alternative method** Successive increments of 10% and 20% = 32%. Then, population will increase by 32% of 18000 = 5760 Population after 2 years will be 18000 + 5760 = 23760

Example 12:

Of the total amount received by Kiran, 20% was spent on purchases and 5% of the remaining on transportation. If he is left with Rs. 1520, the initial amount was

Solution:

Let 100 be the initial amount with Kiran. 20% is spent on purchases. Hence, we are left with 80%. Five percent of 80% is 4%. Hence, the remaining is 76%. We are given that the remaining is 1520. Here, 76% corresponds to 1520 and hence, 100%

corresponds to $\dfrac{100 \times 1520}{76} = 2000$.

Example 13:

5% of income of A is equal to 15% of income of B and 10% of income of B is equal to 20% of income of C. If income of C is Rs. 2,000, then total income of A, B, and C is

Solution:

$$\dfrac{5}{100}A = \dfrac{15}{100}B \text{ and } \dfrac{10}{100}B = \dfrac{20}{100}C$$

$\therefore$ A = 3B and B = 2C = 2 × 2000 = 4000

$\therefore$ A = 3 × 4000 = 12000

$\therefore$ A + B + C = (12000 + 4000 + 2000) = 18000

Example 14:

Arvind spends 75% of his income. His income is increased by 20% and he increases his expenditure by 10%. His savings are increased by how many percent?

Solution:

Let the income be 100. Expenditure = 75 and savings = 25; New income = 120

$$\text{New expenditure} = \left(\dfrac{110}{100} \times 75\right) = \dfrac{165}{2};$$

$$\text{New savings} = \left(120 - \dfrac{165}{2}\right) = \dfrac{75}{2}$$

$$\text{Increase in savings} = \left(\dfrac{75}{2} - 25\right) = \dfrac{25}{2};$$

$$\text{Percentage increase} = \left(\dfrac{25}{2} \times \dfrac{1}{25} \times 100\right) = 50\%$$

Example 15:

Two numbers are respectively 19% and 70% more than a third number. What percentage is the first number out of the second?

Solution:

Let the third number be 100.

Then, the first number is 100 + 19 = 119 and the second number is 170.

$\therefore$ The first is $\dfrac{119}{170} \times 100 = 70\%$ of the second.

Short cut:

First number is

$$\left(\dfrac{100+19}{100+70}\right) \times 100 = 70\% \text{ of the second.}$$

Example 16:

Salaries of A, B and C are in the ratio 1 : 2 : 3. Salary of B and C together is Rs. 6,000. By what percent is salary of C more than that of A?

Solution:

Let A = x; B = 2x and C = 3x

Then, 2x + 3x = 6000 $\Rightarrow$ x = 1200

$\therefore$ A = 1200 and C = 3600

$$\text{Required excess} = \left(\dfrac{2400}{1200} \times 100\right) = 200\%$$

Alternative Method:

If salary of A = x, then salary of C = 3x, hence, salary of C is 2x more than A, So, C is

$$\dfrac{2x}{x} \times 100 = 200\% \text{ more than A.}$$

Example 17:

A cricket team won 40% of the total number of matches it played during a year. If it lost 50% of the matches played and 20 matches were drawn, the total number of matches played by the team during the year was

Solution:

40% of x + 50% of x + 20 = x, where x = Total number of matches

$$\Rightarrow \dfrac{40}{100}x + \dfrac{50}{100}x + 20 = x \text{ or } x = 200$$

Profit, Loss and Discount

This is the other major application area for percentages. If you happen to be a shopping freak, this is a topic you must be glued into. This will enable you to be ahead of the shopkeeper and find out the real discount. Get your concepts right and you will be 'cash positive'.

Suppose that you are selling some article. You can sell that article at the price you bought, more than that or less than that, means in any such transaction three cases will arise.

   a. Cost price (C.P) > selling price (S.P.)
   b. Cost price (C.P) < selling price (S.P.)
   c. Cost price (C.P) = selling price (S.P.)

As a result either you will have profit (P) or loss (L) or no profit-no loss.

Profit or loss can be defined in two ways:

   a. In terms of absolute amount:
      Suppose that the C.P. of an article is Rs.200 and S.P. is Rs. 300. So profit is SP − CP = 300 − 200 = Rs. 100.

   b. In terms of percentage:
      Whenever you want to calculate profit or loss in terms of percentage, it is always calculated on the basis of C.P. In the above example the profit is Rs.100 on C.P. of Rs.200, so the profit percentage is 50%.

Marked price: The price which is marked or listed on / against the item is called the marked price. It may be more than or less than the S.P. or C.P.

Discount: Sometimes the shopkeeper gives a certain discount to attract the customers.

Discount can be expressed in two ways:

a. In terms of absolute number:
     For example, Purchase 5 trousers and get a trouser of same kind free.

b. In terms of percentage:
     For example,
     If you purchase 6 trousers, you will get 16.67% discount.
     The percentage discount is always calculated on the basis of M.P.

$$\text{Percentage Discount} = \frac{(\text{M.P.} - \text{S.P.})}{\text{M.P.}} \times 100$$

Formulae

1. Profit percentage

$$= \frac{(\text{S.P.} - \text{C.P.})}{\text{C.P.}} \times 100 = \frac{\text{Profit}}{\text{C.P.}} \times 100$$

$$= \left(\frac{\text{S.P.}}{\text{C.P.}} - 1\right) \times 100$$

2. Loss percentage

$$= \frac{(\text{C.P.} - \text{S.P.})}{\text{C.P.}} \times 100 = \frac{\text{Loss}}{\text{C.P.}} \times 100$$

$$= \left(1 - \frac{\text{S.P.}}{\text{C.P.}}\right) \times 100$$

3. $\text{S.P.} = \dfrac{(100 + \text{profit percentage} \times \text{C.P.})}{100}$

$$= \frac{(100 - \text{loss percentage}) \times \text{C.P.}}{100}$$

4. If marked price is M.P. and discount percentage is d, then

$$\text{S.P.} = \frac{\text{M.P.} (100 - d)}{100}; \quad \text{M.P.} = \frac{100 \times \text{S.P.}}{(100 - d)}$$

5. $\text{M.P} \xrightarrow{-\,\text{Discount}} \text{S.P.} \xleftarrow{+\,\text{Profit}} \text{C.P.}$

6. If 2 items are sold, each at Rs. X, one at a gain of P % and the other at a loss of P %, then overall loss percentage

$$= \frac{P^2}{100}\% \quad \text{and Loss (in rupees)} = \frac{2\,P^2 X}{100^2 - P^2}$$

Example 18:

A boy buys eggs at 10 for Rs. 1.80 and sells them at 11 for Rs. 2. What is his profit or loss percent?

Solution:

To avoid fractions, let the number of eggs purchased be
LCM of 10 and 11 = 110

$$\text{C.P. of 110 eggs} = \frac{110 \times 1.80}{10} = \text{Rs. 19.80}$$

$$\text{S.P. of 110 eggs} = \frac{110 \times 2.00}{11} = \text{Rs. 20.00}$$

$$\text{Profit percentage} = \frac{0.20 \times 100}{19.80} = 1.01\%$$

Example 19:

A woman buys apples at 15 for a rupee and the same number at 20 a rupee. She mixes and sells them at 35 for 2 rupees. What is her gain or loss percentage?

Solution:

Suppose the woman buys (LCM of 15, 20 and 35) 420 apples each at 15 apples a rupee and 20 apples a rupee.
Cost at the rate of 15 per rupee = Rs. 28
Cost at the rate of 20 per rupee = Rs. 21
Total cost for 840 apples   = Rs. 49

$$\text{S.P. for 840 apples} = \frac{840 \times 2}{35} = 48;$$

$$\text{Loss percentage} = \frac{(49 - 48) \times 100}{49} = 2.04\%$$

	Types of questions	Examples	Approach to the question
1.	If A sells to B at a profit of x%; B sells to C at a profit of y% and C pays Rs. P for it, find the cost for A.	A sells a cycle to B at a profit of 10%, B sells to C at a profit of 20%. If C pays Rs. 264 for it, how much did A pay for it?	$\text{C.P.}_A = \dfrac{100+x}{100} \times \dfrac{100+y}{100} \times P$ where x and y are the % profits or A and B, and P is the cost for C $\therefore \dfrac{110}{100} \times \dfrac{120}{100} \times P = 264$ P = Rs. 200
2.	If cost price of A articles is equal to the selling price of B articles, find the profit percentage.	The C.P. of 10 articles is equal to the S.P. of 9 articles. Find the profit percentage.	C.P. of 10 units = S.P. of 9 units = Rs. 90 (say) $\therefore$ C.P. of 1 unit = 9 S.P. of 1 unit = 10 $\therefore$ Profit % $= \dfrac{10-9}{9} = 11.11\%$ Alternatively, on selling 9 items, profit equal to C.P. of 1 item is made $\therefore$ Profit % $= \dfrac{1}{9} \times 100 = 11.11\%$
3.	The cost price of two articles is same. If one is sold at a X% profit and the other at a loss of X%, find the profit or loss percentage.	Amit buys 2 cows for Rs. 200 each. He sells one at a profit of 10% and the other at a loss of 10%. Find his profit or loss percentage.	For same cost price and equal profit and loss percentage, there is no profit or no loss.
4.	The selling price of two articles is same. If one is sold at X% profit and the other at loss of X%, find his profit or loss percentage.	Amit sells 2 cows for Rs. 200 each. On one he gets a profit of 10%, while losing 10% on the other. What is his overall profit or loss percentage?	Loss % $= \dfrac{X^2}{100}\% = \dfrac{10^2}{100} = 1\%$ $\text{S.P.} = \text{MP}\left(\dfrac{100-x}{100}\right) = \text{C.P.}\left(\dfrac{100+y}{100}\right)$
5.	If x% discount on an article is given on cash payment, find the percentage that should be marked above the cost price so as to make a profit of y%.	A dealer allows a discount of 7% for cash payment. How much percentage above the cost price should he mark his goods to make a profit of 10%.	$\therefore \dfrac{\text{MP}}{\text{C.P.}} = \dfrac{100+y}{100-x} = \dfrac{110}{93} = 1.182$ $\therefore \dfrac{\text{MP} - \text{C.P.}}{\text{C.P.}} = (1.182 - 1) \times 100 = 18.2\%$ **Alternatively,** $P = m - d - \dfrac{md}{100} \qquad \therefore 10 = m - 7 - 0.07\,m$ $\therefore m = \dfrac{17}{0.93} = 18.28$
6.	If a dealer sells goods at cost price but uses faulty weight, find his gain percentage.	A dishonest dealer professes to sell his goods at cost price, but he uses a weight of 960 g for 1 kg. Find his profit percentage.	$\text{Profit \%age} = \dfrac{x}{T-x} \times 100$ where x is the error and T is the true value. $\therefore \dfrac{40}{1000-40} \times 100 = 4.16\%$

Example 20:

A man bought 80 kg of rice for Rs. 88 and sold it at a loss of as much money as he received for 20 kg. At what price did he sell it?

Solution:

C.P. of 80 kg – S.P. of 80 kg = S.P. of 20 kg
S.P. of 100 kg = C.P. of 80 kg = 88
S.P. of 1 kg = 88 paise
He sold it at 88 paise per kg.

Example 21:

Goods are purchased for Rs. 450 and one-third is sold at a loss of 10%. At what profit percentage should the remainder be sold so as to gain 20% on the whole transaction?

Solution:

Total cost price of goods = Rs. 450

$$\text{S.P. of total goods} = \frac{120}{100} \times 450 = \text{Rs. } 540$$

$$\text{C.P. of one-third goods} = \frac{450}{3} = 150$$

$$\text{S.P. of one-third goods} = \frac{90}{100} \times 150 = \text{Rs. } 135$$

S.P. of remaining goods = (540 – 135) = Rs. 405
C.P. of remaining(two-third) goods = Rs. 300

$$\text{Hence, profit percentage} = \frac{405 - 300}{300} \times 100$$

$$= \frac{105}{300} \times 100 = 35\%$$

Alternative method:

Applying weighted average, in one-third of quantity there is a loss of 10% (or a profit of –10%) and the balance two-third gives a profit of x%.
Hence, overall profit is given by

$$\frac{1}{3}\,(-10\%) + \frac{2}{3}x = 20,$$

thus x = 35%.

Example 22:

A reduction of 10% in the price of sugar enables a man to buy 25 kg more for Rs. 225. What is the original price of sugar (per kg)?

Solution:

Let original price be x.

$$\text{Original quantity} = \frac{225}{x}$$

$$\text{New price} = 0.9x; \text{ New quantity.} = \frac{225}{0.9x}$$

$$\text{Equating } \frac{225}{0.9x} - \frac{225}{x} = 25 \Rightarrow x = \text{Re. } 1$$

Example 23:

A man sells an article at a profit of 25%. If he had bought it at 20% less and sold it for Rs. 10.50 less, he would have gained 30%. Find the C.P. of the article.

Solution:

Let C.P. = Rs. x ; S.P. = 1.25x
New C.P. = 0.8x ;   New S.P. = 1.25x – 10.50
But new S.P. = 130% of new C.P. = 1.3 x 0.8x
Therefore, 1.3 × 0.8x = 1.25x – 10.50
$\Rightarrow$ x = Rs. 50.

Example 24:

A vendor bought bananas at 6 for 5 rupees and sold at 4 for 3 rupees. Find his gain or loss percentage.

Solution:

Let number of bananas be 12(LCM of 6 and 4)

$$\text{Cost Price} = \frac{12}{6} \times 5 = \text{Rs. } 10$$

$$\text{Selling Price} = \frac{12}{4} \times 3 = \text{Rs. } 9$$

$$\text{Loss percentage} = \frac{1}{10} \times 100 = 10\%$$

Example 25:

If a commission of 10% is given on the marked price of an article, the gain is 25%. Find the gain percentage, if the commission is increased to 20%.

Solution:

Let marked price = Rs. 100
Commission = Rs.10

$$\text{S.P.} = \text{Rs. } 90; \text{C.P.} = \frac{90}{125} \times 100 = \text{Rs. } 72$$

New commission = Rs. 20; New S.P. = Rs 80.

$$\text{Gain percentage} = \frac{8 \times 100}{72} = 11.1\%$$

Example 26:

Peanuts are sold at 60 per rupee. If the vendor decides to hike the S.P. by 20%, how many peanuts can be bought per rupee?

Solution:

S.P. of 1 peanut = Re. $\dfrac{1}{60}$;

New S.P. = $\dfrac{1.2}{60}$ = Re. $\dfrac{1}{50}$

Therefore, 50 peanuts can be bought per rupee.

Example 27:

Sumit buys 9 books for Rs. 100 but sells 8 for Rs. 100. What is the net percentage of profit?

Solution:

S.P. of 8 books = Rs. 100

$\therefore$ S.P. of 1 book = $\dfrac{100}{8}$ = Rs. 12.50

$\therefore$ S.P. of 9 books = 12.50 × 9 = Rs. 112.50

$\therefore$ Profit percentage = 12.5%

Alternative method:

C.P. of 9 books = S.P. of 8 books

C.P. of 8 books + C.P. of 1 book = S.P. of 8 books

C.P. of 1 books = S.P. of 8 books – C.P. of 8 books

Profit = C.P. of 1 book

Profit percentage

$\quad$ = $\dfrac{\text{C.P. of 1 book}}{\text{C.P. of 8 books}} \times 100 = 12.5\%$

Example 28:

If by selling an article for Rs. 100, a man gains Rs. 15, then find his profit percentage.

Solution:

S.P. = Rs. 100, gain = Rs. 15.

So, C.P. = S.P. – Gain

$\therefore$ Gain percentage = $\left(\dfrac{15}{85} \times 100 \right)\% = 17\dfrac{11}{17}\%$

Example 29:

A grain dealer cheats to the extent of 10% while buying as well as selling by using false weights. What is his total profit percentage ?

Solution:

Here grain dealer gains 10% while buying as well as selling which is equivalent to two successive gains of 10%. Hence total gain

$= 10 + 10 + \dfrac{10 \times 10}{100} = 21\%$

Example 30:

A person earns 15% on an investment but loses 10% on another investment. If the ratio of the two investments be 3 : 5, what is the gain or loss on the two investments taken together?

Solution:

Let the investments be 3x and 5x.

Then, the total investment = 8x

Total receipt = (115% of 3x + 90% of 5x)

= (3.45x + 4.5x) = 7.95x

$\therefore$ Loss = $\left(\dfrac{0.05x}{8x} \times 100 \right)\% = 0.625\%$

Example 31:

Vivek purchased 120 tables at a price of Rs. 110 per table. He sold 30 tables at a profit of Rs. 12 per table and 75 tables at a profit of Rs. 14 per table. The remaining tables were sold at a loss of Rs. 7 per table. What is the average profit per table?

Solution:

Total C.P. = Rs. (120 × 110) = Rs. 13,200

Total S.P.= (30 × 110 + 30 × 12) + (75 × 110 + 75 × 14) + (15 × 110 – 15 × 7) = Rs. 14,505

Average profit = Rs. $\left(\dfrac{14505 - 13200}{120} \right)$

= Rs. $\dfrac{1305}{120}$ = Rs. 10.88

Alternative method:

Total profit = (30 × 12) + (75 × 14) – (15 × 7) = 1305

Hence, average profit = $\dfrac{1305}{120}$ = Rs. 10.88

Partnerships

When two or more persons invest money in a common business, they are called *partners* and the business relation is called *partnership*.

In a partnership business, every partner invests two entities:

i. Time

ii. Money

It follows quite easily that different partners may invest different amounts of money. What may not follow that easily is that even the time for which the money is invested by the partners could be different. Now what is meant by that? It only means that partners join the business at different points of time. For example consider a business in which A, B and C are partners. Suppose A and B invested amounts a and b at the start of the business. Three months after that, C joined as a partner investing an amount c. At the end of the first year A and B have invested their respective amounts for one full year but C has invested his amount for 9 months only.

Hence, it follows that a partner's Investment is a product of the time and the money:

Investment = Time × Money

How to share a Profit (or a Loss)?

The total profit or loss is distributed among the different partners in direct proportion of their investments. So if three partners A, B and C have invested amounts a, b and c for time periods t_A, t_B and t_C then the profit (or loss)

p_A, p_B and p_C are such that:

$$p_A : p_B : p_C :: t_A \times a : t_B \times b : t_C \times c$$

It follows that if $t_A = t_B = t_C$ then

$$p_A : p_B : p_C :: a : b : c$$

Example 32:

A, B and C invested Rs. 1,000, Rs. 600 and Rs. 400 respectively to start a business. The profit is Rs. 200 which is to be divided among A, B and C in the ratio of their capital invested. What share does each of them get?

Solution:

As nothing specific is given about the time periods of their investments, we will assume that each of them invested for an equal time period. Now, the ratio of the investments of A, B & C is the same as the ratio of the money that each of them invested or $p_A : p_B : p_C = 1000 : 600 : 400 = 5 : 3 : 2$

A's share of profit = $\dfrac{5}{10}$ × 200 = Rs. 100

B's share of profit = $\dfrac{3}{10}$ × 200 = Rs. 60

C's share of profit = $\dfrac{2}{10}$ × 200 = Rs. 40

Example 33:

Ram, Sham and Pran share profits in the ratio of 12 : 1 : 5. If Pran's share is Rs. 12,500, what was their total profit?

Solution:

Pran's share = 12500

$= \dfrac{5}{18}$ of total profit

Total profit $= \dfrac{12500 \times 18}{5}$

= Rs. 45,000

Example 34:

A, B and C enter into a partnership with an amount of Rs. 10,000 each. After 4 months, A invests an additional Rs. 2,000. Three months later, B invests Rs.4,000, and C at the same time withdraws Rs.2,000. Profit at the end of the year is Rs. 2,17,000. What are their respective shares if C is to be allowed to draw Rs. 2,000 as monthly salary from profits at the end?

Solution:

A's capital investment in that year.
= 10000 × 4 + 12000 × 8 = 1,36,000
B's capital investment in that year.
= 10000 × 7 + 14000 × 5 = 1,40,000
C's capital investment in that year.
= 10000 × 7 + 8000 × 5 = 1,10,000
Ratio in which profits are to be shared
= 68 : 70 : 55
Annual Salary of C = 2000 × 12 = Rs. 24,000
Profit to be shared = 217000 − 24000 = 193000

Rs. A's share = $\dfrac{193000 \times 68}{193}$ = Rs. 68,000

B's share = Rs. 70,000,
C's share = 55,000.

Example 35:

A, B and C enter into partnership. A invests 3 times as much as B invests and B invests two - third of what C invests. At the end of the year, the profit earned is Rs 6600. What is the share of B?

Solution:

Let C's capital = Rs x.

Then B's capital $= Rs \dfrac{2}{3} x$

A's capital $= Rs \left(3 \times \dfrac{2}{3} x \right) = Rs 2x$

$\therefore$ Ratio of their capitals $= 2x : \dfrac{2}{3} x : x = 6 : 2 : 3$

Hence, B's share $= Rs \left(6600 \times \dfrac{2}{11} \right) = Rs 1200.$

Example 36:

Four milkman rented a pasture. A grazed 24 cows for 3 months; B 10 cows for 5 months; C 35 cows for 4 months and D 21 cows for 3 months. If A's share of rent is Rs 720, find the total rent of the field.

Solution:

Ratio of shares of A, B, C, D = (24 × 3) : (10 × 5) : (35 × 4) : (21 × 3) = 72 : 50 : 140 : 63

Let total rent be Rs. x

Then, A's share $= Rs. \dfrac{72x}{325}$

$\therefore \dfrac{72x}{325} = 720 \Leftrightarrow x = \dfrac{720 \times 325}{72} = 3250$

Hence, total rent of the field is Rs. 3250.

Simple Interest and Compound Interest

This is one of the two main areas in which the concept of percentages is applied. This is also a topic relevant to most people in real life – whether calculating bank interest or buying a car / house on loan and calculating EMI. As the names suggest, simple interest is 'simple' and compound interest is 'complex'.

Simple Interest

Principal (P): The amount of money invested in the beginning of a particular time period.

Rate (R): It is a condition on which money is borrowed or lent.

For example an interest rate of 10% per annum means on every sum of Rs. 100 lent or borrowed and extra sum of Rs. 10 will be given or taken every year.

Time(T): It is the duration for which money is lent or borrowed.

Amount(A): It is the sum of principal and interest.

In simple interest principal is constant and interest for each time period is calculated on the same principal. The interest payable on the principal is known as simple interest.

Formula for simple Interest (S.I.) is $= \dfrac{P \times R \times T}{100}$

Where,

    P = principal or sum being borrowed.

    R = Rate of interest per year.

    T = Time period for which the amount is borrowed.

Amount = Principal + Simple Interest

(If T is not a whole number, then the period is represented as a fraction of year, i.e., 1 Month $= \dfrac{1}{12}$ th of a year.)

The principal grows at a constant rate in absolute terms.

Example 37:

What shall be the interest to be paid on a principal of Rs. 14,000 borrowed at a rate of 15% per annum for a period of 3 years and 6 months?

Solution:

$S.I. = \dfrac{P \times R \times T}{100}$

P = 14,000, R = 15 and T = 3.5 year

So, $S.I. = \dfrac{(14000 \times 15 \times 3.5)}{100} = Rs. 7,350$

Example 38:

At what simple rate of interest shall a sum of money double itself in 4 years?

Solution:

Important point to be noted is that the amount received by the lender is double the amount given, which means Interest = Principal

So, if x is the Principal, then x is the Simple Interest.

Or, $x = \dfrac{(x \times R \times 4)}{100}$ Or, $R = \dfrac{100}{4} = 25\%$

Example 39:

If a certain sum amounts to Rs. 108 in 2 years, Rs. 112 in 3 years, find the principal and rate of interest (simple).

Solution:

Amount after 2 years = Rs. 108.
Amount after 3 years = 112.
In S.I., interest amount remains the same for every year.
Therefore, interest for 1 year = Rs. 4.
Hence, principal = 108 – 2(4) = 100.

Rate of interest $= \dfrac{4 \times 100}{100 \times 1} = 4\%$

Example 40:

For how many years should Rs. 600 be invested at 10% p.a. at S.I., in order to earn the same interest as earned by investing Rs. 800 at 12% p.a. for 5 years at S.I.?

Solution:

Interest required = Rs. $\left(\dfrac{800\times12\times5}{100}\right)$ = Rs. 480

Time = $\left(\dfrac{100\times480}{600\times10}\right)$ = 8 years

Example 41:

Prabhat took a certain amount as a loan from a bank at the rate of 8% p.a. S.I. and gave the same amount to Ashish as a loan at the rate of 12% p.a. If at the end of 12 years, he made a profit of Rs. 320 in the deal, what was the original amount?

Solution:

Let the original amount be Rs. x. Then,

$$\frac{x\times12\times12}{100}-\frac{x\times8\times12}{100}=320$$

$$\Rightarrow x=\frac{2000}{3}=\text{Rs. }666.67$$

Alternative Method:

Prabhat gave at the rate of 12% and took at the rate of 8%. Here his net profit is 12 − 8 = 4%.

If the original sum = x, $\dfrac{x\times12\times4}{100}=320$ and

x = Rs. 666.67

Example 42:

If the sum of money at simple interest doubles in 6 years, it will become 4 times in how many years?

Solution:

Let sum be Rs. x. Then S.I. = Rs.

$\therefore$ Rate = $\left(\dfrac{100\times x}{x\times6}\right)\% = \dfrac{50}{3}\%$

Now sum is x and S.I. is 3x, Rate = $\dfrac{50}{3}\%$.

$\therefore$ Time = $\dfrac{100\times3x}{x\times\dfrac{50}{3}}=18$ years

Alternative Method:

Let principal be P, thus amount is 2P after 6 years.
Interest in 6 years = 2P − P = P.
To become 4 times, interest = 4P − P = 3P.
When interest is P, time taken = 6 years
When interest is 3P, time taken = 3 × 6
= 18 years.

Example 43:

The rate of interest on a sum of money is 4% p.a. for the first 2 years, 6% p.a. for the next 3 years and 8% p.a. for the period beyond 5 years. If the simple interest accrued for a total period of 8 years is Rs. 1,280 then what is the sum?

Solution:

Let the sum be Rs. x. Then,

$$\frac{x\times4\times2}{100}+\frac{x\times6\times3}{100}+\frac{x\times8\times3}{100}$$
= 1280 or 50x = 1280 × 100
$\therefore$ x = Rs. 2,560

Example 44:

Vinod Kumar invested Rs. 1,600 for 3 years and Rs. 1,100 for 4 years at the same rate of simple interest. If the total interest from these investments is Rs. 506, find the rate of interest.

Solution:

$$\frac{1600\times3\times R}{100}+\frac{1100\times4\times R}{100}=506\text{ or }92R$$

= 506 or R = $5\dfrac{1}{2}\%$

Example 45:

A man invests an amount of Rs. 15,860 in the name of his three sons A, B and C in such a way that they get the same amount after 2, 3 and 4 years, respectively. If the rate of interest is 5% p.a., then what is the ratio of amounts invested in the name of A, B and C?

Solution:

Let the amounts invested be x, y, z respectively.

Then, $\dfrac{x\times2\times5}{100}=\dfrac{y\times3\times5}{100}=\dfrac{z\times4\times5}{100}=k$

$\therefore x = 10k,\ y = \dfrac{20k}{3}$ and z = 5k

So, x : y : z = 10k : $\dfrac{20k}{3}$: 5k

= 30 : 20 : 15 = 6 : 4 : 3

Example 46:

The rates of simple interest in two banks A and B are in the ratio 5 : 4. A person wants to deposit his total savings in two banks in such a way that he receives equal half yearly interest from both. In what ratio, he should deposit his savings in banks A and B?

Solution:

Let the savings be X and Y and the rates of simple interest be 5x and 4x respectively. Then,

$$X \times 5x \times \frac{1}{2} \times \frac{1}{100} = Y \times 4x \times \frac{1}{2} \times \frac{1}{100}$$

or $\dfrac{X}{Y} = \dfrac{4}{5}$ i.e. X : Y = 4 : 5

Compound Interest

While computing compound interest the amount received at the end of 1st year becomes principal for 2nd year, and so on. The principal grows at an increasing rate in absolute terms. The interest is calculated on the new principal at the end of every time period. Here for each time period principal keeps changing. The amount (A) for the previous time period becomes the principal (P) for the next time period. Formula for Compound Interest:

$$(C.I) = P\left(1 + \frac{r}{100}\right)^n - P$$

Where,

P = Principal; r = Rate of Interest;

n = Time period and Amount $= P\left(1 + \dfrac{r}{100}\right)^n$

The following table compares the interests accrued for a principal of Rs.100 and at a rate of 10% p.a. under S.I. and C.I.

Year	S.I			C.I		
	Principal (end of year)	S.I. @ 10%	Total Int.	Principal (end of year)	C.I. @ 10%	Total Int.
1	100	10	10	100	10	10
2	100	10	20	110	11	21
3	100	10	30	121	12.10	33.10

Non annual compounding

	Compounding done in a year	Interest added to principal after every
Annually	1	1 year
Semi - Annually	2	6 months
Quarterly	4	3 months
Monthly	12	1 month

Note:

1. If the word interest is given and nothing else is specified, the interest is considered as S.I.

2. If the interest is given by bank and nothing is specified, it is always C.I.

3. Population growth is always taken on compounding basis.

You may encounter the following types of questions in the examination.

Types of questions	Examples	Approach to the question
1. Given Interest amount for n years at rate r%. What is the principal?	A certain sum earns a simple interest of Rs. 250 in 4 years at 5% p.a. Find the principal.	$P = \dfrac{I}{R \times T} \times 100$ $= \dfrac{250}{4 \times 5} \times 100 = \text{Rs. } 1250$
2. Which option would lead to a higher amount ? 1. r_s% simple interest for t_s time. 2. r_i% compound interest for t_c time.	Mr. Sharma wants to choose a investment plan 1. 15% for 5 years. (SI) 2. 20% for 3 years (CI) Which plan will result in higher amount?	<u>Compare</u> 1. 15 × 5 ⇒ 75% of interest on investment 2. $(1.20)^3 - 1 \Rightarrow 1.728 - 1$ ⇒ 72.8% of interest on investments. Thus option 1 will result in higher amount.
3. The C.I. in nth year is Rs. X and C.I. in (n + 1)th year is Rs. Y. What is the rate of interest?	C.I. earned in 7th year is Rs. 600 and in 8th year is Rs. 660. Find the rate of interest.	$R = \dfrac{Y - X}{X} \times 100$ $= \dfrac{60}{600} \times 100 = 10\%$

Types of questions	Examples	Approach to the question
4. The total S.I. in first two years is Rs. X and total C.I. in first two years is Rs. Y. What is the principal and rate of interest, if they are same for S.I. and C.I.?	Total S.I. for first two years is Rs. 600. If same amount was kept at C.I. at same rate, total C.I. would have been Rs. 660. What is the principal and the rate of interest?	$R = \dfrac{Y-X}{X/2} \times 100$ $= \dfrac{60}{300} \times 100 = 20\%$ Since interest for first years $= \dfrac{SI}{2} = \dfrac{600}{2} = 300$ and if Principal is P, then $P \times \dfrac{20}{100} \times 1 = 300$ or P = 1500
5. A principal amounts to X times in T years at S.I. In how many years will it become Y times?	Amount becomes 3 times in 5 years. In how many years will it become 9 times? (Assume S.I.)	$\text{Years} = \left(\dfrac{Y-1}{X-1}\right) \times T$ $= \left(\dfrac{9-1}{3-1}\right) \times 5 = 20$ years
6. Same as above but with C.I.	Same as above but assume C.I.	Years = T × n where n is given by $X^n = Y$ Years = 5 × 2 = 10 years

Example 47:

What shall be the amount for a sum of Rs.1,000 at 10% for 3 years compounded annually?

Solution:

Amount at the end of year 1 is

$$A_1 = \frac{(P \times R \times T)}{100} + P_1$$

$$= \frac{1000 \times 10 \times 1}{100} + 1000 = Rs.\ 1,100$$

This shall be the principal for year 2.

$$A_2 = \frac{(1100 \times 10 \times 1)}{100} + 1100 = Rs.\ 1,210$$

$$A_3 = \frac{(1210 \times 10 \times 1)}{100} + 1210 = Rs.\ 1,331$$

So amount at the end of 3 years in case of Compound Interest (C.I.) is Rs. 1,331, while in the case of S.I., it shall be Rs. 1,300 (at 10%).

Alternative Method:

Amount can also be calculated directly by using the formula.

Amount

$$= P\left(1 + \frac{R}{100}\right)^n = 1000\left(1 + \frac{10}{100}\right)^3 = Rs.\ 1,331$$

Where, P = Principal or sum being borrowed

R = Rate of interest

n = Time period for which the amount is borrowed

Example 48:

Find the C.I. on Rs. 5,000 at 8% p.a. for 2 years, compounded annually.

Solution:

P = Rs. 5000 , R = 8% and N = 2 years

$$5000\left(1 + \frac{8}{100}\right)^2 = \text{Amount} = Rs.\ 5832.$$

C.I. = Amount − Principal
= Rs. (5832 − 5000) = Rs. 832

Alternative method:

The Compound Interest on the given sum is nothing but two successive increment of 8%, i.e.

$$8 + 8 + \frac{8 \times 8}{100} = 16.64\% \left[\text{using } x + y + \frac{xy}{100} \text{ formula}\right]$$

Hence, Compound Interest $= \dfrac{16.64}{100} \times 5000$

= Rs. 832

Example 49:

Find amount for Rs. 80,000 at 20% per annum, compounded semi-annually for 2 years.

Solution:

Here n = (2 years) × 2 = 4 periods

Similarly, R = $\dfrac{20}{2}$ = 10% per time period

(As interest compounded semi-annually)
P = 80000
A = 80000

$\left(1+\dfrac{10}{100}\right)^4 = 80000 \times 1.4641$

= Rs. 117128

Example 50:

Find C.I. on Rs. 10,000 at 10% for 9 months compounded quarterly.

Solution:

n = 3 periods, R = 2.5% per period and
P = Rs. 10,000

Amount = $10000\left(1+\dfrac{2.5}{100}\right)^3$ = Rs. 10,769 (approx.)

C.I. = Amount – Principal
= 10769 – 10000 = Rs. 769

Example 51:

The difference between the C.I. and S.I. on a certain amount at 10% per annum for 2 years, compounded annually is Rs. 372. Find the principal.

Solution:

Let the principal be P.

S.I. = $P \times 10 \times \dfrac{2}{100} = \dfrac{P}{5}$ and

C.I. = Amount – P = $P\left(1+\dfrac{10}{100}\right)^2 - P = \dfrac{21P}{100}$

C.I. – S.I. = Rs. 372

$\dfrac{21P}{100} - \dfrac{P}{5}$ = Rs. 372

∴ P = Rs. 37,200

Alternative Method:
You need to understand the fact that for 1st period,
S.I. = C.I.

The difference between the values of C.I. and S.I. is because of accumulated interest building on interest which is reinvested. Therefore, for period 2, the difference between C.I. and S.I. is the interest on the interest for period 1.

In the above example, the difference being 372 is the interest generated on interest for period 1 on the principal.

Interest for period 1 = Rs. 372 × $\dfrac{100}{10}$

= Rs. 3,720

Therefore, Principal = Rs. 3720 × $\dfrac{100}{10}$

= Rs. 37,200

Example 52:

Ram invested a particular sum at 12% per annum with Shyam and an equal amount in bank which pays interest at 12% p.a. compounded semi-annually. The difference between the amounts received after 1 year was Rs. 1,800. Find the total sum invested by Ram.

Solution:

Following the argument in the previous example, we have the difference equal to the interest on the interest paid on the principal for 6 months.

(Rate of interest becomes $\dfrac{12}{2}$ = 6%).

Interest paid for first 6 months by the bank

= Rs. $1800 \times \dfrac{100}{6}$ on principal = Rs. 30,000.

Principal = Rs. $30,000 \times \dfrac{100}{6}$ = Rs. 5,00,000.

Total sum invested = Rs. 5,00,000 + Rs. 5,00,000
= Rs. 10,00,000.

Example 53:

If the C.I. on a certain sum for 3 years at 20% p.a. is Rs. 728, what is the sum invested?

Solution:

C.I. = 728 = $P\left(1+\dfrac{20}{100}\right)^3 - P$

$\Rightarrow P(1.2)^3 - P = 728$
$P(1.728 - 1) = 728$
$P (0.728) = 728$
P = Rs. 1000

Note: When rates are different for different years, say r_1, r_2, and r_3 for different years 1, 2 and 3 respectively, then amount

$$A = P\left(1+\frac{r_1}{100}\right)\left(1+\frac{r_2}{100}\right)\left(1+\frac{r_3}{100}\right)$$

Example 54:

Find the amount after 3 years if the principal is Rs. 10,000 and rates are 10%, 8%, 12% for those three years in that order.

Solution:

$$\text{Amount } A = 10{,}000\left(1+\frac{10}{100}\right)\left(1+\frac{8}{100}\right)\left(1+\frac{12}{100}\right)$$

$$= \text{Rs. } (10{,}000 \times 1.1 \times 1.08 \times 1.12)$$
$$= \text{Rs. } 13{,}305.60$$

Example 55:

The value of a machine depreciates at the rate of 10% every year. It was purchased three years ago. If its present value is Rs. 8,748, its purchase price was

Solution:

Let the purchase price be P.
Rate of depreciation = 10%

$$P\left(1-\frac{10}{100}\right)^3 = 8748$$

$$\Rightarrow P = \left(8748 \times \frac{10}{9} \times \frac{10}{9} \times \frac{10}{9}\right)$$

$$= \text{Rs. } 12{,}000$$

Exercise

Exercise – I

1. What is the $18\frac{3}{4}$ % of 2000?
   (1) 300   (2) 400
   (3) 390   (4) 375

2. What percent of 48 is 26?
   (1) 54.16%   (2) 184.6%
   (3) 56.33%   (4) 57.16%

3. What is $33\frac{1}{3}$ % of 972?
   (1) 332   (2) 411
   (3) 348   (4) 324

4. What percent of 60 is 37?
   (1) 60%   (2) 61.66%
   (3) 65.66%   (4) 70%

5. The population of a town increases from 6500 to 7475. What is the percentage increase?
   (1) 10%   (2) 12%
   (3) 15%   (4) 20%

6. What is 90% of 90% of 100?
   (1) 80   (2) 100
   (3) 90   (4) 81

7. 50 min is what percent of an hour?
   (1) 83.33%   (2) 50%
   (3) 90%   (4) 87.66%

8. If A's income is 25% more than B's, then B's income is what percent of A's income?
   (1) 75%   (2) 80%
   (3) 90%   (4) 125%

9. In an examination passing percentage is 40. A obtained 72 out of 200. By what percent did he fail?
   (1) 8%   (2) 5%
   (3) 4%   (4) 16%

10. A 50 L mixture of milk and water has 35% water. What is the quantity of milk in it?
    (1) 27.5 L   (2) 15 L
    (3) 31.5 L   (4) 32.5 L

11. If A is increased by 10%, A^2 is increased by
    (1) 20%   (2) 21%
    (3) 100%   (4) 19%

12. A is what percent of $\left(\frac{9}{15}\right)$A?
    (1) 60%   (2) 100%
    (3) 133%   (4) 166%

13. If the length and breadth of a rectangle are decreased by 10%, then by what percent does the area decrease?
    (1) 19%   (2) 25%
    (3) 10%   (4) 20%

14. What is 30% of 55% of 100?
    (1) 25   (2) 16.5
    (3) 85   (4) 11.5

15. Which one of the following is the largest?
    (1) 66%   (2) $\frac{3}{5}$ (3) 0.65   (4) $\frac{16}{25}$

16. In a town, there are 2500 men and 2500 women. If men increased by 20% and women decreased by 20%, women as a percent of men now is:
    (1) 60%   (2) 66.66%
    (3) 80%   (4) 83.33%

17. If the numerator of a fraction is increased by 25% and denominator decreased by 20%, the new value is $\frac{5}{4}$. What was the original fraction?
    (1) $\frac{3}{5}$ (2) $\frac{4}{5}$ (3) $\frac{7}{8}$ (4) $\frac{3}{7}$

18. A 'laddoo' is made of 70% flour, 20% sugar and the rest is 'ghee'. What is the quantity of 'ghee' in two kg laddoos?
    (1) 200 gm   (2) 2 kg
    (3) 100 gm   (4) 400 gm

19. Raman's salary was decreased by 50% and subsequently increased by 50%. He has a loss of
    (1) 0%   (2) 25%
    (3) 0.25%   (4) 2.5%

20. The population of a town increases 20% annually. What will be the population after 2 years, if present population is 2500?
(1) 3250 (2) 3500
(3) 3600 (4) 3700

21. If 37% of a number is 990.86, what will be approximately 19% of that number?
(1) 600 (2) 500
(3) 450 (4) 700

22. I bought 20 kg of mango, out of which 16 kg were fine and rest were rotten. What is my percentage of loss, if I bought them for Rs. 30 per kilogram?
(1) 33% (2) 40%
(3) 15% (4) 20%

23. Y is a% of X. If X is 120% of Y, then find a?
(1) 83.33% (2) 80%
(3) 75% (4) 86.66%

24. The price of rice increased from Rs.15 by 15% and then reduced by 30 paise. What was the net increase?
(1) 10% (2) 12%
(3) 13% (4) 28%

25. If 20% of a number exceeds 16% of the same number by 16, then what is the number?
(1) 4 (2) 40
(3) 4000 (4) 400

Exercise – 2

1. In order to increase sales, price of a product was decreased by 20%. The total revenue is increased by 28%. What is the percentage increase in number of units sold?
(1) 48% (2) 50%
(3) 60% (4) 83%

2. If 28% of a number is less than 43% of the same number by 75. What is 30% of that number?
(1) 120 (2) 105
(3) 180 (4) 150

3. In an examination, it is required to get 45% marks to pass. A student got 138 marks and failed by 15% of the total marks. What were the maximum marks?
(1) 400 (2) 450
(3) 460 (4) 500

4. Design requirement demands that an angle should be $37\frac{1}{2}°$. Upon construction, the same angle was found to be only 36°, as built. The error percent is:
(1) $1\frac{1}{2}\%$ (2) 3%
(3) 4% (4) $4\frac{1}{6}\%$

5. An increase of Rs. 60 in the monthly salary of Madan made it 50% of the monthly salary of Kamal. What is Madan's present monthly salary?
(1) Rs. 180
(2) Rs. 200
(3) Rs. 300
(4) Cannot be determined

6. The salaries of A and B together amount to Rs. 2,000. A spends 95% of his salary and B spends 85% of his salary. If their savings are the same, then what is A's salary?
(1) Rs. 1,500 (2) Rs. 1,250
(3) Rs. 750 (4) Rs. 1,600

7. In an examination, A got 10% marks less than B, B got 25% marks more than C and C got 20% less than D. If A got 360 marks out of 500, the percentage of marks obtained by D was:
(1) 70% (2) 75%
(3) 85% (4) 80%

8. In an examination, 80% of the students passed in English. 85% in Mathematics and 75% in both English and Mathematics. If 40 students failed in both the subjects, the total number of students is:
(1) 200 (2) 400
(3) 600 (4) 800

9. p is six times as large as q. The percent that q is less than p, is
(1) 83.33% (2) 16.66%
(3) 90% (4) 60%

10. In an election involving two candidates, 68 votes were declared invalid. The wining candidate got 52% of the votes and won by 98 votes. The total number of votes polled was
(1) 2500 (2) 2450
(3) 2382 (4) 2518

11. The price of oil is increased by 25%. If the expenditure is not allowed to increase, the ratio between the reduction in consumption and the regular consumption is:
(1) 1 : 3   (2) 1 : 4
(3) 1 : 5   (4) 1 : 6

12. The current birth rate per thousand is 32, whereas corresponding death rate is 11 per thousand. The net growth rate in terms of population increase in percent is
(1) 0.021%   (2) 0.0021%
(3) 21%   (4) 2.1%

13. The length of a rectangle is increased by 60%. By what percent would the width have to be decreased to maintain the same area?
(1) 30%   (2) 60%
(3) 75%   (4) 37.5%

14. In a class of 300 students, the number of boys is twice that of girls. If 50% of boys and 48% of girls appear in examination, how many students did not appear?
(1) 152   (2) 160
(3) 16   (4) 148

15. If 1 L of water is added to 5 L of a 20% solution of sugar in water, what is the strength of the solution now?
(1) 12.66%   (2) 10%
(3) 8.33%   (4) 16.66%

16. Al Pacino invested 40% of his money in shares, 20% of rest in property and lost 25% of the remaining in a casino. What percent of the original sum he was left with?
(1) 15%   (2) 40%
(3) 42%   (4) 36%

Directions for questions 17 to 19: Answer the questions on the basis of the following information.
In an election, there were only 2 candidates. The losing candidate received $66\frac{2}{3}$% of the votes the winner got.
The votes polled in favour of the loser were 60 less than that of the winner.

17. How many votes did the loser get?
(1) 200   (2) 150   (3) 120   (4) 100

18. How many votes were cast in total?
(1) 200   (2) 300   (3) 400   (4) 500

19. What percent of the total votes did the winner get?
(1) 60%   (2) 50%
(3) 80%   (4) 66.66%

20. A shopkeeper made 10% profit if the S.P. of the product is Rs. 121. What would be the percentage loss / profit, if the S.P. is reduced by Rs. 11?
(1) Loss of 10%   (2) Gain of 5%
(3) Loss of 5%   (4) No profit, no loss

21. Due to an increase of 30% in price of eggs, 3 eggs less are available for Rs. 7.80. The present rate of eggs per dozen is:
(1) Rs. 7.20   (2) Rs. 8.64
(3) Rs. 8.88   (4) Rs. 9.36

22. Avinash spends 30% of his income on petrol, $\frac{1}{4}$th of the remaining on house rent and the balance on food. If he spends Rs. 300 on petrol, then what is the expenditure on house rent?
(1) Rs. 525   (2) Rs. 1,000
(3) Rs. 675   (4) Rs. 175

23. If x% of a is the same as y% of b, then z% of b is

(1) $\dfrac{yz}{x}$ % of a

(2) $\dfrac{xy}{z}$ % of a

(3) $\dfrac{x}{zy}$ % of a

(4) $\dfrac{xz}{y}$ % of a

24. The price of sugar is increased by 20%. As a result, a family decreases its consumption by 25%. The expenditure of the family on sugar will be decreased by:
(1) 10%   (2) 5%
(3) 14%   (4) 15%

25. A man's basic pay for a 40-hour week is Rs. 20. Overtime is paid for at 25% above the basic rate. In a certain week, he worked overtime and his total wage was Rs. 25. He, therefore, worked for
(1) 45 hrs   (2) 48 hrs
(3) 47 hrs   (4) 50 hrs

Exercise – 3

1. Cost of 3 balls = Cost of 2 pads. Cost of 3 pads = Cost of 2 gloves. Cost of 3 gloves = Cost of 2 bats. If the bat costs Rs. 54, what is the cost of the ball?
    (1) Rs.12 (2) Rs.14
    (3) Rs.16 (4) Rs. 18

2. If books bought at prices ranging from Rs. 200 to Rs. 350, are sold at prices ranging from Rs. 300 to Rs. 425, then what can be the maximum possible profit?
    (1) Rs. 400
    (2) Rs. 600
    (3) Rs. 800
    (4) Cannot be determined.

3. The cost price of 20 articles is the same as the selling price of 15 articles. The profit percentage is
    (1) 25 (2) 30
    (3) 35 (4) 33.33

4. If the selling price of an article is $\dfrac{4}{3}$ times its cost price, then the profit percent is
    (1) $33\dfrac{1}{3}$ (2) $25\dfrac{1}{4}$ (3) $20\dfrac{1}{2}$ (4) $20\dfrac{1}{3}$

5. A dealer who professes to sell his goods at cost price uses a 900 gm weight for a kg. His gain percentage is
    (1) 9 (2) 10 (3) 11 (4) 11.11

6. A dealer professes to sell his goods at cost price, but he uses a false weight and gains $6\dfrac{18}{47}$ %. For a kg, he uses a weight of
    (1) 953 gm (2) 960 gm
    (3) 940 gm (4) 947 gm

7. A man sells 2 cows for Rs. 4,000 each, neither gaining nor losing in the deal. If he sells one cow at a gain of 25%, then the other cow must have sold at a loss of
    (1) 16.66%
    (2) 18.22%
    (3) 25%
    (4) 30%

8. Two horses were sold for Rs. 12,000 each, one at a loss of 20% and the other at a gain of 20%. The entire transaction resulted in
    (1) No loss, no gain
    (2) Loss of Rs. 1,000
    (3) Gain of Rs. 1,000
    (4) Gain of Rs. 2,000

9. Successive discounts of 30%, 20% and 10% are equivalent to a single discount of
    (1) 50% (2) 40%
    (3) 39.4% (4) 49.6%

10. The difference between the discounts of 40% on Rs. 500 and two successive discounts of 36% and 4 % on the same price is
    (1) Nil (2) Rs. 2
    (3) Rs. 7.20 (4) Rs. 1.93

11. At what percentage above the cost price must an article be marked so as to gain 33% after allowing a discount of 5%?
    (1) 38% (2) 40%
    (3) 43% (4) 48%

12. A trader allows two successive discounts of 20% and 10%. If he sells the article for Rs.108, then the marked price of the article is
    (1) Rs. 150 (2) Rs. 148
    (3) Rs. 142 (4) Rs. 140

13. A merchant gives a discount of 10% on tea, but uses a weight of 900 gm per kg. Find his net profit / loss percentage.
    (1) No profit, no loss (2) 2.05
    (3) 4.67 (4) 3.33

14. If the cost price of 12 books is the same as the selling price of 16 books, the loss percentage is
    (1) 15% (2) 25%
    (3) 20% (4) 30%

15. A man loses the selling price of 4 apples on selling 36 apples. His loss percentage is
    (1) 12.5% (2) 11.11%
    (3) 10% (4) 9%

Exercise – 4

1. By selling a table, Aditya earned a profit equal to one fourth of the price for which he bought it. If he sold it for Rs. 375, what was the cost price?
    (1) Rs. 281.75 (2) Rs. 300
    (3) Rs. 312.50 (4) Rs. 350

2. A man bought a number of bananas at 3 for a rupee and an equal number at 2 for a rupee. At what price per dozen should he sell them to make a profit of 20%?
(1) Rs. 4   (2) Rs. 5
(3) Rs. 8   (4) Rs. 6

3. A man buys two types of equal number of oranges, one at Rs. 5 a dozen and an other at Rs. 2 a dozen. He sells them at Rs. 5.50 a dozen and makes a profit of Rs. 50. How many oranges (in dozens) did he buy?
(1) 25   (2) 40
(3) 50   (4) 60

4. A tea merchant blends two varieties of tea costing Rs. 18 per kg and Rs. 20 per kg in the ratio of 5 : 3. If he sells the blended variety at Rs. 21 per kg, what is his gain percentage?
(1) 10%   (2) 22%
(3) 19%   (4) 12%

5. By selling toffees at 20 for a rupee, a man loses 4%. To gain 20%, for a rupee he must sell
(1) 16 toffees
(2) 20 toffees
(3) 24 toffees
(4) 25 toffees

6. A man gains 10% by selling an article for a certain price. If he sells it at double the price, the profit is
(1) 20%   (2) 120%
(3) 100%   (4) 140%

7. 'A' bought a cycle and spent Rs. 110 on its repairs. He then sold it to 'B' at a profit of 20%. 'B' sold it to 'C' at a loss of 10%. 'C' sold it at a profit of 10% for Rs. 1,188. How much did 'A' buy it for?
(1) Rs. 850   (2) Rs. 870
(3) Rs. 930   (4) Rs. 890

8. A vendor has 24 kg of apples. He sells part of these at a 20% gain and the balance at 5% loss. If on the whole he earns a profit of 10%, the part of apples sold at a loss is
(1) 6 kg   (2) 4.6 kg
(3) 9.6 kg   (4) 11.4 kg

9. The cost price of an article is 40% of the selling price. The percent that the selling price is of cost price is
(1) 250%   (2) 240%
(3) 60%   (4) 40%

10. By selling an article, there is a loss of 2.5%. By selling it at Rs. 6 more, there is a gain of 5%. Find the cost price of the article.
(1) Rs. 78   (2) Rs. 81
(3) Rs. 82   (4) Rs. 80

11. Profit after selling goods for Rs. 425 is the same as the loss after selling it at Rs. 355. What is its cost price?
(1) Rs. 390   (2) Rs. 385
(3) Rs. 395   (4) Rs. 400

12. The profit earned by selling a table for Rs. 900 is double the loss incurred when it is sold for Rs. 450. At what price should it be sold to make a 25% profit?
(1) Rs. 600   (2) Rs. 650
(3) Rs. 800   (4) Rs. 750

13. A merchant intends to offer a discount of 10% but would like to maintain the current selling prices. By what percentage should he increase the list price?
(1) 10%   (2) 9.09%
(3) 11.11%   (4) 12.5%

14. A trader buys 78 kg of wheat for Rs. 492. He sells 40% of this at a loss of 20%. What should be the percentage mark up on the remaining so as to gain an overall 25%?
(1) 40%   (2) 55%
(3) 28%   (4) 45%

15. By selling 25 L of milk at Rs. 50 per litre, a merchant earns a profit equivalent to the cost price of 5 L. Find the profit percentage.
(1) 15%   (2) 25%
(3) 20%   (4) 18%

16. A man bought 100 kg of rice for Rs. 1,100 and sold it at a loss of as much money as he received for 20 kg rice. At what unit price did he sell the rice?
(1) Rs. 9   (2) Rs. 10.50
(3) Rs. 10   (4) Rs. 9.16

17. Ram purchased 35 kg rice at Rs. 9.50 per kilogram and another 30 kg at Rs. 10.50 per kilogram and mixed them. At what price (per kilogram) should he sell the mixture to gain 35%?
(1) Rs. 12   (2) Rs. 12.50
(3) Rs. 13   (4) Rs. 13.50

18. Peter bought an item at 25% discount on its original price. He sold it with 40% increase on the price he bought it. The new sale price is by what percent more than the original price?
(1) 7.5%   (2) 8%
(3) 10%   (4) 12%

19. Had the C.P. been 10% less and S.P. been 10% more, profit %age would have been double than that of earlier case. What is the profit %age in original case?
(1) 20%
(2) 28.56%
(3) 14.28%
(4) Can't be determined

20. By selling 20 kgs of mangoes the profit is equal to C.P. of 5 kgs of mangoes. Find the profit percentage?
(1) 20%   (2) 15%
(3) 25%   (4) 40%

Exercise – 5

1. A, B and C join a partnership contributing Rs. 2,000, Rs. 1,500 and Rs. 1,250 respectively. What is A's share if total profit is Rs. 3,610?
(1) Rs. 1,500   (2) Rs. 2,290
(3) Rs. 1,870   (4) Rs. 1,520

2. A, B and C joins a partnership. A invested Rs. 16,000 for 6 months, B invested Rs. 12,000 for $\frac{2}{3}$rd year and C invested Rs. 1,000 for 12 months. Calculate their profit sharing ratio.
(1) 8 : 8 : 1   (2) 10 : 8 : 7
(3) 6 : 8 : 12   (4) 8 : 7 : 10

3. A starts a business with Rs. 4,000. B joins him after 3 months with Rs. 8,000. C puts a sum of Rs. 12,000 in the business for 2 months only in the same year. At the end of the year, the business generated a profit of Rs. 5,200. Find the share of B.
(1) Rs. 1,500   (2) Rs. 1, 800
(3) Rs. 2,600   (4) Rs. 4,000

4. In a partnership business, A, B and C invest money in the ratio 8 : 7 : 5. A withdraws half her money after 5 months. If the profit is Rs. 26,500 for the year, find B's share.
(1) Rs. 9,800   (2) Rs. 10,200
(3) Rs. 10,500   (4) Rs. 12,600

5. Arun, Kamal and Vinay invested Rs. 8000, Rs. 4000 and Rs. 8000 respectively in a business. Arun left after six months. If after eight months, there was a gain of Rs. 4005, then what will be the share of Kamal?
(1) Rs. 890   (2) Rs. 1335
(3) Rs. 1602   (4) Rs. 1780

6. A, B and C enter into a partnership. A initially invests Rs. 50,000 and adds another Rs.20,000 after one year. B invests Rs. 70,000 and withdraw Rs. 10,000 after 2 years and C invests Rs. 60,000. In what ratio should the profits be divided at the end of 3 years?
(1) 10 : 10 : 9   (2) 20 : 20 : 19
(3) 20 : 19 : 18 (4) None of these

7. A, B, C hired a motorboat for Rs. 480 and used it for 7, 8 and 9 hours respectively. Hire charges paid by B were:
(1) Rs. 140   (2) Rs. 160
(3) Rs. 180   (4) Rs. 220

8. A, B and C enter into a partnership and their shares are in the ratio $\frac{1}{2} : \frac{1}{3} : \frac{1}{4}$. After 2 months, A withdraws half of his capital and there after 10 months later a profit of Rs. 378 is divided among them. What is B's share?
(1) Rs. 129   (2) Rs. 144
(3) Rs. 156   (4) Rs. 168

9. A started a business with Rs. 21,000 and is joined afterwards by B with Rs. 36,000. After how many months did B join if the profits at the end of the year are divided equally?
(1) 3   (2) 4   (3) 5   (4) 7

10. A and B are partners in a business. A contributes $\frac{1}{4}$th of the capital for 15 months and B received $\frac{2}{3}$ of the profit. For how long B's money was used?
(1) 6 months   (2) 9 months
(3) 10 months   (4) 1 year.

11. A and B invest in a business in the ratio 3 : 2. If 5% of the total profit goes to charity and A's share is Rs.. 855, the total profit is:
(1) Rs. 1425   (2) Rs. 1500
(3) Rs. 1537.50   (4) Rs. 1575

12. In a business, A and C invested amounts in the ratio 2 : 1, whereas the ratio between amounts invested by A and B was 3 : 2. If Rs. 1,57,300 was their profit, how much amount did B receive?
(1) Rs. 24,200　　　　(2) Rs. 36,300
(3) Rs. 48,400　　　　(4) Rs. 72,600

13. Arun started a business with Rs. 1,00,000. Sanjay joined him 4 months later with Rs. 1,50,000. After 2 months Arun withdraw Rs. 25,000 of his capital and 2 more months later Sanjay brought in Rs. 1,00,000 more. At the end of the year what should be ratio in which they should share the profits?
(1) 21 : 32　　　　(2) 32 : 21
(3) 2 : 3　　　　(4) 3 : 2

14. The working partner of a business gets as his commission 20% of the profits left after his commission is paid. If working partner's commission is Rs. 10,000 then, find the total profit.
(1) Rs. 3,30,000　　　　(2) Rs. 60,000
(3) Rs. 10,000　　　　(4) Rs. 1,00,000

15. X, Y and Z invest in a partnership in the ratio 3 : 5 : 8. If in the end, the profit was distributed in the ratio 24 : 35 : 56, then find the ratio of the time for which they were invested.
(1) 1 : 2 : 1　　　　(2) 1 : 1 : 2
(3) 7 : 8 : 8　　　　(4) 8 : 7 : 7

16. A and B enter into a partnership with Rs. 50,000 and Rs. 60,000 respectively. C joins them after x months contributing Rs. 70,000 and B leaves x months before the end of the year. If they share the profit in the ratio of 20 : 18 : 21 find the value of x.
(1) 9　　　　(2) 8
(3) 4　　　　(4) 3

17. A and B enter into a partnership contributing Rs. 93,000 and Rs. 1,02,000 respectively. A is entitled to a salary of Rs. 500 per month from the profit. If at the end of the year, they earn Rs. 45,000 as profit, what is the difference of earnings of A and B?
(1) Rs. 4,200　　　　(2) Rs. 7,800
(3) Rs. 4,500　　　　(4) Rs. 6,000

18. Three partners Rohan, Mohan and Sohan starts a business. Thrice of Rohan's capital is equal to twice of Mohan's capital, which is then equal to four times of Sohan's capital. Find the share of Rohan out of total profit of Rs. 52,000.

(1) Rs. 11,000　　　　(2) Rs. 10,000
(3) Rs. 16,000　　　　(4) Rs. 8,000

19. A and B start a business with respective investments of Rs. 20,000 and Rs. 30,000. After some period C joins them with a capital of Rs. 40,000. If the share of C in the annual profit of Rs. 14,000 is Rs. 4,000 after how many months did C join?
(1) 3　　　　(2) 9　　　　(3) 8　　　　(4) 6

20. Arun, Keshav and Jiten start a business with investments of Rs. 1,640, Rs. 32,80 and Rs. 1,230 respectively. After x months. Arun withdraws his capital and after x more months, Jiten withdraws his capital. If at the end of one year, they share the profits in the ratio 4 : 24 : 6, what is the value of x?
(1) 6　　　　(2) 4
(3) 3　　　　(4) 2

Exercise – 6

1. A sum of Rs. 3,500 is lent for 5 years at 5% p.a. The S.I. and amount respectively are
(1) Rs. 785, Rs. 4,375
(2) Rs. 875, Rs. 3,675
(3) Rs. 500, Rs. 4,375
(4) Rs. 875, Rs. 4,375

2. In what time, a sum of money will triple itself at the rate of 20% p.a., interest calculated as S.I.
(1) 5 years　　　　(2) 10 years
(3) 15 years　　　　(4) 20 years

3. What will be the C.I. on Rs. 1,000 for 3 yrs at 10% p.a.?
(1) Rs. 331　　　　(2) Rs. 330
(3) Rs. 300　　　　(4) Rs. 361

4. If C.I. for a certain sum for 2 years at 2% p.a. be Rs. 1,010, what is the principal?
(1) Rs. 20,000　　　　(2) Rs. 25,000
(3) Rs. 25,250　　　　(4) Rs. 27,500

5. At what rate per cent, the interest on Rs. 1,125 will be Rs. 225 in 4 years?
(1) 4%
(2) 5%
(3) $6\frac{2}{3}\%$
(4) Can't be determined

6. In what time will Rs. 36 become Rs. 45 at 6.25% p.a. simple interest?
   (1) 2 years   (2) 3 years
   (3) 4 years   (4) 8 years

7. The simple interest on Rs. 400 for 8 months at the rate of 5 paise per rupee per month is:
   (1) Rs. 120   (2) Rs. 160
   (3) Rs. 200   (4) Rs. 400

8. If Re. 1 becomes Rs. 10 in 50 years at simple interest, the rate percent per annum is
   (1) 15%   (2) 18%
   (3) 20%   (4) 24%

9. The difference between the interests received from two different banks on Rs. 500 for 2 years is Rs. 2.50. Find the difference between their rates. (Assume S.I.)
   (1) 1%   (2) 2.5%
   (3) 0.25%   (4) 0.5%

10. Find the difference between S.I. and C.I. on Rs. 700 at the rate of 10% for 3 yrs.
    (1) Rs. 20.90   (2) Rs. 21.00
    (3) Rs. 21.70   (4) Rs. 24.00

11. S.I. on a sum of money is one fourth of principal. The number of years is equal to the rate of interest. Find the rate of interest.
    (1) 2.5%   (2) 7.5%
    (3) 6%   (4) 5%

12. What is the sum which when lent at 5% S.I. for 2 years would yield Rs. 154?
    (1) Rs. 1,450   (2) Rs. 1,540
    (3) Rs. 1,650   (4) Rs. 1,480

13. I owe you Rs. 1,500 to be payable 4 years from now. What is the equivalent cash payment that I can make now (S.I. prevailing being 6.25% p.a.)?
    (1) Rs. 1,000   (2) Rs. 800
    (3) Rs. 1,400   (4) Rs. 1,200

14. I buy a watch for Rs. 400 and sell it for Rs. 460 at a credit of 8 months. What is my gain percent considering interest rate to be 15% p.a.?
    (1) 4.54%   (2) 6.66%
    (3) 7.5%   (4) 8%

15. If I lend Rs. 5,000 for 3 years in two schemes
    I.   11% S.I.
    II. 10% C.I.

Which scheme is more profitable and by what amount?
   (1) I, Rs. 150   (2) I, Rs. 50
   (3) II, Rs. 5   (4) II, Rs. 50

Execise – 7

1. A sum was put at simple interest at a certain rate for 2 years. Had it been put at 3% higher rate, it would have fetched Rs. 72 more. The sum is
   (1) Rs. 1,200   (2) Rs. 1,500
   (3) Rs. 1,600   (4) Rs. 1,800

2. If a sum of money doubles itself in 8 years at simple interest, the rate percent per annum is
   (1) 11.5%   (2) 12.5%
   (3) 12%   (4) 12%

3. A man lends Rs. 10,000 in four parts and gets 8% on Rs. 2,000, 7.5% on Rs. 4,000 and 8.5 % on Rs. 1,400. What percent must he get for the remainder, if his average annual interest is 8.13%?
   (1) 9%   (2) 9.25%
   (3) 10.5%   (4) 7%

4. If the difference between the compound interest compounded half-yearly and the simple interest on a sum at 10% per annum for one year is Rs. 25, the sum is
   (1) Rs. 9,000   (2) Rs. 9,500
   (3) Rs. 10,000   (4) Rs. 10,500

5. A man borrowed Rs. 800 at 10% per annum simple interest and immediately lent the whole sum at 10 % per annum compound interest. How much does he gain at the end of 2 years?
   (1) Rs. 6   (2) Rs. 8
   (3) Rs. 10   (4) Rs. 12

6. A sum of money amounts to Rs. 4,624 in 2 years and to Rs. 4,913 in 3 years at compound interest. The sum is:
   (1) Rs. 4,096
   (2) Rs. 4,260
   (3) Rs. 4,335
   (4) Rs. 4,360

7. A sum of Rs. 12,000 deposited at compound interest becomes double after 5 years. After 20 years it will become ________.
   (1) Rs. 1,20,000
   (2) Rs. 1,92,000
   (3) Rs. 1,24,000
   (4) Rs. 96,000

8. The least number of complete years in which a sum of money put out at 20% compound interest will be more than doubled is
(1) 3   (2) 7
(3) 5   (4) 4

9. A tree increases annually by one eighth of its height. To what height will it be after 2 years, if today it stands 64 cm high?
(1) 72 cm   (2) 74 cm
(3) 75 cm   (4) 81 cm

10. At what rate of compound interest per annum will a sum of Rs. 1,200 become Rs. 1,348.32 in 2 years?
(1) 7%   (2) 6%
(3) 7.5%   (4) 6.5%

11. A sum of money invested at compound interest amounts to Rs. 800 in 3 years and Rs. 840 in 4 years. What is the rate of interest p.a.?
(1) 2%   (2) 4%
(3) 5%   (4) 10%

12. Simple interest on a certain sum is (9/25) of the sum. Find the rate percent and time, if both are numerically equal.
(1) 6%, 6 yrs.   (2) 6%, 8 yrs.
(3) 8%, 6 yrs.   (4) 8%, 8 yrs.

13. The simple interest on a sum of money for 3 years is Rs. 360 and the compound interest on the sum at the same rate for 2 years is Rs. 270. The interest rate per annum is
(1) 25%   (2) 50%
(3) 60%   (4) 80%

14. A man lent Rs. 400 and Rs. 600 for 3 years at the same rate at simple interest and received only Rs. 90 as interest. What was the rate percent per annum?
(1) 1%   (2) 2%
(3) 4%   (4) 3%

15. If C.I. for a certain sum at 3% for 2 years is Rs. 203, what would be the S.I.?
(1) Rs. 210   (2) Rs. 207.50
(3) Rs. 213.33   (4) Rs. 200

16. A sum of Rs. 1,550 was partly lent at 5% and 8% p.a. simple interest. The total interest received after 3 years was Rs. 300. The ratio of the money lent at 5% to that lent at 8% is
(1) 8 : 5   (2) 5 : 8
(3) 31 : 6   (4) 16 : 15

17. A man invested one third of his capital at 7% p.a., one fourth at 8% p.a. and the remainder at 10% p.a. simple interest respectively. If his annual income from interest earned is Rs. 561, then the capital is
(1) Rs. 5,400   (2) Rs. 6,000
(3) Rs. 6,600   (4) Rs. 7,200

18. Rs. 2,189 is divided into three parts and invested such that their amounts after 1, 2 and 3 years respectively are equal. The rate of simple interest is 4% p.a. in all cases. Find the smallest part.
(1) Rs. 703   (2) Rs. 389
(3) Rs. 756   (4) Rs. 398

19. If the simple interest on a sum of money for 3 years at 5% per annum is Rs. 1,200, then the compound interest for the same period at the same rate is
(1) Rs. 1,260   (2) Rs. 1,216
(3) Rs. 1,264   (4) Rs. 1, 261

20. The simple interest on Rs. 1,820 from March 9, 1994 to May 21, 1994 at 7.5% rate will be
(1) Rs. 29   (2) Rs. 28.80
(3) Rs. 27.30   (4) Rs. 22.50

Time, Work and Distance **4**

Time and Work

Problems involving the concepts of time and work have been increasingly gaining importance in various aptitude exams conducted by different organisations. There is a rich variety of questions covered under this topic.

Following are the **most popular types** based on which questions are asked in various examinations:

i. Time taken to do a certain job by a certain number of workers.

ii. The change in the number of hours required to do a job if the number of workers is changed.

iii. The number of hours required to do the same job by different workers if their speeds are different.

iv. Problems on wages earned by various workers executing a certain work in proportion with the amount of work done by each worker.

v. Work done by various people in alternate intervals.

vi. Time taken by pipes/taps/leakages to fill/empty tanks/cisterns, etc.

There are certain points that are to be kept in mind while solving problems. They are:-

i. A person does the same amount of work everyday (unless specified in the problem).

Note:

(a) **If A can do a piece of work in 'n' days, then the amount of work done by A in one day is $\dfrac{1}{n}$.**

(b) **Conversely, if A's 1 day's work = $\dfrac{1}{n}$, then A can finish the work in 'n' days.**

ii. If there are more than one person involved carrying out the work collectively, it is assumed that the working capacity of each person is the same (unless specified in the problem).

iii. **Mandays:** If 'm' men worked for 'd' days to finish a job, then we can say **m × d Mandays** are required to finish the job. Mandays required to finish a job remains constant while number of men or number of days needed to complete the job can vary, e.g. if 20 men finish a job in 5 days, then Mandays = 20 × 5 = 100 (constant).
Now, if number of men are reduced to 10, then number of days to finish the job

$$= \frac{\text{Mandays}}{\text{Number of Men}} = \frac{100}{10} = 10 \text{ days}$$

Similarly, 50 men will finish the same job in 2 days.

iv. **Manhours:** If 'm' men worked for 'h' hours to finish a job, then we can say **m × h Manhours** are required to finish the job. Manhours required to finish a job remains constant while number of men or number of hours needed to complete the job can vary, e.g. if 25 men finish a job in 4 hours, then Manhours = 25 × 4 = 100 (constant).
Now, if the number of men are reduced to 20, then number of hours to finish the job

$$= \frac{\text{Manhours}}{\text{Number of Men}} = \frac{100}{20} = 5 \text{ hours}$$

Similarly, 10 men will finish the same job in 10 hours.

In general we can say that,

> If 'w_1' work is done by 'm_1' men working 'h_1' hours per day in 'd_1' days and 'w_2' work is done by 'm_2' men working 'h_2' hours per day in 'd_2' days, then
> $$\frac{m_1\, d_1\, h_1}{w_1} = \frac{m_2\, d_2\, h_2}{w_2}$$

Let us solve some examples.

Example 1:

5 men can pack 10 boxes in 6 days, working 6 hours a day. Then in how many days can 12 men pack 16 boxes working 8 hrs a day?

Solution:

We know that, $\dfrac{m_1\, d_1\, h_1}{w_1} = \dfrac{m_2\, d_2\, h_2}{w_2}$.

$$\therefore\ d_2 = \frac{5 \times 6 \times 6 \times 16}{12 \times 8 \times 10} = 3 \text{ days}.$$

Example 2:

40 men can cut 30 trees in an 8 hour shift. If 8 men leave the job, how many trees will be cut if the shift is extended by 4 hours?

Solution:

40 men working 8 hrs can cut 30 trees

or, 1 man working 1 hr can cut $\dfrac{30}{40 \times 8}$ trees.

Thus, 32 men working 12 hrs will be able to cut

$$\frac{30 \times 32 \times 12}{40 \times 8} = 36 \text{ trees.}$$

Generally, the following types of questions are asked in examinations.

Type of question	Example	Approach to question
1. Calculate the time taken by two persons working together to finish a work.	A can complete a piece of work in 10 days which B alone can complete in 12 days. In how many days can they finish the work if they both work together?	$T = \dfrac{XY}{X+Y}$, where X and Y are the time taken by A and B individually. $T = \dfrac{10 \times 12}{10 + 12} = \dfrac{120}{22} = 5\dfrac{5}{11}$ days.
2. Calculate the time taken by three persons working together to finish a work.	A can complete a piece of work in 5 days which B alone can complete in 6 days. If C, who can complete the work in 12 days, joins them, how long will they take to complete the work?	$T = \dfrac{XYZ}{XY + YZ + ZX}$, where X, Y and Z are the time taken by A, B and C individually. $= \dfrac{5 \times 6 \times 12}{5 \times 6 + 6 \times 12 + 12 \times 5} = \dfrac{360}{162}$ $= 2\dfrac{2}{9}$ days.
3. If one worker is 'm' times as efficient as another worker and takes 'D' days less than the other person, then in how many days can both finish the work working together?	A is thrice as efficient as B and takes 60 days less than B for finishing a job. Find the time in which they can finish the work together.	$T = \dfrac{m \times D}{m^2 - 1}$ $= \dfrac{3 \times 60}{9 - 1} = \dfrac{180}{8} = \dfrac{45}{2}$ days $= 22.5$ days
4. One pipe can fill a cistern in T_1 mins and another pipe in T_2 mins. If both the pipes are opened together, find the time taken to fill the cistern.	A pipe can fill a cistern in 30 min and another can fill it in 40 min. If both are opened simultaneously, find the time taken to fill the cistern.	$T = \dfrac{T_1 \times T_2}{T_1 + T_2}$, where T_1 and T_2 are the time taken by each pipe individually. $= \dfrac{30 \times 40}{30 + 40} = \dfrac{1200}{70} = 17\dfrac{1}{7}$ mins.
5. One tap can fill a cistern in T_1 mins and another tap can empty it in T_2 mins. If both the taps are opened together, find the time taken to fill the cistern.	A cistern is filled by a tap A in 10 hrs and emptied by tap B in 12 hrs. If both the taps are opened simultaneously, find the time taken to fill the cistern.	$T = \dfrac{T_1 \times T_2}{T_2 - T_1}$, where T_1 and T_2 are the time taken by each tap individually to fill and empty the cistern respectively. $= \dfrac{10 \times 12}{12 - 10} = \dfrac{120}{2} = 60$ hrs.

Example 3:

A can do a piece of work in 5 days, and B can do it in 6 days. How long will it take to finish the work if they both work together?

Solution:

'A' can do $\dfrac{1}{5}$ work in 1 day.

'B' can do $\dfrac{1}{6}$ work in 1 day.

Thus 'A' and 'B' can do $\left(\dfrac{1}{5} + \dfrac{1}{6}\right)$ work in 1 day.

$\therefore$ 'A' and 'B' can do the work in $\dfrac{1}{\dfrac{1}{5} + \dfrac{1}{6}}$ days

$= \dfrac{30}{11} = 2\dfrac{8}{11}$ **days.**

Example 4:

To do a piece of work Ram would take three times as long as Rohan and Raj together, and Raj will take twice as long as Rohan and Ram together. The three boys together complete the work in 10 days. How long would each boy alone take to complete the work?

Solution:

3 times Ram's daily work = (Rohan + Raj)'s daily work.

Add Ram's daily work to both the sides.

$\therefore$ 4 times Ram's daily work

= (Rohan + Ram + Raj)'s daily work = $\dfrac{1}{10}$

$\therefore$ Ram's daily work = $\dfrac{1}{40}$

Also, 2 times Raj's daily work = (Rohan + Ram)'s daily work. Add Raj's daily work to both the sides.

$\therefore$ 3 times Raj's daily work = (Rohan + Ram +

Raj)'s daily work = $\dfrac{1}{10}$

$\therefore$ Raj's daily work = $\dfrac{1}{30}$

Now Rohan's daily work $= \dfrac{1}{10} - \left(\dfrac{1}{40} + \dfrac{1}{30} \right) = \dfrac{1}{24}$

$\therefore$ Rohan, Ram and Raj can do the work in 24, 40 and 30 days respectively.

Example 5:

Two men and 3 boys can do a piece of work in 10 days while 3 men and 2 boys can do the same work in 8 days. In how many days can 2 men and 1 boy do the same work?

Solution:

Let 1 man's 1 day's work = x
Let 1 boy's 1 day's work = y

$\Rightarrow 2x + 3y = \dfrac{1}{10}$ and $3x + 2y = \dfrac{1}{8}$

On solving the above equations, we get

$x = \dfrac{7}{200}$ and $y = \dfrac{1}{100}$

$\therefore$ (2 men + 1 boy's) 1 day's work

$= 2 \times \dfrac{7}{200} + 1 \times \dfrac{1}{100} = \dfrac{16}{200} = \dfrac{2}{25}$

Thus, 2 men and 1 boy can finish the work in $\dfrac{25}{2}$ days.

Alternative Method:

Two men and three boys can do a piece of work in 10 days.

Hence, in one day the number of men and boys required to finish the job = (2m +3b) × 10 ... (1)

Similarly, if three men and two boys can do a piece of work in 8 days, then in one day the number of men and boys required to finish the job = (3m + 2b) × 8.   ... (2)

By equating eqn. (1) and (2), we get

(2m + 3b) × 10 = (3m + 2b) × 8.

20m + 30b = 24m + 16b

$4m = 14b \Rightarrow m = \dfrac{7}{2}b$

Now, $2m + 3b = 2 \times \dfrac{7}{2}b + 3b = 10b$.

Hence, $2m + 1b = 2 \times \dfrac{7}{2}b + 1b = 8b$

By unitary method,

$10b \longrightarrow 10$ days

$8b \longrightarrow 10 \times \dfrac{10}{8} = 12.5$ days.

Example 6:

Ashok and Arun working alone can do a piece of work in 9 and 12 days respectively. They work for a day alternately, beginning with Ashok. In how many days will they complete the work?

Solution:

(Ashok + Arun)'s 2 days' work $= \left(\dfrac{1}{9} + \dfrac{1}{12} \right) = \dfrac{7}{36}$.

Work done in 5 pairs of days $= \left(5 \times \dfrac{7}{36} \right) = \dfrac{35}{36}$.

Remaining work $= \left(1 - \dfrac{35}{36} \right) = \dfrac{1}{36}$.

On 11th day, it is Ashok's turn and he can complete $\dfrac{1}{9}$ work in a day.

$\therefore$ Ashok will complete $\dfrac{1}{36}$ work in $\left(9 \times \dfrac{1}{36} \right) = \dfrac{1}{4}$ day.

$\therefore$ Total time taken $= \left(2 \times 5 + \dfrac{1}{4} \right)$ days

$= 10\dfrac{1}{4}$ days.

Example 7:

Ramesh and Suresh can do a work in 45 and 40 days respectively. They began the work together, but Ramesh left after some time and Suresh finished the remaining work in 23 days. After how many days did Ramesh leave?

Solution:

Suresh works alone for 23 days.

$\therefore$ Work done by Suresh in 23 days $= \dfrac{23}{40}$ work

$\therefore$ Work done by (Ramesh + Suresh) together

$= 1 - \dfrac{23}{40} = \dfrac{17}{40}$ work

Now, (Ramesh + Suresh) can complete the work

in $\dfrac{40 \times 45}{40 + 45} = \dfrac{40 \times 45}{85}$ days.

$\therefore$ Time taken by (Ramesh + Suresh) to do

$\dfrac{17}{40}$ work $= \dfrac{40 \times 45}{85} \times \dfrac{17}{40} = 9$ days.

Hence, Ramesh left after 9 days.

Example 8:

Rakesh, Sandeep and Prakash can do a work in

16 days, $12\dfrac{4}{5}$ days and 32 days respectively.

They started the work together but after 4 days Rakesh left. Sandeep left the work 3 days before completion of the work. In how many days was the work completed?

Solution:

Suppose the work is completed in x days,
Rakesh's 4 day's work + Sandeep's (x – 3) day's work + Prakash's x day's work = 1

or, $\dfrac{4}{16} + \dfrac{(x-3)5}{64} + \dfrac{x}{32} = 1$

or, $\dfrac{16 + 5x - 15 + 2x}{64} = 1$

or, 7x + 1 = 64

$\therefore$ x = 9 days.

Efficiency

Efficiency is also known as rate of work done

If A is taking less number of days with respect to B to complete the same work, we can say that the efficiency of A is more efficient than B.

In general time and efficiency are correlated as follows:

i. If efficiency of A is x% more than the efficiency of B and B takes 'D' days to complete the work, then A will take $\left(\dfrac{D}{100 + x} \times 100\right)$ days to complete the same work.

ii. If efficiency of A is x% less than the efficiency of B and B takes 'D' days to complete the work, then A will take $\left(\dfrac{D}{100 - x} \times 100\right)$ days to complete the same work.

With this, it can also be observed that if work is constant then time taken is inversely proportional to efficiency.

Example 9:

Sony is thrice as efficient as Rakesh and hence completes a work in 60 days less than the number of days taken by Rakesh. In how many days will the work finish if both of them work together?

Solution:

Since Sony is thrice as efficient as Rakesh, so the number of days taken by him will be 1/3rd the number of days taken by Rakesh. If Sony is taking x days, then Rakesh will take 3x days to complete the same work.
Now, 3x – x = 2x = 60 days
So, x = 30 days and 3x = 90 days
Let us assume that the total work = 90 units (LCM of 30 and 90)
So, the total work done by both of them in one day = 3 + 1 = 4 units of work.
So, the total number of days required to finish the

work $= \dfrac{90}{4}$ days $= 22.5$ days

Example 10:

Hemant is twice as good a workman as Devendra and together they finish a piece of work in 18 days. In how many days will Hemant alone finish the work?

Solution:

(Hemant's 1 day's work) : (Devendra's 1 day's work) = 2 : 1.

(Hemant + Devendra)'s 1 day's work $= \dfrac{1}{18}$.

Divide $\dfrac{1}{18}$ in the ratio 2 : 1.

$\therefore$ Hemant's one day's work $= \left(\dfrac{1}{18} \times \dfrac{2}{3}\right) = \dfrac{1}{27}$

Hence, Hemant alone can finish the work in 27 days.

Example 11:

Rahul can finish a work in 15 days working 8 hours a day. Sunil can finish it in $6\dfrac{2}{3}$ days working 9 hours a day. In how many days can they finish the work by working together 10 hours a day?

Solution:

First suppose each of them works for only one hour a day.

Then, Rahul can finish the work in 15 × 8 = 120 hours and Sunil can finish the work in

$$\dfrac{20}{3} \times 9 = 60 \text{ hours}$$

Now, both together can finish the work in

$$\dfrac{120 \times 60}{120 + 60} = 40 \text{ hours.}$$

But here we are given that they work 10 hrs a day. Hence, they can finish the work in 4 days.

Work and Wages

In general, money earned should be shared by people doing the work together in the ratio of the work done by each of them (unless specified in the given problem).

Example 12:

A, B and C can do a work in 3, 4 and 6 days respectively. Doing that work together they get an amount of Rs 450. What is the share of B in that amount?

Solution:

A's one day's work $= \dfrac{1}{3}$

B's one day's work $= \dfrac{1}{4}$

C's one day's work $= \dfrac{1}{6}$

A's share: B's share: C's share $= \dfrac{1}{3} : \dfrac{1}{4} : \dfrac{1}{6}$

$= 4 : 3 : 2$

$\therefore$ B's share $= \dfrac{450}{9} \times 3 = \text{Rs } 150.$

Example 13:

A and B agreed to do a work for Rs 112. A alone can do it in 7 days and B alone in 8 days. If with the help of a boy they finish the work in 3 days, then what amount does the boy gets?

Solution:

A's 3 days' work + B's 3 days' work + Boy's 3 day's work = 1

Or, $\dfrac{3}{7} + \dfrac{3}{8} + $ Boy's 3 day's work = 1

Or, Boy's 3 day's work $= 1 - \left(\dfrac{3}{7} + \dfrac{3}{8}\right) = \dfrac{11}{56}$

Ratio of shares $= \dfrac{3}{7} : \dfrac{3}{8} : \dfrac{11}{56} = 24 : 21 : 11$

$\therefore$ Boy's share $= \dfrac{112}{24 + 21 + 11} \times 11 = \text{Rs } 22.$

Example 14:

Wages for 9 women amount to Rs 15525 in 48 days. How many men must work for 16 days to receive Rs. 5750, the daily wages of a man being double those of a woman?

Solution:

Wage of a woman for a day $= \dfrac{15525}{9 \times 48} = \text{Rs } \dfrac{575}{16}$

Thus, wage of a man for a day $= 2 \times \dfrac{575}{16} = \text{Rs } \dfrac{575}{8}$

Now, number of men

$$= \dfrac{\text{Total wage}}{\text{No. of days} \times 1 \text{man's 1 day's wage}}$$

$$= \dfrac{5750 \times 8}{16 \times 575} = 5 \text{ men.}$$

Example 15:

A fort accommodating 60 men has a food reserve for 28 days. 8 days later reinforcements arrive leaving the number of days the food would last to 15 days. What was the strength of the reinforcement?

Solution:

Originally, the food would have lasted for 28 days. After 8 days the food would have lasted for 20 days.

Let the reinforcement number be x.

The food that would have been consumed by 60 men in 20 days was consumed by (60 + x) men in 15 days.

$\Rightarrow 60 \times 20 = (60 + x)\,15$

$x = 20$.

The strength of the reinforcement was 20 men.

Pipes and Cisterns

Pipes and cisterns is just another application of the concept of time and work. While we see only +ve work being done in normal cases of time and work, in case of pipes and cisterns, –ve work is also possible.

Given that pipes A and B can fill a tank in 20 mins and 25 mins individually is similar to "A can do a work in 20 mins and B can do the same work in 25 mins."

Again, given that pipe C can empty a tank in 40 mins we can say this statement is similar to "C can demolish a wall in 40 mins.

Example 16:

Two pipes A and B can fill a tank in 4 hours and 5 hours respectively. If both the pipes are opened simultaneously, how much time will be taken to fill the tank?

Solution:

Part filled by A alone in 1 hours $= \dfrac{1}{4}$

Part filled by B alone in 1 hour $= \dfrac{1}{5}$

$\therefore$ Part filled by (A + B) in 1 hour $= \left(\dfrac{1}{4} + \dfrac{1}{5}\right) = \dfrac{9}{20}$

Hence, both the pipes together will fill the tank in $\dfrac{20}{9} = 2\dfrac{2}{9}$ **hours.**

Example 17:

Pipe A can fill a tank in 20 hours while pipe B alone can fill it in 30 hours while pipe C can empty the full tank in 40 hours. If all the pipes are opened together, how much time will be needed to fill the tank if the tank is initially empty?

Solution:

Net part filled in 1 hour $= \left(\dfrac{1}{20} + \dfrac{1}{30} - \dfrac{1}{40}\right) = \dfrac{7}{120}$

$\therefore$ The tank will be full in $\dfrac{120}{7}$ i.e. $17\dfrac{1}{7}$ hours.

Example 18:

A and B are two taps which can fill a tank individually in 10 min and 20 min respectively. However, there is a leakage at the bottom, which can empty a filled tank in 40 min. If the tank is empty initially, how much time will both the taps take to fill the tank (leakage is still there)?

Solution:

Let us assume the units of work
$= $ LCM of (10, 20, 40) = 40 units

Work done by Tap A/min
$= 4$ units/min (Positive work)

Work done by Tap B/min
$= 2$ units/min (Positive work)

Work done by leakage/min
$= 1$ unit/min (Negative work)

Net work done/min = 4 + 2 − 1 = 5 units/min

Hence, time taken to fill the tank $= \dfrac{40}{5} = 8$ mins.

Example 19:

Two pipes can fill a cistern in 14 hours and 16 hours respectively. The pipes are opened simultaneously and it is found that due to leakage in the bottom it took 32 minutes more to fill the cistern. In how much time can the leak empty the whole cistern?

Solution:

Work done by the two pipes in 1 hour

$= \left(\dfrac{1}{14} + \dfrac{1}{16}\right) = \dfrac{15}{112}.$

$\therefore$ Time taken by these pipes to fill the tank

$= \dfrac{112}{15}\,\text{hrs} = 7$ hrs and 28 min.

Due to leakage, time taken = 7 hrs 28 min + 32
= 8 hrs

$\therefore$ Work done by (two pipes + leak) in 1 hour $= \dfrac{1}{8}.$

Work done by the leak in 1 hour

$= \left(\dfrac{15}{112} - \dfrac{1}{8}\right) = \dfrac{1}{112}$

$\therefore$ Leak will empty the full cistern in 112 hours.

Example 20:

Two pipes A and B can fill a tank in 24 mins and 32 mins respectively. If both the pipes are opened simultaneously, after how much time should B be closed so that the tank is full in 18 minutes?

Solution:

Let B be closed after x minutes. Then, part filled by (A + B) in x min. + part filled by A in (18 − x) min. = 1

$$\therefore x\left(\frac{1}{24}+\frac{1}{32}\right)+(18-x)\times\frac{1}{24}=1$$

$$\Leftrightarrow \frac{7x}{96}+\frac{18-x}{24}=1$$

$$\Leftrightarrow 7x+4(18-x)=96$$

Hence, B must be closed after 8 minutes.

Time Speed and Distance

Time, speed and distance (TSD) is one of the most popular topics in aptitude tests. Every year almost 5-10% questions in the paper are asked from this chapter. Further, this concept is extensively used in questions covering other topics.

Some of the most popularly known question types are based on:

1. Basic relationship between time, speed and distance.
2. Calculation of average speed.
3. Questions on relative speed which can be further bifurcated in:
   i. Questions on speed of trains, length of trains crossing each other, etc.
   ii. Questions on speed of boats travelling upstream/ downstream, speed of streams, etc.
   iii. Questions on various types of linear races.
4. Circular motion which covers races on circular tracks. (Do you know that in conventional analog clocks, a race is going on between hour-hand and minute-hand?)

Distance: When an object is moving with a certain speed in a particular time, the travel of the object is called the distance.

Most commonly used units of distance are **kilometer (km)** and **meter (m)**. However, mile, feet, inch, yard and nauts also represents distance but generally they do not make an appearance in questions asked in examinations.

Time: Time is the duration of happening of any event. If we do not have the concept of time, we would not be able to know in what period or in what order something took place.

Generally used units of time are **second** and **hour.** However, day or minute are also the units but less used.

Speed: Speed is defined as the distance covered per unit time. In other words, it is the rate at which distance is covered. Though we commonly take **km/hour** and **meter/sec** as the units of speed still any unit of distance upon any unit of time can be taken as unit of speed for fastly solving the questions.

Conversion of m/s to km/h and vice-versa: If the speed is given in m/s and it is required to convert it into km/hr, then we multiply it by $\frac{18}{5}$ and when speed is given in km/h and we need to convert it into m/s, we multiply it by $\frac{5}{18}$.

$$36 \text{ km/h} = 36 \times \frac{5}{18} = 10\text{m/s}$$

Similarly,

$$20\text{m/s} = 20 \times \frac{18}{5} = 72 \text{ km/h}$$

Relationship between Time, Speed and Distance.

Time, Speed and Distance are related as

Distance = Speed × Time.

It means that if a person is walking at 5 km/h and he walks for 2 hours, then he will be covering a total of 10 kms.

From the relation distance (d) = speed (s) × time (t), we can deduce three important relations:

i. When Distance (d) is constant,

   then s × t = k (constant)

   $$\therefore s = \frac{k}{t} \text{ or } s \propto \frac{1}{t}$$

   Hence, more the speed, lesser is the time taken and more the time taken, lesser is the speed at which distance is travelled.

ii. When Time (t) is constant, then

   $$\frac{d}{s}=k \,(\text{Constant})$$

   $$\Rightarrow d = ks \text{ or } d \propto s.$$

   Hence, higher is the speed, the more will be the distance covered and lower the speed, the lesser will be the distance covered.

iii. When Speed (s) is constant, then

   $$\frac{d}{t}=k\,(\text{Constant})$$

   $$\Rightarrow d = kt \text{ or } d \propto t.$$

   Hence, if a person is running at a constant speed, then the ratio of distance covered in one hour to distance covered in three hours will be 1 : 3.

Example 21:

A scooterist covers a certain distance at 36 km/hr. How much distance does he cover in 3 min?

Solution:

Speed = 36 km/hr = $36 \times \dfrac{5}{18} \times$ m/s = 10 m/s

Thus, the distance covered in 3 min
= (10 × 3 × 60)
= 1,800 m.

Example 22:

Walking at $\dfrac{3}{4}$ of his usual speed a man is $1\dfrac{1}{2}$ hr late in reaching his office from home. Find his usual travel time.

Solution:

Let usual time be t hours. Since the distance travelled in the same.

Hence, $s \propto \dfrac{1}{t}$

New speed = $\dfrac{3}{4}$ old speed (given)

∴ New time = $\dfrac{4}{3}$ old time

$\Rightarrow \dfrac{4}{3} \times t = t + \dfrac{3}{2}$; t = 4.5 hr.

Alternative method:

$st = \dfrac{3s}{4}\left(t + \dfrac{3}{2}\right)$

4st = 3st + 4.5 s
t = 4.5 hr.

Example 23:

Two cyclists cover the same distance in 15 km/hr and 16 km/hr, respectively. Find the distance travelled by each, if one takes 16 min longer than the other.

Solution:

Let the required distance be x km.

$\dfrac{x}{15} - \dfrac{x}{16} = \dfrac{16}{60}$

or 16x − 15x = 64 or x = 64
Hence, the required distance = 64 km.

Example 24:

While covering a distance of 24 km, a man notived that after walking for 1 hour and 40 minutes, the distance covered by him was $\dfrac{5}{7}$ of the remaining distance. What was his speed in metres per second?

Solutions:

Let the speed be x km/hr
Then, distance covered in 1 hr 40 min.

i.e., $1\dfrac{2}{3}$ hrs = $\dfrac{5x}{3}$ km

Remaining distance $= \left(24 - \dfrac{5x}{3}\right)$ km.

$\therefore \dfrac{5x}{3} = \dfrac{5}{7}\left(24 - \dfrac{5x}{3}\right) \Leftrightarrow \dfrac{5}{x} = \dfrac{5}{7}\left(\dfrac{72 - 5x}{3}\right)$

$\Rightarrow 7x = 72 - 5x$

$\Leftrightarrow 12x = 72 \Leftrightarrow x = 6$
Hence, speed = 6km/hr

$= \left(6 \times \dfrac{5}{18}\right)$ m/sec $= \dfrac{5}{3}$ m/sec $= 1\dfrac{2}{3}$ m/sec

Example 25:

A man covers a certain distance between his house and office on scooter. Having an average speed of 30 km/hr, he is late by 10 min. However, with a speed of 40 km/hr, he reaches his office 5 min earlier. Find the distance between his house and office.

Solution:

Let the distance be x km.

Time taken to cover x km at 30 km/hr $= \dfrac{x}{30}$ hrs.

Time taken to cover x km at 40 km/hr $= \dfrac{x}{40}$ hrs.

Difference between the time taken = 15 min $= \dfrac{1}{4}$ hr.

$\therefore \dfrac{x}{30} - \dfrac{x}{40} = \dfrac{1}{4}$ or, 4x − 3x = 30 or, x = 30
Hence, the required distance is 30 km.

Example 26:

A car completes a journey in 10 hrs, the first half at 21 km/hr and the second half at 24 km/hr. Find the distance.

Solution:

Let the distance be x km.

Then $\dfrac{x}{2}$ km is travelled at a speed of 21 km/hr and

$\dfrac{x}{2}$ km at a speed of 24 km/hr.

Then, time taken to travel the whole journey

$$= \dfrac{x}{2 \times 21} + \dfrac{x}{2 \times 24} = 10 \text{ hrs}$$

$$\text{So, } x = \dfrac{2 \times 10 \times 21 \times 24}{21 + 24} = 224 \text{ km}.$$

Example 27:

Excluding stoppages, the speed of a bus is 40 km/hr and including stoppages it is 30 km/hr. For how long does the bus stop per hour?

Solution:

Let the total distance be x km.

Time taken at the speed of 40 km/hr $= \dfrac{x}{40}$ hrs.

$\therefore$ he rested for $= \left(\dfrac{x}{30} - \dfrac{x}{40} \right)$ hrs $= \dfrac{x}{120}$ hrs

$\therefore$ His rest per hour $= \dfrac{x}{120} \div \dfrac{x}{30} = \dfrac{1}{4}$ hrs

= 15 minutes.

Example 28:

A man rode out a certain distance by scooter at the rate of 25 km an hour and walked back at the rate of 4 km per hour. The whole journey took 5 hours and 48 minutes. What is the total distance he covered?

Solution:

Let the distance be x km.

Then time spent in journey by train $= \dfrac{x}{25}$ hrs.

And time spent in journey by walking $= \dfrac{x}{4}$ hrs.

$\therefore \dfrac{x}{25} + \dfrac{x}{4} = 5 \text{ hrs } 48 \text{ minutes}$

or, $\dfrac{29x}{100} = 5\dfrac{48}{60} = \dfrac{29}{5} \therefore x = \dfrac{100}{5} = 20 \text{ km}$

Example 29:

A man travels 360 km in 4 hours, partly by air and partly by train. If he had travelled all the way by air, he would have saved $\dfrac{4}{5}$ of the time he was in train and would have arrived at his destination 2 hours early. Find the distance he travelled by air and train.

Solution:

$\dfrac{4}{5}$ of total time in train = 2 hours.

$\therefore$ Total time in train $= 2 \div \dfrac{4}{5} = \dfrac{5}{2}$ hrs.

$\therefore$ Total time spent in air $= 4 - \dfrac{5}{2} = \dfrac{3}{2}$ hrs.

If 360 km is covered by air, then time taken is $(4 - 2 =)$ 2 hrs.

$\therefore$ When $\dfrac{3}{2}$ hrs is spent in air, distance covered

$= \dfrac{360}{2} \times \dfrac{3}{2} = 270$ km.

$\therefore$ Distance covered by train = 360 − 270 = 90 km.

Example 30:

A started walking in a straight line from a point P to Q. At the same time B started walking from the point Q to P. After passing each other they complete their journeys in 9 and 16 hours respectively. At what rate does B walks if A walks at 16 km per hour?

Solution:

<pre>
A ⟶   ⟵ B
●─────────────●──────────●
P   R   Q
</pre>

Let the speed of A be s_A and speed of B be s_B. Also, let R be the point at which they pass each other after time t.

$\Rightarrow PR = s_A t = s_B \times 16 \qquad \ldots (1)$

Also, $QR = s_B t = s_A \times 9 \qquad \ldots (2)$

Dividing (1) by (2), we get

$$\dfrac{s_A}{s_B} = \dfrac{16 s_B}{9 s_A} \Rightarrow \dfrac{s_A^{\,2}}{s_B^{\,2}} = \dfrac{16}{9}$$

$$\Rightarrow s_B = s_A \sqrt{\dfrac{9}{16}} = \dfrac{3}{4} s_A = \dfrac{3}{4} \times 16 = 12 \text{ km/hr}.$$

Average Speed

$$\text{Average speed} = \frac{\text{Total distance travelled}}{\text{Total time taken}}$$

Suppose, a man covers a distance d_1 kms at s_1 km/hr and a distance d_2 kms at s_2 km/hr, then

$$\text{Average speed of the whole travel} = \frac{d_1 + d_2}{\dfrac{d_1}{s_1} + \dfrac{d_2}{s_2}} \text{ km/hr}$$

If the distances are equal, then

$$\text{Average speed} = \frac{d + d}{\dfrac{d}{s_1} + \dfrac{d}{s_2}} = \frac{2s_1 s_2}{s_1 + s_2} \text{ km/hr}$$

Example 31:

A car during its journey travels 30 minutes at a speed of 40 km/hr, another 45 minutes at a speed of 60 km/hr and 2 hours at a speed of 70 km/hour. Find the average speed of the car.

Solution:

Average speed

$$= \frac{\left(\dfrac{30}{60} \times 40\right) + \left(\dfrac{45}{60} \times 60\right) + (2 \times 70)}{\dfrac{30}{60} + \dfrac{45}{60} + 2} = 63 \text{ km/hr.}$$

Example 32:

What is the average speed if a person travels from A to B and back to A from B at the speed of 10 km/hr and 20 km/hr, respectively
a. for equal intervals of time.
b. for equal distances.

Solution:

a. The concept of weighted average can be used here.

$$\text{The average speed} = \frac{(10 + 20)}{2} = 15 \text{ km/hr}$$

Note:
For equal intervals of time, the average speed is given as

$$\frac{S_1 + S_2 + S_3 + \ldots + S_n}{n}, \text{ where } S_1, S_2, S_3, \ldots, S_n$$

are the speeds and 'n' is the number of observations.

b. The weighted average concept cannot be applied here, because we do not know the fractions of time spent travelling the two distances. **It would be a mistake** to calculate the average speed as

$$\frac{(10 + 20)}{2} = 15 \quad \text{km/hr.}$$

$$\text{Total time taken} = \left(\frac{D}{10}\right) + \left(\frac{D}{20}\right) = T$$

Total distance travelled = 2D.

$$\text{So, average speed} = \frac{2D}{T}$$

$$= \frac{2D}{\left(\dfrac{D}{10} + \dfrac{D}{20}\right)} = \frac{2D}{D\left(\dfrac{1}{10} + \dfrac{1}{20}\right)} = 13\frac{1}{3} \text{ km/hr.}$$

Example 33:

When a man travels equal distance at speed s_1 and s_2 km/hr, his average speed is 4 km/hr. But when he travels at these speeds for equal times his average speed is 4.5 km/hr. Find the value of speeds s_1 and s_2.

Solution:

Suppose the equal distance = d km
Then time taken with s_1 and s_2 speeds are

$$\frac{d}{s_1} \text{ hrs and } \frac{d}{s_2} \text{ hrs respectively.}$$

$$\therefore \text{ average speed} = \frac{\text{Total distance}}{\text{Total time}} = \left(\frac{2d}{\dfrac{d}{s_1} + \dfrac{d}{s_2}}\right)$$

$$= \left(\frac{2s_1 s_2}{s_1 + s_2}\right) = 4 \text{ km/hr}$$

In second case,

$$\text{average speed} = \left(\frac{s_1 + s_2}{2}\right) = 4.5 \text{ km/hr}$$

That is; $(s_1 + s_2) = 9$ and $(s_1 s_2) = 18$
Now, $(s_1 - s_2)^2 = [(s_1 + s_2)^2 - 4s_1 s_2]$
$= 81 - 72 = 9$
$\therefore (s_1 - s_2) = 3$ km/hr and $s_1 + s_2 = 9$ km/hr
$\therefore s_1 = 6$ km/hr and $s_2 = 3$ km/hr.

Relative Speed

If two bodies are moving (in the same direction or in the opposite direction), then the speed of one body with respect to the other is called its relative speed.

Relative speed is a phenomenon that we observe everyday. Suppose you are travelling in a train and there is a second train coming in the opposite direction on parallel track, then it seems that the second train is moving much faster than actual. If both the trains were moving in the same direction on parallel tracks at same speeds, they seem to be stationary if seen from one of these trains, even though they might actually be at a speed of 100 km/hr each. So what you actually observe is your speed relative to the other.

Concepts

1. If two objects are moving in opposite directions towards each other or away from each other on a straight-line at speeds u and v, then they seem to be moving towards each other or away from each other at a relative speed = Speed of first + Speed of second = **u + v.**
2. If the two objects move in the same direction with speeds u and v, then relative speed = difference of their speeds = **u − v.**
    This is also the speed at which the faster object is either drawing closer to the slower object or moving away from the slower object as the case may be.

Example 34:

A thief is spotted by a policeman at a distance of 200 m. If the speed of the thief be 10 km/hr and that of the policeman be 12 km/hr, then how for will the thief runs before the policeman catches him?

Solution:

Relative speed of the policeman = 2 km/hr
Time taken by the policeman to cover the

additional 200 m = $\dfrac{200}{1000} \times \dfrac{1}{2}$ hr = $\dfrac{1}{10}$ hr.

In this time, the thief covers = $10 \times \dfrac{1}{10}$ = 1 km.

Example 35:

A train running at 54 km/hr takes 20 s to cross a platform and 12 s to pass a man walking in the same direction at a speed of 6 km/hr. Find the length of the train and the platform.

Solution:

Let the length of the train = x m. Let the length of the platform = y m.
Speed of the train relative to the man = 48 km/hr

$= \dfrac{40}{3}$ m/s

In passing the man, the train covers its own length with relative speed.

Length of the train = $\dfrac{40}{3} \times 12$ = 160 m. Since

speed of train = 54 km/hr = 15 m/s

$\dfrac{x+y}{15}$ = 20 or x + y = 300   or   y = 140.

Length of the platform = 140 m.

Example 36:

A hare makes 9 leaps in the same time as a dog makes 4. But the dog's leap is $2\dfrac{1}{3}$ m while hare's is only 1 m. How many leaps will the dog have to make before catching up with the hare if the hare has a head start of 16 m?

Solution:

Distance covered by dog in 4 leaps = $4 \times \dfrac{7}{3}$

$= \dfrac{28}{3}$ m

Distance covered by hare in 9 leaps = 9 × 1 = 9 m

Distance gained by the dog in 4 leaps = $\dfrac{1}{3}$ m.

Hence, for 1 m gain he has to make 12 leaps.
Number of leaps required by the dog to gain 16 m
= 12 × 16 = 192 leaps.

Example 37:

Sanjay leaves a point A and reaches the point B in 4 hours. Rahul leaves the point B 2 hours earlier and reaches the point A in 4 hours. Find the time in which Sanjay meets Rahul.

Solution:

Let the distance AB = d km
And they meet t hrs after Sanjay starts.

Average speed of Sanjay $= \dfrac{d}{4}$ km/hr

Average speed of Rahul $= \dfrac{d}{4}$ km/hr

Distance travelled by Sanjay $= \dfrac{dt}{4}$ km

They meet t hrs after Sanjay starts. Rahul meets after (t + 2) hrs from his start. Therefore, the distance travelled by Rahul $= \dfrac{d(t+2)}{4}$ km

Now, $= \dfrac{dt}{4} + \dfrac{d(t+2)}{4}$ km = d

2t + 2 = 4

∴ t = 1hr

Example 38:

Two guns were fired from the same place at an interval of 13 minutes but a person in a train approaching the place hears the second sound 12 minutes 30 seconds after the first. Find the speed of the train, supposing that sound travels at 330 metres per second

Solution:

Distance travelled by the train in 12 min. 30 seconds could be travelled by sound in (13 min – 12 min 30 seconds) = 30 seconds

$\Rightarrow$ train travels 330 × 30 metres in $12\dfrac{1}{2}$ min

∴ Speed of the train per hour $= \dfrac{330 \times 30 \times 2 \times 60}{25 \times 1000}$

$= 47\dfrac{13}{25}$ km/hour.

Boats and Streams

Downstream motion of a boat is its motion in the same direction as the flow of the river.

Upstream motion of a boat is its motion in the opposite direction as the flow of the river.

There are two parameters in these problems.

1. **Speed of the stream or river (R):** This is the speed with which the river flows.

2. **Speed of the boat in still water (B):** If the river is still, this is the speed at which the boat would be moving.

   The effective speed of a boat while moving upstream = B – R

   The effective speed of a boat while moving downstream = B + R

3. The speed of the boat in still water is given as **B** $= \dfrac{1}{2}(d + u)$, and the speed of the river **R** $= \dfrac{1}{2}(d - u)$,

where, d and u are the downstream and upstream speeds, respectively.

Example 39:

A man rows 27 km downstream and 18 km upstream taking 3 hr each. What is the velocity of the current?

Solution:

Rate downstream $= \dfrac{27}{3}$ = 9 km/hr

Rate upstream $= \dfrac{18}{3}$ = 6 km/hr

Velocity of current = 0.5 (9 – 6) = 1.5 km/hr.

Example 40:

A man can row upstream at 7 km/hr and downstream at 10 km/hr. Find his rate in still water and the rate of the current.

Solution:

Rate in still water = 0.5 (10 + 7) = 8.5 km/hr

Rate of current = 0.5 (10 – 7) = 1.5 km/hr

Example 41:

A man can row a boat 30 km upstream and 44 km downstream in 10 hrs. Also, he can row 40 km upstream and 55 km downstream in 13 hrs. Find the rate of the current and the speed of the boat in still water.

Solution:

Let, upstream rate = x k/hr and downstream rate = y km/hr

Then, $\dfrac{30}{x} + \dfrac{44}{y} = 10$ and $\dfrac{40}{x} + \dfrac{55}{y} = 13$

or 30u + 44v = 10

40u + 55v = 13

Where u $= \dfrac{1}{x}$ and v $= \dfrac{1}{y}$

∴ x = 5 and y = 11

∴ rate in still water $= \dfrac{5 + 11}{2} = 8$ km/hr

Rate of current $= \dfrac{11 - 5}{2} = 3$ km/hr

Example 42:

A man can row 6 km/hr in still water. If the river is running at 2 km/hr, it takes 3 hours more in upstream than to go downstream for the same distance. How far is the place?

Solution:

Let the distance of the place be d km.
According to the question,

$$\frac{d}{6-2} - \frac{d}{6+2} = 3$$

or, $\dfrac{d}{4} - \dfrac{d}{8} = 3$

$\therefore$ d = 8 × 3 = 24 km

Races on linear tracks

A contest of speed is called a race. Racing events takes place in various activities like running, riding, driving, walking, rowing, etc. A basic assumption is that contestants cover the race course at uniform speed unless specified in the problem.

Let us get used to the various terminologies used in a race:

1. **Race course:** The path on which race takes place is called race course.

2. **Starting point:** The point of beginning of the race is called the starting point.

3. **Finishing Point:** The point where the race finishes is called the finishing point.

4. **Dead Heat Race:** If two or more than two contestants finish the race in exactly the same time and there can be no single winner of the race, then the race is said to be a dead heat race.

5. **"A beats B by 20m"** means that A has reached the finishing point while B is still 20m behind the finishing point.

6. **"A beats B By 5 seconds"** means that A has reached the finishing point while B will still take another 5 seconds to reach the finishing point.

7. **"A gives B a start of 40m"** means that while A starts the race from the starting point while B starts at a point 40m ahead of the starting point.

8. **"A gives B a start of 5 seconds"** means that A starts the race when B had already ran for 5 seconds.

Example 43:

In a km race A beats B by 25 meters or by 5 seconds. Find the time taken by A to complete the race.

Solution:

A beats B by 25 m or by 5 seconds means that B will take 5 seconds to complete the last 25 m of the race course.

$\Rightarrow$ B's speed = $\dfrac{25}{5}$ = 5 m/s

$\Rightarrow$ Time taken by B to finish the race

$= \dfrac{\text{Total race course}}{\text{Speed of B}}$

$= \dfrac{1000}{5}$ = 100 secs

$\Rightarrow$ Time taken by A to finish the race = Time taken by B − 5 seconds = 200 − 5 = 195 secs

Example 44:

In a race of 100 m, Ajay gives a start of 10 m to Vijay. Despite this, Ajay wins the race by 20 m. What is the ratio of the speed of Ajay and Vijay?

Solution:

Time taken by Ajay to cover 100 m
= Time taken by Vijay to cover 70 m.

$\Rightarrow \dfrac{100}{\text{Ajay's speed}} = \dfrac{70}{\text{Vijay's speed}}$

$\Rightarrow$ Ajay's speed : Vijay's speed = 10 : 7

Example 45:

Sunny, Monty and Bunty are three contestants in a 1 km race. If Sunny can give a start of 40 m to Monty and a start of 64 m to Bunty and finally the race ends in a dead heat, where Sunny, Monty and Bunty finish the race at the same time then over the same race course, how many metres of start can Monty give to Bunty such that race again ends in a dead heat while Sunny doesn't participates in the race?

Solution:

While Sunny covers 1000m, Monty covers (1000 − 40)m = 960 m and Bunty covers (1000 − 64)m = 936m.
Hence, when Monty covers 960 m, Bunty covers 936 m.
So, when Monty covers 1000m, Bunty will cover

$$\left(\frac{936}{960} \times 1000\right)m = 975m$$

$\therefore$ Monty can give Bunty a start of (1000 − 975) = 25 m

Example 46:

Sonu beats Munnu by 40 m and Chunnu by 50 m in a 200 m race, while Munnu beats Chunnu by 2 seconds in the same race. How long does each take to run 400 m?

Solution:

While Sonu ran 200 m, Munnu ran 160 m and Chunnu ran only 150 m.

$\Rightarrow$ Sonu's speed : Munnu's speed : Chunnu's speed = 200 : 160 : 150

= 20 : 16 : 15

$\therefore$ Munnu's speed = 16x m/s

and Chunnu's speed = 15x m/s

Also, time taken by Munnu to complete the race = time taken by Chunnu – 2 secs

$$\Rightarrow \frac{200}{16x} = \frac{200}{15x} - 2$$

$$\Rightarrow x = \frac{100}{15 \times 16}$$

$$\Rightarrow \text{Sonu's speed} = 20x = 20 \times \frac{100}{15 \times 16} \text{ m/s}$$

$$\Rightarrow \text{Time taken by Sonu to cover 400 m} = \frac{400}{20x}$$

$$= \frac{400 \times 15 \times 16}{20 \times 100} = 48 \text{ secs}$$

Similarly, time taken by Munnu and Chunnu to cover 400 m is 60 secs and 64 secs, respectively.

Circular Motion

The problems we have encountered till now covered **motion in straight line**, where the path is not closed i.e. **open**. In linear motion, we observed that, if two bodies moved with different speed in one direction and the body with faster speed overtook the body with slower speed, then the bodies never meet again. However, if the same bodies move on a circular track, then the bodies are bound to meet again since the track is enclosed (by virtue of being circular).

The problems in circular motion deal with races on a circular track to calculate the time of meeting at the starting point or anywhere else on the track.

Concepts

1. If two people A and B start from the same point, at the same time and move in the same direction along a circular track and take x minutes and y minutes respectively to come back to the starting point, then they would meet for the first time at the starting point according to the formula:

First time meeting of A and B at the *starting* point = (LCM of x and y)

Note: This formula would remain the same even if they move in the opposite directions.

2. If two people A and B start from the same point with speeds m km/hr and n km/hr respectively, at the same time and move in the same/opposite direction along a circular track, then the two would meet for the first time by the formula given below:

Time of the first meeting

$$= \frac{\text{Circumference of the track}}{\text{Relative speed}}.$$

Please Remember:

1. The same approach is followed in solving the question if more than two persons (or bodies) are involved. You'll get more clarity in some of the examples that are illustrated ahead.

2. The same approach is followed in solving the question even if the path is not circular but is closed i.e. if the path is triangle, a quadrilateral, a pentagon or a hexagon, etc. The same approach will work to calculate the time of meeting at starting point or at any other point on the track.

3. Our conventional analog clock is a typical example of two runners i.e. hour hand and minute hand running in the same direction on a circular track. Minutes hand covers 360° in 1 hour, i.e., in 60 mins. Hence, speed of minutes hand is 6° per min. Similarly, hours hand covers 360° in 12 hours. Hence, speed of hour hand is 30° per hour or $\frac{1}{2}^{\circ}$ per min.

Therefore, relative speed of the two hands

$$= 6 - \frac{1}{2}^{\circ} = 5\frac{1}{2}^{\circ} \text{ per min.}$$

Some examples are illustrated ahead to get the basic understanding of the concept. However, the student may note that **CLOCKS** is comprehensively covered in **Analytical Ability** and therefore students should refer that chapter in order to have a thorough understanding of the topic.

Example 47:

Ashish and Prashant as a warm up exercise are jogging on a circular track. Prashant is a better athlete and jogs at 18 km/hr, while Ashish jogs at 9 km/hr. The circumference of the track is 500 m. They start from the same point and in the same direction. When will they be together again for the first time? (The same problem could be rephrased as: In what time would Prashant take a lead of 500 m over Ashish?)

Solution:

Since Prashant is faster than Ashish he will take a lead and as they keep running, the gap between them will also keep widening. Unlike on a straight track they would meet again.

Every second, Prashant is taking a lead of

$$\left[18 \times \frac{5}{18} - 9 \times \frac{5}{18}\right] m = 2.5 \text{ m over Ashish.}$$

Hence, he takes $\dfrac{500}{2.5} = 200 \text{ s}$ to take a lead of 500 m over Ashish. Hence, they would meet for the first time after 200 s.

Alternative method:

For every round that Ashish makes, Prashant would have made 2 rounds because the ratio of their speeds is 1 : 2. Hence, when Ashish has made one full round, Prashant would have taken a lead of one round. Therefore, they would meet after

$$\frac{500}{2.5} \text{s, i.e. } \left[\frac{1 \text{ round}}{\text{Ashish's speed}} = \frac{500}{2.5}\right] = 200 \text{ s}$$

$$\left[\text{Here, } 9 \times \frac{5}{18} = 2.5 \text{ m/s is Ashish's speed.}\right]$$

Example 48:

Suppose, in the earlier problem, when would the two meet for the first time if they are moving in the opposite directions?

Solution:

If the two are moving in the opposite directions, then relative speed = 2.5 + 5 = 7.5 m/s
Hence, time for the first meeting

$$= \frac{\text{Circumference}}{\text{Relative speed}} = \left(\frac{500}{7.5}\right) = \left(\frac{200}{3}\right) s = 66.66 \text{ s.}$$

Example 49:

If the speeds of Saurav and Sachin were 8 km/hr and 5 km/hr, then after what time will the two meet for the first time at the starting point if they start simultaneously? The length of the circular track is 500 m.

Solution:

Let us first calculate the time Saurav and Sachin take to make one full circle.

$$\text{Time taken by Saurav} = \frac{500}{\left(8 \times \frac{5}{18}\right)} = 225 \text{ s.}$$

$$\text{Time taken by Sachin} = \frac{500}{\left(5 \times \frac{5}{18}\right)} = 360 \text{ s.}$$

Hence, after every 225 s, Saurav would be at the starting point and after every 360 s, Sachin would be at the starting point. The time, when they will be together again at the starting point simultaneously for the first time, would be the smallest multiple of both 225 and 360, which is the LCM of 225 and 360.
Hence, they would both be together at the starting point for the first time after LCM (225, 360) = 1800 s. Thus, every half an hour, they would meet at the starting point.
From the solution you could realize that it is immaterial whether they move in the same direction or in the opposite.

Example 50:

Rohan, Mohan and Sohan with respective speeds of 9, 18, 36 km/hr, run around a circular track 1200 m long. If they started at the same time from the same point and run in the same direction, when will they meet for the first time?

Solution:

L = 1200 m

$$\text{Speed of Rohan (a)} = 9 \times \frac{5}{18} = 2.5 \text{ m/se}$$

$$\text{Speed of Mohan (b)} = 18 \times \frac{5}{18} = 5 \text{ m/sec}$$

$$\text{Speed of Sohan (c)} = 36 \times \frac{5}{18} = 10 \text{ m/sec}$$

They will meet for the first time at a time which is

the LCM of $\dfrac{L}{(b-a)}$ and $\dfrac{L}{(c-b)}$

$$\frac{L}{(b-a)} = \frac{1200}{(5-2.5)} = 480 \text{s}$$

$$\frac{L}{(c-b)} = \frac{1200}{(10-5)} = 240 \text{s}$$

$\therefore$ They will meet for the first time after 480 seconds i.e., 8 minutes after they start.

Example 51:

A, B and C run around a circular track 1200 m long at respective speeds of 9, 18 and 27 km/hr. If they start at the same point and at the same time in the same direction, when will they meet again at the starting point?

Solution:

L = 1200 m

Speed of A (a) = $9 \times \dfrac{5}{18}$ = 2.5 m/sec

Speed of B (b) = $18 \times \dfrac{5}{18}$ = 5 m/sec

Speed of C (c) = $27 \times \dfrac{5}{18}$ = 7.5 m/sec

They will meet for the first time at a time which is the LCM of $\dfrac{L}{a}$, $\dfrac{L}{b}$ and $\dfrac{L}{c}$.

$\dfrac{L}{a} = \dfrac{1200}{2.5}$ = 480s

$\dfrac{L}{b} = \dfrac{1200}{5}$ = 240s

$\dfrac{L}{c} = \dfrac{1200}{7.5}$ = 160s

LCM of 480, 240, 160 is 480s.

Hence they will meet for the first time at the starting point 8 minutes from the time they start.

Example 52:

When do the hands of a clock coincide between 4 and 5?

Solution:

At 4 the minute hand is 4 × 30° = 120° behind the hour hand.

The minute hand takes a lead of $5\left(\dfrac{1}{2}\right)^{\circ}$ every minute over the hour hand.

The time it takes to catch up 120° = $\dfrac{120}{\dfrac{11}{2}} = \dfrac{240}{11}$

min after 4.

This is when they would coincide.

Example 53:

At 3:45, what is the (acute) angle between the hands of a clock?

Solution:

At 3 o' clock, the minute hand of a clock would be 90° behind the hour hand.

In 45 min, the minute hand of a clock would move (45° × 6) = 270° forward.

The hour hand would move $\left(\dfrac{1}{2} \times 45°\right) = \left(22\dfrac{1}{2}^{\circ}\right)$ forward.

Hence, the angle between the hands would be

$$270° - \left(90° + 22\dfrac{1}{2}^{\circ}\right) = 157\dfrac{1}{2}^{\circ}$$

Example 54:

Consider a square ABCD. X starts from A and travels continuously along the path ABDCA and Y starts from B and continuously moves along path BCADB. If speed of X and Y are equal, how many times would they have met when X has completed 10 laps and reached the starting point A again?

Solution:

When X reaches B, Y would have reached C. Now both would move along the diagonal and would meet at the intersection of the diagonals. Beyond this when X reaches D, Y reaches A. Further when X reaches C, Y would reach D and again after this they would move along the diagonals and would once again meet at the intersection of diagonals. After this they would reach the starting points once again. Thus in every one lap, they meet twice. Thus in 10 laps they would have met 20 time.

Example 55:

Two men Ashok and Birju run a 4 km race on a course 250 m round. If their rates be 5 : 4, how often does the winner pass the other?

Solution:

Ashok's rate : Birju's rate = 5 : 4

⇒ When Ashok makes 5 rounds, Birju makes 4 rounds.

⇒ When Ashok covers $\dfrac{5 \times 250}{1000} = \dfrac{5}{4}$ km

Birju covers $\dfrac{4 \times 250}{1000} = 1$ km

⇒ Ashok passes Birju each time when Ashok makes 5 rounds.

⇒ In covering $\dfrac{5}{4}$ km, Ashok passes Birju 1 time.

So, in covering 4 km Ashok passes Birju

$$1 \times \dfrac{4}{5} \times 4 = 3\dfrac{1}{5} = 3 \text{ times}$$

 **Exercise**

Exercise – I

1. A can do a piece of work in 7 days working 9 hours a day and B can do it in 6 days working 7 hours a day. How long will they take to finish the work, working together $\dfrac{42}{5}$ hours a day?
   (1) 3 days
   (2) 4 days
   (3) 4.5 days
   (4) 6 days

2. A can do a piece of work in 80 days. He works for 10 days and then B alone finishes the remaining work in 42 days. They together could complete the work in:
   (1) 24 days
   (2) 25 days
   (3) 30 days
   (4) 29 days

3. A and B can do a piece of work in 45 days and 40 days respectively. They begin together but A leaves after some days and B completes the rest in 23 days. For how many days did A work?
   (1) 6 days
   (2) 9 days
   (3) 8 days
   (4) 12 days

4. A and B can do a job in 25 days and 20 days, respectively. A started the work and was joined by B after 10 days. The total number of days taken to complete the work is
   (1) 12.5 days
   (2) 14.22 days
   (3) 15 days
   (4) 16.66 days

5. A and B can finish a piece of work in 72 days, B and C in 120 days while A and C can finish it in 90 days. In what time can A finish it alone?
   (1) 150 days
   (2) 120 days
   (3) 100 days
   (4) 80 days

6. A and B together can do a job in 12 days and B and C together can do it in 16 days. First A and B works for 5 days, then B and C works for 7 days and thereafter, C finally finishes the rest of work in 7 days. In how many days can C do the work alone?
   (1) 24 days
   (2) 30 days
   (3) 36 days
   (4) 48 days

7. Twelve men can do a job in 8 days. Six days after they start, 4 more men join them. How many more days will it take to do the job?
   (1) 2.5 days
   (2) 1 day
   (3) 1.5 days
   (4) 4 days

8. A job can be done by 10 men in 20 days or by 20 women in 15 days. How many days will it take for 5 men and 10 women to finish the work?
   (1) $17\dfrac{1}{2}$ days
   (2) $17\dfrac{1}{7}$ days
   (3) 17 days
   (4) $17\dfrac{1}{20}$ days

9. R and S can do a job in 8 days and 12 days respectively. If they work on alternate days with R beginning the work, then in how many days will the work be finished?
   (1) $9\dfrac{1}{2}$ days
   (2) $9\dfrac{1}{3}$ days
   (3) $9\dfrac{1}{24}$ days
   (4) $10\dfrac{1}{3}$ days

10. A, B and C can do a job in 11, 20 and 55 days respectively. On the first day A is assisted by B and on the second day by C. How soon can the work be completed if A is assisted by B and C on alternate days?
    (1) 7 days
    (2) 9 days
    (3) 8 days
    (4) 10 days

11. Machines A and B produce 8,000 clips in 4 hr and 6 hr respectively. If they work alternately for 1 hr, A starting first, then 8,000 clips will be produced in
    (1) 4.33 hr
    (2) 5.66 hr
    (3) 5.33 hr
    (4) 4.66 hr

12. A does half as much work as B, while C does half as much work as A and B together in the same time. If C alone can do the work in 40 days, all of them can together will finish the work in
    (1) 13 days
    (2) 15 days
    (3) 20 days
    (4) 13.33 days

13. A and B can do a piece of work in 10 days and 20 days respectively. Both starts the work together but A leaves the work 5 days before its completion time. Find the time in which work is finished?
(1) 20 days   (2) 15 days
(3) 25 days   (4) 10 days

14. 24 men can complete a work in 16 days. 32 women can complete the same work in 24 days. 16 men and 16 women started working and worked for 12 days. How many more men are to be added to complete the remaining work in 2 days?
(1) 48   (2) 24
(3) 36   (4) None of these

15. 25 men and 15 women can complete a piece of work in 12 days. All of them start working together and after working for 8 days the women stopped working. 25 men completed the remaining work in 6 days. In how many days can one woman complete the job?
(1) 60 days
(2) 36 days
(3) 94 days
(4) None of these

16. 10 men and 15 women finish a work in 5 days. One man alone finishes that work in 100 days. In how many days will a woman finish the work?
(1) 125 days   (2) 150 days
(3) 90 days   (4) 225 days

17. A can do a piece of work in 12 days, B can do the same work in 8 days, and C can do the same job in $\frac{4}{5}$ th time required by both A and B together.

A and B work together for 3 days, then C completes the job. How many days did C work?
(1) 8   (2) 6
(3) 3   (4) None of these

18. 12 men take 18 days to complete a job whereas 12 women in 18 days can complete $\frac{3}{4}$ of the same job. How many days will 10 men and 8 women together take to complete the same job?
(1) 6   (2) $13\frac{1}{2}$
(3) 12   (4) None of these

19. A and B can complete a work in 10 and 15 days respectively. B starts the work and after 5 days A also joins him. In all, the work would be completed in:
(1) 9 days   (2) 7 days
(3) 11 days   (4) None of these

20. A does half as much work as B in three-fourth of the time. If together they take 18 days to complete a work, how much time shall B take to do it?
(1) 40 days   (2) 35 days
(3) 30 days   (4) None of these

21. Ram can mow his lawn in x hours. After 2 hours it begins to rain. The unmoved part of the lawn is ______.
(1) $\frac{2}{x}$ (2) $\frac{2-x}{2}$
(3) $\frac{x}{2}$ (4) $\frac{x-2}{x}$

22. If factory A turns out $\frac{x}{2}$ cars an hour and factory B turns our y cars every 2 hours, the number of cars which both factories turn out in 8 hours is ___.
(1) $8(x + y)$ (2) $8x+\frac{y}{2}$
(3) $16(x + y)$ (4) $4(x + y)$

23. Ramesh can finish a job in 20 days. He worked for 10 days alone and completed the remaining job working with Dinesh in 2 days. How many days would Dinesh take to complete the entire job?
(1) 4   (2) 5
(3) 10   (4) 12

24. A can do a piece of work in 12 days. B is 60% more efficient than A. The number of days, it takes B to do the same piece of work, is:
(1) $7\frac{1}{2}$ (2) $6\frac{1}{4}$
(3) 8   (4) 6

25. 12 men can complete a work within 9 days. 3 days after they started the work, 6 more men joined them while 2 men felt ill and hence didn't work at all. How many days will it take to complete the remaining work?
(1) 2   (2) 3
(3) 4   (4) $4\frac{1}{2}$

26. A is 4 times as fast as B and is therefore able to finish a work in 45 days less than B. Find the time in which they can finish it working together?
(1) 12 days
(2) 16 days
(3) 8 days
(4) 20 days

27. A can complete a certain job in 12 days. B is 100% more efficient than A; B can complete the work alone in
(1) 6 days
(2) 6.25 days
(3) 7 days
(4) 7.5 days

28. A is twice as good a worksman as B and together they finish a job in 14 days. A will finish the work alone in
(1) 11 days
(2) 21 days
(3) 28 days
(4) 42 days

29. A father can do a job twice as fast as his two sons working together. If one of the sons does the work in 3 hr and the other in 6 hr, in how many hours can the father do the work?
(1) 1 hr
(2) 2 hr
(3) 3 hr
(4) 4 hr

30. A can do a work in 6 days and B can do the same work in 5 days. The contract for the work is Rs. 220. How much shall B get if both of them work together?
(1) Rs. 100
(2) Rs. 120
(3) Rs. 80
(4) Rs. 140

31. A man can do a work in 10 days. With the help of a boy he can do the same work in 6 days. If they get Rs. 50 for that work, what is the share of that boy?
(1) Rs. 10
(2) Rs. 30
(3) Rs. 50
(4) Rs. 20

32. 3 men and 4 boys can earn Rs. 756 in 7 days. 11 men and 13 boys can earn Rs. 3008 in 8 days. In what time will 7 men with 9 boys earn Rs. 2480?
(1) 15 days
(2) 20 days
(3) 10 days
(4) 5 days

33. A , B and C together earn Rs. 1350 in 9 days. A and C together earn Rs. 470 in 5 days. B and C together earn Rs. 760 in 10 days. Find the daily earning of C.
(1) Rs. 20
(2) Rs. 10
(3) Rs. 15
(4) Rs. 25

34. Pipes A, B and C take 20, 15 and 12 min to fill a cistern. In how much time will they fill the cistern together?
(1) 15 min
(2) 10 min
(3) 12 min
(4) 5 min

35. A cistern can be filled in 9 hr but it takes 10 hr due to a leak. In how much time will the leak empty the full cistern?
(1) 60 hr
(2) 70 hr
(3) 80 hr
(4) 90 hr

36. Two pipes can fill a tank in 10 hr and 12 hr, while a third can empty it in 20 hr. If all the three pipes are opened, then in how much time will the cistern be completely filled?
(1) 7 hr
(2) 8 hr
(3) 7.5 hr
(4) 8.5 hr

37. If two pipes A and B operate simultaneously, the tank will be filled in 12 hrs. If B takes 10 hrs less than A, how much time does A take to fill the tank?
(1) 25 hr
(2) 28 hr
(3) 30 hr
(4) 35 hr

38. Taps A and B can fill in a tank in 12 and 15 min respectively. If both are opened and A is closed after 3 min, how long will it take for B to fill in the tank?
(1) 8 min 15 s
(2) 7 min 15 s
(3) 8 min 5 s
(4) 7 min 45 s

39. A and B can fill a tank in 6 hrs and 4 hrs respectively. If they are opened for alternate hours and A is opened first, then how many hours will it take to fill the tank?
(1) 4 hr
(2) 5 hr
(3) 4.5 hr
(4) 5.5 hr

40. A leak in the bottom of a tank can empty it in 6 hr. A pipe fills in the tank at the rate of 4 litres per minutes. When the tank is full, the inlet is opened but due to the leak, the tank is emptied in 8 hr. What is the capacity of the tank?
(1) 5760 L
(2) 5670 L
(3) 5846 L
(4) 6970 L

Exercise – 2

1. A man walks at 36 km/hr. In what time will he cover one-tenth of a kilometre?
(1) 12 s
(2) 10 s
(3) 15 s
(4) 8 s

2. A car can finish a journey in 10 hr at a speed of 48 km/hr. To cover the same distance in 8 hr, the speed must be increased by:
   (1) 10 km/hr (2) 12 km/hr
   (3) 16 km/hr (4) 18 km/hr

3. Tarun can cover a certain distance in 1 hr 24 min by covering $\frac{2}{3}$ of the distance at 4 km/hr and the rest at 5 km/hr. The total distance is:
   (1) 9 km (2) 6 km
   (3) 5 km (4) 4.5 km

4. The difference in times, when a man covers a certain distance at 10 km/hr and 20 km/hr, is 45 min. What would the difference be if the same distance is covered with speeds 25 km/hr and 40 km/hr?
   (1) 20 min. (2) 12.5 min.
   (3) 15 min. (4) 13.5 min.

5. A man covers a distance at 75 km/hr and returns to the starting point at 50 km/hr. What is his average speed?
   (1) 75 km/hr (2) 45 km/hr
   (3) 30 km/hr (4) 60 km/hr

6. A man goes uphill at 24 km/hr and comes down at 36 km/hr. What is his average speed?
   (1) 30.1 km/hr (2) 29.2 km/hr
   (3) 31.2 km/hr (4) 28.8 km/hr

7. A plane travels 2,500 km, 1,200 km, 500 km at the rate of 500 km/hr, 400km/hr, 250 km/hr respectively. The average speed is
   (1) 420 km/hr (2) 400 km/hr
   (3) 450 km/hr (4) 425 km/hr

8. A car has to cover 80 km in 10 hr. If it covers half the journey in three-fifths of the time, what should be its speed for the remaining journey?
   (1) 8 km/hr (2) 10 km/hr
   (3) 12 km/hr (4) 15 km/hr

9. Two persons start from A and B with the speeds of 25 km/hr and 49 km/hr respectively towards each other. After they cross each other, the person from B covers 145 km to reach A. What is the distance AB?
   (1) 437.1 kms (2) 428.4 kms
   (3) 429.2 kms (4) 441.2 kms

10. Two cities P and Q are 110 km apart. Person A started from city P at 7 a.m. at 20 km/hr and B started from city Q at 8 a.m. at 25 km/hr. At what time will they meet?
    (1) 10 a.m. (2) 11 a.m.
    (3) 1 p.m. (4) 12 noon.

11. Walking at three-fourths of his normal speed, a man is late by 2.5 hr. The usual time is:
    (1) 4.5 hr (2) 6 hr
    (3) 7.5 hr (4) 9 hr

12. If a boy walks from his house at 4 km/hr, he reaches school 10 min early. If he walks at 3 km/hr, he reaches 10 min late. What is the distance from his house to school?
    (1) 2 km (2) 4 km
    (3) 8 km (4) 16 km

13. A, who is travelling at 3.5 km/hr, starts 2.5 hr before B who travels at 4.5 km/hr in the same direction as A. In how much time will B overtake A?
    (1) 9.25 hr (2) 8.75 hr
    (3) 9.75 hr (4) 8.5 hr

14. A thief, who had escaped at 7 p.m, was followed by a policeman at 9 p.m. at the rate of 6 km/hr. At what time will the policeman overtake him, supposing the thief runs at 4.5 km/hr?
    (1) 2 a.m. (2) 3 a.m.
    (3) 4 a.m. (4) 1 a.m.

15. Mohan goes to school at a speed of 3 km/hr and return to home at a speed of 2 km/hr. If he takes 5 hrs in all, what is the distance between home and school?
    (1) 6 km (2) 7.5 km
    (3) 4.5 km (4) 5 km

16. Two men A and B walk from P to Q, a distance of 21 km, at 3 and 4 km an hour respectively. B reaches Q, returns immediately and meets A at R. Find the distance from P to R.
    (1) 18 km (2) 12 km
    (3) 16 km (4) 21 km

17. Excluding stoppages, the speed of a bus is 54 km/hr and including stoppage, it is 45 km/hr. For how long does the bus stop per hour?
    (1) 20 min. (2) 15 min.
    (3) 12 min. (4) 10 min.

18. The driver of a car sees a bus 40 m ahead of him. After 20 s, the bus is 60 m behind. If the speed of the car is 30 km/hr, what is the speed of the bus?
(1) 6 km/hr
(2) 12 km/hr
(3) 9 km/hr
(4) 24 km/hr

19. A man on a platform notices that a train going in one direction takes 10 s to pass him, and a train of same length going in the opposite direction takes 15 s to pass him. What is the time taken by the two trains to pass one another if the length of the trains is 200 m each?
(1) 15 s
(2) 12 s
(3) 18 s
(4) 24 s

20. A train leaves A at 40 km/hr. At the same time, another train departs from B at a speed of 60 km/hr. They reach the respective destinations and turn back immediately towards the starting points. Now if they meet at a distance of 200 km from A, what is the distance between A and B?
(1) 275 kms
(2) 125 kms
(3) 250 kms
(4) 300 kms

21. The speeds of A and B are in the ratio 3 : 4. A takes 30 min more than B to reach the destination. How much time does A take to reach the destination?
(1) 1 hr
(2) 2 hr
(3) 1 hr 30 mins.
(4) 2 hr 30 mins.

22. A man sees a train passing over a bridge 1 km long. The length of the train is half that of the bridge. If the train clears the bridge in 2 min, the speed of the train is
(1) 45 km/hr
(2) 60 km/hr
(3) 30 km/hr
(4) 90 km/hr

23. Two trains travel in opposite directions at 36 km/hr and 45 km/hr respectively. A man sitting in the slower train passes the faster train in 8 s. The length of the faster train is
(1) 180 m
(2) 150 m
(3) 210 m
(4) 175 m

24. A train 110 m long is travelling at a speed of 58 km/hr. What is the time in which it will pass a man walking in the same direction at 4 km/hr?
(1) 6.33 s
(2) 9.33 s
(3) 8.33 s
(4) 7.33 s

25. A man rows 13 km upstream and 28 km downstream in 5 hr each. The velocity of the stream is
(1) 2.5 km/hr
(2) 2.0 km/hr
(3) 1.5 km/hr
(4) 3 km/hr

26. A stream runs at 1 km/hr. A boat goes 35 km upstream and come back again in 12 hr. The speed of the boat in still water is
(1) 6 km/hr
(2) 15 km/hr
(3) 9 km/hr
(4) 4.5 km/hr

27. A man rows a distance downstream in 45 min and the same distance upstream in 75 min. What is the ratio of speed of the stream to the boat in still water?
(1) 1 : 4
(2) 2 : 5
(3) 2 : 3
(4) 1 : 2

28. A boat is moving downstream and reaches its destination in 25 hrs while moving at a speed of 50 km/hr (given speed is in still water). One particular day due to engine problem at mid-point and ship's speed reduction by 20% of the original, it reaches its destination 2.5 hrs late. Find out the speed of the river. [Assume its speed to be uniform]
(1) 12 km/hr
(2) 15 km/hr
(3) 20 km/hr
(4) None of these

29. In a race of 100 metres. Pawan beats Arun by 4 metres and Pawan beats Rahul by 2 metres. By how many metres would Rahul beat Arun in a 100 metre race?
(1) 4.18 m
(2) 2.04 m
(3) 2.12 m
(4) 3.36 m

30. A is twice as fast as B. If A gives B a start of 60 metres, how long should the racecourse be so that both of them reach at the same time?
(1) 150 m
(2) 120 m
(3) 180 m
(4) 90 m

31. Krishna beats Arjun by 31 m and Virat by 18 m in a race of 200 m. By how many metres will Virat beat Arjun in a race of 350 m?
(1) 15 m
(2) 20 m
(3) 25 m
(4) 30 m

32. In a 500 m race, the ratio of speeds of two runners A and B is 3 : 4. A has a start of 140 m. Then A wins by __________.
(1) 15 m
(2) 45 m
(3) 30 m
(4) 20 m

33. Bhim and Arjun were exercising during their Vanvaas. They start running on a circular track simultaneously and in the same direction. If Bhim takes 4 min to complete one full round, and Arjun takes 7 min to complete one full round after how much time will they meet for the first time?
(1) 9 min. 40 secs.
(2) 9 min. 10 secs.
(3) 9 min. 30 secs.
(4) 9 min. 20 secs.

34. Bhim and Arjun were exercising during their Vanvaas. They start running on a circular track simultaneously and in the same direction. If Bhim takes 4 min to complete one full round, and Arjun takes 7 min to complete one full round after how much time will they meet for the first time at the starting point?
(1) 21 min.
(2) 24 min.
(3) 32 min.
(4) 28 min.

35. The speeds of three athletes A, B and C, who are racing on a circular track of length 200 m, are 20 m/s, 23 m/s and 27 m/s respectively. They do not rest until all of them meet at a place. When they stop, what is the ratio of the distances travelled by each?
(1) 20 : 23 : 27
(2) 27 : 23 : 20
(3) 20 : 27 : 23
(4) 23 : 20 : 27

36. When will the hour hand and the minute hand of a clock be together between 1 a.m. and 2 a.m?
(1) 1 hour and $6\frac{6}{11}$ min s.
(2) 1 hour and $6\frac{5}{11}$ min s.
(3) 1 hour and $5\frac{5}{11}$ min s.
(4) 1 hour and $5\frac{6}{11}$ min s.

37. A takes a puff for 2 s and B takes a puff for 3 s. Rate of burning during puffing is 3 mm/s while the ordinary rate of burning is 1 mm/s. After how much time will the cigarette be completely burnt if its length is 63 mm excluding the stub and there is a gap of 3 s between each puff? It is given that starting with A, both A and B puff alternately.
(1) 30 s
(2) 33 s
(3) 36 s
(4) 39 s

38. A candle of 8 cm long burns at the rate of 3 cm in 3 hr, whereas another one of 10 cm long burns at the rate of 3 cm in 2 hr. What are the lengths of the candles when they are of the same length? (Assume the rate of burning is constant in both the cases.)
(1) 4 cm
(2) 8 cm
(3) 6 cm
(4) 2.5 cm

39. Munna Bhai travels 280 km from Mudhuvani to Darbhanga, partly by bus and partly by Jeep. Both the vehicles move in the given fashion.

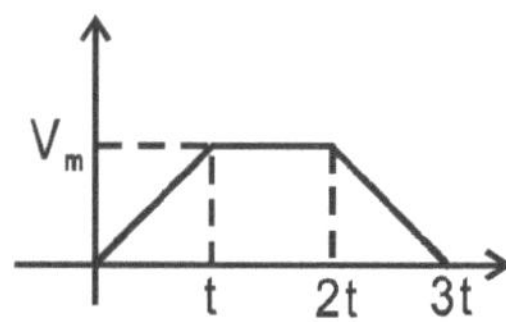

V_m = Maximum speed
But their maximum speeds differ by 10 km/hr. Both the vehicles travel for 6 hr each. Find out their respective maximum speeds. There is no fine gap between movement of both vehicles. [Assume that the bus is moving first and faster than the Jeep].
(1) 60 km/hr, 50 km/hr
(2) 30 km/hr, 20 km/hr
(3) 40 km/hr, 30 km/hr
(4) 45 km/hr, 35 km/hr

40. What is the average speed of the jeep in question number 39?
(1) 25 km/hr
(2) 15 km/hr
(3) 20 km/hr
(4) 10 km/hr

Quantitative Ability

Geometry **5**

Introduction

Plane geometry is a fundamental strand of elementary mathematics. It deals with different simple and complex plane figures. You need to understand the properties of these figures and applying these properties to solve problems related to different dimensions of these figures.

Geometry is basically the study of different properties of point, line and plane.

Right angle: An angle of 90° is called a right angle.

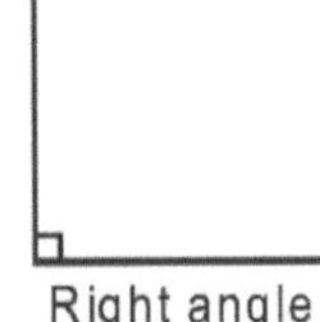

Right angle

Acute angle: An angle of less than 90° is called an acute angle

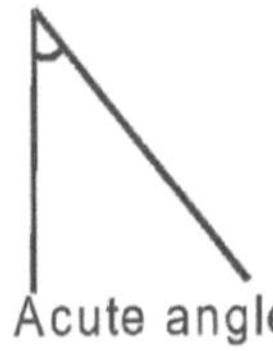

Acute angle

Obtuse angle: An angle of greater than 90° is called an obtuse angle.

Obtuse angle

Reflex angle: An angle of greater than 180° is called reflex angle.

Reflex angle

Complementary angles: If the sum of the two angles is 90° then they are called complementary angles.

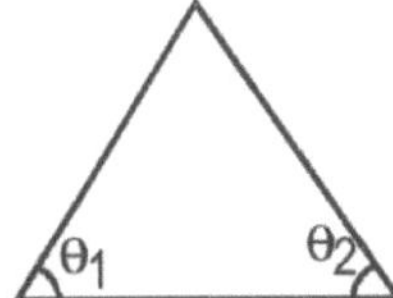

θ_1 and θ_2 and complimentary as $\theta_1 + \theta_2 = 90°$

Supplementary angles: If the sum of the two angles is 180° then they are called supplementary angles.

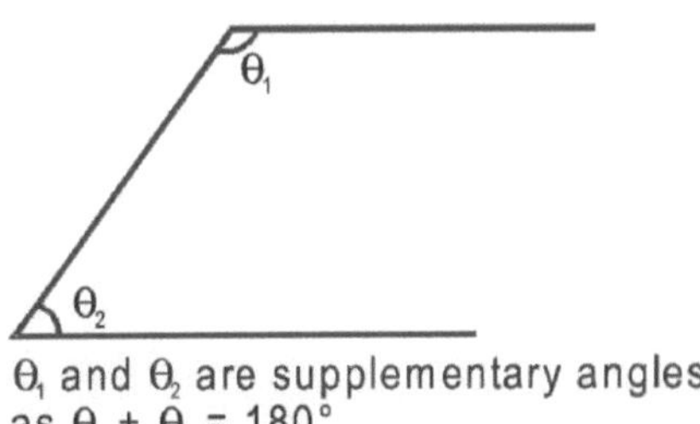

θ_1 and θ_2 are supplementary angles
as $\theta_1 + \theta_2 = 180°$

Vertically opposite angles: If two lines intersect each other then the vertically opposite angles are equal.
$\angle a = \angle c$ and $\angle b = \angle d$
a, c and b, d are vertically opposite angles.

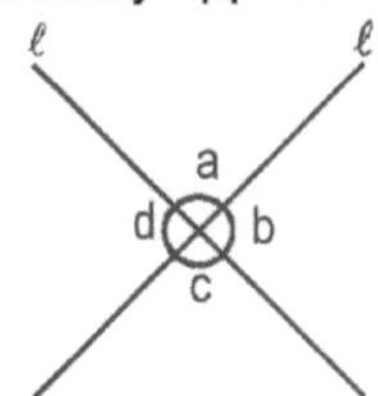

Angles in parallel lines: If a transversal intersects two parallel lines

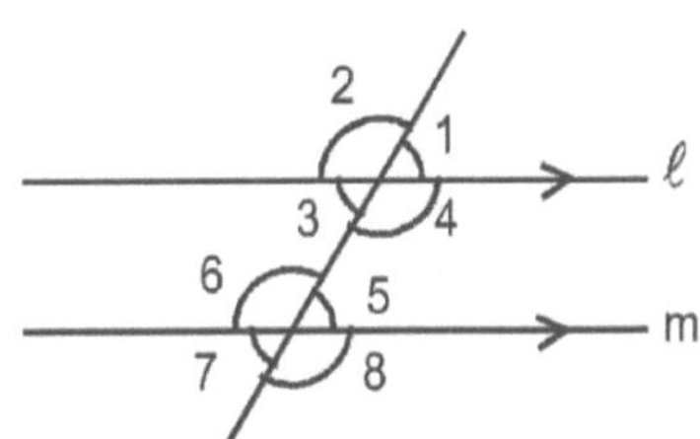

a. each pair of consecutive interior angles are supplementary

$\angle 4 + \angle 5 = 180°$

$\angle 3 + \angle 6 = 180°$

b. each pair of alternate interior angles are equal

$\angle 5 = \angle 3,\ \angle 6 = \angle 4$

$\angle 7 = \angle 5 = \angle 3 = \angle 1$

$\angle 8 = \angle 6 = \angle 4 = \angle 2$

Collinear:

Three or more than three points are said to be collinear, if there is a line which contains all of them.

Concurrent:

Three or more than three lines are said to be concurrent, if there is a point which lies on all of them.

Triangle is a closed figure made by three straight lines.

Types of triangles

1. **Equilateral triangle:** A triangle whose all three sides are equal is called an equilateral triangle. An equilateral triangle is also known as equi angles triangle.

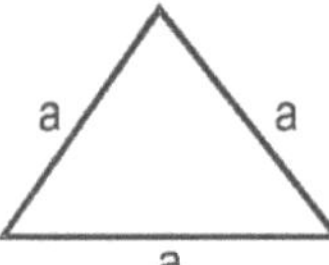

2. **Isosceles triangle:** A triangle whose two and only two sides are equal is called an isosceles triangle.

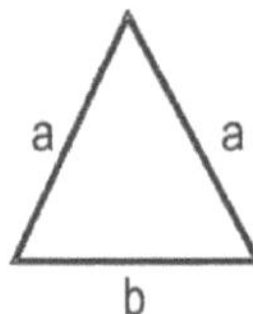

3. **Scalene triangle:** A triangle whose all sides are of different length is called scalene triangle.

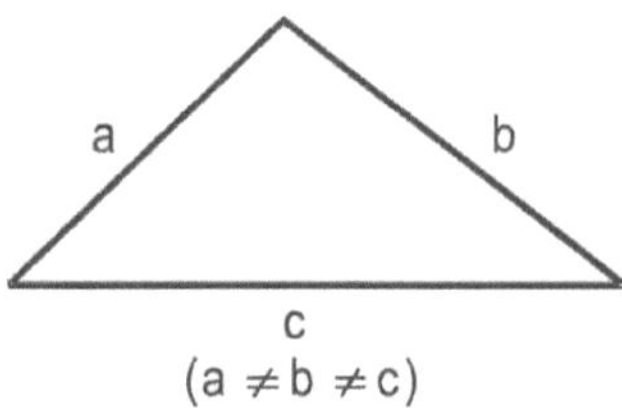

$(a \neq b \neq c)$

4. **Right-angled triangle:** A triangle whose one angle is of 90° is called a right-angled triangle.

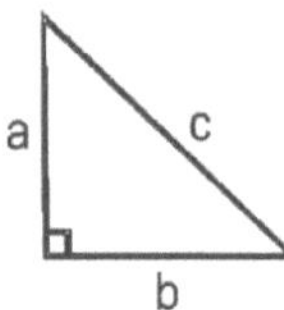

In a right angled triangle the longest side is called the hypotenuse. Here 'c' is the length of the hypotenuse of the triangle.

Triangle and angle

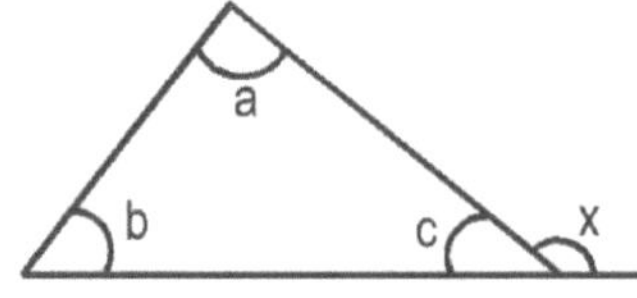

1. The sum of three interior angles of a triangle is 180°.
   $\angle a + \angle b + \angle c = 180°$.

2. The exterior angle of a triangle is equal to the sum of the two interior opposite angles.
   $\angle x = \angle a + \angle b$

3. Sum of lengths of any two sides of a triangle is always greater than or equal to the length of the third side.

If in two triangles corresponding angles are equal or their corresponding sides are in proportion then the triangles are said to be similar to each other.

Condition for similarity

1. **AA condition**

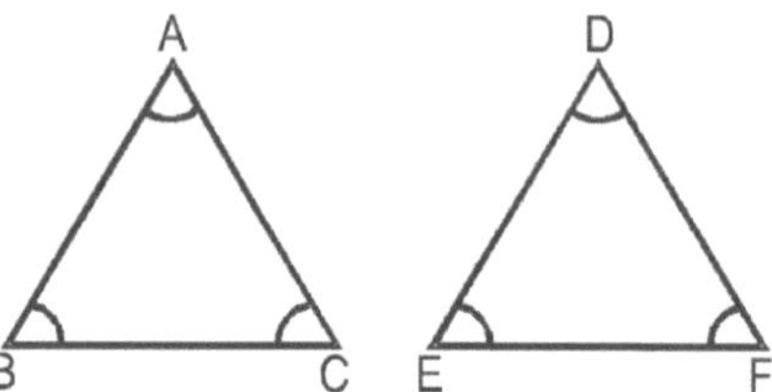

If any two angles of a triangle is equal to the corresponding angles of the other triangle, then both the triangles are similar.
If $\angle A = \angle D$, $\angle B = \angle E$, then $\triangle ABC \approx \triangle DEF$

2. **SSS condition**

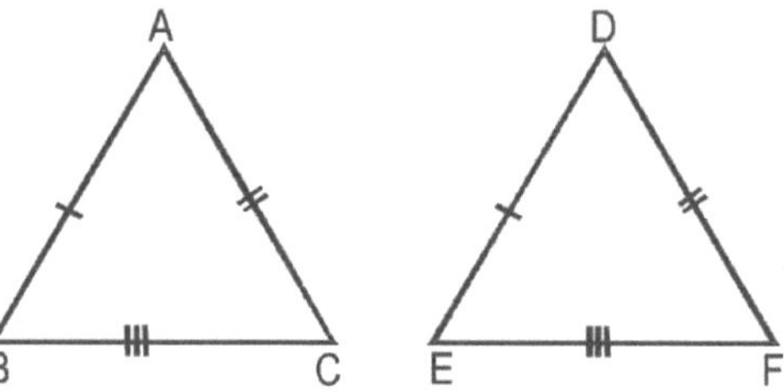

If all the three sides of a triangle is in proportion with the corresponding three sides of the other triangle, then both the triangles are similar to each other.

If $\dfrac{AB}{DE} = \dfrac{AC}{DF} = \dfrac{BC}{EF}$ then $\triangle ABC \approx \triangle DEF$

3. **SAS condition**

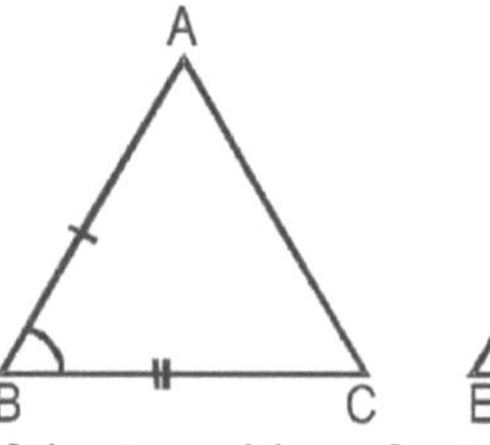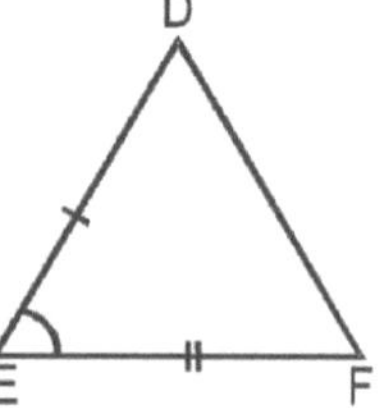

If the two sides of a triangle is in proportion with the corresponding two sides of the other triangle and the included angle of one triangle is equal to the included angle of the other triangle, then the triangles are similar to each other.

If, $\dfrac{AB}{DE} = \dfrac{AB}{EF}$ and $\angle B = \angle E$,

then $\triangle ABC \approx \triangle DEF$

Two triangles are said to be congruent to each other, if both triangles are equal in shape and size.

Condition for congruency

1. SAS condition

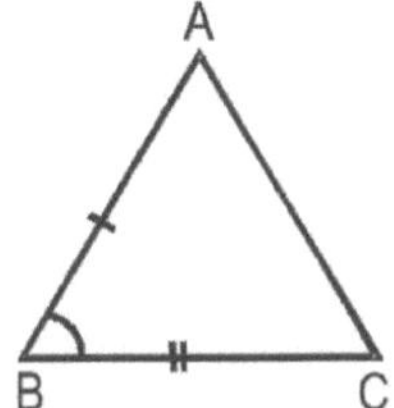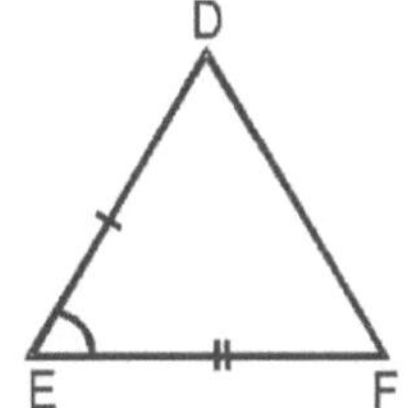

If two sides and the included angle of one triangle is equal to the corresponding sides and included angle of the other triangle, then both triangles are congruent.

AB = DE, BC = EF and $\angle B = \angle E$, then

$\triangle ABC \cong \triangle DEF$

2. ASA condition

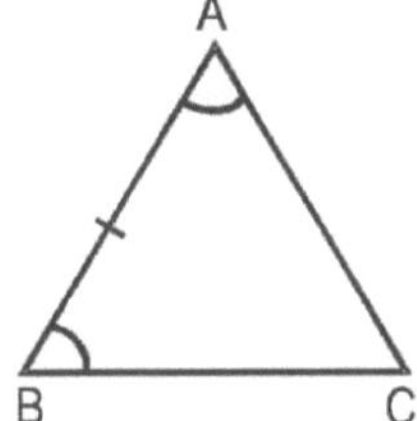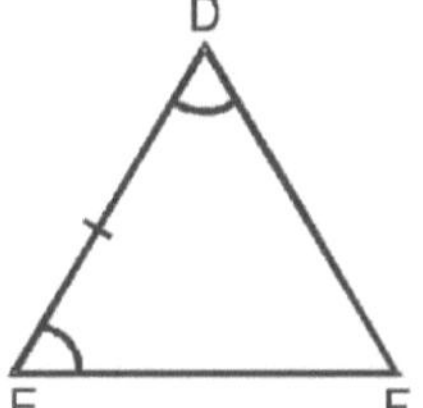

If two angles and the included side of one triangle is equal to the corresponding two angles and the included side of the other triangle, then both triangles are congruent.

If $\angle A = \angle D$, $\angle B = \angle E$ and AB = DE, then

$\triangle ABC \cong \triangle DEF$

3. SSS condition

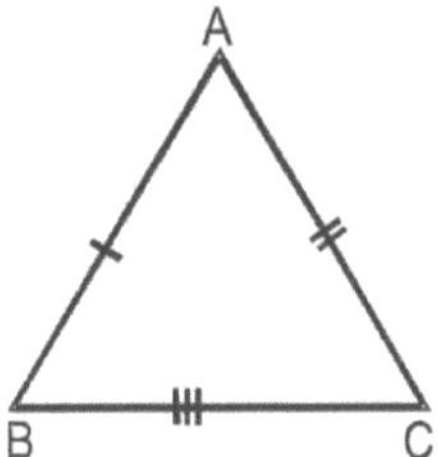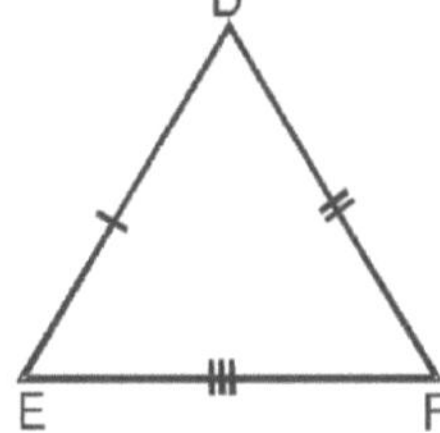

If three sides of one triangle is equal to the corresponding three sides of other triangle then both triangles are congruent.

If AB = DE, AC = DF and BC = EF, then

$\triangle ABC \cong \triangle DEF$

4. RHS Condition

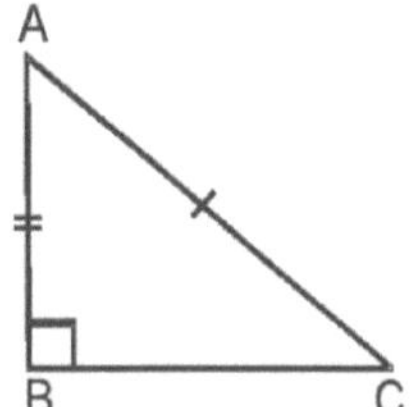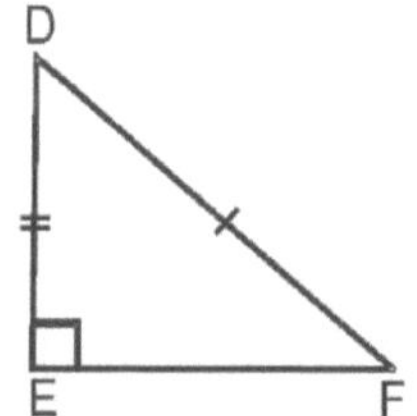

If the two triangles are right-angled and hypotenuse and one side of one triangle is equal to the hypotenuse and corresponding side of the other triangle, then both the triangles are congruent.

If $\angle B = \angle E = 90°$, AC = DF and AB = DE or BC = EF, then $\triangle ABC \cong \triangle DEF$

Note:

i.   All the congruent triangles are similar but all similar triangles are not congruent.

ii. The ratio of the areas of two similar triangles is equal to the ratio of the squares of any two corresponding sides.

Pythagoras' theorem: In a right angle triangle the square of the hypotenuse is equal to the sum of the squares of other two sides.

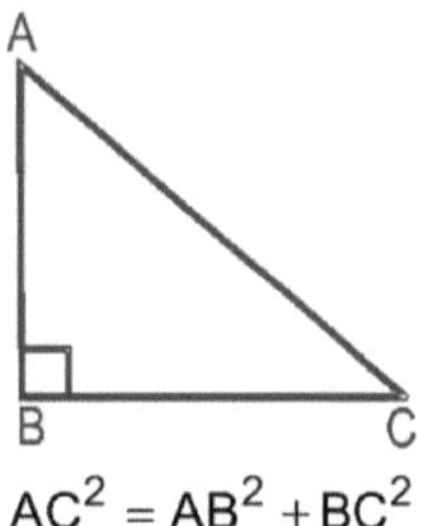

$$AC^2 = AB^2 + BC^2$$

Pythagorean triplet: There are certain triplets which satisfy the pythagoras theorem and are commonly, called pythagorean triplet.

For example:

3, 4, 5; 5, 12, 13; 24, 10, 26; 24, 7, 25; 17, 8, 15

Pythagorean triplet: $(5^2 = 4^2 + 3^2)$

A polygon is a closed figure in a plane formed by three or more line segments which meet only at their end points.

For a 'n' sided polygon.

Sum of the interior angles of a polygon = $(2n - 4) \times 90°$

Regular polygon: A polygon with all sides of equal length.

In a regular polygon, Interior angle = $\dfrac{(2n-4) \times 90°}{n}$

Exterior angle = $\dfrac{360°}{n}$

Number of diagonals in a polygon

$$= {}^nC_2 - n = \frac{n(n-3)}{2}$$

Parallelogram

1. The opposite sides are parallel and equal.
2. Opposite angles are equal.
3. The diagonals bisect each other. [$\angle 1 = \angle 3$, $\angle 2 = \angle 4$]
   (The diagonals need not be equal in length and do not necessarily bisect at right angles.)
4. Sum of two adjacent angles = 180°
   [$\angle 1 + \angle 4 = 180°$, $\angle 1 + \angle 2 = 180°$,
   $\angle 2 + \angle 3 = 180°$ and $\angle 3 + \angle 4 = 180°$]
5. Each diagonal of a parallelogram divides it into two congruent triangles.
6. A parallelogram that is inscribed in a circle is a rectangle.
7. A parallelogram that is circumscribed about a circle is a rhombus.
8. Area of a parallelogram = base × height of the parallelogram.

Rhombus

1. If all the sides of a parallelogram are equal then it is called a rhombus.
2. Opposite angles are equal.
3. Diagonals are not necessarily equal but they bisect each other at 90°.
4. Area of a rhombus = $\frac{1}{2}$ × product of the lengths of its diagonals.

Rectangle

1. Opposite sides are equal and parallel.
2. Every angle is a right angle.
3. Diagonals bisect each other.
4. The area of a rectangle = length × breadth

Square

1. It is a rectangle with all sides equal.
2. Every angle is a right angle.
3. Diagonals are equal and they bisect each other at 90°.
4. The area of a square = (side)^2.
5. The diagonal of a square = $\sqrt{2}$ side.

Trapezium

1. Only one pair of sides are parallel.
2. Area of a trapezium = $\frac{1}{2}$ (sum of the parallel sides) × height.

Cyclic quadrilateral

1. The four vertices of the quadrilateral lie on a circle.
2. Opposite angles are supplementary to each other.
   ∠DAB + ∠BCD = 180°
   ∠ADB + ∠ABC = 180°

Circle

1. If two circles have equal radii then both circles are congruent.
2. The perpendicular drawn from the centre of a circle to chord bisects the chord.

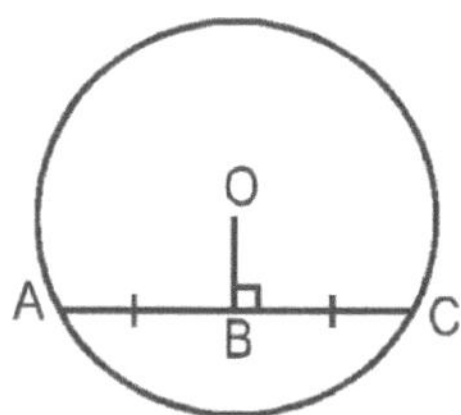

3. Equal chords of a circle are equidistant from the centre.
4. Equal chords of a circle subtend equal angles on the centre.
5. The angle subtended by an arc of a circle at the centre is double the angle subtended by it on the circle in the same segment.

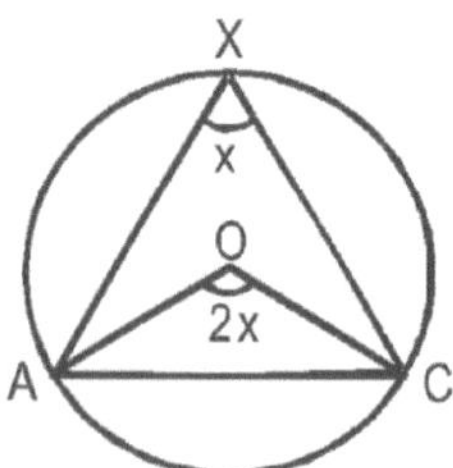

6. Angles subtended by a chord in the same segment are equal.
7. The angle in a semi circle is 90°.

8. Tangent is a line that touches the circle at only one point.

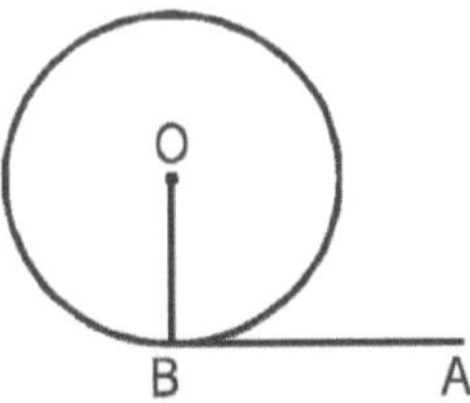

Here AB is a tangent to the circle with centre O.

9. The length of the two tangents that can be drawn from an external point are equal.
PA = PB.

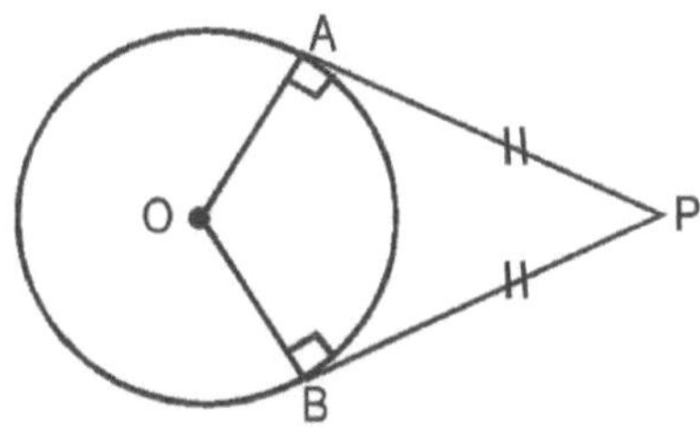

10. The angle made by a chord and tangent to the circle is equal to the angle made by the chord in the alternate segment.
∠BPC = ∠BAP and ∠APD = ∠ABP

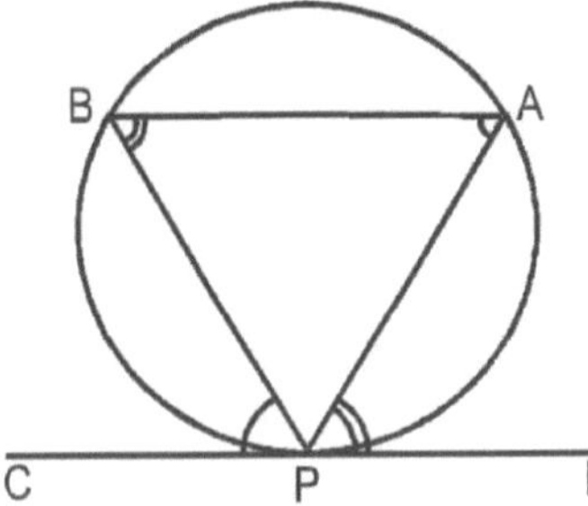

11. If two chords AB and CD intersect each other internally at a point P, then PA × PB = PC × PD

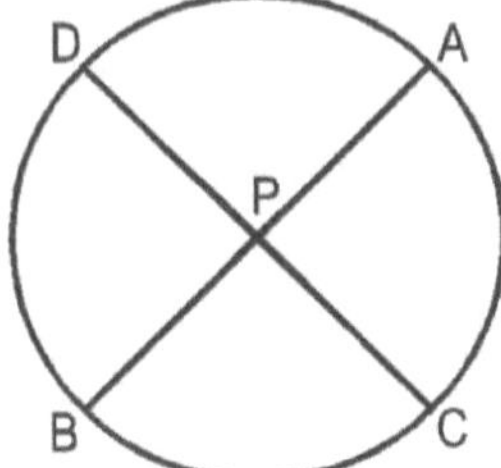

12. If two segments PA and PC intersect each other externally at point P, then PA × PB = PC × PD

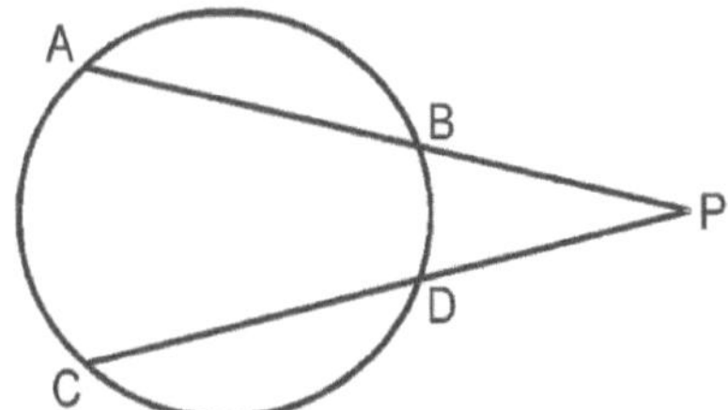

13. If PBA is a secant and PT is a tangent segment, then PA × PB = PT^2

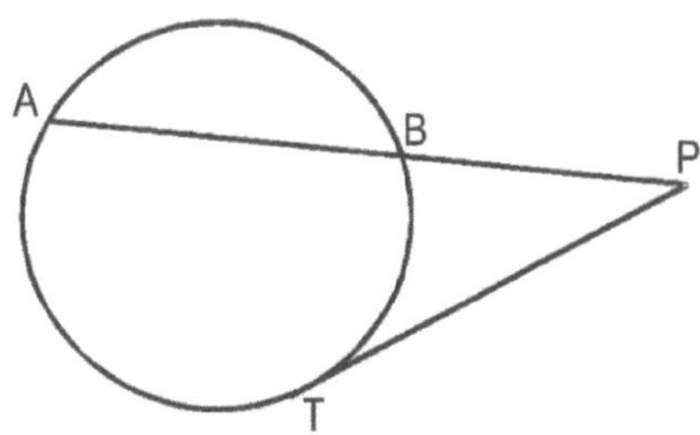

14. If the bisector of ∠ABC and ∠BCA of a △ABC intersect each other at O, then

$$\angle BOC = 90° + \frac{1}{2} \angle BAC$$

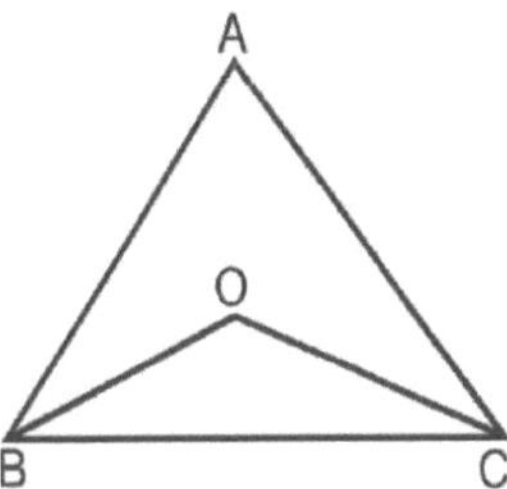

Example 1:

If the two sides of triangle are 10 m and 20 m then the third side of the triangle must be lying between

Solution:

We know that sum of any two sides of a triangle is always greater than the third side, so the third side must be smaller than 10 + 20 = 30 m and greater than 20 – 10 = 10 m

Example 2:

Find the sum of the interior angles of a hexagon.

Solution:

The sum of interior angles of a polygon
= (n – 2) × 180°
where n = number of sides in the polygon so sum of interior angles = (6 – 2) × 180° = 720°

Example 3:

In the given figure OD = 4 cm, OC = 6 cm, OA = 8 cm, find OB.

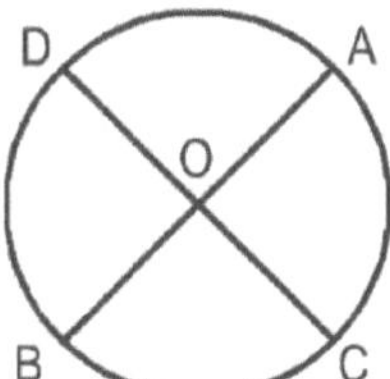

Solution:

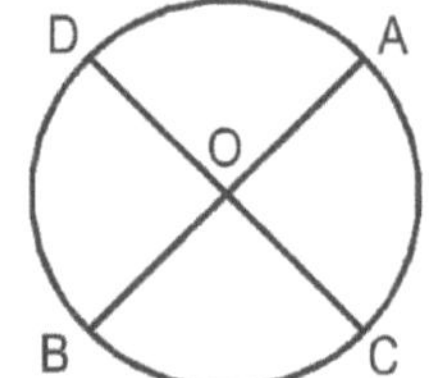

$\because$ AO × OB = OC × OD

$\Rightarrow$ 8 × OB = 6 × 4 $\therefore$ OB = 3 cm

Example 4:

In the given figure A is the centre of the circle and AO is perpendicular on BC. If BC = 12 cm, then find the length of OB.

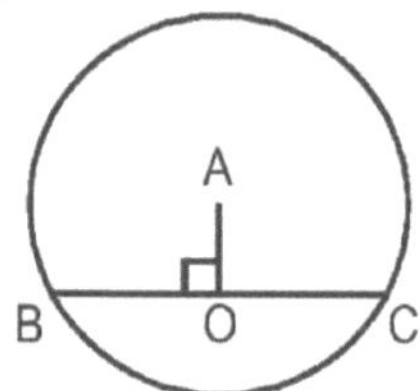

Solution:

Perpendicular from the centre on the chord bisects the chord.

$$\Rightarrow OB = \frac{1}{2}BC = \frac{1}{2} \times 12 = 6 \text{ cm}$$

Example 5:

In the given figure AB = 6 cm, AO = 2 cm and AC = 3 cm. Find the length of CD.

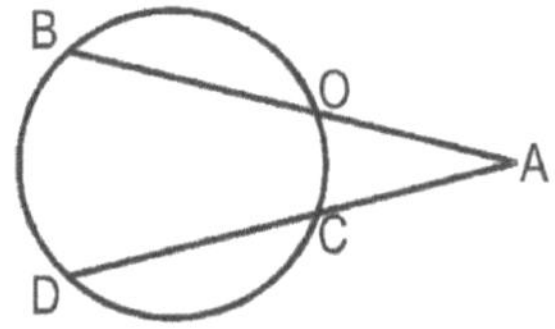

Solution:

AO × AB = AC × AD

$\Rightarrow$ 2 × 6 = 3 × AD

$\therefore$ AD = 4 cm

$\because$ AC = 3 cm,

so CD = 4 – 3 = 1 cm

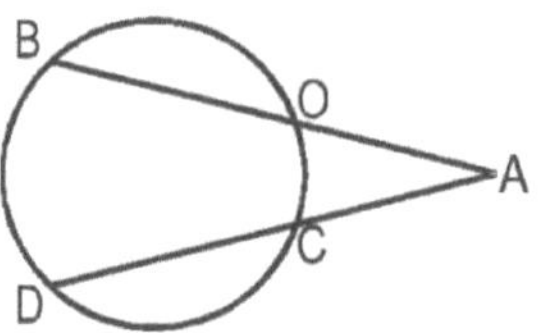

Example 6:

In the given figure AB is the diameter, find $\angle$ACB and $\angle$ADB.

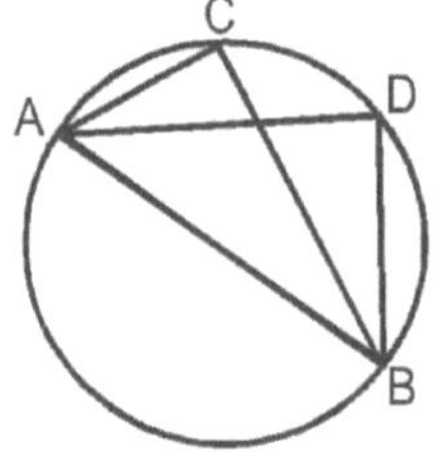

Solution:

$\angle$ACB = $\angle$ADB = 90°

The angle subtended by the diameter on the circumference is always 90°.

Example 7:

In the given figure AB is a tangent to the circle at point C and $\angle$DCB = 60°. Find the measure of $\angle$CED.

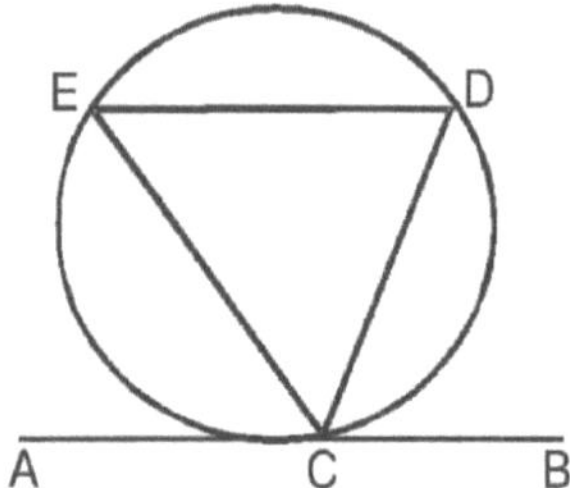

Solution:

$\angle$DCB = 60° then by alternate angle theorem $\angle$CED is also 60°

Example 8:

In the adjoining figure, find the measure of $\angle$DAB + $\angle$DCB.

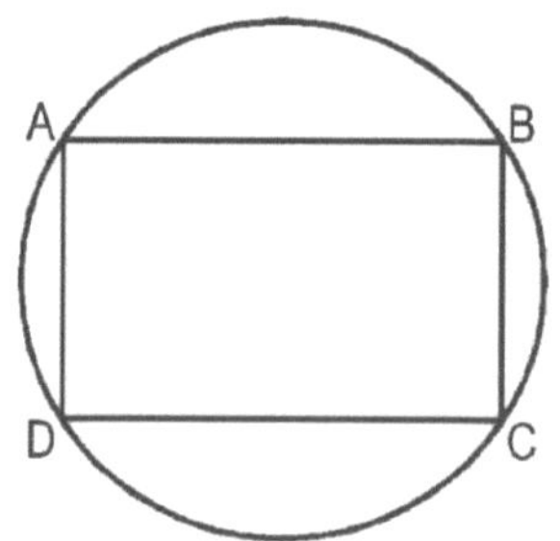

Solution:

ABCD is a cyclic quadrilateral and in the cyclic quadrilateral the sum of the opposite angles is 180°

Example 9:

From a given point how many tangents can be drawn to a circle?

Solution:

A Maximum of two tangents can be drawn from any point to a circle.

Example 10:

Find the measure of an exterior angle of a regular pentagon.

Quantitative Ability

Solution:

Exterior angle of a polygon is

$180° -$ interior angle $= 180 \times \dfrac{(n-2)}{n}$

Interior angle of a regular pentagon

$= \dfrac{180 \times (n-2)}{n} = \dfrac{180 \times (5-2)}{5} = 108°$

So the exterior angle is $(180 - 108°) = 72°$

Example 11:

In the adjoining figure $\angle ABO = \angle OBC$ and $\angle ACO = \angle OCB$.
If $\angle BAC = 60°$, then find the measure of $\angle BOC$.

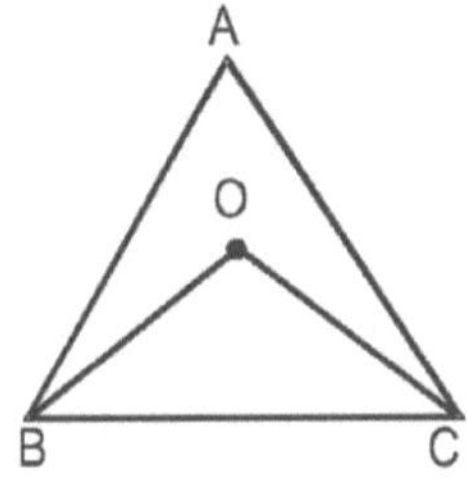

Solution:

Since OB and OC are bisectors of $\angle B$ and $\angle C$

$\therefore \angle BOC = 90° + \dfrac{1}{2}\angle BAC$

$= 90° + \dfrac{1}{2} \times 60° = 90° + 30° = 120°$

Example 12:

The angle in a major segment of a circle is

Solution:

The angle in the Major segment of a circle is obtuse.

Example 13:

ABCD is cyclic quadrilateral such that $\angle ADB = 40°$ and $\angle DCA = 70°$, find the value of $\angle DAB$.

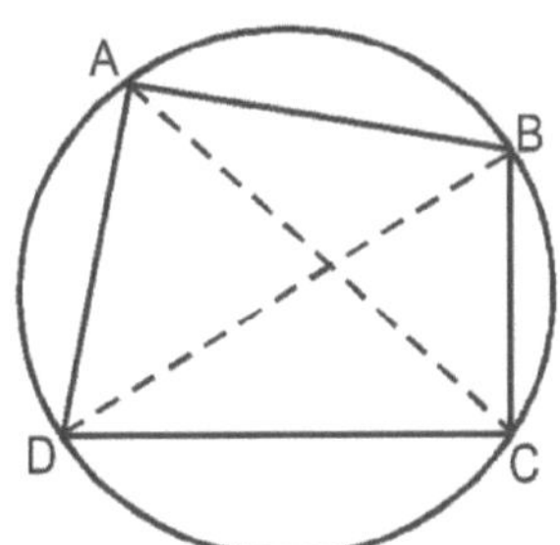

Solution:

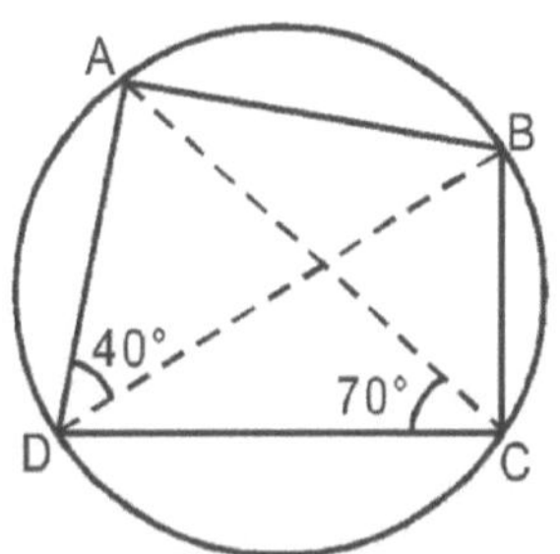

$\angle BCA = \angle ADB = 40°$
(Angle subtended by chord on same arc)
$\therefore \angle DCB = \angle ACD + \angle BCA$
$\qquad = 70° + 40° = 110°$
$\therefore \angle DAB + \angle DCB = 180°$
$\therefore \angle DAB = 180° - \angle DCB$
$\qquad = 180° - 110° = 70°$

Example 14:

A point A is 10 cm from the centre of the circle. The length of the tangent drawn from A to the circle is 8 cm. Find the radius of circle.

Solution:

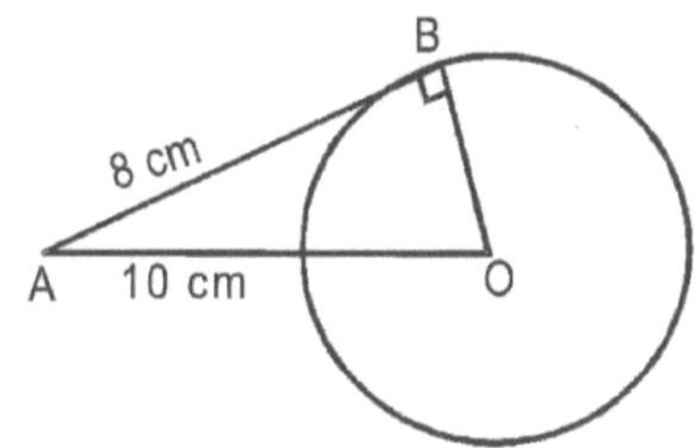

$\triangle ABO$ is right-angled at point B.
OB is the radius of the circle.

$\therefore OA^2 = OB^2 + AB^2 \Rightarrow 10^2 = 8^2 + OB^2$

$\Rightarrow OB^2 = \sqrt{36} \Rightarrow OB = \sqrt{36} = 6$ cm

Example 15:

If one of the angles of cyclic quadrilateral is four times its opposite angle, then find the measure of the larger of the two angles.

Solution:

Let the angle be A. we know that opposite angles of cyclic quadrilateral are supplementary.
$\therefore A = 4(180° - A)$
$A = 720° - 4A$
$5A = 720° \Rightarrow A = 144°$

Example 16:

The angles of a triangle are in the ratio of 2 : 3 : 5. Find the value of the largest angle.

Solution:

Let the angles of triangle be $2x°$, $3x°$, $5x°$.

$\therefore\ 2x + 3x + 5x = 180$

$\Rightarrow 10x = 180$

$\Rightarrow x = 18$

Largest angle = $5x = 5 \times 18 = 90°$

Example 17:

Find the interior angle of a regular polygon having 9 sides.

Solution:

Number of sides = 9

$\therefore$ Number of exterior angles = 9

$$\text{Each exterior angle} = \frac{360}{\text{number of sides}}$$

$$= \frac{360}{9} = 40$$

Each interior angle = $180°$ – exterior angle

= $180° - 40° = 140°$

Alternate method:

$$\text{Interior angle} = \frac{180 \times (n-2)}{n}$$

$$= \frac{180 \times (9-2)}{9} = 140°$$

Example 18:

In the given triangles $\angle A = \angle P$ and $\angle B = \angle C$. Find length of RQ.

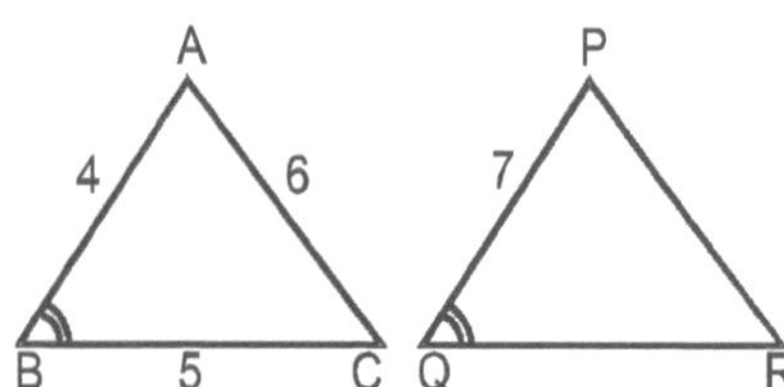

Solution:

Since the angles of two triangles are equal they are similar.

$\therefore \Delta ABC \approx \Delta PQR$

$$\therefore\ \frac{AB}{PQ} = \frac{BC}{QR} \Rightarrow RQ = \frac{5 \times 7}{4} = \frac{35}{4}\ cm$$

Mensuration

Mensuration deals with measurements of various shapes. This would come naturally to students in science and technology. However, it would be important to realise that it has a lot of importance to be able to measure the area and volume of various shapes in our day-to-day life. Much of it appears to be committed to memory. However, it can come to you quite easily provided you practice a number of problems.

Example 19:

A rectangular plot has an area of 490 m^2. If the length of the rectangular plot is 24.5 m, then find the perimeter of the rectangular plot.

Solution:

The perimeter of a rectangle = $2(l + b)$

Here $l = 24.5$ and the area is 490 m^2.

Suppose its breadth is 'y' m, then

$l \times y = $ area

$\Rightarrow 24.5 \times y = 490$

$$\Rightarrow y = \frac{490}{24.5} = 20\ m$$

So the perimeter = $2(l + b) = 2(24.5 + 20)$

= $2 \times 44.5 = 89$ m.

Example 20:

There is a large room of size 24 ft × 32 ft. The floor of the room is to be paved with square tiles of the same dimension. Find out (i) the minimum number of tiles required and its size and (ii) the maximum number of tiles required.

Solution:

(i) Since the floor of the room is to be paved with minimum number of square tiles, so the size of the square tiles must be maximum. Since the size of the tile is square, so the maximum dimension of each tile is 8 ft × 8 ft (HCF of 24 and 32). And the number of tiles required

$$= \frac{\text{Area of the floor}}{\text{Area of 1 tile}} = \frac{24 \times 32}{8 \times 8} = 12$$

(ii) It's answer is infinity! How? Think over it.

Example 21:

There is a rectangular field having dimension 20 m × 30 m. There is a jogging track inside the field along its perimeter. The width of the track is uniform and it is equal to 2 m. Find the total perimeter of the jogging track and the area of the jogging track.

Part – I: Plane Figures

S.No.	Name	Figure	Perimeter	Area	Nomenclature
1.	Rectangle	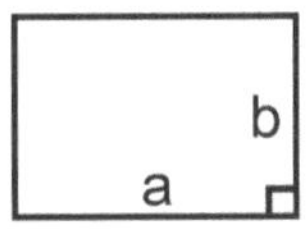	$2(a + b)$	ab	a = Length b = Breadth
2.	Square	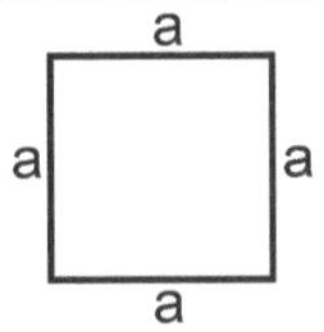	$4a$	a^2	a = Side
3.	Triangle	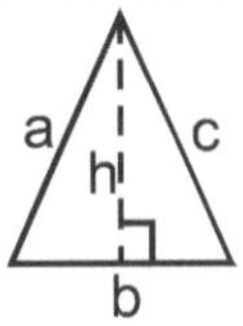	$a + b + c = 2s$	1. $= \dfrac{1}{2} b \times h$ 2. $= \sqrt{s(s-a)(s-b)(s-c)}$	b is the base and h is the altitude. a, b, c are three sides of $\triangle$ and s is the semiperimeter
4.	Right angled triangle	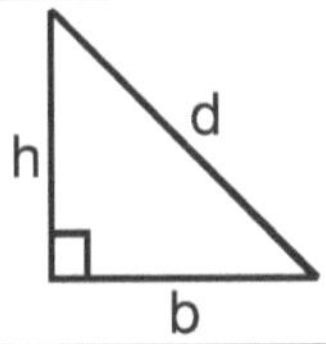	$b + h + d$	$\dfrac{1}{2} bh$	d (hypotenuse) $= \sqrt{b^2 + h^2}$
5.	Equilateral triangle	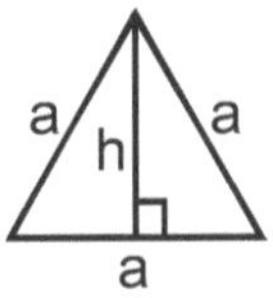	$3a$	1. $\dfrac{1}{2} ah$ 2. $\dfrac{\sqrt{3}}{4} a^2$	a = side h = Altitude $= \dfrac{\sqrt{3}}{2} a.$
6.	Isosceles triangle	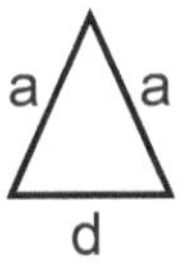	$2a + d$	$\dfrac{1}{2}\sqrt{4a^2 - d^2}$	a = length of two equal side d = length of unequal side
7.	Parallelogram	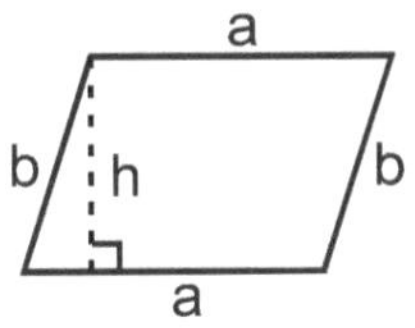	$2(a + b)$	ah	a = Side b = Side adjacent to a h = Distance between the parallel sides (a) and (b)
8.	Rhombus	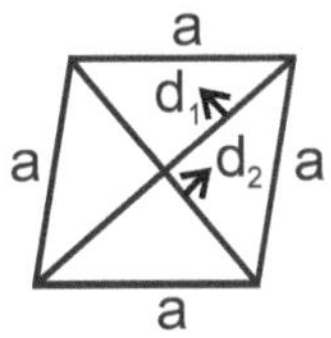	$4a$	$\dfrac{1}{2} d_1 d_2$	a = Side of rhombus d_1, d_2 are the two diagonals.

S.No.	Name	Figure	Perimeter	Area	Nomenclature
9.	Quadrilateral		Sum of the length of its four sides	$\frac{1}{2}(AC)(h_1+h_2)$	AC is one of its diagonals and h_1, h_2 are the altitudes on AC from D and B respectively.
10.	Trapezium		Sum of the length of its four sides	$\frac{1}{2}h(a+b)$	a, b are the length of parallel sides and h is the perpendicular distance between parallel sides.
11.	Circle		$2\pi r$	πr^2	r = Radius of the circle $\pi = \frac{22}{7}$ or 3.1416 (approx.)
12.	Semicircle		$\pi r + 2r$	$\frac{1}{2}\pi r^2$	r = Radius of the circle
13.	Ring (shaded region)		----	$\pi(R^2 - r^2)$	R = Outer radius r = Inner radius
14.	Sector of a circle		$l + 2r$ where $l = (\theta/360) \times 2\pi r$	$\theta/360° \times \pi r^2$	θ = Central angle of the sector r = Radius of the sector l = Length of the arc
15.	Segment of a circle		$(\theta/360°) \times 2\pi r + 2r\sin(\theta/2)$	Area of segment ACB (Minor segment) $= r^2\left[\dfrac{\pi\theta}{360°} - \dfrac{\sin\theta}{2}\right]$	r = Radius θ = Angle of the related sector AOB.

Solution:

ABCD is the rectangular region field and the shaded in it is the jogging track.

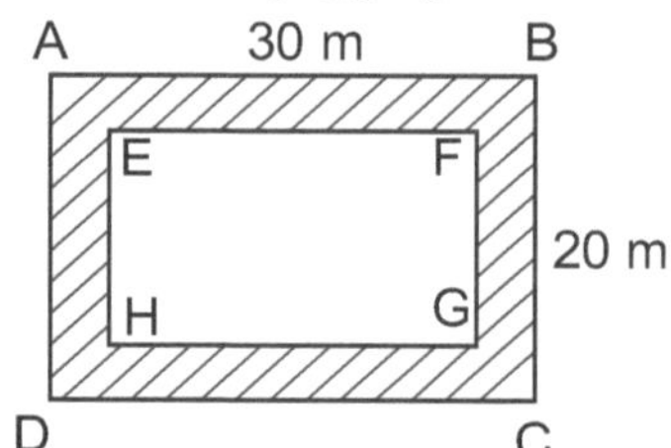

Perimeter of the jogging track = Perimeter of ABCD + Perimeter of EFGH

EF = 30 – (2 × 2) = 26 m because the width of the track is 2 m on either side.

Similarly, FG = 20 – (2 × 2) = 16

Perimeter = 2(30 + 20) + 2(26 + 16)

= 100 + 84 = 184 m

Area of the jogging track

= Area of ABCD – Area of EFGH

= (30 ×20) – (26 × 16) = 600 – 416

= 184 m^2

Part – II: Solids

S. No.	Name	Figure	Lateral/curved surface area	Total surface area	Volume	Nomenclature
1.	Cuboid	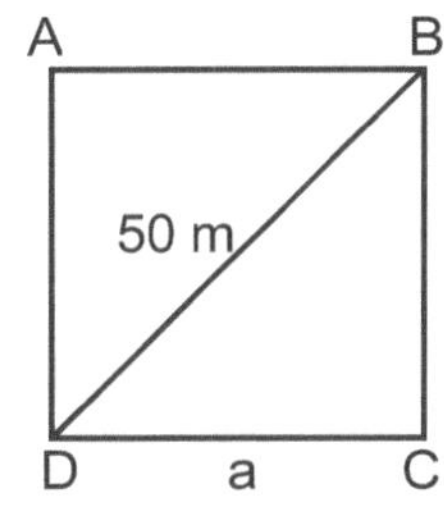	$2h(l+b)$	$2l(b+bh+lh)$	lbh	l=Length b=Breadth h=Height
2.	Cube		$4a^2$	$6a^2$	a^3	a = Edge
3.	Right circular cylinder		$2\pi rh$	$2\pi r(r+h)$	$\pi r^2 h$	r = Radius of base h = Height of the cylinder
4.	Right circular cone		πrl	$\pi r(l+r)$	$\dfrac{1}{3}.\pi r^2 h$	h = Height r =Radius l=Slant height
5.	Sphere		–	$4r^2\pi$	$\left(\dfrac{4}{3}\right)\pi r^3$	r = Radius
6.	Hemisphere		$2\pi r^2$	$3\pi r^2$	$\left(\dfrac{2}{3}\right)\pi r^3$	r = Radius

Note: Here it is just a chance that the answer of the perimeter and the area of jogging track is coming same.

Example 22:

The diagonal of a square is 50 m. Find the length of its side?

Solution:

We know that diagonal of a square

$= \sqrt{2} \times$ side

So, BD $= \sqrt{2}a = 50$

$\Rightarrow a = \dfrac{BD}{\sqrt{2}} = \dfrac{50}{\sqrt{2}} = 25\sqrt{2}$ m

Example 23:

There is a flower bed in the shape of trapezium. The length of its parallel sides are 60 m and 80 m. If the distance between them is 20 m, then find the area of the flower bed.

Solution:

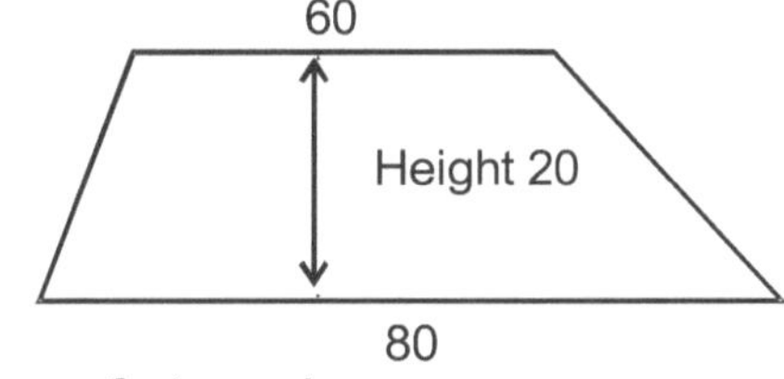

Area of a trapezium

$= \dfrac{1}{2}$ (sum of the parallel sides) × height

$$= \frac{1}{2}(60+80) \times 20 = \frac{1}{2} \times 140 \times 20$$

$$= 1400 \text{ m}^2$$

Example 24:

If the area of square is $3\sqrt{3}$ times the area of an equilateral triangle, then find the ratio of the sides of the square to the side of equilateral triangle.

Solution:

Let the side of the square be 'x' m and the side of the equilateral triangle be 'y' m, then

$\therefore$ Area of the square x^2 and area of the equilateral triangle $= \dfrac{\sqrt{3}}{4}y^2$

$$\Rightarrow x^2 = 3\sqrt{3}\left(\frac{\sqrt{3}}{4}y^2\right)$$

$$\Rightarrow \frac{x^2}{y^2} = \frac{3\sqrt{3} \times \sqrt{3}}{4} = \frac{3 \times 3}{4} = \frac{9}{4}$$

$$\Rightarrow \frac{x}{y} = \sqrt{\frac{9}{4}} = \frac{3}{2}.$$

So, ratio of the length of side of a square to the length of side of an equilateral triangle is 3 : 2.

Example 25:

If the length of the rectangle is increased by 100% and the width is increased by 200%, what is the percentage change in the area of the rectangle?

Solution:

Let the length of the rectangle be 'x' m and the width of the rectangle be 'y' m. Area of the rectangle is xy m^2.

Its new length is 2x and new width is 3y, so its new area is 2x × 3y = 6xy m^2

So, percentage change in area of the rectangle

$$= \left(\frac{6xy - xy}{xy}\right) \times 100 = \frac{5xy}{xy} \times 100 = 500\%$$

Alternate approach: For successive percentage change we can use the formula

$$a + b + \frac{a \times b}{100}$$

$$= 100 + 200 + \frac{100 \times 200}{100}$$

$$= 300 + 200 = 500\%$$

Example 26:

There is a rope of length 44 m. A circle is made by this rope. Find the diameter of the circle formed.

Solution:

Perimeter of the circle formed = length of the rope
$2\pi r = 44$, where 'r' is the radius of the circle

$$\Rightarrow 2 \times \frac{22}{7} \times r = 44$$

$$\Rightarrow r = \frac{44 \times 7}{22 \times 2} = 7$$

$\therefore$ Diameter = 2r = 2 × 7 = 14 m

Example 27:

There are 2 spherical balls, each having a radius of 4 m. By melting both balls a bigger spherical ball is made. Find the radius of the new ball.

Solution:

Total volume (of 2 balls)

$$= 2 \times \frac{4}{3} \times \pi(4)^3 = \frac{2}{3} \times \pi(4)^4$$

So, $\dfrac{2}{3} \times \pi(4)^4$ is the volume of the bigger ball.

Let the radius of the bigger ball be 'r' m.

$$\Rightarrow \frac{4}{3}\pi r^3 = \frac{2}{3}\pi(4)^4$$

$$\Rightarrow 2r^3 = 4 \times 4 \times 4 \times 4$$

$$\Rightarrow r^3 = 2 \times 64 \text{ and } r = \sqrt[3]{128} = 4\sqrt[3]{2} \text{ m}$$

Example 28:

There is a cylindrical pipe. Its height is 20 m, outer radius is 2 m and inner radius is 1.5 m. Find the volume of the metal used in the pipe.

Solution:

Let the inner radius of the pipe be r and the outer radius of the pipe be R.

So the required volume = Total volume of the cylinder – Volume of hollow cylinder

$$= \pi R^2 h - \pi r^2 h = \pi h\left(R^2 - r^2\right)$$

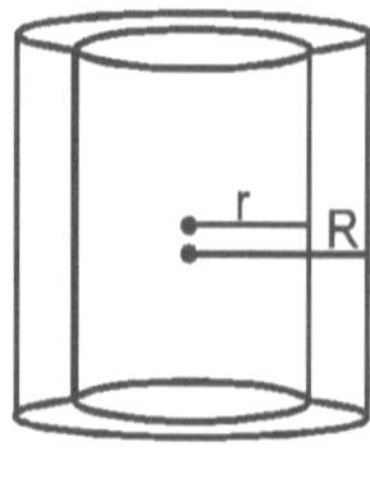

$$= \pi 20\,[(2)^2 - (1.5)^2]$$

$$= \pi 20(2 + 1.5)(2 - 1.5)$$

$$= \pi 20 \times 3.5 \times 0.5 = 35\pi$$

$$= 35 \times \frac{22}{7} = 110 \text{ m}^3$$

Example 29:

A field is in the form of a rectangle having length 20 m and breadth 15 m. There is a square pit having dimension 15 m × 15 m. This pit is to be filled uniformly upto a height of 4 m by the soil taken out by digging the rectangular field. Find out the depth upto which the rectangular field must be dig if the soil is taken out uniformly?

Solution:

To fill the pit, the volume of soil required
$= 15 \times 15 \times 4 = 900$ m^3
Let 'h' be the depth upto which the rectangular field is dug.
$\therefore 20 \times 15 \times h = 900$

$$\Rightarrow h = \frac{900}{20 \times 15} = 3 \text{ m}$$

Example 30:

The slant height and diameter of a conical tomb is 13 m and 10 m respectively. Find the cost of constructing tomb at the rate of Rs. 2 per m^3.

Solution:

Height of the cone

$$= \sqrt{AB^2 - BC^2} = \sqrt{13^2 - 5^2}$$
$$= \sqrt{144} = 12 \text{ m}$$

Volume of the cone

$$= \frac{1}{3}\pi r^2 h = \frac{1}{3}\pi \times 5 \times 5 \times 12$$

$$= 100\pi m^3$$

So, the cost of construction

$$= 100 \times \frac{22}{7} \times 2 = \text{Rs. } 628.57$$

Example 31:

Find the area of a rectangle whose area is equal to the area of a circle with perimeter equal to 24π.

Solution:

Let the radius of the circle be 'r'
$\Rightarrow 2\pi r = 24\pi \Rightarrow r = 12$
Area of the circle $= \pi(12)^2$
$=$ Area of the rectangle $= 144\pi$

Example 32:

The side of a hollow cube is 4 m. What is the length of the largest pole that can be fit into it?

Solution:

The length of the largest pole
$=$ largest diagonal of cube,
i.e. AB

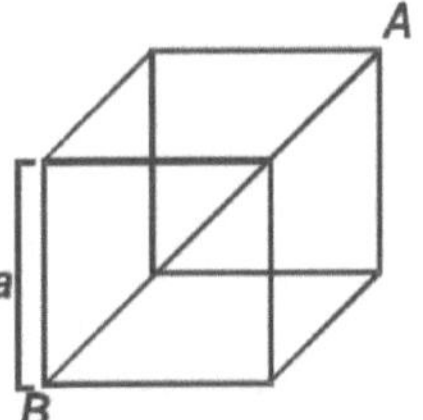

$$AB = \sqrt{a^2 + a^2 + a^2}$$

$$= \sqrt{3a^2} = a\sqrt{3} = 4\sqrt{3} \text{ m}.$$
Where a = side of cube.

Example 33:

Three cubes of sides 4 cm, 5 cm and 6 cm are melted together and a bigger cube is made. Find the side of the new cube?

Solution:

Total volume of the cubes $= 4^3 + 5^3 + 6^3$
$= 64 + 125 + 216 = 405$ cm^3

Side of the new cube $= \sqrt[3]{405}$

$$= \sqrt[3]{3 \times 3 \times 3 \times 3 \times 5}$$

$$= 3\sqrt[3]{15} \text{ cm}$$

Example 34:

A wire bent in the form of a circle of radius 2 cm is cut and bent in the form of a square. Find the ratio of the area of the circle to the area of the square.

Solution:

Area of the circle $= \pi r^2 = \pi(2)^2$

The circle is cut to make a square, so the side of the square 's'

$$= \frac{2\pi r}{4} = \frac{2 \times \pi \times 2}{4} = \pi \text{ cm}$$

Area of the square $= \pi \times \pi = \pi^2$ cm^2
Ratio of the area of the circle and square

$$= \frac{\pi(2)^2}{\pi^2} = \frac{4}{\pi}$$

Example 35:

A spherical copper ball, whose diameter is 14 cm, is melted and converted into a wire having diameter equal to 14 cm. Find the length of the wire.

Solution:

Volume of the ball $= \dfrac{4}{3}\pi r^3 = \dfrac{4}{3}\pi \times 7 \times 7 \times 7$

Let the length of the wire be 'h' m

$\Rightarrow \dfrac{4}{3}\pi \times 7 \times 7 \times 7 = \pi \times 7 \times 7 \times h \; \left(\pi r^2 h\right)$

$\therefore h = \dfrac{28}{3}$ cm

Example 36:

Two cylindrical jars have their diameter in the ratio 2 : 3 and their heights are in the ratio 3 : 2. Find the ratio of their volumes.

Solution:

Volume of a cylinder $= \pi r^2 h$

So ratio of their volumes $= \dfrac{\pi r_1^{\,2} h_1}{\pi r_2^{\,2} h_2}$

$= \dfrac{\pi(2)^2 \times 3}{\pi(3)^2 \times 2} = \dfrac{12\pi}{18\pi} = \dfrac{2}{3}$

Example 37:

The volume of the metal used in a hollow cylindrical pipe is 3300 cm^3. If its length is 28 cm and external radius is 21 cm, then find the thickness of the cylindrical pipe.

Solution:

Volume of the metal $= \pi h\left(R^2 - r^2\right)$

$= \dfrac{22}{7} \times 28\left\{(21)^2 - (r)^2\right\} = 3300$

$\Rightarrow 21^2 - r^2 = 37.5$

$\Rightarrow r = 20$ cm (approx.)

$\therefore$ the thickness of the cylinder

$= R - r = 21 - 20$

$= 1$ cm (approx.)

Example 38:

There is a room having dimensions 10 m × 15 m × 20 m. Find the cost of painting the four walls at the rate of Rs. 2.5 per m^2.

Solution:

Total area of the four walls $= 2(l + b)h$
$= 2(10 + 15) \times 20 = 1000$ m^2
So, total cost $= 1000 \times 2.5 =$ Rs. 2500

Example 39:

A horse is tied with a rope of length 7 m at one corner of a square field having side equal to 10 m. Find the minimum possible area of the square field that is left ungrazed.

Solution:

Total area of the field $= 10 \times 10$
$= 100$ m^2
The area of the field grazed by the horse

$= \dfrac{90°}{360°} \times \pi \times 7 \times 7$

$= \dfrac{1}{4} \times \dfrac{22}{7} \times 7 \times 7 = \dfrac{77}{2}$ m^2

So area of the ungrazed part of the field = Area of the shaded region

$= 100 - \dfrac{77}{2} = \dfrac{123}{2} = 61.5$ m^2

Example 40:

The length of a rectangular field is 3 times its width. If the perimeter of the field is 24 m, then find the area of the field.

Solution:

Perimeter $= 2(l + b) = 24$
$\Rightarrow 2(3b + b) = 24$
$\Rightarrow 8b = 24$
$\therefore b = 3$ and $l = 9$
So area of the field $= l \times b$
$= 3 \times 9 = 27$ m^2

Exercise

1. In the adjoining figure, find the measure of ∠c.

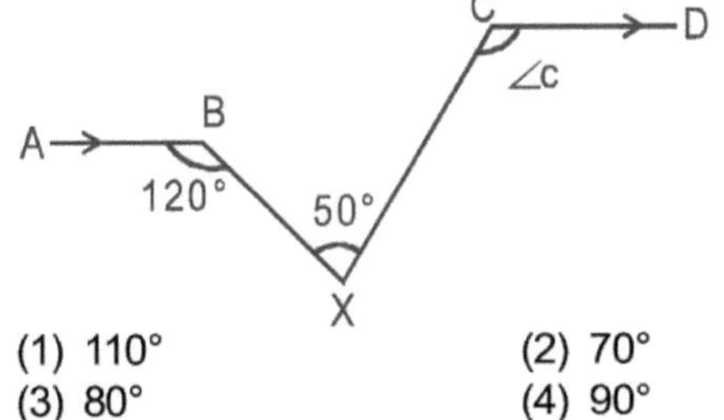

(1) 110° (2) 70°

(3) 80° (4) 90°

2. In the given figure XY || BC. Find the length of XY.

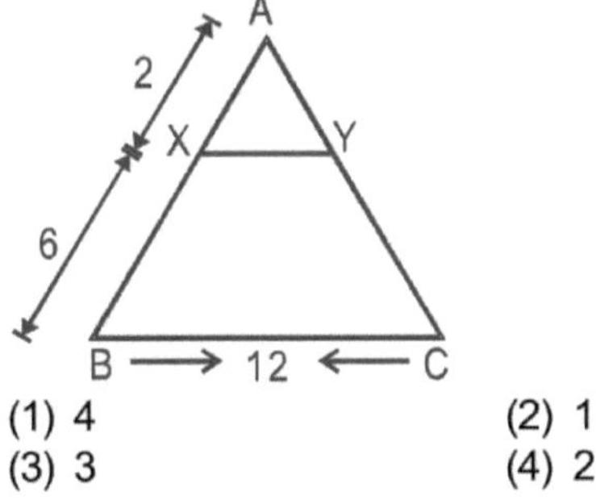

(1) 4 (2) 1

(3) 3 (4) 2

3. Find the value of x°.

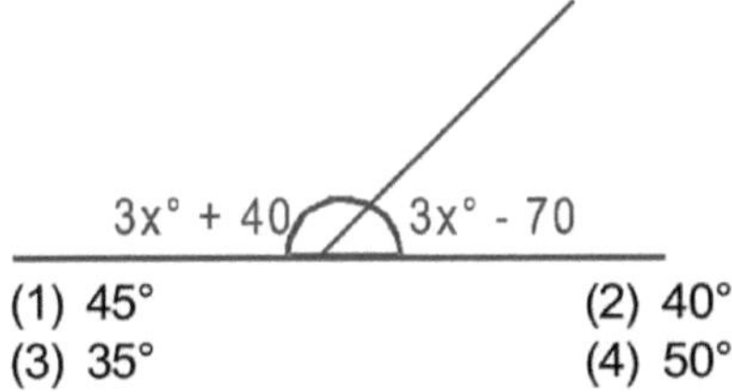

(1) 45° (2) 40°

(3) 35° (4) 50°

4. Find the angle that is equal to one fourth of its supplement.

(1) 45° (2) 40°

(3) 30° (4) 36°

5. In the adjoining figure, find the value of x. ['O' is the centre of the circle].

(1) 170°

(2) 180°

(3) 80°

(4) 160°

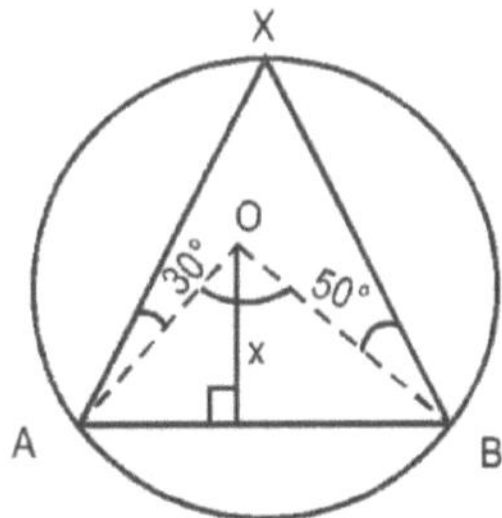

6. In the adjoining figure O is the centre of circle. Find the measure of ∠ATS .

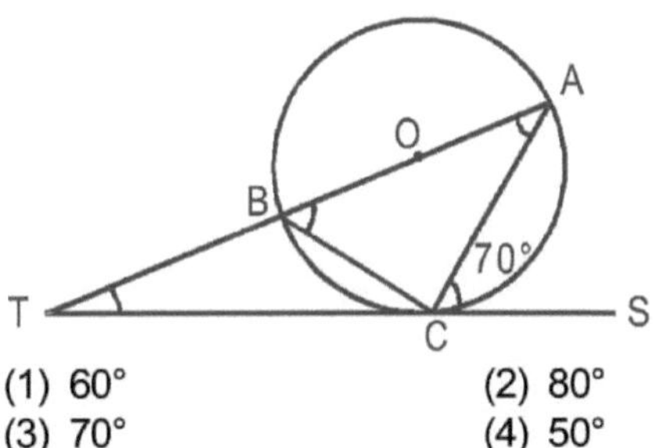

(1) 60° (2) 80°

(3) 70° (4) 50°

7. In the adjoining figure O is the centre of circle. Find the length of PC.

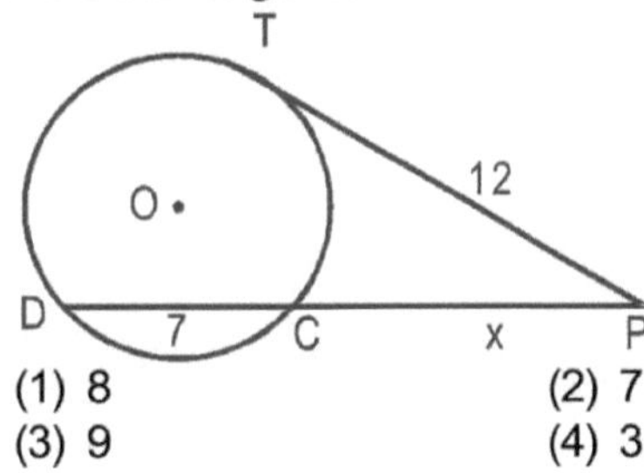

(1) 8 (2) 7

(3) 9 (4) 3

8. In the following diagram ∠B : ∠C = 3 : 4 . Find the measure of ∠B .

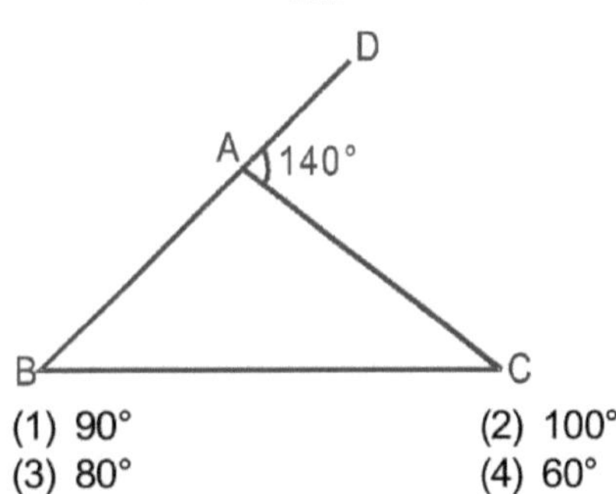

(1) 90° (2) 100°

(3) 80° (4) 60°

9. Find the value of x in the following figure.

(1) 70°

(2) 80°

(3) 110°

(4) 120°

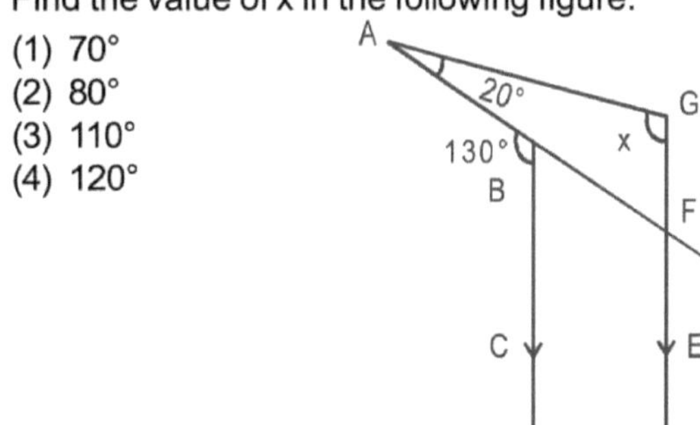

10. In △ABC, right angled at A, AD is perpendicular to BC and ∠B = 45°. If AB = x, find the length of AD in terms of x.

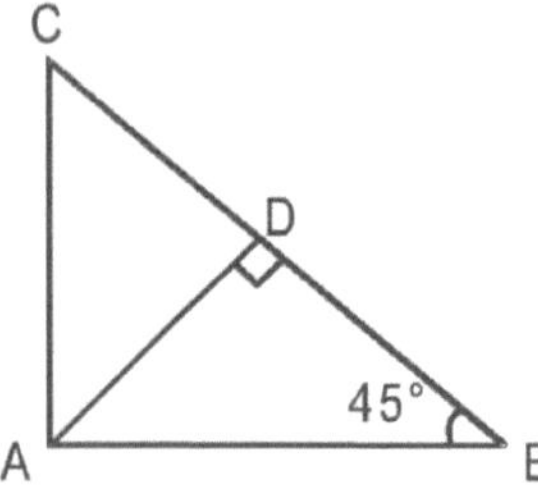

(1) $\dfrac{x}{\sqrt{2}}$

(2) 3x

(3) $x\sqrt{2}$

(4) 2x

11. In the given figure, if ∠DBG is equal to 55° and ∠CBF is equal to 115°, then find the measure of ∠GBE.

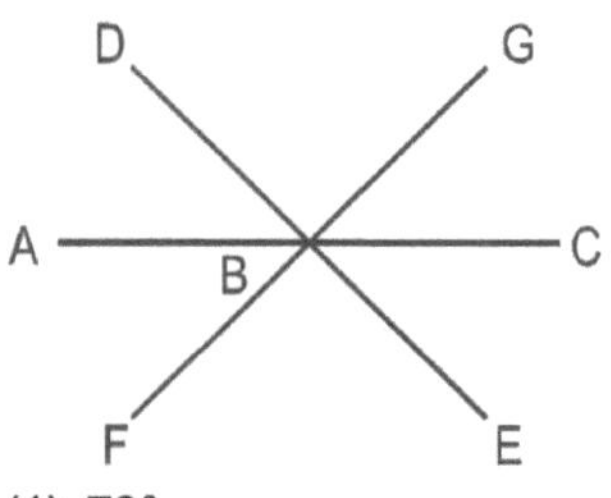

(1) 70°

(2) 125°

(3) 80°

(4) 30°

12. What is the value of d in given figure?

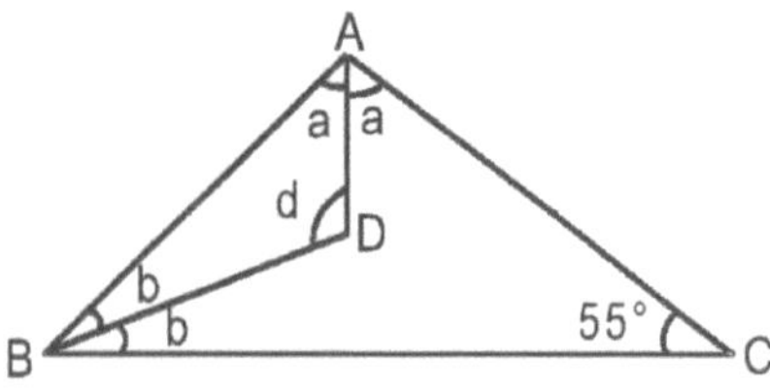

(1) 107.5°

(2) 220°

(3) 100°

(4) 117.5°

13. In the given figure, chord AB = chord CD, ∠AOB = 60° and ∠BOC = 15° then. Find the measure of ∠BOD

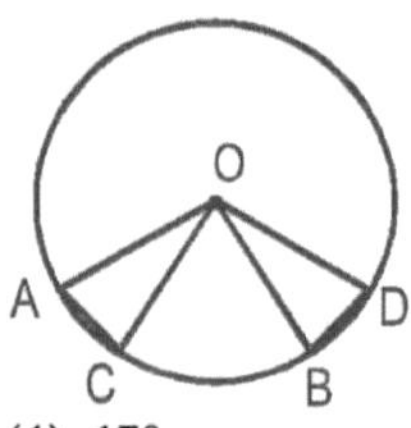

(1) 45°

(2) 50°

(3) 40°

(4) 120°

14. The diagonals AC and BD of a parallogram ABCD intersect at O. If ∠DAC = 30°, ∠AOB = 80° then find the measure of ∠DBC.

(1) 150°

(2) 50°

(3) 120°

(4) 100°

15. Triangle ABC and DEF are similar. If their areas are 64 cm^2 and 49 cm^2 and if AB is 7. Find the value of DE. (Assume AB and DE are the corresponding sides in the similar triangle.)

(1) 50 cm

(2) $\dfrac{25}{3}$ cm

(3) $\dfrac{50}{4}$ cm

(4) $\dfrac{49}{8}$ cm

16. In the given figure, ∠DBE = 36° and ∠DBC = 72°. Find the measure of ∠BDE.

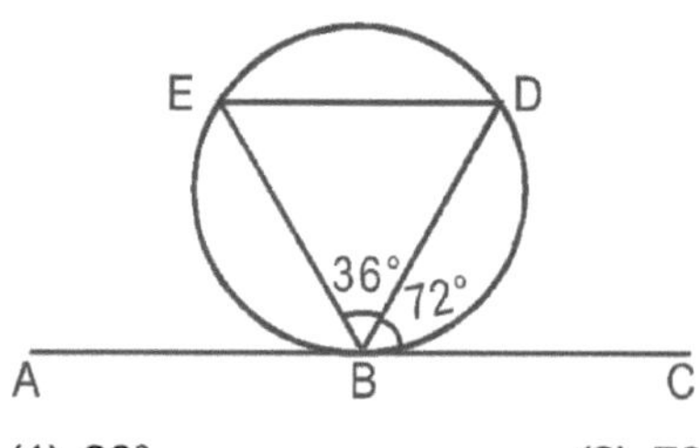

(1) 36°

(2) 70°

(3) 72°

(4) 18°

17. In the given circle, O is the centre of circle and ∠AOB = 132°. Find the measure of ∠ABO.

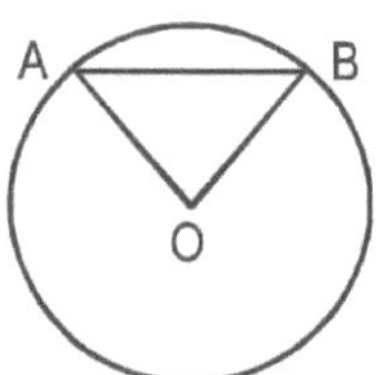

(1) 72°

(2) 24°

(3) 20°

(4) 30°

18. In the given figure AB || QR. Find the length of PB.

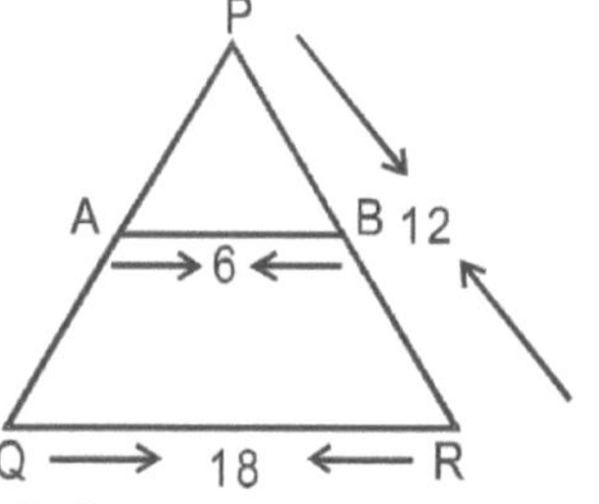

(1) 1

(2) 6

(3) 5

(4) 4

19. In the given figure AB || MN. If PA = x – 3, PM = x, PB = x – 2 and PN = x + 4, then find the value of x.

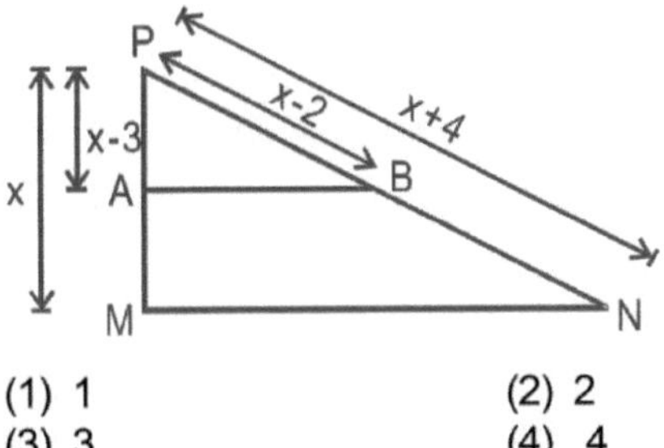

(1) 1   (2) 2
(3) 3   (4) 4

20. In $\triangle$ABC, DE || BC. If AD = x, DB = x – 2, AE = x + 2 and EC = x – 1, then find the value of x.

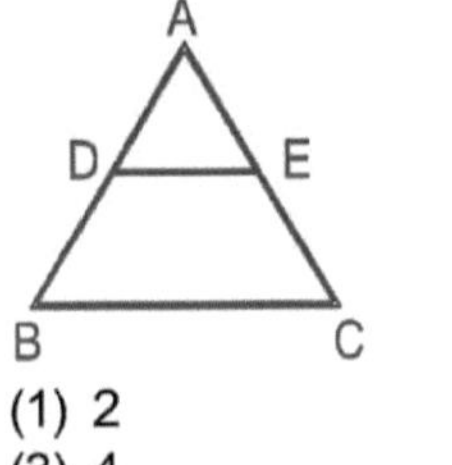

(1) 2   (2) 3
(3) 4   (4) 5

21. In the given figure AD is the bisector of $\angle$BAC meeting BC, at D. If AB = 16 units and AC = 8 units, then find BD : CD.

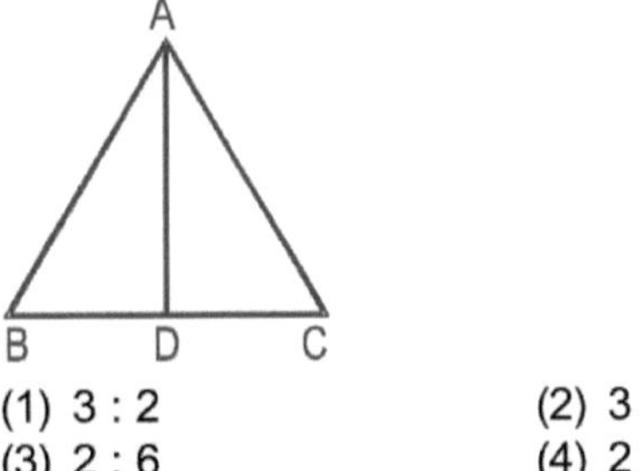

(1) 3 : 2   (2) 3 : 1
(3) 2 : 6   (4) 2 : 1

22. In the given figure, AD is the bisector of $\angle$BAC. If BD = 2 cm, DC = 3 cm and AB = 5 cm, then find the length of AC.

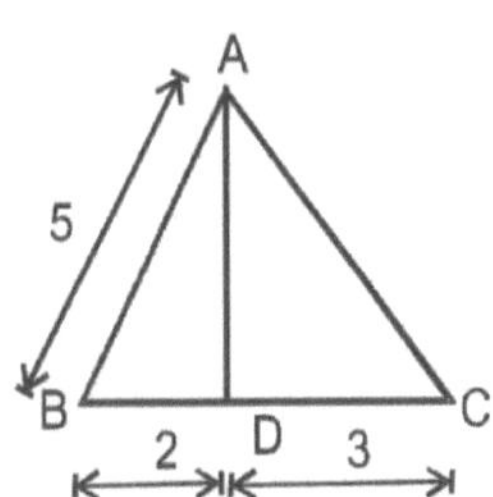

(1) 7 cm   (2) 8 cm
(3) 9 cm   (4) 7.5 cm

23. Find the value of x in the given figure.

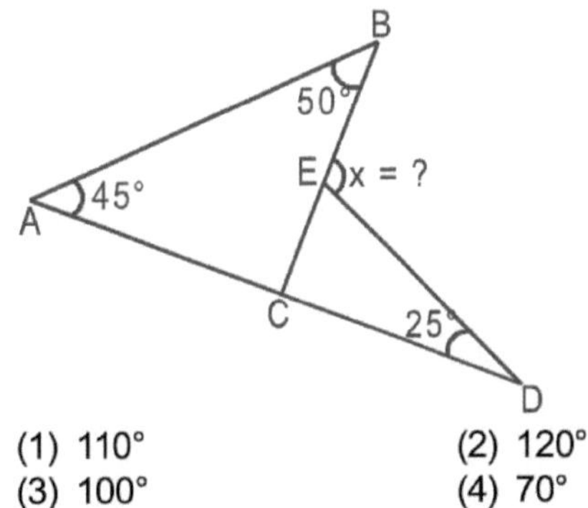

(1) 110°   (2) 120°
(3) 100°   (4) 70°

24. Find the perimeter of triangle ABC, if A = 90°, AB = 8 and AC = 6 cm.
(1) 24 cm   (2) 22 cm
(3) 20 cm   (4) 18 cm

25. In an equilateral triangle, the circumcentre, orthocentre and incentre is __.
(1) coplanar   (2) concurrent
(3) colinear   (4) Coincident

Exercise – 2

1. If the diagonal of a square field is 60 m, then find the area of the square.
(1) 800 m^2 (2) 1200 m^2
(3) 1600 m^2 (4) 1800 m^2

2. The perimeter of a square is (8x + 40) m. Find the length of its diagonal in metres.
(1) $\sqrt{2}(2x + 10)$ (2) $\sqrt{2}x$
(3) $\sqrt{2}x + 40$ (4) 2x

3. The area of a triangle is 32 cm^2. Its base is 8 cm. What is the length its altitude?
(1) 6 cm   (2) 10 cm
(3) 12 cm   (4) 8 cm

4. An isosceles right-angled triangle has an area equal to 800 cm^2. What is the length of its hypotenuse?
(1) 44 cm   (2) $40\sqrt{2}$ cm
(3) $30\sqrt{2}$ cm   (4) 65 cm

5. Find the area of the triangle whose sides are 6 cm, 7 cm, and 11 cm.
(1) 10 cm^2 (2) 14 cm^2
(3) $6\sqrt{10}$ cm^2 (4) $9\sqrt{2}$ cm^2

6. The side of equilateral triangle is 4a units. Find the length of its altitude.

(1) $\dfrac{a}{2}$ units (2) $\sqrt{2}a$ units

(3) $\sqrt{3}a$ units (4) $2\sqrt{3}a$ units

7. Find the area of a right-angled triangle if the radius of its circumcircle is 3 cm and the length of altitude drawn to the hypotenuse of the triangle is 2 cm.

(1) 4 cm^2 (2) 4.5 cm^2
(3) 5.2 cm^2 (4) 6 cm^2

8. Find the area of a rhombus whose diagonals are of length are 10 cm and 8 cm.

(1) 40 cm^2 (2) 39 cm^2
(3) 32 cm^2 (4) 54 cm^2

9. The radius of a circle is 14 cm. Find the length and area of the arc of the sector with central angle equal to 18°.
(1) 2.2 cm, 30 cm (2) 4.4 cm, 30.8 cm
(3) 3 cm, 31 cm (4) 3.2 cm , 32 cm

10. Find the length of the side of a cube whose total surface area is equal to 150 m^2.
(1) 10 m (2) 8 m
(3) 7 m (4) 5 m

11. Find the perimeter of a square if the sum of the lengths of its diagonals is 196 cm.
(1) 196 cm (2) 204 cm

(3) $196\sqrt{2}$ cm (4) 216 cm

12. The cost of levelling a square ground at the rate of Re. 0.80 per 100 m^2 is Rs. 28.80. Find the cost of fencing the same square ground at Re. 0. 60 per metre.
(1) Rs. 144 (2) Rs. 196
(3) Rs. 225 (4) Rs. 250

13. A chessboard contains 64 equal squares and the area of each square is 2.56 cm^2. Find the length of the side of the chessboard.
(1) 3.5 cm (2) 4 cm
(3) 12.8 cm (4) 8 cm

14. A lawn is in the shape of a rectangle of length 80 m and width 40 m. Outside the lawn there is a footpath of uniform width 3 m. Find the area of the path.
(1) 775 m^2 (2) 800 m^2
(3) 825 m^2 (4) 756 m^2

15. The perimeter of a triangle is 240 m and its sides are in the ratio 6 : 8 : 10. Find its area.
(1) 220 m^2 (2) 2400 m^2
(3) 250 m^2 (4) 300 m^2

16. A wire is in the form of a circle of radius 28 cm. It is cut and bent to form a square. Find the side of square.
(1) 23 cm (2) 63 cm
(3) 44 cm (4) 75 cm

17. A paper is in the form of rectangle ABCD, where AB = 30 cm and BC = 14 cm. A semicircular portion having diameter equal to the width of the rectangle is cut. Find the area of the remaining portion.
(1) 250 cm (2) 343 cm
(3) 243 cm (4) 543 cm

18. A park is in the form of rectangle 150 m × 120 m. In the centre of the park, there is a circular lawn. The area of the park excluding the lawn is 5500 m^2. Find the radius of the circular lawn.
(1) 70 m (2) 65 m
(3) 60 m (4) 63.06 m

19. A circular disc of 16 cm radius is divided into 3 sectors with central angle 80°, 140° and 160° respectively. Find the ratio of areas of three sectors.
(1) 5 : 7 : 8
(2) 6 : 7 : 8
(3) 2 : 7 : 8
(4) Data inconsistent

20. Find the length of the longest pole that can be placed in a room of size 20 m × 10 m × 5 m.

(1) $\sqrt{500}$ m (2) $\sqrt{600}$ m

(3) 30 m (4) $\sqrt{525}$ m

21. What is the volume of a cube, the length of whose largest diagonal is $8\sqrt{3}$ cm cm.

(1) 500 cm^3 (2) 508 cm^3
(3) 512 cm^3 (4) 600 cm^3

22. If the ratio of the volume of the sphere to the surface area of sphere is 5 cm, then find the radius of the sphere.
(1) 15 cm
(2) 6 cm
(3) 7 cm
(4) 8 cm

23. If the height and radius of the base of a cylinder are both increased by 200%, then find the increase in volume of the cylinder.
   (1) Twice
   (2) Thrice
   (3) 30 times
   (4) 27 times

24. A metal sphere of radius 10 cm is beated and drawn into wire of radius 0.1 cm. Find the length of the wire.
   (1) 1400 m
   (2) 1500 m
   (3) 1333.33 m
   (4) 1430 m

25. Find the height of water on a rectangular field of size 150×25 m, if the volume of water accumulated on the rectangular field is 2250 m^3.
   (1) 80 cm
   (2) 60 cm
   (3) 100 cm
   (4) 120 cm

26. Find the volume of the cube whose surface area is equal to 216 m^2.
   (1) 216 m
   (2) 280 m
   (3) 300 m
   (4) 180 m

27. A circular wire of radius 28 cm is cut and bent in form of a square. Find the ratio of the area of the circle to the area of the square.
   (1) 21 : 28
   (2) 14 : 15
   (3) 20 : 21
   (4) 14 : 11

28. Find the area of the largest circle that can be inscribed in a rectangle of length 16 cm and breadth 8 cm.
   (1) 20π cm^2
   (2) 16π cm^2
   (3) 22π cm^2
   (4) 24π cm^2

29. The length of a rectangle is increased by 60% and its width remains the same. What is the ratio of the new area to the old area of the rectangle?
   (1) 5 : 8
   (2) 3 : 5
   (3) 5 : 3
   (4) 8 : 5

30. If both the length and the width of a rectangle are increased by 10% and 20% each, then by what percentage does the area of the resulting rectangle exceeds the original rectangle?
   (1) 32%
   (2) 30%
   (3) 10%
   (4) 0%

31. Find the percentage change in volume of a cylinder, if its radius and height are increased by 10% and 20%, respectively.
   (1) 37%
   (2) 36%
   (3) 40%
   (4) 45.2%

32. Find the ratio of volume a cube to that of a sphere inscribed in the same cube.
   (1) 5 : 3
   (2) 6 : π
   (3) π : 6
   (4) 3 : 5

33. The three sides of a triangle are represented by 3 consecutive odd numbers. If the perimeter of the triangle is 27 cm, then find the length of its side.
   (1) 5, 6, 7
   (2) 9, 11, 13
   (3) 7, 9, 11
   (4) 5, 7, 9

34. Two cones of equal volume have their radii in the ratio 2 : 3. Find the ratio of their heights.
   (1) 3 : 2
   (2) 2 : 3
   (3) 9 : 4
   (4) 4 : 9

35. If the length of one side and the diagonal of a rectangle is 8 cm and 10 cm respectively, then find the area of the rectangle.
   (1) 40 m^2
   (2) 48 m^2
   (3) 60 m^2
   (4) 75 m^2

Introduction

The concepts of higher maths are normally perceived to be difficult and many students leave out these topics without even attempting it. It will make sense to try and understand the basics of these concepts. The level of questions asked from these topics in many cases is low and hence will be easy to crack!

Factorial:

Factorial of a natural number is defined as the product of all the consecutive natural numbers from 1 to that particular number. For example factorial of 5 is $1 \times 2 \times 3 \times 4 \times 5$. 'Factorial' word is represented with a symbol '!'. or 'L'. For example factorial of 5 is written as $L5$ or $5!$.

Example: $\dfrac{10!}{8!} = ?$

$$\dfrac{10!}{8!} = \dfrac{10 \times 9 \times 8!}{8!} = 10 \times 9 = 90 .$$

Note: Factorial of zero is 1 ($0! = 1$)

Basic principle of counting

To make the counting simpler there are two basic principles

1. Basic principle of multiplication:

Suppose that there are two ways of reaching the railway station from your home and from the railway station there are three ways of reaching the airport. So the total number of ways of reaching the airport from your home is $2 \times 3 = 6$.

If a function can be done in x ways and for each of these functions the other function can be done in y ways then both the functions together can be done in $(x \times y)$ ways.

Example:

There are 10 boys and 8 girls in a school. For the post of class monitor the teacher has to select one boy and one girl. In how many ways the class monitor can be selected?

Solution:

For every boy the teacher can select any one of the 8 girls. So for one boy the teacher has 8 choices.

So for 10 boys, the teacher has 10×8 = 80 choices.

2. Basic principle of addition:

Suppose you are at the railway station and you want to go to either the airport or your home. So this can be in 2 ways (if you are going home) + 3 ways (if you are going airport) = 5 ways.

If a function can be done in x ways and the other function can be done in y ways then either of the function can be done in $(x + y)$ ways.

Example 1:

There are 10 boys and 8 girls in a class . For the post of class monitor, the teacher wants to select either a boy or a girl. In how many ways can he do this function?

Solution:

He can select one boy out of 10 boys in 10 ways. He can select one girl out of 8 girls in 8 ways. He can select either a boy or a girl in 10 + 8 = 18 ways.

Note:

1. If all the functions are correlated, then basic principle of multiplication is used
2. If all the functions are independent, then basic principle of addition is used.

Example 2:

How many three digit numbers are there?

Solution:

We know that there are 10 digits 0, 1, 2, 3, 4, 5, 6, 7, 8, 9
'0' cannot be at the hundreds place
So, 100th place can be filled in 9 ways.
Tens place can be filled in 10 ways.
Units place can be filled in 10 ways.
So the total number of three digit numbers
= $9 \times 10 \times 10 = 900$

Example 3:

How many three digit numbers are there in which all the digits are distinct?

Solution:

100th place can be filled in 9 ways.

10th place can be filled in 9 ways.

Units place can be filled in 8 ways because all the digits should be distinct.

So the total number of three digit numbers in which all digits are distinct = 9 × 9 × 8 = 648

Example 4:

There are 5 multiple choice questions in an examination. First three questions have 4 choices each and the remaining two questions have 5 choices each. How many sequences of answers are possible?

Solution:

Each one of the first three questions can be solved in 4 ways, and each one of the last two questions can be solved in 5 ways.

So the total number of different sequences of answers are

$4 \times 4 \times 4 \times 5 \times 5 = 4^3 \times 5^2 = 1600$

Example 5:

How many even numbers less than 1000 can be formed by using the digits 2, 4, 3 and 5, if repetition of the digits is allowed?

Solution:

All the numbers of one digit, two digits and three digits are less than 1000. So take these cases one by one

1. Single digit even numbers are 2 and 4

2. Two digit even numbers:

   Unit's place can be filled in 2 ways, by 2 and 4 because unit's place digit must be an even number

   Ten's place can be filled in 4 ways.

   So the total number of two digit even numbers
   = 2 × 4 = 8

3. Three digit even numbers

   Unit's place can be filled in 2 ways.

   Ten's place can be filled in 4 ways.

   Hundred's place can be filled in 4 ways

   So the total number of three digit even numbers
   = 2 × 4 × 4 = 32

   Total number of three digit even numbers (by using the digits 2, 4, 3 and 5) less then 1000
   = 2 + 8 + 32 = 42

Permutations

Suppose there are three persons A, B and C contesting for the post of president and vice president of an organization and we have to select two persons. We can do it in 3 ! ways. For example, (A, B), (B, C), (A, C) (B, A), (C, B) and (C, A). Here, the first person can be the president and the second person can be the vice president, means here we are talking about the order of arrangement.

The arrangements of a number of things taking some or all of them at a time are called **permutations**.

For example, if there are 'n' number of persons and we have to select 'r' persons at a time, then the total number of permutations is denoted by $^{n}P_r$ or by P(n, r).

First person can be selected in 'n' ways. Second person can selected in 'n −1' ways. Third person can be selected in 'n − 2' ways.

Similarly, the rth person can be selected in 'n − (r −1)' = '(n − r + 1)' ways.

∴ Total number of ways of arranging these 'r' selected persons

$$= n \times (n-1) \times (n-2) \times .... (n-r+1)$$

$$= \frac{n \times (n-1)(n-2) \times ....1}{(n-r)(n-r-1) \times ....1} = \frac{n!}{(n-r)!}$$

$$\therefore{}^{n}P_r = \frac{n!}{(n-r)\ !} \ .$$

Example 6:

There are four persons A, B, C and D and at a time we can arrange only two persons. Find the total number of arrangements.

Solution:

Total number of arrangements (**permutations**) is AB, BA, AC, CA, AD, DA, BC, CB, CD, DC, BD and DB or we can say that out of 4 persons we have to arrange only 2 at a time, so the total number of permutations is $^{4}P_2$

$$^{4}P_2 = \frac{4!}{(4-2)\ !} = \frac{4!}{2!} = \frac{4 \times 3 \times 2}{2!} = 12$$

Example 7:

In the above question, if all the persons are selected at a time, then how many arrangements are possible?

Solution:

We have to arrange 4 persons, so this can be

$$^{4}P_4 = \frac{4!}{(4-4)\ !} = \frac{4!}{0!} = \frac{4!}{1}$$

$$= 4 \times 3 \times 2 \times 1 = 24$$

Example 8:

There are 4 flags of different colours. How many different signals can be given, by taking any number of flags at a time?

Solution:

Signals can be given either taking all or some of the flags at a time.

Number of signals that can be given by taking 1 flag $= {}^4P_1$

Number of signals that can be given by taking 2 flags $= {}^4P_2$

Number of signals that can be given by taking 3 flags $= {}^4P_3$

Number of signals that can be given by taking 4 flags $= {}^4P_4$

So the total number of signals

$$= {}^4P_1 + {}^4P_2 + {}^4P_3 + {}^4P_4$$

$$= \frac{4!}{(4-1)!} + \frac{4!}{(4-2)!} + \frac{4!}{(4-3)!} + \frac{4!}{(4-4)!}$$

$$= 4 + 12 + 24 + 24 = 64$$

Example 9:

Find the number of ways in which 5 boys and 5 girls be seated in a row so that:

I.   All the boys sit together and all the girls sit together.
II. Boys and girls sit at alternate positions.
III. No two girls sit together.
IV. All the girls always sit together.
V.   All the girls are never together.

Solution:

I.   All the boys can be arranged in 5! ways and all the girls can be arranged in 5! ways.
     Now we have two groups (boys, girls) and these 2 groups can be arranged in 2 ! ways.
     [boys–girls and girls–boys]
     So total number of arrangements is 5! × 5! × 2! = 28,800

II. Boys and girls sit alternately, this can be arranged like this
     B G B G B G B G B G or G B G B G B G B G B
     B
     In the first case boys can be arranged in 5! and girls can be arranged in 5! ways.
     In the second case also, the number of arrangement is same as first case
     So the total number of arrangement = 5! × 5! + 5! × 5! or

$${}^5P_5 \times {}^5P_5 + {}^5P_5 \times {}^5P_5$$

$$= 120 \times 120 + 120 \times 120$$
$$= 14,400 + 14,400 = 28,800 \text{ ways}$$

III. No two girls sit together - In this case
     _ _B_ _B_ _B_ _ B_ _B_ _ there are 6 spaces where a girl can find her seat.

5 girls can be arranged in ${}^6P_5$

$$\frac{6!}{(6-5)!} = 6 \times 5 \times 4 \times 3 \times 2$$

$$= 720 \text{ ways}$$

5 boys can be arranged in

$${}^5P_5 = 5 \times 4 \times 3 \times 2 \times 1 = 120 \text{ ways}$$

Total number of arrangements
$$= 720 \times 120 = 86,400$$

IV. When all the girls are always together, then treat them as one group. So now we have 5 boys and 1 group of 6 girls and this can be permutated in 6! ways at the same time 5 girls in the group can be permutated in 5 ! ways, so total number of required ways is 6 ! × 5 ! = 720 × 120 = 86400

V.   All the girls are never together
     Total number of arrangements of 5 boys and 5 girls is 10!
     Number of arrangements in which all the girls are always together

$$= B_1, B_2, B_3, B_4, B_5 \text{ [All 5 girls]}$$

$$= 6! \times 5! = 8,64,00$$

So number of arrangements in which all the girls are never together = total arrangement – number of arrangements when girls are always together.

$$= 10! - (6! \times 5!) = 3,54,2400$$

Example 10:

Find the number of permutation of the letters of the word FOLDER taking all the letters at a time?

Solution:

Number of letters in the word FOLDER is 6
So the number of arrangements

$$= {}^6P_6 = 6!$$

Alternate method:

First place can be filled by any one of the six letters. The second place can be filled by any one of the five remaining letters, the third place can be filled by any one of the four remaining letters and so on.
So the total number of arrangements is
6 × 5 × 4 × 3 × 2 × 1 = 720.

Example 11:

How many four digit numbers greater than 5000 can be formed by using the digits 4, 5, 6 and 7? (Repetition of the digits is not allowed.)

Solution:

Total number of arrangements possible is $^4P_4 = 4!$

Total number of arrangements by using the digits 5, 6 and 7 is $= 3!$

So the total number of required arrangements is $4! - 3! = 24 - 6 = 18$

Alternative method:

Thousand's place can be filled in 3 ways.
Hundred's place can be filled in 3 ways.
Ten's place can be filled in 2 ways.
Unit's place can be filled in 1 ways.
So total number of arrangements
$= 3 \times 3 \times 2 \times 1 = 18$

Example 12:

In Q. 11, find the number of four digit numbers that can be formed if the repetition of digits is allowed.

Solution:

If the repetition is allowed then the total number of arrangements is $4 \times 4 \times 4 \times 4 = 256$ ways
Because on the first place any one of the four number can come, similarly on the 2nd, 3rd and 4th place also.
Total number of arrangements beginning with 4 is $4 \times 4 \times 4 = 64$
So, total number of required arrangements
$= 256 - 64 = 192$

Alternative method:

Thousand's place can be filled in 3 ways
Hundred's place can be filled in 4 ways.
Ten's place can be filled in 4 ways.
Unit's place can be filled in 4 ways. So the total number of arrangements $= 3 \times 4 \times 4 \times 4 = 192$

Combinations

Suppose three persons A, B and C are contesting for the post of president and vice president of an organization and we have to select two persons. We can select either (a, b) or (b, c) or (a, c) = 3 ways because here we are talking about the selection, not about the order. Whether 'a' is a president or 'b' is a vice president or vice-versa, doesn't matter.

Suppose there are 10 persons in class and we have to select any 3 persons at a point regardless of the order, it is a case of combination.

If there are n number of things and we have to select some or all of them it is called **combinations**.

If out of n things we have to select r things ($1 \leq r \leq n$), then the number of combinations is denoted by

$$^nC_r = \frac{n!}{(n-r)! \, r!}$$

We already know that the number of arrangements of 'r'

things out of the 'n' things is given by $^nP_r = \dfrac{n!}{(n-r)!}$

Combination does not deal with the arrangements of the selected things.

$\therefore$ 'r' selected things can be arranged in r! ways.

$$\therefore (r!) \times \left(^nC_r\right) = {}^n P_r$$

$$\Rightarrow {}^n C_r = \frac{^nP_r}{r!} = \frac{n!}{r!(n-r)!}$$

Difference between permutations and combinations

Suppose that there are five persons A, B, C, D and E and we have to choose two persons at a time then in

Permutation

Number of required ways $= {}^5P_2$

$$= \frac{5!}{(5-2)!} = \frac{5!}{3!} = 5 \times 4 = 20$$

Combinations

Number of required ways $= {}^5C_2$

$$= \frac{5!}{2! \, (5-2)!} = \frac{5!}{2! \times 3!} = \frac{5 \times 4}{2} = 10$$

So it is clear that in permutations (rearrangement) order matters but in combinations (selections) order does not matter.

Example 13:

In a class there 5 boys and 6 girls. How many different committees of 3 boys and 2 girls can be formed?

Solution:

Out of 5 boys we have to select 3 boys, this can be done in $^5C_3$ ways.

Out of 6 girls we have to select 2 girls, this can be done in $^6C_2$ ways.

So, selection of 3 boys and 2 girls can be done in $\left(^5C_3\right)\times\left(^6C_2\right)$ ways

[Basic rule of multiplication]

$$= \left(\frac{5!}{3!(5-3)!}\right)\times\left(\frac{6!}{2!\,(6-2)!}\right)$$

$$= \left(\frac{5\times4}{2}\right)\times\left(\frac{6\times5}{2}\right) = 10\times15$$

$$= 150 \text{ ways}$$

Example 14:

If there are 10 persons in a party, and each person shakes hands with all the persons in the party, then how many hand shakes took place in the party?

Solution:

It is very obvious that when two persons shake hands, it is counted as one handshake. So we can say that there are 10 hands and every combination of 2 hands will gives us one handshake.

So the number of handshakes

$$= {}^{10}C_2 = \frac{10!}{2!\,(10-2)\,!}$$

$$= \frac{10\times9\times8!}{2!\ \times\ 8!} = 45$$

Example 15:

For the post of Maths faculty in Career Launcher there are 6 vacant seats. Exactly 2 seats are reserved for MBA's. There are 10 applicants out of which 4 are MBA's. In how many ways the selection can be made?

Solution:

There are 4 MBA's and 6 other candidates.

So we have to select 2 candidates out of the 4 MBA's and the rest 4 candidates out of 6 other candidates.

So the total number of ways of selection

$$= \left(^4C_2\right)\times\left(^6C_4\right)$$

$$= \left(\frac{4!}{2!\times(4-2)\,!}\right)\times\left(\frac{6!}{4!(6-4)\,!}\right)$$

$$= \left(\frac{4\times3\times2!}{2\times1\times2!}\right)\times\left(\frac{6\times5\times4!}{4!\times2\times1}\right)$$

$$= 6\times15 = 90 \text{ ways}$$

Example 16:

There are 10 points out of which no three are collinear. How many straight lines can be formed using these 10 points?

Solution:

By joining any two points we will get one line.

So the total number of lines formed

$$= {}^{10}C_2 = \frac{10\times9\times8!}{2\times(10-2)\ !} = \frac{10\times9\times8!}{2\times8!} = 45$$

Example 17:

Find the number of diagonals that can be drawn by joining the vertices of a decagon.

Solution:

In decagon there are 10 vertices and by joining any two vertices we will get one line.

So in a decagon total number of lines formed

$$= {}^{10}C_2 = \frac{10!}{2!\,(10-2)!} = \frac{10\times9\times8!}{2!\times8!} = 45$$

But out of these 45 lines, 10 lines will be the sides of the decagon. So total number of diagonals = 45 − 10 = 35

Example 18:

In the above question how many triangles can be formed?

Solution:

We know that in a triangle there are three vertices and by joining any three points we will get a triangle.

So number of triangles formed

$$= {}^{10}C_3 = \frac{10\times9\times8\times7!}{3!\times(10-3)!} = \frac{10\times9\times8\times7!}{3!\times7!} = 120$$

Example 19:

There are 5 boys and 6 girls. A committee of 4 is to be selected so that it must consist at least one boy and at least one girl?

Solution:

The different possibilities are

I.   1 boy and 3 girls
II. 2 boys and 2 girls
III. 3 boys and 1 girl

In the first possibility total number of combinations is $^5C_1 \times {}^6C_3$

In the second possibility total number of combinations is $^5C_2 \times {}^6C_2$

In the third possibility total number of combinations is $^5C_3 \times {}^6C_1$

So the total number of combinations are

$$^5C_1 \times {}^6C_3 + {}^5C_2 \times {}^6C_2 + {}^5C_3 \times {}^6C_1 = 310$$

Circular combination

If n persons are seated around a circular table then they can be arranged in $(n-1)!$ ways.

For example: If three persons are there they can be arranged in $(3-1)!$

$= 2!$ ways. [We fix the position of 1 person and then arrange the remaining $(n-1)$ persons.]

Probability

Suppose a magician approaches you and says that he has a dice and if he throws that dice number greater than 5 comes on the top, he will give you Rs. 20 otherwise you will have to give Rs. 10 to him. What will you do? Here is an application of probability which deals with uncertainties. It has nothing to do with actual happenings. It just talks about the possibilities.

To know about the probability in a better way just take the above example.

When a dice is thrown then on the top either 1, 2, 3, 4, 5 or 6 can come. So we can say there are a total of six possibilities. Out of these 6 numbers, greater than 5 is only one number that is 6. So in your favour there is only 1 number that is 6 and against our (or our opponent) favour there are 5 numbers 1, 2, 3, 4 and 5. This indicates that your chance of losing is five times than your chance of winning. It means this game is not in your favour.

Probability is defined as

Probability of a event

$$= \frac{\text{Number of favourable events}}{\text{Total number of possible events}}$$

Like in the example given above

Probability of your winning $= \dfrac{1}{6}$

Probability of your losing $= \dfrac{5}{6}$

Possible events (sample space): It means all those events which can occur in that scenario.

For example: If we have one dice and one coin then the possible outcomes are

H1, H2, H3, H4, H5, H6, T1, T2, T3, T4, T5, T6

Note: Probability of an event cannot be less than 0 and at the same time it cannot be more than 1.

Addition rule

Events: Each possible outcome is called an event. Like the events of throwing a dice are 1, 2, 3, 4, 5 and 6.

Mutually exclusive events: When a particular event occurs and the other particular event cannot occur, then they are called mutually exclusive events.

For example:
In the experiment of throwing a dice the event that a possible outcome is an odd number and the event that possible outcome is an even number, are mutually exclusive (Because there is no number which is odd as well as even).
Here, the probability of such event is given by
$P(E) = P(A) + P(B)$
where
$P(E)$ = Probability of occurence of such mutually exclusive event.
$P(A)$ = Probability of occurence of event A
$P(B)$ = Probability of occurence of event B

Non mutually exclusive events: When a particular event occurs and a particular event may also occur and vice versa or you can say that both events can occur simultaneously, then they are called non mutually exclusive events.

For example:
In the experiment of throwing a dice the event that a possible outcome is an odd and the event that a possible outcome is a prime number are not mutually exclusive, because there are certain numbers (like 3 and 5) which are both odd as well as prime, so the probability of such an event is given by
$P(E) = P(A) + P(B) - P(C)$
where
$P(E)$ = Probability of occurrence of any or both of A and B
$P(A)$ = Probability of occurrence of event A
$P(B)$ = Probability of occurrence of event B
$P(C)$ = Probability of occurrence of event C, which is an intersection of A and B. (Intersection of A and B means that outcomes in which the number is odd as well as prime. For example, the numbers 3 and 5 which are both prime as well as odd).

Example 20:

In a single throw of a fair dice what is the probability that the number the appearing on the top face of the dice is more than 2?

Solution:

In a dice there are 6 faces numbered 1, 2, 3, 4, 5 and 6.
So, the total number of possible events are 1, 2, 3, 4, 5 and 6 = 6
and the total number of favourable events are 3, 4, 5 and 6 = 4

So, the required probability is $\dfrac{4}{6} = \dfrac{2}{3}$

Example 21:

If two fair dice are thrown simultaneously, then what is the probability that the sum of the numbers appearing on the top faces of the dice is less than 4?

Solution:

Total number of possible events = (1, 1), (1, 2), (1, 3), (1, 4), (1, 5), (1, 6), (2, 1), (2, 2) ….and so on. There will be 6 × 6 = 36 possible events.
Number of favourable events = (1, 1), (1, 2) and (2, 1) = 3 events

So, the required probability = $\dfrac{3}{36} = \dfrac{1}{12}$

Example 22:

If out of the first 20 natural numbers Mr. X selects a number at random, then what is the probability that this number will be a multiple of 4?

Solution:

Total number of possible events = 1, 2, 3, …, 20 = 20 such numbers
Total number of favourable events = 4, 8, 12, 16 and 20 = 5 such numbers

So, the required probability = $\dfrac{5}{20} = \dfrac{1}{4}$

Example 23:

In the example 22, what is the probability that this number will be a multiple of 4 or 7?

Solution:

Total number of possible events
= 1, 2 … 20 = 20 such numbers
Numbers divisible by 4 = 4, 8, 12, 16, 20 = 5 such numbers
Number divisible by 7 = 7 and 14
= 2 such numbers
Since from 1 to 20 there is no number which is divisible by both 4 and 7. It is a case of mutually exclusive events.
So number of possible outcomes = 5 + 2 = 7

So, the required probability is = $\dfrac{7}{20}$

Example 24:

In the example 22, what is the probability that the selected number is divisible by 2 and 4?

Solution:

The total number of possible events = 20 such numbers
Number divisible by 2 and 4 means the number should be divisible by 4 (LCM of 2 and 4 is 4) = 4, 8, 12, 16, 20 = 5 such numbers

So, the required probability is $\dfrac{5}{20} = \dfrac{1}{4}$

Example 25:

In the example 22, what is the probability that this number is divisible by 2 or 4?

Solution:

The total number of possible outcomes = 20 in number
Number divisible by 2 = 2, 4, 6, 8, 10, 12, 14, 16, 18, 20 = 10 such numbers
Number divisible by 4 = 4, 8, 12, 16 and 20 = 5 such numbers
There are certain numbers which are divisible by both 2 and 4, so it is case of non mutually exclusive events.
Number divisible by both 2 and 4 are 4, 8, 12, 16 and 20 = 5 such number
So, the required probability = P(A) + P(B) – P(C)

$$= \dfrac{10}{20} + \dfrac{5}{20} - \dfrac{5}{20} = \dfrac{10}{20} = \dfrac{1}{2}$$

# Exercise

Exercise – I

1. Find the value of $^8P_6$
   (1) 33425　　　　(2) 20160
   (3) 18972　　　　(4) 6625

2. Find the value of $^8C_6$
   (1) 33　　　　(2) 32
   (3) 30　　　　(4) 28

3. Find the number of ways in which the letters of the word BIHAR can be rearranged.
   (1) 99　　　　(2) 129
   (3) 119　　　　(4) 125

4. Find the number of ways in which the letters of the word AMERICA can be rearranged.
   (1) 2519　　　　(2) 2620
   (3) 1250　　　　(4) 2500

5. Find the number of ways in which the letters of the word CALCUTTA can be rearranged.
   (1) 3000　　　　(2) 5009
   (3) 5029　　　　(4) 5039

6. In how many ways can you arrange the letters of the word AKSHAY such that vowels do not start the words?
   (1) $\dfrac{6!}{2!}-1$　　　　(2) $\dfrac{6!}{2!}-2$
   (3) $2 \times 5!$　　　　(4) 240

7. How many distinct 4 letter words can be formed by using the letters a, b, c and d? (Repetition of the letters is allowed).
   (1) 296　　　　(2) 346
   (3) 440　　　　(4) 256

8. How many numbers greater than 4000 can be made by using the digits 2, 3, 4 and 5? (Repetition of the digits is not allowed).
   (1) 12　　　　(2) 14
   (3) 20　　　　(4) 24

9. How many numbers greater than 4000 can be made by using the digits 2, 3, 4 and 5? (Repetition of digits is allowed).
   (1) 120　　　　(2) 128
   (3) 138　　　　(4) 130

10. A bag contains 6 white balls and 4 red balls. Three balls are drawn one by one with replacement. What is the probability that all the 3 balls are red?
    (1) $\dfrac{8}{125}$　　(2) $\dfrac{1}{20}$　　(3) $\dfrac{1}{30}$　　(4) $\dfrac{1}{120}$

11. In the above question, if 3 balls are drawn one by one with replacement, then what is the probability that 2 balls are white and 1 ball is red?
    (1) $\dfrac{54}{125}$　　(2) $\dfrac{1}{4}$　　(3) $\dfrac{1}{3}$　　(4) $\dfrac{1}{2}$

12. In question 10, if the balls are drawn without replacement, wat is the probability that 2 balls are red and 1 ball is white?
    (1) 0.1　　　　(2) 0.2
    (3) 0.3　　　　(4) 0.4

13. The probability that A will pass the examination is $\dfrac{1}{3}$ and the probability that B will pass the examination is $\dfrac{1}{2}$. What is the probability that both A and B will pass the examination?
    (1) $\dfrac{1}{6}$　　(2) 1　　(3) $\dfrac{2}{3}$　　(4) $\dfrac{3}{2}$

14. In Q. No. 13, what is the probability that only one person [either A or B] will pass the examination?
    (1) 1　　(2) $\dfrac{1}{2}$　　(3) $\dfrac{1}{3}$　　(4) $\dfrac{2}{3}$

15. In Q. No. 13, what is the probability that at least one person will pass the examination?
    (1) 1　　(2) $\dfrac{1}{2}$　　(3) $\dfrac{1}{3}$　　(4) $\dfrac{2}{3}$

16. In Q. No. 13, what is the probability that no one will pass the examination?

(1) 1

(2) $\dfrac{1}{2}$

(3) $\dfrac{1}{4}$

(4) $\dfrac{1}{3}$

17. Two cards are drawn together from a pack of 52 cards at random. What is the probability that both the cards are spades?

(1) $\dfrac{^{4}C_2}{^{52}C_2}$

(2) $\dfrac{^{13}C_2}{^{52}C_2}$

(3) $\dfrac{^{26}C_2}{^{52}C_2}$

(4) $\dfrac{^{8}C_2}{^{52}C_2}$

18. In question number 17, what is the probability that both the cards are kings?

(1) $\dfrac{^{8}C_2}{^{52}C_2}$

(2) $\dfrac{^{13}C_2}{^{52}C_2}$

(3) $\dfrac{^{26}C_2}{^{52}C_2}$

(4) $\dfrac{^{4}C_2}{^{52}C_2}$

19. In question number 17, what is the probability that one card is a spade and one card is a heart?

(1) $\dfrac{^{13}C_1 \times {}^{13}C_2}{^{52}C_2}$

(2) $\dfrac{^{13}C_1 \times {}^{26}C_1}{^{52}C_2}$

(3) $\dfrac{13}{52} \times \dfrac{13}{52}$

(4) $\dfrac{^{13}C_1 \times {}^{13}C_1}{^{52}C_2}$

20. In question number 17, what is the probability that exactly one card is a king ?

(1) $\dfrac{^{52}C_1}{^{52}C_2}$

(2) $\dfrac{4}{^{58}C_2}$

(3) $\dfrac{^{4}C_1 \times {}^{48}C_1}{^{52}C_2}$

(4) $\dfrac{1}{2}$

Data Based Reasoning   7

Data Interpretation

Data is just like loads of ammunition with you. It can come to your aid or else may overwhelm you in a negative manner. Just as a tool is just as good as the craftsman, data itself is of no use unless we cannot interpret it meaningfully to gather valuable information.

Though the interpretation would depend on the actual data given, this chapter tackles some of the common interpretations handy across any set of data.

For a person to gather worthwhile information from an overwhelming amount of data, the data needs to be presented in a lucid and concise manner. Duplicating data has to be avoided and at the same time no detail has to be lost out. The data should be able to provide an immediate overall scenario and also should be sufficient to compute any detailed information. This is where data representation plays a very important role. While there can be any number of ways a data can be represented, in this chapter we will look at the standard ones.

A table is one of the simplest and most convenient tools used for summarizing data. In a table, data is systematically arranged in columns and rows. All the columns and the rows have a particular heading that defines the information contained in the columns and the rows. The column and row heading also may define the units of measurements, if any. While a tabular data can offer a lot of information, it lacks a pictorial representation and may demand some time (and calculation) to give an idea of the overall scenario.

Annual Sales of 2-wheelers in India, 2000 – 2004
Figures in '000s

	Number of vehicles sold in year				
	2000	2001	2002	2003	2004*
Mopeds	580	490	450	380	330
Scooters	520	640	720	680	830
Motorcycles	460	540	750	840	930
Total	1560	1670	1920	1900	2090

* Figures for 2004 are projected numbers

While reading a table, or for that matter any representation of data, it is imperative that you read everything about the data i.e. the heading for the data, the column headings, any foot notes, units of the data, etc. and not just give a cursory glance to the actual numbers. e.g. on reading the head note to the data, it should be kept in mind that the data is about sales and not production. Thus any information on production cannot be understood from this unless further data is given. Another point to note is that the figures correspond to only India and only of 2-wheelers and not all automobiles. The units suggest that the sale of mopeds in year 2000 is not 580 but 580,000. The column heading should have made it clear that the data refers to the number of vehicles and not the revenue generated through sales (erroneous interpretation would have been to consider 580 as Rs. 580,000). The actual number of mopeds sold in 2004 is NOT 300. This is clear as the figures for 2004 are projections and not actual, as stated in the foot-note.

The same data as given in the above table could have been shown as a line graph as follows:

Annual Sales of 2-wheelers in India, 2000 – 2004

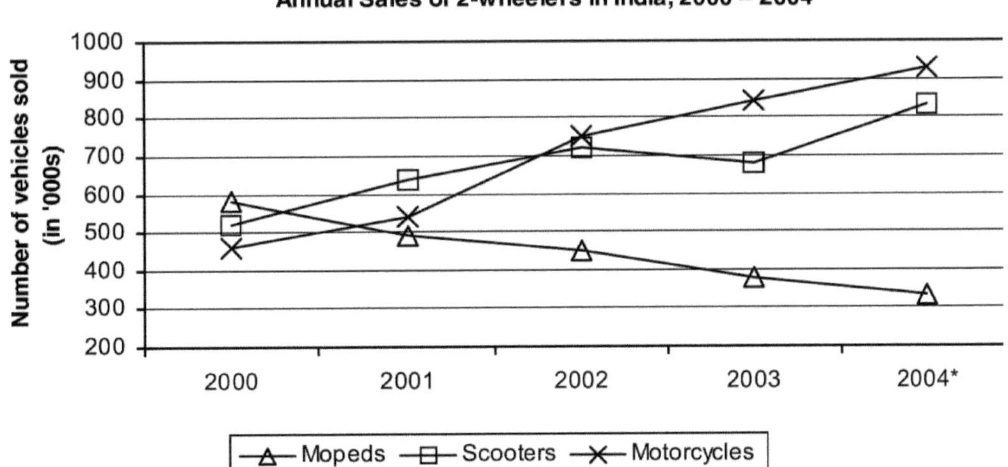

* Figures for 2004 are projected numbers

What a line graph achieves over a table is that it is a pictorial representation and hence can give an immediate overall picture. Thus it is very obvious that the sales of mopeds have continuously decreased over the period whereas the sales of motorcycles have shown the highest growth rate over the period. Not only this, it is also immediately clear that the highest growth rate in any year, by any product group is shown by motorcycles in the period 2001-2002 as the line is the steepest in this period. What is lost out in the process is the accuracy as one would have to ascertain the value of any point looking at the scale of the Y axis. However the actual values could also be mentioned in the graph adding accuracy but making the graph look more cluttered. Apart from these differences, any minute information that could be calculated using the data in table or this data in line graph remain the same as the underlying data is same. Thus all questions that could have been asked on the tabular data can also be asked on this representation.

Bar graph is very similar to a line graph and can appear in various forms as shown below :

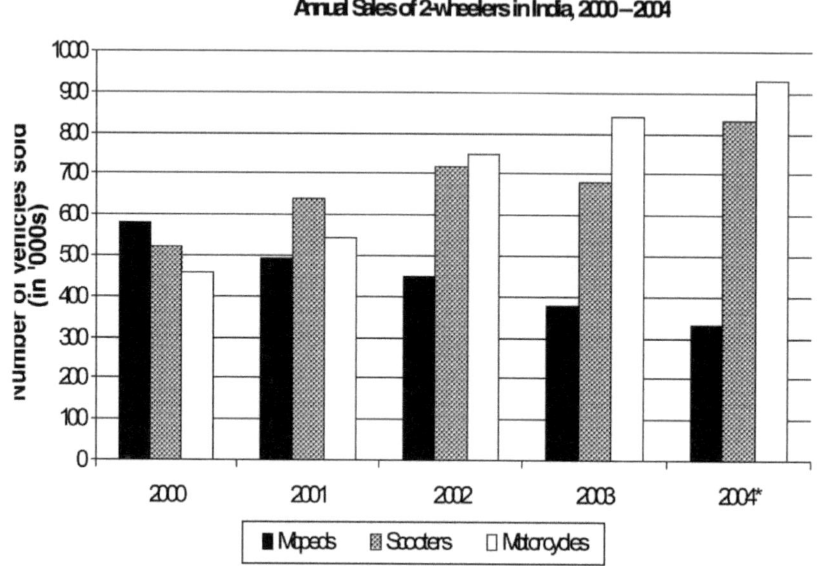

This type of graph is more correctly called a column chart rather than a bar chart. As the underlying data is exactly same as the tabular data and the line graph, there is no information lost and any of the three representations can be used interchangeably. Lest you start wondering why then are there so many varied ways of representations, a moments glance can help you understand that this type of graph is more visually appealing when we have to compare the sales across product groups in any particular year whereas the line graph was more visually appealing for the growth rates or trends across years for a particular product group.

Please note that in such a graph, it is only the height of the bar that matters and the width of the bar does not hold any significance.

The cumulative bar graph of the percent contribution of each category introduced the idea of a percent share of the total. A more appropriate graph to depict this is the pie chart. The name itself suggests that this graph basically shows the manner in which an entire pie is divided among different groups.

Share of 2-wheelers sold (volumes) in India for 2003 and 2004

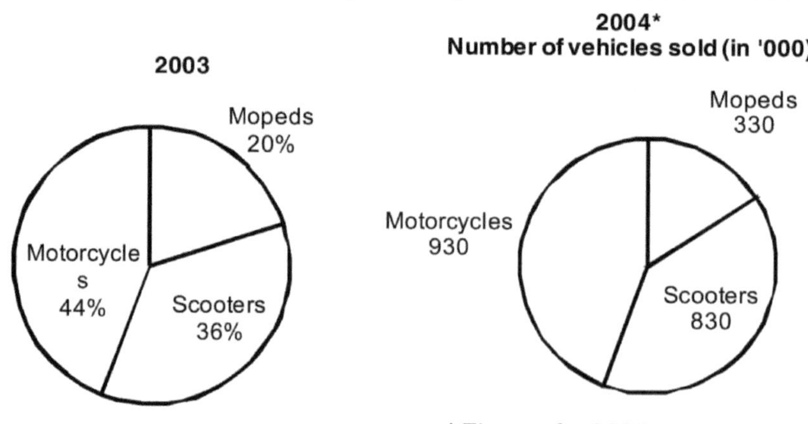

* Figures for 2004 are projected numbers

Thus when using pie-charts, each pie corresponds to a particular year. Also worth noting is that the pie on the left has just the percentages whereas the pie on the right has the actual sales figures given. Thus for the year 2003, we cannot find the actual sales figures as the total value of the pie (cumulative sales of the three product groups) is not known for 2003. But for 2004, we can calculate the expected share of each product group in percentage as we can sum the individual figures to know the total sales of 2-wheelers.

Pie charts are more amenable to compare the share of various product groups, visually. Thus it is very clear just by visual observations that the share of mopeds has declined at the expense of an increase in share of scooters, with the share of motorcycles remaining almost the same.

Any of the above graphs types can be combined to form a combination graph. An example of a combination graph is shown below. The line graph shown has additional data of the average price of a product group.

Number of 2-wheelers sold and the Average Price

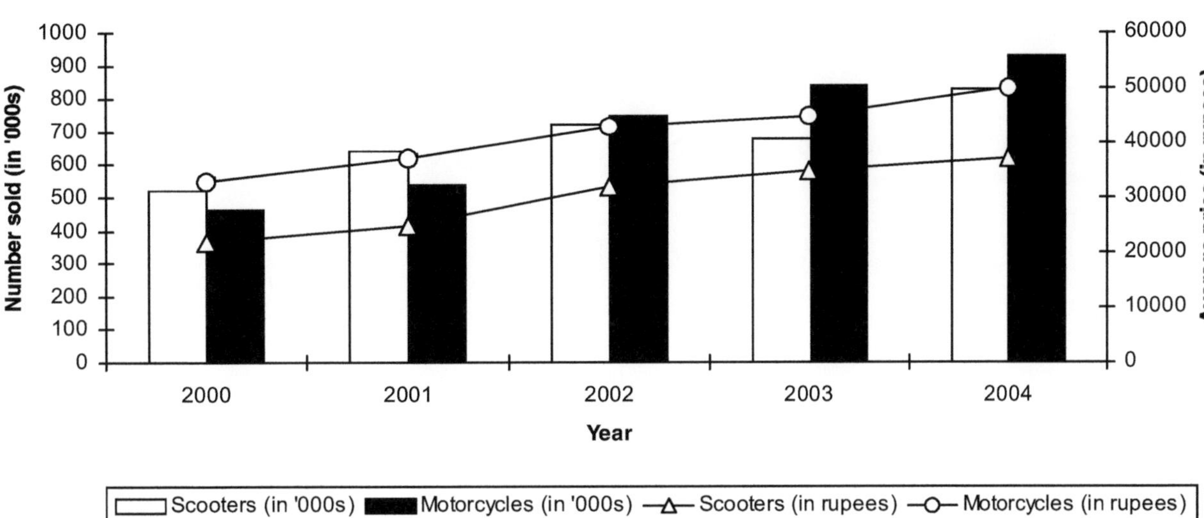

The chapter here has discussed only the standard types of data representation. Data can be represented in many more unusual ways. Irrespective of the type of graph, if one reads the instructions, head notes and foot notes carefully, one can very easily decipher the graphs.

Solved Examples

Directions for questions 1 to 6: Refer to the underlying tabulated data on production of seven crops in tonnes.

Year	Wheat	Sugar	Cotton	Rice	Maize	Bajra	Pulse
1994-95	6124	978	570	84	305	418	214
1995-96	7004	908	600	60	306	420	224
1996-97	7216	904	780	64	210	670	226
1997-98	7060	990	1114	42	204	314	250
1998-99	6950	730	1170	90	220	370	318
1999-00	6916	830	1454	114	164	304	405
2000-01	7620	816	1464	76	220	264	450

Example 1:
In 1997-98, which crop recorded the maximum increase in production over the previous year?

Solution:

Rice and Bajra production fell and sugar recorded increase but not as much as cotton.

Therefore, cotton recorded maximum increase in production.

Example 2:

What is the average yield of pulses during the period 1994-95 to 2000-01?

Solution:

$$\text{Average} = \frac{214 + 224 + 226 + 250 + 318 + 405 + 450}{7}$$

$$= 298.14.$$

Example 3:

During 1999-2000, the production of rice was how many times to that in 1997-98?

Solution:

$$\text{Ratio} = \frac{\text{Production of rice (1999-2000)}}{\text{Production of rice (1997-1998)}}$$

$$= \frac{114}{42} = 2.7$$

Example 4:

During 2000-01, in which group was there a minimum decrease in production in comparison to the previous year?

Solution:

Sugar dipped by $830 - 816 = 14$ units.

Therefore, sugar shows the minimum decrease in production in comparison to the previous year.

Example 5:

In which year, deficiency in wheat production started?

Solution:

The first fall from 7216 to 7060 in 1997-98.

Example 6:

How many crops showed an increasing trend throughout the given period i.e. 1994-95 to 2000-01?

Solution:

Two crops showed an increasing trend. The crops are cotton and pulse.

Directions for questions 7 to 11: Study the data given below carefully and answer the following questions.

Observations on the pattern of blood groups (in per cent)								
	A^+	B^+	O^+	AB^+	A^-	B^-	O^-	AB^-
Asia	24.7	23.2	19.5	1.2	9.7	10.3	10.8	0.6
Europe	19.5	23.5	20.7	2.8	5.6	12.1	14.3	1.5
America	18.9	20.6	25.3	5.0	8.5	12.9	7.9	0.9
Africa	24.2	26.1	22.9	2.3	6.7	8.8	7.8	1.2

Pattern of number of registered blood donors across the four continents

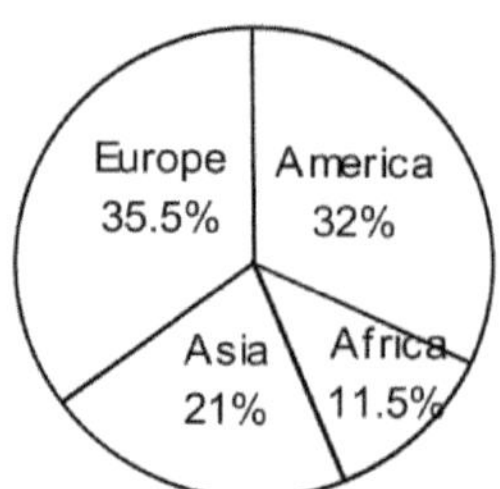

Example 7:

Which continent has the highest proportion of Rh⁻ blood donors?

Solution:

$A^- + B^- + O^- + AB^-$

Asia $= 9.7 + 10.3 + 10.8 + 0.6 = 31.4$

Similarly, Europe $= 33.5$

America $= 30.2$

Africa $= 24.5$

Therefore, Europe has the highest proportion of Rh⁻.

Example 8:

If a person donates blood anywhere in the world, what is the probability of his blood group being AB? (assume that each continent has equal population)

Solution:

$AB^- = AB^-$ (Asia) $+ AB^-$ (Europe) $+ AB^-$ (Africa) $+ AB^-$ (America)

AB^- (Total) $= 4.2\%$

Example 9:

What proportion of the population world over have A^- blood group?

Solution:

From the given data, 30.5 portion of the population have A^- blood group.

Example 10:

In Asia, which blood group has the highest factor of Rh^+ to Rh^- ratio?

Solution:

$$\text{Ratio for } A^+ \text{ to } A^- = \frac{24.7}{9.7} = 2.55$$

$$\text{Similarly, ratio for B} = \frac{23.2}{10.3} = 2.25$$

$$\text{Similarly, ratio for O} = \frac{19.5}{10.8} = 1.80$$

$$\text{And AB} = \frac{1.2}{0.6} = 2.$$

Example 11:

It was found that in Europe, there were 40,000 registered donors of AB^+ blood group, how many registered donors were there in Africa?

Solution:

The pie chart gives us the breakup of the number of registerd blood donors continent wise and not on the basis of blood group. Thus if the total number of blood donors in a continent is given we can calculate the number of registered blood donors in the other continents, but not the number of blood donors based on the blood groups. Hence, the answer is data insufficient.

Directions for questions 12 to 16: Study the following graph and answer the following questions.

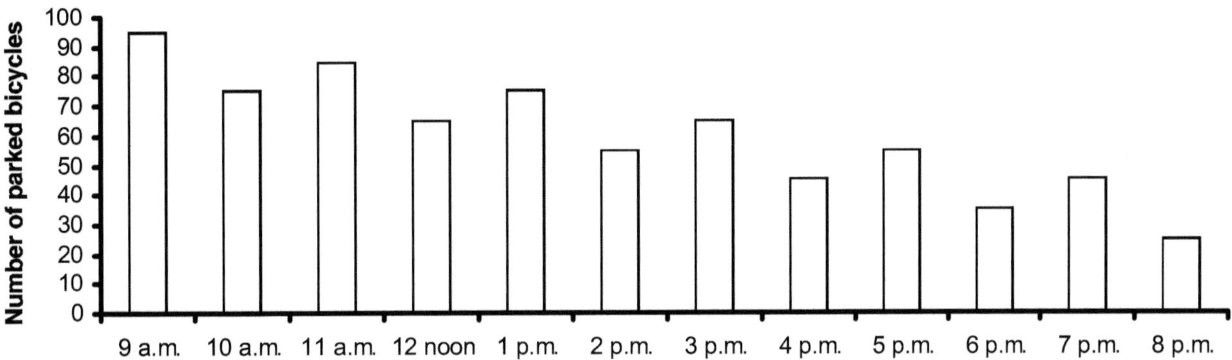

The above graph gives the number of bicycles parked in the parking space of Shatabdi Hall at various points of time. Charges for parking is Re. 1 per hour.

Example 12:

What will be the total collection from 9 a.m. to 8 p.m.?

Solution:

Total collection = {95 + 75 + 85 + 65 + 75 + 55 + 65 + 45 + 55 + 35 + 45} = 695. (Please note that the last column cannot be included.)

Example 13:

From 9 a.m. to 2 p.m., 80 bicycles left. How many more bicycles were parked between 2 p.m. and 3 p.m.?

Solution:

Just because we know the starting and ending number of bicycles, we cannot say the number which came and left during the hour.

Example 14:

What is the highest percentage decrease in the number of parked bicycles in a given hour?

Solution:

$$\text{Highest percentage decrease is } \frac{20}{45} = 44.4.$$

Example15:

At how many of the times mentioned in the graph is the number of parked bicycles above average?

Solution:

$$\text{Average is } \frac{720}{12} = 60.$$

So, for 6 times, number of parked bicycles is above average.

Example 16:

If the charge is increased to Rs. 2 for the time period 9 a.m. to 4 p.m., what will be the total collection?

Solution:

The number of bicycles between 9 a.m. and 4 p.m. is 515.
The number of bicycles between 4 p.m. and 9 p.m. is 205. So, total collection is 515 × 2 + 205
= 1030 + 205 = Rs. 1,235.

Directions for questions 17 to 20: Study the graph and answer the following questions.

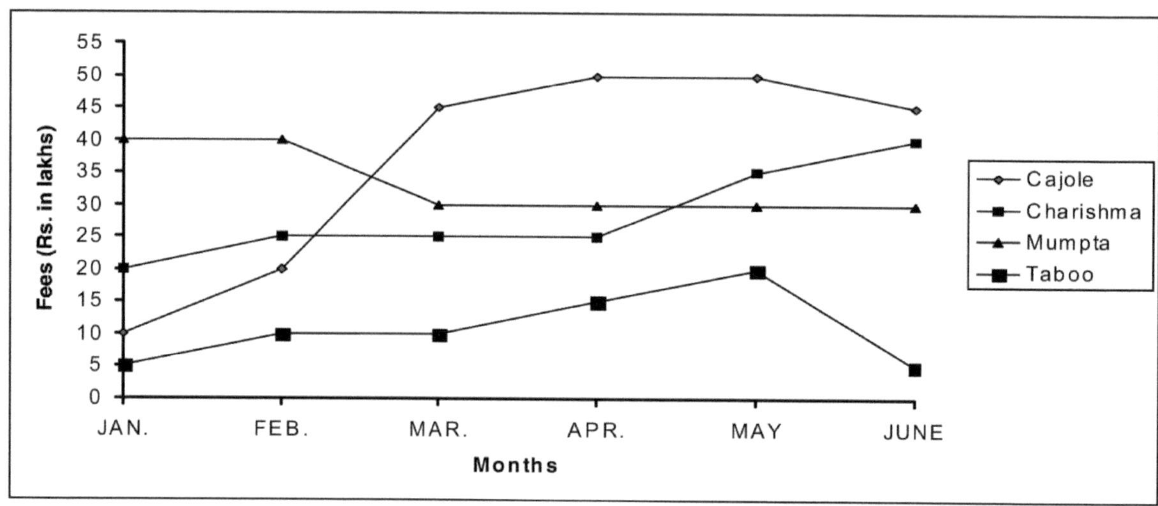

The graph shows the fees per film of major Jollywood stars from January to June.

Example 17:

In which month was the greatest percentage increase in market value for any star recorded?

Solution:

Cajole's price skyrocketed from Rs. 20 lakh to Rs. 45 lakh, i.e. by 125%.

Example 18:

Who showed the greatest percentage decrease in market value for any particular month?

Solution:

Taboo: Between May and June.

Example 19.

A producer replaced Mumpta and Taboo by Charishma and Cajole respectively due to date hassles in January. In which month would his losses, due to market value fluctuations, be the most?

Solution:

	T-M	C-C
Jan	45	30
Feb	50	45
March	40	70

	T-M	C-C
April	45	75
May	50	85
June	45	95

The maximum difference between C - C and T - M is in June: 95 − 45 = Rs. 50 lakh.
Therefore, the answer is June.

Example 20:

In which month was the greatest absolute change in market value for any star recorded?

Solution:

March: Cajole's price increased by Rs. 25 lakh.

Quantitative Ability

Data sufficiency (DS) form of questions are introduced in this section. The sufficiency check for the data given in the problem is tested in these questions. Therefore, these questions require maximum clarity of fundamentals. The techniques introduced in this chapter provide you the guideline to approach DS questions of two-statement type, most effectively.

The Data Sufficiency Format

A data sufficiency (DS) question consists of three parts. The actual question is called the question stem. e.g.

Is P > 1?

That's all you will be given. Sometimes the question is literally a question, like the preceding example. Sometimes the 'question' is actually a statement, telling you to do something. e.g.

Mr Prasad drives at 80 mph in 5 hr. Find the distance that Mr Prasad drives.

Or, like this: Find the rate at which oil flows into a container.

While the question form is far more common, do not be surprised if you get a statement form.

The second part of the DS question contains statement 1 and statement 2. It may be like this:

1. q > 1
2. p + q > 1

   or

1. Mr Prabhu drives thrice as far as his sister, but at half her speed.
2. Mr Prabhu starts 300 miles east of the point at which his sister started.

   or

   The third part of the question is statement 2. It may be like this:

1. The container has a capacity of 15,000 gallons.

2. The container is $\dfrac{3}{8}$ full by evening.

You need to decide whether the data (the information) is sufficient to answer the question and hence the title, Data Sufficiency. No answer choices are given at the end of the DS questions. Instead, instructions are given at the beginning of the section as illustrated below.

Elaboration of Various Choice Types

Data Sufficiency as a subject is completely based on the set of choices and instructions given, which should be read carefully before starting to answer the questions.

In various entrance tests across the country, the combinations of four of five out of the following choice bits is taken in the set of instructions.

1. Statement I alone is sufficient but statement II alone is not sufficient to answer the question.
2. Statement II alone is sufficient but statement I alone is not sufficient to answer the question.
3. Both statements I and II together are sufficient, but none of the two statements alone is sufficient to answer the question.
4. Both statements together are also not sufficient and additional data is required to answer the question.
5. Either/each of the statements alone is sufficient to answer the question.
6. Only one of the two statements alone is sufficient to answer the question.

Over the past so many ICET exams, the favourite set of the paper setter has been the combination of the first four choices. To answer the questions in examples and exercises, we will consider this set while arriving at the answer.

The following problems illustrate the meanings of the six answer categories.

1. **Choice (1)**

   In any problem, the answer choice is (1) if statement I alone is sufficient to answer the question but statement II alone is not sufficient to answer the question.

   Here is an example: Is Raja older than Ramu?

   I.   Sita is 4 years younger than Raja and 2 years younger than Ramu.

   II. The average age of Raja and Ramu is 21 years.

   Statement I by itself is sufficient to answer the question. If Sita is 4 years younger than Raja and 2 years younger than Ramu, then Raja must be two years older than Ramu. Statement II, however, is not by itself sufficient to answer the question. From the statement about the average of their ages, you can't draw any conclusion about their respective ages. Since statement I alone is sufficient, but statement II is not, the correct answer is choice (1).

2. **Choice (2)**

In any problem, the answer will be choice (2) if statement II alone is sufficient to answer the question, but statement I alone is not sufficient to answer the question.

Example: If x, y and z are consecutive positive integers, is y even?

I.   x < y < z

II. xz is an odd integer.

Statement I is not sufficient to answer the question. Although statement I describes the order of the integers, it provides no information about which integers of the sequence are even and which are odd. Statement II, however, by itself is sufficient to determine whether or not y is even. If xz is odd, then both x and z must be odd integers. In the series of three consecutive integers, at least one of the integers must be even. Therefore, y must be even. Since statement II alone is sufficient to answer the question, but statement I alone is not, the correct answer is choice (2).

3. **Choice (3)**

In any problem, the answer will be choice (3) if each statement alone is not sufficient to answer the question but the two statements when taken together are sufficient to answer the question.

Example: How many students are enrolled in Madam Vidya's English class?

I.   If three more students sign up for the class and none drop out, then more than 35 students will be enrolled in the class.

II. If four students drop out of the class and no more sign up, then fewer than 30 students will be enrolled in the class.
     Statement I alone is not sufficient to answer the question, but I does imply that at least 33 students are enrolled in the class. Statement II alone is not sufficient to answer the question asked, but II does imply that no more than 33 students are enrolled in the class. Although neither statement alone is sufficient to answer the question, the two statements when taken together are sufficient to answer the question that the number of students enrolled in the class is 33. Since neither statement alone is sufficient to answer the question but both together are sufficient, the correct answer choice is (3).

4. **Choice (4)**

In any problem, the answer choice is (4) if the two statements are not capable of answering the question asked, either alone or when taken together.

Example: Is u < v?

I.   – 0.25 < u < 0.4

II. 0.10 < v < 0.38

Statement I alone is not sufficient to answer the question asked. Although statement I defines a range for u, the statement provides no information about v. Similarly, statement II alone is not sufficient to answer the question asked. Statement II defines a range for v but provides no information about u. Since the two statements, even when taken together, do not provide enough information to answer the question asked, the correct answer choice is (4).

5. **Choice (5)**

In a problem, choice (5) becomes the answer if each statement alone is sufficient to answer the question, in it's own way, as shown in the illustration below.

Example: What is the area of the circular region O?

I.   The circular region has a circumference of 4π.

II. The circular region has a diameter of 4.

Statement I alone is sufficient to answer the question. Since the circumference of a circle is equal to 2π times its radius, a circle with a circumference of 4π has a radius of 2, and a circle with a radius of 2 has an area of 4π. Statement II is also, by itself, sufficient to answer the question. A circle with a diameter of 4 has a radius of 2 and an area of 4π. Since each statement by itself is sufficient to answer the question, hence choice (5) is the correct answer.

6. **Choice (6)**

If, it is given as "Only one of the two statements alone is sufficient to answer the question", it means that either of the choices is 'NOT' sufficient to answer the question. In short, this choice clubs choices (1) and (2), where only one statement alone is sufficient and the other is not sufficient to answer the question.

Exercise

Directions for questions 1 to 5: Answer the questions based on the following information.

The pie chart gives the marks scored by a student in different subjects. English, Hindi, Mathematics, Science and Social Science in an examination. Assuming that the total marks obtained in the examination are 540, answer the following questions 1 to 6.

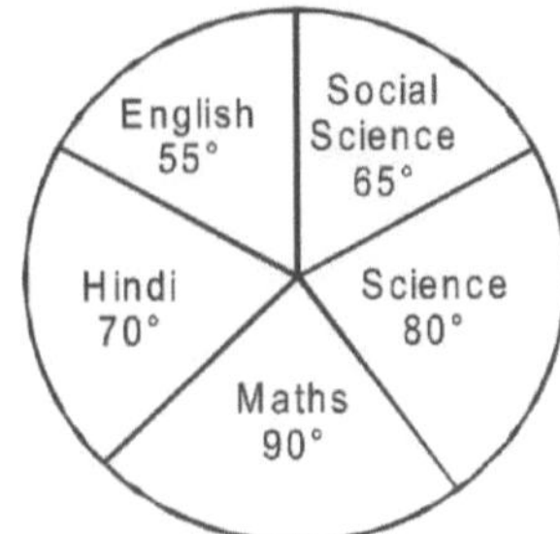

1. The marks scored in Hindi and Mathematics exceed the marks scored in English and Social Science by ___.
   (1) 60　　　　　　　(2) 75
   (3) 40　　　　　　　(4) 30

2. The subject in which the student scored 22.2% marks is ___.
   (1) Hindi　　　　　　(2) Science
   (3) Social Science　　(4) English

3. The subject in which the student scored 105 marks is ___.
   (1) Mathematics　　　(2) Science
   (3) Hindi　　　　　　(4) English

4. The marks obtained in the three subjects: English, Science and Social Science are what per cent of the total?
   (1) 45　　　　　　　(2) $44\dfrac{9}{4}$
   (3) 55　　　　　　　(4) $55\dfrac{5}{9}$

5. The marks scored in Mathematics is what per cent of the total marks?
   (1) 20　　　　　　　(2) 30
   (3) 35　　　　　　　(4) 25

Directions for questions 6 to 9: Refer to the pie chart given below which represents the portion of wage-earners engaged in various occupations in a city.

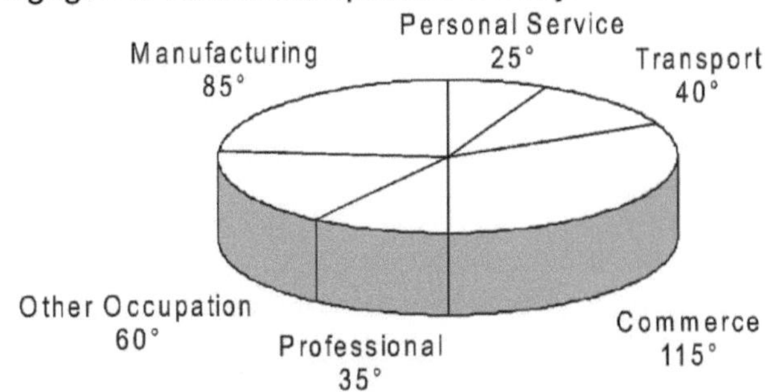

6. If the average earning of a wage-earner from personal service was twice that from transportation, the ratio of total earnings from these occupation is___.
   (1) 3 : 4　　(2) 4 : 5　　(3) 5 : 4　　(4) 4 : 3

7. If total earning from commerce is twice that from transportation, the ratio of average wages in these occuptions is___.
   (1) 16 : 23　(2) 23 : 16　(3) 5 : 4　　(4) 23 : 4

8. If the total number of wage-earners exceeds by 10% and the number of wage-earners engaged in commerce by 15% in the next year, the nearest central angle of commerce in pie chart for that year would be___.
   (1) 120°　　(2) 125°　　(3) 130°　　(4) 135°

9. What per cent of wage-earners in the city are engaged in manufacturing?
   (1) 8.6　　(2) 23.6　　(3) 18.6　　(4) 13.6

Directions for questions 10 to 14: Answer the questions based on the following information.

Gurvinder Singh, the bright new star on the internet horizon starts his dotcom project in the year 1997. In his first year of operations, he gets a revenue of Rs. 10,000, which is also the cost to him for the next year. The amount of profit remains the same in both the years. In 1999, the revenue increased by Rs. 3,000 over the previous year but the profit could increase by only 50% from the profit of last year. The revenue for the year 2000 could increase by only 20% over the previous year because of the Y2K problem, but so did his costs. The revenue for 1998 was Rs. 12,000.

10. What was the profit for the year 1997?
    (1) Rs.1,000   (2) Rs. 2,000
    (3) Rs. 3,000   (4) Rs. 4,000

11. What was the cost for the year 1999?
    (1) Rs. 10,000   (2) Rs. 12,200
    (3) Rs. 14,000   (4) Rs. 12,000

12. What was the cost for the year 2000?
    (1) Rs. 10,000   (2) Rs. 12,000
    (3) Rs. 14,000   (4) Rs. 14,400

13. Which year has the maximum increase in profit percentage?
    (1) 1998   (2) 2000   (3) 1999   (4) 1997

14. In which year was the percentage increase in cost the highest?
    (1) 1998   (2) 2000
    (3) 1999   (4) 1998 and 2000

Directions for questions 15 to 19: Answer the questions based on the following table.

The table gives the production of major agricultural products in Million Tonnes (MT).

Year	Wheat	Rice	Sugar cane	Pulses
1997	100	91	15	71
1998	120	88	18	75
1999	125	97	21	79
2000	131	107	25	88

15. The agro product which witnessed the highest growth rate in production from 1997 to 2000 is _____.
    (1) wheat   (2) rice
    (3) sugar cane   (4) pulses

16. Pulses production in 1998 is what per cent of the total production of rice in the given 4-year period?
    (1) 19.13   (2) 19.58   (3) 20.38   (4) 19.38

17. By what percent is the average wheat production more than the average sugar cane production for the given 4-year period?
    (1) 535   (2) 529   (3) 629   (4) 502

18. The simple annual growth rate of wheat from 1997-2000 is:
    (1) 8.23%   (2) 9.65%   (3) 10.33%   (4) 11.33%

19. What would be the actual production of wheat in 2001 if the growth in 2001 is the same as the average growth for the period?
    (1) 140 MT   (2) 144.5 MT
    (3) 141.3 MT   (4) 145 MT

Directions for questions 20 to 24: Answer the questions based on the data represented in the charts given below.

Soft drink market share (value basis) for 1998 and 1999

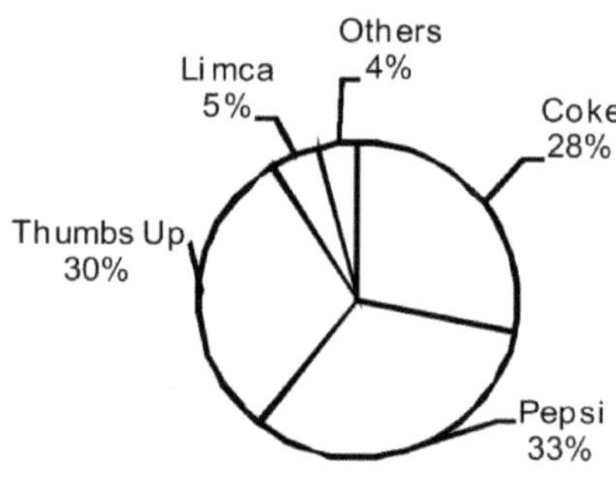

Market for soft drinks-1998

20. If in 1998, Coke sold soft drinks worth Rs. 196 crore, then what would be the revenue from soft drinks for Pepsi (Rs. in crore)?
    (1) 221   (2) 226   (3) 241   (4) 231

21. In 1998, if the total market for soft drinks were Rs. 550 crore. and in 1999, it grew to Rs. 650 crore, then what is the percentage increase in revenue for Coke?
    (1) 33   (2) 37   (3) 35   (4) 34

22. Using data from question 12, what would be the percentage increase in revenue for Pepsi in 1999?
    (1) 4.2   (2) 3.2   (3) 3.8   (4) 4.5

23. Using data from question 12, what would be the revenue from soft drinks for Thumbs Up (Rs. crore) in 1998?
    (1) 160   (2) 162   (3) 165   (4) 170

24. Given that the total market size was Rs.600 cr in 1998 and Rs. 650 cr in 1999, what is the difference between the value of sales of Pepsi in 1998 and that of Coke in 1999?
    (1) Rs. 9.5 cr   (2) Rs. 9 cr
    (3) Rs.10 cr   (4) Rs.10.5 cr

Directions for questions 25 to 29: Answer the questions based on the following information.

As an investor, I have been studying the financial performance of the four companies. I invest in AAA Ltd, BB Ltd, CC Ltd, and DDD Ltd. I notice a few interesting things. Sales of AAA Ltd are Rs.100,000, which is equal to the costs of CC Ltd. As for companies BB Ltd, and DDD Ltd, their asset-turnover ratio (ratio of sales to assets) is the same, i.e. 3; however, the sales of BB Ltd are half that of DDD Ltd. The profit of CC Ltd is 25%, which is equal to two-thirds of the profits of AAA Ltd. The profits of BB Ltd are equal to that of AAA Ltd which amount to 25% of BB Ltd's sales. The last thing I noticed was that the costs of DDD Ltd is twice the sales of CC Ltd.

25. What are CC Ltd's sales?
    (1) Rs. 2,50,000　　　　(2) Rs. 1,00,000
    (3) Rs. 1,25,000　　　　(4) Rs. 75,000

26. What are AAA Ltd's costs?
    (1) Rs. 60,500　　　　(2) Rs. 37,500
    (3) Rs. 25,000　　　　(4) Rs. 62,500

27. What are BB Ltd's sales?
    (1) Rs. 1,25,000　　　　(2) Rs. 1,50,000
    (3) Rs. 2,50,000　　　　(4) Rs. 1,75,000

28. What are DDD Ltd's assets?
    (1) Rs. 3,00,000　　　　(2) Rs. 1,00,000
    (3) Rs. 2,00,000　　　　(4) Rs. 4,00,000

29. Which company is the most profitable, using the criterion of profit percentage on sales?
    (1) AAA Ltd　　　　(2) BB Ltd
    (3) CC Ltd　　　　(4) DDD Ltd

Directions for questions 30 to 35: Answer the questions based on the following information.

The table below gives population data for a few states in India. It divides the country in two categories — urban and rural. The table gives the number of urban and rural villages, towns and cities and their total population. In the questions below, villages, towns and cities are all referred to as towns.

States	Urban		Rural	
	Number	Population	Number	Population
Maharashtra	15489	1224122	68003	355900
Tamil Nadu	13800	938970	133807	536381
Uttar Pradesh	9862	797101	247907	348908
Gujarat	10881	707150	94870	276955
Karnataka	5724	415072	88513	244039
Punjab	6136	401632	138337	206209
Madhya Pradesh	3489	414183	184245	158808
Kerala	3422	259238	86595	169309
Rajasthan	3089	259980	64437	122550
Haryana	3162	241884	79953	105656
Goa	207	17314	5381	19935

30. What is the average population per urban town for Punjab, Madhya Pradesh and Kerala together?
    (1) 97　　　　(2) 82　　　　(3) 113　　　　(4) 75

31. By how much does the average population per urban town exceed the average population per rural town for Rajasthan (approximately)?
    (1) 82　　　　(2) 74　　　　(3) 45　　　　(4) 104

32. Which of the following has the maximum population per urban town?
    (1) Maharashtra　　　　(2) Goa
    (3) Haryana　　　　(4) Gujarat

33. Which of the following has the minimum population per rural town?
    (1) Maharashtra　　　　(2) Goa
    (3) Haryana　　　　(4) Gujarat

34. Which of the given states has the maximum literacy rate?
    (1) Delhi
    (2) Rajasthan
    (3) Goa
    (4) Cannot be determined

35. For Uttar Pradesh, the population per urban town exceeds the same for Tamil Nadu by ______.
    (1) 29%　　　　(2) 19%　　　　(3) 26%　　　　(4) 11%

Exercise – 2

Directions for questions 1 to 20: Each question is followed by two statements, I and II. Answer each question using the following instructions.
Mark:
1. if the question can be answered using statement I alone, but cannot be answered using statement II alone.
2. if the question can be answered using statement II alone, but cannot be answered using statement I alone.
3. if the question can be answered using both the statements together, but cannot be answered using either statement alone.
4. if the question cannot be answered even using both the statements together.

1. Is 'g' greater than 'h'?
   I. g^2 is greater than h^2.
   II. The cube of 'g' is greater than the cube of 'h'.

2. If Jeevan can paint a house in 15 days working alone, how many days will it take if he does the same job together with Raju?
   I. Working together with Jeevan, Raju does $\frac{3}{7}$th of the total work, when the job is completed.
   II. Raju is 3 times older than Jeevan.

3. What is the sum of 2 numbers?
   I.   The L.C.M. of the numbers is 51.
   II. One of the numbers is 17.

4. Two teams S and U were playing a basketball match. What was the final score?
   I.   Team S scored 16 points more during the 2nd half of the game than it scored during the 1st half.
   II. At the end of the 1st half the score was tied and team U won the game by 3 points.

5. What are the distinct integers A and B?
   I.   The product of A and B is 4.
   II. A and B are both positive.

6. There are 85 people in the town who attend either meeting X or meeting Y or both. How many attend meeting X?
   I.   35 of them attend meeting X only.
   II. 47 of them attend meeting Y only.

7. The number of people who can vote in an election is 78% of the population. How many of them actually cast their vote?
   I.   The population of the town is 89000.
   II. 64% of the eligible men and 56% of the eligible women voted.

8. A, B and C take 25 days to complete a piece of work. How many days will A take to do it alone?
   I.   A and B together take 35 days for the same work.
   II. A and C together take 35 days for the same work.

9. What is the divisor?
   I.   Two different numbers when divided by this divisor, leave remainders 11 and 21.
   II. The divisor is greater than 2.

10. What is the remainder when the square of N is divided by 5?
    I.   N divided by 5 leaves a remainder 3.
    II. N is an even number.

11. L.C.M. of two numbers is 630. What is the absolute difference between them?
    I.   H.C.F. is 9.
    II. Sum of the 2 numbers is 153.

12. Are two triangles congruent?
    I.   Both triangles are right-angled.
    II. Both triangles have the same perimeter.

13. Is it Friday today?
    I.   21st February of this year was a Wednesday.
    II. Today is 18th March.

14. What is the distance between A and B?
    I.   The distance between A and C is 50 km more than that between A and B.
    II. To cover the distance between A and C in the same time that a person takes to cover the distance between A and B, his speed must be higher by 0.5 km/min.

15. The investments of P, Q and R were in the proportion 2 : 2 : 3 in the 2nd year. What was investment ratio of P to Q in the 1st year?
    I.   In the 2nd year the profit was Rs. 7,000.
    II. P and Q reinvest their profits every year.

16. Jack has certain number of coins in his pocket. If at least one of them has to be 10-paise, find the total number of 10-paise coins.
    I.   He has 65-paise in coins in his pocket.
    II. At least two of the coins in his pocket are 25-paise coins.

17. Eight litres of water is drawn from a vessel full of water and is replaced with 8 litres of pure milk. Again 8 litres of the mixture is drawn and by pure milk. What is the capacity of the vessel?
    I.   Vessel now contains water and milk in the ratio 9 : 16.
    II. The capacity of the vessel is an even number.

18. What is the area of right angled triangle ABC?
    I.   Length of AB is 5 cm.
    II. Length of BC is 12 cm.

19. Subhash ordered certain number of books from Bhadra Publishers. If he had to make a total payment of Rs. 73.80 which includes postage charges and sales tax, how much did each book cost him?
    I.   He paid Rs. 1.75 as postage per book.
    II. The sales tax for each book is 9%.

20. If after 7 years a man gets an interest of Rs. 576 on his investment, what is the rate at which the interest is charged ?
    I.   The amount after 7 years is Rs. 3,849.
    II. Had he invested Rs. 463 more, the bank would have offered him 8% rate of interest.

PART - 2
REASONING

Number Series

Generally, two kinds of series are asked in the examination. One is based on numbers and the other based on alphabet.

In questions based on series, some numbers or alphabets are arranged in a particular sequence. You have to decipher that particular sequence of numbers or alphabets and on the basis of that deciphered sequence, find out the next number or alphabet in the series which will logically follow in the same sequence. Although there is no limit for patterns which can be used to build a series, here are some important examples which highlight some of the types of series asked in the examination.

Types

I. Prime Number Series:

Example 1:

2, 3, 5, 7, 11, 13, ...
(1) 15   (2) 17   (3) 18   (4) 19

Solution. (2)

The given series is prime number series . The next prime number is 17.

Example 2:

2, 5, 11, 17, 23, ... 41.
(1) 29   (2) 31   (3) 37   (4) 39

Solution. (2)

The prime numbers are written alternately. The alternate prime number after 23 is 31.

II. Difference Series:

Example 3:

2, 5, 8, 11, 14, 17, ..., 23.
(1) 19   (2) 21   (3) 20   (4) 18

Solution. (3)

The difference between the consecutive numbers is 3.
(17 + 3 = 20)

III. Multiplication Series:

Example 5:

2, 6, 18, 54, 162, ..., 1458.
(1) 274   (2) 486   (3) 1236   (4) 1032

Solution. (2)

Each number is multiplied with 3 to get the next number. (162 × 3 = 486).

IV. Division Series:

Example 6:

720, 120, 24, ..., 2, 1.
(1) 12   (2) 18   (3) 20   (4) 6

Solution. (4)

Starting with 720, the numbers are divided by 6, 5, 4, 3, and so on. 720/6 = 120, 120/5 = 24, <u>24/4 = 6</u>, 6/3 = 2, 2/2 = 1.

V. n^2 Series:

Example 7:

1, 4, 9, 16, 25, ..., 49.
(1) 28   (2) 30   (3) 32   (4) 36

Solution. (4)

The series is $1^2, 2^2, 3^2, 4^2, 5^2, ...$ The next number in the sequence is $6^2 = 36$.

Example 8:

0, 4, 16, 36, 64, ... 144.
(1) 100   (2) 84   (3) 96   (4) 120

Solution. (1)

The series is $0^2, 2^2, 4^2, 6^2$, etc. The next number is $10^2 = 100$.

Example 4:

45, 38, 31, 24, 17 , ..., 3.
(1) 12   (2) 14   (3) 10   (4) 9

Solution. (3)

The difference between the consecutive numbers is 7.
(17 − 7 = 10).

VI. $n^2 - 1$ Series:

Example 9:
> 0, 3, 8, 15, 24, 35, 48, ...
> (1) 60   (2) 62   (3) 63   (4) 64

Solution. (3)
> The series is $1^2 - 1$, $2^2 - 1$, $3^2 - 1$, and so on. The next number in the sequence is $8^2 - 1 = 63$.
> Another logic : Difference between numbers is 3, 5, 7, 9, 11, 13, etc (odd numbers).
> The next number is (48 + 15 = 63).

VII. $n^2 + 1$ Series:

Example 10:
> 2, 5, 10, 17, 26, 37, ..., 65.
> (1) 50   (2) 48   (3) 49   (4) 51

Solution. (1)
> The series is $1^2 + 1$, $2^2 + 1$, $3^2 + 1$, and so on. The required number is $7^2 + 1 = 50$.

VIII. $n^2 + n$ Series (or) $n^2 - n$ Series:

Example 11:
> 2, 6, 12, 20, ..., 42.
> (1) 28   (2) 30   (3) 32   (4) 36

Solution. (2)
> The series is $1^2 + 1$, $2^2 + 2$, $3^2 + 3$, $4^2 + 4$, and so on. The required number is $5^2 + 5 = 30$.
> Another Logic : The series is 1×2, 2×3, 3×4, 4×5. The next number is $5 \times 6 = 30$.
> Another Logic : The series is $2^2 - 2$, $3^2 - 3$, $4^2 - 4$, $5^2 - 5$. The next number is $6^2 - 6 = 30$.

IX. n^3 Series:

Example 12:
> 1, 8, 27, 64, 125, 216, ...
> (1) 256   (2) 343   (3) 365   (4) 400

Solution. (2)
> The series is 1^3, 2^3, 3^3, and so on. The missing number is $7^3 = 343$.

X. $n^3 + 1$ Series:

Example 13:
> 2, 9, 28, 65, 126, 217, 344, ...
> (1) 513   (2) 500   (3) 428   (4) 600

Solution. (1)
> The series is $1^3 + 1$, $2^3 + 1$, $3^3 + 1$, and so on. The missing number is $8^3 + 1 = 513$.

XI. $n^3 - n$ Series:

Example 14:
> 0, 6, 24, 60, 120, 210, ...
> (1) 280   (2) 336   (3) 343   (4) 350

Solution. (2)
> The series is $1^3 - 1$, $2^3 - 2$, $3^3 - 3$, and so on. The missing number is $7^3 - 7 = 336$.
> Another Logic : The series is $0 \times 1 \times 2$, $1 \times 2 \times 3$, $2 \times 3 \times 4$, etc.
> The missing number is $6 \times 7 \times 8 = 336$.

XII. $n^3 + n^2$ Series:

Example 15:
> 2, 12, 36, 80, 150, ...
> (1) 250   (2) 252   (3) 276   (4) 300

Solution. (2)
> The series is $1^3 + 1^2$, $2^3 + 2^2$, $3^3 + 3^2$ and so on. The missing number is $6^3 + 6^2 = 252$.

XIII. xy, $x + y$ Series:

Example 16:
> 48, 12, 76, 13, 54, 9, 32, ...
> (1) 14   (2) 5   (3) 7   (4) 10

Solution. (2)
> $4 + 8 = 12$, $7 + 6 = 13$, $5 + 4 = 9$
> $\therefore 3 + 2 = 5$.

XIV. Image Series or (Interchange Series):

Example 17:
> 34, 81, 72, 47, 74, 27, 18, ...
> (1) 9   (2) 21   (3) 43   (4) 34

Solution. (3)
> (47, 74), (72, 27), (81, 18), are images.
> $\therefore$ Image of 34 is 43.

 # Exercise

Directions for questions 1 to 60: In this type of questions, usually a sequence of numbers is given. The candidate should carefully read the sequence and find out the particular order followed by the numbers. Based on the deciphered pattern, mark the right option which should fit in the sequence.

1. 4, 16, 36, ___, 100, 144
   (1) 72   (2) 68   (3) 81   (4) 64

2. 4, 25, 64, 121, 196, ___
   (1) 384   (2) 256   (3) 225   (4) 289

3. 0, 1, 8, 27, 64, ___
   (1) 91   (2) 125   (3) 128   (4) 256

4. 8, 27, 125, 343, ___
   (1) 729   (2) 512   (3) 1331   (4) 1000

5. 1, 1, 2, 4, 3, 9, 4, 16, 5, 25, 6, ___
   (1) 35   (2) 42   (3) 49   (4) 36

6. 2, 3, 5, 7, 11, ___, 17
   (1) 14   (2) 13   (3) 10   (4) 12

7. 3, 5, 7, 9, 11, 13, 15, 17, ___
   (1) 14   (2) 19   (3) 15   (4) 21

8. 2, 5, 10, 17, ___
   (1) 34   (2) 24   (3) 20   (4) 26

9. 5, 6, 9, 14, 21, ___
   (1) 31   (2) 29   (3) 28   (4) 30

10. 2, 6, 12, 20, 30, ___
   (1) 44   (2) 40   (3) 36   (4) 42

11. 5, 15, 35, 75, 155, ___
   (1) 275   (2) 300   (3) 310   (4) 315

12. 4, 7, 12, 19, ___
   (1) 25   (2) 26   (3) 27   (4) 28

13. 17, 21, 29, 45, ___
   (1) 49   (2) 53   (3) 61   (4) 77

14. 9, 11, 15, 23, ___
   (1) 25   (2) 21   (3) 39   (4) 31

15. 5, 9, 15, ___, 33, 45, 59
   (1) 24   (2) 22   (3) 20   (4) 23

16. 81, 72, 63, ___, 45
   (1) 56   (2) 54   (3) 52   (4) 49

17. 8, 8, 10, ___, 20, 28
   (1) 14   (2) 15   (3) 16   (4) 12

18. 1, 2, 6, 15, 31, 56, 92, ___
   (1) 150   (2) 128   (3) 141   (4) 149

19. 8, 9, 11, 15, 16, 18, ___
   (1) 21   (2) 22   (3) 23   (4) 24

20. 6, 9, 27, 30, 90, 93, ___
   (1) 181   (2) 160   (3) 279   (4) 198

21. 35, 30, 25, 20, 15, 10, ___
   (1) 15   (2) 10   (3) 5   (4) 2

22. 7, 13, 21, ___, 43, 57
   (1) 23   (2) 27   (3) 31   (4) 35

23. 27, 24, 20, 15, 9, ___
   (1) 2   (2) 4   (3) 6   (4) 8

24. 5, 9, 15, 23, 33, 45, 59, ___
   (1) 54   (2) 95   (3) 78   (4) 75

25. 5, 6, 9, 18, 45, ___
   (1) 67.5   (2) 81   (3) 54   (4) 126

26. 3, 15, 35, ___, 99, 143
   (1) 63   (2) 77   (3) 69   (4) 81

27. 4, 10, 22, 46, ___
   (1) 56   (2) 66   (3) 76   (4) 94

28. 84, 64, 46, 30, ___
   (1) 14   (2) 16   (3) 18   (4) 20

29. 15, 20, 27, 36, 47, ___
(1) 64 (2) 70 (3) 66 (4) 60

30. 6, 14, 26, 42, 62, 86, ___
(1) 114 (2) 115 (3) 116 (4) 118

31. 11, 13, 17, 19, ___, 25, 29
(1) 21 (2) 24 (3) 20 (4) 23

32. 5, 14, 27, 44, 65, ___
(1) 88 (2) 90 (3) 109 (4) 130

33. 0, 5, 22, 57, 116, ___
(1) 205 (2) 216 (3) 192 (4) 207

34. 7, 24, 75, 228, ___
(1) 684 (2) 686
(3) 688 (4) None of these

35. 4, 5, 6, 9, 8, 13, 10, ___
(1) 11 (2) 12 (3) 15 (4) 17

36. 1, 8, 9, 64, 25, 216, ___, ___
(1) 49, 64 (2) 343, 64 (3) 343, 81 (4) 49, 512

37. 4, 11, 7, 14, 10, 17, ___
(1) 24 (2) 13 (3) 20 (4) 21

38. 5, 7, 8, 11, 13, 17, ___
(1) 24 (2) 20 (3) 18 (4) 26

39. 5, 6, 8, 9, 11, ___
(1) 15 (2) 12 (3) 17 (4) 20

40. 6, 9, 7, 10, 8, 11, ___
(1) 12 (2) 13 (3) 16 (4) 9

41. 8, 15, 9, 14, 10, 13, ___
(1) 12 (2) 9 (3) 11 (4) 15

42. 4, 4, 12, 16, 36, 36, 108, ___
(1) 64 (2) 66 (3) 82 (4) 86

43. 5, 18, 7, 21, 9, 24, 11, 27, 13, 30, 15, ___
(1) 33 (2) 40 (3) 43 (4) 35

44. 4, 7, 10, 11, 22, 17, 46, 25, ___
(1) 58 (2) 69 (3) 86 (4) 94

45. 19, 11, 30, 22, 41, 33, ___
(1) 44 (2) 52 (3) 56 (4) 60

46. 7, 11, 16, 23, 25, 35, ___
(1) 34 (2) 36 (3) 38 (4) 42

47. 2, 2, 4, 4, 6, 8, 8, ___
(1) 10 (2) 12 (3) 14 (4) 16

48. 2, 3, 4, 7, 13, 12, 12, 23, 20, 17, 33, 28, ___
(1) 22 (2) 29 (3) 30 (4) 32

49. 12, 11, 10, 13, 18, 17, 14, 25, 24, 15, 32, 31, ___
(1) 15 (2) 34 (3) 16 (4) 38

50. 5, 7, 9, 11, 14, 16, 20, 22, 27, 29, ___
(1) 38 (2) 31 (3) 34 (4) 35

51. 3, 12, 8, 5, 14, 12, 8, 16, 17, 12, 18, 23, ___
(1) 32 (2) 17 (3) 46 (4) 28

52. 1, 2, 5, 10, 13, ___
(1) 16 (2) 26 (3) 39 (4) 29

53. 5, 10, 15, 25, 40, 65, ___
(1) 95 (2) 100 (3) 110 (4) 105

54. 5, 10, 15, 25, 40, 65, 105, 170, ___
(1) 290 (2) 275 (3) 205 (4) 180

55. 3, 9, 36, 180, ___
(1) 1080 (2) 900 (3) 720 (4) 850

56. 17, 17, 68, 612, ___
(1) 9792 (2) 9700 (3) 9820 (4) 8945

57. 4, 8, 24, 12, 24, 72, 36, 72, ___
(1) 248 (2) 216 (3) 288 (4) 108

58. 64, 32, 92, 46, 102, 51, 122, 61, 148, ___
(1) 74 (2) 78 (3) 82 (4) 88

59. 6, 9, 27, 30, 90, 93, ___
(1) 181 (2) 160 (3) 279 (4) 198

60. 20, 17, 34, 31, 62, 59, ___
(1) 95 (2) 118 (3) 110 (4) 128

The alphabet series is based almost on the similar patterns as those in the number series, except that instead of numbers, we now have alphabets forming a series.

Important Points

1. Letters in the alphabet are represented by the following numbers as their place values.

A → 1	B → 2	C → 3
D → 4	E → 5	F → 6
G → 7	H → 8	I → 9
J → 10	K → 11	L → 12
M → 13	N → 14	O → 15
P → 16	Q → 17	R → 18
S → 19	T → 20	U → 21
V → 22	W → 23	X → 24
Y → 25	Z → 26	

2. The numbering continues in the following manner:

A $\xrightarrow{\text{to}}$ Z $\xrightarrow{\text{to}}$ A,

i.e. if we want to know the alphabet representing 28, then it will be B: as Z = 26, A = 27 and B = 28. This means that while assigning place values to the letters, we must consider the cyclic nature of the alphabet.

There are two ways of splitting the letter series:

I. Corresponding letters from the two ends:

A B C D E F G H I J K L M

Z Y X W V U T S R Q P O N

The Alphabet are split into two equal halves:

From left to Right:

Half 1 → From A(1) to M(13); Half 2 → From Z(26) to N(14).

The two halves are placed in front of each other in such a way so as to indicate for any letter, the same positioned letter corresponding from the opposite end.

For Example: The first letter from the <u>left</u> of the alphabet is A, and the first letter from the <u>right</u> of the alphabet is Z.

Hence, A and Z correspond to each other from the two ends of the alphabet.

Similarly, B corresponds to Y, C corresponds to X, and so on.

Note: It is suggested to remember the place values of every letter in the alphabet. This way, it will be faster to find out the corresponding letter from the other end.

This is because of the fact that **the sum of the place values of the corresponding letters from the two ends is always 27.**

For example: In the alphabet, the place value of A is 1 and that of Z is 26. The sum 1 + 26 is 27. Similarly I(9) and R(18) correspond to each other from the two ends of the alphabet.

II. Corresponding letters in the two halves:

A B C D E F G H I J K L M

N O P Q R S T U V W X Y Z

Here again, the alphabet are split into two equal halves, from left to right:

Half 1 → From A(1) to M(13); Half 2 → From N(14) to Z(26)

Here, A is the first letter in the first half and N is the first letter in the second half. Hence, A and N are the corresponding letters in the two halves of the alphabet.

Note: It is suggested that the student should remember the place values of every letter in the alphabet, for faster results.

This is because of the fact that the **difference between the place values of the corresponding letters in the two halves is always 13.**

For example: Letter A(1) and N(14) correspond to each other in the two halves. The difference between their place values, 1 and 14, is 13. Similarly, letters R(18) and E(5) correspond to each other in the two halves. The difference between their place values, 18 and 5, is 13.

▮ Vowels and Consonants

The English alphabet has 5 vowels and 21 consonants. The 5 vowels are A, E, I, O and U. The rest of the letters are termed as consonants.

Types of Letter Series

Type 1: Single Letter Series :

Given below are some of the types and examples to illustrate this type of series.

Example 1:
A, C, E, G, I, ...
(1) J (2) K (3) L (4) M

Solution. (2)

The series is (+2) i.e, A + 2 = C; C + 2 = E; E + 2 = G; G + 2 = 1.
The missing letter is I + 2 = K.
Another Logic : Skip one letter to get the next letter.
After I skip J to get K. The missing letter is K.

Example 2:
A, B, D, G, K, ...
(1) P (2) N (3) O (4) L

Solution. (1)

The series is +1, +2, +3, etc.
The missing letter is (K + 5) = P.
Skip Process : First no letter is skipped, then 1, 2, 3, etc. number of letters are skipped to get the next letter. Skip 5 letters after 'K' to get 'P'.

Type 2: Double Letter Series:

In a series which consists of pairs of letters, the first letters of the pairs follow one pattern and the second letters follow another pattern. Also, the letter in a pair are connected together based on a logic, thus forming a pattern for the letters in the other pairs.

Example 3:
AM, BN, CO, DP, EQ, ...
(1) FG (2) FR (3) GR (4) ER

Solution. (2)

The first letters in each pair are A,B,C,D,E,F and the second are M,N,O,P,Q and R.

Example 4:
AB, DE, GH, JK, MN, ...
(1) OP (2) NO (3) PQ (4) RS

Solution. (3)

After every set of letters one letter is skipped. Skip O to get next two letters PQ.

Type 3: Three Letter Series:

This sequence consists of 3 letters in each group of letters. The first letters of each group are in a series, based on some logic or pattern, the second letters follow a different pattern and the third letters follow yet another pattern, (or it could be that all the three terms may form a series based on the same logic).

Example 5:
CKZ, DLY, EMX, FNW,..........
(1) GOV (2) GOU (3) GNU (4) GNV

Solution. (1)

The first letters form a continuous alphabet series of C, D, E, F, G, and so on.
The second letters form a series of K, L, M, N, O, and so on, and the third letters form a series of Z, Y, X, W, V, and so on.

Type 4: Multiple blank series:

Sometimes, the following type of series were asked in the examination:

Example 6:
a _ b c c _ d _ d _ e _ _ e _
(1) accddeef (2) bcddeee
(3) acdefff (4) bcdeeff

Solution.

Here, we should use the choices to fill in the blanks and then observe the appropriateness of the series.
a b b c c c d d d d e e e e e
Here 'a' occurs once, 'b' occurs twice, 'c' thrice, 'd' 4 times and 'e' 5 times – as per the count of their place values in the alphabet.
Hence, choice (2) makes the question series appropriate.

Example 7:
a _ _ a b _ _ b c a _ c
(1) b b a a c (2) a b a c b
(3) b c c a b (4) a c c a b

Solution.

When we fill the letters of choice (3), we observe the following:
a b c | a b c | a b c | a b c
Here, the group 'abc' is repeating itself. Hence, choice (3) fills in the blanks appropriately.

In addition to the above types, many more different types and varieties can be observed. The exercise provides the student with a thought pattern and insight into the topic.

Reasoning

Exercise

Directions for questions 1 to 50: In each question given below, there is a series of letters following some pattern. Which among the following choices would follow the same pattern?

1. A, C, E, G, I , ____
   (1) H   (2) J   (3) K   (4) L

2. Y, W, U, S, Q, ____
   (1) A   (2) P   (3) O   (4) B

3. Z, X, U, Q, L, ____
   (1) F   (2) K   (3) G   (4) E

4. A, H, N, S, W, ____
   (1) A   (2) Y   (3) B   (4) Z

5. C, F, K, R, ____
   (1) G   (2) A   (3) B   (4) D

6. X, A, D, G, J, ____
   (1) N   (2) O   (3) M   (4) P

7. T, V, Z, B, F, ____
   (1) G   (2) H   (3) K   (4) J

8. Z, X, U, S, P, ____
   (1) L   (2) M   (3) N   (4) K

9. Q, T, V, Y, A, ____
   (1) B   (2) C   (3) D   (4) F

10. H, L, P, T, X, ____
    (1) A   (2) B   (3) C   (4) D

11. AZ, BY, DW, GT, ____
    (1) JQ   (2) KQ   (3) KP   (4) JP

12. AG, LR, WC, HN, ____
    (1) SX   (2) RY   (3) SY   (4) TX

13. LO, IL, FI, CF, ____
    (1) ZB   (2) AB   (3) ZC   (4) ZO

14. AH, DL, GP, JT, ____
    (1) MY   (2) NX   (3) MX   (4) NY

15. AF, EJ, IN, OT, ____
    (1) UX   (2) UY   (3) UN   (4) UZ

16. TYU, NSO, HMI, ____
    (1) AGC   (2) CGC   (3) GBC   (4) BGC

17. ZSD, YTC, XUB, WVA, ____
    (1) VZZ   (2) ZVX   (3) VWZ   (4) VZX

18. CIR, GMV, KQZ, OUD, ____
    (1) YSH   (2) SHR   (3) SYH   (4) SRY

19. KTE, SBM, AJU, IRC, ____
    (1) KZQ   (2) ZRL   (3) QZK   (4) LYJ

20. ZYX, BAZ, DCB, FED, ____
    (1) GHF   (2) FGH   (3) FFG   (4) HGF

21. RML, VIJ, ZFH, DDF, ____
    (1) HDC   (2) CHI   (3) HCD   (4) DIC

22. HEJ, JGL, LIN, NKP, ____
    (1) MOR   (2) PNS   (3) PMR   (4) NPT

23. YAL, TCP, OET, JGX, ____
    (1) EIC   (2) FIA   (3) EJD   (4) EIB

24. LRX, DJP, VBH, NTZ, ____
    (1) ELS   (2) FMR   (3) GKS   (4) FLR

25. ATL, BUM, CVN, DWO, ____
    (1) EZP   (2) EYQ   (3) EFP   (4) EXP

26. AZ, BY, CX, DW, ____
    (1) EU   (2) EV   (3) FV   (4) EW

27. IR, KP, NM, RI, ____
    (1) VE   (2) WC   (3) WD   (4) VF

28. AN, BO, CP, DQ, _____
   (1) ES   (2) FR   (3) ET   (4) ER

29. TG, VI, YL, CP, _____
   (1) HU   (2) GU   (3) GT   (4) HT

30. ZAN, XCP, VER, TGT, _____
   (1) RHV   (2) SHU   (3) RIV   (4) RIU

31. NAZ, REV, VIR, BOL, _____
   (1) GTG   (2) HUE   (3) HTG   (4) HUF

32. MNA, OPC, QRE, STG, _____
   (1) UVH   (2) UVI   (3) TUV   (4) VUH

33. FUX, VEI, LOT, ZAG, _____
   (1) RIP   (2) NMU
   (3) RIQ   (4) None of these

34. AEIO, UEOA, IAOE, UOIE, _____
   (1) A E I O   (2) A I A E
   (3) AAAA   (4) None of these

35. ACG, MOS, YAE, KMQ, _____
   (1) W V C   (2) X Z D   (3) V Y C   (4) WYC

36. AZ, BO, DW, HU, _____
   (1) N O   (2) M N
   (3) PC   (4) None of these

37. PKF, JQM, RIF, _____
   (1) K P K   (2) L K P
   (3) LOM   (4) None of these

38. a _ c _ b _ a _ c c b _
   (1) b a c b a   (2) a b c c b
   (3) b c a b a   (4) b b a c a

39. a _ c b _ b _ d c b c _ e d _
   (1) b c c d e   (2) b a c d c
   (3) b a c d e   (4) b c e d c

40. _ b b _ a _ a _ a _ b a a _ a b
   (1) a a b b b b   (2) a b a a b b
   (3) b a a a b b   (4) b a b a b a

41. j, z, i, y, h _____
   (1) a   (2) x   (3) u   (4) z

42. a, e, i, m, q _____
   (1) v   (2) w   (3) n   (4) u

43. a, b, d, g, k, p _____
   (1) t   (2) j   (3) x   (4) v

44. z, y, x, a, b, c, w, v, u, d, e, f, t, s, r, g, h _____
   (1) i   (2) m   (3) r   (4) p

45. a, z, e, y, i, x, o, w _____
   (1) g   (2) v   (3) p   (4) u

46. a, 1, c, 9, f, 36, b, 4, h _____
   (1) 81   (2) 64   (3) k   (4) 7

47. a, w, e, q, i, l, o, h, _, __
   (1) v, e   (2) v, f
   (3) u, f   (4) None of these

48. a, f, k, p, u _____
   (1) z   (2) a   (3) x   (4) w

49. b, c, d, f, g, h, j, k, l, n, o, __
   (1) r   (2) s   (3) o   (4) p

50. t, u, w, z, d, i, _____
   (1) l   (2) m   (3) n   (4) o

Analogies   **3**

▌ Introduction

These types of questions are similar to word analogy. The numbers in the questions follow some logic based on some arithmetic rules. Find the rule or logic in one part of the question and apply the same logic to the second part of the problem.

An analogy is represented as below:

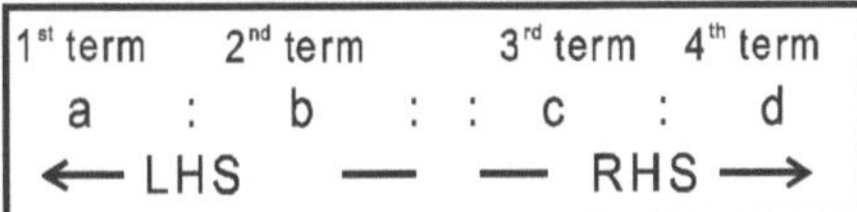

As is the relationship between the first two terms on the LHS, the same relationship is followed between the two terms on the RHS. Also, the 1ˢᵗ term and the 3ʳᵈ term follow the same pattern. Similarly, the 2ⁿᵈ term and the 4ᵗʰ term follow the same pattern.

There are three types of questions in analogies
  (i) Number Analogy
  (ii) Letter Analogy
  (iii) Verbal Analogy

(i) NUMBER ANALOGY:

Examples 1:
  30 : 130 : : 56 : _______
  (1) 156
  (2) 234
  (3) 350
  (4) Verbal Analogy

Solution: (4)
  Due to choice (4), which says "All follow", we will have to check each of the choice seperately.
  Choice (1). We know that 30 **+ 100** = 130.
  Similarly, 56 **+ 100** = 156.
  Choice (2). We know that 30 **× 4 + 10** = 130.
  Similarly, 56 **× 4 + 10** = 234
  Choice (3).

$$30 \quad : \quad 130 \quad : \quad 56 \quad : \quad 350$$
$$\downarrow \qquad \downarrow \qquad \downarrow \qquad \uparrow$$
$$5^2+5 \quad\; 5^3+5 \quad\; 7^2+7 \quad\; \mathbf{7^3+7}$$
$$(n^2+n) \quad (n^3+n) \quad (n^2+n) \quad \mathbf{(n^3+n)}$$

  Hence, choice (4) follows as the answer.

(ii) LETTER ANALOGY:

Example 2:
  A : C : : E : _______
  (1) G
  (2) O
  (3) K
  (4) All follow

Solution. (4)
  The place value of A is 1 and of C is 3.
  Now (A) 1 + 2 = 3 (C). Hence, (E) 5 + 2 = 7(G)
  Now (A) 1 × 3 = 3 (C). Hence, (E) 5 × 3 = 15(O)
  Now (A) 1 + next no. 2 = 3 (C). Hence, (E)
  5 + next no. 6 = 11 (K).
  Hence, (1) , (2) and (3) follow.

Example 3:
  NAZ : QDW : : TGT : _______
  (a) WJW
  (b) WJQ
  (c) XKQ
  (d) None of these

Solution. (2)
  N and Z are the corresponding letters for A in the other half and from the other end, respectively. (A)1 + 3 = 4(D), for which Q and W are the corresponding letters in the other half and from the other end of the alphabet, respectively. Similarly, T is the corresponding letter for G in the other half and from the other end of the alphabet. Now, (G)7 + 3 = 10(J), and for J, W and Q are the corresponding letters in the other half and from the other end of the alphabet, respectively. Hence, WJQ is the correct answer.

(iii) VERBAL ANALOGY:

Example 4:
  Chair : Sit : : Bicycle : _______
  (1) Wheels
  (2) Ride
  (3) Vehicle
  (4) None of these

Solution. (2)
  The purpose of a "Chair" is to "Sit" on it. Similarly, the purpose of a "Bicycle" is to "Ride" it.

Exercise

Directions for questions 1 to 50: In each of the following questions, there is a space mark and only one of the four alternatives given under the questions bears the same reltionship as is found between the two groups of the sign :: given in the question. Find the correct alternative in each quetion.

1. 18 : 27 : : 22 : ____
   (1) 42   (2) 39   (3) 33   (4) 54

2. 14 : 20 : : 16 : ____
   (1) 23   (2) 10   (3) 48   (4) 32

3. 8 : 27 : : 64 : ____
   (1) 277   (2) 125   (3) 250   (4) 99

4. 1/7 : 1/14 : : 1/9 : ____
   (1) 1/88   (2) 1/80   (3) 1/81   (4) 1/18

5. 0.16 : 0.0016 : : 1.02 : ____
   (1) 10.20   (2) 0.102   (3) 0.0102   (4) 1.020

6. 5 : 24 : : 8 : ____
   (1) 65   (2) 63   (3) 62   (4) 64

7. 12 : 54 : : 8 : ____
   (1) 28   (2) 36   (3) 58   (4) 48

8. 7 : 28 : : 2 : ____
   (1) 8   (2) 16   (3) 24   (4) 12

9. 65 : 30 : : 44 : ____
   (1) 79   (2) 62   (3) 28   (4) 16

10. 99 : 76 : : 24 : ____
    (1) 1   (2) 13   (3) 9   (4) 7

11. 11 : 35 : : 17 : ____
    (1) 3   (2) 22   (3) 53   (4) 10

12. 663 : 884 : : 221 : ____
    (1) 332   (2) 554   (3) 773   (4) 442

13. 43 : 34 : : 52 : ____
    (1) 49   (2) 25   (3) 36   (4) 64

14. 30 : 42 : : 56 : ____
    (1) 92   (2) 21   (3) 38   (4) 72

15. 190 : 10 : : 102 : ____
    (1) 4   (2) 7   (3) 3   (4) 5

16. 4 : 36 : : 6 : ____
    (1) 63   (2) 54   (3) 35   (4) 30

17. 6 : 12 : : 20 : ____
    (1) 50   (2) 30   (3) 42   (4) 38

18. 6 : 18 : : 4 : ____
    (1) 2   (2) 6   (3) 8   (4) 16

19. 10 : 20 : : 30 : ____
    (1) 45   (2) 60   (3) 50   (4) 70

20. 63 : 9 : : 49 : ____
    (1) 12   (2) 3   (3) 36   (4) 7

21. 2 : 11 : : 3 : ____
    (1) 27   (2) 30   (3) 33   (4) 36

22. 357 : 73 : : ____
    (1) 429:94   (2) 201:21   (3) 138:38   (4) 93:39

23. 36 : 18 : : 72 : ____
    (1) 164   (2) 134   (3) 94   (4) 14

24. 162 : 9 : : 310 : ____
    (1) 33   (2) 27   (3) 16   (4) 4

25. 13 : 17 : : 15 : ____
    (1) 19   (2) 11   (3) 21   (4) 16

26. 225 : 15 : : 256 : ____
    (1) 26   (2) 16   (3) 20   (4) 28

27. 33 : 36 : : 21 : _____
   (1) 9   (2) 18   (3) 24   (4) 32

28. 19 : 39 : 42 : _____
   (1) 60   (2) 83   (3) 85   (4) 91

29. 5 : 45 : : 2 : _____
   (1) 40   (2) 36   (3) 20   (4) 18

30. 123 : 149 : : 201 : _____
   (1) 202   (2) 404   (3) 401   (4) 226

31. 11 : 101 : : 73 : _____
   (1) 153   (2) 330   (3) 543   (4) 703

32. 4 : 32 : : 8 : _____
   (1) 34   (2) 68   (3) 92   (4) 128

33. 94 : 26 : : 62 : _____
   (1) 16   (2) 22   (3) 39   (4) 48

34. 12 : 18 : : 32 : _____
   (1) 92   (2) 64   (3) 124   (4) 98

35. 6 : 21 : 14 : _____
   (1) 82   (2) 75   (3) 60   (4) 41

36. A : E : : I : _____
   (1) O   (2) N
   (3) S   (4) All the above.

37. G : T : : L : _____
   (1) Y   (2) O
   (3) I   (4) All the above.

38. B : D : : C : _____
   (1) F   (2) I
   (3) E   (4) All the above.

39. I : R : : P : _____
   (1) K   (2) O
   (3) F   (4) Both (1) and (3)

40. IQ : RJ : : LW : _____
   (1) OD   (2) XJ
   (3) YD   (4) None of these

41. HK : SV : : _____ : QT
   (1) JG   (2) JM
   (3) OP   (4) None of these

42. FJ : IM : : PT : _____
   (1) SV   (2) US   (3) SW   (4) QS

43. FLY : GNB : : RIG : _____
   (1) SKW   (2) IRT   (3) SJH   (4) SJW

44. PAIR : NXEM : : GROW : _____
   (1) ETKY   (2) IUSB
   (3) ETQY   (4) EOKR

45. BEAR : DBFK : : KILL : _____
   (1) MFPG   (2) MFQE
   (3) NKNO   (4) MEQG

46. AJMER : ELJIV : : DELHI : _____
   (1) HGILO   (2) FGOKL
   (3) FIILO   (4) None of these

47. SUITE : WAOXI : : EQUAL : _____
   (1) IWAEP   (2) IUAEO
   (3) IVBDO   (4) IUAEP

48. PCX : SFU : : _____ : DQJ
   (1) MNA   (2) ANK   (3) ANM   (4) MAN

49. CAB : FCH : : DIP : _____
   (1) GKU   (2) HRF   (3) GLV   (4) HAL

50. PIN : OQHJMO : : DUB : _____
   (1) CETUAD   (2) CETVAC
   (3) BFUVDE   (4) None of these

In competitive examinations, the examiner also likes to check whether the candidate has the skills to classify or segregate information. For this, he uses the "Odd Man Out" kind of problems, in which there are four choices given. The candidate must link three choices which have some common characteristic or property amongst them so as to form a group of alike things. The remaining choice, which does not share that common characteristic with the others is considered to be the "Odd Man Out" or the "Odd thing out". Thus, this item stands apart from the group.

There are three classifications for such kind of questions.

1. Number Odd Man Out
2. Letter Odd Man Out
3. Word Odd Man Out

I. Number Odd Man Out:

In these type of problems, three of the four given numbers share a common property, say, they are squares, or cubes, or primes, or based on some pattern like $n^2 \pm n$, $n^3 \pm n$, $n^3 \pm n^2$, etc. The number which does not have that common property is the odd one out.

Example 1:

    (1) 2   (2) 3   (3) 5   (4) 7

Solution. (1)

Here, although each of the four choices is a prime number, the numbers 3, 5 and 7 form the group of odd numbers and the number 2, which is an even number, does not belong to that group. Hence, by virtue of this 2 is the odd man out.

Example 2:

    (1) 16   (2) 25   (3) 38   (4) 49

Solution. (3)

Here, each of 16, 25 and 49 is a perfect square ($16 = 4^2$; $25 = 5^2$; $49 = 7^2$), whereas 38 is not a perfect square. Hence, 38 is the odd man out.

II. Letter Odd Man Out:

In these kind of problems, the letters share some characteristic in common, say they are vowels or consonants, or belong to any of the two halves or are corresponding from the ends or in the two halves, etc. Once again, the letter which does not have that characteristic, as the others in the group, is considered to be the odd man out.

Example 3:

    (1) A   (2) E   (3) I   (4) L

Solution. (4)

Here, A, E and I form the group of vowels (Common shared property), whereas 'L' does not belong to that group. Hence, 'L' is the odd man out.

Example 4:

    (1) AC   (2) BE   (3) DF   (4) HJ

Solution. (2)

Here, in each of the groups AC, DF and HJ the difference between the place values is 2 i.e, A(1) + 2 = (3) C; D (4) + 2 = (6) F; H (8) + 2 = (10) J.

But in BE, B(2) + 2 = (4) D, not E. Hence, BE is the odd man out. Alternately, in AC, DF and HJ one letter is skipped in the alphabet to the get the second letter i.e. A (skip B) C; D (skip E) F; H (skip I) J. But in BE, two letters are skipped from B to get E(skip C and D), which makes it different from the other three.

III. Word Odd Man Out:

As in the other two types, there will be four words, out of which three share some common characteristic, and the fourth one which does not possess that characteristic is the odd man out.

Example 5:

    (1) Chair   (2) Sofa
    (3) Table   (4) Window

Solution. (4)

Here, chair, sofa and table are furniture items, whereas window is not.

Example 6:

    (1) Sun   (2) Earth
    (3) Mars   (4) Saturn

Solution. (1)

Here, earth, mars and saturn are planets, whereas 'Sun' is not (it is a star).

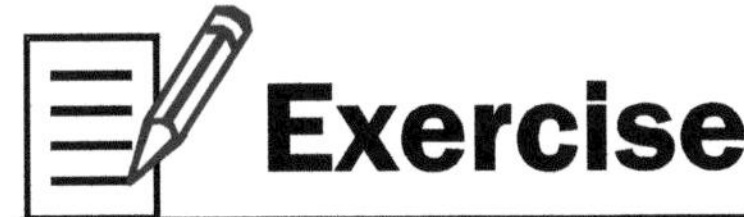# Exercise

Directions for questions 1 to 35: Each of the following questions has four numbers out of which three are similar due to some common characteristic. Find the odd one out which does not share that common characteristic with the other three.

1. (1) 12   (2) 84   (3) 44   (4) 124

2. (1) 24   (2) 22   (3) 21   (4) 20

3. (1) 47   (2) 45   (3) 43   (4) 41

4. (1) 256   (2) 324   (3) 432   (4) 504

5. (1) 1225   (2) 625   (3) 125   (4) 25

6. (1) 28   (2) 33   (3) 35   (4) 42

7. (1) 15   (2) 56   (3) 35   (4) 77

8. (1) 8   (2) 16   (3) 25   (4) 49

9. (1) 64   (2) 125   (3) 216   (4) 324

10. (1) 1   (2) 64   (3) 125   (4) 729

11. (1) 1331   (2) 729   (3) 343   (4) 125

12. (1) 961   (2) 1089   (3) 841   (4) 529

13. (1) 1561   (2) 1089   (3) 1225   (4) 1369

14. (1) 26   (2) 50   (3) 10   (4) 38

15. (1) 62   (2) 98   (3) 38   (4) 14

16. (1) 333   (2) 264   (3) 150   (4) 205

17. (1) 1139   (2) 1423   (3) 1008   (4) 1278

18. (1) 210   (2) 342   (3) 156   (4) 274

19. (1) 28   (2) 125   (3) 9   (4) 344

20. (1) 730   (2) 511   (3) 215   (4) 63

21. (1) 520   (2) 68   (3) 1005   (4) 219

22. (1) 508   (2) 7   (3) 213   (4) 60

23. (1) 2758   (2) 4114   (3) 2210   (4) 3390

24. (1) 1210   (2) 504   (3) 2184   (4) 350

25. (1) 970   (2) 2702   (3) 30   (4) 110

26. (1) 2236   (2) 1030   (3) 74   (4) 756

27. (1) 150   (2) 350   (3) 810   (4) 1452

28. (1) 2028   (2) 294   (3) 100   (4) 1220

29. (1) 1234   (2) 2468   (3) 3456   (4) 5678

30. (1) 2456   (2) 3578   (3) 2467   (4) 4689

31. (1) 6587   (2) 8769   (3) 5476   (4) 3245

32. (1) 824   (2) 623   (3) 553   (4) 414

33. (1) 10   (2) 28   (3) 327   (4) 464

34. (1) 48   (2) 16   (3) 72   (4) 32

35. (1) 169   (2) 324   (3) 961   (4) 196

Directions for questions 36 to 60: Each of the questions given below consists of four words / letters / numbers. Three out of the four are similar due to a common characteristic.

Find the odd one amongst the choices.

36. (1) I   (2) A   (3) D   (4) E

37. (1) A   (2) E   (3) I   (4) O

38. (1) M   (2) N   (3) P   (4) Q

39. (1) A   (2) B   (3) C   (4) D

40. (1) P   (2) E   (3) Y   (4) I

41. (1) AZ   (2) IR   (3) OL   (4) UE

42. (1) FS   (2) HU   (3) JQ   (4) LY

43. (1) KPC   (2) JWD   (3) DQJ   (4) FSH

44. (1) VXCE   (2) FHMU   (3) LNSO   (4) RTWI

45. (1) WURM   (2) LMQV   (3) PNKF   (4) TROJ

46. (1) MAP   (2) CAP   (3) SIP   (4) GAP

47. (1) LAJNIRB   (2) OTATOP
    (3) OTAMOT   (4) AVAUG

48. (1) Microsoft   (2) Infosys
    (3) IBM   (4) Oracle

49. (1) Car   (2) Television
    (3) Refrigerator   (4) Washing Machine

50. (1) Leopard   (2) Tiger
    (3) Wolf   (4) Lion

51. (1) Eagle   (2) Ostrich
    (3) Sparrow   (4) Pigeon

52. (1) Child   (2) Parent
    (3) Spouse   (4) Sister

53. (1) Violin   (2) Sitar
    (3) Flute   (4) Guitar

54. (1) India   (2) Japan
    (3) China   (4) Spain

55. (1) Cricket   (2) Lawn Tennis
    (3) Badminton   (4) Hockey

56. (1) Bay   (2) Lake
    (3) Ocean   (4) Sea

57. (1) 2 : 8   (2) 3 : 27
    (3) 4 : 16   (4) 5 : 125

58. (1) 123 : 6   (2) 234 : 24
    (3) 345 : 60   (4) 456 : 110

59. (1) 16 : 16   (2) 25 : 32
    (3) 36 : 32   (4) 49 : 128

60. (1) 12 : 144   (2) 31 : 169
    (3) 17 : 982   (4) 25 : 526

Coding is a method of transmitting a message from one place to the other. ***Decoding*** is the ability to decipher a certain code.

In this type of questions, certain code values are assigned to a word or a group of words and you have to find out the original words.

Various types of coding-decoding questions are asked in the examination. Some of them are given in the following pages.

■ Type – I: Solved Examples

In this type of questions, you have to find out the correct answer code from the given alternatives.

Example 1:

If NUMERICAL is written as MVLFQJBBK, then how ASTROLOGY will be written in this code?
(1) BRSTMNNHX   (2) ZTSSNMNHX
(3) ZTUSPMPEZ   (4) BRSSNKNHX

Solution. (2)

First, third, fifth, seventh and ninth letters have preceding letters as their code and the remaining ones have next letter as their code. Hence, the answer is (2).

Example 2:

If IMPORT is written as USPQNJ, then how CAPITAL will be written in this code?
(1) MBUJQBD   (2) KZSHOZB
(3) MUBJBDQ   (4) MBQJUBD

Solution. (1)

Reverse the word and use next letters as codes. Hence, the answer is (1).

Exercise

Directions for questions 1 to 15: In each of the following questions, certain code values are assigned to a word and you have to find out the code which will be used for the given word, from the given options.

1. If MAN is written as NZM, then how GIRL will be written in this code?
(1) HHQK   (2) RTIO   (3) HJLM   (4) GIKL

2. If COBRA is written as BOCAR, then how GROUP will be written in this code?
(1) ORPGU   (2) OGRPU
(3) ORTAU   (4) ORGPU

3. If SPECIAL is coded as KZHBDOR, then ORDINARY would be coded as
(1) ZQBMHCSX   (2) XQZOHCQN
(3) XQZMHCQN   (4) ZQBHOBQZ

4. If GOOD is written as HQRH, how will you write DREAM?
(1) ESPBN   (2) ETHER
(3) ETHPQ   (4) ESHDR

5. If CONSULTS is written as OCSNLUST, then ADVICE will be written as
(1) DVIACE   (2) DAVCEI
(3) DAVICE   (4) DAIVEC

6. In a certain code, PAINTER is written as NCGPRGP, then REASON would be written as:
(1) PCYQMN   (2) PGYQMN
(3) PGYUMP   (4) PGYUPM

7. If in a certain code SOCIAL is TQFMFR, then DIMPLE would be:
(1) EKPUQK   (2) EKPQPJ
(3) EKPSPJ   (4) EKPTQK

8. If JAPAN is coded as KCSES, then the code for CASTLE will be:
(1) DIJOBK   (2) DJKRQX
(3) DKMGQX   (4) DCVXQK

9. If TRAIN is coded as RPYGL, the code for SCOOTER would be:
(1) QAMMRCP   (2) QBNNRCP
(3) QAMMSBP   (4) QBNNSBP

10. If the word RADIO is written as PYBGM, then how the word SCHOOL would be written in that code?
(1) USQOON   (2) QAFMMJ
(3) PTFNNO   (4) QYFMMT

11. If the word PEARL is written as MBXOI, then how the word DIAMOND would be written in that code?
(1) BFXKLNA   (2) AFXJKLA
(3) AFXKLNA   (4) AFXJLKA

12. If the word MENTAL is written as LNDFMOSUZBKM, then how would the word TEST be written in that code?
(1) UVFGTIIV   (2) RSCDQRRS
(3) SUDFQRSM   (4) SUDFRTSU

13. In a certain code MOTHER in coded LPSIDS. How will FATHER be written in that code?
(1) ESDSIS   (2) EBSIDS
(3) EBISDS   (4) EBSDIS

14. If PREPARE is coded PEAE then the code for REASONING will be _____ .
(1) RSOIG   (2) RAOIG
(3) REOLG   (4) RANIG

15. If OPPOSITE is coded PRSSXOAM, then the code for PROPER will be _____ .
(1) QTRTJX   (2) QTRTJS
(3) QTTRJX   (4) QTRTPX

Type – 2: Solved Examples

In this type of questions, either numerical code values are assigned to a word or alphabetical code values are assigned to the numbers. You have to analyse the code as per the directions.

Example 1:

If in a certain language, A is coded as 1, B is coded as 2, and so on, how will FADCCBM coded in that language?
(1) 61433213   (2) 13233416
(3) 6243313   (4) 51433123

Solution. (1)

As given, the letters are coded as:

A B C D E F G H I J K L M
1 2 3 4 5 6 7 8 9 10 11 12 13

So, in FADCCBM, F is coded as 6, A as 1, D as 4, C as 3, B as 2 and M as 13. Thus, FADCCBM is coded as 61433213. Hence, the answer is (1).

Example 2:

If in a certain code, BEAUTIFUL is coded as 573041208, BUTTER as 504479, how is FUTURE coded in that code?
(1) 201497   (2) 204097
(3) 704092   (4) 204079

Solution. (2)

As given, the letters are coded as:

B E A U T I F L R
5 7 3 0 4 1 2 8 9

So, in FUTURE, F is coded as 2, U as 0, T as 4, R as 9 and E as 7. Therefore, FUTURE is coded as 204097. Hence, the answer is (2).

Example 3:

In a certain language, 5 is coded as Z, 7 as E, 2 as S, 9 as T, and 4 as W. How is 977452 coded in that language?
(1) SEEWZT   (2) TEEWZS
(3) ZEEWST   (4) WEEZST

Solution. (2)

977452 is coded as TEEWZS. Hence, the answer is (2).

Example 4:

In a certain code, 98602 is coded as MANGO, 0139867 as GERMANY, then how is 9868013 coded as?
(1) MANEGER   (2) MENEGER
(3) MENAGAR   (4) MANAGER

Solution. (4)

As given, the numbers are coded as:

9 8 6 0 2 1 3 7
M A N G O E R Y

Thus, 9868013 is coded as MANAGER. Hence, the answer is (4).

Example 5:

If CAT is coded as 24, what will be the code number for BAT?
(1) 32   (2) 21   (3) 23   (4) 42

Solution. (3)

Add up the position numbers - B-2, A-1, T-20. ∴ Total = 23. Hence, the answer is (3).

Exercise

Directions for questions 1 to 10: Read the given information carefully and answer the questions that follow.

1. If in a certain language, A is coded as 1, B is coded as 2, and so on, how is STAR coded in that language?
(1) 1810291   (2) 9120118
(3) 1920118   (4) 1920811

2. If in a certain language, BOX is coded as 213, BITTER as 207749, how is BOXER coded in that language?
   (1) 21359   (2) 23159
   (3) 23149   (4) 21349

3. In a certain language, C is coded as 0, E as 7, T as 4, I as 9, P as 1, R as 3 and U as 5. How is 1904537 coded in that language?
   (1) PICTRUE   (2) PICTURE
   (3) PITUPRE   (4) PCTUREI

4. In a certain language, 123 is coded as OX, 21 1 29 as FOR and 23 12 12 9 as DOOR, then how is 21 12 3 12 9 23 coded?
   (1) DOXFOR   (2) FORDOX
   (3) OXFORD   (4) FOXORD

5. In a certain language, 2468 is coded as PART, 8136 as TOUR, then how is 246618 coded?
   (1) PORRAT   (2) TARROP
   (3) PAROUT   (4) PARROT

6. In a certain language, 13352 is coded as OFFER, 795 as ICE, then how is 1337952 coded?
   (1) FICEROF   (2) CIFFOER
   (3) OICFFER   (4) OFFICER

7. In a certain language, 1223 is coded as BOOK, 627962 as TOMATO, then how is 126627 coded?
   (1) BOTTOM   (2) MOTTOB
   (3) TOBOMT   (4) BOMOTT

8. If BOOK is coded as 43, what will be the code number for PEN?
   (1) 53   (2) 33
   (3) 35   (4) 43

9. If TOWER is coded as 81, what will be the code number for POWER?
   (1) 75   (2) 55
   (3) 18   (4) 77

10. If MAN is coded as 28, what will be the code number for CHILD?
    (1) 25   (2) 36
    (3) 49   (4) 64

▌Type – 3: Solved Examples

In these type of questions, some particular objects are assigned with code names and then a question is asked, that is to be answered in the code language.

Example 1:

If 'orange' is called 'butter' , 'butter' is called 'soap', 'soap' is called 'ink', 'ink' is called 'honey' and 'honey' is called 'orange', which of the following is used for washing clothes?
(1) Honey   (2) Butter
(3) Orange   (4) Ink

Solution. (4)

Clearly, 'soap' is used for washing clothes and as given soap is called 'ink'. So, 'ink' is used for washing clothes. Hence, the answer is (4).

Example 2:

If 'water' is called 'food', 'food' is called 'tree', 'tree' is called 'sky', 'sky' is called 'wall', on which of the following grows a 'fruit'?
(1) Water   (2) Food
(3) Tree   (4) Sky

Solution. (4)

Clearly, a fruit grows on a 'tree' and as given 'tree' is called 'sky'. So, a fruit grows on 'sky'. Hence, the answer is (4).

Exercise

Directions for questions 1 to 5: Read the given information carefully and answer the questions that follow.

1. If light is called 'dark', dark is called 'green', green is called 'blue', blue is called 'red', red is called 'white' and white is called 'yellow', what is the colour of 'blood'?
   (1) Red   (2) Dark
   (3) White   (4) Yellow

2. If water is called 'black', black is called 'tree', tree is called 'blue', blue is called 'rain', rain is called 'pink' and pink is called 'fish' in a certain language, what will the colour of 'sky' be in that language?
   (1) Blue   (2) Fish
   (3) Rain   (4) Pink

3. If the animals which can 'walk' are called 'swimmers', animals which can 'crawl' are called 'flying', those which live in water are called 'snakes', the 'snakes' are called 'fish' and those which fly in the sky are called 'hunters', then what will a 'lizard' be called?
   (1) Swimmer   (2) Snake
   (3) Hunter   (4) Flying

4. If 'pen' is called 'pencil', 'pencil' is called 'scale', 'scale' is called 'bag' and 'bag' is called 'book', which is used to carry the 'books'?
    (1) Scale   (2) Pen
    (3) Book   (4) Bag

5. If 'paper' is called 'eraser', ' eraser' is called 'bag', 'bag' is called 'scale', 'scale' is called 'pencil' and 'pencil' is called 'paper', what will a person 'write' with?
    (1) Pencil   (2) Scale
    (3) Eraser   (4) Paper

Type – 4: Solved Examples

In these type of questions, few complete messages are given in the coded language and the code for a particular word or sentence is asked.

Example:

In a certain code language 'nee po tam' means 'boys are studying', 'me tam sam' means 'grapes are sour' and 'ism po me' means 'boys eat grapes'. Which of the following is the code for 'sour' in that language?
(1) ism   (2) tam
(3) me   (4) None of these

Solution:

We are required to find the code for 'sour', for this we try to find out the code for 'grapes' and 'are' first, and then eliminate the corresponding codes for them. The remaining code would be the representative code for 'sour'.

On comparing codes 'nee po tam' and 'me tam sam' we get 'tam' as the code for word 'are'. Similarly on comparing codes 'me tam sam' and 'ism po me', we get 'me' as code for 'grapes'. Now as 'grapes are sour' coded as 'me tam sam', and 'me' and 'tam' represent 'grapes' and 'are', therefore 'sam' represents the code for 'sour'.

Exercise

Directions for questions 1 to 5: Read the given information carefully and answer the questions that follow.

1. In a certain code language, 'Col tip mot' means 'singing is appreciable', 'mot baj min' means 'dancing is good' and 'tip nop baj' means 'singing and dancing'. Which of the following means 'good' in that code language?
    (1) mot   (2) min   (3) baj   (4) nop

2. In a certain code language, 'dom pul ta' means 'bring hot food', 'pul tir sop' means 'food is good' and 'tak da sop' means 'good bright boy'. Which of the following does mean 'is' in that language?
    (1) dom   (2) pul   (3) ta   (4) tir

3. In a certain code language, 'pul tir fin' means 'good sweet fruit', 'tie dip sig' means 'beautiful red rose', 'sig lon fin' means 'rose and fruit'. Which of the following stands for 'and' in that language?
    (1) pul   (2) tir   (3) lon   (4) sig

4. In a certain code language, 'pul ta nop' means 'fruit is good', 'nop ko tir' means 'tree is tall' and 'pul ho sop' means 'eat good food'. Which of the following means 'fruit' in that language?
    (1) pul   (2) ta   (3) nop   (4) sop

5. In a certain code language, '3a, 2b, 7c' means 'truth is eternal', '7c 9a, 8b, 3a' means 'enmity is not eternal', '9a, 4d, 2b, 8b' means 'truth does not perish'. Which of the following means 'eternal ' in that language?
    (1) 3a
    (2) 2b
    (3) 7c
    (4) Cannot be determined

Type – 5: Solved Examples

In this type of questions, few complete messages are given in the coded language and the code for a particular word or sentence is asked.

Example 1:

In a certain code language, '289' means 'read from paper', ' 276' means 'tea from field' and '85' means 'wall paper'. Which of the following is the code for 'paper'?
(1) 2   (2) 8   (3) 9   (4) 7

Solution. (2)

From first and last statements, 8 = paper
Hence, the answer is (2).

Exercise

Directions for questions 1 to 5: Read the given information carefully and answer the questions that follow.

1. In a certain code language, '246' means 'He is cool', '653' means 'Cool and bright' and '849' means 'India is hot', then code for 'is' in that language would be:
    (1) 2   (2) 6   (3) 4   (4) 8

2. In a certain code language, '123' means 'hot filter coffee', '356' means 'very hot day' and '589' means 'day and night'. Which digit in that language means 'very'?
(1) 8   (2) 6   (3) 9   (4) 5

3. In a certain code language, '721' means 'good college life', '526' means 'you are good' and '257' means 'life are good'. Which digit stands for 'you' in the code?
(1) 6   (2) 5   (3) 7   (4) 2

4. In a certain code language, '357' means 'get me toy', '843' means 'bring good toy' and '746' means 'bring me water'. Which of the following digits represents 'good' in that code?
(1) 7   (2) 6
(3) 4   (4) None of these

5. In a certain code language, '786' means 'bring me apple', '958' means 'peel green apple' and '645' means 'bring green fruit', which of the following is the code for 'me'?
(1) 8   (2) 6
(3) 7   (4) Data inadequate

Directions

6

Introduction

Around one to three questions are asked from this topic. This topic is quite easy. The best way of solving these questions is to follow the instructions given in the question carefully and make a diagram accordingly with the help of which the question can be solved.

Points to remember:

The following basics must be taken into consideration while solving the questions.

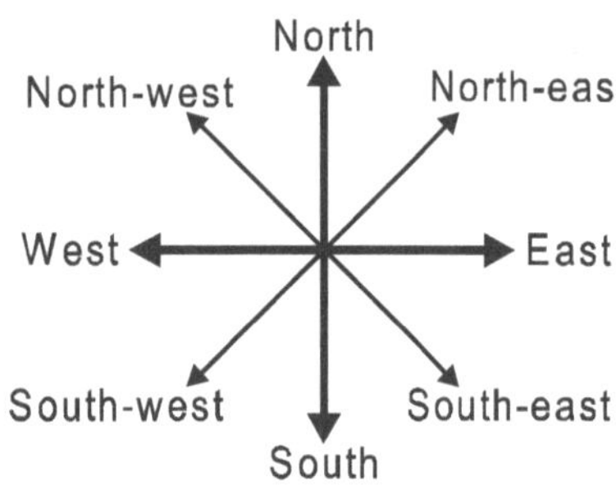

i. There are four major directions viz., **NORTH, EAST, WEST** and **SOUTH** (NEWS), called the **Primary directions**.

ii. There are four minor directions viz., **North-east, North-west, South-east** and **South-west**, called the **Secondary directions**.

iii. You are always facing North by default when solving a question.

iv. The questions should be solved by adopting the diagramatic approach.

v. Whenever you represent a distance with an inclined line, take it's vertical and horizontal components to get a right-angled triangle and apply the PYTHAGOROS THEOREM.

vi. For shadow based problem, always consider the direction in which the source of light is located. If the source of light is SUN, then in the morning the sun is in the EAST and in the evening, the sun redundant is in WEST and at noon it is overhead.

Now let us observe the application of these concepts in the following examples.

Example 1:

I walk 5 kms East, then turn right and walk another 8 kms. Then I turn left and walk 5 kms and then I turn left and walk 8 kms. At what distance am I from the starting point?

(1) 10 kms   (2) 8 kms   (3) 6 kms   (4) 7 kms

Solution. (1)

The movement is

The required distance OD is OA + AD, where AD = BC = 5 kms.

Hence,

OD = 5 kms + 5 kms

= 10 kms.

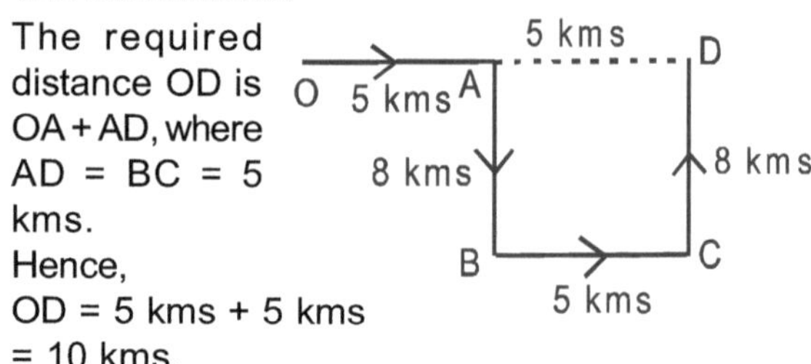

Example 2:

One fine evening, my girlfriend and I were walking on the Juhu beach. If my girlfriend's shadow fell exactly to her left, then towards which direction were we walking?

(1) North   (2) South
(3) East   (4) West

Solution. (2)

It was evening and the shadow of my girlfriend fell on her left side. This means that the Sun was towards our right. During evenings, the sun is in the West.

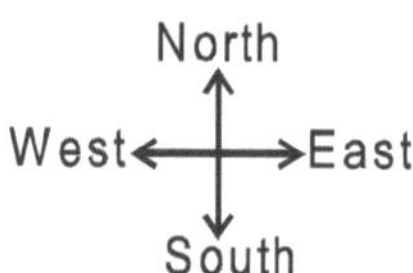

We were walking towards the South.

Example 3:

A clock is placed in such a way at 9'O clock, that the minute-hand points towards South-West. In which direction does the hour-hand point at 12'O clock?

(1) South-West   (2) South-East
(3) North-East   (4) South

Solution. (1)

Clock is placed, in such a way that the minute-hand points towards South-West at 9 p.m.

So, at 12'O clock hour-hand also points towards South-West.

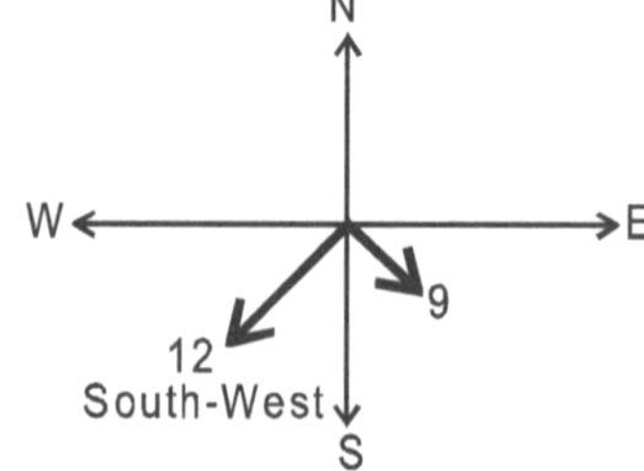

Example 4:

Swati travelled 100 kms towards South, then she took three turns of 45° each in clockwise direction and then she took two turns of 45° each in anti-clockwise direction. In which direction was she travelling finally?

(1) West   (2) South-East

(3) South-West   (4) North-East

Solution. (3)

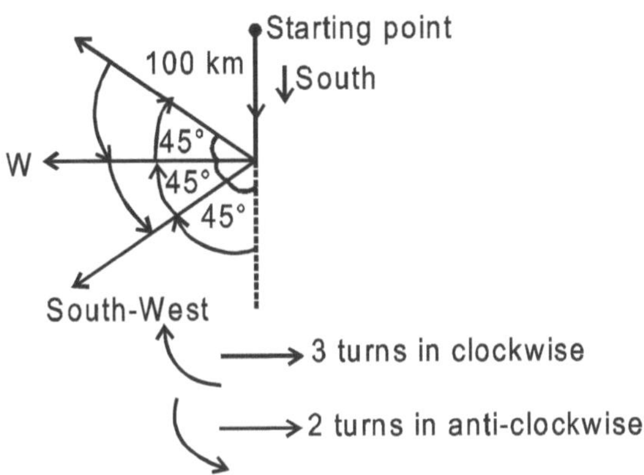

Finally, Swati is travelling towards the South-West.

Exercise

Directions for questions 1 to 21: Answer each of the following questions independently.

1. A man walks 2 kms southward and takes a right turn and walks 5 kms and then turns left and walks 3 kms and again turning left, walks 5 kms. In which direction is he now from the starting point?
   (1) South-east   (2) South
   (3) East   (4) West

2. Bantu walks southwards, then takes a half-right turn and then a left turn. In which direction is he walking now?
   (1) South   (2) East
   (3) South   (4) South-east

3. Aditya faces North and covers 24 kms, turns West and covers 12 kms, then turns South and covers 6 kms and turns West again and covers 12 kms. How far is he from the starting point and in which direction?
   (1) 10 kms South-east   (2) 20 kms North-east
   (3) 30 kms North-west   (4) 40 kms South-west

4. Pradeep walks 10 m West, then turns left and walks 10 m. He then again turns left and walks 10 m.

He takes a 45 degrees turn rightwards and walks straight. In which direction is he walking now?
   (1) South   (2) South-west
   (3) East   (4) South-east

5. City 'K' is situated to the West of city 'L'. City 'M' is situated to the North of city 'L'. City 'N' is situated towards the South of city 'M'.
   In which direction is city 'L' situated with respect to city 'N'?
   (1) North
   (2) South
   (3) North-east
   (4) Cannot be determined

6. Which of the following turning sequences will make one who started walking towards East, walk towards South?
   (1) Left, Left, Left   (2) Left, Right, Left
   (3) Right, Right, Right   (4) All of these

7. Ashok is standing at a point P. He walks 10 m towards the South, then he walks 20 m towards the West then he walks 10 m towards the South, then he walks 20 m towards the East, then he walks 5 m towards the North and reached Q. What is the distance between P and Q?
   (1) 20 m   (2) 25 m   (3) 15 m   (4) 5 m

8. Mr Mehta is facing North. Before reaching his destination he takes a total of 40 turns, 20 left turns and 20 right turns. Which direction is he facing now?
   (1) West   (2) North   (3) South   (4) East

9. I am facing east. I turn 180° in the clockwise direction and then 135° in the anti-clockwise direction. Which direction am I facing now?
   (1) East   (2) South-east
   (3) West   (4) South-west

10. I am facing North. I turn 90° in the anti-clockwise direction and walk 30 m and then turning South I walk 40 m and then turning East I go 60 m. Then turning right I walk 80 m. How far am I from my starting point?
   (1) $10\sqrt{153}$ m   (2) 15 m
   (3) 11.12 m   (4) $11\sqrt{21}$ m

11. Ram went to his office which is 8 kms towards the South from his hostel. HIs roommate Meghal went to a clinic which is 6 kms towards the West from the hostel. What is the shortest distance between the clinic and Ram's office?
(1) 12 kms (2) 10 kms (3) 14 kms (4) 10 m

12. One fine evening, an elephant was facing a man. The shadow of the man fell exactly to the elephant's right. Which direction was the elephant facing?
(1) South (2) North (3) East (4) West

13. One evening, Suraj and Dhiraj were talking facing each other. If Suraj's shadow was exactly to his right, then which direction was Dhiraj facing?
(1) South (2) East (3) North (4) West

14. One fine morning, Rajeev was walking in a garden. He sees that a man is coming towards him from the opposite direction. When the man reaches near Rajeev, the man's shadow is falling to the left of Rajeev. In which direction would Rajeev be walking, if he takes a right turn ahead?
(1) West (2) South (3) East (4) North

15. A clock is placed in such a way at 3 a.m. that the minute-hand points towards North. In which direction does the hour-hand point at 6'O clock?
(1) North (2) West (3) South (4) East

16. A watch shows 5:45. If the minute hand points towards the North-west, then in which direction will the hour-hand point?
(1) North (2) South-east
(3) East (4) South-west

17. Priyanka started running from her house towards South. While running she turns 135° clockwise and 45° anti-clockwise. Which direction is she facing now?
(1) North (2) East (3) South (4) West

18. Ajay started moving towards South. After taking 128 turns in clockwise direction towards his right. Which will be the opposite direction at the end of Ajay's facing?
(1) South (2) West (3) North (4) East

19. Radha and Sita are standing 10 m apart and Radha is towards Sita's left. Both start travelling towards North, walk for about 30 m and then turn right to travel 40 m further. Radha, then takes a left turn, travels 20 m and stops but Sita takes a right turn to travel 10 m. Sita again turns right, travels 10 m and stops. How far are they from each other?
(1) 10 m (2) 20 m (3) 30 m (4) 50 m

20. A is to the East of B but to the South-east of C. C is to the North-east of B. D is to the North-east of C and to the North of A but in line with B and C. In which direction of B is D located?
(1) North-east (2) North
(3) East (4) North-west

21. The town of Paranda is located on Green Lake. The town of Akram is West of Paranda. Tokhada is East of Akram but West of Paranda, Kakran is East of Bopri but West of Tokhada and Akram. If they are all in the same district, which town is the farthest west from Paranda?
(1) Green Lake (2) Kakran
(3) Akram (4) Bopri

Directions for questions 22 to 25: Read the information given carefully and answer the questions the follow.

'A', 'B', 'C', 'D', 'E', 'F', 'G', and 'O' are 8 cities. 'A' is to the West of 'C' but not to the West of 'D'. 'D' is to the west of 'C'. 'B' is to the 'West' of 'C' but not to the West of 'O'. 'O' is to the East of 'A' but not to the East of 'B'. 'E' and 'G' are 15 kms Northwards from 'A' and 'B' respectively. 'F' is 15 km Southwards from 'O'.

22. Which city is situated on the extreme West?
(1) D (2) C (3) A (4) O

23. What is the position of 'G' with respect to 'D'?
(1) North-west (2) North-east
(3) South-east (4) South

24. If the distance between 'A' and 'E' is equal to the distance between 'A' and 'D', then what is the shortest distance between 'E' and 'D' ?
(1) $\sqrt{12}$ kms (2) $\sqrt{200}$ kms
(3) $15\sqrt{2}$ kms (4) Both (1) and (2)

25. If the compass becomes defective and it's, needle turns in a such a manner that the needle initially pointing towards North now points towards East. Now, what is the position of 'F' with respect to 'D'?
(1) South-east (2) North-east
(3) South-west (4) South

Introduction

In this type of questions, generally some relations between the members of a particular community is given and you are supposed to find out the missing relations which are there between them, but in the hidden form. Before proceeding any further, here is a list of the **important** relations that are mostly asked in the examinations.

1.	Brother	Son of Mother or Father
2.	Sister	Daughter of Mother or Father
3.	Aunt	Sister of Mother or Father
4.	Uncle	Brother of Mother or Father
5.	Cousin	Son of Uncle or Aunt **OR** Daughter of Uncle or Aunt
6.	Grandmother	Mother of Father or Mother
7.	Grandfather	Father of Father or Mother
8.	Niece	Daughter of Brother or Sister
9.	Nephew	Son of Brother or Sister
10.	Brother-in-law	Sister's Husband or Brother of Wife or Husband
11.	Sister-in-law	Brother's Wife or Sister of Wife or Husband
12.	Daughter-in-law	Wife of Son

Example 1:

If Teena's mother is Uday's mother's daughter, how is Uday related to Teena?
(1) Grandfather   (2) Brother
(3) Grandson   (4) Maternal uncle

Solution. (4)

Uday's mother's daughter would be Uday's sister. So, Teena's mother is Uday's sister. Hence, Uday is maternal uncle of Teena.

Example 2:

Hema, who is Sahil's daughter, tells Anjali ,"Your mother Rekha is the younger sister of my father, who is the third child of Captain Rathore". How is Captain Rathore related to Anjali?
(1) Father   (2) Grandfather
(3) Father-in-law   (4) Brother

Solution. (2)

Anjali's mother Rekha is sister of Hema's father. So, Anjali and Hema are cousins. Captain Rathore is Rekha's father. So, he is Hema's and hence Anjali's grandfather.

Example 3:

How is Suresh's brother's grandmother's only daughter's child related to Suresh?
(1) Brother
(2) Cousin
(3) Sister
(4) Cannot determined

Solution. (2)

Suresh's brother's grandmother is Suresh's grandmother, either maternal or paternal. Suresh's grandmother's only daughter has only one child. Therefore, she has to be Suresh's only paternal aunt. So, Suresh's aunt's only child is Suresh's cousin.

Example 4:

Pointing towards a person in a photograph, Aruna said, "He is the only son of the father of my sister's brother". How is that person related to Aruna?
(1) Maternal Uncle   (2) Son
(3) Father   (4) Brother

Solution. (4)

The person is brother of Aruna as he is the only son of Aruna's father.

Example 5:

Pointing to a photograph, a woman says, "This man's son's sister is my mother-in-law." How is the woman's husband related to the man in the photograph?
(1) Son-in-law   (2) Son
(3) Grandson   (4) Nephew

Solution. (3)

The man's daughter is the woman's mother-in-law. Hence, the woman's husband should be the man's grandson.

Example 6:

If A + B means 'A is the brother of B'; A × B means 'A is the mother of B'; and A ÷ B means 'A is the sister of B', then which of the following would mean 'X is the uncle of Y'?
(1) X × A + Y   (2) X × Y + A
(3) X + A × Y   (4) X ÷ A × Y

Solution. (3)

X is the uncle of Y means X is the brother of Y's mother. According to the given expressions, it must be X + A × Y, which is choice 3.

Directions for questions 7 to 10: Read the given information carefully and answer the questions that follow.

A family consists of 5 members P, Q, R, S and T. T has two sons, an unmarried daughter and only one daughter-in-law. P is the brother-in-law of the above-mentioned daughter-in-law. Q's sister is not happy with Q's wife. But P and his father support Q's wife S.

7. Who is the daughter of T?
(1) P   (2) Q
(3) R   (4) S

8. How is P related to S?
(1) Brother   (2) Brother-in-law
(3) Sister-in-law   (4) Sister

9. How is T related to Q?
(1) Father   (2) Brother
(3) Father-in-law   (4) Sister-in-law

10. Who is the wife of Q?
(1) P   (2) R
(3) S   (4) T

Solutions for questions 7 to 10: From the given information, we can conclude the following :

'T' has two sons. That means out of P, Q, R, S two are sons of T. T has an unmarried daughter. That means out of P, Q, R, S one is his daughter. T has a daughter-in-law. That means one of the sons is married; the other one is unmarried. S, who is supported by P and T, is the daughter-in-law of T and wife of Q and the sister-in-law of P. On the basis of this if we can draw the following family tree.

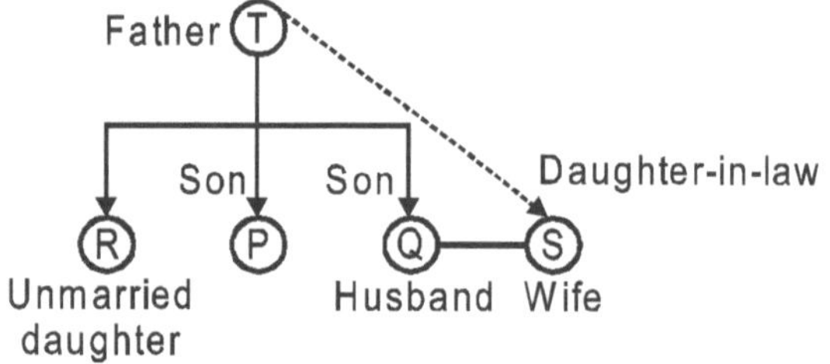

Hence, based on the above diagram and our conclusions, we can answer the questions as below.

7. 3 R is the daughter of T.

8. 2 P is the brother-in-law of S.

9. 1 T is the father of Q.

10. 3 S is the wife of Q.

Exercise

Directions for questions 1 to 11: Answer each of the following questions independently.

1. If Akshay is the brother of the son of Sunil's son, then how is Akshay related to Sunil?
(1) Grandson   (2) Brother
(3) Cousin   (4) Nephew

2. A is the mother of B. B's father C has 3 children. Based on this information, state which of the following statements is definitely true?
(1) C has 3 daughters   (2) C has 3 sons
(3) B is a male child   (4) A has 3 children

3. R told S that T is his father's nephew. U is R's cousin but not brother of T. How is U related to T?
(1) Mother   (2) Father
(3) Aunt   (4) Sister

4. Ashish said to Himani, "Your only brother's son is my wife's brother". How is Himani related to wife of Ashish?
(1) Sister   (2) Aunt
(3) Mother   (4) Daughter

5. Pointing to a man, a lady says that his father is the third son of her grandmother. How is the lady related to that man?
(1) Cousin   (2) Sister
(3) Brother   (4) Either (1) or (2)

6. Pointing towards a man in a photograph, a woman said, "He is the father of the brother of my father". How is the man related to the woman?
(1) Father   (2) Uncle
(3) Grandfather   (4) Uncle or Father

7. Pointing towards a lady in a photograph, a girl said, "She is the sister of my mother's husband". How is the girl related to the lady?
   (1) Daughter   (2) Niece
   (3) Sister   (4) Daughter or niece

8. A woman while looking at the photograph of a man said, "He is the maternal grandfather of children of my husband's sister". How is the man related to the woman?
   (1) Father   (2) Father-in-law
   (3) Grandfather   (4) Brother-in-law

9. A lady while looking at a photograph said, "This person is the brother of the daughter of the wife of my brother." How is the person in the photograph related to the lady?
   (1) Sister   (2) Brother
   (3) Nephew   (4) Niece

10. A girl while pointing at a man in the photograph, says to her mother, "The man's sister is the daughter of your father-in-law." How is the girl related to the man in the photograph?
   (1) Niece   (2) Daughter
   (3) Sister   (4) Niece or Daughter

11. A girl while looking at a photograph of a man said, "He is the only son of the father-in-law of my mother." How is the man related to the girl?
   (1) Uncle   (2) Father
   (3) Brother   (4) Grandfather

Directions for questions 12 to 14: Read the following information carefully and answer the questions that follow.
   X – Y means X is the husband of Y.
   X + Y means X is the daughter of Y.
   X × Y means X is the brother of Y.

12. If A + B × C, then which of the following is true?
   (1) A is the daughter-in-law of C.
   (2) A is the aunt of C.
   (3) A is the niece of C.
   (4) A is the daughter of C.

13. If A + B – C, then which of the following is true?
   (1) C is the mother-in-law of A.
   (2) C is the aunt of A.
   (3) C is the mother of A.
   (4) C is the sister-in-law of A.

14. If A × B + C, then which of the following is true?
   (1) A is the father of C.
   (2) A is the uncle of C.
   (3) A is the brother of C.
   (4) A is the son of C.

Directions for questions 15 to 17: Answer the questions based on following information.
   I.   'P × Q' means 'P is the brother of Q'.
   II. 'P + Q' means 'P is the father of Q'.
   III. 'P ÷ Q' means 'P is the sister of Q'.

15. Which of the following represents 'P is the uncle of Q'?
   (1) P + D ÷ Q   (2) P × D + Q
   (3) P + D × Q   (4) P ÷ D + Q

16. Which of the following statements is superfluous to answer the above question?
   (1) Only III   (2) Only II or III
   (3) Only I   (4) Only II

17. A is the brother of B. C is the sister of B. How is A related to C?
   (1) Uncle   (2) Sister
   (3) Brother   (4) Data insufficient

Directions for questions 18 and 19: Read the information carefully and answer the following questions.

A family consists of six persons. A is E's grandfather; E is the niece of B and D. A has three children, a daughter and two sons. B is F's sister-in-law. D is unmarried. C is also a member of this family.

18. How is F related to C ?
   (1) Husband   (2) Wife
   (3) Brother-in-law   (4) Brother

19. How is B related to A ?
   (1) Son   (2) Daughter
   (3) Sister   (4) Brother

Directions for questions 20 and 21: In a family of seven persons there are people belonging to three generations who live together. S is married in the family. V is the grand-daughter of P. R, who is unmarried, is the son of T. U is Q's son. Q is R's sister. There are four male and three female members in the family. There are two married couples.

20. How is P related to U?
   (1) Grandfather
   (2) Grandmother
   (3) Mother
   (4) Cannot be determined

21. How is S related to V?
   (1) Father
   (2) Mother
   (3) Uncle
   (4) Cannot be determined

Directions for questions 22 to 26: These questions are based on the information given below:

A family consists of six members L, M, N, O, P and Q. O is the only child of L. Q is the sister of the son of M. L is the wife of N's son. N is the mother of 'P' and 'Q'.

22. How many male members are there in the family?
   (1) 1
   (2) 2
   (3) 3
   (4) Cannot be determined

23. How is 'O' related to Q?
   (1) Nephew   (2) Cousin
   (3) Niece   (4) either (1) or (2)

24. How is the son of the father of L related to O?
   (1) Paternal Uncle (2) Cousin
   (3) Maternal Uncle (4) Can't say

25. How is L related to Q?
   (1) Sister   (2) Mother
   (3) Sister-in-law   (4) Mother-in-law

26. How is N related to O?
   (1) Grandfather   (2) Mother
   (3) Grandmother   (4) Mother-in-law

Directions for questions 27 to 30: These questions are based on the information given below:

A family consists of eight persons P, Q, R, S, T, U, V & W. P is a doctor. R is a Computer Engineer and is the wife of Q, who is a Mechanical Engineer. V is the father-in-law of T, a Teacher. R and U are the daughters of V, a Scientist. W is the wife of V and grandmother of P and S. P is the cousin of S and the son of the Mechanical Engineer. U is the wife of the Teacher. S is a Student.

27. How is the Student related to the Computer Engineer?
   (1) Nephew
   (2) Son
   (3) Niece
   (4) Cannot be determined

28. How is the Scientist related to S?
   (1) Father   (2) Grandfather
   (3) Cousin   (4) Can't be determined

29. How many female members are there in the family?
   (1) 4   (2) 2
   (3) 3   (4) Either (1) or (3)

30. How is T related to R?
   (1) Father   (2) Father-in-law
   (3) Brother-in-law (4) Either (2) or (3)

Directions for questions 31 to 35: These questions are based on the information given below:

Mr. Reddy has three children Usha, Ram and Sunil. Sunil married Rita, the eldest daughter of Mr. and Mrs. Mathur. The Mathur married their youngest daughter to the eldest son of Mr. and Mrs. Rao, and they had two children named Sanjay and Sunita. The Mathur have two more children, Rakesh and Bindu, both elder than Shanti. Sonu and Surinder are sons of Sunil and Rita. Lata is the daughter of Sanjay.

31. What is the surname of Lata?
   (1) Rao   (2) Mathur
   (3) Sanjay   (4) Reddy

32. What is the surname of Sonu?
   (1) Rao   (2) Mathur
   (3) Reddy   (4) Sunil

33. How is Mrs. Mathur related to Sunil?
   (1) Aunt   (2) Mother-in-law
   (3) Mother   (4) Sister-in-law

34. How is Sunil related to Rakesh?
   (1) Brother   (2) Father
   (3) Son   (4) Brother-in-law

35. How is Mr. Rao related to Lata?
   (1) Grandfather   (2) Great grandfather
   (3) Father   (4) Brother-in-law

Analytical Reasoning   8

Various Types and Solved Examples

There are variety of problems under Analytical Reasoning. Broadly, they can be categorised under the following headings.

1. **Seating Arrangements**
   (a) In a row
   (b) Around a table
      (i) Circular
      (ii) Any other shape (square, rectangular, etc.)
2. **Sequencing**
3. **Combinations**
4. **Comparisons**
5. **Selections**
6. **Series-based**
7. **Ranking**

Let us discuss and understand the details involved under each of these categories.

I. SEATING ARRANGEMENT

In these kind of problems, some people are sitting in a row or around a table in a desired formation. The conditions provide clues towards the actual arrangement and you have to make use of these clues to reach to the final arrangement.

(a) Seating arrangement in a row :

Let us understand the type with the help of the following example.

Directions for questions 1 to 5: Answer the questions based on the following information.

  i. A, B, C, D, E, F and G are sitting on a bench and all of them are facing East.

  ii. C is to the immediate right of D, but not next to F.

  iii. B is at the extreme end and has E as his neighbour.

  iv. G is between E and F.

  v. D is sitting third from the South end.

1. Who is sitting to the right of E?
   (1) A   (2) C
   (3) D   (4) None of these

2. Which of the following pairs is sitting at the extreme ends?
   (1) A, B   (2) A, E   (3) C, B   (4) F, B

3. The person sitting third from the North end is ____.
   (1) E   (2) F   (3) G   (4) D

4. Between which of the following pairs is D sitting?
   (1) A, C   (2) A, F   (3) C, E   (4) C, F

5. Which of the conditions from i to v given above is not required to find out the place where A is sitting?
   (1) i   (2) ii
   (3) iii   (4) All are required.

Solutions for questions 1 to 5:

From (i): A, B, C, D, E, F, G are sitting on a bench and all of them are facing East.

$$\_\_\_\_\_\_\_\_\_\_\_\_\_\_\_ \uparrow East$$

From (ii): $\underline{D}\ \underline{C}$

From (iii): $\underline{B}\ \underline{E}\ \_\_\_\_\_\_$
   OR
$\_\_\_\_\_\_\ \underline{E}\ \underline{B}$

From (iv): $\underline{E}\ \underline{G}\ \underline{F}$ or $\underline{F}\ \underline{G}\ \underline{E}$

From (v): $\_\_\_\_\ \underline{D}\_\_$ East ↑ → South

Let us start with the arrangement obtained from condition (v).

$$\_\ \_\ \_\ \_\ \overset{D}{\_}\ \_\ \_ \quad East$$
$$1\ 2\ 3\ 4\ 5\ 6\ 7\ \ \uparrow$$

Now, from (ii), we get that C will occupy seat 6. From (iii). B and E will occupy seats 1 and 2, respectively. From (iv), G and F will occupy 3 and 4 and finally the last seat 7 will be occupied by the remaining person A. From the above reasoning, we get the following final arrangement.

$$\boxed{\underline{B}\ \ \underline{E}\ \ \underline{G}\ \ \underline{F}\ \ \underline{D}\ \ \underline{C}\ \ \underline{A}\ \ \uparrow East}$$

1. 4   G is sitting to the right of E.

2. 1   A and B are sitting at the extreme ends.

3. 3   G is sitting 3rd from the North end.

4. 4   D is sitting between C and F.

5. 4   All are required.

(b) Seating arrangement around a table:

Let us consider the following example for circular arrangements.

Directions for questions 6 to 10: Read the given information carefully and answer the questions given below:

Six persons A, B, C, D, E and F are sitting around a circular table facing the centre.
   i. C is sitting exactly between A and F.
  ii. B is sitting two places to the left of E.
 iii. D is sitting two places to the right of F.

6. Between which two persons is D sitting?
   (1). F – B   (2) E – B   (3) C – B   (4) A – B

7. Who is sitting opposite A?
   (1) F   (2) C
   (3) E   (4) None of these

8. Which of the following is A's neighbour to his right?
   (1) C   (2) F   (3) B   (4) D

9. Who is sitting opposite E?
   (1) A   (2) B   (3) C   (4) F

10. Between which of the two persons is F sitting?
    (1) C – D   (2) C – A   (3) D – A   (4) C – B

Solutions for questions 6 to 10:

Start with any fixed position. Statement i does not give any fixed position since the order could be A-C-F or F-C-A. Starting with ii, we will have the positions of B and E. Now, C has to be in between A and F in such an order that D is two places to the right of F. The order in the clockwise direction has to be F-C-A, else A will fall 2 places to the right of F.

Thus, we have the arrangement as shown below.

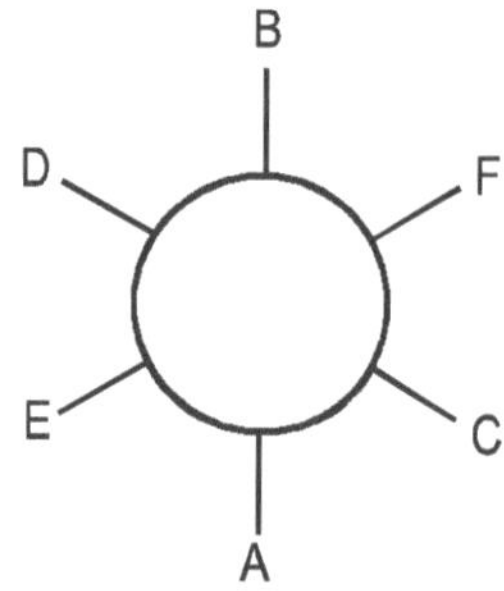

6. 2 D is sitting between E and B.

7. 4 B is sitting opposite A.

8. 1 C is to the immediate right of A.

9. 4 F is sitting opposite E.

10. 4 F is sitting between C and B.

2. SEQUENCING

In such type of problems, certain things or events have to be arranged in a sequence or an order as per the conditions. Let us look at the following example for better understanding.

Directions for questions 11 to 14: Read the following information carefully and answer the questions given below:
   i. Seven meetings - A, B, C, D, E, F, and G are to be scheduled, one on each day of a week that begins on Monday.
  ii. Meeting A must take place on Monday and meeting B on the last day.
 iii. Meeting B immediately takes place after meeting C which is scheduled immediately after meeting D.
 iv. Meeting E, F and G must take place on three consecutive days, in that order.

11. Which is the earliest day of the week on which meeting C can take place?
    (1) Wednesday   (2) Thursday
    (3) Friday   (4) Saturday

12. Which of the following must be true about the order of meetings?
    (1) C takes place immediately after A.
    (2) C takes place immediately after F.
    (3) E takes place immediately after A.
    (4) E takes place immediately after G.

13. If meeting A is on Wednesday, which is the first day that meeting B must take place on?
    (1) Tuesday   (2) Wednesday
    (3) Thursday   (4) Friday

14. Which of the following represents a possible order of meetings on three consecutive days?
    (1) ADB   (2) BCF
    (3) DEA   (4) AEF

Solution:

The given information can be summarized as follows:

Days	Meetings	
1 – Monday — A	...from statements (i) and (ii)	
2 – Tuesday— E		
3 – Wednesday— F	... from the statement (iv)	
4 – Thursday — G		
5 – Friday — D	... from statement (iii)	
6 – Saturday — C		
7 – Sunday — B	...from statements (i) and (iii)	

11. 4 — Saturday

12. 3 — E takes place immediately after A.

13. 1 — From statement (ii), we know that meeting A takes place on Monday i.e., the first day, and B takes place on the last day i.e., Sunday. If the first day changes from Monday to Wednesday, then the last day becomes Tuesday.

14. 4 — AEF, as can be observed from the arrangement.

Directions for questions 15 and 16: These questions are based on the following information.

Five friends - Hemant, Ram, Krishna, Pramod and Mahesh participated in a race. Ram finished the race before Krishna but after Hemant. Hemant finished the race before Mahesh and Pramod. Pramod finished the race after Krishna but before Mahesh.

15. Who finished the race in the fourth position?
    (1) Krishna   (2) Mahesh
    (3) Pramod   (4) Ram

16. Who was the first person to finish the race?
    (1) Hemant   (2) Pramod
    (3) Ram   (4) Mahesh

Solution:

Ram finished the race before Krishna but after Hemant who finished the race before Mahesh and Pramod means Hemant must finished the race first. Pramod finished the race after Krishna but before Mahesh.

So, the order we get in ranks is as follows.

Hemant	Ram	Krishna	Pramod	Mahesh
1	2	3	4	5

15. 3   Pramod finished the race in the fourth position.

16. 1   Hemant finished the race first.

3. COMBINATIONS

Here, the elements in some groups are to be combined, as per the given conditions. In the following example, the groups are of (a) Men, (b) Professions and (c) Musical Instruments. As per the conditions, these are mixed and matched.

Let us look at the following example.

Directions for questions 17 to 21: Read the following information carefully and answer the questions given below:

  i. Five gentlemen (Mr. Ajay, Mr. Bijay, Mr. Vinay, Mr Sanjay and Mr. Akshay) are practising five different professions (Engineering, Medical, Law, Chartered Accountancy and Architecture). Each one can play only one of the five different instruments: Tabla, Violin, Sarod, Sitar and Flute.

  ii. Mr Ajay is a Doctor and can play Sarod.

  iii. The Sitarist is not an Engineer.

  iv. Mr Vinay and Mr Bijay are not Architects and Vinay cannot play Tabla.

  v. Mr Bijay can play Violin.

  vi. Mr Akshay is a Lawyer and can play Flute.

17. Which instrument does Mr. Vinay play?
    (1) Sarod   (2) Sitar   (3) Violin   (4) Flute

18. What is the profession of Mr. Bijay?
    (1) Architect   (2) Doctor
    (3) Lawyer   (4) Engineer

19. Who is an Architect?
    (1) Mr. Ajay   (2) Mr. Akshay
    (3) Mr. Bijay   (4) Mr. Sanjay

20. What is the profession of Mr. Vinay?
    (1) Doctor   (2) Engineer
    (3) Lawyer   (4) CA

21. Which instrument can the Doctor learn from the Architect?
    (1) Flute   (2) Sitar
    (3) Tabla   (4) Sarod

Solution:

Let us represent the three groups in a table. By taking the group of gentlemen as the base, because most of the information given is with regard to the gentlemen, we will try filling in the other details/elements of the other two groups in the table, as shown below.

From ii, we get the combination Ajay-Doctor-Sarod.

From iii, we get to know that Sitar ≠ Engineer.

From iv, (Vinay, Bijay) ≠ Architects and Vinay ≠ Tabla.

From v, Bijay = Violin.

From vi, we get the combination Akshay - Lawyer -Flute.

Putting the above details in the table as shown below.

Gentlemen	Profession	Instrument
Ajay	Doctor	Sarod
Bijay	×Architect	Violin
Vinay	×Architect	×Tabla
Sanjay		
Akshay	Lawyer	Flute

Now, here we observe that neither Bijay nor Vinay is the Architect, hence the remaining person Sanjay is the Architect. Similarly, Sanjay plays Table and hence Vinay plays Sitar. This means that Bijay is the Engineer (from iii) and Vinay is the CA.

We get the final arrangement as shown below :

Gentlemen	Profession	Instrument
Ajay	Doctor	Sarod
Bijay	Engineer	Violin
Vinay	CA	Sitar
Sanjay	Architect	Tabla
Akshay	Lawyer	Flute

Now, based on the above table, let us answer the questions.

17. 2 Mr. Vinay plays Sitar.

18. 4 Mr. Bijay is the Engineer.

19. 4 Mr. Ajay is the Architect.

20. 4 Mr. Vinay is the CA.

21. 3 The Doctor can learn Tabla from the Architect.

4. COMPARISONS

In such kind of problems, some elements are compared with each other in terms of measurables (like height, weight, speed, size, marks, etc.). Let us have a look at the following example.

22. Among five boys, Vasant is taller than Manohar, but not as tall as Raju. Jayant is taller than Dutta, But shorter than Manohar. Who is the tallest in the group?
    (1) Raju
    (2) Manohar
    (3) Vasant
    (4) Can't be determined

Solution:

Arranging the given information, we get

Raju > Vasant > Manohar > Jayant > Dutta

So, Raju is the tallest.

5. SELECTIONS

In these problems, some teams are made from the given people in accordance with the conditions. The most common statements are: 1. A and B are in the same team. 2. A and B cannot be in the same team. 3. A and B are in different teams. Let us look at the following example.

23. Two teams of three members each, have to be selected from among six persons - P, Q, R, S, T and U. P and R cannot be in the same team. Q and S must be in the same team. R and T cannot be in the same team. Which of the following must be one of the two teams selected?
    (1) P, T and U   (2) P, Q and T
    (3) P, S and R   (4) Q, R and T

Solution:

As P and R can not be in the same team and R and T cannot be in the same team, R must be with Q and S. Hence, the other team is P, T and U.

6. SERIES-BASED

In these kind of problems, you'll see a series consisting of numbers, letters or symbols as the elements. Any one of these is selected and the following type of questions are posed.

(i) How many X are such that each is immediately preceded by Y and immediately followed with Z_x?

(ii) How many X and are such that each is immediately preceded by Y but not immediately followed with Z?

(iii) How many X are such that each is not immediately preceded by Y but immediately followed with Z?

(iv) How many X are such that each is neither immediately preceded by Y nor immediately followed with Z?

Let us look at the following example.

24. How many 6's are there in the following series of numbers which are preceded by 7 but not immediately followed by 9?
6 7 9 5 6 9 7 6 8 7 6 7 8 6 9 4 6 7 7 6 9 5 6 7 6 3
(1) one   (2) two
(3) three   (4) four

Solution:

All the 6's that satisfy the given condition are underlined in the series.
6 7 9 5 6 9 <u>7 6</u> 8 <u>7 6</u> 7 8 6 9 4 6 7 7 6 9 5 <u>7 6</u> 3
So, in above series, 3 times, 6's are preceded by 7 but not immediately followed by 9.

7. RANKING

Here, a student may have a rank from the top or bottom of the result ranking list. The following generalisation can be used while solving such questions.

$$T = R_T + R_B - 1$$

where,

$T \rightarrow$ Total number of students in the class.
$R_T \rightarrow$ Rank from the top of the ranking list.
$R_B \rightarrow$ Rank from the bottom of the ranking list.

Let us look at the following example for better clarity.

25. In a class, Krishna is ranked 8th from the top and 48th from the bottom. How many students are there in his class?
(1) 56   (2) 55
(3) 57   (4) None of these

Solution: 2

Using the formula $T = R_T + R_B - 1$, we get
$T = 8 + 48 - 1 = 55$. Hence, there are 55 students in Krishna's class.

Now, please solve questions in the exercise based on the concepts discussed.

Exercise

Directions for questions 1 to 5: Answer the questions based on the following information.
  i. There are five friends.
  ii. They are standing in a row facing north.
  iii. Jayesh is to the immediate right of Alok.
  iv. Pramod is exactly between Bhagat and Subodh.
  v. Subodh is exactly between Jayesh and Pramod.

1. Who is at the extreme left end?
(1) Alok   (2) Bhagat
(3) Subodh   (4) Jayesh

2. Who is in the middle?
(1) Bhagat   (2) Jayesh
(3) Pramod   (4) Subodh

3. To find the answer to the above two questions, which of the given statements can be dispensed with?
(1) None   (2) Only ii
(3) Only iii   (4) Only iv

4. If five of them were to stand in a circle with the same arrangement, between which two people would Bhagat stand?
(1) Alok and Subodh   (2) Jayesh and Pramod
(3) Subodh and Pramod   (4) Alok and Pramod

5. If a new friend Sukhdev joins the group, and is standing to the right of Bhagat, who is his other neighbour (in the original linear arrangement)?
(1) Jayesh   (2) Pramod
(3) Subodh   (4) None of these

Directions for questions 6 to 10: Study the following information carefully and answer the questions given below it.
  i. Eleven students A, B, C, D, E, F, G, H, I, J and K are sitting in the first row of the class facing the teacher.
  ii. D, who is to the immediate left of F, is second to the right of C.
  iii. A is second to the right of E, who is at one of the ends.
  iv. J is the immediate neighbour of A and B and third to the left of G.
  v. J is second to the left of I.

6. Who is sitting in the middle of the row?
(1) C   (2) I   (3) B   (4) G

7. Which of the following group of friends could be sitting to the right of G?
(1) IBJA   (2) ICHDF   (3) CHDF   (4) CKDE

8. In the above seating arrangement, which of the following statements is superfluous?
   (1) I
   (2) II
   (3) III
   (4) None of superfluous

9. Which of the following statements is TRUE in the context of the above seating arrangement?
   (1) There are three students sitting between D and G.
   (2) G and C are neighbours sitting to the immediate right of H.
   (3) B is sitting between J and I.
   (4) K is between A and J.

10. If E and D, C and B, A and H and K and F interchange their positions, which of the following pairs of students is sitting at the ends?
    (1) D and E
    (2) E and F
    (3) D and K
    (4) K and F

Directions for questions 11 to 15: Read the given information carefully and answer the questions given below:

Eight persons L, M, N, P, Q, R, S and T are sitting for a round table conference facing the centre.
   i. R sits between L and S.
   ii. S, who is the neighbour of Q, sits 3 places to the right of T.
   iii. Q sits 2 places to the right of T.
   iv. M sits 3 places to the left of R.

11. Who sits opposite M?
    (1) P
    (2) L
    (3) Q
    (4) T

12. Between which two persons is S sitting?
    (1) L – Q
    (2) M – Q
    (3) R – Q
    (4) L – M

13. Who sits opposite S?
    (1) N
    (2) P
    (3) T
    (4) Either N or P

14. Who among the following is Q's neighbour?
    (1) P
    (2) R
    (3) L
    (4) S

15. Who Is L's neighbour on his left?
    (1) R
    (2) S
    (3) Q
    (4) T

Directions for questions 16 to 20: Answer the questions based on the following information.

B, C, D, E, F and G are to be seated at a round table. The following apply to the seating arrangement.

   i. D must sit next to F.
   ii. B cannot sit next to F.
   iii. C cannot sit next to G.

16. If D is one of the two people who sit next to E, then which of the following can sit next to E?
    (1) B
    (2) C
    (3) G
    (4) Either C or G

17. Who must sit on the chairs on either side of E, if B sits next to D and C sits next to F?
    (1) B and G
    (2) B and C
    (3) B and F
    (4) C and G

18. Who must sit directly across the table from F, if C sits next to D and E sits next to F?
    (1) C
    (2) B
    (3) D
    (4) E

19. If C sits to the immediate left of F, what is the total number of seating arrangements possible?
    (1) 1
    (2) 2
    (3) 3
    (4) 4

20. Who must sit in the chairs on either side of G, if C sits directly across the table from E?
    (1) C and D
    (2) D and E
    (3) E and F
    (4) B and E

Directions for questions 21 to 25: Read the information given carefully and answer the questions that follow.

Eight persons L, M, N, P, Q, R, S and T are sitting around a square table such that there are two on each side and they are all facing the centre of the table.
   i. P sits exactly between L and S.
   ii. Q sits two places to the left of L.
   iii. R and T are sitting along one side of the square table. R sits opposite L.
   iv. M sits two places to the left of R.

21. Who sits opposite P?
    (1) S
    (2) M
    (3) N
    (4) T

22. Who sits two places to the right of S?
    (1) P
    (2) M
    (3) T
    (4) L

23. Between which two persons is L sitting?
    (1) M-P
    (2) N-P
    (3) N-R
    (4) T-Q

24. Which of the following is a neighbour of L?
    (1) S
    (2) Q
    (3) P
    (4) R

25. Who sits opposite Q?
    (1) S
    (2) P
    (3) T
    (4) M

Directions for questions 26 to 30: Read the given information carefully and answer the questions given below:

Five books A, B, C, D and E have to be proofread in 6 hours where one hour needs to be spent per book.

   i. A break of one hour has to be taken in the third or the fourth hour.
   ii. The proofreading cannot start with A and has to end in C.
   iii. D has to immediately follow B with no break in-between.
   iv. A cannot be done immediately after D.
   v. A has to immediately precede E with no break in-between.

26. Which hour is the break?
   (1) Sixth   (2) Fourth   (3) Fifth   (4) Third

27. Which is the first book to be proofread?
   (1) D   (2) A   (3) B   (4) C

28. Which book is to be proofread immediately after the break?
   (1) D   (2) A   (3) B   (4) C

29. Which book is to be proofread immediately after D?
   (1) B   (2) E
   (3) C   (4) None of these

30. Which book is to be proofread immediately after E?
   (1) A   (2) E   (3) C   (4) B

Directions for questions 31 to 35: Read the given information carefully and answer the questions given below:

Six lectures on 6 different subjects Physics, Chemistry, Biology, Algebra, Geometry and Astronomy have to be scheduled (one on each day) across 7 days starting Sunday and ending Saturday. The schedule has to be drawn out for the subjects such that

   i. One day has to be a holiday and it can be neither Sunday nor Saturday.
   ii. Geometry has to be scheduled immediately after Algebra.
   iii. Physics cannot start the series in the week and has to be done exactly 2 days before Astronomy.
   iv. Biology has to be scheduled for Thursday and cannot immediatly follow Physics.

31. What subject will start the series of lectures?
   (1) Algebra   (2) Chemistry
   (3) Physics   (4) Biology

32. Which of the following days is a holiday?
   (1) Monday   (2) Tuesday
   (3) Wednesday   (4) Thursday

33. On which day is the lecture in Physics scheduled?
   (1) Monday   (2) Tuesday
   (3) Wednesday   (4) Friday

34. On which day is the lecture in Geometry scheduled?
   (1) Monday   (2) Tuesday
   (3) Wednesday   (4) Saturday

35. How many days after Physics is Biology scheduled?
   (1) One   (2) Three
   (3) Four   (4) Two

Directions for questions 36 to 40: Read the following information carefully and answer the questions given below.

   i. There are seven teachers 'A', 'B', 'C', 'D', 'E', 'F' and 'G' in a college. Each one of them teaches a different subject.
   ii. There are three female and four male teachers, and out of these, there are two pairs of couples.
   iii. 'C' who teaches Social Sciences is married to the teacher who teaches Chemistry.
   iv. 'E' and 'G' are female teachers who teach Zoology and Physics respectively.
   v. 'A' teaches Mathematics, and his wife does not teach Physics.
   vi. 'B' does not teach Chemistry or Commerce.
   vii. 'F' and 'D' are male teachers. 'F' is unmarried.

36. Which subject does 'F' teach?
   (1) Mathematics
   (2) Chemistry
   (3) Commerce
   (4) Social Sciences

37. Which subject does 'B' teach?
   (1) Physics
   (2) Commerce
   (3) Social Sciences
   (4) Cannot be determined

38. Which of the following are two pairs of couples?
    (1) DC and AE
    (2) AC and DE
    (3) GA and CD
    (4) Cannot be determined

39. Which subject does A's wife teach?
    (1) Chemistry
    (2) Zoology
    (3) Social Sciences
    (4) Cannot be determined

40. Who among the following are the males among
    the two couples?
    (1) AC
    (2) AE
    (3) AD
    (4) Cannot be determined

Directions for questions 41 to 45: Read the information given carefully and answer the questions that follow.

Amit, Bharati, Cheryl, Deepak and Eric are five friends sitting in a restaurant. They are wearing caps of five different colours – yellow, blue, green, white and red. Also, they are eating five different snacks – burgers, sandwiches, ice-cream, pastries and pizza.
  i.   The person wearing a red cap is eating pastries.
  ii. Amit does not eat icecream and Cheryl is eating sandwiches.
  iii. Bharati is wearing a yellow cap and Amit is wearing a blue cap.
  iv. Eric is eating pizza and is not wearing a green cap.

41. What is Amit eating?
    (1) Burgers   (2) Sandwiches
    (3) Ice cream   (4) Pastries

42. Who is wearing the green cap?
    (1) Amit   (2) Bharati
    (3) Cheryl   (4) Deepak

43. Who is eating icecream?
    (1) Amit   (2) Bharati
    (3) Cheryl   (4) Deepak

44. Which colour cap is Eric wearing?
    (1) Yellow   (2) Blue
    (3) Green   (4) White

45. Which of the following combinations is not correct?
    (1) Yellow cap + ice cream
    (2) Red cap + pastries
    (3) White cap + pizza
    (4) Bharati + burger

46. Ramesh is taller than Vinay, who is not as tall as Karan. Sanjay is taller than Anupam but shorter than Vinay. Who among them is the tallest?
    (1) Ramesh
    (2) Karan
    (3) Vinay
    (4) Cannot be determined

47. Among A, B, C and D, it is known that B is heavier than A and C but C is taller than B. D is not as tall as C, while A is the shortest. C is not as heavy as A. D is heavier than B but shorter than him. Who are the heaviest and the tallest, respectively?
    (1) B, C   (2) A, D
    (3) D, C   (4) C, D

48. A ranks 5th from the top in the class. B is 8th from the last. If C is ranked 6th after A and just in the middle of A and B, how many students are there in the class?
    (1) 25   (2) 26
    (3) 23   (4) 24

49. Three girls P, Q and R played 3 games of carrom. Each player is ranked in each game according to the points earned in that game. A player with the highest point is ranked first, and so on. Each girl got a different rank in each game. P got the second rank in the first game and R got the first rank in the second game, then who got the 3rd rank in the third game?
    (1) P
    (2) Q
    (3) R
    (4) Can't determined

50. Six students are sitting in a row. K is sitting exactly between V and R. V is sitting next to M. M is sitting next to B, who is sitting on the extreme left end and Q is sitting next to R. Who are sitting adjacent to V?
    (1) Q and K   (2) R and Q
    (3) B and M   (4) M and K

51. Six persons A, B, C, D, E and F are sitting around a circle facing towards centre. B is sitting exactly between F and C. A is sitting exactly between E and D. F is to the left of D. Who is sitting between A and F?
(1) B　　(2) C　　(3) D　　(4) E

52. Six books are kept one above the other. History book is just above the Computer book. The Math book is between the Civics book and the Physics book. The English book is between the History book and the Civics book, then which subject book is at the bottom of the pile of books?
(1) History　　(2) Physics
(3) Computer　　(4) Civics

53. In a concert, a musician had sung four classical Raagas viz. Bhairavi, Kedar, Todi and Durbari. Durbari was not sung before Bhairavi. Kedar was sung before Bhairavi. Todi was sung immediately after Durbari, then which Raaga was sung immediately after Bhairavi?
(1) Todi　　(2) Kedar
(3) Durbari　　(4) Can't say

54. Three students are to be selected in a team, from a group of six students - Ram, Shyam, Raju, Amit, Rohit and Dinesh - by satisfying the following conditions.
i.　Ram and Shyam cannot be in the same team.
ii.　Raju and Amit must be selected together.
iii.　Rohit and Dinesh cannot be in the same team.
Who among the following must be in the team?
(1) Ram　　(2) Shyam
(3) Amit　　(4) Dinesh

55. Three persons must be selected from among five persons - A, B, C, D and E. A and B cannot be together. A and D cannot be together. B and C must be together. Which of the following is the correct team?
(1) B, A and E　　(2) A, B and C
(3) A, D and B　　(4) B, C and F

56. If it is possible to make a meaningful word with the third, sixth and ninth letters of the word RESTAURANT, then what will be the first letter of the word? If no such word is possible, mark 'X' as your answer. If more than one such words are possible, mark 'M' as your answer.
(1) U　　(2) M
(3) S　　(4) X

57. If starting from the left, the first and the seventh, the second and the eighth, the third and the ninth ... and so on, letters of the word RELATIONSHIP are interchanged; what will be the third letter from the right, if the second half of the new word, thus formed is reversed?
(1) T　　(2) L
(3) A　　(4) E

58. How many pairs of letters are there in the word NECESSARY which have as many letters between them in the word as there are between them in the alphabet and in the same order?
(1) One　　(2) Two
(3) Three　　(4) Nill

59. How many numbers are there in the given series which are preceded by the number which can be divided by 3 and followed by the number which is divided by 2?
1 3 4 6 7 5 4 6 9 8 3 5 6 9 1 7 3 6 5 8 5 6
(1) 1　　(2) 4
(3) 2　　(4) Nill

60. How many A's are there in the following sequence which are immediately followed by B as well as immediately preceded by Z?
A M B Z A B M N A B Z A B A Z B A M Z B A B Z A B
(1) 1　　(2) 3
(3) 2　　(4) 4

Calendars

Introduction

The questions on this topic are very common in various competitive exams. The method of solving such questions lies in the concept of obtaining the number of **odd days.** Before jumping to the topic, let us review some of the basic concepts.

(1) Whenever the number of year is exactly divisible by 4 (except the century years), then it is a Leap year.

(2) Whenever the number of year is not divisible by 4, then it is an Ordinary year.

(3) In case of the century years, if the number of year is exactly divisible by 400, then it is a Leap year.

(4) In case of the century years, whenever the number of year is not divisible by 400, then it is an Ordinary year.

Ordinary year: An ordinary year can be defined as the year having 365 days which is equal to 52 weeks and an extra day.

Century year: A year is a century year if it is divisible by 100.

Non-Century year: A year is a non-century year if it is not a century year.

Leap year: A year is a leap year if it is a non-century year that is divisible by 4, or a century year that is divisible by 400.

How to find the number of odd days?

The total number of days for a specific period of time is when divided by 7, the remainder obtained in such a case is termed as the odd day(s).

Counting of Odd days:

i. 1 ordinary year = 365 days = 52 weeks + 1 odd day

ii. 1 leap year = 366 days = 52 weeks + 2 odd days

iii. 1st century years = 100 years = 76 ordinary years + 24 leap years = 76 + 2 × 24 = 124 odd days = 5 odd days

Now, based on the above fact, we can conclude that the number of odd days in

(i)   100 years = 5   (ii)   200 years = 3
(iii) 300 years = 1   (iv) 400 years = 0

The following points have been observed:

The following table is based on the fact that 1st January, 1 A.D. was a Monday. This table is helpful in solving the question which assumes the given information.

No. of odd days	1	2	3	4	5	6	7 or 0
Days	Mon.	Tue.	Wed.	Thu.	Fri.	Sat.	Sun.

(2) In an Ordinary year, the calendar for the month of January is the same as the calendar for the month of October. In short, **In an Ordinary year, January = October**.

(3) In a Leap year, the calendar for the month of January is the same for the month July. In short, **In a Leap year, January = July.**

Example 1:

Find the day of the week on 16th July, 1776.

Solution:

16th July, 1776 means
(1775 years + 6 months + 16 days)
Now, 1600 years have 0 odd days.
100 years have 5 odd days.
75 years contain 18 leap and 57 ordinary years and therefore, (36 + 57) or 93 or 2 odd days.
∴ 1775 years give 0 + 5 + 2 = 7 and so 0 odd days.
Also, number of days from 1st Jan, 1776 to 16th July, 1776
Jan.   Feb.   Mar.   Apr.   May   Jun.   Jul.
31 + 29 + 31 + 30 + 31 + 30 + 16
= 198 days = 28 weeks + 2 days = 2 odd days.
∴ Total number of odd days = 0 + 2 = 2.
Hence, the day on 16th July, 1776 was Tuesday.

Example 2 :

January 1, 1992 was a Wednesday. What day of the week was January 1, 1993?

Solution:

1992 being a leap year, it has 2 odd days. So, the first day of the year 1993 will be two days beyond Wednesday. i.e., it was Friday.

Example 3 :

On January 12, 1980, it was Saturday. The day of the week on January 12, 1979 was:

Solution:

The year 1979 being an ordinary year, it has 1 odd day. So, the day on 12th January 1980 is one day beyond the day on 12th January, 1979.

But, January 12, 1980 being Saturday, January 12, 1979 was Friday.

Example 4:

February 20, 1999 was Saturday. What day of the week was on December 30, 1997?

Solution:

The year during this interval was 1998 and it was not a leap year. Now, we calculate the no. of odd days in 1999 up to February 19:

January 1999 gives	3 odd days
19 February 1999 gives	5 odd days
1998, being ordinary year, gives	1 odd day
In 1997, December 30 and 31 give	2 odd days

∴ Total number of odd days = 3 + 5 + 1 + 2 = 11 days = 4 odd days.

Therefore, December 30, 1997 was 4 days before Saturday i.e., on Tuesday.

Example 5:

The year next to 1987 having the same calendar as that of 1987 is:

Solution:

Starting with 1987, we go on counting the number of odd days till the sum is divisible by 7.

Number of odd days = 1(1987) + 2(1988) + 1(1989) + 1(1990) + 1(1991) + 2(1992) + 1(1993) + 1(1994) + 1(1995) + 2(1996) + 1(1997) = 14/7 = 0 odd days.

So, the year next to 1987 having the same calendar as that of 1987 is 1998.

 **Exercise**

1. The first Republic Day of India was celebrated on 26th January, 1950. What was the day of the week on that date?
   (1) Wednesday   (2) Thursday
   (3) Friday   (4) Saturday

2. Mahatma Gandhi was born on 2nd October, 1869. The day of the week was
   (1) Wednesday   (2) Thursday
   (3) Friday   (4) Saturday

3. India got Independence on 15th August 1947. What was the day of the week ?
   (1) Wednesday   (2) Thursday
   (3) Friday   (4) Saturday

4. Smt Indira Gandhi died on 31st October, 1984. The day of the week was:
   (1) Monday   (2) Tuesday
   (3) Wednesday   (4) Friday

5. What day of the week was 20th June, 1837?
   (1) Monday   (2) Tuesday
   (3) Thursday   (4) Friday

6. If 23rd April, 1984 was a Monday, which day of the week was 15th August in that year?
   (1) Monday   (2) Wednesday
   (3) Tuesday   (4) Thursday

7. If 3rd March, 1984 was a Sunday, then which day of the week was 13th July, 1987?
   (1) Monday   (2) Sunday
   (3) Saturday   (4) Tuesday

8. If 10th April, 1883 was a Wednesday, then which day of the week was 23rd August, 1879?
   (1) Sunday   (2) Tuesday
   (3) Monday   (4) Friday

9. January 16, 1997 was a Thursday. What day of the week was January 4, 2000?
   (1) Monday   (2) Sunday
   (3) Tuesday   (4) Wednesday

10. March 5, 1999 was on Friday, what day of the week was March 5, 2000?
    (1) Friday   (2) Tuesday
    (3) Monday   (4) Sunday

11. Monday falls on 4th April, 1988. What was the day on 3rd November, 1987?
    (1) Tuesday   (2) Sunday
    (3) Monday   (4) Wednesday

12. The year after 1991 having the same calendar as that of 1991 is:
    (1) 1998   (2) 2001   (3) 2002   (4) 2003

13. Which year will have the same calendar as that of 2004?
    (1) 2008   (2) 2012   (3) 2032   (4) 2030

14. If a year starts and ends with Monday, then how many Mondays, are there in that year?
    (1) 51   (2) 53
    (3) 52   (4) Can't say

15. Which dates of April, 2012 will be a Sunday?
    (1) 1, 8, 15, 22, 29   (2) 3, 10, 17, 24, 31
    (3) 2, 9, 16, 23, 30   (4) Can't say

Clocks **10**

Introduction

Many a times, questions appear on clocks in certain exams. Here, we discuss some concepts related to clocks covering all type of questions asked.

The dial of a clock is a circle whose circumference is divided into 12 parts, called **hour spaces**. Each hour space is further divided into 5 parts, called **minute spaces**. This way, the whole circumference is divided into 12 × 5 = 60 minute spaces.

The time taken by the hour hand (smaller hand) to cover a distance of an hour space is equal to the time taken by the minute hand (longer hand) to cover a distance of the whole circumference. Thus, we may conclude that **in 60 minutes, the minute-hand gains 55 minutes over the hour-hand.**

Note: The above statement (given in bold) is very much useful in solving the problems in this chapter, so it should be remembered. The above statement wants to say that: "In an hour, the hour-hand moves a distance of 5 minute spaces whereas the minute-hand moves a distance of 60 minute spaces. Thus, the minute-hand remains 60 – 5 = 55 minute spaces ahead of the hour-hand."

Some other facts :

1. In every hour, both the hands coincide once.
2. When the two hands are at right angle, they are 15 minute spaces apart. This happens twice in every hour.
3. When the hands are in opposite directions, they are 30 minute spaces apart. This happens once in every hour.
4. The hands are in the same straight line when they are opposite each other.
5. The hour hand moves around the whole circumference of clock once in 12 hours. So, the minute-hand is twelve times faster than the hour-hand.
6. The clock is divided into 60 equal minute divisions.
7. 1 minute division $= \dfrac{360°}{60} = 6°$ apart.
8. The clock has 12 hours numbered from 1 to 12 serially arranged.
9. Each hour number is evenly and equally separated by five minute divisions (= 5 × 6°) = 30° apart.
10. In one minute, the minute-hand moves one minute division or 6°.
11. In one minute, the hour hand moves $\dfrac{1°}{2}$.
12. In one minute the minute-hand gains $5\dfrac{1°}{2}$ more than the hour-hand.
13. When the hands are together, they are 0° apart. Hence,

θ	Formed in 12 hours	Formed in 24 hours
0° or 180°	11	22
90° or any other angle	22	44

As per the required angle difference between the minute-hand and the hour-hand and the initial (or starting) position of the hour-hand, different formulae are used to find out the required time. Now consider the **Rules (Quicker Methods)** given in the following pages.

Variants in a Clock: It is evident that the two hands of a clock will subtend an angle 'θ' between them. At any time, the same can be found out using the following formula:

$$\theta = \frac{11}{2}m - 30h \quad \left(\text{when } \frac{11}{2}m > 30h\right)$$
$$\text{or}$$
$$\theta = 30h - \frac{11}{2}m \quad \left(\text{when } 30h > \frac{11}{2}m\right)$$

(here m = minutes and h = hours)

Example 1:

At what time between 3 O'clock and 4 O'clock, will the minute-hand and the hour-hand of a clock coincide with each other?

Solution:

When the two hands of a clock coincide with each other the angle between them is 0°.

$$\theta = \frac{11}{2}m - 30h$$

Here,

$\theta = 0°$ and h = 3

$\therefore O = \dfrac{11}{2}m - 30h \qquad\qquad \therefore \dfrac{11}{2}m = 30 \times 3$

$\therefore m = \dfrac{90 \times 2}{11} = 16\dfrac{4}{11}$ min.

Therefore, the two hands of the clock are coincide at $16\dfrac{4}{11}$ min. past 3.

Example 2 :

At what time between 4 O'clock and 5 O'clock will the hands of a clock be in the same straight line but not together?

Solution:

When the two hands of the clock are in the same straight line but not together then the angle between them is 180°.

$$\boxed{\theta = \frac{11}{2}m - 30h}$$

Here, h = 4 and $\theta = 180°$

$$180 = \frac{11}{2}m - 30 \times 4$$

$$\therefore m = \frac{(180 + 30 \times 4) \times 2}{11} = 54\frac{6}{11} \text{min.}$$

Therefore, the hands of the clock are on the same straight line at 4 hours $54\frac{6}{11}$ min.

Example 3:

What is the angle between the minute-hand and the hour-hand of a clock at 3 hrs. 20 min.?

Solution:

$$\boxed{\theta = \frac{11}{2}m - 30h}$$

θ = angle   m = minutes   h = hours

Here, m = 20 and h = 3

$$\theta = \frac{11}{2} \times 20 - 30 \times 3 = 110 - 90 = 20°$$

$$\boxed{\therefore \theta = 20°}$$

Gain or Lose: In a correct clock hands of a clock coincide every $65\frac{5}{11}$ min.

If hands of a clock coincide in less than $65\frac{5}{11}$ min. then clock gains time and if hands of a clock coincide in more than $65\frac{5}{11}$ min. then clock loses time.

Example 4:

The minute-hand of a clock overtakes the hour-hand at intervals of 65 minutes of the correct time. How much in a day does the clock gain or lose?

Solution:

In a correct clock, the hands of a clock coincide every $65\frac{5}{11}$ minutes. But in this case they are

together again after 65 minutes, hence clock gains time.

$$\text{Gain in 65 minutes} = \left(65\frac{5}{11} - 65\right) = \frac{5}{11} \text{ minutes.}$$

$\therefore$ Gain in one day (24×60 min.)

$$= \frac{5}{11} \times \frac{60}{65} \times 24 = \frac{5 \times 288}{143} \text{ min.} = 10\frac{10}{143} \text{min.}$$

Too Fast And Too Slow:

If a watch indicates 9.20, when the correct time is 9.10, it is said to be 10 minutes too fast. And if it indicates 9.00, when the correct time is 9.10, it is said to be 10 minutes too slow.

Example 5:

A watch, which gains uniformly, was observed to be 5 minutes, slow at 10 a.m. on a Tuesday. On the next day at 11 a.m. it was noticed that watch was 5 minutes fast. When did the watch show the correct time?

Solution:

Total hours from 10 a.. Tuesday to 11 a.m. on next day = 25 hours.
The watch gains (5 + 5) = 10 minutes in 25 hours.
The watch gains 5 min. in

$$\left(\frac{25}{10} \times 5\right) = \frac{125}{10} \text{hrs.} = 12\frac{1}{2} \text{hrs.}$$

$$= 12\frac{1}{2} \text{hours from 10 a.m. Tuesday}$$

$$= 10 : 30 \text{ p.m. Tuesday}$$

Example 6:

There are two clocks, both set to show the correct time at 10 p.m. One clock gains one minute in an hour while the other gains 2 minutes in one hour, then by how many minutes do the two clocks differ at 10 a.m. on the next day?

Solution:

Difference in minutes between the two clocks in one hour = 1 minute. Total number of hours (10 p.m to 10 a.m. on next day) = 12 hours. The two clocks differ by = 1 × 12 = 12 minutes

Example 7:

If the time in a clock is 8 hours 20 minutes, then what time does it show on the mirror?

Solution:

The time shown by the clock, when seen in the mirror is
= 12 hours – 8 hours 20 minutes
= 3 hours 40 minutes

Exercise

1. A clock is started at noon. By 10 minutes past 5, the angle that the hour-hand has turned through is:
   (1) 145° (2) 150° (3) 155° (4) 160°

2. An accurate clock shows 8 O'clock in the morning. Through how many degrees will the hour-hand rotate when the clock shows 2 O'clock in the afternoon ?
   (1) 144° (2) 150° (3) 168° (4) 180°

3. At what time between 9 O'clock and 10 O'clock will the hands of a watch coincide?

   (1) 10 hrs. $49\frac{1}{11}$ min. (2) 9 hrs. $49\frac{1}{11}$ min.

   (3) 11 hrs. $49\frac{1}{11}$ min. (4) 9 hrs. $59\frac{1}{11}$ min.

4. The angle between the minute-hand and the hour-hand of a clock when the time is 8 : 30, is:
   (1) 80° (2) 75° (3) 60° (4) 105°

5. At what time between 5 and 6 O'clock are the hands of a clock 3 minutes apart?

   (1) 24 min. past 5 (2) $30\frac{6}{11}$ min. past 5
   (3) 30 min. past 5 (4) Both (1) and (2)

6. How many times do the hands of a clock coincide in a day?
   (1) 20 (2) 21 (3) 22 (4) 24

7. The minute-hand of a clock overtakes the hour-hand at interval of 64 minutes of the correct time. How much does the clock gain or lose in a day?

   (1) $32\frac{8}{11}$ min. (2) $36\frac{5}{11}$ min.
   (3) 90 min. (4) 96 min.

8. The minute-hand of a clock overtakes the hour-hand at intervals of 67 minutes of a correct time. How much in a day does the clock gain or lose?

   (1) $53\frac{169}{187}$ minutes (2) $53\frac{168}{186}$ minutes
   (3) $53\frac{170}{187}$ minutes (4) $54\frac{169}{187}$ minutes

9. A watch which gains uniformly is 2 minutes slow at noon on Monday and is 4 min. 48 sec fast at 2 p.m. on the following Monday. When did it show the correct time?
   (1) 2 p.m. on Tuesday
   (2) 2 p.m. on Wednesday
   (3) 3 p.m. on Thursday
   (4) 1 p.m on Friday

10. A watch which gains 5 seconds in 3 minutes was set right at 7 a.m. In the afternoon of the same day, when the watch indicated quarter past 4 O'clock, the true time is :

    (1) $59\frac{7}{12}$ min. past 3 (2) 4 p.m.

    (3) $58\frac{7}{12}$ min. past 3 (4) $2\frac{3}{11}$ min. past 4

11. A watch, which gains uniformly is 6 minutes slow at 4 p.m. on a Sunday and $10\frac{2}{3}$ minutes fast on the following Sunday at 8 a.m. When did it show the correct time?
    (1) 2 : 00 a.m. on Monday
    (2) 1 : 36 a.m. on Tuesday
    (3) 1 : 36 a.m. on Wednesday
    (4) 1 : 36 a.m. on Thursday

12. A clock gains 10 minutes in every 24 hours. It is set right on Monday at 8 a.m. What will be the correct time on the following Wednesday, when the watch indicates 6 p.m.?
    (1) 5 : 30 p.m. (2) 5 : 24 p.m
    (3) 5 : 36 p.m. (4) 5 : 20 p.m.

13. A clock is set right at 5 a.m. The clock loses 16 min. in 24 hrs. What will be the true time when the clock indicates 10 p.m. on the 4th day?
    (1) 12 p.m. (2) 11 a.m.
    (3) 11 p.m. (4) 10 a.m.

14. There are two clocks, both set to show the correct time at 10 a.m. One clock gains two minutes in one hour while the other gain one minute in one hour. If the clock which gains 2 minute shows the time as 22 minute past 9 p. m. On the same day, then what time the other watch show?
    (1) 9 hrs. 33 min. (2) 9 hrs. 12 min.
    (3) 9 hrs. 11 min. (4) 9 hrs. 23 min.

15. If the time in a clock is 6 hours 45 minutes, then what time does it show on the mirror?
    (1) 4 hrs. 15 min. (2) 5 hrs. 45 min.
    (3) 5 hrs. 15 min. (4) 5 hrs. 30 min.

Introduction

This variety of question - type was introduced in an aptitude test years back and was later on seen repeated in other aptitude tests as well. Not much explanatory material or elaborate descriptive explanations are made available by any book or institute, to counter such problems. Here, we will help the student develop his insight into this type of questions, and enable him solve any problem, how so ever twisted it may seem.

As the topic name suggests, we will have to ascertain the status of a statement - whether the statement is true or it is false.

Usually, there are three categories, which are defined as below.

  (i) **THE TRUTH - TELLER:** This is a person who always tells the truth and is to be believed. In short all his statements hold good as true statements.

  (ii) **THE LIAR:** This is a person who always tells a lie and is NOT to be believed. In short, all his statements are always false.

  (iii) **THE ALTERNATOR:** This is a person who always alternates between the truth and lie, in any order. If an alternator makes two statements, then one statement is true and the other statement is false. The order of the status could be **True - False** or **False - True**.

Following are some of the types of questions that have been asked in various aptitude tests.

Type A : When the status of a statement becomes evident.

Type B : When the status of a statement is determined by assumption.

Let us understand each of these types with the help of some examples.

Type A : Some of the statements, as shown below, are self - descriptive and their actual status can be known, thus giving a head-start in cracking the question.

Statement : I am the liar.

Now who would say that? A truth - teller?

No, a truth - teller won't say that he is the liar. Instead, he would say that I am the truth - teller. Then? Will a liar

make such a statement? Not at all. A liar won't tell you the truth by admitting that he is a liar. Instead, he would say that he is NOT a liar. Now, that leaves us with the third category - The alternator. The status of the statement will be FALSE, as the alternator is making a false statement by saying that he is the liar. This means his other statement must be true.

So, whenever you see the statement "I am the liar", please know that it is spoken by only an alternator and the statement is false.

Statement : I am not the truth - teller.

This statement, again, can be spoken only by an alternator and is true.

There are many such statements, depending on the categories mentioned in the question, whose status becomes evident.

Type B : The status of a statement, whether it is true or false, can be found out by initially assuming the status. If the assumption gives rise to ambiguity, then it is ignored and the next set of statements are subjected to an assumption.

It depends on what categories are given in a question. If a truth - teller is mentioned in the questions, then one - by - one each person should be assumed to be a truth - teller, which will get you the actual truth - teller, whenever the assumption fits in the arrangement and no statement in the question seems violated.

Let us view some of the examples.

Example 1:
Three persons - A, B and C - were asked a question. "Who among you is the lawyer?". Each of them gave the following replies.
A : I am the lawyer.
   B is the liar.
B : I am the lawyer.
   C is the alternator.
C : A is the liar.
   I am the lawyer.

It is known that there is only one truth - teller, one liar and one alternator amongst these three. If only one of them is a lawyer, who is the lawyer?
(1) A   (2) B
(3) C   (4) Cannot be determined

Solution: 2

Let us first assume that A is the truth - teller. By assessing his statements, we get the following arrangement.

Persons	Statements		Lawyer
	I	II	
A	T	T	√
B	F	(F)	x
C			x

When we assume A as the truth - teller, we consider both his statements to be true - by virtue of which A is the lawyer (and nobody else is the lawyer) and B is the liar. This means that the remaining person C should be the alternator, which creates ambiguity as this was spoken by B, whose statement should have been false as according to A, he is the liar.

Hence, we ignore this assumption and now assume B to be the truth - teller, to get the following arrangement.

Persons	Statements		Lawyer
	I	II	
A	F	F	x
B	T	T	√
C	T	F	x

As the arrangement does not violate any statement, this means that B is the truth - teller, A is the liar and C is the alternator. Hence, B is the lawyer.

Example 2:

Three alternators - X, Y and Z - were asked a question, "Who among you is the doctor?". Following were their replies.

X : I am the doctor.

   Z is the engineer.

Y : X is the engineer.

   I am the doctor.

Z : X is the broker.

   Y is the engineer.

It is know that each has only one profession out of doctor, engineer and broker. Which of the following gives the complete and correct list of the person and his profession?

(1) X - Broker, Y - Engineer, Z - Doctor

(2) Y - Doctor, X - Broker, Z - Engineer

(3) Z - Engineer, Y - Broker, X - Doctor

(4) None of the above

Solution: 2

As each of them is an alternator, let as assume X's first statement to be true and second to be false, to get the following arrangement.

Persons	Statements		Professions
	I	II	
X	T	F	Dr.
Y	(F)	(F)	Er.
Z			X Er.

Here, the ambiguity arises for Y's statements. This means that our initial assumption, that X's first statement is true and second is false, is incorrect. Hence, now we will assume X's first statement to be false and second to be true, to get the following arrangement.

Persons	Statements		Professions
	I	II	
X	F	T	Broker
Y	F	T	Dr.
Z	T	F	Er.

Here, the arrangement is valid, as it does not violate any of the given statements. Hence, choice (2) gives the correct arrangement.

Let us solve the exercise based in the concepts learned so far.

Exercise

Directions for questions 1 to 4: These questions are based on the following data.

There are three friends-Ajay, Vijay and Mahesh-each always makes two statements. Exactly one among them is the truth-teller, one is liar and one always alternates between the truth and lie, in any order. When each was asked "What is your profession?," following were there replies.

Mahesh	: I am an Engineer.
	Vijay is the Doctor.
Vijay	: I am a Scientist.
	Ajay is the Doctor.
Ajay	: Mahesh is the Doctor.
	Vijay is the Scientist.

Each of them has a different profession among Doctor, Engineer and Scientist.

1. Who is the Scientist?
   (1) Mahesh   (2) Vijay
   (3) Ajay   (4) None of the above.

2. Who is the truth-teller?
   (1) Ajay   (2) Mahesh
   (3) Vijay   (4) None of the above.

3. Who is the lier?
   (1) Ajay   (2) Vijay
   (3) Mahesh   (4) None of the above.

4. What is the profession of Ajay?
   (1) Engineer   (2) Scientist
   (3) Vijay   (4) None of the above.

Direction for questions 5 to 7: These questions are based on the following information.

In 'Ha-Na' village, people always make two statements while replying to any question, one of which is always true and other one is always false. One day I met three people Krishna, Dinesh and Anuj of 'Ha-Na' Village. Each is a professor for a different subject amongst Biology, Chemistry and Maths. When asked about them, the following were their replies.

Krishna : I am a Biology Professor.
Anuj is the Chemistry Professor.

Dinesh : I am a Biology Professor.
Krishna is the Chemistry Professor.

Anuj : I am a Biology professor.
Krishna is the Maths professor.

5. Who is the Chemistry professor?
   (1) Anuj   (2) Krishna
   (3) Dinesh   (4) None of the above

6. Who is the Biology professor?
   (1) Krishna   (2) Dinesh
   (3) Anuj   (4) None of the above

7. Who is the Maths professor?
   (1) Anuj   (2) Dinesh
   (3) Krishna   (4) None of the above

Directions for questions 8 to 11: These question are based on the following data.

There are three friends - Sania, Megha and Manasi. Each of them likes a different colour among blue, red and green, not necessarily in the same order. When asked about the colour each likes, each of them gives two replies. Exactly two of them are alternators and one is the truth-teller.

The following were their replies:

Sania : I like blue colour.
Megha likes red colour.

Megha : I like green colour.
Sania likes red colour.

Manasi : I do not like blue colour.
Sania does not like green colour.

8. Who is the truth-teller ?
   (1) Sania   (2) Manasi
   (3) Megha   (4) None of the above

9. Who likes Red colour ?
   (1) Megha   (2) Sania
   (3) Manasi   (4) None of the above

10. Which colour does Sania like ?
    1. Blue
    2. Green
    3. Red
    4. None of the above

11. Which colour does Megha like ?
    (1) Blue   (2) Green
    (3) Red   (4) None of the above

Direction for question 12 to 15 : These questions are based on the following data.

There are three players - Ram, Sachin and Rahul. Each of them plays exactly one game among Chess, Carrom and Cricket. Each of them always gives three statements while replying to any question. Out of these three players, exactly one is the truth-teller, exactly one is liar and exactly one is alternator. When I asked them "Which game do you play?", the following were their replies.

Ram : I play chess.
Rahul does not play carrom.
Sachin plays carrom.

Sachin : I play chess.
Ram plays carrom.
Rahul does not play carrom.

Rahul : Sachin plays carrom.
Ram plays chess.
I do not play cricket.

12. Who among the three players is a liar ?
    (1) Rahul   (2) Sachin
    (3) Ram   (4) None of the above

13. Who among the three players is the truth - teller ?
    (1) Rahul   (2) Sachin
    (3) Ram   (4) None of the above

14. Who plays chess ?
    (1) Ram   (2) Rahul
    (3) Sachin   (4) None of the above

15. Who plays cricket ?
    (1) Sachin
    (2) Ram
    (3) Rahul
    (4) None of the above

Directions for questions 16 to 20: Answer the following questions.

16. In 'T - F' city there are two type of peoples- truth-tellers and liars. One day I met two people Raj and Nilesh of 'T - F' city and when I asked them, "Who among you is the truth-teller?", their replies were as follows:

    Raj   :   Nilesh is a truth-teller.
    Nilesh   :   Raj is not a liar.

    Who is the truth - teller ?
    (1) Only Raj
    (2) Only Nilesh
    (3) Both are truth-tellers or both are liars.
    (4) None of the above

17. In 'Ha - Na' village there are two types of peoples - truth-tellers and liars. One day I met three people Ajay, Ravi and Krishna of 'Ha - Na' village and when I asked them 'Who among you is the truth-teller ?', their replies were as follows.

    Krishna   :   Ravi is a truth-teller.
    Ravi   :   Krishna is not a liar.
    Ajay   :   I am not a liar.

    It is known that only one among Krishna, Ravi and Hemant is the truth teller?
    Who could be the truth-teller?
    (1) Ajay   (2) Krishna
    (3) Ravi   (4) None of these

18. Amit, Mohit and Manish are three friends. When asked, "Who among you is the heaviest?", following were their replies.

    Amit   :   I am the heaviest.
                      Mohit is the lightest.
    Mohit   :   I am the heaviest.
                      Amit is not the heaviest.
    Manish   :   Mohit is the heaviest.
                      Amit is the lightest.

    It is known that one among them is the truth-teller, other two are liars.

    Who is the truth-teller ?
    (1) Amit   (2) Manish
    (3) Mohit   (4) None of the above

19. There are three friends - Amit, Raja and Albert amongst when there is only one singer. Exactly one among them is the truth-teller, one is liar and one is the alternator. When I asked them "Who among you is the singer?", their replies were as follows.

    Amit   :   I am not the singer.
                      Raja is the singer.
    Raja   :   I am not the singer.
                      Amit and Albert are the singers.
    Albert   :   Amit is the not singer.
                      Raja is not the singer.

    Who is the singer ?
    (1) Amit   (2) Albert
    (3) Raja   (4) None of these

20. Three friends P, Q and R - always make two statements while replying to any question. One of them is the truth-teller, one is liar and one is alternator. When I asked them "Who among you is the thief?", their replies were as follows:

    P   :   Q is the thief.
                      R is the liar.
    Q   :   I am the thief.
                      P is the liar.
    R   :   I am the thief.
                      Q is the liar.

    If only one among P, Q and R is the thief, then who is the thief?
    (1) P   (2) Q
    (3) R   (4) None of these

Reasoning

Introduction

A cube is a solid which has 6 faces, 8 corners and 12 edges.

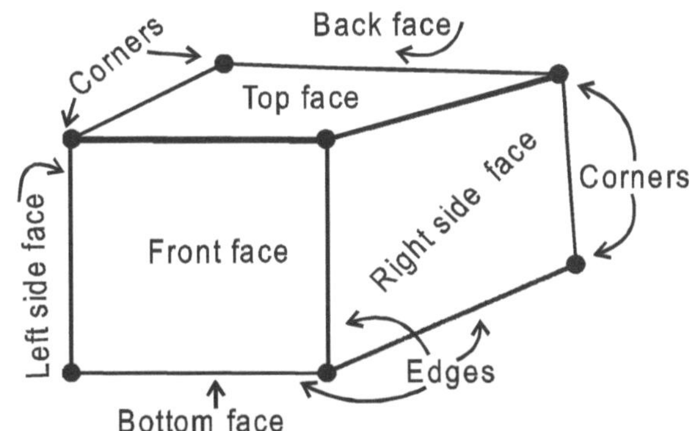

Following are some of the important types based on which questions have been asked in various aptitude tests.

(i) Number of cuts given to a cube is given, find the **maximum** number of identical pieces that can be produced.

(ii) Number of pieces a cube is cut into is given, find the **least** number of cuts required to produce these many pieces.

(iii) Miscellaneous types.

It must be remembered that in order to obtain the maximum number of pieces, the cuts given to a large cube must be divided as equally as possible in three different directions.

Let us discuss each of these types with the help of examples.

(i) **Number of cuts = given;**
Maximum number of pieces = ?

(a) Whenever the number of cuts made to a cube is a multiple of 3.

If 'n' is the number of pieces along each edge,

and $n = \left(\dfrac{\text{Total cuts}}{3}\right) + 1$, then

Maximum number of identical pieces = n^3
Number of pieces with 3 faces visible = 8
Number of pieces with 2 faces visible = $12(n-2)$
Number of pieces with 1 face visible = $6(n-2)^2$
Number of pieces with no face visible = $(n-2)^3$

Let us take an example where 30 cuts are made to a large cube to get the maximum number of pieces. Here,

the value of 'n' will be $\dfrac{30}{3} + 1 = 11$. Then,

- Maximum number of pieces = $n^3 = 11^3 = 1331$.
- Number of 3 - face visible pieces = 8.
- Number of 2 - faces visible pieces = $12(n-2)$ = $12(11-2) = 108$.
- Number of 1- face visible pieces = $6(n-2)^2$ = $6(11-2)^2 = 486$.
- Number of no face visible pieces = $(n-2)^3$ = $(11-2)^3 = 729$.

(b) Whenever the number of cuts made to the large cube is NOT a multiple of 3.

In such a case, there is no direct formula for finding out the 2 - faces visible, 1 - face visible or no face visible pieces, but the maximum number of pieces produced can be found out.

Let us consider that a large cube is given 4 cuts. Now 4 cuts are divided into three directions as 1 cut, 1 cut, 2 cuts. We know that the number of pieces along each edge is one more than the number of cuts along that edge (when all cuts are made in the same direction - parallel to the same pair of faces). We can represent the above as shown below:

$$
\begin{array}{ccccc}
1 & & 1 & & 2 \\
+1 & & +1 & & +1 \\
\hline
2 & \times & 2 & \times & 3
\end{array} = 12 \text{ pieces.}
$$

Similarly, 11 cuts will give us maximum 100 pieces, as shown below:

$$
\begin{array}{ccccc}
3 & & 4 & & 4 \\
+1 & & +1 & & +1 \\
\hline
4 & \times & 5 & \times & 5
\end{array} = 100 \text{ pieces.}
$$

(ii) **Number of pieces = given,**
Least number of cuts = ?

We use the reverse process. To get the least number of cuts to produce 100 pieces, factorise 100 into 3 factors with least difference between them, and then subtract one from each of them, as shown below:

$$
\begin{array}{ccccc}
100 = & 4 & \times & 5 & \times & 5 \\
& -1 & & -1 & & -1 \\
\hline
& 3 & + & 4 & + & 4 & = 11 \text{ cuts}
\end{array}
$$

(iii) **Miscellaneous types:**

Apart from the above two types, a cube can be coloured with one, two or more colours, and then is given some number of cuts.

Let us study and practice each of the above types with the questions given in the exercise.

Exercise

1. Maximum number of identical pieces a cube can be cut into by 6 cuts are ____
   (1) 32   (2) 30   (3) 27   (4) 24

2. Maximum number of identical pieces a cube can be cut into by 4 cuts are ____
   (1) 12   (2) 11   (3) 10   (4) 9

3. Maximum number of identical pieces a cube can be cut into by 17 cuts are ____
   (1) 294   (2) 258   (3) 230   (4) 268

4. Maximum number of identical pieces a cube can be cut into by 27 cuts are ____
   (1) 1000   (2) 1020   (3) 980   (4) 1050

5. What is the least number of cuts required to cut a cube into 100 identical pieces?
   (1) 10   (2) 9   (3) 11   (4) 8

6. What is the least number of cuts required to cut a cube into 48 identical pieces?
   (1) 8   (2) 4   (3) 6   (4) 5

7. There is a cube of 64 identical pieces. How many more such small cubes will be required to cover this cube completely?
   (1) 150   (2) 151   (3) 152   (4) 48

8. If a cube is cut into identical pieces by giving 8 cuts, each parallel to the same pair of faces, then maximum number of identical pieces that can be obtained by making two more cuts are ____
   (1) 30   (2) 24   (3) 32   (4) 28

Directions for questions 9 to 12: These questions are based on the given data.

A cube consisting of 216 identical smaller cubes is painted on all six faces.

9. How many of the smaller cubes have no face painted at all?
   (1) 64   (2) 56   (3) 50   (4) 50

10. How many of the smaller cubes have one face painted?
    (1) 90   (2) 80   (3) 96   (4) 76

11. How many of the smaller cubes have two faces painted?
    (1) 68   (2) 36   (3) 48   (4) 50

12. How many of the smaller cubes have exactly three faces painted?
    (1) 16   (2) 24   (3) 8   (4) 6

Directions for questions 13 to 16: These questions are based on the given data.

A large cube painted on all six faces is cut into 64 smaller but identical pieces.

13. How many of the smaller cubes have no faces painted at all?
    (1) 6   (2) 16   (3) 8   (4) 12

14. How many of the smaller cubes have exactly one face painted?
    (1) 32   (2) 27   (3) 24   (4) 16

15. How many of the smaller cubes have exactly two faces painted?
    (1) 30   (2) 36   (3) 24   (4) 27

16. How many of the smaller cubes have exactly three faces painted?
    (1) 6   (2) 12   (3) 8   (4) 16

Directions for questions 17 to 20: These questions are based on the given data.

A large cube is painted on all six faces and then cut into identical cubes. Among these smaller cubes, there were six cubes which had exactly one face painted.

17. How many smaller cubes was the original large cube cut into?
    (1) 125   (2) 36   (3) 27   (4) 64

18. How many smaller cubes have exactly two faces painted?
    (1) 12   (2) 8   (3) 10   (4) 6

19. How many smaller cubes have exactly three faces painted?
    (1) 10   (2) 8   (3) 12   (4) 6

20. How many smaller cubes have no faces painted at all?
    (1) 1   (2) 3   (3) 2   (4) 4

Reasoning

Venn Diagrams **13**

Introduction

Venn Diagrams are pictorial representation of sets making use of geometrical figures (generally circles). The number of sets for which the Venn Diagrams are to be drawn could be two, three or four sets.

1. Venn Diagrams for two sets:

If X and Y are two sets, then the following Venn diagram can be used to represent the two sets, their intersection and the universal set.

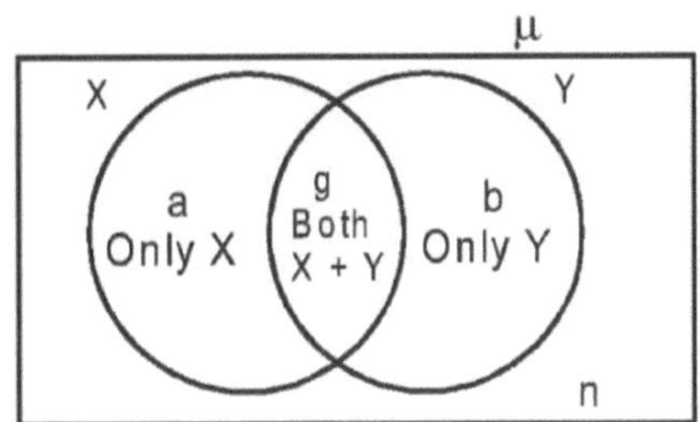

The following conclusions can be drawn from the above diagram.

(a) $\boxed{T = a + b + g}$, where T = those elements which are present in at least one of the two sets.

(b) $\boxed{\mu = T + n}$, where μ = Universal set or total number of samples; n = those elements which are present in none of the two sets.

(c) $\boxed{X + Y = T + g}$

Let us take an example. In a class of 100 students (μ), 70 pass in maths (X), 50 pass in English (Y) and 10 fail in both (n). Now, the following questions can be asked.

How many students ..

  (i) ... pass in at least one subject?

  (ii) ... pass in both the subjects?

  (iii) ... pass in only Maths?

  (iv) ... pass in only English?

  (v) ... fail in English?

  (vi) ... fail only in English?

  (vii) ... fail in Maths?

  (viii) ... fail only in Maths?

  (ix) ... pass in only one subject?

  (x) ... fail in only one subject?

Let us draw a Venn diagram to represent the above information.

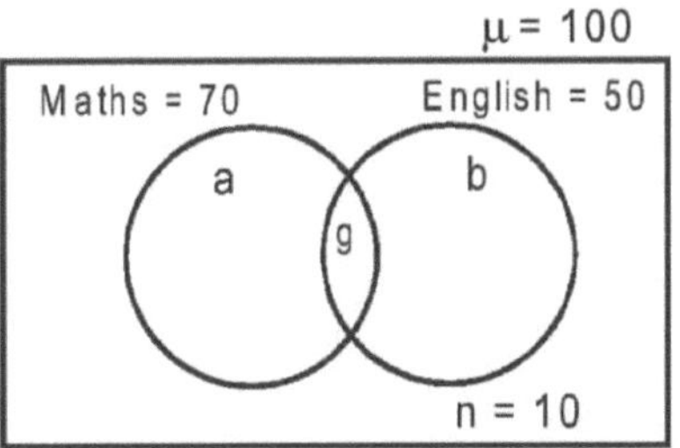

(i) $\mu = T + n \Rightarrow T = \mu - n = 100 - 10 = \mathbf{90}$.

(ii) $X + Y = T + g \Rightarrow 70 + 50 = 90 + g \Rightarrow g = \mathbf{30}$.

Now, let us fill in the remaining details i.e., 'a' and 'b' in the Venn diagram.

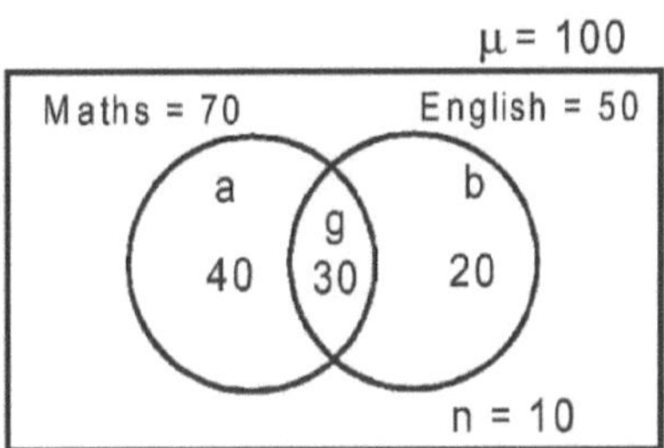

(iii) No. of students who **pass only in Maths** = a = **40**.

(iv) No. of students who **pass only in English** = b = **20**.

(v) No. of students who **fail in English** = a + n = 40 + 10 = **50**.

(vi) No. of students who **fail ONLY in English** = a = **40**.

(vii) No. of students who **fail in Maths** = b + g = 20 + 10 = **30**.

(viii) No. of students who **fail ONLY in Maths** = b = **20**.

(ix) No. of students who **pass in only one subject** = a + b = 40 + 20 = **60**.

(x) No. of students who **fail in only one subject** = a + b = 40 + 20 = **60**.

2. Venn Diagrams for three-sets:

If X, Y and Z are three sets, then the following Venn diagram can be used to represent the three sets and their intersections (intersections of two sets and of all the three sets).

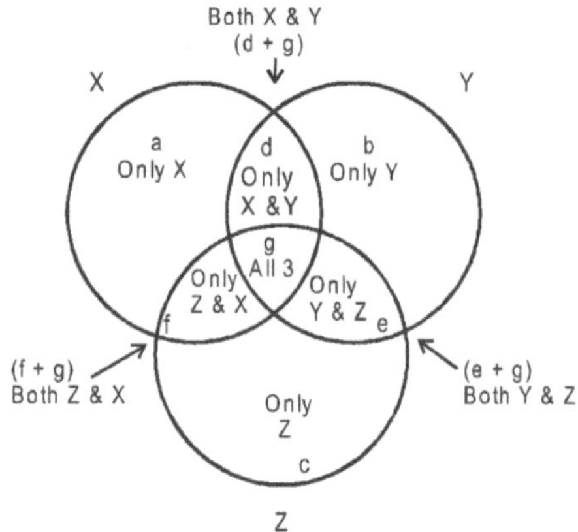

Following formulae are useful while solving questions.

(a) $\mu = T + n$

$$T = \underbrace{(a + b + c)}_{} + \underbrace{(d + e + f)}_{} + \underbrace{g}_{}$$

(b) At least = (Only one) + (Only two) + All 3
    one

(c) $X + Y + Z = T + (d + e + f) + 2g$

(d) $X + Y + Z = T(d + g) + (e + g) + (f + g) - g$

(e) $X + Y + Z = (a + b + c) + 2(d + e + f) + 3g$

(f) Neither X nor Y = $c + b$

(g) Neither Y nor Z = $a + n$

(h) Neither Z nor X = $b + n$

(i) Either X or Y = $T - c$

(j) Either Y or Z = $T - a$

(k) Either Z or X = $T - b$

(l) At least two = $(d + e + f) + g$

(m) At most two = $T + n - g = \mu - g$

(n) At most one = $n + (a + b + c)$

3. Venn diagrams for four-sets:

The four sets can be represented in the following way.

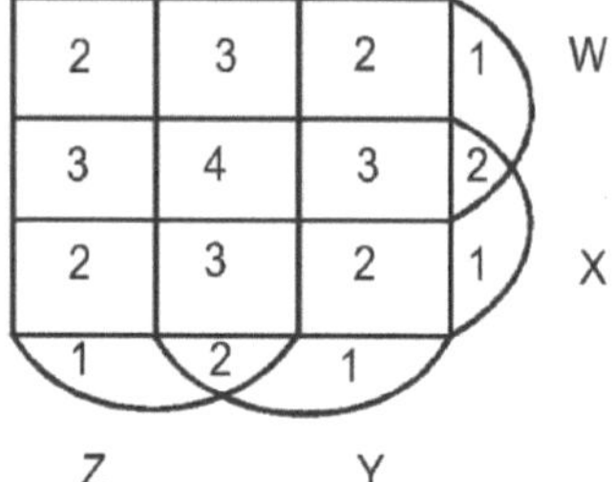

Where various regions are represented as below:

1s → No. of elements belonging to exactly one set.
2s → No. of elements belonging to exactly two sets.
3s → No. of elements belonging to exactly three sets.
4s → No. of elements belonging to all the four sets.

Let us solve questions from the exercise that follows, applying the concepts learnt so far.

 **Exercise**

Directions for questions 1 to 4: These questions are based on the following data.

In a class of 100 students, 50 students like Cricket, 30 students like Football and 20 students like both Cricket and Football.

1. How many students like only Cricket ?
    (1) 50   (2) 40
    (3) 30   (4) 20

2. How many students like only Football ?
    (1) 10   (2) 30
    (3) 20   (4) 50

3. How many students like neither Football nor Cricket?
    (1) 40   (2) 30
    (3) 50   (4) 20

4. How many students like at least one of Football or Cricket ?
    (1) 80   (2) 60
    (3) 40   (4) 30

Directions for questions 5 to 8 : These questions are based on the following data.

There are 120 workers in a company. 40% of the workers own a car, 20% of the workers own a bike and 10% of the workers own both bike and car.

5. How many workers own only a car ?
   (1) 36   (2) 24
   (3) 48   (4) 12

6. How many workers own only a bike ?
   (1) 24   (2) 36
   (3) 48   (4) 12

7. How many workers own at least a bike or a car ?
   (1) 80   (2) 60
   (3) 70   (4) 40

8. How many workers own neither a bike nor a car?
   (1) 72   (2) 24
   (3) 60   (4) 48

Directions for questions 9 to 12 : These questions are based on the following data.

In a class of 150 students, 85 students passed in Maths, 95 students passed in English and 120 students passed in Marathi. 65 students passed both in Maths and English, 60 students passed both in Maths and Marathi and 70 students passed in both English and Marathi. 50 students passed in English, Marathi and Maths.

9. How many students passed only in Maths ?
   (1) 10   (2) 30
   (3) 20   (4) 40

10. How many students passed only in Marathi?
    (1) 50   (2) 55
    (3) 60   (4) 40

11. How many students passed in both Marathi and English but not in Maths ?
    (1) 20   (2) 40
    (3) 30   (4) 50

12. How many students passed in both Maths and English but not in Marathi ?
    (1) 30.   (2) 15
    (3) 25   (4) 20

Directions for questions 13 to 17 : These questions are based on the following data.

In a class, students play three games, namely Cricket, Football and Hockey. 50 students play only one game, 25 students play exactly two games and 10 students play all the three games. All the students in a class play atleast one game.

13. How many students are there in the class ?
    (1) 85   (2) 95
    (3) 75   (4) 100

14. How many students play atleast two games?
    (1) 30   (2) 35
    (3) 45   (4) 40

15. How many students play cricket ?
    (1) 50
    (2) 25
    (3) 15
    (4) Cannot be determined

16. What is the percentage of students who plays exactly two games to that of students who play atleast one game ?
    (1) 42%   (2) 52%
    (3) 30%   (4) 60%

Direction for questions 17 to 20 : These questions are based on the following data.

In a certain club, 50% of the members like red colour, 28% like blue colour, 48% like green colour and 5% like all the three colours. Also, 10% of the members like both red and blue , 15% like both blue and green and 12% like both green and red. There are 12 members who do not like any colour.

17. How many members are there in the club ?
    (1) 100   (2) 200
    (3) 150   (4) 250

18. How many members like exactly two colours?
    (1) 20   (2) 66
    (3) 44   (4) 88

19. How many members like exactly one colour?
    (1) 110   (2) 124
    (3) 114   (4) 134

20. What is the percentage of the members who like only blue to those who like only red ?
    (1) 10%   (2) 30%
    (3) 20%   (4) 25%

In a certain locality, 200 people own Innova, 150 people
own Scorpio, 175 people own Maruti and 145 people own
Mercedez. 26% of the people do not own any of the above
mentioned cars. 40 people own all the four cars. The
number of people owning exactly two cars for any two of
the above mentioned cars is 30. Nobody owns exactly
three cars out of the four cars.

21. How many people own exactly two cars ?
    (1) 180   (2) 220
    (3) 200   (4) 240

22. How many people own exactly one car ?
    (1) 300   (2) 280
    (3) 150   (4) 160

23. How many people do not own even one car ?
    (1) 130   (2) 170
    (3) 120   (4) 180

24. What is the percentage of the people who own all
    the four cars to those who own atleast one car ?
    (1) 20%   (2) 21.1%
    (3) 30%   (4) 10.8%

Directions for questions 25 to 28 : Read the given data
and answer the given questions.

In a class, there are 72 students. For every 6 students
who like Maths there are 3 students who like English.
For every 12 students who like Maths there are 6 students
who like Maths and English and 6 students like neither
Maths nor English.

25. How many students like only Maths ?
    (1) 25   (2) 16
    (3) 24   (4) 20

26. How many students like only English ?
    (1) 20   (2) 24
    (3) 16   (4) None

27. How many students like both English and Maths?
    (1) 8   (2) 16
    (3) 12   (4) 24

28. What percentage of total number of students like
    only Maths ?
    (1) 10%   (2) 33%
    (3) 20%   (4) 40%

Directions for questions 29 and 30: Answer the
following questions.

29. In a class of 100 students, 50 take Marathi, 30
    take English and 20 take both English and
    Marathi. How many students take only English ?
    (1) 20   (2) 30
    (3) 10   (4) 40

30. In a group of 100 people, 20% read The Hindu,
    60% read The Times of India and 10% read both
    The Hindu and The Times of India. How many
    people read only one newspaper ?
    (1) 30   (2) 60
    (3) 40   (4) 70

Series

Here you are given a set of figures that depict a serial progression of a theme. You have to figure out the next figure in the series or sequence. For example:

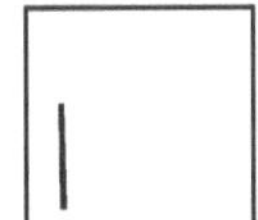 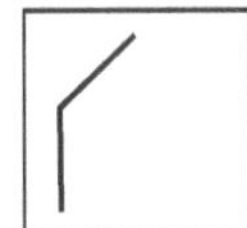   

In the first figure, we have one line. The next has two lines, the third has three lines, the fourth has one more line; so the next logical figure in the series should have five lines. Also, the lines sequentially form a pentagon. Therefore, the answer is:

Sounds really simple, doesn't it? Well, once the logic is known, getting the answer is simple. The difficult part, most often, is to identify the logic. For now, let us examine the sub-categories within 'Series' questions.

'WHAT'S NEXT?' SERIES

In this kind of question, you are given a few figures. You are then required to find out the next figure as a continuation of the sequence. The figure in question is always the last one, i.e. the question mark appears at the end of the series. For example:

'WHAT'S FIRST?' SERIES

This kind of question is the reverse of a 'What's Next' series. You are given a set of four or five figures and asked to find the first figure of the series. The first figure should have a sequential link with the later figures given in the question. The question mark appears at the beginning of the series. Though, this question should be as easy to solve as the 'Find Next' series, we have found that usually, students use the first figure as the benchmark for understanding the series. As a result, when the first figure itself is missing, it becomes a task to figure out the logic and then 'go back' to the first figure. However, with some practice this problem should be taken care of. The best method is to treat this series as 'What's Next' series and move backwards starting from the last figure. For example:

'WHAT'S IN-BETWEEN?' SERIES

So, guess what this kind of question is all about? Like the name suggests, the question mark appears in the middle of the series. The logic of the series needs to be maintained throughout and the figure in question should contribute in continuing the series. For example:

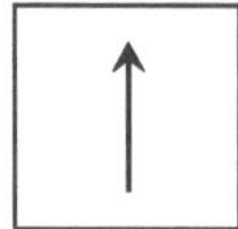    

The three examples given above are the same, and hence use the same logic. Regardless of whether you need to find the first, last or in-between figure, the logic in the above questions is that *Every consecutive figure has one arrow more than the previous one. New arrows appear first pointing the top right, then the top left, then the top right , then the top left ....*

Odd Man Out

Another category of questions within visual reasoning is the 'pick odd man out' question, or 'find the odd figure' question. Out here, you would be given a set of four or five figures. The question would be to locate the figure that does not logically fit in with the others. Here is an example of pick the odd one out.

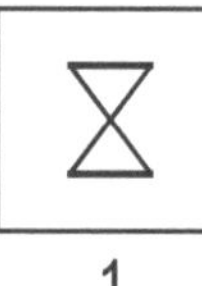   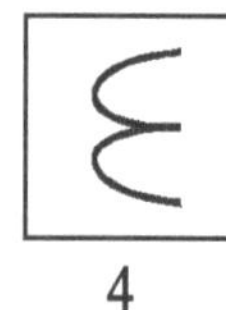 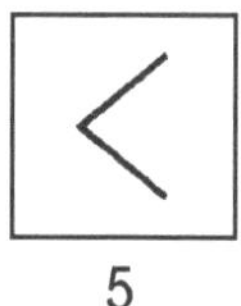

1   2   3   4   5

In this set of five figures, you have various characteristics shown by each figure. Your job is to find a figure whose characteristics are not matching with any other figure.

Let us begin by using the method of elimination. Figure 1 has two enclosed spaces, so, maybe, number of enclosed spaces will lead to an answer. However, figures 4 and 5 do not have any enclosed space. So, this is not the logic.

Figure 2 is a curved figure. But then, so is figure 4. So this logic is disqualified too.

If you notice carefully, all figures (except one of them) can be folded into exact halves along its horizontal axis at the centre. Figure 3 cannot be folded on its horizontal axis into perfect halves. In fact it can be folded on its vertical axis. Hence, the odd one out is figure 3.

Reasoning

Series-based Questions :

1. **Question Figures**

   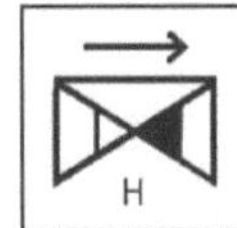 

Answer Figures

 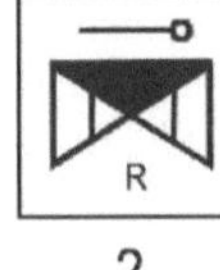 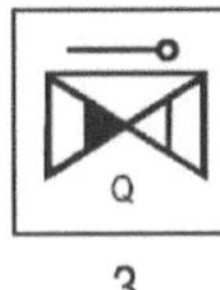 

   1   2   3   4

2. **Question Figures**

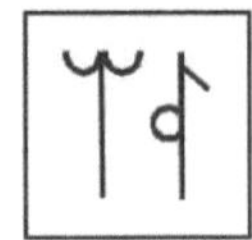 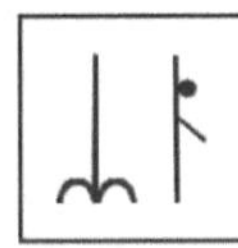 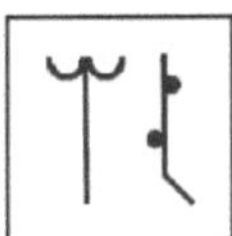 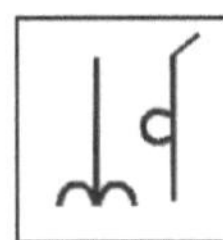 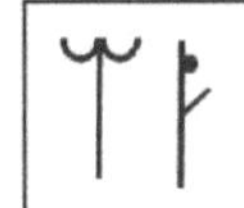 

Answer Figures

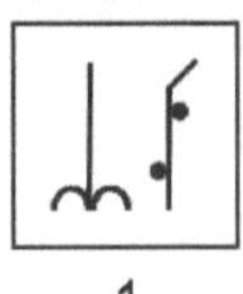 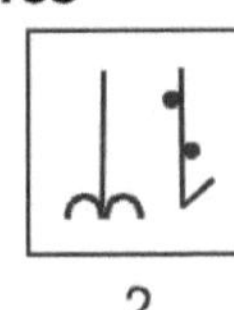 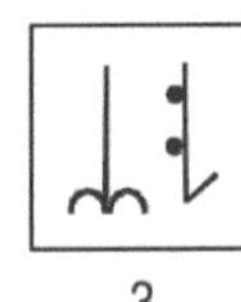 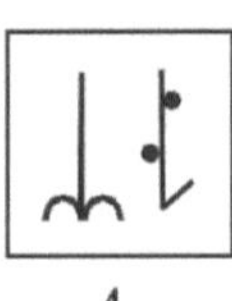

   1   2   3   4

3. **Question Figures**

    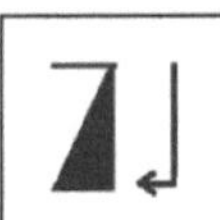 

Answer Figures

   1   2   3   4

4. **Question Figures**

   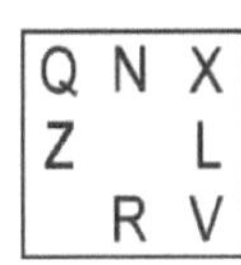 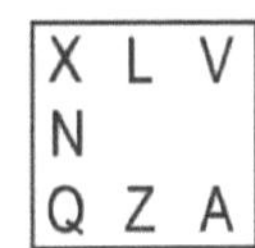 

Answer Figures

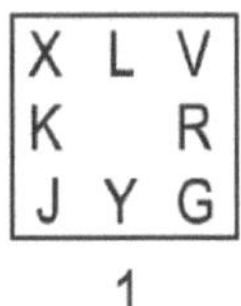  

   1   2   3   4

5. **Question Figures**

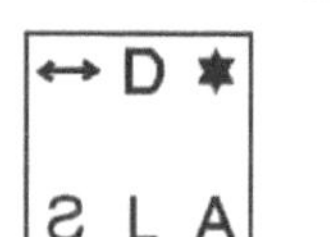 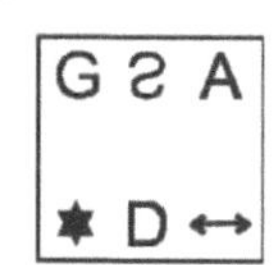  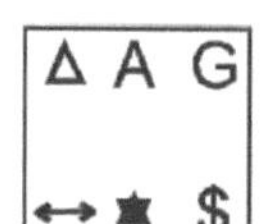 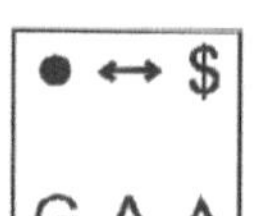 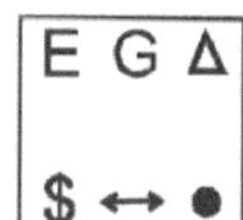

Answer Figures

 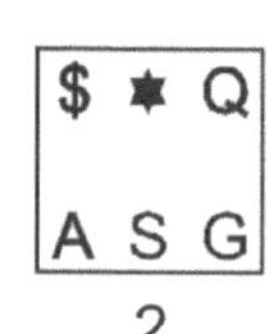 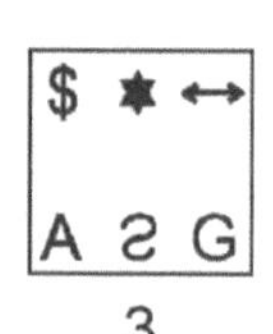 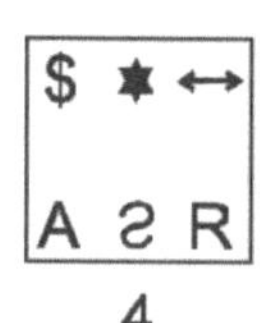

  1   2   3   4

6. **Question Figures**

 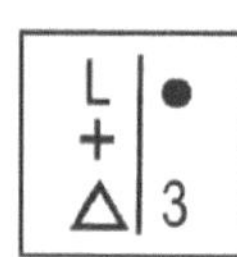 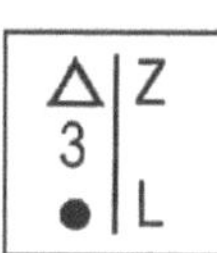  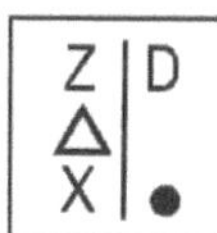 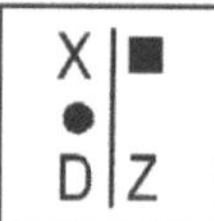

Answer Figures

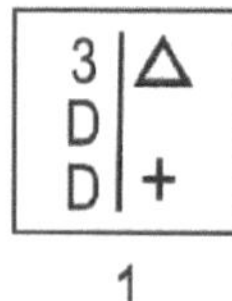 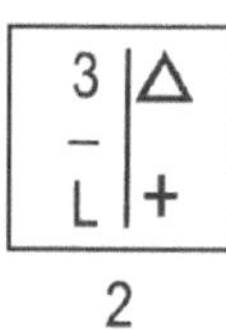 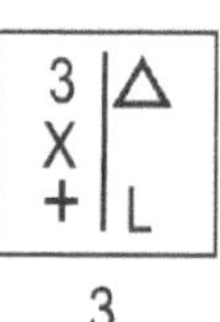 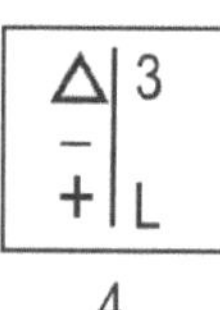

  1   2   3   4

7. **Question Figures**

   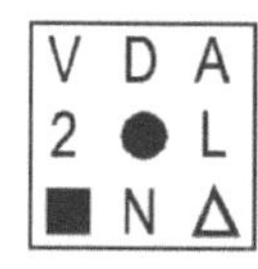  

Answer Figures

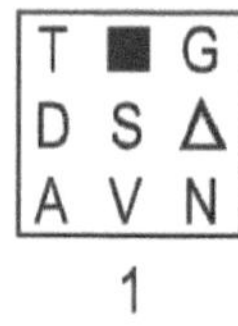 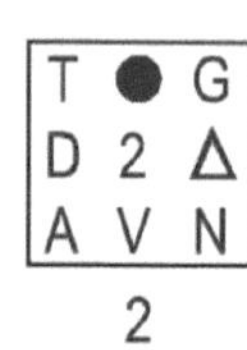 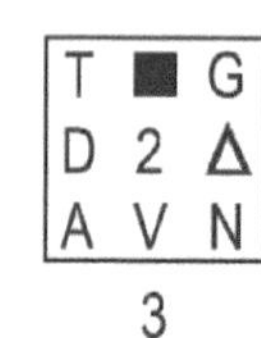 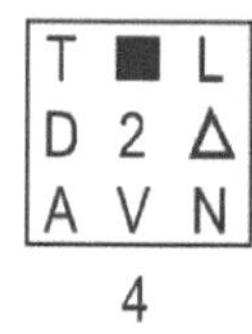

  1   2   3   4

8. **Question Figures**

Answer Figures

  1   2   3   4

9. Question Figures

  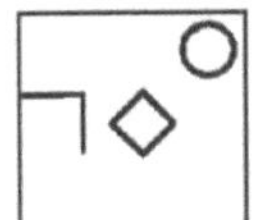 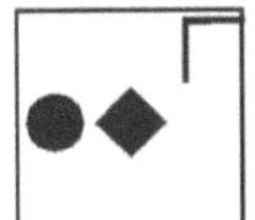  

Answer Figures

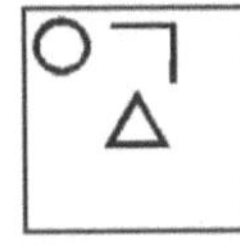 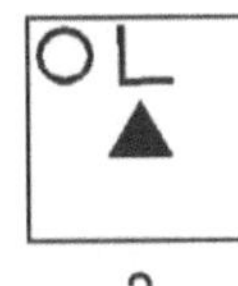 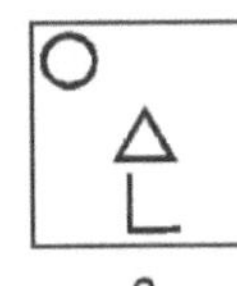 

   1   2   3   4

10. Question Figures

Answer Figures

   1   2   3   4

11. Question Figures

Answer Figures

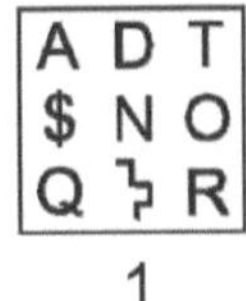 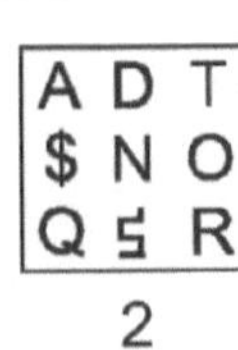 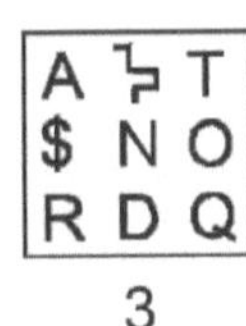 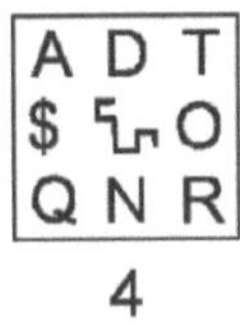

   1   2   3   4

12. Question Figures

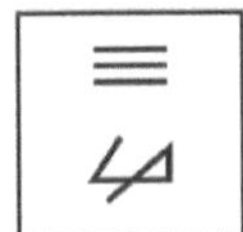 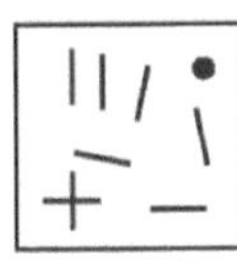 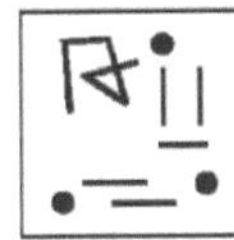 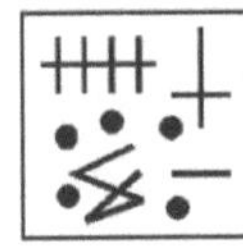 

Answer Figures

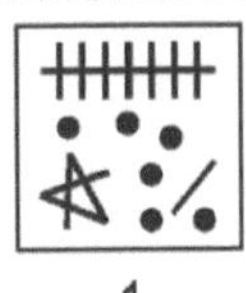 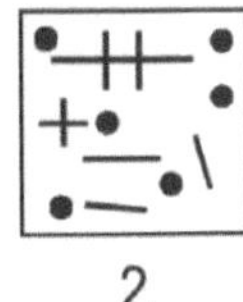  

   1   2   3   4

13. Question Figures

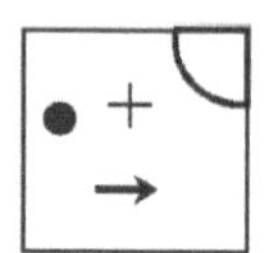 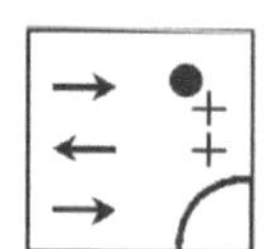 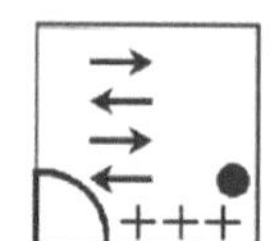 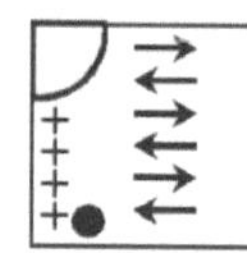 

Answer Figures

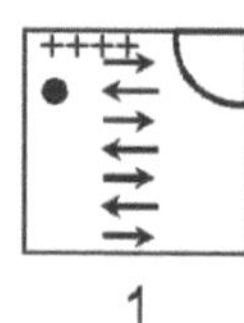 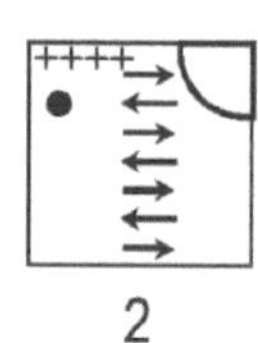 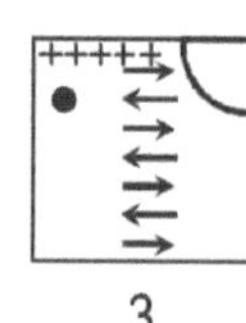 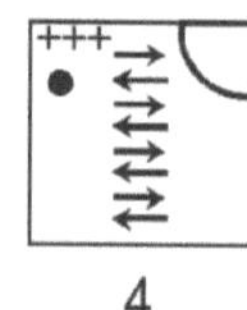

| 1 | 2 | 3 | 4 |

14. Question Figures

 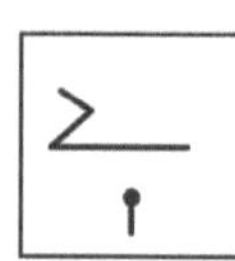 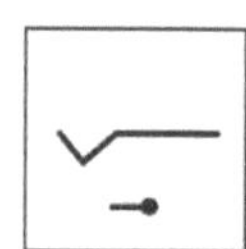 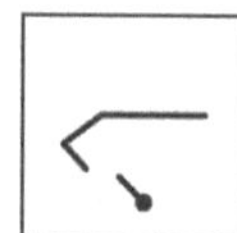 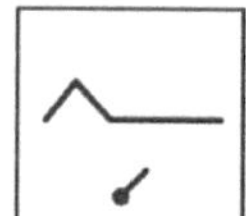

Answer Figures

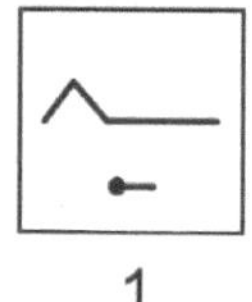 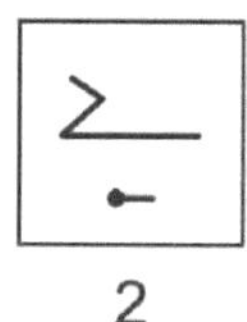 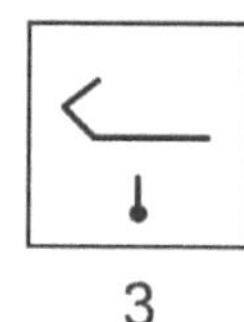 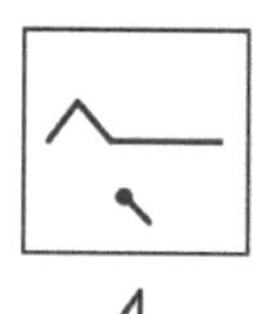

| 1 | 2 | 3 | 4 |

15. Question Figures

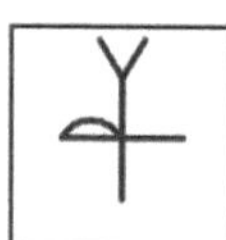  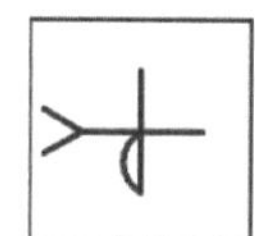 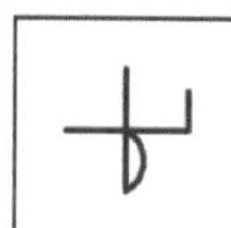 

Answer Figures

 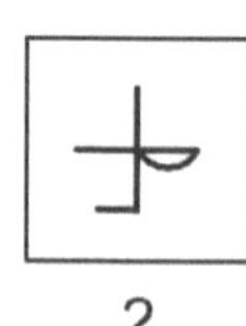  

| 1 | 2 | 3 | 4 |

16. Question Figures

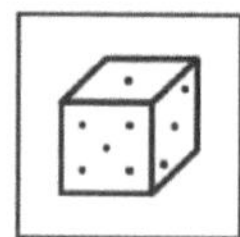 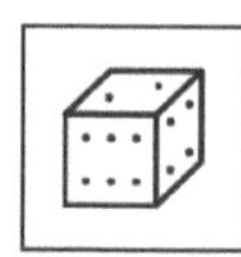 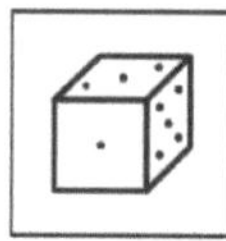 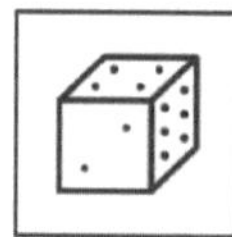 

Answer Figures

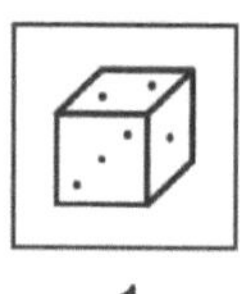 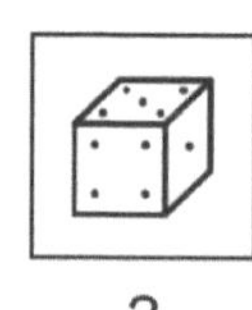 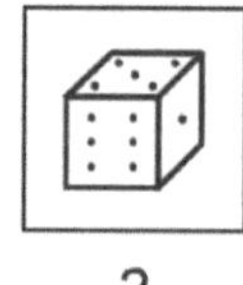 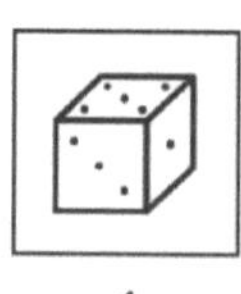

| 1 | 2 | 3 | 4 |

17. **Question Figures**

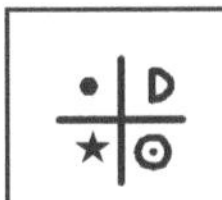

Answer Figures

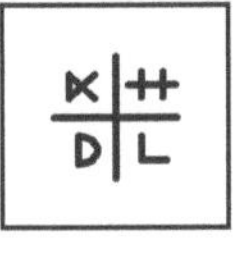 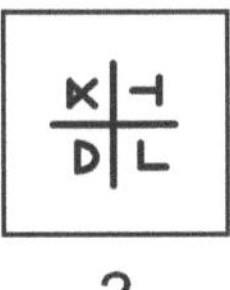 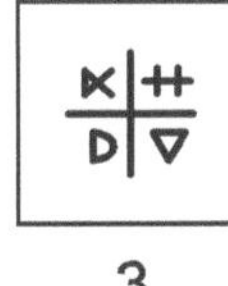

1   2   3   4

18. **Question Figures**

Answer Figures

1   2   3   4

19. **Question Figures**

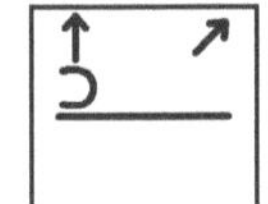 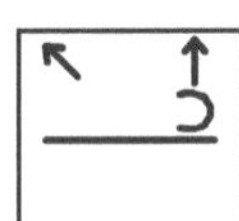  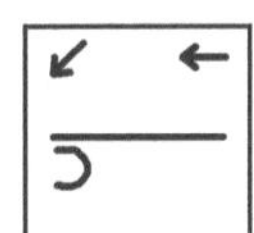 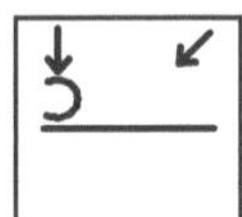

Answer Figure

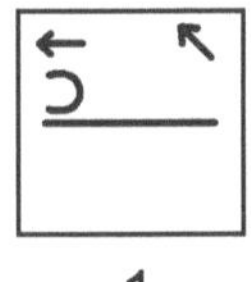 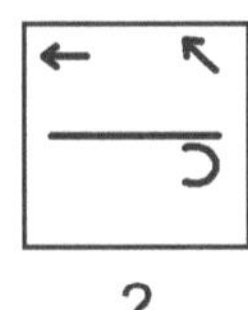 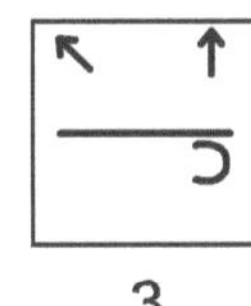 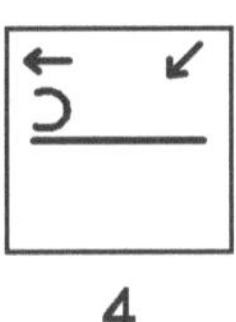

1   2   3   4

20. **Question Figures**

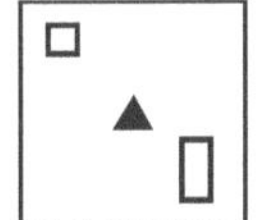 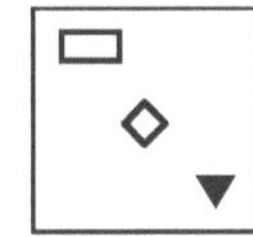  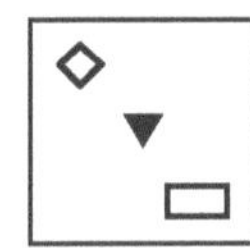 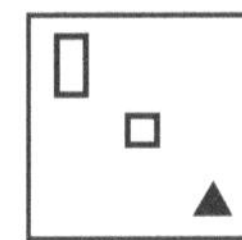

Answer Figures

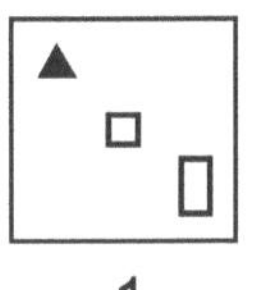 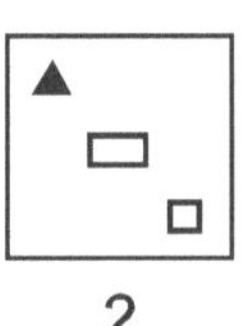 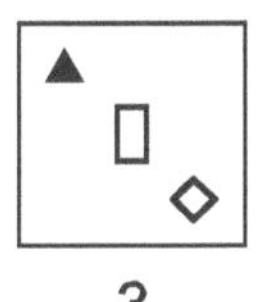 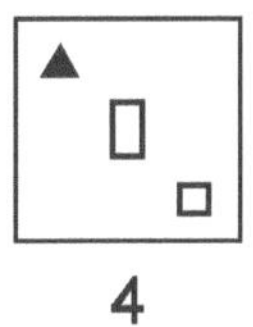

1   2   3   4

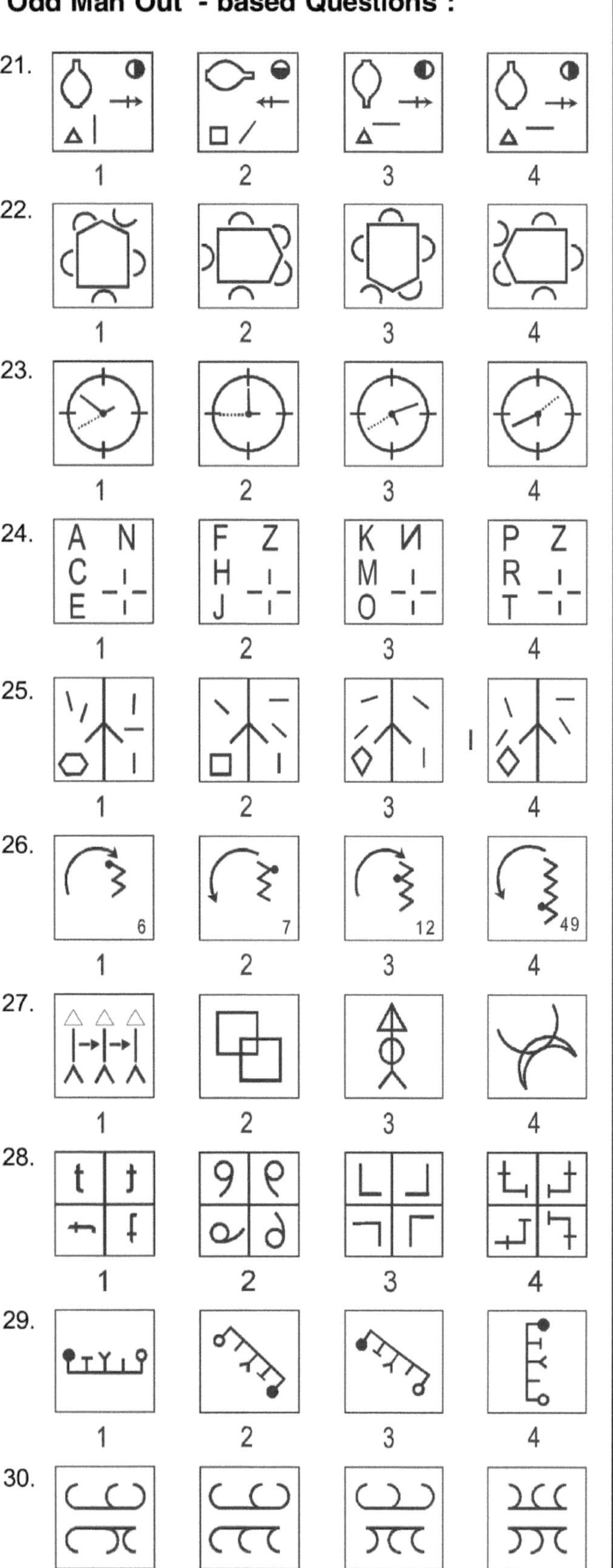

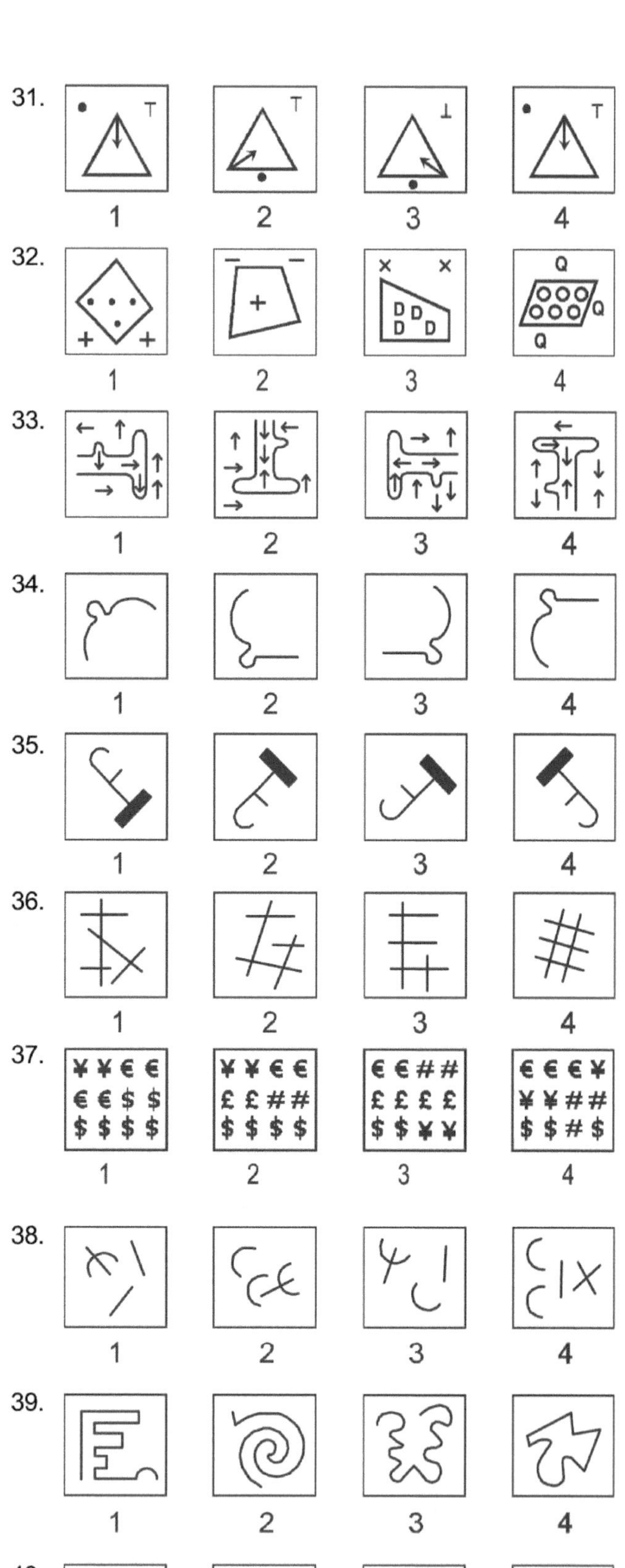

Reasoning

Logical Deductions & Connectives **15**

Logical Deductions or Syllogism

A syllogism is a deductive argument relating two premises and a conclusion, all of which are quantified propositions, i.e. propositions joining concepts by using words such as 'all' or 'some'.

Deductive logic is used to derive conclusions from premises where the truth of the conclusion must always be contained in the truth of the premises. Although, the questions can be answered by representing the given statements by Venn Diagrams, we will look at arriving at the deduction by using some simple rules in syllogism.

Let us try to understand some terms with help of examples.

All pen are pencils.   ...(i)
All pencils are erasers.   ...(ii)
All pens are erasers.   ...(iii)

Statements (i) and (ii) are called '**premises**'.

Statement (iii) is the '**conclusion**'.

The premises normally start with the words All, No, Some and Some not.

The word "All" has synonyms as — Each, Any, Every, whereas the word "Some" can be substituted by Many, Few, Most of, at least, etc.

These words are referred to as **quantifiers**.

A premise consists of a subject and a predicate. In the premise (i) "All pens are pencils", the first term 'pens' is called the subject and the second term 'pencils' is called the predicate. Similarly, in premise (ii) 'pencils' becomes the subject and 'erasers' is the predicate.

The word that occurs in both the premises is known as the '**middle term**' i.e. 'pencils'. Usually, the conclusion consists of the other two words 'pens' and 'erasers'. The middle term may or may not be present in the conclusions, as per the directions or instructions for the question.

According to the quantifier used, the premise can be classified into

(1) Universal statements — The statements where "All" is used.

(2) Particular statements — The statements where "Some" is used.

Also, premises can be divided into
(1) Affirmative Statements
(2) Negative Statements — These are the statement which have negative terms like "no" or "not".

The combination of the above two different categories leads to four different premises as given in the table.

	Universal	Particular
Affirmative	All	Some
Negative	No	Some not

In a premise, the subject or predicate can be distributed ⊘ or not distributed ⊗ according to the kind of premise.

The distribution pattern is as follows:

Premise	Subject	Predicate
All	⊘	⊗
No	⊘	⊘
Some	⊗	⊗
Some not	⊗	⊘

Example: Some apples⊗ are oranges⊗.

In the above premise, subject 'apples' is not distributed. Also, predicate 'oranges' is not distributed.

Rules for Syllogism

1. There should be exactly three terms for each deduction in two premises.
2. If the middle term is not distributed in atleast one of the premise, then a conclusion cannot be drawn.
3. If one of the two premises is negative, then conclusion, if at all it exists, must be negative.
4. If one of the two premises is particular, then conclusion, if at all it exists, must be particular.
5. If both the premises are negative, then a conclusion cannot be drawn.
6. If both the premises are particular, then a conclusion cannot be drawn.
7. If a term is not distributed in any of the two premises, it cannot be distributed in the conclusion.

From the above rules, we now list some of the combinations of quantifiers in which a conclusion can be obtained (provided the middle term is distributed)

(1)   All + All = All/Some

Example: All boys are men.   ...(i)
                 All men are wise.   ...(ii)

We can see that the middle term i.e. 'men' is distributed in statement (ii), so a conclusion can be drawn. We can draw three conclusions.

Conclusions: (I)   All boys are wise.
                     (II) Some boys are wise.
                     (III) Some wise are boys.

(2)   All + All = Some

Example :   All men are boys.
                  All men are wise.

Conclusions :   (I) Some men are wise.
                      (II) Some wise are men.

(3)   All + Some = Some

Example: All men are boys.
                 Some men are wise.

Conclusions :   (I) Some boys are wise.
                      (II) Some wise are boys.

(4)   All + No = No/Some not.

Example: All boys are men
                 No man is wise

Conclusions :   (I)   No boy is wise.
                      (II) No wise is boy.
                      (III) Some boys are not wise.
                      (IV) Some wise are not boys.

(5)   All + No = Some Not.

        All men are boys
        No men are wise

Conclusions :   Some boys are not wise.

Note: The conclusion "Some wise are not boys" cannot be drawn because as per rule [7] 'boys' is not distributed in the premise, so 'boys' can not be distributed in the conclusion.

(6)   All + Some not = Some not.

        All men are boys
        Some men are not wise.

Conclusions: Some boys are not wise.

(7)   Some + No = Some not

        Some boys are men
        No men are wise

Conclusions :   Some boys are not wise.

The combination of quantifiers in which no conclusion can be drawn are as follows:

(1) Some + Some
(2) Some + Some not   (As per rule [6] two particular statements can't yield a conclusion)
(3) Some not + Some not
(4) Some not + No   (As per rule [5] two negative statements can't yield a conclusion)
(5) No + No

Interchangeability of the terms:

The terms can be interchanged for two quantifiers — 'No' and 'Some'. This means that 'No A is B' is same as 'No B is A'.

Similarly, 'Some A is B' is same as 'Some B is A'.

Inferred quantifiers:

From a universal quantifiers, we can always infer a particular quantifier. For example, whenever we say 'All A are B,' we can always infer 'Some A are B' or 'Some B are A'. Similarly, whenever we say 'No A is B', we can always infer 'Some A are not B' or 'Some B are not A'.

Logical Connectives:

In logical connectives, the basic constituents are simple propositions which are combined into more complex propositions by means of logical words, like 'not', 'and', 'or', 'if', etc.

Reasoning

Consider the following example.

Ram is in the room when Piyush is in the hotel. Can Ram be in the room when Piyush is not in the hotel?

The answer is YES.

The condition given in the first statement is that if Piyush is in the hotel, then Ram definitely has to be in the room. Ram can be in the room otherwise also, i.e. when Piyush is not in the hotel.

The valid conclusions you can make about the main statement given are :

   (i) Piyush is in the hotel. Ram is in the room (straight logic).

   (ii) Ram is not in the room, Piyush is not in the hotel (straight negation).

Statement (ii) above is also correct because at any given time Ram and Piyush have two possible positions each, i.e.

     Ram can be in the room or outside.

     Piyush can be in the hotel or outside.

When Ram is not in the room, Piyush has two options of either being in the hotel or outside. However it can be said definitely that Piyush is not in the hotel because if Piyush is the hotel, then Ram would be in the room, but Ram is outside. So Piyush has to be outside.

Let us understand the implications of various connectives connecting two statements 'p' and 'q'.

Note: ~ p stands for negation p
       ~ q stands for negation q.

S. No	Connectives	Implications
1	If p, then q or q, if p	(i) $p \Rightarrow q$ (ii) $\sim q \Rightarrow \sim p$
2	Whenever p, then q or q, whenever p	(i) $p \Rightarrow q$ (ii) $\sim q \Rightarrow \sim p$.
3	Either p or q	(i) $\sim p \Rightarrow q$ (ii) $\sim q \Rightarrow p$
4	Unless p, q or q, unless p	(i) $\sim p \Rightarrow q$ (ii) $\sim q \Rightarrow p$
5	Only if p, then q or q, only if p	(i) $q \Rightarrow p$ (ii) $\sim p \Rightarrow \sim q$
6	If and only if p, q or q, if and only if p	(i) $p \Rightarrow q$ (ii) $q \Rightarrow p$ (iii) $\sim p \Rightarrow \sim q$ (iv) $\sim q \Rightarrow \sim p$.

Example:

   "If p, then q" or "q, if p".

            q   q

If $\boxed{\text{labour works hard}}$, then $\boxed{\text{the boss is happy}}$.

It is always better to mark the statments as p and q and then proceed.

Conculsions:

   (i) $p \Rightarrow q$ i.e. the labour works hard, implies the boss is happy.

   (ii) $\sim q \Rightarrow \sim p$ i.e. The boss is not happy, implies the labour has not work hard.

Students are advised to stick to the rules and therefore mark only those options which adhere to the implications given in the table before.

Example:

   "Either p or q".

              p   q

Either $\boxed{\text{Raman is happy}}$, or $\boxed{\text{Raghu is crazy}}$.

Conculsions:

   (i) $\sim p \Rightarrow q$ i.e. Raman is not happy, implies Raghu is crazy.

   (ii) $\sim q \Rightarrow p$ i.e. Raghu is not crazy, implies Raman is happy.

Example:

   "Only if p, then q".

Only   if $\boxed{\text{Ram runs fast}}$, then

$\boxed{\text{he'll reach on time}}$.

Note: "Only if p, then q" is not the same as "If p, then q".

Conclusions:

   (i) $q \Rightarrow p$ i.e. Ram reaches on time, implies Ram ran fast.

   (ii) $\sim p \Rightarrow \sim q$ i.e. Ram didn't run fast, implies Ram didn't reach on time.

 **Exercise**

Logical Deductions

Directions for questions 1 to 25: Given in each question below are two statements followed by two conclusions numbered I and II. Decide which of the two conclusions follows logically from the two given statements.
Mark your answer:
(1) If only conclusion (I) follows;
(2) If only conclusion (II) follows;
(3) If both (I) and (II) follow; and
(4) If neither (I) nor (II) follows.

1. **Statements :** All cakes are icecreams.
   All ice creams are toffees.

   Conclusion : (I) All cakes are toffees.
   (II) All toffees are icecreams.

2. **Statements :** All pens are pencils.
   All pencils are erasers.

   Conclusion : (I) Some erasers are pens.
   (II) All pens are erasers.

3. **Statements :** All bottles are cans.
   All bottles are tanks.

   Conclusion : (I) Some cans are not tanks.
   (II) Some tanks are cans.

4. **Statements :** All gold is silver.
   Some gold is copper.

   Conclusion : (I) All silver is copper.
   (II) All copper is silver.

5. **Statements :** All fools are men.
   Some fools are wise.

   Conclusion : (I) Some wise are men.
   (II) All wise are not men.

6. **Statements :** All teachers are professors.
   No professor is principal.

   Conclusion : (I) No teacher is principal.
   (II) Some principal are teachers.

7. **Statement :** All cows are animals.
   No animal is herbivorous.

   Conclusion : (I) All cows are herbivorous.
   (II) All cows are not herbivorous.

8. **Statement :** All heros are popular.
   No hero is kind.

   Conclusion : (I) Some kind are not popular.
   (II) Some popular are not kind.

9. **Statement :** All coats are bags.
   No bags are toys.

   Conclusion : (I) No coats are toys
   (II) No toys are coats.

10. **Statement :** Some men are brave
    No brave is warrior.

    Conclusion : (I) Some warriors are not men.
    (II) Some men are not warriors.

11. **Statement :** No locks are keys.
    Some locks are spoons.

    Conclusion : (I) Some spoons are not keys.
    (II) All spoons are not keys.

12. **Statement :** All dogs are cows.
    Some horses are not cows.

    Conclusion : (I) Some dogs are horses.
    (II) Some horses are not dogs.

13. **Statement :** Some clips are not rocks.
    All stones are rocks.

    Conclusion : (I) Some clips are not stones.
    (II) Some stones are not clips.

14. **Statement :** Some females are girls.
    Some girls are angels.

    Conclusion : (I) Some females are angels.
    (II) Some angels are females.

15. **Statement :** Some men are helpful.
    Some helpful are kind.

    Conclusion : (I) All kind are men.
    (II) Some men are kind.

16. **Statement :** Some cars are scooters.
    Some trains are not scooters.

    Conclusion : (I) Some cars are not trains.
    (II) Some trains are cars.

17. **Statements :** Some children are intelligent.
Some naughty are intelligent.

Conclusion: (I) Some children are not naughty.
(II) Some naughty are children.

18. **Statement:** Some authors are not teachers.
Some teachers are not writers.

Conclusions: (I) Some authors are writers.
(II) Some authors are not writers.

19. **Statements :** No train is a bus.
Some buses are not trucks.

Conclusion : (I) No train is a truck.
(II) Some trucks are not trains.

20. **Statements :** No watch is a pen.
No pen is a bracelet.

Conclusion : (I) All watches are bracelets.
(II) All watches are not bracelets.

21. **Statement :** All books are pages.
All letters are pages.

Conclusion : (I) All books are letters.
(II) Some letters are not books.

22. **Statements :** All apples are oranges.
Some oranges are bananas.

Conclusion : (I) Some apples are not bananas.
(II) Some apples are bananas.

23. **Statement :** All rocks are knights.
Some pawns are knights.

Conclusion : (I) Some rocks are pawns.
(II) All rocks are not pawns.

24. **Statements :** All terrorists are murderers.
Some murderers are not saints.

Conclusion : (I) Some terrorists are not saints.
(II) Some saints are not terrorists.

25. **Statement :** All ministers are thieves.
Some thieves are not policemen.

Conclusion : (I) All ministers are policemen.
(II) Some policemen are not ministers.

Logical Connectives

Directions for questions 26 to 40 : Each question ahead consists of a main statement followed by four numbered statements. From the numbered statements, select the one that logically follows the main statement.

26. If it rains, then i'll wear a raincoat.
    (1) I wear a rain coat, implies it is raining.
    (2) It is raining, implies i'll wear a raincoat.
    (3) I am not wearing a raincoat, implies it is not raining.
    (4) Both (2) and (3)

27. If gold is silver, then copper is bronze.
    (1) Copper is not bronze, implies gold is not silver.
    (2) Copper is bronze, implies gold is not silver.
    (3) Gold is not silver, implies copper is not bronze.
    (4) None of the above

28. The ground is wet, if the water is in abundance.
    (1) The water is in abundance, implies the ground is not wet.
    (2) The ground is not wet, implies the water is not in abundance.
    (3) Both (1) and (2)
    (4) Neither (1) nor (2)

29. Whenever Rahul is hungry, Rahul eats.
    (1) Rahul is not hungry, implies Rahul does not eat.
    (2) Rahul does not eat, implies Rahul is not hungry.
    (3) Rahul eats implies Rahul is hungry.
    (4) Both (1) and (3)

30. The minister is elected, whenever he wins the elections.
    (1) The minister is elected, implies he wins the elections.
    (2) The minister loses the elections means he is not elected.
    (3) The minister loses the elections means he is elected.
    (4) The minister wins the elections, implies the minister is elected.

31. Either the pen is heavy or the pencil is light.
    (1) The pencil is not light, implies the pen is heavy.
    (2) The pen is not heavy, implies the pencil is light.
    (3) The pen is heavy and the pencil is light.
    (4) Both (1) and (2)

32. Either the tank is empty or the plug is short.
    (1) The tank is empty implies the plug is not short.
    (2) The tank is empty implies the plug is short.
    (3) The tank is not empty implies the plug is not short.
    (4) None of the above

33. Unless Dhoni is the captain, India will lose all its matches.
    (1) Dhoni is not the captain, implies India will lose all it matches.
    (2) India wins all its matches, implies Dhoni is the captain.
    (3) Dhoni is the captain, implies India will lose all its matches.
    (4) Both (1) and (2)

34. Unless the tea is hot, Rohan will eat cake.
    (1) Tea is not hot implies Rohan will eat cake.
    (2) Tea is hot implies Rohan will eat cake.
    (3) Rohan will not eat the cake implies tea is not hot.
    (4) Both (1) and (3)

35. Sonu will play cricket, unless it rains.
    (1) Sonu will play cricket, implies it is raining.
    (2) It is not raining, implies Sonu will play cricket.
    (3) It is raining, hence Sonu will play cricket.
    (4) None of the above

36. He drinks tea, only if she drinks coffee.
    (1) He drinks tea, implies she drinks coffee.
    (2) She does not drinks coffee implies he does not drink tea.
    (3) Both (1) and (2)
    (4) None of the above

37. Only if he wins the race, he will win a gold medal.
    (1) He did not win the race implies he did not win the gold medal.
    (2) He did not win the race implies he won the gold medal.
    (3) He won the gold medal implies he did not win the race.
    (4) Both (1) and (3)

38. Only if Sunil's parents are with him, he will go to circus.
    (1) Sunil does not go to circus, implies his parents are not with him.
    (2) Sunil does not go to circus, implies his parents are with him.
    (3) Sunil goes to circus, implies his parents are with him.
    (4) None of the above

39. Amit dances, if and only if Rohit sings.
    (1) Rohit sings implies Amit dances.
    (2) Amit dances implies Rohit sings.
    (3) Amit does not sing implies Amit does not dance.
    (4) All of the above

40. Ajay is honest, if and only if Raja is dishonest.
    (1) Ajay is dishonest implies Raja is dishonest.
    (2) Raja is honest implies Ajay is honest.
    (3) Raja is dishonest implies Ajay is honest.
    (4) None of the above

Reasoning

PART - 3

VERBAL ABILITY / GRAMMAR & RC

Parts of Speech **1**

English words belong to eight parts of speech:
They are:
1. Noun
2. Pronoun
3. Adjective
4. Verb
5. Adverb
6. Preposition
7. Conjunction
8. Interjection

1. NOUN

A Noun is a word which is the name of a person, thing, place or quality.

Name of things:
table, chair, book, pen, pencil, tree, flower, plant, water, milk, gold, silver, paper, wood, iron, stone, hill, sky, sun, moon, earth, river, door, window, bicycle, etc.

Name of Places:
street, lane, village, town, city, room, state, district, country, continent, world, field, ground, class, school, college, university, Mamilla gudem, Gandh Chowk, Kothagudem, India, Andhra Pradesh, Asia etc.

Name of Persons:
boy, girl, mother, father, brother, sister, man, woman, king, queen, master, servant, doctor, actor, collector, teacher, student, clerk, officer, Ram Chandra, Lalitha, Ambica, Keats, Tagore, Shakespeare etc.

Qualities:
honesty, sincerity, patience, beauty, strength, courage, weakness, knowledge, power, cleverness, poverty, cruelty, kindness, sympathy etc.

Names are mainly of two types:
- A. Concrete Noun
- B. Abstract Noun.

A. CONCRETE NOUN: Concrete Noun is one which can be seen and touched.
Eg: chair, table, house, boy, girl, water etc.

B. ABSTRACT NOUN: An abstract noun is one which cannot be seen and touched but that can be thought of.

Eg: god, death, air, honesty, sound, pain, patience, wisdom, pity, bravery, beauty, knowledge, cruelty, joy, liberty, kindness, perseverance, youth etc.
Note: We must not write any article before abstract nouns.
Eg:
1. Death is inevitable.
2. I always pray to God.

Note: We can write article 'the' before an abstract noun when the name of particular person is given.
Eg:
1. The honesty of Gandhi is admirable.
2. The death of Subhash Chandra Bose is heroic.

B. CONCRETE NOUN:
Concrete Noun is of four types.
- i. Proper Noun
- ii. Common Noun
- iii. Collective Noun
- iv. Material Noun.

I. PROPER NOUN:
A proper noun is the name of a particular person, place or thing. The names of days, months, rivers, seas and oceans, mountains, languages, islands etc., are also proper nouns. Proper Noun begin with a capital letter.

Names of particular persons:
Rama, Krishna, Saleem, Robert etc.

Names of particular places:
Kakinada, Andhra University, New York etc.

Names of particular things:
Ford (car), Brooke Bond (tea), Philips (radio), Colgate (paste), Prestige (cooker) and Onida (T.V) etc.

Names of rivers:
Krishna, Godavari, Nile, Ganges and Thames etc.

Names of seas and oceans:
Indian ocean, Arabian sea, Pacific ocean etc.

Names of days and months:
Friday, May, September etc.

Names of languages:
Telugu, Hindi, English, Sanskrit etc.

Names of mountains and islands:
Himalayas, Everest Alps, Sri Lanka, Andamans etc.

2. COMMON NOUN:

A common noun is the name of a person or a thing in general.

Eg: Boy, girl, woman, man, village, town, country, table, chair, book, doctor, student, teacher, flower, cow, tree, city and hill etc.

Note: Generally article is not used before a proper noun. But we can use article 'the' before a proper noun when it is used as a common noun.

Eg:
1. Kalidas is the Shakespeare of India.
2. Mussolini is the Hitler of Italy.
3. Kode Rama Murthy is the Bhima of modern times.
4. Krishna is the James Bond of Andhra.
5. Chiranjeevi is the Bruce Lee of Andhra.
6. Krishna Sastry is the Shelly of Andhra.
7. Bombay is the Manchester of India.

But….
1. He is a Hitler.
2. Krishna is a James Bond.
3. She is a Savitri.

3. COLLECTIVE NOUN:

A collective Noun is group of persons or things used as a single unit.

Eg: Group, crowd, team, family, committee, bunch, gang, union, fleet, squadron, flock, herd, poetry, scenery, machinery, jury, stationery, army etc.
A flock of sheep and birds.
A fleet of ships.
A team of players.
A bunch of flowers and keys.
A bouquet of flowers.
A squadron of aeroplanes.
An army of soldiers etc.

4. MATERIAL NOUN:

A material noun is the name of some matter or substance.
Eg: Gold, silver, copper, iron, lead, glass, wood, wool, cotton, clay, paper, stone, marble etc.,
(We must not write any article before material nouns. We can write <u>a</u> or <u>an</u> before these material nouns when they are used as adjectives).

Eg:
1. Gold is a precious metal.
2. Silver is a bright metal.

3. Iron is a useful metal.
4. This is made of marble.
5. This bottle is made of glass.
6. This pot is made of clay.
7. These doors are made of wood.

But….
1. It is an iron box.
2. It is a gold ring.
3. It is a paper boat.
4. It is a silver coin.

2. PRONOUN

A pronoun is a word used instead of a noun.
Eg:
1. Gopal painted a picture. He gave it to Sita.
2. Radha bought a box yesterday. She gave it to Krishna.

Pronouns are of nine types:
1. Personal pronoun
2. Reflexive pronoun
3. Emphatic pronoun
4. Demonstrative pronoun
5. Indefinite pronoun
6. Interrogative pronoun
7. Distributive pronoun
8. Reciprocal pronoun
9. Relative pronoun

1. PERSONAL PRONOUN:
Personal pronouns are those which stand for three persons.

A. Person: The first person stands for the speaker.
Eg: I, me, my, mine, we, us, our, and ours
B. Person: The second person stands for the person spoken to.
Eg: you, your and yours
C. Person: The third person stands for anyone or anything elsewhere.
Eg: He, him and his
She, her and hers
It, It and Its
They, them, their and theirs

The passive forms my, our, your, his, her and their etc. are used before a noun.
Eg:
1. This is my hat.
2. That is your pen.

3. It is their house.
4. This is our garden.
5. That is his book or that is her book.

The forms mine, ours, yours, his, hers and theirs etc. are used after a noun.

Eg:
1. This hat is mine.
2. That pen is yours.
3. The house is theirs.
4. This garden is ours.
5. That book is hers or that book is his.

II. REFLEXIVE PRONOUN:

Reflexive pronoun is generally preset after the verb. In the reflexive pronoun, the subject and the object are the same persons. The objects have <u>self</u> forms.

A. Person: Myself and ourselves.
B. Person: Yourself and yourselves.
C. Person: Himself, Herself, Itself and Themselves.

Eg:
1. I have taught myself.
2. We knew ourselves.
3. He told himself that he had done it.
4. She washed herself.
5. They helped themselves.

III. EMPHATIC PRONOUN:

Emphatic pronoun is one in which the reflexive pronoun is used for the sake of emphasis. Emphatic pronouns are used immediately after the subjects or the objects.

Eg:
1. I myself did it.
2. She herself cooked it.
3. They themselves admitted it.
4. You yourself can explain it.
5. The house itself has fallen down.

IV. DEMONSTRATIVE PRONOUN:

Demonstrative pronoun is one which points out the particular persons or things.
Eg: This, that, these, those, such and yonder.
Eg:
1. This is my book.
2. That is Mohan's room.
3. These are your books.
4. Those were the good old days.
6. Such is the position.

V. INDEFINITE PRONOUN:

The indefinite pronoun is one which doesn't point out any person or thing in particular. One, nobody, none (not one), somebody, everybody, some, someone, anybody, something, all, any, many, other, anything, anyone, and another etc. are indefinite pronouns.

Eg:
1. One should love one's country.
2. None of his friends have come forward to help him.
3. Nobody came to see me.
4. Somebody has come for you.
5. Everybody is dissatisfied with this.

VI. INTERROGATIVE PRONOUN:

Interrogative pronoun is one which is used for asking questions. Who, whom, whose, which and what etc. are interrogative pronouns.

Eg:
1. Who is he?
2. What is he?
3. Which is your book?
4. Whose is this pen?
5. Whom do you want?

VII. DISTRIBUTIVE PRONOUN:

Distributive pronoun is one which refers to persons or things taken one at a time. Distributive pronouns are always singular and are so followed by singular verbs. Each, either, and neither are distributive pronouns.

Eg:
1. Each of us will get a share.
2. Either of these girls has got more marks.
3. Neither of these men has passed the exam.

VIII. RECIPROCAL PRONOUN:

Reciprocal pronoun is one which expresses a mutual relationship. Each other and one another are reciprocal pronouns.

Eg: The two rivals hated <u>each other</u>.
We must all love <u>one another</u>.
The two friends always quarrel with <u>each other</u>.
The three sisters quarreled with <u>one another</u>.

IX. RELATIVE PRONOUN:

A relative pronoun is one which relates or refers to a noun that has gone before it. It is also called conjunctive pronoun.
Eg: I have found the pen which I lost yesterday.
I saw a beggar who was deaf and dumb.

This is the woman whose husband was killed in the accident.
Here is the boy who is good at sports
This is the book that you gave me yesterday.

The table showing the format of personal pronouns :

Person	Nominative Case	Objective case	Possessive case
I person	I	Me	My, Mine
	We	Us	Our, Ours
II person	You	You	You/ Yours
III person	He	Him	His
	She	Her	Her, Hers
	It	It	Its
	They	Them	Their, theirs

REFLEXIVE PRONOUNS
I.	Person	: Myself, Ourselves
II.	Person	: Yourself, Yourselves
III.	person	: Himself, Herself, Itself, Themselves

3. ADJECTIVES

An adjective is a word which qualifies a noun and shows the quality, quantity, number etc., of a noun.
Eg:
1. She is a clever girl.
2. Gita is beautiful
3. The sky is blue.

There are six types of Adjectives:
1. Adjectives of quality
2. Adjectives of quantity
3. Adjectives of number (numeral adjectives)
4. Demonstrative adjectives
5. Distributive adjectives
6. Interrogative adjectives

A. ADJECTIVES OF QUALITY:

Adjectives of quality show the quality of a person or thing.
Eg:
1. He is a good player.
2. She is a young girl.
3. Calcutta is a large city.

Note: Sometimes the present and past participles of verbs can be used as adjectives. They are called participle adjectives.
Eg:
1. She has a smiling face.
2. He gave me a visiting card.

B. ADJECTIVES OF QUANTITY:

Adjectives of quantity show how much of a thing is meant.
Eg:
1. He drank little water.
2. Don't waste much money.

C. ADJECTIVES OF NUMBER:

Adjectives of Number show how many persons or things are meant.
1. Definite numeral adjectives:
Eg:
1. There are fifty students in the class.
2. I have taken five rupees from him.
3. He was the first man to become a doctor in the family.
Eg:
1. Many people were killed in the accident.
2. Do you have any books?
3. All students have gone out of the class.
4. I want the help of a few students.

D. DISTRIBUTIVE ADJECTIVES:

Distributive adjectives refer to each one of a number.
Eg:
1. Each man must know his responsibility.
2. Every man must work hard.
3. Either side may win.

E. DEMONSTRATIVE ADJECTIVES:

Demonstrative adjective point out which person or thing is meant.
Eg: That man is bad.
This boy is very active.
Those people are very cruel.
These mangoes are very sweet.

F. INTERROGATIVE ADJECTIVES:

An interrogative adjectives is one which is used with a noun to ask question.
Eg: What type of man is he?
Which way shall we go?
Whose daughter is she?

4. VERB

A verb is a word which shows the action done by the subject. Verb tells us not only about an action but also about existence and possession.
Eg:
1. I gave a pen to him.
2. He was in Bangalore last week.

3. There are fifty students in the class.
4. A cat is on the wall.

Verbs are of two types:
1. Transitive verbs
2. Intransitive verbs

1. TRANSITIVE VERBS:
Transitive verb is one which is immediately followed by an object. After transitive verbs, we must not write prepositions.
Eg:
1. I saw a film last week.
2. She wrote a letter yesterday.

2. INTRANSITIVE VERBS:
Intransitive verb is one which is not immediately followed by an object.
Eg:
1. She ran on the road.
2. I listened to a song.
3. She suffered from typhoid.

Verbs are of two types:
1. Finite verbs
2. Non-finite verbs

1. FINITE VERBS:
A finite verb is one which is controlled by person and number of the subject.
Eg:
1. I go to temple every evening.
2. She goes to temple every evening.
3. They go to temple every evening.

2. NON-FINITE VERBS:
A Non-finite verb is one which is not controlled by the person and number of the subject.
Eg:
1. I wanted to write a letter.
2. She wanted to write a letter.
3. They wanted to write a letter.

Non finite verbs are of three types:
1. Infinitive Verbs
2. Participle Verbs and
3. The Gerund (Verbal noun)

INFINITIVE VERBS: Infinitive verbs are of two types:
1. To-infinitive and
2. Bare infinitive (plain infinitive)

To – infinitive:
Eg:
1. I want to write a letter
2. He used to do exercise in his youth.
3. She decided to marry him.
4. They tried to insult us.

Bare- infinitive : (plain infinitive)
Bare infinitives are used after the modal auxiliaries.
Eg:
1. I shall write a letter.
2. He shall do it tomorrow.
3. You should respect the teachers.

PARTICIPLE VERBS: Participle verbs are of two types
1. Present Participle and
2. Past participle
   (A participle is a word which is partly a verb and partly an adjective.)

PRESENT PARTICIPLE:
Present participle refers to an action going on and which is incomplete.
Eg:
1. They are playing well.
2. They were repairing the road.
3. We have been living here for two years.
4. Our mother will be coming tomorrow by this time.
5. I saw a boy running on the road.

GERUND: (Verbal Noun)
Gerund is one which does the work of a noun. Gerund does the work of work of a subject or an object.
Eg:
1. Smoking is a bad habit.
2. Singing is his hobby.
3. Swimming is a good exercise.

5. ADVERB

An adverb is a word which qualifies a verb or adjective or another adverb.

A. Adverbs qualifying verbs:
Eg:
1. She sang <u>sweetly.</u>
2. Rama runs <u>quickly.</u>

B. Adverbs qualifying another adverb:
Eg:
1. She sang <u>very</u> sweetly.
2. He ran <u>very</u> quickly.

C. **Adverbs qualifying adjectives:**
Eg:
  1. She is a <u>very</u> beautiful girl.
  2. He is a <u>very</u> cruel man.

There are three kinds of adverbs:
  1. Simple adverbs
  2. Interrogative Adverbs
  3. Relative Adverbs

SIMPLE ADVERBS: There are again many types of adverbs:

1. Adverbs of time:
Eg:
  1. He came late.
  2. Let us start now.

2. Adverbs of number:
Eg:
  1. They always play tennis.
  2. I often go there.

3. Adverbs of place: here, everywhere, nowhere, there etc.
Eg:
  1. He lives here.
  2. I looked for him everywhere.
  3. I found him nowhere.

4. Adverbs of manner or quality:
Eg:
  1. She sings sweetly.
  2. He fought bravely.

5. Adverbs of quantity:
Eg:
  1. The girl is very beautiful.
  2. She is a very beautiful girl.

6. Adverbs of reason:
Eg:
  1. Therefore they decided to kill him.
  2. Hence I am unable to help you.
  3. Consequently I refused to go.

7. Adverbs of affirmation and negation:
Eg:
  1. He is certainly right.
  2. You are surely mistaken.
  3. She is a fool indeed.
  4. He is not right.
  5. I do not know him.

FORMATION OF ADVERBS:
1. By adding 'ly' to an adjective.
Eg: (nicely, actively, quickly, slowly, lovingly, rashly, ably, rapidly, deeply, carefully, sorrowfully, joyfully, silently, excellently, calmly, loudly, highly, greatly, strongly, cheerfully, probably, handsomely, selfishly, happily, kindly, readily, heavily, doubly, cleverly, wisely, foolishly, beautifully and sweetly etc.)

2. By using wise, ways, ward and wards:
Eg: (Clock-wise, backwards, upwards, sideways and onward, forward)

3. Some of the Adverbs:
Eg: Asleep, ahead, away, today, tomorrow, abroad, along, behind, below, beyond, across, around and besides etc. Hereafter, hereby, thereby, herewith, within, without, before, beneath, herein, wherein, hitherto, therefore, and henceforth etc.

Now and then, again and again, by and by, far and wide, far and near, first and foremost, off and on, out and out, through and through, to and fro, up and down, over and above, over and over etc.

6. PREPOSITION

Prepositions carry significant importance in most of the ICET papers and hence they have been dealt in this book as a separate chapter.

7. CONJUNCTION

A conjunction is a word which combines two words or two clauses.
Eg:
  1. Sita and Gita are my sisters.
  2. You are strong and active.
  3. He worked patiently and carefully.
  4. Though he worked hard, he failed in the examination.
  5. Gopal or Govind is going to college.
  6. Prasad as well as Venu might do it.
  7. He was hungry, so he ate all cakes.
  8. If you come regularly, you will understand the lessons.

(And, or, if unless, as, so, as well as, but although, because, till, until, before, after, as soon as, no sooner-than, as far as, that, both-and, not only-but also, either-or, neither-nor, yet, for, since, which, who, what, whose, whom, why, while, when and whereas etc.)

Conjunctions are two types:
1. Coordinating Conjunctions
2. Subordinating Conjunctions

1. Coordinating Conjunction:

Coordinating conjunction is one that joins together sentence or clauses of equal rank. The main coordinating conjunctions are and, but, or, yet, so, either-or, neither-nor, as well as etc.

Eg:
1. The cow got up and slowly walked away.
2. She was both clever and beautiful.
3. She is poor, but she is honest.
4. You must run or you can't catch the train.
5. Something certainly fell in, for I heard a noise.
6. He is very wealthy, yet he is unhappy.
7. Either Sita or Gita should do it.
8. Neither Prasad nor Kumar has come here.

2. Subordinating Conjunction:

The chief subordinating conjunctions are after, because, if, unless, though (although), till, until, before, as, when and where.

Eg:
1. I think that he is a gentleman.
2. I don't know whether he will come.
3. I don't care if he comes or not.
4. I don't know where you are going.
5. Do you know when the Krishna Express arrives.
6. I don't understand why he was punished.
7. Tell me how you managed it.

8. INTERJECTION

An Interjection is a word which expresses a sudden feeling.

Eg: Hurrah! Sirrah! Alas! Hello! Oh! Hush! Good Heavens! Good God!

Prepositions 2

A Preposition is a word placed before a noun or a pronoun to show its relation to some other word in the sentence.

FOR:

Eg:

1. I have got some good news for you.
2. Drinking wine is bad for your health.
3. We are going to colleges for nothing.
4. He was given a little for his services to the country.
5. I cannot speak for others.
6. We have been waiting for twenty minutes.
7. There is no house for two kilometers.
8. Gandhiji fought with the English for freedom.
9. Abraham Lincoln strove for the abolition of slavery in the United States.
10. I bought it for ten rupees.
11. We paid ten rupees for it.
12. Red for danger.
13. She has won the prize for the third time.
14. For all his wealth; he had no happiness.
15. There are some apples for you.
16. It is a custom for the Hindus to burn dead bodies.
17. I am waiting for my wife.
18. Here is a letter for you.
19. She made some coffee for use.
20. They chose him for their leader.

OF:

Eg:

1. He spoke to us of his experiences.
2. She is fond of children.
3. I am fond of teaching.
4. It is very kind of you to invite me.
5. She had the sweetest of smiles.
6. What are you thinking of?
7. In course of time he saw his mistake.
8. There is a big tree in front of his house.
9. He walked to the end of the street.
10. He is capable of anything.
11. He is desirous of visiting Agra.
12. Children are fond of sweets.
13. The country suffers for want of skilled labour.
14. He is confident of securing the first prize.
15. Remember the duty of helping the poor.

TO:

Eg:

1. The mother sang her baby to sleep.
2. He tore the letters to pieces.
3. To whom did you give it?
4. I didn't stay to the end of the meeting.
5. I prefer walking to running.
6. The picture is true to life.
7. To my surprise he failed in the examination.
8. To my shame, I completely forgot the date.
9. He wants to go.
10. They came to help me.
11. I am ready to help.
12. The book is easy to understand.
13. She is too young to marry.
14. I will come with you to the bus stop.
15. We should not be cruel to animals.

WITH:

Eg:

1. Indians are acquainted with the art of painting.
2. I acted with him.
3. I met with an accident last night.
4. I have no money with me.
5. A tree's shadow moves with the sun.
6. We can't do anything with him.
7. His face was red with anger.
8. Her eyes were dim with tears.
9. The church was decorated with flowers.
10. She was in love with a doctor.
11. She fell in love with a black man.
12. I could not agree with you.
13. A new man came with the milk this morning.
14. We rose with the sun.
15. Times change and we must change with them.

AT:

Eg:

1. He charges interest at five percent.
2. He had to guess at the meaning.
3. He left school at the age of fifteen.
4. Mr.Kumar is at the office.
5. I will meet you at the railway station.
6. I first met him at a dinner party.
7. How many people were there at the lecture?
8. At last we have arrived at our destination.
9. I am good at Chess.

Verbal Ability / Grammar & RC

10. The boy is clever at Mathematics.
11. The policeman looked at us suspiciously.
12. Cars are parked at their owners risk.
13. The manager is at lunch.
14. The two tribes were constantly at war.
15. I wondered at his behaviour.

BY:

Eg:

1. She sat by the fire and told me a tale.
2. Come and sit by me.
3. My house is by the river.
4. It is useful to have a good dictionary by you, when you are reading.
5. Did you come by the nearest road?
6. It is no use trying to escape by day light.
7. Can you finish the work by tomorrow?
8. By the time you get there, it will be dark.
9. This temple was designed by Mr.Shanker.
10. He makes a living by teaching.
11. By the time you get there, it will be dark.
12. I swear by Almighty God.
13. The new library was opened by the collector.
14. I shall go by the 10-30 train.

ON:

Eg:

1. Let us move on.
2. The book lies on the table.
3. He sat on a stool.
4. Put it on.
5. The actor stepped on the stage.
6. The dog was sleeping on the mat.
7. She knocked on the window.
8. London stands on the Thames.
9. On his doctor's advice, he took rest.
10. They lived mostly on vegetables from their garden.
11. The two men were arrested on a charge of theft.
12. Have you any idea on the subject?
13. He lives on others.
14. He had no mercy on his victims.
15. I have had second thought on that matter.

IN:

Eg:

1. There is a cow in the field.
2. In case of need, phone to me.
3. Has he come in?
4. Is he in his room?
5. She sat in a corner.
6. We all went in.
7. He is in the room.
8. She is in America.
9. They live in Delhi.
10. He did not succeed in his life.
11. She excels in dancing.
12. He dipped his pen in the ink.
13. Cut the apple in two.
14. They fell in love.
16. I shall be back in a short time.

FROM:

Eg:

1. How far is it from here?
2. From what I know of him I hesitate to trust him.
3. His skill comes from practice.
4. She will go to school from tomorrow.
5. The income derived from the ownership of land is called rent.
6. Man is entirely different from other animals.
7. They were prohibited from entering the village.
8. Steel is made from iron.
9. Wine is made from grapes.
10. Take that knife away from the baby.
11. The train for Calcutta leaves from platform three.
12. My brother came from Guntur.
13. Tea comes from India and China.
14. Many English words are derived from Latin.
16. Shakespeare lived from 1564 to 1616.

OVER:

Eg:

1. She spread a cloth over the table.
2. They hung a curtain over the picture.
3. I have two people over me.
4. The thief threw the purse over the bush.
5. It is no use crying over spilt milk.
6. The sky is over our heads.
7. There was a lamp over the table.
8. He has no command over himself.
9. Snow is falling over the north of England.
10. He is famous all over the world.
11. He has travelled all over Europe.
12. He stayed in London over a month.

DURING:

Eg:

1. During the winter, we play foot ball.
2. The theft occurred during the night.
3. The fire started during the dinner hour.
4. He called to see me during my absence.
5. The sun gives us light during the day.

AGAINST:

Eg:
1. Public opinion was against the proposal.
2. She was married against her will.
3. I voted against the party.
4. He hit his head against the wall.
5. Place the ladder against the tree.
6. My father was against giving votes to women.

OFF:

Eg:
1. He cut himself off from the rest of the people.
2. The examinations were put off.
3. They got off the bus.
4. I went to the airport to send him off.
5. The picture fell off the wall.

AFTER:

Eg:
1. I do not know what to do in after years.
2. He fell ill on Sunday and died three days after.
3. I shall arrive after you leave.
4. Shut the door after he comes.
5. 'Against' comes after 'again' in the dictionary.
6. The policeman ran after the thief.

ACCORDING TO:

Eg:
1. According to the Bible, God created the world in six days.
2. Take one to three tablets according to the severity of the pain.
3. According to the weather forecast, we shall have rain tomorrow.
4. He will be punished according to the seriousness of his crime.
5. The books are placed on the shelves according to the authors.

ABOVE:

Eg:
1. The shelf should be six feet above the level of the floor.
2. As a scholar he is far above me.
3. The water came above our knees.
4. She married above her position.
5. This book is above me.
6. We flew above the Sahara.

ABOUT:

Eg:
1. Don't leave waste paper and empty bottles about in the park.
2. People are sitting about on the grass.
3. There is no one to talk about.
4. He was walking about the town.
5. He has traveled about the world.

ACROSS:

Eg:
1. I have never come across such an idiot.
2. He swam across the river.
3. She walked across the street.
4. He sat with his arms across his chest.
5. At one point the railway line goes across the road.

ALONG:

Eg:
1. We walked along the road.
2. There are trees all along the river banks.
3. He comes along here. (in this direction)
4. The small boy was dragging his coat along the ground.

Exercise [On Prepositions]

Directions for questions 1 to 100: Fill in the blanks with the appropriate choice of prepositions.

1. He wanted to talk to me but I kept ___ working and refused to listen.
   (1) on   (2) up
   (3) out   (4) back

2. She is a good secretary but she is kept ___ by her ignorance of languages.
   (1) on   (2) up
   (3) out   (4) back

3. The country was in a state of rebellion and was only kept ___ by repressive measures.
   (1) on   (2) down
   (3) out   (4) back

4. Look ___ the baby while I am out.
   (1) on   (2) up
   (3) after   (4) back

5. She kept the children ___ all day because it was so wet and cold.
   (1) on   (2) in
   (3) out   (4) back

6. You must look ___ and make plans for the future.
   (1) on   (2) up
   (3) ahead   (4) back

7. "Keep ___!" he said. "Don't come any nearer."
   (1) on   (2) up
   (3) out   (4) back

8. If you look ___ it carefully, you will see the mark.
   (1) on   (2) at
   (3) out   (4) back

9. I told the children to keep ___ the room that was being painted.
   (1) on   (2) up
   (3) out of   (4) back

10. Looking ___ , I see now all the mistakes I made when I was younger.
    (1) on   (2) up
    (3) out   (4) back

11. I have started getting ___ at 5 a.m. to study but I don't know if I can keep this up.
    (1) on   (2) up
    (3) out   (4) back

12. He had an unhappy childhood and he never looks ___ on it with any pleasure.
    (1) on   (2) up
    (3) out   (4) back

13. The man walked so fast that the child couldn't keep ___ him.
    (1) on   (2) up with
    (3) out   (4) back

14. She looked ___ to see who was following her.
    (1) on   (2) up
    (3) out   (4) back

15. There were so many panes of glass broken that the windows couldn't keep ___ the rain.
    (1) on   (2) up
    (3) out   (4) back

16. I' ve been looking ___ a cup to match the one I broke.
    (1) on   (2) up
    (3) out   (4) for

17. Look ___ me at the station. I'll be at the bookstall.
    (1) on   (2) up
    (3) out for   (4) back

18. Look ___ ! You nearly knocked my cup out of my hand.
    (1) on   (2) up
    (3) out   (4) back

19. He was kept ___ in his research by lack of money.
    (1) on   (2) up
    (3) out   (4) back

20. Tom is looking ___ his first trip abroad.
    (1) on   (2) foward to
    (3) out   (4) back

21. Look ___ on your way home and tell me what happened.
(1) on　　　　　　　　(2) up
(3) out　　　　　　　　(4) in

22. Before putting any money into the business, we must look very carefully ___ the accounts.
(1) on　　　　　　　　(2) up
(3) into　　　　　　　　(4) back

23. I look ___ her as one of the family.
(1) on　　　　　　　　(2) up
(3) out　　　　　　　　(4) back

24. My windows look ___ the garden.
(1) on　　　　　　　　(2) on to
(3) out　　　　　　　　(4) back

25. He asked me to look ___ the document and then sign it.
(1) on　　　　　　　　(2) up
(3) over　　　　　　　　(4) back

26. He looked ___ the book to see if he had read it before.
(1) on　　　　　　　　(2) up
(3) out　　　　　　　　(4) through

27. If you can afford a new car, your business must be looking ___ .
(1) on　　　　　　　　(2) up
(3) out　　　　　　　　(4) back

28. You can always look ___ her address in the directory if you have forgotten it.
(1) on　　　　　　　　(2) up
(3) out　　　　　　　　(4) back

29. He looked me ___ and ___ before he condescended to answer my question.
(1) on ... on　　　　　　(2) up ... down
(3) up ... up　　　　　　(4) back ... front

30. I am looking ___ seeing your new house.
(1) foward to　　　　　　(2) up to
(3) out to　　　　　　　(4) back to

31. Children have a natural inclination to look ___ their parents.
(1) foward to　　　　　　(2) up to
(3) out on　　　　　　　(4) back to

32. You will see I am right if you look ___ the matter from my point of view.
(1) on　　　　　　　　(2) at
(3) down　　　　　　　(4) back

33. He looks ___ me because I spend my holidays in Bournemouth instead of going abroad.
(1) down at　　　　　　(2) down on
(3) out of　　　　　　　(4) back on

34. If he doesn't know the word he can look it ___ in a dictionary.
(1) on　　　　　　　　(2) up
(3) out　　　　　　　　(4) back

35. The crowd looked ___ while the police surrounded the house.
(1) on　　　　　　　　(2) up
(3) out　　　　　　　　(4) at

36. Since our quarrel, she looks ___ me whenever we meet.
(1) at　　　　　　　　(2) up to
(3) down　　　　　　　(4) through

37. It was some time before he came ___ after being knocked out.
(1) round　　　　　　　(2) up
(3) on　　　　　　　　(4) back

38. I had to wait for permission from the Town Council before I could go ___ with my plans.
(1) round　　　　　　　(2) up
(3) on　　　　　　　　(4) back

39. He came ___ to my way of thinking after a good deal of argument.
(1) round　　　　　　　(2) up
(3) on　　　　　　　　(4) back

40. The guard dog went ___ the intruder and knocked him down.
(1) round　　　　　　　(2) for
(3) on　　　　　　　　(4) back

41. He had a sandwich and a cup of coffee, then went ___ working.
(1) out　　　　　　　　(2) up
(3) on　　　　　　　　(4) back

42. It's no use trying to keep it secret; it's sure to come ___ in the end.
(1) out　　　　　　　　(2) up
(3) on　　　　　　　　(4) back

43. I went ___ the proposal very carefully with my solicitors and finally decided not to accept their offer.
(1) over   (2) up
(3) on   (4) off

44. The gun went ___ by accident and wounded him in the leg.
(1) over   (2) up
(3) on   (4) off

45. The question of salary increases will come ___ at the next general meeting.
(1) out   (2) up
(3) on   (4) off

46. Wearing black for mourning went ___ many years ago.
(1) out   (2) up
(3) on   (4) off

47. She went ___ a beauty contest and got a prize.
(1) in for   (2) up for
(3) on for   (4) off

48. Those rust marks will come ___ if you rub them with lemon.
(1) out   (2) up
(3) on   (4) off

49. The price of tomatoes usually goes ___ in summer in England.
(1) out   (2) down
(3) on   (4) off

50. If there isn't enough soup to go ___, just put some hot water in it.
(1) out   (2) round
(3) on   (4) off

51. Seeing me from across the room she came ___ me, and said that she had a message for me.
(1) out to   (2) up to
(3) on to   (4) off to

52. The early colonists of Canada went ___ many hardships.
(1) out   (2) to
(3) through   (4) off

53. You can't go ___ on your promise now; we are depending on you.
(1) out   (2) back
(3) up   (4) down

54. I have changed my mind about marrying him; I simply can't go ___ with it.
(1) on   (2) up
(3) through   (4) off

55. The aeroplane crashed and went ___ in flames.
(1) out   (2) up
(3) on   (4) off

56. He came ___ to a fortune last year.
(1) up   (2) in
(3) on   (4) off

57. Wait till prices come ___ again before you buy.
(1) low   (2) up
(3) on   (4) down

58. I refuse to go ___ now. I'm going on.
(1) out   (2) up
(3) on   (4) back

59. They have gone ___ all the calculations again but they still can't find the mistake.
(1) out   (2) over
(3) on   (4) off

60. The party went ___ very well; we all enjoyed ourselves.
(1) out   (2) up
(3) on   (4) off

61. Come ___ ! It's far too cold to wait here any longer.
(1) out   (2) up
(3) on   (4) off

62. Mary went ___ in such a hurry that she left her passport behind.
(1) out   (2) up
(3) on   (4) off

63. The handle of the tea-pot came ___ in my hand as I was washing it.
(1) out   (2) up
(3) on   (4) off

64. Why don't you go ___ for stamp collecting if you want a hobby?
(1) out   (2) up
(3) in   (4) off

65. I came ___ a vase exactly like yours in an antique shop.
(1) out   (2) upon
(3) on   (4) off

66. Her weight went ___ to 70 kilos when she stopped playing tennis.
(1) out   (2) up
(3) on   (4) off

67. Don't go ___ food if you want to economize. Just drink less.
(1) without   (2) no
(3) on   (4) off

68. The sea has gone ___ considerably since last night's gale.
(1) out   (2) down
(3) on   (4) off

69. I'm at home all day. Come ___ whenever you have time.
(1) out   (2) up
(3) on   (4) round

70. She went ___ with her work after the interruptions.
(1) out   (2) up
(3) on   (4) off

71. She goes ___ a lot. She hardly ever spends an evening at home.
(1) out   (2) up
(3) on   (4) off

72. I suggested that we should all take a cut in salary. Naturally this didn't go ___ very well .
(1) out   (2) up
(3) down   (4) off

73. I couldn't take ___ the lecture at all. It was too difficult for me.
(1) out   (2) in
(3) on   (4) off

74. He is inclined to let his enthusiasm run ___ with him.
(1) out   (2) up
(3) away   (4) off

75. When he offered me only $3, I was too taken ___ to say a word.
(1) out   (2) back
(3) on   (4) aback

76. He has already run ___ the money his father left him two years ago.
(1) out   (2) through
(3) on   (4) off

77. Now he is catching ___ because he wants to pass.
(1) out   (2) up
(3) on   (4) off

78. She took ___ riding because she wanted to lose weight.
(1) out   (2) up
(3) on   (4) off

79. I can't start the car; the battery has run ___ .
(1) out   (2) up
(3) down   (4) off

80. The policeman ran ___ the thief.
(1) out   (2) up
(3) on   (4) after

81. He takes ___ his mother; he has blue eyes and fair hair.
(1) out   (2) up
(3) on   (4) after

82. I forgot to turn off the tap and the wash basin ran ___ .
(1) out   (2) up
(3) over   (4) off

83. That blouse is easy to make. You could run it ___ in an hour.
(1) out   (2) up
(3) on   (4) off

84. I am sorry I called you a liar. I take it ___ .
(1) out   (2) back
(3) on   (4) off

85. Reformers usually run ___ against opposition from all kinds of people.
(1) out   (2) up
(3) on   (4) off

86. He took ___ going for a walk every night before he went to bed.
(1) to   (2) up
(3) on   (4) off

87. Don't run ___ with the idea that Scotsmen are mean. They just don't like wasting money.
(1) out   (2) away
(3) on   (4) off

Verbal Ability / Grammar & RC

88. I wish we could sell the grand piano; it takes ___ too much space here.
(1) out   (2) up
(3) on   (4) off

89. She is always running ___ her friends behind their backs. She soon won't have any friends left.
(1) out   (2) up
(3) down   (4) off

90. You'd better take ___ your coat if you're too hot.
(1) out   (2) up
(3) on   (4) off

91. Just run ___ the music of this song for me.
(1) out   (2) over
(3) on   (4) off

92. We took ___ each other the first time we met and have been friends ever since.
(1) to   (2) over
(3) on   (4) off

93. When his father died, Tom took ___ the business.
(1) out   (2) up
(3) over   (4) off

94. What I saw in the water was only an old tree, I took it ___ the Loch Ness Monster.
(1) out   (2) for
(3) on   (4) off

95. I ran ___ to an old school friend in the tube today.
(1) in   (2) up
(3) on   (4) off

96. I can't go more than 50 km/hr as this is a new car and I am still running it ___ .
(1) out   (2) up
(3) in   (4) off

97. People often take me ___ my sister. We are very much like each other.
(1) out   (2) for
(3) about   (4) off

98. My neighbour is always running ___ of bread and borrowing some from me.
(1) out   (2) up
(3) on   (4) off

99. He always takes ___ his false teeth before he goes to bed.
(1) out   (2) up
(3) off   (4) on

100. I took ___ Tom at chess and beat him
(1) out   (2) up
(3) on   (4) off

Tenses 3

Tense: Tense is the form of a verb which shows the time of an action. Tenses are mainly of three types.
I.   Present Tense
II. Past Tense
III. Future Tense

I. PRESENT TENSE
Present Tense shows the action of the present time.
Eg:
1. I go to college by bus every morning.
2. I am reading a book
3. He has come just now.
4. We have been living in this house for the last four years.

1. SIMPLE PRESENT TENSE:
Simple present tense shows a daily action. When the subject is in the third person singular (he, she and it) and the verb is in simple present tense, we must add 's' or 'es' to the verb.

Simple present tense is used to express habitual actions. It is used with the expressions showing a daily action like

Always, daily, regularly, everyday, every night, generally, every morning, often, frequently, usually, rarely, seldom etc.,
Eg:
1. He drinks tea every morning.
2. I get up every day at 5 O' clock.

Simple present Tense is used to express general truths or universal truths.
Eg:
1. The sun rises in the east.
2. The earth moves round the sun.

Simple present tense is used in the verbs expressing possession like have, possess, own, consist, belong to, comprise, contain etc.,
Eg:
1. We have three daughters and two sons.
2. He owns two shops.

Simple Present Tense is used in the verbs that express feelings like love, like, hate, dislike, remember, want, wish feel, think, hope, believe, agree, disagree, know, consider, prefer, suppose, taste, smell understand, imagine etc.,

Eg:
1. I love my parents.
2. I remember the address.

Simple Present Tense is used in the verbs of appearance like appear, look, seem etc.,
Eg:
1. He seems to be a gentle man.
2. She looks like an angel.
3. You appear to be good students.

Simple present tense is also used to indicate future event that is part of a plan or arrangement.
Eg:
1. Our college reopens on 12th June.
2. The Chief Minister returns from Delhi next Thursday.
3. The Prime Minister visits U.S.A. in June.
4. We dine at the Taj tonight.

Simple present tense is used to refer to what happens at the time of speaking.
Eg:
1. Here comes the bus.
2. There goes the ball.

Simple present tense is also used to express a certain capability.
Eg:
1. He speaks three languages.
2. She cooks well.

Simple present tense is used in a quotation.
Eg:
1. Shakespeare says, "Love is blind."
2. Keats says, "A thing of beauty is a joy forever."

After the expressions like accustomed to, habituated to, averse to, addicted to, look forward to, used to, became used to etc., we must use verbal noun or continuous form of the verb.
Eg:
1. She is habituated to singing.
2. They are addicted to drinking wine.

2. PRESENT CONTINUOUS TENSE
The –ing form of the verb or 'verbal noun' is used as an object after some verbs like avoid, stop, start, like, love, hate, finish, begin, enjoy, miss etc.,

Verbal Ability / Grammar & RC

Eg:
1. She avoids seeing/meeting him.
2. I love swimming in the sea.
3. I hate dancing in the rain.
4. I begin singing at 4 a.m.
5. I enjoy reading at a cafe.

The verbs see, hear, feel, notice, watch, find, observe, keep, catch etc., are used with an object followed by 'ing' form.

Eg:
1. We saw Gopal crossing the bridge.
2. I heard somebody knocking at the door.
3. He felt his heart beating.
4. They kept her waiting.
5. We observed her dancing
6. We watched them playing
7. She found him running on the road.
8. She caught him cheating in the exam.

3. PRESENT PERFECT TENSE:

Present Perfect tense shows an action that has just completed.

It is formed with have or has followed by the past participle of the verb. It is used with the expressions like just, just now, till now, so far, yet, already, recently, never, ever, before etc., (for & since also)

Eg:
1. He has just come here
2. My father has gone out just now.
3. Gauri has just undergone an operation.
4. She has just finished her report.
5. Ramu has already begun his preparations.

4. PRESENT PERFECT CONTINUOUS TENSE:

It shows an action that began in the past and is still continuing. It is formed with <u>have</u> or <u>has</u> + <u>been</u> + <u>continuous</u> form of the verb. It is used with prepositions like <u>for</u> and <u>since</u> which show the time.

For is used for period of time.

Eg: They have been discussing the marketing plan for the last three hours.

II. PAST TENSE

Past tense shows the action of the past time. Past tense has four forms. They are

1. Simple past tense
2. Past continuous tense
3. Past perfect tense and
4. Past perfect continuous tense.

1. SIMPLE PAST TENSE:

Simple past tense shows a single past action.

It is used with the expressions showing past action like <u>yesterday, last week, last night, last year, four days ago, once upon a time, long long ago, in 1996, last Monday</u> etc.,

Eg:
1. We saw a film last night.
2. They gave me a book last year.

Simple past tense is used when since is used as a conjunction.

Eg:
1. I have not played cricket since I left college.
2. She has not seen films since her husband died.
3. Twenty years have passed since we first met.
4. I have not seen him since I left for England.

Simple past tense is used in the clause after the expressions like <u>high time, it is time, would rather, I wish, as if</u> and <u>suppose</u> in the imaginary type.

Eg:
1. It is high time that we left.
2. I would rather you stayed at home.
3. It is time we left.
4. I wish I were rich.
5. Suppose we went to a show.
6. She walks as if she were a queen.
7. If I were a poet, I would write many poems.

2. PAST CONTINUOUS TENSE:

It shows an action going on in the past. It is formed with was or were followed by the continuous form of the verb.

Eg:
1. When the principal went to the college yesterday, all the students were quarrelling.
2. When he came to our house yesterday, I was sleeping.
3. When I went to the playground last evening, my friends were playing cricket.
4. While he was going through the forest, a tiger jumped on him.
5. He was in a meeting when we went near him.
6. The boy fell while he was running.
7. I was having a bath when the phone rang.
8. Mother was cooking when the bell rang.
9. While we were watching television, the power failed.
10. The light went out, while I was reading.
11. When I saw him, he was playing chess.

Note: When there is a past tense in the subordinate clause, then we must write past continuous tense (not present continuous tense) in the main clause.

3. PAST PERFECT TENSE:

It shows two past actions which happened one after the other. The action which happened first must be in the past perfect tense and the action which happened next must be in the simple past tense. It is formed with <u>had</u> followed by the past participle of the verb. When there is a single past action, we must write only simple past tense, but not past perfect tense.

Eg:
1. Before I reached the station, the train had left the platform.
2. Before the teacher entered the class, all the students had gone out.
3. After we had finished our lunch, the guests came to our house.
4. Before he arrived. I had written the letter.
5. She had passed B.A., before she got a job.
6. When I reached the station, the train had started.
7. They went home, after they finished their work.

4. PAST PERFECT CONTINUOUS TENSE:

It shows an action that began before a certain point in the past and was continuing still in the past. It is formed with <u>had + been + continuous of the verb.</u>

Eg:
1. The old man had been exercising in his youth.
2. Gavaskar had been batting very well in his youth.

Note: When there is a past tense in the reported part, we must write past perfect continuous tense, but not past continuous tense in the indirect part in which for and since are used before time expressions.

Eg:
1. He said, "I have been suffering from fever for three days."
2. He said that he had been suffering from fever for three days.

III. FUTURE TENSE

1. SIMPLE FUTURE TENSE:

It shows a single future action. It is formed with <u>shall</u> or <u>will</u> followed by infinitive. Even after the helping verbs like <u>shall, should, will, would, can, could, may, might, ought to, must</u> etc., we must write only infinitive.

The difference between shall and will is as follows:
1. I person + shall _____________ definite future action.
2. I person + will _____________ only future action.
3. II & III persons + will _________ only future action.
4. II & III persons + shall _________ definite future action.

Generally after first person, we use <u>shall</u> and after second and third persons, <u>will.</u>

Eg:
1. I shall do it tomorrow. (definite future action).
2. We will do it tomorrow. (Only future action)
3. You will come to our house tomorrow. (only future action)
4. He shall come to our house tomorrow. (definite future action).

Note: The simple future tense is not used in clauses of time and condition. The simple present tense is used in clauses of time and condition beginning with when, before, till until, that, as long as, as soon as, if, unless etc.

Eg:
1. I will stay here till you return.
2. He won't pass the examination unless he works hard.
3. I shall wait here till you finish your lunch.
4. I shall go there if he calls me.
5. He will pay the bill when he comes.
6. Please see me before you leave the office.
7. We shall leave the place an soon as you are ready.
8. There will be no poverty as long as we work hard.
9. He will wire before he arrives.

2. FUTURE CONTINUOUS TENSE:

It shows an action going on in the future. It is formed with <u>shall</u> or <u>will + be + continuous form of the verb.</u>

Eg:
1. We shall be witnessing the cricket match tomorrow by this time.
2. They will be coming to our house tomorrow by this time.
3. When he goes home, his wife will be waiting for him at the door.

Note: When there is simple present tense in the subordinate clause, in the main clause we must write future continuous tense, but not present continuous tense.

3. FUTURE PERFECT TENSE:

It shows completion of an action by a certain time in the future. It is formed with shall or will + have + past participle of the verb;

Eg:

1. Before you reach the station, the train will have left the platform.
2. Before you go to see him, he will have left the place.
3. They will have built the dam by next year.
4. He will have written his second novel by next May.

Note: When there is simple present tense in subordinate clause, then we must write future perfect tense, (not simple future tense) in the main clause.

4. FUTURE PERFECT CONTINUOUS TENSE:

It shows an action that will start in the future and will be going on in the future. It is formed with will or shall + have + been + continuous form of the verb.

Eg:

1. We shall have been living together.
2. His daughter will have been leading her life with her husband.
3. I shall have been doing the job in this office.

TENSES IN CONDITIONAL SENTENCES

Conditional sentences have 2 parts. They are

1. The if-clause 2. The main – Clause

Eg: If you come regularly.

If – clause

You will understand the lessons.

Main – clause

There are three types of conditional sentences. They are :

1. Type (probable condition)
2. Type (Improbable condition or imaginary type)
3. Type (Unfulfilled condition)

EACH OF CONDITIONAL SENTENCES HAS DIFFERENT PART OF TENSES

No.	If-Clause	Main – clause
1. Type	Simple present Tense	Future tense (Shall or will or may or can + infinitive)
2. Type	Simple past Tense	Should or would or could or might +infinitive
3. Type	Past perfect tense	Should or would or could or might + (had +past participle of the verb) have + past participle of the verb

1. Type (Probable Condition):

In the I Type of conditional sentences, something will happen if a certain condition is fulfilled. In the if-clause, simple present tense is used.

Eg:

1. If you work hard, you will get more marks.
2. If you come regularly, you will understand the lessons.
3. If I am a rich man, I shall help the poor.
4. If the students have patience, they can achieve anything.
5. If it rains, I won't go out.

2. Type (Improbable condition or Imaginary type)

In the second type of conditional sentences, anything will not happen and everything is purely imaginary. In the if – clause we must write simple past tense and in the main clause we must use should or would or could or might + infinitive.

Eg:

1. If I had more money, I would buy a car.
2. If I married her, I would get all her property.
3. If I were a poet, I would write many poems.
4. If I were a rich man, I would help the poor.
5. If I had wings, I would fly.

3. Type (Unfulfilled condition):

In this type, something did not happen in the past, because a certain condition was not fulfilled. In the in-clause we must write past perfect tense and in the main clause we must use should or would or could or might +have + past participle of the verb.

Eg:

1. If you had gone by taxi, you would have caught the train.
2. If you had come regularly at the beginning, you would have understood the lessons.
3. If I had come earlier, I would have met him.
4. If he had worked hard, he would have passed the examination.
5. If she had played well, she would have got a prize.

If I have more money, I will buy a car. (1 Type)

If I had more money, I would buy a car (2 Type)

If I had more money, I would have bought a car. (3 Type)

If you work hard, you will get more marks. (1 Type)

If you worked hard, you would get more marks. (2 Type)

If you had worked, you would have got more marks. (3 Type).

Structures 4

1. **Simple Present Tense :** Do, Does
   I, We, You, They ....do
   He, She, It, Rama ....does
   Subject + Verb + Object
   I   Write   a letter

2. **Present Continuous Tense :** Am, Is and Are
   I .... am
   We.......... are
   You .... are
   He, She, It, Rama .... is
   They ....are
   Subjects + am/is/are + Verb+ing.form + Object
   I   am   writing   a letter

3. **Present Perfect Tense :** Have , has
   I, We, You, They .... have
   He, She, It, Rama........... has
   Subject + have / has + Past participle of the verb + Object
   I   have   written   a letter

4. **Present Perfect Continuous Tense:** Have been
   I, We, You, They .... have been
   He, She, It, Rama........... have been
   Subject + have / has + Past participle of the verb + Object
   I   have been   writing   a letter

5. **Simple Past Tense:** Did
   I, We, You, They, He, She, It, Rama ....did
   Subject + Past Tense of the verb + Object
   I   wrote   a letter

6. **Past Continuous Tense:** Was, were
   I, We, You, They........were
   He, She, It, Rama....... was
   Subject + Was/were + Verb+ing.form + Object
   I   was   writing   a letter

7. **Past Perfect Tense :** Had
   I, We, You, They, He, She, It, Rama ....had
   Subject + had + Past participle of the Verb + Object
   I   had   written   a letter

8. **Past Perfect Continuous Tense :** had been
   I, We, You, They, He, She, It, Rama........had been
   Subject + Had been + verb+ing.form + Object
   I   had been   writing   a letter

                                          Verbal Ability / Grammar & RC

9. **Simple Future Tense :** Shall, will

I, We, …….. shall

You, He, She, It, Rama, They ……….will

Subject   +   Shall/will   +   Infinitive   +   Object

I   Shall   Write   a letter

10. **Future Continuous Tense :** Shall be, will be

I, we ……….. shall be

You, He, She, It, They……. will be

Subject   +   shallbe/will be   +   verb +ing. Form   +   Object

I   shall be   writing   a letter

11. **Future Perfect Tense :** Shall have, will have

I, We……….. Shall have

You, He, She, It, Rama, They …… will have

Subject   +   Shall have / will have   +   past participle of the verb   +   Object

I   Shall have   written   a letter

12. **Future Perfect Continuous Tense :** Shall have been, will have been

I, We…….. shall have been

You, He, She, It, Rama, They…….. will have been

Subject   +   shall have been / will have been   +   Verb +ing. Form   +   object

I   shall have been   writing   a letter

Examples:

I am a student	:	Please give me your pen.
We are workers	:	They invited us to the party.
You are a clerk	:	He called you.
He is a teacher	:	I know him well.
She is a nurse	:	Do you know her?
It is a book	:	Take it.
They are doctors	:	Tell them to wait here.

This is my hat.
This is our garden.
That is your pen.
This is his book
That is her bag.
It is their house.

This book is mine.
This garden is ours.
That pen is yours.
This shop is his.
That bag is hers.
This car is theirs.

I have taught myself.
We knew ourselves.
You said it yourself.
He told himself that he had done it.
He told himself that he had done it.
She hurt herself.
The house itself has fallen down.
They helped themselves.

VERBAL FORMS

A. ALL THREE VERBAL FORMS ARE IDENTICAL :

Present Tense	Past Tense	Past Participle
Bet	Bet (Betted)	Bet (Betted)
Bid	Bid	Bid
Broadcast	Broadcast	Broadcast
Cast	Cast	Cast
Burst	Burst	Burst
Cost	Cost	Cost
Cut	Cut	Cut
Hit	Hit	Hit
Hurt	Hurt	Hurt
Knit	Knit (Knitted)	Knit (Knitted)
Let	Let	Let
Put	Put	Put
Quit	Quit (Quitted)	Quit (Quitted)
Read	Read	Read
Set	Set	Set
Shut	Shut	Shut
Split	Split	Split
Spread	Spread	Spread
Shed	Shed	Shed
Slit	Slit	Slit

B. TWO PARTS (MAINLY PAST AND PAST PARTICIPLE) ARE IDENTICAL:

Present Tense	Past Tense	Past Participle
Beat	Beat	Beaten
Come	Came	Come
Become	Became	Become
Bend	Bent	Bent
Present Tense	**Past Tense**	**Past Participle**
Bind	Bound	Bound
Bleed	Bled	Bled
Bring	Brought	Brought
Buy	Bought	Bought
Build	Built	Built
Burn	Burned (Burnt)	Burned (Burnt)
Bowl	Bowled	Bowled
Beseech	Besought	Besought
Catch	Caught	Caught
Cling	Clung	Clung
Creep	Crept	Crept
Call	Called	Called
Act	Acted	Acted
Colour	Coloured	Cloured
Cough	Coughed	Coughed
Dig	Dug	Dug
Dream	Dreamt (Dreamed)	Dreamt (Dreamed)
Drag	Dragged	Dragged
Dare	Dared	Dared
Deal	Dealt	Dealt

Dwell	Dwelt	Dwelt
Dive	Dived	Dived
End	Ended	Ended
Endeavour	Endeavoured	Endeavoured
Feed	Fed	Fed
Feel	Felt	Felt
Fight	Fought	Fought
Find	Found	Found
Flee	Fled	Fled
Flow	Flowed	Flowed
Frame	Framed	Framed
Get	Go	Got
Forget	Forgot	Forgotten
Grind	Ground	Ground
Hand (for men)	Hanged	Hanged
Hang (for things)	Hung	Hung
Have	Had	Had
Hear	Heard	Heard
Hold	Held	Held
Hope	Hoped	Hoped
Hop	Hopped	Hopped
Keep	Kept	Kept
Kneel	Knelt (Kneeled)	Knelt (Kneeled)
Kill	Killed	Killed
Kiss	Kissed	Kissed
Lay	Laid	Laid
Lie	Lied	Lied
Present Tense	**Past Tense**	**Past Participle**
Leap	Leapt	Leapt
Learn	Learnt (learned)	Learnt (learned)
Lend	Lent	Lent
Light	Lit (Lighted)	Lit (Lighted)
Lose	Lost	Lost
Make	Made	Made
Mean	Meant	Meant
Meet	Met	Met
Mark	Marked	Marked
Manage	Managed	Managed
Miss	Missed	Missed
Need	Needed	Needed
Overcome	Overcome	Overcome
Open	Opened	Opened
Pay	Paid	Paid
Prove	Proved	Proved
Run	Ran	Run
Say	Said	Said
Seek	Sought	Sought
Shoot	Shot	Shot
Sit	Sat	Sat
Sleep	Slept	Slept
Slide	Slid	Slid
Smell	Smelt (Smelled)	Smelt (Smelled)

Speed	Sped	Sped
Spell	Spelt (Spelled)	Spelt (Spelled)
Spill	Spilled	Spilled
Understand	Understood	Understood
Stick	Stuck	Stuck
Strike	Struck	Struck
String	Strung	Strung
Swing	Swung	Swung
Spoil	Spoilt (Spoiled)	Spoilt (Spoiled)
Shine	Shone	Shone
Spit	Spat	Spat
Spin	Spun	Spun
Sling	Slung	Slung
Sting	Stung	Stung
Teach	Taught	Taught
Tell	Told	Told
Weep	Wept	Wept
Win	Won	Won
Wind	Wound	Wound
Wish	Wished	Wished
Withhold	Withheld	Withheld
Withstand	Withstood	Withstood
Whisper	Whispered	Whispered

C.   ALL VERBAL FORMS ARE DIFFERENT

Present Tense	Past Tense	Past Participle
Arise	Arose	Arisen
Awake	Awoke	Awoken (awaked)
Be (am, is, are)	Was, Were	Been
Bear	Bore	Born (Borne)
Break	Broke	Broken
Choose	Chosen	Chosen
Do	Did	Done
Draw	Drew	Drawn
Drink	Drank	Drunk
Eat	Ate	Eaten
Fly	Flew	Flown
Give	Gave	Given
Go	Went	Gone
Grow	Grew	Grown
Know	Knew	Known
Mistake	Mistook	Mistaken
Ride	Rode	Ridden
Ring	Rang	Rung
Rise	Rose	Risen
Sow	Sowed	Sown
See	Saw	Seen

Verbal Ability / Grammar & RC

Degrees of Comparison 5

Adjectives and adverbs have degrees of comparison. There are three kinds of degrees of comparison.

They are :
1. Positive degree
2. Comparative Degree
3. Superlative degree

Generally we can form comparative degree by adding 'er' to the positive and superlative by adding 'est' to the positive.

Positive	Comparative	Superlative
High	Higher	Highest
Big	Bigger	Biggest
Small	Smaller	Smallest
Kind	Kinder	Kindest
Great	Greater	Greatest
Tall	Taller	Tallest
Clever	Cleverer	Cleverest

Exceptions:

Good	Better	Best
Bad	Worse	Worst
Little	Less	Least
Beautiful	More beautiful	Most beautiful
Active	More active	Most active

(A) Comparison between two persons or two things:

When there is a comparison between two things or two persons, there will be no superlative degree.

Eg:

1. Sita is taller than Gita (Comparative)
Ans: Gita is not so tall as sita. (Positive)

2. Mumbai is bigger than Hyderabad. (Comparative)
Ans: Hyderabad is not so big as Mumbai. (Positive)

3. Chennai is hotter than Hyderabad. (Comparative)
Ans: Hyderabad is not so hot as Chennai. (Positive)

4. A deer runs faster than a horse. (Comparative)
Ans: A horse does not run so fast as a deer. (Positive)

5. Gold is more precious than silver. (Comparative)
Ans: Silver is not so precious as gold. (Positive)

6. It is more difficult to learn Sanskrit than to learn English (Comparative)
Ans: To learn English is not so difficult as to learn Sanskrit. (Positive)

7. Sita is not taller than Rajani. (Comparative)
Ans: Rajani is as tall as Sita. (Positive)

8. It is not so easy to understand women as to understand men. (Positive)
Ans: To understand men is easier than to understand women. (Comparative)

9. Ravi runs faster than Sarath. (Comparative)
Ans: Sarath does not run so fast as Ravi. (Positive)

10. My pen is not so good as yours. (Positive)
Ans: Your pen is better than mine. (Comparative)

11. I am not so strong as he. (Positive)
Ans: He is stronger than I. (Comparative)

12. I am as strong as he. (Positive)
Ans: He is not stronger than I. (Comparative)

B. Comparison among more than two persons or things:

I Model: No other (so-as) ....positive
Than any other or..........comparative
Than all over
The or of all.............. Superlative

1. Bharath is the cleverest boy in the class. (Superlative)
Or
Bharath is the cleverest of all boys in the class.
Ans: Bharath is cleverer than any other boy in the class (Comparative)
No other boy in the class is so clever as Bharath (Positive)

2. Everest is higher than all other peaks. (Comparative)
Ans: Everest is the highest peak. (Superlative)
No other peak is so high as Everest. (Positive)

3. No other building in our town is so old as this. (Positive)
Ans: This is older than any other building in our town. (Superlative)

II Model: <u>Very few (as..as)</u>....... Positive
<u>Than most other</u> or ...... Comparative
<u>Than many other</u>
<u>One of the</u> ....Superlative

1. The Hindu is one of the best newspapers. (Superlative)
Ans: The Hindu is better than most other newspapers. (Comparative)
Very few newspapers are as good as the Hindu. (Positive)

2. Akbar was greater than most other kings. (Comparative)
Ans: Akbar was one of the greatest kings. (Superlative)
Very few kings were as great as Akbar. (Positive)

3. Taj Mahal is one of the most beautiful buildings in India. (Superlative)
Ans: Taj Mahal is more beautiful than most other buildings in India. (Comparative)
Very few buildings in India are as beautiful as Taj Mahal.

III Model: Some other – at least (as—as) ....positive
Not – than some other ....comparative
Not the ....superlative

1. Mumbai is not the biggest city in the world. (Superlative)
Ans: Mumbai is not bigger than some other cities in the world (Comparative)
Some other cities in the world are at least as big as Mumbai.

2. Some other boys are at least as industrious as Kiran. (Positive)
Ans: Kiran is not the most industrious boy. (Comparative)
Kiran is not more industrious than some other boys. (Comparative)

3. Radha is not taller than some other girls in the class. (Comparative)
Ans: Radha is not taller than some other girls in the class. (Comparative)
Some other girls in the class are at least as tall as Radha. (Positive)

Verbal Ability / Grammar & RC

Voice is that form of a verb which shows whether the subject does something or something is done to the subject.

Eg:

1. The hunter has killed a lion.
   (Here, the subject has done something.)
2. A lion has been killed by the hunter.
   (Here, something is done by the subject.)

There are two types of voice. They are

1. The Active Voice (and)
2. The Passive Voice

1. **Active Voice:** Active voice is one in which subject is active or subject is the doer of action.
   Eg: Tagore wrote this play.

2. **Passive Voice:** Passive Voice is one in which the subject is the sufferer or receiver of the action.
   Eg: Ravana was killed by Rama.

3. **From Active voice into Passive voice :**
   Rules:
   1. The subject in the active voice will become object in the passive voice and vice versa.
      Eg: The cat killed a rat.
      A rat was killed by the cat.
   2. In the passive voice, there must be a 'be' form followed by the past participle of the main verb. Generally the preposition 'by' is used after the past participle.

S.No.	Tense	'be' Forms
1.	Present Tense	is, are and am
2.	Past Tense	was and were
3.	Future Tense	be
4.	Continuous Tense	being
5.	Perfect Tense	been

Subject	Object
I	Me
We	Us
You	You
He	Him
She	Her
It	It
They	Them

1. **PRESENT TENSE:** In the present tense, the 'be' forms are is, am and are.

Eg:

1. Sita loves Rama. (Active Voice)
Ans: Rama is loved by Sita.

2. Mr.Krishna teaches English.
Ans: English is taught by Mr.Krishna.

3. They sell T.V.s here.
Ans: T.V.s are sold here by them.

4. People speak English all over the world.
Ans: English is spoken all over the world.

5. Bees make honey.
Ans: Honey is made by bees.

6. We prohibit smoking.
Ans: Smoking is prohibited by us.

7. Carpenters make chairs and tables.
Ans: Chairs and tables are made by carpenters.

8. She brings water from the Krishna river.
Ans: Water is brought from the Krishna river by her.

9. We use milk for making butter and cheese.
Ans: Milk is used for making butter and cheese.

10. People always admire this picture.
Ans: This picture is always admired.

2. **PAST TENSE:** In past Tense, the 'be' forms are <u>was</u> and <u>were</u>.

Eg:

1. Columbus discovered America.
Ans: America was discovered by Columbus.

2. They offered me a passport.
Ans: I was offered a passport by them.

3. They painted the house green.
Ans: The house was painted green by them.

4. Shaw wrote this play.
Ans: This play was written by Shaw.

5. The police arrested him on a charge of theft.
Ans: He was arrested on a charge of theft by the police.

6. Somebody left the dog in the park.
Ans: The dog was left in the park.

7. They told me to go away.
Ans: I was told to go away.

8. They told me the truth.
Ans: I was told the truth by them.

9. Gandhiji taught us the doctrine of non-violence.
Ans: We were taught the doctrine of non-violence by Gandhiji.

10. They elected Mr.Johnes as President of the Board.
Ans: Mr. Johnes was elected as President of the Board.

3. **FUTURE TENSE:** In future tense, the 'be' form is <u>be</u>. When the helping verbs like <u>shall, should, can, could, may, might, will, would, must, ought to, need</u> etc. are present, the 'be' is also be.

Eg:
1. He will do it tomorrow.
Ans: It will be done tomorrow by him.

2. You ought to do your duties.
Ans: Your duties ought to be done.

3. We should respect teachers.
Ans: Teachers should be respected by us.

4. I will examine the proposal carefully.
Ans: The proposal will be examined carefully.

5. Somebody must send for a doctor at once.
Ans: A doctor must be sent for at once.

6. No one can gain anything without effort.
Ans: Nothing can be gained without effort.

7. We should always keep promises.
Ans: Promises should always be kept.

4. **CONTINUOUS TENSE:** In the continuous tense, the 'be' form is 'being'

Eg:
1. He is selling rice.
Ans: Rice is being sold by him

2. A judge is inquiring into the incident at Besant Nagar.
Ans: The incident is being inquired into at Besant Nagar.

3. The woman is milking the cow.
Ans: The cow is being milked by the woman.

4. They were sending goods.
Ans: Goods were being sent by them.

5. They were repairing the road.
Ans: The road was being repaired by them.

6. She is laughing at them.
Ans: They are being laughed at by her.

Note: The verbs in 'Present Perfect Continuous Tense', 'Past Perfect Continuous Tense' 'Future continuous Tense' can't be changed into passive voice.

5. **PERFECT TENSE:** In the perfect Tense, the 'be' form is '<u>been</u>'.

Eg:
1. Mary has written this essay.
Ans: This essay has been written by Mary.

2. Someone has stolen her watch.
Ans: Her watch has been stolen.

3. The enemy have defeated our army.
Ans: Our army have been defeated by the enemy.

4. Some one has picked my pocket.
Ans: My pocket has been picked.

5. I have read the story.
Ans: The story has been read by me.

6. Seetha had told him about the incident.
Ans: He had been told about the incident by Seetha.

7. Kumar will have read the book by this evening.
Ans: The book would have been read by the evening by Kumar.

8. Kalidasa had created many a work of art.
Ans: Many a work of art had been created by Kalidasa.

9. Somebody has put off the light.
Ans: The light has been put off.

6. **Questions in Active Voice:**
Eg:
1. Are you singing a song?
Ans: Is a song being sung by you?

2. Have you seen the film?
Ans: Has the film been seen by you?

3. s the doctor examining the patients?
Ans: Are the patients being examined by the doctor?

4. Did you write the essay?
Ans: Was the essay written by you?

5. Must I do this work?
Ans: Must this work be done by me?

6. Will they sing a song?
Ans: Will a song be sung by them?

7. Do you speak English well?
Ans: Is English spoken well by you?

8. Can you speak Sanskrit?
Ans: Can Sanskrit be spoken by you?

9. Does she make chairs?
Ans: Are chairs made by her?

10. Why have you done this work?
Ans: Why has this work been done by you?

7. 'Who' in Active Voice:

Eg:
1. Who wrote this poem?
Ans: By whom was this written?

2. Who is opening the doors?
Ans: By whom were the doors being opened?

3. Who can do this work?
Ans: By whom can this work be done?

4. Who can break these toys?
Ans: By whom can these toys be broken?

5. Who drew this picture on the wall?
Ans: By whom was this picture drawn on the wall?

8. The Question 'what' in the Active Voice:

Eg:
1. What did you buy yesterday?
Ans: What was bought yesterday by you?
(Here the question 'What' is the object in the sentence. The same will become the subject in the Passive Voice).

2. What will you eat in the food?
Ans: What would be eaten in the food by you?

3. What has she seen in the market?
Ans: What has been seen in the market by her?

9. Imperative sentences in Active Voice (Orders and requests)

When there is an imperative sentence, we must start the passive voice with 'let', After 'let' the subject should be in the objective form. The 'be' form. The 'be' form is 'be'.

Eg:
1. Post this letter.
Ans: Let this letter be posted.

2. Open the door.
Ans: Let the door be opened.

3. Give the order.
Ans: Let the order be given.

4. Take away these books.
Ans: Let these books be taken away.

(If the imperative sentences have order without an object, the Passive Voice starts with 'you are ordered').

1. Sit down there.
Ans: You are ordered to sit down there.

2. Go away from the class.
Ans: You are ordered to go away from the class.

3. Don't talk in the class.
Ans: You are ordered not to talk in the class.

(If the imperative sentences have requests or advice, passive voice will start with 'you are requested' or 'you are advised'.)
1. Please come here.
Ans: You are requested to come here.

2. Read well.
Ans: You are advised to read well.

3. Please sing a song.
Ans: You are requested to sing a song.

4. Please don't come late.
Ans: You are requested not to come late.

5. Take proper medicine.
Ans: You are advised to take proper medicine.

10. 'Let' in the Active Voice:
When there is 'let' in the active voice, the 'to' form is 'be' in the passive voice.

1. Let him read the book.
Ans: Let the book be read by him.

2. Let them watch the T.V.
Ans: Let the T.V. be watched by them.

3. Let her sing a song.
Ans: Let a song be sung by her.

There are two ways of relating the words of the speaker. They are:

1. Direct Speech
2. Indirect Speech

1. **DIRECT SPEECH:** Direct speech is one in which the actual words of a person are quoted. Here, the exact words of the speaker are put within quotation marks or inverted commas. A comma is placed before a remark.

   Eg: He said, "I am very busy now".

2. **INDIRECT SPEECH:** (Reported speech): In indirect speech, the words of the speaker are not quoted but indirectly reported so as to convey the meaning. Here some conjunction is used before the indirect statement. Pronoun is changed. Verb is changed. Quotation marks are removed.

   Eg: He said that he was very busy then.

A. From Direct into Indirect:

The following are the changes to be noticed while changing direct into indirect speech, if the reporting verb is in the past tense.

Changes in tenses:

No	Direct	Indirect
1.	Simple Present Tense	Simple Past Tense
2.	Present Continuous Tense	Past Continuous Tense
3.	Present Perfect Tense	Past Perfect Tense
4.	Simple Past Tense	Past Perfect Tense
5.	Past Continuous Tense	Past Perfect Continuous Tense
6.	Present Perfect Continuous Tense	Past Perfect Continuous Tense
7.	Shall	Should or would
8.	Will	Would
9.	Can	Could
10.	May	Might
11.	Must	Had to
12.	Come	Go

B. Other Changes:

Word expressing nearness are changed into words expressing distance

No	Direct	Indirect
1.	This	That
2.	These	those
3.	Here	There
4.	Now	Then
5.	Ago	Before
6.	Thus	So
7.	Today	That day
8.	Tomorrow	The next day
9.	Yesterday	The previous day
10.	Last night	The previous night
11.	Hence	Thence
12.	Last year	The previous year
13.	Hereby	Thereby
14.	Tonight	That night
15.	Sir or Madam	Respectfully
16.	Hurrah	Gladly
17.	Alas	Sadly
18.	Yes	Positively
19.	No	Negatively

When the reporting verb is in the present or present perfect or future tense, there will be no change in tense.

Eg:
1. He says, "I am coming" (Direct Speech)

Ans: He says that he is going (Indirect speech)

2. He has said to her, "I am writing a letter". (Direct speech)

Ans: He has told her that he is writing a letter. (Indirect speech)

3. He will say, "I am right". (Direct speech)

Ans: He will say that he is right (Indirect speech)

(The simple present tense in the direct speech does not change when a general truth is mentioned.)

Eg: The teacher said, "The earth moves round the Sun". (Direct speech)

The teacher said that the earth moves round the Sun. (Indirect speech)

Statement Sentences: Statements in indirect speech are generally introduced by the conjunction 'that'; after the reporting verb. 'said to' will become 'told'. Pronouns change according to the context.

Eg:
1. He said, "My father is ill". (Direct speech)

Ans: He said that his father was ill. (Indirect speech)

2. He said, "I am writing to my uncle". (Direct speech)

Ans: He said that he was writing to his uncle. (Indirect speech)

3. "I have bought this pen" Sita said. (Direct speech)

Ans: Sita said that she had bought that pen. (Indirect speech)

4. She said, "Hari took my pen yesterday". (Direct speech)

Ans: She said that Hari had taken her pen the previous day. (Indirect speech)

5. She said "My brother will do it tomorrow". (Direct speech)

Ans: She said that her brother would do it the next day. (Indirect speech)

6. He said to me, "I will meet you again". (Direct speech)

Ans: He told me that he would meet me again. (Indirect speech)

7. She said to him, "I will meet you again". (Direct speech)

Ans: She told him that she would meet him again. (Indirect speech)

8. I said to him, "I will meet you again". (Direct speech)

Ans: I told him that I would meet him again (Indirect speech)

9. On Sunday last he said, "My brother is coming today". (Direct speech)

Ans: On Sunday last he said that his brother was going that day. (Indirect speech)

10. He said, "You are a gentleman". (Direct speech)

Ans: He told me that I was gentleman. (Indirect speech).

Questions in Direct Speech: In indirect speech, the question form changes to the statement form. If the question in direct speech begins with a question work. (Eg; who, why, where, when, how etc.,) This question word serves as a conjunction, if the question has no question word, we can use the conjunction <u>whether</u> or <u>if</u>.

As the indirect speech is statement form, full stop is used at the end of the sentence. <u>"Said to"</u> will become asked or <u>enquired.</u>

Eg:
1. He said to her, "Where are you going"? (Direct speech)

Ans: He asked her where she was going. (Indirect speech)

2. He said, "How are you"? (Direct speech)

Ans: He asked me how I was. (Indirect speech)

3. "When did she visit you?", said Sarma. (Direct speech)

Ans: Sarma asked me when she had visited me. (Indirect speech)

4. "Do you know Telugu?", she said. (Direct speech)

Ans: She asked me whether I knew Telugu. (Indirect speech)

5. "Will you come if it rains?", she said to him. (Direct speech)

Ans: She asked him whether he would go if it rained. (Indirect speech)

6. He said to her, "Did you visit Golconda Fort when you were in Hyderabad last month?" (Direct speech)

Ans: He asked her whether she had visited Golconda Fort when she had been in Hyderabd the previous month. (Indirect speech)

7. "Why are you talking?", said the teacher (Direct speech)

Ans: The teacher asked the student why he was talking (Indirect speech)

Exclamatory Sentences: The conjunction is 'that!'. 'said' will become 'exclaimed', 'said to' will become 'told'. The exclamatory sentence in direct speech must be changed into statement form.

Eg:
1. He said, "How clever I am!" (Direct speech)

Ans: He exclaimed that he was very clever (Indirect speech)

2. "What a lovely garden you have!", she said. (Direct speech)

Ans: She exclaimed that I had a very lovely garden. (Indirect speech)

3. He said to her, "What a beautiful girl you are!" (Direct speech)

Ans: He told her that she was a very beautiful girl. (Indirect speech)

4. "What a nice boy you have!" said she. (Direct speech)

Ans: She told me that I had a very nice boy. (Indirect speech)

Imperative sentences (orders and requests): The conjunction is 'that'. 'Said to' will become ordered or requested or advised or asked or prayed (in wishes).

Eg:

1. He said to his servant, "Post these letters". (Direct speech)

Ans: He ordered his servant to post those letters. (Indirect speech)

2. "Read this book", he said. (Direct speech)

Ans: He advised me to read that book. (Indirect speech)

3. She said, "Have a cup of coffee". (Direct speech)

Ans: She asked me to have a cup of coffee. (Indirect speech)

4. He said, "May God pardon this sinner". (Direct speech)

Ans: He prayed that God might pardon that sinner. (Indirect speech)

5. He said to her, "Please wait till return". (Direct speech)

Ans: He requested her to wait till her returned. (Indirect speech)

Verbal Ability / Grammar & RC

Simple, Complex, Compound Sentences **8**

Simple Sentence : A simple sentence is one which contains only a main clause and may have a phrase.
Eg: Inspite of my hard work, I failed.

Complex Sentence: A complex sentence is one which contains a main clause and one or more subordinate clauses.
Eg: Though I worked hard, I failed in the examination.

Compound Sentence: A compound sentence is one which contains two or more main clauses and may have one or more subordinate clauses.
Eg: I worked hard, but I failed in the examination.

A. From Simple into Complex: A simple sentence can be changed into a complex sentence by turning a phrase into a subordinate clause.
1. He admitted his guilt. (Simple)
Ans: He admitted that he was guilty (Complex)

2. I hoped to succeed. (Simple)
Ans I hoped that I would succeed. (Complex)

3. I was sorry to hear the news. (Simple)
Ans: I was sorry when I heard the news. (Complex)

B. From Simple into Compound: We can convert a simple sentence into a compound sentence by turning a phrase into a main clause.
1. On hearing the teacher's footsteps, the boys kept silent. (Simple)
Ans: The boys heard the teacher's footsteps and kept silent. (Compound)

2. Inspite of his hard work, he failed. (Simple)
Ans: He worked hard, but failed. (Compound)

3. Owing to illness, he could not attend the meeting. (Simple)
Ans: He was ill, so he could not attend the meting. (Compound) Or
He was ill and so he could not attend the meeting. (Compound)

C. Compound into Complex: We can convert a compound sentence into a simple one by turning a main clause into a phrase.
1. I went to the college and met the Principal. (Compound)
Ans: Having gone to the college, I met the Principal. (Simple)

2. It was raining, but they went out. (Compound)
Ans: Inspite of the rain, they went out. (Simple)

3. She was hungry, so she ate all the cakes. (Compound)
Ans: Owing to her hunger, she ate all the cakes. (Simple).

D. Complex into Simple: We can turn a complex sentence into a simple one by changing a subordinate clause into a phrase.
1. I don't know when he will arrive. (Complex)
Ans: I don't know the time of his arrival. (Simple)

2. He did it when I was absent. (Complex)
Ans: He did it in my absence. (Simple)

3. He failed to prove that he was innocent. (Complex)
Ans: He failed to prove his innocence. (Simple)

4. Though he is poor, he is honest (Complex)
Ans: Inspite of his poverty, he is honest. (Simple)

E. Complex sentence into compound: We can turn a complex sentence into a compound one by changing a subordinate clause into a main clause.
1. Though he is poor, he is honest. (Complex)
Ans: He is poor, but he is honest. (Compound)

2. We can prove that the earth is flat. (Complex)
Ans: The earth is flat and we can prove it. (Compound)

3. If you do not work hard, you will fail. (Complex)
Ans: You must work hard or you will fail. (Compound)

4. He is more a statesman than a politician. (Complex)
Ans: He is something of a politician, but he is rather more a statesman. (Compound)

IMPORTANT MODELS

No	SIMPLE	COMPLEX	COMPOUND	
1.	Inspite of	Though (although)	Even though	But (yet)
2.	Ing	When	And	
3.	Owing to	As (Since or because)	So (therefore)	
4.	In case of not	Unless (if not)	Or	
5.	Besides also	As well as	Not only, but	
6.	Immediately	After	As soon as	And at once
7.	Soon after	No sooner than	And at once	

I.   Model: Inspite of – Though – But

1. He worked hard, but he failed in the examination. (Compound)

Ans: Though he worked hard, he failed in the examination. (Complex)

Inspite of his hard work, he failed in he examination. (Simple)

2. Though he was hungry, he did not eat anything. (Complex)

Ans: He was hungry, but he did not eat anything. (Compound)

Inspite of his hunger, he did not eat anything. (Simple)

3. Inspite of her honesty, she was not recognized by the people.

Ans: She was honest, but she was not recognized by the people. (Compound)

Though she was honest, she was not recognized by the people. (Complex)

II.   Model: Ing – When – and

1. I went to the college and met the principal. (Compound)

Ans: When I went to the college, I met the principal. (Complex)

Having gone to the college, I met the principal. (Simple)

2. When the boys heard the teacher's footsteps, they kept silent. (Complex)

Ans: On hearing the teacher's footsteps the boys kept silent. (Simple)

The boys heard the teacher's footsteps and kept silent. (Compound)

3. On seeing the police, the thief ran away. (Simple)

Ans: The thief saw the police and ran away. (Compound)

When the thief saw the police, he ran away. (Complex)

III.   Model: Owing to – as (Since or because) – so (therefore)

1. He was poor, so he could not afford to buy books. (Compound)

Ans: As he was poor, he could not afford to buy books. (Complex)

Owing to his poverty, he could not afford to buy books. (Simple)

2. As she was ill, she could not attend the classes. (Complex)

Ans: She was ill, so she could not attend the classes. (Compound)

Owing to her illness, she could not attend the classes. (Simple)

3. Owing to their sincerity, they became rich. (Simple)

Ans: As they were sincere, they became rich. (Complex)

They were sincere, so they became rich. (Compound)

IV.   Model : In case of not – Unless (if not) – or

1. You must work hard or you can't get more marks. (Compound)

Ans: Unless you work hard, you can't get more marks. (Complex) or

If you do not work hard, you can't get more marks. (Simple)

2. Unless you run, you won't catch the train. (Complex)

Ans: You must run or you won't catch the train. (Compound)

In case of not running, you won't catch the train. (Simple)

3. In case of not coming regularly, you can't understand the lessons. (Simple)

Ans: You must come regularly or you can't understand the lessons. (Compound)

Unless you come regularly, you can't understand the lessons. (Complex)

Verbal Ability / Grammar & RC

V.   Model : Besides – as well as – not only – but also

1. He not only stole the jewels but also murdered her. (Compound)

Ans: He stole he jewels as well as murdered her. (Complex)
Besides stealing the jewels, he (also) murdered her. (Simple)

2. He scolded me as well as beat me. (Complex)

Ans: He not only scolded me but also beat me. (Compound)
Besides scolding me, he (also) beat me. (Simple)

3. Besides robbing the poor child, he (also) murdered her. (Simple)

Ans: He not only robbed the poor child, but also murdered her. (Compound)
He robbed the child as well as murdered her. (Complex)

VI.   Model: Immediately after – as soon as – and at once:

1. The bell rang and at once the boys ran to the playground. (Compound)

Ans: As soon as the bell rang, the boys ran to the playground. (Complex)
Immediately after the ringing of the bell, the boys ran to the playground. (Simple)

2. As soon as the teacher came the students stood up. (Complex)

Ans: The teacher came and at once the students stood up. (Compound)
Immediately after the coming of the teacher, the students stood up. (Simple)

3. Immediately after the completion of his work, he left the office. (Simple)

Ans: He completed his work and at once he left the office. (Compound)
As soon as he completed his work, he left the office. (Complex).

VII.   Model: soon after – no sooner than – and at once

1. The bell rang and at once the boys ran to the playground. (Compound)

Ans: No sooner had the bell rung than the boys ran to the playground. (Complex)
Soon after the ringing the bell, the boys ran to the playground. (Simple)

2. No sooner had the teacher come than the students stood up. (Complex)

Ans: The teacher came and at once the students stood up. (Compound)
Soon after the coming of the teacher, the students stood up. (Simple)

3. Soon after the completion of his work, he left the office. (Simple)

Ans: He completed his work and at once he left the office. (Compound)
No sooner had he completed his work than he left the office. (Complex).

OTHER MODELS

As soon as – no sooner than; Scarcely when (hardly – when)

1. As soon as the teacher entered the class, the students went out. (Complex)

Ans: No sooner had the teacher entered the class than the students went out. (Complex)
Scarcely had the teacher entered the class when the students went out. (Complex)
Hardly had he teacher entered the class when the students went out. (Complex)

Too.........To.........So that not:

1. She is too weak to walk. (Simple)

Ans: She is so weak that the can not walk. (Complex)-No compound

2. I am too poor to buy a pen.

Ans: I am so poor that I can not buy a pen.

3. He was too lazy to work.

Ans: He was so lazy that he could not work.

4. The river is too deep to swim.

Ans: The river is so deep that we can not swim

5. The atom is too small to be seen.

Ans: The atom is so small that is can not be seen.

Unless – If not:

1. Unless you work hard, you will fail.

Ans: If you do not work hard, you will fail.

2. Come tomorrow unless I phone.

Ans: Come tomorrow if I do not phone.

3. I will take the job, unless the pay is low.

Ans: I will take the job, if the pay is not low.

4. Unless you run, you can not catch the train.

Ans: If you do not run, you can not catch the train.

5. Unless you read well, you will not pass the examination.

Ans: If you read well, you will pass the examination.

Articles

9

'A', 'an' and 'the' are called articles. They are actually adjectives.

'A' and 'an' (Indefinite articles): 'A' or 'an' must be used before a singular noun. The difference between them is in the sound a word is pronounced.

I. THE USE OF 'AN':

(1) 'An' is used before a singular noun which is pronounced with a vowel sound. (a vowel which does not have a 'y' or a 'w' sound).

Examples:

An umbrella, an elephant, an animal, an interesting story, an intelligent boy, an unhappy man, an asset, an ugly girl, an old man, an aeroplane, an open secret, an onion, an American, an Indian, an English man, an Australian, an Irish man, an industrious boy, an apple, an orange, an island, an ink bottle, an ear, an eye, an active man, an unmarried man, an accident, an Ice-cream, an enemy, an ass; such an occasion, an urgent telegram, an upper class, an idiot, an Italian, an apple, an Indian poet, many an accident.

(2) 'An' is used before a singular noun in which 'h' is silent:

Examples:

An honest man, an honourable man, an hour, an honour, an heir, such an honour, sixty miles an hour. (but a hint, a horse)

(3) It is used before a consonant in an abbreviation which begins with a vowel sound.

Examples:

An M.A., an M.Sc., an M.B.B.S., an M.L.A., an M.P. (but a B.A., a B.Sc)

II. THE USE OF 'A':

(1) 'A' is used before a singular noun beginning with a consonant sound.

Examples: A good man, a boy, a girl, a young woman, a youth, a doctor, a cat, a man, a mat, a monkey, a pen, a king, a queen, a public meeting, a year, a few, a few students, such a man, a horse, a little monkey, a yard, a hole, a lot of money, many a boy, half a rupee, a cup and saucer, a knife and fork etc. He is a Hitler; a headache; all of a sudden; a bad cold, at a time, twice a month, wait a minute, a hundred rupees, a yard, a film star, a friend of yours, a little ship, a Hindu, a Muslim, a rupee note, a few friends, a little time, many a boy, such a fool, a dozen pencils etc….,

(2) It is used before a singular noun beginning with a vowel which has a 'w' consonant sound.

Examples:

A one eyed man, a one rupee note, a one man committee, a one – side argument, a one – way road.

(3) It is used before a singular noun beginning with a vowel which has a 'y' consonant sound.

Examples:

A university, a union, a uniform, a European, a useful animal, a unicorn, a unit, a utensil etc.

III. THE USE OF 'THE': (Definite article):

1. 'The' is used before a definite person.

Examples:

The President, the Prime Minister, the Secretary, the Chief Minister, the Collector, the Principal, the Manager, the Chairman, the Head Master, the Post Master etc.,

2. It is used when the same noun is repeated for the second time.

Examples:

i. There was an old man. The old man had a dog. The dog jumped upon a boy and killed him.

ii. There was a prince. The prince married a princess. They were happy.

iii. There is a duster on my desk. Get me the duster.

iv. One night a wolf fell in with a dog. The wolf was all skin and bones, while the dog was very fat.

3. It is used before unique things.

Examples:

The earth, the sun, the moon, the east, the south, the west, the Tajmahal, the sky, the world, the road, the sea, the ocean, the world (the universe) etc.

4. It is used before ranks.

Examples:

The first, the second, the third, the last, the next, the letter, the former etc.

5. It is used before superlative degrees.

Examples

The best, the worst, the least, the highest, the tallest, the cleverest, the most beautiful etc.,

Verbal Ability / Grammar & RC

i. It is <u>the</u> worst for a long time.

ii. Everest is <u>the</u> highest mountain in the world.

iii. Sita is <u>the</u> shortest girl in the class.

iv. We are <u>the</u> best of friends.

6. It is used before holy books.

   Examples:

   The Ramayana, The Mahabharta, The Vedas, The Gita, The Bible, The Upanishads, The Koran etc.

   1. I read the Ramayana.

   2. I read Valmiki's Ramayana.

7. It is used before the names of rivers, seas, oceans, mountain ranges, groups of islands, canals, valleys deserts and gulfs.

   Examples:

   i. The Ganges, the Krishna, the Nile, the Amazon, the Thames, the Indus etc.,

   ii. The Himalayas (Everest or Mount Everest) the Vindyas, the Alps. the Andes etc....

   iii. The Indian ocean, the Pacific Ocean etc.

   iv. The Buckingham canal, the Suez Canal etc.

   v. The Kashmir Valley, the Araku Valley etc.

   vi. The Andamans, the West Indies, the Philippines, the Netherlands etc.

8. It is used before the names of the countries consisting of the words like Union, United Kingdom, Republic, United States and Provinces and Federation.

   Examples:

   The Union of India, the United States of America, the U.S.S.R., the U.K., the Arab Republic, the Punjab, the Indian Republic, the Deccan etc.

9. It is used when a singular noun represents the whole class.

   Examples:

   i. The cow is a useful animal.

   ii. The rose is a beautiful flower.

   iii. The honest man is a noble creature.

   iv. The lion is a dangerous animal.

   v. The dog is a faithful animal.

10. It is used when two comparatives are in a single sentence.

    Examples:

    i. The older we grow, the wiser we become.

    ii. The higher we climb, the colder it gets.

    iii. The more we get, the more we want.

11. It is used before a proper noun when it is used as a common noun .

    Examples:

    i. Kalidasa is the Shakespeare of India.

    ii. Bombay is the Manchester of India.

    iii. Mussolini is the Hitler of Italy.

    (But **1.** He is a Hitler **2.** She is a Savithri)

12. It is used before an adjective when the noun is understood.

    Examples:

    i. This is a school for <u>the</u> blind.

    ii. <u>The</u> rich are proud.

    iii. <u>The</u> English have good sense of humour.

    iv. We must help <u>the</u> poor.

    v. <u>The</u> good lives on after a man dies.

13. It is used before an abstract noun when the name of a particular person is given.

    Examples:

    i. The honesty of Gandhi must be admired.

    ii. The patience of J.P. is admirable.

    iii. We must admire the bravery of Netaji Bose. (Honesty is the best policy)

14. It is used before the name of a person with its plural form representing the whole family.

    Examples:

    i. The Kennedys are royal.

    ii. The Smiths.

    iii. The Tagores etc.

15. It is used before the names of shops, industries, banks, hotels, government departments, clubs etc.,

    Examples:

    The ministry of Education, the India Bank, the Union Bank, the War Office, the Grand Hotel, The Lion's Club, the King's Restaurant etc.

16. It is used before the names of ships and trains, aeroplanes etc.

    Examples:

    The Howrah and Madras Express, the Godavari Expres, The Minar Express, The Queen Elizabeth – II (Ship), the Vaijayanti (ship).

17. It is used before the names of musical instruments.

    Examples:

    The Sitara, the Guitar, the Veena, the Drums, the Voilin, the Piano etc.

    i. He plays <u>the</u> violin, but I play <u>the</u> trumpet.

    ii. Do you play the piano?

18. It is used before three types of forces.

    Examples:

    The Naval force, the Army force, the Air force etc.,

19. It is used before stations.

    Examples:

    The Railway Station, the Post Office, the Radio Station, the Police Station etc.

20. It is used before a comparative degree used with <u>'of the two'</u>.

    Examples:

    1. Gita is <u>the</u> tailor of the two sisters.

    2. Mohan is <u>the</u> stronger of the two friends.

IV. OMISSION OF ARTICLES:

1. Article is generally omitted before an abstract noun.
    (1) ___________ Patience is a great virtue.
    (2) ___________ Honesty is the best policy.
    (3) We must worship ____________ beauty.
    (4) ___________ Wisdom is the gift of heaven.
    (But the wisdom of Solomon is well-known)

2. Article is omitted before proper nouns.
    (Names of persons, places and languages)
    (1) ____________ Newton is a great scientist.
    (2) ____________ He stayes in India.
    (3) He speaks _____________ English but not ___________ Hindi.
    (4) ___________ India is a great country.
    (5) ____________ Tagore is a great poet.

3. Article is not used after the expressions like type of, sort of, kind of, manner of etc.,
    What kind of ____________ man is he?
    (What a man he is!)

4. Article is not used before a noun giving the widest sense.
    (1) Man is mortal.
    (2) Woman is selfish.
    (3) Woman is man's companion is life.
    (4) Science tried to discover the laws of nature.

5. Article (especially a or an) is not used before uncountable nouns like news, advice, business, soap, paper, work, chalk rice, bread, sand, soil, sugar, marble, iron, gold, coal, silver etc.,
    (We must not write the plural form of these uncountable nouns.)

Grammar Review Exercise – 1

Directions for questions 1 to 50: Fill in the blanks with the most appropriate words from the options given below the sentences.

1. 'Waiter, bring me a …………cup of tea.
   (1) thick   (2) strong
   (3) heavy   (4) sold

2. I drove through ……… traffic.
   (1) strong   (2) heavy
   (3) big   (4) solid

3. They are all ……. a film on the T.V.
   (1) seeing   (2) watching
   (3) looking at   (4) observing

4. If you…….to be successful in life, work hard.
   (1) want   (2) wanted
   (3) will want   (4) waiting

5. They …..me a poet.
   (1) consider   (2) considers
   (3) will consider   (4) have considered

6. I shall go and see him before he ……this place.
   (1) will leave   (2) is leaving
   (3) leave   (4) leaves

7. Please call me when the dinner……ready.
   (1) is   (2) was
   (3) will be   (4) has been

8. You must avoid …..friendship with bad people.
   (1) make   (2) making
   (3) made   (4) will make

9. They stopped ………..to go home.
   (1) work   (2) worked
   (3) working   (4) to work

10. I …………..him since last Monday.
    (1) am not seeing   (2) did not see
    (3) have not seen   (4) do not see

11. She…….only two letters to me so far.
    (1) wrote   (2) had written
    (3) has written   (4) is writing

12. She…………..anybody yet.
    (1) did not marry   (2) will not marry
    (3) have not married   (4) has not married.

13. I ……….ill since last week.
    (1) is   (2) was
    (3) have been   (4) had been

14. The boy……..from fever since yesterday.
    (1) is suffering   (2) was suffering
    (3) suffered   (4) has been suffering

15. She has not seen films since her husband………….
    (1) would die   (2) died
    (3) has died   (4) had died

16. They are accustomed to…………
    (1) drink   (2) drank
    (3) drinks   (4) drinking

17. I shall wait here till you………..your lunch.
    (1) will finish   (2) finish
    (3) will have finished   (4) finished

18. She looks forward to ……..him.
    (1) see   (2) seeing
    (3) saw   (4) sees

19. Unless every man works hard, he …………… become prosperous in his life.
    (1) can   (2) could not
    (3) cannot   (4) is not

20. Man …………….mortal.
    (1) was   (2) is
    (3) will be   (4) has been

21. We…………..in Vizag for ten years.
    (1) had been living   (2) had lived
    (3) live   (4) have been living

22. It is high time……………
    (1) that we left   (2) that we have left
    (3) that we had left   (4) that we leave

23. I wish I ………rich.
    (1) were   (2) am
    (3) was   (4) have been

24. They said that they………..the Taj Mahal soon.
    (1) will visit   (2) would visit
    (3) are visiting   (4) may visit.

25. He said that he................from fever.
    (1) is suffering (2) has been suffering
    (3) was suffering (4) has been suffering

26. I told him that I ....a book.
    (1) am reading (2) will be reading
    (3) was reading (4) were reading

27. Before you go to see him, he..............the place.
    (1) will leave (2) leave
    (3) left (4) will have left

28. If I ....the time, I shall visit the zoo.
    (1) had (2) have
    (3) will have (4) had been.

29. When I go home, my children.................
    (1) are playing (2) will be playing
    (3) will play (4) have been playing

30. If I.............the money, I shall lend it to you.
    (1) am (2) was
    (3) were (4) have

31. If we............. the time, we would visit the Zoo.
    (1) have (2) had
    (3) will have (4) have had

32. He talks as if he ....here.
    (1) was (2) were
    (3) is (4) has been

33. Before I went to the college the bell..............
    (1) rang (2) has rung
    (3) had rung (4) was ringing

34. She asked me whether I ....the film the previous night.
    (1) have seen (2) was seeing
    (3) have been seeing (4) had seen

35. If you had worked hard, you..................rich.
    (1) will become (2) would become
    (3) would have become (4) became

36. If I were a king, I ....you my queen.
    (1) will make (2) make
    (3) made (4) would make

37. If he comes to me, I...............him.
    (1) help (2) would help
    (3) shall help (4) must help

38. I did not go and ....the Principal yesterday.
    (1) met (2) meet
    (3) had met (4) meeting

39. She has not ....there yet.
    (1) go (2) went
    (3) gone (4) going

40. You need not............home.
    (1) coming (2) to come
    (3) come (4) came

41. Nehruji used to................with children.
    (1) played (2) play
    (3) playing (4) rained

42. If it................. I shall not go to college.
    (1) rain (2) rains
    (3) will rain (4) rained

43. My father..............a watch to me if I get first class.
    (1) will present (2) shall present
    (3) would present (4) present

44. I will help only...............
    (1) if I will have time (2) if I shall have item
    (3) if I had time (4) if I have time

45. Do you know.................
    (1) to swim (2) how to swim
    (3) swimming (4) to floating

46. Babar.............the Moghul Empire.
    (1) founded (2) has founded
    (3) has found (4) has discovered.

47. You should work hard lest you..............fail.
    (1) might (2) will
    (3) should (4) should not

48. His daughter enjoys................a lot.
    (1) singing (2) to sing
    (3) to singing (4) sing

49. I have not seen him.........
    (1) since we have left college
    (2) since we left college
    (3) since we had left college
    (4) since college having been left by us.

50. If I ....a bird, I should fly away.
    (1) were (2) was
    (3) am (4) have been

Grammar Review Exercise – 2

Directions for questions 1 to 10: Fill in the blanks with suitable phrasal verbs from the given choices.

1. He became so furious that he ___________ his opponent with a baseball.
   (1) came around   (2) knocked out
   (3) dropped out   (4) wiped out

2. He ___________ that he was a good basketball player but actually he could not even dribble properly.
   (1) got behind   (2) made out
   (3) kept in   (4) talked about

3. She fainted in the afternoon but soon ___________
   (1) wiped on   (2) pulled out
   (3) came around   (4) caught up

4. They did not find the deal favourableand so they decided to ___________ it.
   (1) pull out of   (2) run over
   (3) look down on   (4) cut of

5. Children should be ___________ home if it rains heavily outside.
   (1) held onto   (2) slipped away into
   (3) fend off to   (4) kept in

6. We ___________ this deal since it is crucial for the company's future.
   (1) hinge on   (2) weigh up
   (3) pick on   (4) hang around

7. In order to help the society in constructing a temple, the residents came together and ___________ for its funds.
   (1) digged in   (2) took over
   (3) put up   (4) raked in

8. By the time we reached there, the boy who was ___________ the cards had gone away.
   (1) let in for   (2) took up on
   (3) fishing out   (4) dishing out

9. You can ___________ at my aunt's house if it does not stop raining till then.
   (1) wind up   (2) wait up
   (3) put up   (4) wake up

10. She was so annoyed after knowing the truth that she ___________ the lamp.
    (1) smashed up   (2) snarled up
    (3) frittered away   (4) hammed up

Directions for questions 11 to 20: The following sentences which are in active voice have to be changed into sentences that are in passive voice. Choose the right option.

11. Hasn't your science teacher taught you about molecules?
    (1) Haven't you been taught about molecules by your science teacher?
    (2) Weren't you taught about molecules by your science teacher?
    (3) Weren't you been taught about molecules by your science teacher?
    (4) Haven't you being taught about molecules from your science teacher?

12. The diffusion process spreads the perfume odour throughout the hall.
    (1) The perfume odour is been spread throughout the hall.
    (2) The perfume odour is being spread by the diffusion process.
    (3) The perfume odour is spread throughout the hall by the diffusion process.
    (4) The perfume odour was been spread throughout the hall by the diffusion process.

13. Her arrogant behaviour annoyed me.
    (1) I was annoyed by her arrogant behaviour.
    (2) I was being annoyed by her arrogant behaviour.
    (3) I have been annoyed by her arrogant behaviour.
    (4) I was been annoyed by her arrogant behaviour.

14. My friends are giving me a birthday present tomorrow.
    (1) I am given a birthday present tomorrow by my friends.
    (2) I will have been given a birthday present tomorrow by my friends.
    (3) I will be given a birthday present tomorrow by my friends.
    (4) I am being given a birthday present tomorrow by my friends.

15. Emily observed the chemical reactions occuring in the jar.
    (1) The chemical reactions that occured in the jar were observed by Emily.
    (2) The chemical reactions occuring in the jar were observed by Emily.
    (3) The chemical reactions occuring in the jar will be observed by Emily.
    (4) The chemical reactions occuring in the jar have been observed by Emily.

16. Anna said, "I can't finish my work by tomorrow."
    (1) Anna said that she can't finish her work by the next day.
    (2) Anna said that she will not finish her work by this day.
    (3) Anna said that she couldn't finish her work by that day.
    (4) Anna said that she will not be able to finish her work by this day.

17. Olena said, "I will ask the teacher to explain the concept again."
    (1) Olena said that she would ask the teacher to explain the concept again.
    (2) Olena said that she will ask the teacher to explain the concept again.
    (3) Olena said that she was going to ask the teacher to explain the concept again.
    (4) Olena said that she had asked the teacher to explain the concept again.

18. Chan said, "My English may improve soon."
    (1) Chan said that her English was going to improve soon.
    (2) Chan said that her English had been able to improve soon
    (3) Chan said that her English improved soon.
    (4) Chan said that her English might improve soon.

19. He said, "I had written a letter to my family yesterday."
    (1) He said that he had written a letter to his family the day before.
    (2) He said that he wrote a letter to his family the day before.
    (3) He said that he was writing a letter to his family the previous day.
    (4) He said that he will write a letter to his family the previous day.

20. Maria said, 'Ambi is fit to win the competition'.
    (1) Maria said that that Ambi will be fit to win the competition.
    (2) Maria said that Ambi should be fit to win the competition.
    (3) Maria said that Ambi has to be fit to win the competition.
    (4) Maria said that Ambi was fit to win the competition.

Directions for questions 21 to 25: Given below are sentences written in direct speech. Choose the option that presents the most appropriate way of writing them in the indirect speech.

21. "Will you help me with my homework?", Neeta asked Raman.
    (1) Neeta asked Raman if he would help her with her homework.
    (2) Raman was asked by Neeta whether he would help her do the homework.
    (3) Neeta asked Raman to help her in doing the homework.
    (4) Neeta asked for Raman's help in doing her homework.

22. "How long have you been studying here?", Ajay asked Seema.
    (1) Seema was asked by Ajay whether she was studying there.
    (2) Ajay asked Seema that how long she had been studying there.
    (3) Ajay asked Seema when she was studying there.
    (4) Ajay asked Seema about how long she had studied there.

23. Chakram said "I went to Honolulu ten years ago".
    (1) Chakram announced that he had been to Honolulu ten years ago.
    (2) Chakram said he has been to Honolulu ten years ago.
    (3) Ten years ago he had been to Honolulu said Chakram.
    (4) Chakram said that he had been to Honolulu ten years ago.

24. Heena said "I'm getting married tomorrow".
    (1) Heena said that she was getting married the day after.
    (2) She was getting married on the day after said Heena.
    (3) Heena said on the day after she was getting married.
    (4) Heena said that on the day after she gets married.

25. Simon said "I like taking photographs and collecting stamps".
    (1) Simon said about his liking for stamp collection and photography.
    (2) Simon likes photography and stamp collection.
    (3) Taking photographs and stamp collection are liked by Simon.
    (4) Simon said that he liked taking photographs and collecting stamps.

Directions for questions 26 to 35: Choose the appropriate article given below and fill in the blank in each of the sentences. In case, the sentence does not require an article, choose 'no article'.

26. __________ event takes place in the second Sunday of June every year.
    (1) a   (2) an
    (3) the   (4) no article

27. Absorption is __________ process where broken food molecules enter cells of the body.
    (1) a   (2) an
    (3) the   (4) no article

28. After staring at __________ menu for five minutes, Jane ordered some food.
    (1) the   (2) a
    (3) an   (4) no article

29. In the human body, the liver is the largest glandular organ with __________ weight of about 1.36 kg.
    (1) the   (2) a
    (3) an   (4) no article

30. __________ used piece of wood can fit in that area.
    (1) the   (2) a
    (3) an   (4) no article

31. It was __________ unusually difficult answer.
    (1) a   (2) an
    (3) the   (4) no article

32. World peace is __________ very commonly debated topic.
    (1) a   (2) an
    (3) the   (4) no article

33. __________ exaggerated statement is called a hyperbole.
    (1) a   (2) an
    (3) the   (4) no article

34. One who gives directions from behind __________ scene is a prompter.
    (1) a   (2) an
    (3) the   (4) no article

35. __________ assistant came up to me and asked me if I needed assistance.
    (1) a   (2) an
    (3) the   (4) no article

Directions for questions 36 to 40: In each of the following sentences, some part of the sentence is underlined. Below each sentence there are four ways of rephrasing the underlined part. Select the answer that produces the most effective sentence.

36. The old man down the street <u>has been selling newspapers for the last ten years</u>.
    (1) has been selling newspapers for the last ten years.
    (2) had to sell newspapers for the last ten years.
    (3) have been selling newspapers for the last ten years.
    (4) will have been selling newspapers for the last ten years.

37. <u>When you had received the invitation tonight</u>, only then we will go together.
    (1) When you had received the invitation tonight
    (2) When you will be receiving the invitation tonight
    (3) When you receive the invitation tonight
    (4) When you received the invitation tonight

38. <u>You were not listening to me</u> when I told you to bring me a cup of tea.
    (1) You were not listening to me
    (2) You had not listened to me
    (3) You would not listen to me
    (4) You had not been listening to me

39. Imagine that you were travelling in a train, in a crowded compartment and <u>one of the passengers will be talking very loudly.</u>
    (1) one of the passengers will be talking very loudly.
    (2) one of the passengers was talking very loudly.
    (3) one of the passengers has talked very loudly.
    (4) one of the passengers had been talking very loudly.

40. I am <u>not to be doing</u> any favours for anyone.
    (1) not to be doing   (2) not to do
    (3) not going to   (4) not going to do

Directions for questions 41 to 50: Fill in the blanks with appropriate choice of prepositions.

41. He wanted to talk to me but I kept ..... working and refused to listen.
    (1) on   (2) up
    (3) out   (4) back

42. She is a good secretary but she is kept ...... by her ignorance of languages.
    (1) on   (2) up
    (3) out   (4) back

43. The country was in a state of rebellion and was only kept .... by repressive measures.
    (1) on   (2) down
    (3) out   (4) back

44. Look .... the baby while I am out.
    (1) on   (2) up
    (3) after   (4) back

45. She kept the children ...... all day because it was so wet and cold.
    (1) on   (2) in
    (3) out   (4) back

46. You must look ..... and make plans for the future.
    (1) on   (2) up
    (3) ahead   (4) back

47. 'Keep ..... !' he said. 'Don't come any nearer'.
    (1) on   (2) up
    (3) out   (4) back

48. If you look ...... it carefully, you will see the mark.
    (1) on   (2) at
    (3) out   (4) back

49. I told the children to abide .... the rules.
    (1) on   (2) in
    (3) by   (4) of

50. Looking .... , I see now all the mistakes I made when I was younger.
    (1) on   (2) up
    (3) out   (4) back

Verbal Ability / Grammar & RC

Grammar Review Exercise – 3

Directions for questions 1 to 5: Choose the appropriate combination of articles (a, an or the) to fill the two blanks in each of the sentences given below.

1. __________ black boy and an emotionally troubled white boy in North Carolina form __________ precarious friendship.
   (1) a, a   (2) the, a
   (3) an, the   (4) a, no article

2. Shayla, __________ aspiring writer, can't figure out __________ new girl next door, Elaine, who tells fantastic stories.
   (1) no article, a   (2) the, a
   (3) an, the   (4) a, no article

3. __________ exercise of restraint is certain to help __________ achievement of peace.
   (1) no article, an   (2) the, the
   (3) a, the   (4) a, no article

4. __________ small patch of bright colour can succeed to brighten __________ otherwise dull interior.
   (1) the, a   (2) no article, an
   (3) a, the   (4) a, an

5. According to Einstein __________ curvature is caused by __________ presence of mass or energy.
   (1) a, no article   (2) the, the
   (3) an, the   (4) no article, the

Directions for questions 6 to 10: Choose the appropriate article to fill in the blanks in each of the sentences given below; In case, the sentence does not require an article, choose 'no article'.

6. __________ car I was talking about is standing outside the mall.
   (1) the   (2) a
   (3) an   (4) no article

7. It is always preferable to study in __________ European University.
   (1) an   (2) the
   (3) a   (4) no article

8. Raj is one of __________ board of directors of the company.
   (1) a   (2) the
   (3) an   (4) no article

9. His courage to confront the minister was termed as __________ audacious act by everybody.
   (1) the   (2) an
   (3) a   (4) no article

10. Everybody nowadays is interested in taking part in __________ theatre.
    (1) the   (2) a
    (3) an   (4) no article

Directions for questions 11 to 15: The following sentences which are in active voice have to be changed into sentences that are in passive voice. Choose the right option.

11. Jack has sent the television for repair.
    (1) The television has been sent for repair by Jack.
    (2) The television is being repaired by Jack.
    (3) The television is being sent for repair by Jack.
    (4) The television will have been sent for repair by Jack.

12. The Chopras are giving their full support to the power project.
    (1) The power project gets its support from the Chopras.
    (2) The power project is being approved by the Chopras.
    (3) The power project is being given full support by the Chopras.
    (4) The power project has been given full support by the Chopras.

13. Can you pass this bill on behalf of the director?
    (1) Can the director pass this bill on your behalf?
    (2) Can the passing of the bill be done by you?
    (3) Can this bill be passed by you on behalf of the director?
    (4) Can you help me out in passing this bill?

14. Who has decided to take the final decision?
    (1) By whom is the final decision being taken?
    (2) Who is taking the final decision nowadays?
    (3) By whom has the final decison been taken?
    (4) The final decsion is taken by who?

15. We should reorganise the entire show.
    (1) The entire show is being reorganised by us.
    (2) The entire show should be reorganised by us.
    (3) The entire show is reorganised by us.
    (4) The entire show has been reorganised by us.

Directions for questions 16 to 20: The following sentences, which are in passive voice have to be changed into sentences that are in active voice. Choose the right option.

16. Before the semester was over, the new nursing program had been approved by the Curriculum Committee and the Board of Trustees.
    (1) Before the semester was over, the Curriculum Committee and the Board of Trustees had approved the new nursing program.
    (2) Before the semester was over the new nursing program was approved by the Curriculum Committee and the Board of Trustees.
    (3) The Board of Trustees approved the new nursing program after the semester was over.
    (4) Once the semester was over the new nursing program had been approved by the Curriculum Committee and the Board of Trustees.

17. The major points of the lesson were quickly learned by the class, but they were also quickly forgotten by them.
    (1) The major points lessons were learnt quickly and forgotten quickly by the class.
    (2) The class quickly learned and then the major points of the lesson were quickly forgotten by them.
    (3) The class quickly learned, and then had quickly forgotten, the lesson's major points.
    (4) The class quickly learned, and then quickly forgot, the lesson's major points.

18. Tall buildings and mountain roads were avoided by Ram because he had such a fear of heights.
    (1) Ram had a fear of heights therefore all buildings and mountain roads were avoided by him.
    (2) A fear of heights led to the avoidance of tall buildings and mountain roads by Ram.

(3) Ram avoided fall buildings and mountain roads because he had such a fear of heights.
(4) Because he had such a fear of heights, tall buildings and mountain roads were avoided by Ram.

19. "The Yellow Wallpaper" was written by Charlotte Perkins Gilman.
    (1) The Yellow Wallpaper had been written by Charlotte Perkins Gilman.
    (2) The Yellow Wallpaper was being written by Charlotte Perkins Gilman.
    (3) Charlotte Perkins Gilman wrote "The Yellow Wallpaper."
    (4) The Yellow Wallpaper was written by Charlotte Perkins Gilman.

20. I was surprised by the teacher's lack of sympathy.
    (1) The teacher's lack of sympathy surprised me.
    (2) Lack of sympathy of teacher surprised me.
    (3) By the lack of sympathy of the teacher I was surprised.
    (4) Surprisingly teacher lacked sympathy for me.

Directions for questions 21 to 25: Given below are sentences written in direct speech. Choose the option that presents the most appropriate way of writing them in the indirect speech.

21. "Will you help me with my homework?", Neeta asked Raman.
    (1) Neeta asked Raman if he would help her with her homework.
    (2) Raman was asked by Neeta whether he would help her do the homework.
    (3) Neeta asked Raman to help her in doing the homework.
    (4) Neeta asked for Raman's help in doing her homework.

22. "How long have you been studying here?", Ajay asked Seema.
    (1) Seema was asked by Ajay whether she was studying there.
    (2) Ajay asked Seema that how long she had been studying there.
    (3) Ajay asked Seema when she was studying there.
    (4) Ajay asked Seema about how long she had studied there.

23. Chakram said "I went to Honolulu ten years ago".
   (1) Chakram announced that he had been to Honolulu ten years ago.
   (2) Chakram said he has been to Honolulu ten years ago.
   (3) Ten years ago he had been to Honolulu said Chakram.
   (4) Chakram said that he had been to Honolulu ten years ago.

24. Heena said "I'm getting married tomorrow".
   (1) Heena said that she was getting married the day after.
   (2) She was getting married on the day after said Heena.
   (3) Heena said on the day after she was getting married.
   (4) Heena said that on the day after she gets married.

25. Simon said "I like taking photographs and collecting stamps".
   (1) Simon said about his liking for stamp collection and photography.
   (2) Simon likes photography and stamp collection.
   (3) Taking photographs and stamp collection are liked by Simon.
   (4) Simon said that he liked taking photographs and collecting stamps.

Directions for questions 26 to 30: Choose the option that correctly converts the given sentence, which is in indirect speech, into direct speech.

26. Shyam asked me whether I was going to help him.
   (1) "Can you help me?" Shyam asked me.
   (2) "Are you going to help me?" Shyam asked me.
   (3) Shyam wanted to know whether I could help him.
   (4) Please help me, Shyam asked me.

27. At a dinner party a female MP once accused Churchill of being drunk.
   (1) At a dinner party a female MP once accused Churchill: "You are drunk!"
   (2) Churchill was accused of being a drunk at a dinner party by a female MP.
   (3) 'Churchill you are drunk' accused a female MP at a dinner party.
   (4) 'Drunk you are, Churchill' at a dinner party a female MP accused.

28. Chakram wanted to know what time the banks closed.
   (1) Chakram asked as to what time the banks closed.
   (2) Chakram asked, "What time do the banks close?"
   (3) What time do the banks close was asked by Chakram.
   (4) What is the closing time for the banks? Asked Chakram.

29. The police officer asked us where we were going.
   (1) 'Where we were going' the police officer asked us.
   (2) Where we were going was asked by the police officer.
   (3) The police officer asked us, 'Where are you going?'
   (4) The police officer asked us as to 'Where are we going?'

30. The doctor told me to stay in bed for a few days.
   (1) The doctor said me, 'Stay in bed for a few days'.
   (2) The doctor said that I need to stay in bed.
   (3) 'Stay in bed for a few days,' the doctor said to me.
   (4) Stay in bed for a few days the said to me.

Directions for questions 31 to 35: Replace the blank with suitable phrasal verbs from the given choices.

31. Doctors find it diificult to _________ to their obese patients that having a healthy body is very necessary in order to avoid any type of critical disease.
   (1) put behind   (2) set up
   (3) get down   (4) get through

32. Rehan _________ the group discussion round although the topic given was very difficult for him.
   (1) muddled through
   (2) played down
   (3) tried on
   (4) ticked off

33. They could not make the mayor _________ regarding the inconvenience caused to the city in the last two days.
   (1) run into   (2) stretch out
   (3) pin down   (4) wrap up

34. It is better to _________ her way as she is a highly aggressive person.
(1) stay off   (2) keep off
(3) beat up   (4) leave off

35. The lecturer _________ the students to carry their class notebooks daily.
(1) hit on   (2) paid off
(3) dawned on   (4) impressed on

Directions for questions 36 to 50: Fill in the blanks with appropriate choice of prepositions.

36. I have started getting .... at 5 a.m. to study but I don't know if I can keep this.
(1) on   (2) up
(3) out   (4) back

37. He had an unhappy childhood and he never looks ...... on it with any pleasure.
(1) on   (2) up
(3) out   (4) back

38. The man walked so fast that the child couldn't keep .... him.
(1) on   (2) up with
(3) out   (4) back

39. She looked ...... to see who was following her.
(1) on   (2) up
(3) out   (4) back

40. There were so many panes of glass broken that the windows couldn't keep ..... the rain.
(1) on   (2) up
(3) out   (4) back

41. I've been looking ..... a cup to match the one I broke.
(1) on   (2) up
(3) out   (4) for

42. Look ...... me at the station. I'll be at the bookstall.
(1) on   (2) up
(3) out for   (4) back

43. Look .... ! You nearly knocked my cup out of my hand.
(1) on   (2) up
(3) out   (4) back

44. He was kept ..... in his research by lack of money.
(1) on   (2) up
(3) out   (4) back

45. Tom is looking .... his first trip abroad.
(1) on   (2) to
(3) forward to   (4) back

46. Look .... on your way home and tell me what happened.
(1) on   (2) up
(3) out   (4) in

47. Before putting any money into the business, we must look very carefully .... the accounts.
(1) on   (2) up
(3) into   (4) back

48. I look .... her as one of the family.
(1) on   (2) up
(3) out   (4) back

49. My windows look .... the garden.
(1) on   (2) on to
(3) out   (4) back

50. He asked me to look ...... the document and then sign it.
(1) on   (2) up
(3) over   (4) back

In this section, a passage is given and you are asked to answer questions based on the information that is specifically given in the passage. So, do not make your own judgement or refer to any matter that you already know.

Why do we need to pay special attention to RC – Reading Comprehension? It is because we are being tested on what we have understood after reading the passage under a time constraint. The reading style for RC varies from the reading style we already use. We have to go through our textbooks very carefully to study everything. We cannot afford to skip a point here or a line there, lest we miss out on that crucial one mark that gives us an edge over the competitor. Nor do we read the passage as we read an Agatha Christie novel, from page to page, word by word, curled up in bed on a nice wintry day.

In RC, we need to keep the time factor in mind and finish off our task within the allotted time. It is seldom advisable to take more than 4 or 5 minutes for a passage; this includes the time to answer the questions. We get marks for answering the questions and not for reading the passage only. But we must bear in mind that if we read the passage smoothly and fast, we can answer almost all the questions confidently.

Is it possible for us to answer the questions without reading the passage? Yes. And we should just search for the answers if we have just a minute or so and no time to read the passage at all. But, we must understand the importance of reading fast and getting the important points without dilly-dallying. This will also help us understand and go through our textbooks, case studies, newspapers and magazines faster and better so that we can improve our personality by talking sense when we meet our friends, instead of just 'what's cool' and 'what's hip'.

There are a few techniques that we can apply to read faster and comprehend better:
- Do not regress while reading. Read right the first time round only, instead of re-reading and re-re-reading and re-re-…. Always read in the forward direction and do not look back at all.
- Concentrate on what you are reading and not on what's there for dinner or what dress to wear for the birthday party.

- Read fast as if you really have an express train running after you.
- Keep the details roughly in mind so that you can search for the answer quickly instead of going on a treasure hunt.
- Do not read aloud or even read word-by-word in your mind, this is because there is really no need to read everything, you can skip a point here and a point there if you feel that they are not important enough to be asked a question about.
- Try to have a picture of what you read so that you can get the whole picture of the passage.
- Try to take in more words at a glance rather than only one word.
  If you can't figure out the meaning of the word, try to guess its contextual meaning by reading the whole sentence.
- Read the editorials in the middle page of your newspaper, they are more or less of the same type as passages and you can even widen your general knowledge.
- Mark the right answer! Do not answer half-heartedly, verify!

Approaches to Reading Comprehension

There are several methods of attempting a Reading Comprehension passage. They are given below:
- Read the passage and answer the questions. This is a good method and can help you get all the answers right, or at least help you guess intelligently.
- Take a glance at the questions first, and then read the passage and answer the questions. This is a smart way to work since you can answer questions as you read the passage and not waste time reading unnecessary things.
- Just read the questions and go searching for the answers. If you do not have any time to read the passage, just go and mark answers to whatever questions you can trace in the passage.
- Read two paragraphs, look up if there are any questions based on it and then read two more paragraphs and answer any questions based on it, and so on…This is a good method too as what ever you have read remains fresh in your mind and you can answer it immediately.

There are various methods that help you improve your reading speed. These are given below:

Underlining Hand Method

In this method, you need to move your finger or pencil under the line that you are reading in the forward direction. This helps you concentrate and keep reading forward.

Vertical Page Motion

In this method, you get focus and concentration by placing your hands on either side of the passage and moving it down as you read along. This method helps as you are able to read more as compared to the previous method. You can take a look at the entire line and a portion below it too.

The Brush Technique

Quite an advanced one, you have to brush your hands diagonally from the north-west corner of the page. It requires a lot of concentration and an attention to detail.

The Mapping Technique

What you do here is to read paragraph by paragraph and make a mental map of what you have read in each paragraph, so that you can search in the exact paragraph, should you wish to search for an answer. Also, you must keep in mind how each paragraph links to the previous one and the one that follows.

Finally, read with enthusiasm, and not in a dejected mood. Positive thinking always leads to outstanding results! Yeah!

Directions for passages 1 to 5: Read the following passages and answer the questions that follow:

Passage – 1

San Francisco, America's romantic city by the bay, has always been for the artists, writers, and lovers who have left at least part of their hearts there. One of the great American romantics, who wrote in San Francisco, was Jack Kerouac. Kerouac rewrote the history of an entire post-war era in 'On the Road'.

Born on March 12, 1922, in Lowell, Massachusetts, to a working class Catholic, French-Canadian family, Kerouac had a typically all American childhood. He played baseball, read pulp fiction, and became a high school football star. He entered Columbia University on a football scholarship, but when a leg injury put him out of action on the grid iron, he chose the literary field of work.

American literature would never be the same. His romanticized autobiographical novels and wayward travels, which were often the basis of his work, made him the unquestioned king of the Beat Generation writers.

Before becoming the father of the San Francisco-based Beat Generation, Kerouac was writing in the bars and basement apartments of New York City's Lower East and Lower West sides. Here he met and worked with William S. Burroughs and Allen Ginsberg before they all took their restless spirits to West and started a literary and cultural revolution.

Kerouac first landed in the San Francisco Bay area in 1947, hoping to get a berth on a merchant marine ship. Here, he soon met his kindred spirit, Neal Cassady, whose frenetic letters and cross-country travels spurred Jack to write *On the Road*, perhaps his pre-eminent work, in one long paragraph during the month of April, 1951.

Since the book was written as a simple personal testament 'in search of his writing soul', Kerouac had no idea that *On the Road* would spur a generation onto the highways and into the tumultuous activism of the Vietnam era, a decade later.

Almost overnight, Kerouac became a media superstar and even a mythical figure himself. But in the end, he could not live with the myth he created. He split from the ranks of his fellow Beat writers, like Ginsberg, and actually voiced support for America's war effort in Vietnam. Later in his life, he moved in back with his mother, drank too much, and became more and more reactionary. His later years were an ironic turn on the life of freedom he wrote about and lived to a great extent. Still, the stories he created live on within the souls of American youth, the lingering American romantics.

1. Jack Kerouac was born
   (1) to a working class family in Massachusetts.
   (2) to a Canadian family.
   (3) to Irish Catholic parents.
   (4) in a sandlot

2. Jack Kerouac relocated to San Francisco in
   (1) 1922
   (2) 1951
   (3) 1947
   (4) the midst of the Vietnam War

3. Kerouac met Neal Cassady at
   (1) French-Canadian Massachusetts.
   (2) San Francisco.
   (3) New York.
   (4) Vietnam.

4. *On the Road* was
   (1) not important to the youth of America.
   (2) a paperback edition.
   (3) Alan Ginsberg's poem.
   (4) one long paragraph.

5. Which of the following is NOT mentioning about Kerouac's life?
   (1) His support for the US war effort in Vietnam.
   (2) His French-Canadian upbringing.
   (3) His leading role in the Beat Generation.
   (4) His unsuccessful marriage.

6. The best title for this passage would be
   (1) Post-war Literature and a New Beginning.
   (2) Kerouac: King of the Beats Opens a New Road.
   (3) San Franciso Writers.
   (4) Vietnam Protests: The Early Years.

Passage – 2

Rock, or rock- and- roll is a form of music that was invented in the United States in the 1950s. It has become popular in the US, Europe, and many other parts of the world. African-American performers like Little Richards, Fats Domino, Ray Charles, and Big Joe Turner were among the first people to come out with true rock-and-roll, a combination of various elements from country and Western, gospel, rhythm and blues, and jazz. The influences of early performers like blues man Muddy Waters, gospel performer Ruth Brown, jazz musician Louis Jordan, on rock-and-roll, are still felt today. For example, the songs of early country legend Hank Williams affected musicians, from early rock star Buddy Holly to 1980s rocker Bruce Springsteen.

In the segregated 1950s, African-American musical forms were not considered appropriate for White audiences. Much of the US population had not been exposed to them. All that changed, when in 1953, Cleveland disc jockey, Alan Freed began to play rhythm and blues to a largely non-African- American audience. Freed was successful and a lot of records were sold. The music spread, and the term that Freed had adopted for the music – rock-and-roll – began to spread as well.

Teenagers and the money they were willing to spend on records provided an impetus for rock-and-roll. On their way to becoming rock stars, many performers copied songs from the original artists. For instance, Pat Boone scored a hit with a toned-down version of Little Richards' song, 'Tutti Frutti', prompting Little Richard to comment, "He goes and outsells me with my song that I wrote". In 1955-56, Chuck Berry, Bill Haley and the Comets, and particularly Elvis Presley became famous for their version of traditional rhythm and blues. Elvis Presley's first television appearance in January 1956 marked rock-and-roll's ascendancy into the world of pop music.

1. What is the main topic of this passage?
   (1) American popular music
   (2) The careers of successful rock musicians
   (3) The musical elements that distinguish pop from classical music.
   (4) The origins of the music that came to be called 'rock-and-roll'.

2. Who is NOT mentioned as an African-American performer who was amongst the first to come out with rock-and-roll?
   (1) Fats Domino   (2) Little Richards
   (3) Elvis Presley   (4) Ray Charles

3. According to the passage, true rock-and-roll is characterized by a combination of which of the following?
   (1) The music of Bruce Springsteen and Hank Williams
   (2) Musical influences from Europe and Asia
   (3) Forms of music heard on most radio stations in the early 1950s
   (4) Country and Western, gospel, rhythm and blues, and jazz

4. In the 1950s rock-and-roll
   (1) was not popular among teenagers.
   (2) was not considered appropriate for White audiences.
   (3) sold few records.
   (4) was invented.

5. Many performers copied songs from ______.
   (1) classical music
   (2) Pat Boone
   (3) original artists
   (4) 'Tutti Frutti'

6. Which of the following is NOT mentioned in the passage as being a factor in the commercial success of early rock-and-roll?
   (1) The purchasing power of early rock enthusiasts.
   (2) The charismatic personality of disc jockey Alan Freed.
   (3) the exposure of a non-African-American audience to African-American musical forms
   (4) rock's popularity with teenage audiences

Passage – 3

Primitive mammals called monotremes are the only living representatives of the subclass Prototheria. This makes them the most likely living representatives of creatures that were part of the evolutionary transition from reptiles to mammals. They share some qualities with reptiles and birds, but are nevertheless true mammals. Like birds and reptiles, monotremes lay eggs rather than give birth. But like other mammals, they have hair, large brains, and mammary glands that produce milk to nourish their offspring.

Their primitive organization and close relation to reptiles is manifested in their uncomplicated brain structure, egg-laying habits and cloaca. (A cloaca is found in amphibians, reptiles, birds, certain fish, and monotremes, but not in placental mammals or most bony fishes. The animal's intestinal, urinary, and genital tracts open into this common cavity, which also functions as an outlet.)

Another feature that indicates they may be related to reptiles is their egg-laying behaviour. Monotremes lay shelled eggs, which are predominantly yolk, like those of reptiles and birds. The young are born in a relatively early stage of development and remain dependent upon the parents. The females have no teats; the milk that they secrete from their mammary glands passes directly through their skin.

There are only three types of monotremes in existence: the duck–billed platypus and two species of spiny echidna, or anteater. The platypus has webbed feet, a flat tail, and a 'bill' like a duck's. The short- and the long-nosed echidnas have spines and tube-like noses. The female echidna lays one egg at a time into a pouch that she develops in her abdomen. Her young will hatch in it and develop for several months.

1. On which of the following aspects of monotremes does the passage focus?
   (1) The food they eat and their behaviour in the wild
   (2) The times of day when they are most active
   (3) Their relationship to both reptiles and mammals
   (4) Their mating behaviour and reproductive organs

2. Which of the following is NOT mentioned as a quality that monotremes share with other mammals?
   (1) hair on the body
   (2) development of mammary glands
   (3) egg-laying
   (4) a large brain

3. The passage states that monotremes are
   (1) extinct
   (2) reptiles and birds
   (3) egg-laying mammals that are related to reptiles and birds
   (4) highly intelligent

4. Monotreme babies are born
   (1) and nurtured in a nest
   (2) fully developed and quickly become independent
   (3) live like the babies of other mammals
   (4) in the early stages of development and must rely on their mothers

5. The duck-billed platypus is
   (1) the tube-like nose of a monotreme
   (2) a subspecies of anteater
   (3) a portion of the monotreme reproductive system
   (4) one of the few surviving species of monotreme

6. According to the passage, where do young echidnas live right after they are hatched?
   (1) in a pouch on their mother's abdomen
   (2) in their mother's cloaca
   (3) in amphibians, birds, reptiles, and certain fish
   (4) in an egg that has a shell and that is predominantly yolk

Passage – 4

Asteroids are rocky, metallic objects that orbit around the Sun, but are too small to be considered planets. The largest known asteroid, Ceres, has a diameter of about 1,000 kilometres. The smallest asteroids are the size of pebbles. Millions are of the size of boulders. Most are irregularly shaped – only a few are large enough for gravity to have made them into spheres. About 250 asteroids in the solar system are 100 kilometres in diameter, and at least 16 have a diameter of 240 kilometres or greater. Their orbits lie in a range that stretches from Earth's orbit to beyond Saturn's orbit. Tens of thousands of asteroids exist in a belt between the orbits of Mars and Jupiter. An asteroid that hits Earth's atmosphere is called a meteor or shooting star, because it burns and gives off a bright flash of light. Whatever does not completely burn falls on Earth as a meteorite. Between 1,000 and 10,000 tons of this material fall on Earth daily. Much is in the form of small grains of dust, but about 1,000 metallic or rocky bits fall on Earth each year.

There has been much speculation about large meteors hitting the Earth. A large asteroid or comet is thought to have landed in Mexico about 65 million years ago. The impact may have led to the extinction of many species, including the dinosaurs, by throwing dust into the atmosphere, blocking the sunlight, and causing a climate change. The period of time between such a large meteor impacts is probably in the millions of years, but smaller meteors such as the one that caused the Metro's Cater in Arizona (about 1.2 kilometres in diameter), may hit the Earth every 50,000 to 100,000 years. There's no historical record of a person being killed by a meteorite. The only reported injury occurred on November 30, 1954, when an Alabama woman was bruised by an eight-pound meteorite that fell on her through the roof of her house.

1. Which of the following assumptions about asteroids is expressed in the passage?
   (1) They rarely become meteorites.
   (2) Most are relatively small.
   (3) Many exist, but few actually fall on Earth.
   (4) They are a major cause of death in some regions.

2. The majority of asteroids are
   (1) of the size of boulders.
   (2) symmetrical.
   (3) about 1,000 kilometres in diameter.
   (4) irregular in shape.

3. Which of the following explains why a meteor is called a shooting star?
   (1) It may have caused the extinction of dinosaurs.
   (2) No one is known to have been killed by one.
   (3) It burns in a flash of light.
   (4) It can be rocky or metallic.

4. In the passage, why does the author mention the Metro's Crater in Arizona?
   (1) To give an example of the impact of a smaller meteor.
   (2) To increase interest in astronomy.
   (3) To close the passage on an interesting note.
   (4) To show how meteors can wipe out animal species.

5. The Alabama woman in the passage is mentioned to
   (1) show that meteorites can kill.
   (2) illustrate the only documented injury of a human being by a meteorite.
   (3) show that meteorites can damage homes.
   (4) warn people of space objects.

Passage – 5

A highly-acclaimed motion picture of 1979 concerned a nearly disastrous accident at a nuclear power plant. Within a few weeks of the film's release, in a chilling coincidence, a real-life accident startlingly similar to the fictitious one occurred at the Three Mile Island plant near Harrisburg, Pennsylvania. The two incidents even corresponded in certain details, for instance, both in the film and in real life, one cause of the mishap was a false meter reading caused by a jammed needle.

Such similarities led many to wonder whether the fictional movie plot had been prophetic in other ways. The movie depicted officials of the power industry as seriously corrupt, willing to lie, bribe, and even kill to conceal their culpability in the accident. Did a similar cover-up occur in the Three Mile Island accident? Perhaps we will never know. We do know that, despite the endeavours of reporters and citizen groups to uncover the cause of the accident, many of the facts remain unknown. Although they declare that the public is entitled to the truth, many of the power industry leaders responsible have been reluctant to cooperate with independent, impartial investigators.

1. The nuclear accident described in the movie
   (1) was successfully concealed by power industry leaders and officials.
   (2) was caused by a series of coincidences.
   (3) as a surprisingly accurate foreshadowing of actual events.
   (4) took place at the Three Mile Island.

2. Officials of the nuclear power industry
   (1) have committed murders to make possible a cover-up of the incident at Harrisburg.
   (2) had predicted that nuclear accidents were likely to occur.
   (3) have cooperated with the film industry.
   (4) have been reluctant to reveal the full story about the Three Mile Island incident.

3. According to the passage, public concern over the accident near Harrisburg
   (1) had no effect on the subsequent investigation.
   (2) was lessened by the quick response of industry leaders and officials.
   (3) prompted widespread panic throughout Pennsylvania.
   (4) persisted as many questions were left unanswered.

4. Reporters looking into the accident at Three Mile Island
   (1) uncovered more facts than did citizen groups.
   (2) did not succeed in uncovering all the facts about the cause of the accident.
   (3) cooperated closely with power industry officials.
   (4) kept documented information from the public.

5. All of the following are true, EXCEPT...
   (1) The movie about a nuclear accident has been praised.
   (2) The Press has sought fuller information about the Three Mile Island mishap.
   (3) A mechanical breakdown was a partial cause of the Harrisburg accident.
   (4) The release of the movie came only weeks after the Three Mile Island accident.

Every passage given in ICET has a specific style of its own.' Style' here refers to the way of writing of an author. It can be known by looking at the sentence structure, usage of words and phrases and formation of paragraphs.

Some of the well - defined styles of passages which are a frequent phenomenon in ICET papers are as follows:

1. **Argumentative style** – These style of passages carry forward a distinct opinion of the author on any significant topic. The author tries to justify his/her individual point of view on a particular issue by giving examples and sometimes the author may also try to impose these views on the reader.

2. **Philosophical style** – Passages based on this style use abstract words, phrases, idioms and they always have a hidden meaning of their own which the reader has to derive in order to understand the main idea and the theme of the passage. Topics related to philosophy, psychology, morality and religion are essentially based on this style.

3. **Factual Style** – These passages are very neutral and objective by nature. They mostly talk about facts and natural occurences which have an existence of their own. They also refer to scientific facts and data in order to support their statements. Such passages do not include the author's opinion at all and they are very unbiased and dispassionate in their theme.

4. **Analytical Style** – These passages have the main idea given in the first paragraph or the last paragraph of the passage. First the main idea is given and then its individual elements are broken down into different parts and each part is analysed in detail in separate paragraphs.

5. **Narrative Style** – Passages based on this style are written in the form of a story with a definite beginning, middle and end.

Argumentative Style Passages

Directions for questions 1 to 15: Read the following passages and answer the questions that follow:

Passage – 1

Genetic engineering enables scientists to create plants, animals and micro-organisms by manipulating genes in a way that does not occur naturally.These genetically modified organisms (GMO) can spread through nature and interbreed with natural organisms, thereby contaminating non 'GE' environments and future generations in an unforeseeable and uncontrollable way.

Their release is 'genetic pollution' and is a major threat because GMOs cannot be recalled once released into the environment. While scientific progress on molecular biology has a great potential to increase our understanding of nature and provide new medical tools, it should not be used as justification to turn the environment into a giant genetic experiment by commercial interests. The biodiversity and environmental integrity of the world's food supply is too important to our survival to be put at risk.

Biological diversity must be protected and respected as the global heritage of humankind and one of our world's fundamental keys to survival. Governments are attempting to address the threat of GE with international regulations such as the Biosafety Protocol.

We believe GMOs should not be released into the environment as there is not adequate scientific understanding of their impact on the environment and human health.We advocate immediate interim measures such as labelling of GE ingredients, and the segregation of genetically engineered crops and seeds from conventional ones.

We also oppose all patents on plants, animals and humans, as well as patents on their genes. Life is not an industrial commodity. When we force life forms and our world's food supply to conform to human economic models rather than their natural ones, we do so at our own peril.

1. How can GMO pollute the nature and non GE environments?
   (1) By using non-renewable resources
   (2) By throwing natural waste injudiciously.
   (3) By violating biological laws.
   (4) By interbreeding with natural organisms

2. Why is genetic pollution seen as a threat?
   (1) Because it causes environment pollution.
   (2) Because GMO violates Biosafety Protocol.

(3) Because GMO cannot be called back if once introduced.
(4) Because GMO is not natural but synthetic.

3. Why is the author against GMOs?
   (1) Because he believes that natural genes should not be tampered with.
   (2) GMOs are a menace to environmental integrity.
   (3) GMOs do not understand nature as it exists.
   (4) GMO are bi-products of industries.

4. What should be seen as a heritage of mankind?
   (1) Nature
   (2) GE ingredients
   (3) Biological diversity
   (4) All of the these.

5. The author preaches for which of the following?
   (1) Ban on the use of GE genes.
   (2) Patents on genes of living organisms.
   (3) Protection of world's food supply.
   (4) labelling GE ingredients and segregating GMOs.

Passage – 2

The African continent has been the location of some of the bloodiest and violent conflicts of recent decades. In Rwanda, for example, there was genocide on an unprecedented scale. In Europe and the USA there has been strong criticism of international organisations such as the United Nations for their slowness in reacting to crisis in Rwanda and Somalia.

But the question to be asked is whether the involvement of other African countries in these conflicts is really this philanthropic. We have seen in places such as the Democratic Republic of the Congo that many countries such as Zimbabwe are involved in the war to procure the diamond mines and other resources in the warzones and thus have a greater vested interest in fuelling the wars over resolving them. The neighbouring countries in Africa rather have their own way than sort the crises which according to them can become international disputes in future. These countries do no better by sending their own troops to stabilize the country and restore the rightful ruler. In fact, the situation degenerates into the civil wars we see elsewhere on the continent.

Just because the intervening country used infantry or tanks instead of negotiation or aerial bombardment (Kosovo), doesn't make it any more likely to restore peace. On a global scale, Vietnam is the classic example of how using infantry to intervene in a guerrilla war is a futile exercise. On an African stage, the infantry intervention by neighbouring countries has only increased the death toll, not the success at ending the war.

6. Which the following places saw genocide?
   (1) Congo
   (2) Zimbabwe
   (3) Rwanda
   (4) Somalia

7. How are the neighboring countries in Africa trying to help those countries which are facing conflicts?
   (1) By educating the citizens of the war-torn areas.
   (2) By providing food supplies to the poor and deprived.
   (3) By negotiating with the conflicting groups.
   (4) By using infantry and tanks to restore peace.

8. Why does the author doubt whether the involvement of Zimbabwe in Congo is really genuine?
   (1) Because Zimbabwe has vested interests in other resources.
   (2) Because it is unable to restore peace.
   (3) Because it is slow in negotiating with other governments.
   (4) Because it hasn't informed UN about the steps it is taking.

9. What is the problem that African countries are facing?
   (1) The Africans are illiterate and uneducated.
   (2) The African government is inefficient.
   (3) There are wars and conflicts causing violence in Africa.
   (4) The United Nations is reluctant to help the poor economies of African countries.

10. Which of the following has been futile attempt in restoring peace in African countries?
    (1) Zimbabwe's intervention
    (2) Guerrilla war of Vietnam
    (3) Infantry intervention and tanks
    (4) Criticism of United Nations by African countries

Passage – 3

Before the rise of the modern animal movement there were societies for the prevention of cruelty to animals, but these organizations largely accepted that the welfare of nonhuman animals deserves protection only when human interests are not at stake. Human beings were seen as quite distinct from, and infinitely superior to, all forms of animal life. If our interests conflict with theirs, it is always their interests which have to give way. In contrast with this approach, the view that I want to defend puts human and nonhuman animals, *as such*, on the same moral footing. That is the sense in which I argued, in *Animal Liberation*, that "all animals are equal."

Obviously nonhuman animals cannot have equal rights to vote and nor should they be held criminally responsible for what they do. That is not the kind of equality I want to extend to nonhuman animals. The fundamental form of equality is *equal consideration of interests*, and it is this that we should extend beyond the boundaries of our own species. Essentially this means that if an animal feels pain, the pain matters as much as it does when a human feels pain—if the pains hurt just as much. How bad pain and suffering are does not depend on the species of being that experiences it.

I have been arguing against the widely accepted idea that we are justified in discounting the interests of an animal merely because it is not a member of the species *Homo sapiens*.Unfortunately a great deal of what Americans do to animals, especially in raising them for food in modern industrialized farms, does inflict prolonged suffering on literally billions of animals each year. Since we can live very good lives without doing this, it is wrong for us to inflict this suffering, irrespective of the question of the wrongness of taking the lives of these animals.

11. The author is fighting for which of the following?
    (1) Cloning of animals
    (2) Beating and ill-treating animals
    (3) Animal Rights
    (4) Protection of animals from poachers

12. Which of the following is used to represent humans in the passage ?
    (1) Homo sapiens
    (2) Anser Indicus
    (3) Phylum Chordata
    (4) Diceros Bicornis

13. Some organisations protect animal rights only when
    (1) they animals are used in industralised farms.
    (2) till the time interest of humans and animals are different.
    (3) the use of animals causes them prolonged illness.
    (4) painful experiments are conducted on domestic animals.

14. What does the author definitely not mean by 'equal consideration of interests' of humans & animals?
    (1) Pain inflicted to humans matters as much as when it is inflicted on animals.
    (2) Animals should not be made to sacrifice their interests for humans.
    (3) Animals should be punished and held responsible for mistakes the same way as humans are.
    (4) Cruelty to animals is unfustified.

15. What causes prolonged suffering on animals?
    (1) Shooting them for pleasure.
    (2) Beating them for carrying load.
    (3) Using them for mechanical jobs.
    (4) Raising them in industrialised farms.

Philosophical Style Passages

Directions for questions 1 to 20: Read the following passages and answer the questions that follow:

Passage – 1

It is truly said that even a holy man cannot live in peace without satisfying his wicked neighbors. It is therefore not a question whether one wants to live in peace; the more important question is whether the wicked will tolerate it. To bring tolerance among the neighbors so that you can live in peace, they demand that you please them. It is natural with them to be jealous of things which you enjoy but which they could not hope to have. Although in theory it sounds good to preach *"live and let live" and "treat thy neighbor as thyself"* in actual practice; it is seldom followed. One thing is clear: that anyone seeking peace, freedom and happiness, must select a suitable neighborhood.

For a society or a country to be well governed, a certain discipline and self-control becomes necessary. Allowing each to live as he likes is sure to lead to chaos as the interests of individuals are likely to conflict. What will follow is violence and untruth. Suffering has been the lot of mankind even after centuries of civilization and culture, and it speaks ill of the society and the world that did not benefit from these.

Have we ever thought why our civilization and culture with all their promises and traditions of religion, science, philosophy, sociology, economics, politics and what else there is - have so far failed to give a positive shape to a normal human society where every one can live in peace, can enjoy happiness and be free? We hardly realize that this is due to the bane of permissive society which is not the product of today as some think but which is an evil that made inroads, though in small measure, right from the beginning of our civilization and culture.

For example, the divine rights of royalty and the might and main of privileged class have scant respect for self-control and discipline. Their behavior pattern was governed by their attitude which held self-control in contempt and discipline as abasement.

In permissive society, exceptions become the rule and the rules remain as mere exceptions. So whatever principles, commandments, rules, etc. were formulated by religion, ethics, sociology, economics, law, etc. have remained operative only for those who respect and obey them. Others who defied the structure and authority behaved cynically. After much deliberation on the issues of right and wrong, a framework of rules, customs and commandments happens to be projected - and do we not find them uniformly good everywhere? - but these, however, fail to be imperative.

1. The primary purpose of the passage is to
   (1) discuss about the tolerance of people in permissive society regarding the wrong doings that are happening in the society.
   (2) discuss about a holy man living in peace with his neighborhood.
   (3) analyse the culture and tradition of a specific society.
   (4) justify the importance of suffering in creating a successful society.

2. The meaning of the word 'abasement' given in the 4th paragraph of the passage is:
   (1) devastation
   (2) reduction
   (3) degradation
   (4) esteem

3. According to the passage
   (1) A suitable neighborhood can be selected easily.
   (2) Each individual should be allowed to live his life in his own way.
   (3) In permissive society, each individual is made to abide by the rules and regulations that are laid down.

(4) The curse of the permissive society has been present since the very beginning of the human civilisation.

4. The author has defined the attitude of the divine rights of royalty as:
   (1) disciplined and rule-oriented
   (2) full of life and happiness
   (3) full of sympathy and compassion
   (4) very less respect for self-control and discipline

5. What does the author imply by the statement 'a holy man cannot live in peace without satisfying his wicked neighbors'?
   (1) Peace and happiness are the secrets of a successful life.
   (2) One cannot live in peace unless the wicked people tolerate this attitude.
   (3) 'Treat thy neighbor as thyself' is seldom followed in real life.
   (4) A society or country cannot be well - governed unless people develop strong interaction with each other.

Passage – 2

A virtue such as honesty or generosity is not just a tendency to do what is honest or generous, nor is it to be helpfully specified as a "desirable" or "morally valuable" character trait. It is, indeed a character trait — that is, a disposition which is well, entrenched in its possessor, something that, as we say "goes all the way down", unlike a habit such as being a tea–drinker — but the disposition in question, far from being a single track disposition to do honest actions, or even honest actions for certain reasons, is multi–track. It is concerned with many other actions as well, with emotions and emotional reactions, choices, value, desires, perceptions, attitudes, interests, expectations, and sensibilities. To possess a virtue is to be a certain sort of person with a certain complex mindset. (Hence the extreme recklessness of attributing a virtue on the basis of a single action.)

The most significant aspect of such a mindset is the wholehearted acceptance of a certain range of considerations as reasons for action. An honest person cannot be identified simply as one who, for example, practices honest dealing, and does not cheat. If such actions are done merely because the agent thinks that honesty is the best policy, or because they fear being caught out, rather than through recognising " To do

Verbal Ability / Grammar & RC

otherwise would be dishonest" as the relevant reason, they are not the actions of an honest person. An honest person cannot be identified simply as one who, for example, always tells the truth, nor even as one who always tells the truth because it is the truth, for one can have the virtue of honesty without being tactless or indiscreet. The honest person recognises "That would be a lie" as a strong (though perhaps not overriding) reason for not making certain statements in certain circumstances, and gives due, but not overriding, weight to "That would be the truth" as a reason for making them.

6. According to the passage, 'honesty' can be defined as
   (1) a 'desirable' or 'morally valuable' character trait
   (2) a particular characteristic that is deeply rooted within a person who follows it
   (3) a single–track disposition to do honest actions
   (4) a tendency to be honest or generous

7. The meaning of the word 'indiscreet' given in the last paragraph of the passage is
   (1) careful
   (2) unclear
   (3) imprudent
   (4) unjustified

8. All of the following are true according to the passage except
   (1) A person can be honest even by being tactful.
   (2) Honesty is a quality or trait of being honest.
   (3) Any person who practices honesty cannot be necessarily qualified as honest.
   (4) An honest person differentiates between a strong or a weak reason for his actions.

9. Any virtue or disposition (like honesty) is not concerned with which of the following?
   (1) desires and attitudes
   (2) emotions and reactions
   (3) interests
   (4) recklessness

10. Possessing a virtue like honesty implies that
    (1) the person never does a dishonest act.
    (2) the person is honest for the sake of being called 'moral'.
    (3) the person is tactless and indiscreet.
    (4) a person has a certain mindset which reasons his honest actions.

Passage – 3

In his book, The Myth of the Framework, Popper stated, "I hold that orthodoxy is the death of knowledge, since the growth of knowledge depends entirely on the existence of disagreement." In short, everything should be open to critical analysis. Nothing is sacred in that regard. Thomas Jefferson said, "Question with boldness even the existence of a God; because, if there be one, he must more approve of the homage of reason, than that of blind-folded fear."

One of Popper's main contributions to political theory was The Open Society and Its Enemies. In it, he reformulates Plato's question of "Who should rule" into "How do we arrange our institutions to prevent rulers (whether individuals or majorities) from doing too much damage." He is probably best known for his principle of falsification. Falsificationism is the idea that science advances by unjustified, exaggerated guesses followed by unrelenting criticism. Only hypotheses capable of clashing with observation reports are allowed to count as scientific. Those that aren't are considered metaphysical and exist outside the realm of science. Faith, for example, is not a matter of science. It's metaphysical in nature. On that basis alone subjects such as creationism don't qualify as science.

11. Which of the following works deals with political theory ?
    (1) The Myth of the Framework
    (2) The Open Society and Its Enemies
    (3) Falsification of Political Principles
    (4) None of the above

12. What is metaphysical and not science ?
    (1) Observation
    (2) Hypothesis
    (3) Faith
    (4) Growth of knowledge

13. According to Popper, what is the relationship between orthodoxy and knowledge?
    (1) Orthodoxy helps in growth of knowledge.
    (2) Orthodoxy and knowledge are two sides of the same coin.
    (3) Knowledge leads to orthodoxy.
    (4) Orthodoxy causes death of knowledge because it does not believe in disagreement.

14. What is the theory of Falsification ?
    (1) Any guess which is substantiated and validated by observation is science.
    (2) Beliefs which are justified by an authority are rational.
    (3) A rationalist is someone who keeps his ideas open to criticism.
    (4) Science adheres to its positions regardless of shifts in reality.

15. Why did Jefferson say that existence of God should be questioned ?
    (1) If God exists, His existence should be critically analysed
    (2) God would approve reasoning of His existence rather than blind belief in Him.
    (3) The debate of His existence is metaphysical and not scientific.
    (4) This helps in increasing our knowledge about God.

Passage – 4

The theory of the mean, which states that virtue is a point between two vices, is still influential in moral philosophy today.

The theory of the mean is one of Aristotle's best-known pieces of ethical thinking. It can be found in his book *The Nicomachean Ethics*. In a nutshell, Aristotle said that virtues are a point of moderation between two opposite vices. For instance, the virtue courage lies between the two vices of cowardice and recklessness. Recklessness is too much confidence and not enough fear, cowardice is too much fear and not enough confidence, courage is just the right amount of both.

Some of the "virtues" may seem a bit odd to those brought up with a post-Christian worldview. Aristotle thinks you should have the "right amount" of pride, depending on your worth, and that humility is a deficiency of proper pride, and therefore a vice.

Aristotle makes it clear that he is not talking about a mathematical middle, but the perfect intermediate point with regard to ourselves. The perfect point might be closer to excess, or closer to deficiency. Courage is closer to recklessness than cowardice, and self-control is closer to lack of sensitivity to one's needs than to self indulgence.

Even if you manage to find the mean, it's not enough just to follow it. You can do good deeds but unless you have a good character yourself, Aristotle says the actions won't be truly virtuous. You have to keep doing the right thing so that your character can become good, through training, and only then will your good deeds actually be good!

16. What is main theme of the passage ?
    (1) The golden rule of mean applies to all spheres of life.
    (2) One should live a life of temperance and self-control.
    (3) Proper emotional response to situations is the highest virtue.
    (4) A virtue is a point of moderation between two vices, which are extremes in opposite directions.

17. What does 'The Nicomachean Ethics' deal with ?
    (1) Virtues and vices
    (2) The theory of mean
    (3) Maintaining dignity
    (4) How to find the mean

18. Who gave the theory of mean of virtue ?
    (1) Aristotle
    (2) Socrates
    (3) Plato
    (4) David Hume

19. With which of the following would Aristotle agree with ?
    (1) One should feel anger to the right extent - neither too little nor too much.
    (2) Being recklessness is better than being a coward.
    (3) Virtues differ from person to person.
    (4) Mean of virtues mean the middle of two virtues.

20. The mean of virtues definitely does not refer to
    (1) the moderate point between vices.
    (2) the middle point between the vices.
    (3) both 1. and 2..
    (4) neither 1. and 2..

Verbal Ability / Grammar & RC

Factual Style Passages

Directions for questions 1 to 15: Read the following passages and answer the questions that follow:

Passage – 1

Earthquakes are the shaking, rolling or sudden shock of the earth's surface. They are the Earth's natural means of releasing stress. More than a million earthquakes rattle the world each year. The West Coast is most at risk of having an earthquake, but earthquakes can happen in the Midwest and along the East Coast. Earthquakes can be felt over large areas although they usually last less than one minute. Earthquakes cannot be predicted - although scientists are working on it! There are about 20 plates along the surface of the earth that move continuously and slowly past each other. When the plates squeeze or stretch, huge rocks form at their edges and the rocks shift with great force, causing an earthquake. Think of it this way: Imagine holding a pencil horizontally. If you were to apply a force to both ends of the pencil by pushing down on them, you would see the pencil bend. After enough force was applied, the pencil would break in the middle, releasing the stress you have put on it. The Earth's crust acts in the same way. As the plates move they put forces on themselves and each other. When the force is large enough, the crust is forced to break. When the break occurs, the stress is released as energy which moves through the Earth in the form of waves, which we feel and call an earthquake. The theory of plate tectonics is an interesting story of continents drifting from place to place breaking apart, colliding, and grinding against each other. The plate tectonic theory is supported by a wide range of evidence that considers the earth's crust and upper mantle to be composed of several large, thin, relatively rigid plates that move relative to one another. The plates are all moving in different directions and at different speeds. Sometimes the plates crash together, pull apart or sideswipe each other. When this happens, it commonly results in earthquakes.

1. Earthquakes are earth's means of:
   (1) rolling around.
   (2) releasing stress.
   (3) shocking the earth.
   (4) shaking the east and west coasts.

2. Earthquakes are felt over large areas although:
   (1) they cannot be predicted.
   (2) they last less than a minute.
   (3) more than a million earthquakes unnerve the world every year.
   (4) the West Coast is most at risk.

3. The pencil acts like the:
   (1) Earth's crust
   (2) Plates
   (3) Shifting rocks
   (4) Released energy

4. The plate tectonics theory is about:
   (1) the violent movement of the earth's surface.
   (2) the forces that manifest in the rocks.
   (3) the continents moving about.
   (4) the collision of continents.

5. The tectonic theory finds support in:
   (1) a wide range of evidence
   (2) the composition of earth's crust
   (3) the crashing of the plates
   (4) the occurrence of the earthquakes

Passage – 2

Education - the pursuit of knowing is an all encompassing process that must lead to the highest realization of our ability. In our conventional language, a person who has specialized knowledge and professional degrees in a particular subject is called educated. This accumulated knowledge helps him to make a successful career in his chosen field and earn a comfortable living. This education indeed is only one dimensional. In this era of overstressing a single dimension we are developing oblivion to the other aspects that are unequivocally important. The process of education begins the moment we are born. As we enter the world, the eyes gaze at the surrounding things and the ears listen to the various sounds. As we grow, we pick up actions and words from those around us. It is obvious that we learn those things quickly and easily to which we are exposed early and frequently. This very nature or tendency of our comprehension forms the foundation of all our learning in all the years to come. Hence it is of utmost value to familiarize a child early with the positive energy of his mind. Our educational syllabi are quite vast and well compiled. We are made aware of the infinite universe, wonders of science and technology, logics of mathematics but we do not find it necessary to explain or be explained the wonders and power of the mind. Mind which is the genesis of all human thoughts and thus the originator of all human creation. This is either the irony of our progressive world or the short sightedness of our educated society.

6. The passage defines education as:
    (1) the pursuit of knowing.
    (2) an encompassing process.
    (3) a gradual realization process.
    (4) the highest realization of one's ability.

7. Traditionally, an educated person is
    (1) a person who explores the various facets of a
        particular subject.
    (2) a person with professional degrees.
    (3) a person with specialized knowledge and
        professional degrees.
    (4) an expert in various subjects.

8. The one dimensional approach results in:
    (1) overstepping a single dimension
    (2) earning a comfortable living.
    (3) gaining success in a chosen field.
    (4) developing oblivion towards other aspects.

9. The foundation of all our learning is:
    (1) early learning through frequent exposure.
    (2) the positive energy of a child's mind.
    (3) the capability to comprehend swiftly.
    (4) picking up actions and words around us.

10. According to the passage, the inadequacy in the
    syllabi is:
    (1) that it is quite vast and not well compiled.
    (2) that it creates awareness of the infinite
    universe.
    (3) that it does not explain the power of the mind.
    (4) that it overlooks the genesis of human thought.

Passage – 3

The first humans evolved in tropical and subtropical
regions of Africa about 2.5 million years ago. Since then,
we have successfully occupied all of the major geographic
regions of the world, but our bodies have remained
essentially those of warm climate animals. We cannot
survive outside of the warmer regions of our planet without
our cultural knowledge and technology. What made it
possible for our ancestors to begin living in temperate
and ultimately subartic regions of the northern hemisphere
after half a million years ago was the invention of efficient
hunting skills, fire use, and, ultimately, clothing, warm
housing, agriculture, and commerce. Culture has been
a highly successful adaptive mechanism for our species.
It has given us a major selective advantage in the
competition for survival with other life forms. Culture has

allowed the global human population to grow from less
than 10 million people shortly after the end of the last ice
age to more than 6.5 billion people today, a mere 10,000
years later. Culture has made us the most dangerous
and the most destructive large animal on our planet. It is
ironic that despite the power that culture has given us,
we are totally dependent on it for survival. We need our
cultural skills to stay alive. Over the last several hundred
thousand years, we have developed new survival related
cultural skills and technologies at a faster rate than natural
selection could alter our bodies to adapt to the
environmental challenges that confronted us. The fact
that cultural evolution can occur faster than biological
evolution has significantly modified the effect of natural
selection on humans. One consequence of this has been
that we have not developed thick fat layers and dense fur
coats like polar bears in the cold regions because our
culture provided the necessary warmth during winter
times.

11. Survival outside the warmer regions will be
    impossible without:
    (1) Suitable climate
    (2) Cultural knowledge and technology
    (3) Warm bodies
    (4) Geographical knowledge

12. Survival, according to the passage, was possible
    in the sub arctic regions because:
    (1) of the evolution in the tropical and the sub
        tropical regions.
    (2) of the invention of efficient hunting skills, fire
        use and commerce.
    (3) of a thorough understanding of other planets.
    (4) our ancestors lived half a million years ago.

13. According to the passage, the growth in population
    can be attributed to:
    (1) competition
    (2) agriculture
    (3) clothing
    (4) civilization or culture

14. Culture has triumphed because
    (1) Cultural skills grew at a faster rate than natural
        selection.
    (2) Culture has deterred natural selection.
    (3) Culture halted the body alteration process.
    (4) Culture helped us develop survival related
        technologies.

Verbal Ability / Grammar & RC

15. The lack of fur coats in humans can be attributed to:
    (1) artistic skills   (2) environment
    (3) culture   (4) artificial coats

Analytical Style Passages

Directions for questions 1 to 15: Read the following passages and answer the questions that follow:

Passage – 1

If you want to incubate an author who will show lifelong sympathy for children and animals, it seems best to sequester him at an early age and then subject him to a long regime of domestic torture. This was the formula that worked so well for Kipling, as evidenced in his frightening autobiographical story, "Baa Baa, Black Sheep," and it is almost uncanny to see how closely Saki's early life followed the same course. Abandoned to the care of cold and neurotic aunts in England while his father performed colonial duties in India, he and his siblings had to learn how to do without affection, and how to resist and outpoint adult callousness and stupidity. But without those terrible women—and the villains in Saki's gem-like tales are almost always female—we might not have had the most-fearsome aunts in fiction, outdoing even Wodehouse's Aunt Agatha or Wilde's Lady Bracknell. As is by no means uncommon in such cases, Saki was of the extreme right, and even an admirer must concede that some of his witticisms were rather labored and contrived as a consequence. Several of his less amusing stories are devoted to ridicule of the women's suffrage movement, which was cresting during his heyday, while a persistent subtext of his work is a satirical teasing of his contemporary and bête noire, the ponderously socialistic Bernard Shaw.

1. Incubation is a basis for:
   (1) authors being subjected to domestic torture.
   (2) authors creating literary masterpieces.
   (3) authors displaying lifelong sympathy for children.
   (4) authors writing historical pieces.

2. According to the passage, 'Baa Baa, Black Sheep' is a
   (1) A nursery rhyme.
   (2) An altruistic poem.
   (3) A satire on sheep.
   (4) An autobiographical piece.

3. Saki and his siblings, according to the passage, were deprived of:
   (1) warmth.
   (2) food
   (3) education
   (4) entertainment

4. The "terrible women" refers to:
   (1) The villains in Saki's stories.
   (2) The aunts who took care of Saki.
   (3) The aunts in Wilde's stories.
   (4) Wodehouse's Aunt Agatha.

5. It can be ascertained from the passage that:
   (1) the main plots in Saki's stories were women dominated.
   (2) the playwright, Bernard Shaw was Saki's arch rival.
   (3) Saki's childhood had robbed him of his innocence.
   (4) the women's suffrage movement was peaking in Saki's time.

Passage – 2

Whether made of highly polished metal or of glass with a coating of metal on the back, mirrors have fascinated people for millennia: ancient Egyptians were often depicted holding hand mirrors. With their capacity to reflect back nearly all incident light upon them and so recapitulate the scene they face, mirrors are like pieces of dreams, their images hyper-real and profoundly fake. Mirrors reveal truths you may not want to see. Give them a little smoke and a house to call their own, and mirrors will tell you nothing but lies. To scientists, the simultaneous simplicity and complexity of mirrors make them powerful tools for exploring questions about perception and cognition in humans and other neuronally gifted species, and how the brain interprets and acts upon the great tides of sensory information from the external world. They are using mirrors to study how the brain decides what is self and what is other, how it judges distances and trajectories of objects, and how it reconstructs the richly three-dimensional quality of the outside world from what is essentially a two-dimensional snapshot taken by the retina's flat sheet of receptor cells. They are applying mirrors in medicine, to create reflected images of patients' limbs or other body parts and thus trick the brain into healing itself. Mirror therapy has been successful in treating disorders like phantom limb syndrome, chronic pain and post-stroke paralysis.

6. Mirrors are made of:
   (1) highly polished metal
   (2) translucent glass
   (3) shining steel
   (4) pieces of wood

7. Which of the following qualities do mirrors possess?
   (1) a dreamy quality.
   (2) an ability to reflect back incident light.
   (3) the power to mask reality.
   (4) the capacity to add glory.

8. Scientists are aided by mirrors in which of the following ways:
   (1) Mirrors assist in investigating questions concerning discernment and cognition.
   (2) Mirrors increase perception and cognition in humans.
   (3) Mirrors are helpful in judging the neurological capacity of an individual.
   (4) Mirrors help in addressing neuron altering problems.

9. Mirror therapy has been successful in healing which of the following:
   (1) vanity   (2) limps
   (3) mild pain   (4) paralysis

10. How, according to the passage, does the brain alter images?
    (1) The brain reconstructs the images.
    (2) The brain retrieves obtuse images.
    (3) The trajectories of the brain are illusive.
    (4) The brain retains only the positive.

Passage – 3

In 1865 Friedrich August Kekulé woke up from a strange dream: he imagined a snake forming a circle and biting its own tail. Like many organic chemists of the time, Kekulé had been working feverishly to describe the true chemical structure of benzene, a problem that continually eluded understanding. But Kekulé's dream of a snake swallowing its tail, so the story goes, helped him to accurately realize that benzene's structure formed a ring. This insight paved the way for a new understanding of organic chemistry and earned Kekulé a title of nobility in Germany. Although most of us have not been ennobled, there is something undeniably familiar about Kekulé's problem-solving method. Whether deciding to go to a particular college, accept a challenging job offer or propose to a future spouse, "sleeping on it" seems to provide the clarity we need to piece together life's puzzles. But how does slumber present us with answers? The latest research suggests that while we are peacefully asleep our brain is busily processing the day's information. It combs through recently formed memories, stabilizing, copying and filing them, so that they will be more useful the next day. A night of sleep can make memories resistant to interference from other information and allow us to recall them for use more effectively the next morning. And sleep not only strengthens memories, it also lets the brain sift through newly formed memories, possibly even identifying what is worth keeping and selectively maintaining or enhancing these aspects of a memory. It can analyze collections of memories to discover relations among them or identify the gist of a memory while the unnecessary details fade—perhaps even helping us find the meaning in what we have learned.

11. The dream helped Kekulé comprehend which of the following?
    (1) That it's best to sleep over a problem.
    (2) That benzene's structure formed a ring.
    (3) That benzene's true chemical structure was like a snake.
    (4) That a snake had come to his assistance.

12. The realization of benzene's structure led to:
    (1) A mature approach to inorganic chemistry.
    (2) A marginal increase in one's belief in dreams.
    (3) A better understanding of organic chemistry.
    (4) Chemists working hard at realizing their goals.

13. According to the passage, the brain, does which of following while we are asleep?
    (1) The brain segregates memories.
    (2) The brain fulfils our wishes.
    (3) The brain handles the day's information.
    (4) The brain weakens bad memories.

14. In the passage, Kekulé's problem-solving technique, offers:
    (1) An ennobling experience
    (2) A familiar condition
    (3) A time tested supposition
    (4) A vague hypothesis

15. How does slumber provide us with the answers?
    (1) It can analyze collections of memories.
    (2) It helps us find meaning in what we have learned.
    (3) By making the redundant details grow fainter.
    (4) By helping us to drop our guard.

Narrative Style Passages

Directions for questions 1 to 10: Read the following passages and answer the questions that follow:

Passage – 1

When I got into Elizabeth town, I was covered with mud up to my knees and almost froze. I fell into several houses and asked them if they would be good enough to let me warm me, but none of them would be good enough. I almost sunk in despair and I thought I would freeze. I fell into a house where there was an old gentleman, and I asked him if he would be good enough to let me come and warm myself, he told me yes he would; my heart leaped for joy, because I was almost chilled through. Aaron says he had two daughters and they were very fine women, and one of them had lived in Missouri for four years, her husband died and she became a widow. It was a very cold windy night, and I asked him if he would be good enough to let me lay down in the kitchen all night by the fire. No you shant lay in the house, he said, but you may go and lay in the barn. And his daughter that had become a widow in Missouri, she kept house for her father, she gave Aaron a first rate of a supper, and a pair of dry trousers to put on, and a good pair of dry socks to put on, and two good blankets and a quilt, and she slipped them to me out of the kitchen window, she told me in the morning when I got up to fetch them down out of the hay loft and put them in the carriage. I did so, I came to the kitchen and she refreshed me with a first rate of a breakfast, and I had long talk with her, she told me after her husband died she went about twelve miles out of the city of St. Louis, and kept school for a planter that owned one hundred and six slaves. She told me that he cut up with his female slaves more than he did with his wife, she said sometimes his poor wife was almost crazy, and he tried to cut up the same capers with me, but he missed of it, and he pretended to be a member of the church too. She told me that when the sinful capers were found out by every one of the Free States, she thought then slavery would be abolished and not before. She told me she came home to her father's house as quickly as she could get away. What a blessed thing it is for any one when they meet with sorrow and afflictions, to have a father's home to go to.

1. The speaker's was in:
    (1) a state of desolation.
    (2) a hysterical state.
    (3) a content state.
    (4) a state of extreme hunger.

2. The person who provided refuge to the speaker was:
    (1) A planter   (2) A slave owner
    (3) A free man   (4) An old man

3. According to the passage, the planter owned :
    (1) Six hundred and one slaves.
    (2) One hundred slaves.
    (3) A hundred and six slaves.
    (4) Six slaves and more to go.

4. What, according to the daughter, was a possible solution to slavery?
    (1) The Free states coming forward.
    (2) The discovery of the wrongdoings by the Free states.
    (3) The slaves coming together in rebellion.
    (4) The planter's wife going to the Free states.

5. The passage ends on a note of:
    (1) remorse   (2) nostalgia
    (3) guilt   (4) pining

Passage – 2

Lately I have felt this disconnect from those closest to me, and often I feel, like I am all alone. There are numerous times I get in my car and I just want to drive and leave this life, in hopes that one day I will find the life that was destined for me. Where would I go? I am not sure, but I would hope that wherever I go, I would find true happiness. Why would I be looking for happiness and not looking for love? I am no longer searching for love (like most people in our world), for I have fully experienced true and unconditional love (if there is such a thing), and love is a luxury (like a new care) that eventually (no matter how hard you work to keep it new and fresh) wears out with time. Though most people will never admit it, seeking love gives one hope that if they don't have it, they will one day be blessed with love from another. And this love will bring happiness to their life or give their life purpose. However the true question is: "What good is true love without true-happiness?" I ask myself this question daily. Maybe it is this world we live in, it seems that nothing is good enough anymore. You must always strive to get more, and more, and more. More money, more cars, more clothes, more shoes, more degrees. The more you have the better you'll feel, right? Well I have a nice house in a great booming neighborhood, a nice car, a great IT career, a wonderful wife and two beautiful children, but the one thing that has eluded me in this life is true happiness. I'm sure there are those that can understand how I feel and those that may think I'm crazy, but I think the first step toward resolving any challenges we are faced with (in life) is to admit there is a problem, and do all that you can to find a solution.........what's my solution? I wish I knew.

6. The reason for the disconnect can be inferred to be:
   (1) A need for solitude.
   (2) A discontented life.
   (3) An ambition gone awry.
   (4) A person gone astray.

7. Why does the author shun love?
   (1) Because she/he has completely experienced true love.
   (2) Because love is a rarity.
   (3) Because love is an opulence.
   (4) Because love is fleeting.

8. The question that the speaker raises to himself:
   (1) That true love is the key to happiness.
   (2) That true love is incomplete without happiness.
   (3) That true love and unhappiness go hand in hand.
   (4) That without happiness man cannot survive.

9. All except which of the following has eluded the speaker?
   (1) A nice house.
   (2) Beautiful children.
   (3) A great career.
   (4) Proper bliss.

10. According to the passage the first step towards resolving any problem is:
   (1) Defining the steps.
   (2) Acknowledging the problem.
   (3) Confronting the hurdles.
   (4) Assessing the situation objectively.

PART - 4
VERBAL ABILITY / VOCABULARY

Vocabulary List **1**

ABANDON: To give up completely
S: Desert, Forsake, Leave
A: Retain, Accept

ABASE: To humiliate
S: Scorn, Belittle, Degrade
A: Exalt, Cherish

ABASH: Confuse
S: Disconcert, Bewilder
A: Hearten, Comfort

ABATE: To lessen
S: Decrease, Alleviate
A: Increase, Aggravate

ABBREVIATE: To shorten
S: Abridge, Condense
A: Expand, Prolong

ABERRATION: Deviation from what is normal
S: Irregularity, Peculiarity
A: Normalcy

ABET: To assist (normally a crime)
S: Conspire, Connive
A: Dissuade, Deter

ABEYANCE: A temporary suspension
S: Adjournment, Suspension
A: Revival, Continuation

ABHOR: Hate
S: Loathe, Detest
A: Enjoy, Relish

ABJECT: Miserable
S: Pitiful, Despicable
A: Noble, Lofty

ABRIDGEMENT: A short summary
S: Outline, Abbreviation, Summary, Abstract
A: Enlargement, Expansion

ABSOLVE: To free from guilt
S: Pardon, Exonerate
A: Accuse, Inculpate

ABSTINENCE: Keeping away from (all food, liquor, etc.)
S: Moderation, Temperance
A: Excess, Wantonness

ABYSMAL: Wretched, Extremely bad
S: Miserable
A: Heavenly

ABYSS: A bottomless pit, Anything too deep to measure, Depth of despair
S: Chasm
A: Summit, Elevation

ACCEDE: Agree to
S: Assent, Concur
A: Refuse, Dissent

ACCOMPLICE: A partner in crime
S: Ally
A: Enemy

ACQUAINT: To inform, To make familiar with
S: Inform, Apprise
A: Mislead, Beguile

ACQUIT: To clear (a person) of a charge
S: Pardon, Free, Absolve, Exonerate
A: Convict, Condemn, Sentence

ACRIMONY: Bitterness or harshness of speech or manner
S: Acerbity, Acridity, Virulence, Causticity
A: Gentleness, Tenderness

ACUMEN: Keenness of mind, Insight
S: Perspicacity, Sagacity
A: Stupidity, Dullness

ADAMANT: Unyielding, Inflexible
S: Stubborn
A: Pliable, Flexible

ADVENT: An arrival
S: Coming
A: Departure

ADVERSARY: Enemy
S: Opponent
A: Ally

ADMONISH: To warn, To reprove mildly
  S: Censure, Rebuke.
  A: Applaud, Praise, Compliment

ADROIT: Skilful and Clever
  S: Proficient, Dexterous
  A: Awkward, Dull, Maladroit

ADULATION: Servile, Flattery
  S: Praise
  A: Contempt, Indifference

ADVERSITY: Misfortune, Troubled state
  S: Distress, Ill luck
  A: Fortune

AEGIS: Shield
  S: Protection
  A: Exposure

AFFABLE: Pleasant, Friendly
  S: Polite, Courteous, Benign
  A: Impolite, Arrogant, Haughty , Disdainful

AFFIRM: To declare positively, To confirm
  S: Assert, Declare, Assure
  A: Deny

AFFRONT: Insult openly
  S: Provoke, Humiliate
  A: Placate, Please, Praise, Flatter

AGAPE: With the mouth open wide with surprise
  S: Astound
  A: Unfazed

AGGRANDIZE: To make greater, more powerful richer
  S: Exalt, Advance
  A: Degrade, Debase

AGILE: Quick and easy movement
  S: Nimble, Alert
  A: Slow, Lazy, Lethargic

AGNOSTIC: One who believes that it is impossible to know if God exists.
  S: Atheist
  A: Theist, Pious

ALACRITY: Eager willingness
  S: Speed, Liveliness
  A: Indolence, Sluggishness

ALIENATE: Cause to make unfriendly, To distance oneself
  S: Estrange
  A: Familiarize, Accost

ALLAY: To calm, To quieten
  S: Soothe, Pacify
  A: Agitate, Kindle

ALLEVIATE: To lessen or relieve
  S: Mitigate, Assuage
  A: Intensify, Heighten, Aggravate

ALLUDE: To refer to indirectly

ALLURE: To tempt with something desirable
  S: Lure, Entice, Inveigle
  A: Repel, Deter, Discourage

ALTERCATION: An angry or heated argument
  S: Controversy, Quarrel, Fracas
  A: Harmony, Peace, Concurrence

ALTRUISM: Unselfish concern for the welfare of others
  S: Unselfishness
  A: Egocentricity, Selfishness

AMBIDEXTROUS: Using both hands with equal ease

AMBIVALENCE: Simultaneous, conflicting feeling
  S: Vacillation, Dilemma
  A: Unequivocal

AMIABLE: Good-natured
  S: Gentle, Pleasing, Charming
  A: Sullen, Churlish, Quarrelsome

AMNESIA: Partial or total loss of memory

AMNESTY: A general pardon (especially for political offences)
  A: Punishment

ANACHRONISM: Anything out of its proper historical time
  S: Old-fashioned, Synchronized
  A: Modernity

ANARCHY: Absence of government, Political disorder
  S: Entropy
  A: Order, Discipline

Verbal Ability / Vocabulary

ANATHEMA: Anything greatly detested
  S: Curse
  A: Adoration

ANNUITY: An investment earning fixed payments (usually per year)

ANNUL: To do away with
  S: Subscribe
  A: Enforce

ANODYNE: A pain-reliever

ANOMALY: Departure from the usual
  S: Abnormality
  A: Normality

ANTAGONISM: Opposition or hostility
  S: Antipathy, Enmity
  A: Harmony, Accord, Agreement

ANTIPATHY: Strong dislike
  S: Hatred, Repugnance, Abhorrence
  A: Honour, Admiration, Love, Esteem, Empathy

APATHY: Lack of emotion
  S: Indifference, Passiveness
  A: Care, Sympathy

APLOMB: Self-confidence
  S: Poise
  A: Diffident

APOGEE: A point farthest from a heavenly body, the earth

APPRAISE: To assess the value, To evaluate
  S: Judge, Gauge

APPRISE: To inform
  S: Notify

ARBOREAL: Of or living on trees

ARCANE: Secret
  S: Mysterious

ARCHAIC: Ancient, Old-fashioned
  A: Modern

ARTICULATE: To express oneself clearly in words
  A: Mince

ASININE: Stupid, foolish, Asslike
  S: Silly
  A: Learned, Knowledgeable

ASPERSION: Damaging or disparaging remark
  S: Slander
  A: Praise, Eulogy

ASSIDUOUS: Diligent
  S: Persevering
  A: Careless, Lazy, Indolent

ASSUAGE: To calm, To make less severe
  S: Soothe
  A: Aggravate

ASTUTE: Shrewd, Crafty
  S: Cunning, Artful
  A: Obtuse, Shallow, Short-sighted

ASUNDER: Into pieces
  S: Apart
  A: United, Harmonious

ATYPICAL: Not typical
  S: Abnormal
  A: Typical, Normal

AUDACIOUS: Bold, Daring
  S: Impudent, Vain, Brazen
  A: Meek, Mild, Gentle, Humble

AUGMENT: To make large in number or size
  S: Increase
  A: Decrease, Lessen

AVARICE: Greed for money
  S: Rapacious
  A: Generosity

AVER: To declare to be true
  S: Assert
  A: Hesitate

AXIOM: A statement universally accepted as true, Maxim

AZURE: Sky-blue

B

BANTER: Playful teasing

BASHFUL: Easily embarrassed
S: Shy, Diffident
A: Bold, Adventurous, Arrogant

BASTION: Any strong defence

BAWDY: Indecent
S: Obscene
A: Decent

BEACON: A light used for warning or guiding

BEATITUDE: Perfect blessedness or happiness
S: Divine
A: Curse, Condemnation

BEDIZEN: Adorn with showy splendour. Deck out gaudily
S: Decorate
A: Sober

BEDLAM: Any place or situation or noise and confusion
S: Chaos
A: Order

BEGUILE: To mislead or deprive of
A: Escort

BELLICOSE: Quarrelsome, Warlike
S: Aggressive
A: Peaceful

BENEDICTION: Blessing, Invocation of a blessing
A: Curse, Malediction

BENEVOLENCE: Kindness
S: Benign, Generosity, Munificence
A: Malignity, Animosity, Churlishness

BENIGN: Good nature, Kindly
S: Kind, Favourable, Beneficial
A: Malignant

BEQUEATH: To leave to another by one's will

BERATE: To scold severely
A: Praise, Eulogize

BEREAVE: To leave in a sad or lonely state, as by death

BERSERK: In or into a violent rage or frenzy
S: Wild, Frenzied
A: Calm, Tranquil

BESIEGE: To overwhelm

BESOTTED: Made silly or stupid by love
S: Infatuated
A: Level-headed

BESTIAL: Like a beast
S: Brutish, Savage, Barbaric
A: Civilized, Cultured, Learned

BETROTHED: Engaged, Pledged to marry

BIGOT: One who holds blindly and intolerantly to a particular opinion
S: Intolerant, Prejudiced, Opinionated
A: Broad-minded

BLASPHEMY: Profane abuse of God or sacred things

BLATANT: Boldly conspicuous or obtrusive
A: Obscure, Subtle, Hidden

BLEARY: Dim
S: Blurred
A: Bright

BLEMISH: To mar or spoil, A defect
S: Flaw, Imperfection
A: Embellishment

BLUDGEON: (N) A short club with a heavy head
(V) To bully or coerce

BLUSTER: To speak in a noisy or a swaggering manner

BOLSTER: Support
A: Deny, Desert

BOUNTEOUS: Generous, Abundant
S: Benevolent, Liberal
A: Miserly

BOVINE: Of an ox or cow, Slow and stupid
S: Dull
A: Sharp, Intelligent

BRAGGART: An offensively boastful person

BRAVADO: Pretended courage or feigned confidence

BRAZEN: Shameless, Bold
- **S:** Daring
- **A:** Submissive, Humble

BREACH: A violation, Gap
- **S:** Rift
- **A:** Bridge

BROACH: To start a discussion of
- **A:** Hesitate

BRUSQUE: Rough and abrupt in manner of speech
- **S:** Curt, Blunt
- **A:** Rambling

BUCOLIC: Rural
- **S:** Rustic
- **A:** Urban

BUOYANT: Having the ability or tendency to float
- **S:** High-spirited
- **A:** Depressed

BUTTRESS: A structure that supports, Support
- **S:** Bolster, Prop-up

CACOPHONY: Harsh, Jarring sound
- **S:** Discord
- **A:** Harmony, Concord, Rhythm

CADENCE: Measured movements especially of sound, rhythm, beat
- **S:** Rhythm
- **A:** Cacophony, Discord

CALLIGRAPHY: Art of producing beautiful handwriting

CALLOUS: Hardened, Unyielding
- **S:** Obdurate, Insensible, Indifferent
- **A:** Compassionate, Sympathetic

CALLOW: Immature, Inexperienced
- **S:** Raw, Unfledged, Inexperienced
- **A:** Mature, Wise, Sagacious

CAMOUFLAGE: A disguise in order to conceal
- **S:** Hide
- **A:** Expose

CANDID: Honest, Frank
- **S:** Truthful, Sincere, Ingenuous
- **A:** Sly, Shrewd, Tricky, Hypocritical

CANARD: A false especially malicious report

CANON: A basic law or principle by which something is judged

CAPACIOUS: Roomy
- **S:** Spacious
- **A:** Narrow, Limited, Confined

CAPITULATE: Surrender
- **A:** Resist

CAPRICIOUS: Subject to caprices (eccentricities), Erratic
- **S:** Fanciful, Odd, Whimsical
- **A:** Staid, Steadfast

CARDINAL: Principal, Chief, Most important
- **S:** Fundamental, Vital
- **A:** Insignificant, Negligible, Minor

CARTEL: An association (business firms, etc.) establishing a national or international monopoly

CASTIGATE: To rebuke severely especially by public criticism
- **S:** Scold
- **A:** Condone, Forgive, Pardon

CATACLYSM: Anything sudden, Violent, Change
- **S:** Catastrophe, Upheaval, Calamity
- **A:** Blessing

CATARACT: A large waterfall, An eye disease

CATASTROPHE: Any sudden great disaster
- **S:** Calamity, Cataclysm
- **A:** Blessing

CAVEAT: Warning
- **S:** Proviso

CAVIL: To object unnecessarily, Find fault
- **A:** Approve

CELERITY: Swiftness, Speed
    S: Alacrity, Haste
    A: Lethargy, Indolence

CELESTIAL: Of the heavens and sky
    S: Heavenly, Divine
    A: Mortal, Earthy, Terrestrial

CELIBACY: The state of being unmarried
    A: Matrimony

CENSURE: Strong disapproval, To condemn as wrong
    S: Condemnation, Criticism, Blame
    A: Praise, Approval, Laudation

CERTITUDE: Sureness
    S: Certainty, Inevitability
    A: Uncertain, Unsure

CHAGRIN: Embarrassment due to disappointment
    S: Failure, Annoyance, Shame
    A: Delight, Glorification

CHARISMATIC: Possessing spiritual grace
    S: Inspiring
    A: Awkward

CHARLATAN: A person who claims to have more skill, knowledge than he really has
    S: Quack, Fraud, Impostor
    A: Genuine

CHAUVINISM: Militant and fanatical patriotism
    A: Cosmopolitan

CHEQUERED: Marked by vicissitudes

CHOLERIC: Easily angered
    S: Irascible, Angry, Fiery
    A: Phlegmatic, Calm, Placed

CIRCUITOUS: Roundabout
    S: Indirect
    A: Straightforward

CIRCUMSPECT: Cautious
    S: Careful, Vigilant, Prudent
    A: Audacious, Careless

CLAIRVOYANCE: Keen ability to perceive things
    S: Exceptional insight, Perception

CLANDESTINE: Secret or hidden
    S: Furtive, Covert, Private
    A: Open, Forthright, Clear

CLAUSTROPHOBIA: Fear of being in an enclosed place

CLEMENT: Lenient
    S: Merciful
    A: Vindictive

CLOISTERED: Secluded
    S: Confined
    A: Freed

COERCE: To compel
    S: Force

COGENT: Convincing
    A: Doubtful

COGITATE: To think deeply about
    S: Ponder

COHERENT: Sticking together, Logically connected
    S: Unity
    A: Separation

COLLATERAL: Parallel or corresponding; Security towards a loan
    S: Secondary, Parallel, Concurrent

COMELY: Pleasing, Attractive
    S: Graceful, Agreeable, Nice
    A: Ugly

COMESTIBLE: Food
    S: Edible
    A: Unedible

COMITY: Courtesy
    S: Friendly
    A: Hostility

COMMISERATE: To feel or show pity for
    S: Condole, Sympathise
    A: Ignore

COMPATIBLE: Getting along or going well together
    S: Friendly
    A: Opposite, Intolerant

COMPLACENCY: Self-satisfaction
    S: Smugness
    A: Discontent

CONCEDE: To admit as true, Accept
  S: Surrender, Admit, Own up
  A: Deny, Refuse, Disagree

CONCISE: Brief and to the point
  S: Compact, Short, Terse
  A: Diffuse, Repetitive, Wordy

CONDIGN: Deserved, said especially of punishment
  S: Adequate, Justifiable, Just, Fit
  A: Undeserved, Inadequate, Inappropriate

CONDONE: To forgive or overlook an offence
  S: Overlook
  A: Punish

CONGENIAL: Kindred, Compatible
  S: Friendly
  A: Unapproachable

CONJECTURE: Inferring or predicting from incom-plete evidence
  S: Guesswork
  A: Affirmation

CONJUGAL: Of marriage or relation between a husband and a wife
  S: Marital

CONJURE: To summon as if by magic

CONNIVE: To pretend not to look (at crime, etc.)
  S: Assist

CONNOISSEUR: One who is an expert in food, wine, art, etc.
  S: Mastery
  A: Boor

CONNUBIAL: Of marriage, Conjugal
  S: Matrimonial

CONSCIENTIOUS: Governed by one's conscience
  S: Scrupulous, Painstaking
  A: Remiss

CONSECRATE: To bring something into religious use by a special ceremony. Devote to a religious purpose

CONSTERNATION: Dismay, Panic
  S: Alarm
  A: Tranquillity, Repose

CONSTRUE: To interpret, To analyse
  S: Translate, Explain

CONSUMMATE: Complete
  S: Perfect
  A: Incomplete, Imperfect, Faulty

CONTEMPTUOUS: Full of contempt
  S: Scornful
  A: Kind

CONTINGENT: A group of people sharing particular characteristics; Dependent; Troops supplied to form part of a larger force.

CONTRITE: Showing regret
  S: Repentant
  A: Callous

CONTROVERT: To argue against, Dispute
  S: Debate
  A: Agree

CONVIVIAL: Cheerful and friendly, Pleasant situation
  S: Sociable, Jovial
  A: Dismal, Staid, Solemn

CONVOKE: To call together
  S: Convene, Assemble, Gather
  A: Dismiss, Prorogue, Dissolve

CORPULENCE: Fatness, Obesity
  S: Fleshy, Stout, Bloated
  A: Thin, Lean, Emaciated

COVERT: Hidden, Secretive
  S: Clandestine, Concealed
  A: Open, Frank, Candid

COVET: To want ardently
  S: Desire
  A: Disown

CRASS: Unrefined
  S: Crude
  A: Elegant

CREDULOUS: Tending to believe too readily
  S: Gullible, Easily deceivable
  A: Wily

CRESCENDO: Gradual increase in intensity
   A: Diminish

CULPABLE: Blameworthy
   A: Praiseworthy

CUMBERSOME: Hard to handle
   A: Facile

CUPIDITY: Strong desire for wealth
   S: Avarice
   A: Lavishness

CYNOSURE: A centre of attention or interest

CONGENITAL: Existing at birth
   A: Acquired

D

DABBLE: To play in water as with hands, Do something superficially
   A: Stalwart

DAFT: Silly, Inane
   S: Idiotic, Foolish
   A: Profound, Wise, Intelligent

DAINTY: Delicately pretty
   S: Nice, Delicate, Sweet
   A: Sour, Bitter, Revolting

DAPPER: Small and active
   S: Trim, Neat
   A: Awkward, Untidy

DASTARDLY: Mean
   S: Cowardly
   A: Heroic

DEBACLE: Crushing defeat
   A: Success

DEBILITATE: To make weak
   S: Enervate
   A: Strengthen, Invigorate

DEBONAIR: Dashing
   S: Courteous
   A: Repulsive

DECADENCE: A process, condition or period or decline, as in morals, art, etc.
   S: Decay
   A: Growth

DECORUM: Appropriate social behaviour
   A: Uncultured

DECREPIT: Broken down or worn out by old age or long use
   S: Weak, Aged
   A: Robust, Agile

DEFER: To postpone, To yield due to respect
   S: Delay, Adjourn
   A: Expedite, Hasten, Quicken

DEFERENTIAL: Very respectful
   S: Obedient, Reverential
   A: Impudent, Defiant

DEFILE: To pollute
   A: Corrupt

DEFRAY: To pay
   S: Settle, Adjust
   A: Decamp, Repudiate, Disown

DEFT: Skilful
   S: Adept, Dexterous, Agile
   A: Awkward, Clumsy, Inept

DEFUNCT: No longer existing
   S: Extinct, Dead
   A: Alive, Fashionable

DEIFY: To look upon as a God
   A: Loathe

DELINQUENT: Said of young people showing a tendency to commit crimes

DELUGE: Great flood

DELUSION: A false belief, the act of deluding
   S: Hallucination, Illusion, Error
   A: Certainty, Reality, Fact

DEMEAN: To degrade
   S: Humble
   A: Honour, Revere

DEMEANOUR: Outward behaviour

DEMUR: To hesitate because of doubt
- **S:** Object, Hesitate
- **A:** Agree, Accept, Consent

DEMURE: Decorous, Modest
- **S:** Coy, Shy
- **A:** Brazen, Impudent, Shameless

DENIGRATE: To blacken or belittle the character of
- **S:** Defame, Slander
- **A:** Glorify, Praise

DENIZEN: An inhabitant or frequenter of a particular place
- **S:** Citizen
- **A:** Alien, Foreigner

DENOUNCE: Condemn publicly
- **A:** Laud

DEPLETE: To use up (resources)
- **S:** Drain, Empty, Exhaust
- **A:** Fill, Strengthen, Enlarge

DEPRECATE: To express disapproval
- **S:** Disapprove, Protest
- **A:** Approve, Endorse, Command

DEPRECIATE: To lesson in value
- **S:** Undervalue, Lower, Decry
- **A:** Boost, Raise, Praise

DERIDE: To ridicule
- **S:** Taunt, Mock, Scorn
- **A:** Encourage, Cheer, Incite

DEROGATORY: Disparaging
- **S:** Insulting, Belittling
- **A:** Glorifying, Eulogizing

DESPICABLE: Deserving scorn
- **S:** Low, Mean, Cowardly
- **A:** High, Noble, Exalted

DESPONDENCY: Dejection
- **S:** Melancholy, Depression
- **A:** Buoyancy, Elation

DESPOT: An absolute ruler
- **S:** Tyrant
- **A:** Democrat

DETENTION: Detaining
- **A:** Free

DETRIMENT: Damage
- **S:** Harm, Hurt, Injury
- **A:** Advantage, Gain, Interest

DEVIOUS: Not direct, Roundabout, Not honest
- **S:** Cunning, Underhand
- **A:** Straight forward, Honest

DEXTERITY: Skill in using one's hands, body or mind
- **S:** Ability, Expertise, Tact
- **A:** Clumsiness, Awkwardness, Blunder

DIATRIBE: A bitter, criticism, in speech/writing
- **S:** Abuse
- **A:** Praise

DILAPIDATED: Falling to pieces
- **S:** Decaying
- **A:** Sturdy

DILIGENT: Hardworking
- **S:** Perseverance, Earnest
- **A:** Lazy, Careless, Lethargic

DISCERN: To perceive or recognize clearly
- **S:** Perceive
- **A:** Overlook, Neglect

DISCONCERT: To upset
- **S:** Embarrass, Confuse
- **A:** Assure, Encourage

DISCONSOLATE: Inconsolable
- **S:** Object, Hesitate
- **A:** Agree, Accept, Consent

DISCORD: Disagreement, Lack of harmony between musical notes
- **S:** Quarrel
- **A:** Agree

DISCRETION: The freedom to make decisions
- **S:** Prudence, Foresight
- **A:** Rashness, Impudence

DISENCHANTED: Disillusioned
- **A:** Hopeful

DISINGENUOUS: Not sincere
- **A:** Candid, Frank, Honest

DISSEMINATE: To scatter, To spread ideas
A: Collect

DISSENT: To disagree
A: Agree

DISSIPATE: To disperse, To waste foolishly
S: Waste
A: Frugal

DISSEMBLE: To hide one's feelings
A: Frank

DISTRAUGHT: Distracted
S: Upset
A: Happy

DIVULGE: Reveal
A: Hide

DOCILE: Easy to discipline
S: Meek, Mild, Gentle
A: Stubborn, Resolute, Wilful

DODDER: To shake or tremble as from old age

DOGMATIC: Insisting that one's beliefs must be accepted

DOLDRUMS: Low spirits
S: Depressed
A: High-spirited

DOLEFUL: Sad
S: Mournful
A: Happy

DOLOROUS: Sorrowful, Sad
S: Grief, Sorrow
A: Happiness, Joy

DOMINEER: To rule in a harsh or arrogant way
S: Haughty, Arrogant, Despotic
A: Humble, Gentle, Mild

DORMANT: Inactive
S: Latent
A: Alive, Vibrant

DOWDY: Not neat or smart in dress
S: Shabby
A: Tidy, Fashionable

DRACONIAN: Cruel
S: Severe
A: Mild

DUBIOUS: Doubtful
A: Certain

EARTHY: Unrefined behaviour
S: Coarse
A: Cultured, Refined

EBULLIENT: Enthusiastic, Vivacious
S: Exuberant, Over-demonstrative
A: Sober, Staid, Dejected

EFFERVESCE: To be lively
S: Buoyant, Gleeful
A: Staid, Sober, Sedate

EFFICACIOUS: That produces the desired effect
S: Effective
A: Futile

EGRESS: Exit
A: Entrance

ELAN: Spirited self-assurance
S: Vivacity, Enthusiasm, Exuberance
A: Sobriety, Depression

ELEGIAC: Sad
S: Mournful
A: Happy

ELUCIDATE: To make something clear
S: Explain, Illustrate, Clarify
A: Obscure, Confuse, Disorder

EMACIATE: To cause to become abnormally lean
S: Weak
A: Strengthen

EMANCIPATE: To set free(a slave etc.)
S: Liberate, Release
A: Suppress, Hold, Restrain

EMANATE: To come forth, issue, as from a source
S: Emerge, Originate
A: Stop

Verbal Ability / Vocabulary

EMBARGO: Any legal restriction of commerce

EMBARK: Begin a journey or endeavour

EMBELLISH: To decorate
    S: Adorn, Deck
    A: Spoil, Injure, Tarnish

EMBEZZLE: To steal (money, etc. entrusted to one)
    S: Purloin, Misuse

EMPATHY: Intellectual or emotional identification with another
    S: Understanding, Compassion, Sensitivity
    A: Apathy

EMPIRICAL: Based on experiment or experience
    S: Practical
    A: Hypothetical

EMULATE: To try to equal or surpass
    S: Copy

ENERVATE: To deprive of strength, force, vigour, etc.
    S: Weaken, Enfeeble, Devitalize
    A: Strengthen, Energize, Enliven

ENIGMA: A riddle
    S: Puzzle, Mystery
    A: Clear, Plain, Specific

ENDEMIC: Prevalent in or restricted to a particular locality
    S: Confined
    A: Pandemic

ENNUI: A feeling of boredom or weariness
    S: Boredom, Languor, Tedium
    A: Enthusiasm, Ebullience, Vigour

ENORMITY: Of great size, number, etc., Huge, A serious crime
    S: Vast, Immense
    A: Smallness, Insignificance

EPHEMERAL: Short-lived
    S: Fleeting, Momentary
    A: Lasting

EPICURE: One who enjoys and has a discriminating taste for fine food and drink
    S: Fastidious, Luxurious, Connoisseur
    A: Ascetic, Puritanical

EQUABLE: Steady, Reasonable
    S: Calm, Serene, Unruffled
    A: Mercuriality, Caprice

EQUITABLE: Fair
    S: Impartial, Fair, Just
    A: Prejudiced, Partial, Biased

EQUIVOCAL: Uncertain, Doubtful
    S: Ambiguous, Indistinct, Dubious
    A: Clear, Plain, Lucid

EQUIVOCATE: To use equivocal terms in order to deceive or mislead
    A: Frankness, Openness, Honesty

ERADICATE: Remove totally
    S: Extirpate, Nullify, Abolish
    A: Implant, Establish, Strengthen

ERRONEOUS: Containing an error
    S: False, Inaccurate, Erring
    A: Accurate, Genuine, Factual

ERUDITE: Learned
    S: Scholarly, Cultured
    A: Unlettered, Illiterate, Uneducated

ESCAPADE: Reckless adventure

ESOTERIC: Understood by only a chosen few
    A: Exoteric, Commonplace

ESPOUSAL: Giving support to a movement or theory
    A: Withdraw

ESTRANGE: To turn from an affectionate attitude to an indifferent or unfriendly one
    S: Alienate, Withdraw, Disagree
    A: Unite, Conjoin, Harmonise

ETHEREAL: Spiritual
    A: Physical

ETIQUETTE: The forms, manners, etc. conventionally acceptable or required in society, profession, etc.

EULOGISE: To praise highly
    A: Criticise

EUPHEMISM: The use of a less direct word or phrase to an unpleasant one
    A: Direct

EUPHORIA: A feeling of well-being
- **S:** Elation
- **A:** Depression

EVANESCENT: Tending to fade from sight
- **S:** Transient, Fleeting, Ephemeral
- **A:** Immortal, Eternal

EXACERBATE: To aggravate (pain, annoyance, etc.)
- **S:** Irritate
- **A:** Placate, Soothe

EXACTING: Making severe demands
- **S:** Strict
- **A:** Lax

EXALT: To praise, To raise in rank
- **S:** Glorify
- **A:** Degrade, Condemn, Despise

EXASPERATE: To irritate
- **S:** Exacerbate, Provoke
- **A:** Mollify, Placate, Conciliate

EXCERPT: A passage or extract from a book, film or piece of music

EXCISION: Pruning
- **A:** Branch

EXCRUCIATING: Intensely painful
- **S:** Agonising, Intense, Severe
- **A:** Soothing

EXCURSIVE: Digressive
- **S:** Rambling, Diverse
- **A:** Similar, Uniform

EXEMPLARY: Serving as a model or example
- **S:** Model, Pattern
- **A:** Mundane

EXIGENCY: A situation calling for immediate attention
- **S:** Emergency, Distress, Crisis
- **A:** Normalcy, Regularity, Commonplace

EXORBITANT: Going beyond what is reasonable just
- **S:** Huge, Enormous, Excessive (grossly)
- **A:** Meagre, Paltry

EXORCISE: To expel (an evil spirit) by incantations
- **A:** Bedevil

EXPEDIENCY: Suitability for a given purpose
- **A:** Tardiness

EXPEND: To spend, To use up
- **S:** Spend
- **A:** Earn, Save

EXPLETIVE: A rude word expressing anger

EXPURGATE: To remove passages considered obscene

EXTEMPORE: Offhand, with little preparation
- **S:** Impromptu, Offhand, Unprepared
- **A:** Prepared, Rehearsed, Formed

EXTORT: To get (money) from someone by force or threats

EXTRANEOUS: Coming from outside, Unrelated
- **S:** Irrelevant
- **A:** Germane

EXTROVERT: An outgoing person
- **A:** Introvert

EXUBERANT: Full of enthusiasm

EXUDE: To pass out in pores, to ooze

FABRICATE: To construct, To make up (a story or lie)
- **S:** Construct, Frame, Compose
- **A:** Wreck, Shatter, Demolish

FARCE: Absurd, Ridiculous
- **S:** Comic, Funny
- **A:** Grave

FASTIDIOUS: Not easy to please
- **S:** Fussy, Squeamish
- **A:** Uncritical

FATUOUS: Stupid
- **S:** Foolish, Idiotic, Imbecile, Inane
- **A:** Sagacious, Perceptive, Intelligent

FAWN: A young deer;
To act slavishly submissive.

Verbal Ability / Vocabulary

FELICITATE: To congratulate
S: Compliment
A: Disparage

FELICITY: Happiness, Bliss
S: Rapture, Ecstasy, Joy
A: Misery, Sadness, Grief

FELONY: A major crime such as murder, etc.

FERRET: A small animal of the weasel family;
To search and drive out.

FETISH: Any object or thing to which one is rationally devoted;
An object with magical power.

FETTER: To put in chains
S: Confine

FIASCO: Total disaster
A: Success

FICKLE: Unstable
S: Uncertain, Wavering, Capricious
A: Stable, Constant, Settled

FICTITIOUS: False, Not genuine
S: False, Fabricated, Spurious
A: Genuine, Factual, Exact

FIEND: Evil, Inhuman
S: Devil
A: Angel, Benevolent, Kind

FINICKY: Fussy
S: Fastidious
A: Indifferent

FLAGELLATE: To whip

FLAGRANT: Outrageous, Scandalous
S: Glaring, Atrocious, Heinous

FLAIR: A natural talent
A: Gaucherie

FLORID: Elaborately ornate, Ruddy
S: Showy
A: Plain

FLOUNDER: To move or struggle in a helpless manner (especially in water), Unable to react because or confusion

FLOURISH: To grow vigorously, To thrive
S: Prosper
A: Decay, Diminish

FLUMMOX: Bewilder, Confuse
S: Disconcert, Confound
A: Clarify, Enlighten

FOMENT: To stir up (trouble)
S: Excite, Fan
A: Allay, Extinguish

FORERUNNER: A sign that tells or warns of something to follow
S: Herald, Harbinger, Predecessor
A: Successor, Offspring

FORFEIT: A fine or penalty for some crime, fault or neglect

FORGERY: The act or crime of forging (falsely duplicating) documents
S: Counterfeit, Copy

FORTHRIGHT: Direct and frank
S: Outspoken, Straightforward
A: Obscure, Veiled

FORTITUDE: Courage
S: Heroism, Spirit
A: Cowardice, Shyness

FRACTIOUS: Irritable, Stubborn
S: Peevish, Snappish, Quick-tempered
A: Meek, Gentle, Submissive

FRAUDULENT: Based on or using fraud
S: Cheating, Deceitful
A: Honest

FRENETIC: Frenzied, Wild
S: Frantic
A: Calm, Composed

FRITTER: To waste (money, time, etc.)
S: Idle
A: Save

FRIVOLOUS: Of little value, Trivial, Silly.
- **S:** Petty, Worthless, Futile
- **A:** Serious, Important, Significant

FRUGAL: Economical
- **S:** Careful, Thrifty, Saving
- **A:** Wasteful, Lavish, Liberal

FULSOME: Disgusting, especially because excessive
- **S:** Gross, Excessive, Disgusting
- **A:** Pleasing, Moderate, Acceptable

FUTILE: Useless
- **S:** Trifling, Trivial, Vain
- **A:** Effective, Satisfactory, Fruitful

GAFFE: A blunder

GAMUT: The entire range or extent
- **S:** Range, Scope, Purview

GARBLE: To distort or confuse so as to mislead
- **S:** Distort, Confuse
- **A:** Clear

GARISH: Gaudy
- **S:** Ostentatious
- **A:** Sober, Modest, Sombre

GARNER: To gather up
- **S:** Store
- **A:** Deplete, Reduce, Dissipate

GARNISH: To decorate
- **S:** Embellish, Adorn, Beautify
- **A:** Spoil, Disfigure, Impair

GARRULOUS: Talking much especially about unimportant things
- **S:** Talkative, Verbose, Loquacious
- **A:** Silent, Reserved, Modest

GAUCHE: Lacking social grace
- **S:** Incept, Awkward, Clumsy
- **A:** Adroit, Skilful, Dextrous

GENEALOGY: Recorded history of one's ancestry

GENESIS: Origin

GENTEEL: Polite or well-bred
- **S:** Polished, Refined, Cultured
- **A:** Rough, Coarse, Ill-bred

GERMANE: Relevant
- **S:** Pertinent
- **A:** Irrelevant

GESTICULATE: To make lively gestures
- **S:** Signal, Pantomime

GLEAN: To collect (facts, etc.) gradually

GLIB: Speaking smoothly
- **A:** Halting

GORGE: A deep valley with steep sides; To eat greedily

GOURMAND: One who likes good food and drink, often in excess

GRANDILOQUENT: Using pompous, bombastic words

GRANDIOSE: Impressive
- **S:** Showy

GREGARIOUS: Fond of the company of others
- **S:** Sociable, Convivial, Companionable
- **A:** Solitary, Unsociable, Unfriendly

GRISLY: Terrifying
- **S:** Horrible, Terrible, Ghastly

GROTESQUE: Distorted in appearance, shape, etc.
- **S:** Bizarre
- **A:** Normal, Usual, Customary

GROVEL: To lie or crawl (lower oneself) to please another
- **S:** Cringe, Fawn, Beseech
- **A:** Command, Lead, Master

GRUELLING: Exhausting
- **S:** Easy

GRUMPY: Peevish
- **S:** Morose, Irritable, Surly
- **A:** Amicable, Gentle

GULLIBLE: Easily duped
- **S:** Credulous
- **A:** Shrewd

GUMPTION: Initiative and courage
   S: Common sense, Sagacity, Acumen
   A: Apathy, Indifference

GUSTO: Zest, Enjoyment
   S: Relish, Pleasure, Enthusiasm
   A: Apathy

GYRATE: To move in a circular or spiral path
   S: Spin, Whirl, Rotate

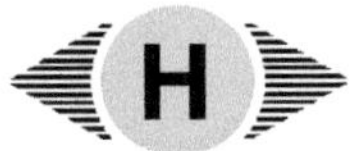

HAGGARD: Having a wild, wasted, worn look
   S: Gaunt, Tired, Weary
   A: Strong, Robust, Exuberant

HALCYON: Tranquil, Happy, Idyllic
   S: Golden, Peaceful
   A: Stormy, Turbulent, Rough

HALLUCINATION: The apparent perception of sights, sounds, etc. that are not actually present
   S: Delusion, Illusion, Mirage

HAPLESS: Unfortunate
   S: Luckless, Unlucky
   A: Fortunate, Successful, Happy

HARBINGER: A forerunner
   S: Herald, Precursor

HARMONIOUS: Having parts arranged in an orderly or pleasing way
   S: Agreeable, Concordant, Congruous
   A: Dissonant, Opposed, Incompatible

HARRIDAN: A disreputable shrewish old woman

HARROWING: Upsetting
   S: Distressing
   A: Pleasant

HEADY: Intoxicating
   S: Giddy
   A: Bland

HEARSAY: Rumour
   S: Gossip
   A: Truth, Fact

HECKLE: To harass (a speaker) with questions or taunts
   A: Enraptured

HEDONISM: The doctrine that pleasure is the principal good
   S: Epicureanism, Sensualism, Debauchery
   A: Slavery, Servility

HEINOUS: Outrageously evil
   S: Atrocious, Flagrant, Terrible
   A: Virtuous, Moral, Meritorious

HERCULEAN: Calling for great strength, size and courage
   S: Rugged, Enduring, Steadfast

HEREDITARY: Of or passed down by inheritance from an ancestor
   S: Inherited, Congenital, Innate

HEYDAY: The time of greater vigour, prosperity, etc.

HIATUS: A gap or break as where a part is missing
   A: Bridge

HIBERNATE: To spend the winter in a dormant state (of animals, especially frog);To be inactive.

HIEROGLYPHIC: A picture or symbol representing a word, sound, etc.

HINDER: To keep back, Stop
   S: Impede, Obstruct, Prevent
   A: Help, Assist, Further

HISTRIONIC: Of acting
   S: Theatrical

HOI POLLOI: The common people
   S: Masses, Crowd, Riff-raff
   A: Elite, Haut monde

HOLOCAUST: Great destruction of life, especially by fire
   S: Conflagration, Devastation, Ruin

HOMICIDE: The killing of one person by another

HOMONYM: A word with the same pronunciation and spelling as another but a different meaning, origin

HOODWINK: Deceive
   S: Fraud
   A: Sincere

HORRENDOUS: Horrible
  S: Frightful, Horrifying, Fearful
  A: Appealing, Pleasant, Charming

HOSTILE: Unfriendly
  S: Belligerent, Antagonistic
  A: Friendly, Devoted, Loyal

HOVEL: Small, miserable dwelling or hut

HUBRIS: Arrogance caused by pride
  A: Simple

HUMANE: Kind, Tender
  S: Benevolent, Compassionate
  A: Barbaric

HUMANISM: Any system of thought based on the interests and ideals of man

HUMDRUM: Dull
  S: Monotonous
  A: Interesting

HUMANITARIAN: A person/activity devoted to promoting the welfare of humanity

HYPERBOLE: Exaggeration for effect, not meant to be taken literally
  A: Depreciating

HYPERCRITICAL: Too critical
  S: Carping, Captious
  A: Apathetic, Indifferent

IDIOSYNCRASY: Any personal peculiarity, mannerism, etc.

IGNORAMUS: An ignorant person
  S: Dunce, Dolt, Dope
  A: Genius, Prodigy, Scholar

ILLEGIBLE: Hard or impossible to read because badly written or printed
  S: Unreadable, Indecipherable
  A: Clear

ILLUSION: An unreal or misleading appearance or image
  S: Fantasy, Image
  A: Reality, Fact

IMMACULATE: Perfectly clean
  S: Unstained, Spotless, Clean
  A: Unclean, Tarnished, Dirty

IMMUNE: Exempt from or protected against something or harmful
  S: Exculpate, Reprieve
  A: Condemn, Convict, Blame

IMPALE: To pierce with a sharp stake through the body

IMPASSE: A situation offering no escape, Dead-end
  S: Deadlock, Stalemate
  A: Progress

IMPECCABLE: Flawless
  S: Immaculate, Faultless, Perfect
  A: Defective, Flawed

IMPECUNIOUS: Having no money
  S: Poor, Bankrupt
  A: Opulent, Rich, Wealthy

IMPEDIMENT: Anything that hinders
  S: Obstacle, Barrier, Obstruction
  A: Aid, Assistance, Help

IMPERIL: To put in danger
  S: Endanger, Hazard, Jeopardize
  A: Safeguard, Protect, Preserve

IMPERIOUS: Arrogant, Domineering
  S: Authoritative, Overbearing, Tyrannical
  A: Subservient, Obsequious, Sycophantic

IMPERTINENT: Disrespectful
  S: Impudent, Rude, Insolent
  A: Polite, Suave, Meek

IMPERVIOUS: Not affected by
  S: Impenetrable, Impermeable, Resistance
  A: Open, Susceptible, Exposed

IMPETUOUS: Acting or done suddenly with little thought
  S: Impulsive
  A: Planned

IMPETUS: Driving force or motive
  S: Force, Momentum, Stimulus
  A: Impediment

Verbal Ability / Vocabulary

IMPIETY: Lack or reverence for God
   S: Ungodliness, Irreverence, Disrespect
   A: Reverence, Godliness, Respect

IMPINGE: To strike, hit, etc. (on or upon)
   S: Strike, Hit
   A: Boomerang

IMPLACABLE: Merciless, Inflexible
   S: Unrelenting, Inflexible, Inexorable
   A: Lenient, Tolerant, Merciful

IMPRECATE: To curse
   S: Oath
   A: Praise

IMPROMPTU: Without preparation
   S: Extempore
   A: Rehearsed, Deliberate, Premeditate

IMPROVISE: To compose and perform without preparation
   S: Extemporize, Invent, Compose
   A: Rehearsed

IMPUDENT: Shamelessly bold
   S: Saucy, Brazen, Audacious
   A: Modest, Humble, Timid

INADVERTENT: Unintentional
   A: Deliberate

INALIENABLE: That cannot be taken away or transferred
   S: Undeniable, Inviolable, Irrevocable
   A: Disputable, Repealable, Alienable

INANE: Silly, Lacking sense
   S: Empty, Pointless, Foolish
   A: Expressive, Meaningful, Significant

INCARCERATE: To imprison
   S: Confine
   A: Release, Free

INCENDIARY: Having to do with the wilful destruction of property by fire, Stirring up trouble
   S: Inflammatory, Fiery, Seditious
   A: Placating

INCEPTION: Act of beginning, Start
   S: Inauguration, Beginning, Origin
   A: Termination, End, Finish

INCERTITUDE: Doubt
   S: Uncertainty
   A: Certainty

INCINERATE: To burn into ashes

INCIPIENT: Just beginning to develop or appear
   S: Initial
   A: Mature, Developed

INCOGNITO: Disguised under an assumed name, rank, etc.
   S: Unidentified

INCOHERENT: Not logically connected, Disjointed
   S: Confused
   A: Clear, Vivid

INCONGRUOUS: Lacking harmony or agreement or parts, etc.
   S: Inappropriate, Absurd, Unsuitable
   A: Accordant, Suitable, Harmonious

INCREDULOUS: Unwilling to believe
   S: Sceptical
   A: Gullible

INDEFATIGABLE: Untiring
   S: Unweary, Vigorous
   A: Fatigued

INDELIBLE: That cannot be erased, blotted out, etc.
   A: Erasable

INDEMNIFY: To insure against damage, etc.
   S: Recompense, Repay, Compensate

INDETERMINATE: Indefinite
   S: Vague
   A: Definite, Clear

INDICT: To charge with a crime
   S: Accuse, Incriminate

INDIGENOUS: Existing or growing naturally in a region or country
   S: Native, Aboriginal, Inherent
   A: Alien, Foreign, Immigrant

INDIGENT: Poor, Needy
   S: Needy, Penniless, Destitute
   A: Opulent, Rich, Wealthy

INDIGNANT: Feeling or expressing anger, especially at unjust or mean action
- **S:** Anger, Wrath, Scorn
- **A:** Calm, Cool, Patient

INDISCREET: Too open to what one says or does
- **S:** Brash, Rash, Reckless
- **A:** Wise

INDOLENT: Idle, Lazy
- **S:** Lethargic
- **A:** Active, Keen, Smart

INDUBITABLE: That cannot be doubted, Certain
- **S:** Indisputable, Undeniable, Positive
- **A:** Dubious, Doubtful, Uncertain

INDUCT: To place formally in an office or a society
- **S:** Install, Initiate

INEBRIATED: Intoxicated
- **S:** Drunk, Tipsy
- **A:** Sober, Teetotaller

INEPT: Unsuitable, Unfit
- **S:** Absurd, Awkward, Foolish
- **A:** Apt, Appropriate, Competent

INFINITESIMAL: Too small to be measured

INFIRM: Weak from age
- **S:** Weak, Languid, Feeble
- **A:** Strong, Powerful, Tough

INFLICT: To cause (wounds, pain, etc.) suffering
- **A:** Mollify

INFRINGE: To break (a law or pact)
- **S:** Transgress, Violate, Trespass

INGENIOUS: Clever, Resourceful
- **S:** Skilful, Awkward, Dull
- **A:** Cunning

INGENUOUS: Frank, Open, Simple
- **S:** Sincere
- **A:** Cunning, Crafty, Deceptive

INHIBITION: Restraint, Reserve
- **S:** Repression, Ban, Opposition
- **A:** Benevolent, Amicable, Affectionate

INIMICAL: Hostile, Unfriendly
- **S:** Harmful
- **A:** Benevolent, Amicable, Affectionate

INKLING: A hint
- **S:** Intimation, Idea

INNATE: Inborn, Natural (an innate sense of style)
- **S:** Intrinsic
- **A:** Extrinsic, Alien

INNOCUOUS: Harmless
- **S:** Harmless, Inoffensive
- **A:** Malignant

INNUENDO: A hint or indirect reference, usually derogatory
- **S:** Insinuation, Intimation, Allusion

INORDINATE: Excessive, Unusual
- **S:** Unlimited, Profuse
- **A:** Meagre, Scanty

INSANE: Mentally ill or deranged, Not sane
- **S:** Mad, Delirious, Frenzied
- **A:** Sound, Sane, Normal

INSATIABLE: That cannot be satisfied
- **S:** Unquenchable, Greedy, Unappeasable
- **A:** Appeasable, Quenchable

INSINUATE: To suggest in an unpleasant or indirect way
- **A:** Forthright

INSIPID: Without flavour, Tasteless, Dull
- **S:** Lifeless, Bland
- **A:** Tasty, Lively

INSOLENT: Boldly disrespectful
- **S:** Impudent, Impertinent, Offensive
- **A:** Polite

INSTIGATE: To provoke, To stir up
- **S:** Incite, Goad, Stimulate
- **A:** Dissuade, Deter, Restrain

INSULAR: Of or like an island, Isolated
- **S:** Narrow-minded
- **A:** Broad-minded

INTER: To put a dead body into a grave or tomb
- **S:** Entomb
- **A:** Exhume, Disinter, Disentomb

INTERIM: The period of time between
- **S:** Intermission, Interlude

INTERPOLATE: To make a remark that interrupts a speech, conversation, To add something to a text, book, etc.

INTERSPERSE: To put here and there, To scatter
- **S:** Diversify
- **A:** Unify, Group

INTERVENE: To come or be between
- **S:** Arbitrate
- **A:** Hedge

INTRACTABLE: Hard to manage, Unruly or stubborn
- **S:** Unruly, Refractory, Disobedient
- **A:** Tractable, Obedient, Submissive

INTREPID: Bold, Fearless
- **S:** Brave, Adventurous
- **A:** Timid, Nervous, Cowardly

INTROSPECTION: Looking into one's own mind

INTROVERT: One who is more interested in his own thoughts, feelings, etc. than in external objects or events
- **S:** Reserved
- **A:** Extrovert

INVIGORATE: To give vigour to
- **S:** Energize, Strengthen, Vitalize
- **A:** Weaken, Enervate, Unnerve

IRASCIBLE: Irritable
- **S:** Quick-tempered
- **A:** Calm, Patient

IRATE: Angry
- **S:** Wrathful, Incensed, Nettled
- **A:** Peaceful

IRIDESCENT: Having or showing an interplay of rainbow-like colours

IRKSOME: Annoying, Tiresome
- **S:** Troublesome, Annoying
- **A:** Pleasant, Gratifying

JADED: Worn-out, Worthless
- **S:** Dull
- **A:** Enthusiastic

JARGON: Specific language of a group

JEOPARDY: Great danger or risk
- **S:** Peril, Hazard
- **A:** Safety, Security, Sanctuary

JEREMIAD: A tale of woe: in allusion to the lamentations of Jeremiah
- **S:** Grief
- **A:** Happiness

JINGOISM: Chauvinistic advocacy of an aggressive, war-like foreign policy
- **A:** Tolerant

JINX: A person or thing supposed to bring bad luck

JOCKEY: To manoeuvre for positions or advantage

JOCOSE: Joking
- **S:** Jocular, Playful
- **A:** Serious, Solemn

JOCULAR: Meant as a joke, Given to joking
- **S:** Jesting, Waggish
- **A:** Serious, Solemn

JUDICIOUS: Having or showing judgement, management
- **S:** Discerning, Wise, Prudent
- **A:** Foolish, Fatuous, Puerile

JUVENILE: Young
- **S:** Immature
- **A:** Experienced

KEN: (Out of or beyond) Range of sight or knowledge; Recognize at sight, Know
- **S:** Knowledge, Range, Purview

KEYNOTE: The basic idea or ruling principle
- **S:** Musical Note

KICKBACK: Payment (gratification) given to a person who has enabled one to make money

KILLJOY: One who destroys or lessens other people's enjoyment
- **S:** Spoilsport
- **A:** Cynosure

KILN: A furnace or oven for drying, burning or baking bricks, pottery, etc.

KIN: Relative, Family related by blood

KLEPTOMANIA: An abnormal, persistent impulse to steal

KNELL: To ring slowly, Omen of death or failure

KUDOS: Credit for achievement, Glory
- **S:** Glory
- **A:** Jeer

LACERATE: To tear roughly
- **A:** Restore, Placate, Sympathise

LACKADAISICAL: Showing lack of interest of spirit
- **S:** Languishing, Indolent, Apathetic
- **A:** Energetic, Lively, Enthusiastic

LACONIC: Terse in expression, Using few words, Concise
- **S:** Brief, Pithy
- **A:** Profuse, Wordy, Discursive

LACUNA: A blank space, especially a missing portion in a text, etc.
- **S:** Gap

LAGGARD: A slow person especially one who falls behind
- **S:** Slowpoke, Dawdler.
- **A:** Leader

LAMENT: To feel or express deep sorrow for
- **S:** Grieve, Mourn
- **A:** Rejoice

LANGUID: Without vigour or vitality
- **S:** Pensive, Drooping, Lethargic
- **A:** Brisk, Lively, Vivacious

LANGUISH: To become weak, Be unhappy
- **S:** Suffer
- **A:** Flourish

LARCENY: The unlawful taking of another's property
- **S:** Theft, Robbery, Plunder
- **A:** Restoration, Compensation, Atonement

LARGESS: Generous giving
- **A:** Selfish

LASCIVIOUS: Characterized by or expressing lust
- **S:** Immoral, Lustful, Lecherous
- **A:** Pure, Chaste, Virtuous

LASSITUDE: Weariness
- **S:** Langour, Weariness, Quickness
- **A:** Energetic

LAUDABLE: Praiseworthy
- **S:** Commendable, Worthy, Deserving
- **A:** Degrading, Depraving, Contemptible

LEVITY: Lightness of body or spirit, Lack of seriousness
- **S:** Inconstancy, Jocularity, Flippancy
- **A:** Gravity, Sobriety, Solemnity

LEWD: Pertaining to lust
- **S:** Obscene, Lustful, Licentious
- **A:** Pure, Chaste

LEXICON: Vocabulary of a person; Dictionary (especially of Greek, Latin or Hebrew)

LIMBER: Easily bent, To exercise in preparation for a sport
- **S:** Flexible
- **A:** Rigid

LIMBO: In an uncertain state
- **A:** Surety

LITHE: Graceful, Flexible
- **S:** Supple, Flexible, Pliant
- **A:** Awkward, Stiff, Wooden

LITIGATE: To consent in a lawsuit

LIVID: Discolored by a bruise, Black and blue, Furiously angry
- **S:** Discolored, Angry
- **A:** Calm

LOATHE: To feel intense dislike or disgust for
- **S:** Detest, Abhor, Abominate
- **A:** Like, Love, Admire

Verbal Ability / Vocabulary

LUCID: Clear, Readily understand
   S: Clear, Intelligible
   A: Incomprehensible, Irrational, Illegible

LUDICROUS: Causing laughter because it is absurd or ridiculous
   S: Absurd, Laughable, Preposterous
   A: Serious

LUMINARY: Natural light giving body like the sun, moon, etc.;
      A person of eminence
   A: Non-entity

LURID: Shocking, Sensational
   S: Violent
   A: Bright, Pleasant

M and N

MACABRE: Gruesome, Grim and horrible, Suggesting death
   S: Ghastly, Morbid
   A: Pleasant

MAGNANIMOUS: Generous
   A: Selfish, Mean, Miserly

MALADY: Disease, Illness
   S: Illness, Disorder, Ailment

MALEDICTION: Curse
   S: Execration, Disparagement
   A: Benediction, Blessing, Benison

MALICE: Active ill-will, Desire to harm another
   S: Spite, Grudge, Hatred
   A: Benevolence, Goodwill, Kindness

MALIGN: To speak evil of
   A: Praise

MALLEABLE: That which can be hammered and pounded without breaking, Adaptable
   S: Pliable, Ductile, Flexible, Tractable
   A: Independent, Intractable

MANDATORY: Authoritatively commanded
   S: Compulsory, Mandatory
   A: Voluntary

MASQUERADE: Disguise

MAUDLIN: Foolishly, Often tearfully sentimental
   S: Sentimental, Emotional, Mushy
   A: Unemotional, Unsentimental

MAVERICK: An unorthodox, Independent-minded person
   S: Nonconformist
   A: Conformist

MEDIOCRE: Ordinary
   S: Average
   A: Extraordinary

MELANCHOLY: Very sad and depressed state
   S: Dispirited, Sorrowful
   A: Happy, Merry

MELEE: A confused fight, Confused crowd of people
   S: Scuffle, Brawl, Affray
   A: Order

MELLIFLUOUS: Sounding sweet and smooth
   S: Dulcet, Melodious
   A: Harsh, Discordant

MENDACIOUS: Not truthful, Lying
   S: Deceitful, False
   A: Honest, Trustworthy

MERCENARY: Working or done for payment only
   S: Venal, Pecuniary, Avaricious
   A: Altruistic

MERCURIAL: Changeable, Erratic
   S: Fluctuating, Inconstant, Volatile
   A: Steady, Stable, Constant

MERETRICIOUS: Alluring but showy
   S: Vulgar, Hashy, Superficial

METEORIC: Momentarily brilliant
   S: Rapid, Transient
   A: Gradual, Dull, Slow

MILLENNIUM: Period of thousand years

MISANTHROPE: One who hates or distrusts all people and human society
   S: Cynic, Pessimist, Grouch
   A: Philanthropist

MISOGYNY: Hatred of women
   A: Chivalrous

MISOGAMIST: One who hates marriage

MITIGATE: To make or become less severe
   S: Assuage, Abate, Lessen
   A: Aggravate, Increase, Intensify

MODULATE: To regulate or adjust
   S: Moderate

MOLLIFY: To soothe, Appease
   S: Calm
   A: Agitate

MORBID: Of or caused by disease, Gruesome
   S: Sickly, Ailing
   A: Healthy, Lively

MORIBUND: Dying
   S: Decaying
   A: Inception

MORTIFY: To humiliate
   S: Embarrass
   A: Please

MUNDANE: Of the world, Worldly
   S: Mortal
   A: Heavenly, Ethereal, Celestial, Spiritual

MYRIAD: A great number of persons or things
   S: Innumerable, Countless, Vast
   A: Determinate, Limited

NADIR: The lowest point
   S: Base
   A: Zenith, Summit, Pinnacle

NAIVE: Unaffectedly simple
   S: Artless, Innocent, Unsophisticated
   A: Cunning, Shrewd, Sly

NAUTICAL: Of sailors, ships or navigation

NECROMANCY: Magic, especially that practised by a witch

NEMESIS: Just punishment, Deserved fate; Goddess of vengeance

NEPOTISM: Favouritism shown by a person in high position to relatives especially in securing jobs
   S: Partial
   A: Impartial

NEXUS: A link or connection or connected series
   S: Connection, Bond, Link
   A: Gaps

NIGGARDLY: A stingy person
   S: Miser
   A: Generous, Spendthrift, Bounteous

NINCOMPOOP: A stupid or silly person, Fool
   S: Simpleton, Stupid, Fool
   A: Genius

NOCTURNAL: Of or in the night
   A: Diurnal

NONCHALANT: Casual
   S: Indifferent, Unconcerned, Negligent
   A: Careful, Considerate, Enthusiastic

NONENTITY: A person or thing of little or no importance

NOTORIOUS: Widely known especially unfavourably
   S: Ill-flamed, Infamous, Dishonourable
   A: Good, Virtuous, Honest

NUMISMATICS: The study or collection of coins, medals, paper money, etc.

NUPTIAL: Of marriage or wedding

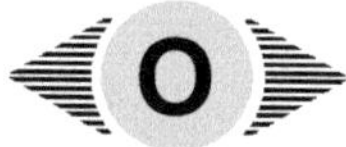

OBESE: Corpulent
   S: Fat
   A: Slim

OBLITERATE: To blot out, To erase
   S: Delete, Raze
   A: Preserve, Build

OBNOXIOUS: Very unpleasant ,Offensive
   S: Repugnant, Odious, Detestable
   A: Pleasurable, Delightful, Attractive

OBSTINATE: Determined to have one's own way, Stubborn
  S: Head-strong
  A: Obliging, Yielding, Flexible

OCCIDENT: West-Europe and countries of the American Continents
  S: West
  A: Orient, Middle East

OCCULT: Hidden, Mysterious; Supernatural, Magical
  S: Latent, Secretive
  A: Plain, Clear, Evident, Worldly

ODIOUS: Disgusting, Offensive
  S: Hateful, Abhorrent, Repellent
  A: Pleasing, Attractive, Inviting

OFFICIOUS: Offering unwanted advice or services
  S: Meddling, Obstructive, Nosey
  A: Indifferent, Apathetic

OLFACTORY: Of the sense of smell

OMINOUS: Of or serving as an evil omen
  S: Threatening, Suggestive, Premonitory
  A: Cheerful, Cheering, Comforting

OMNIPOTENT: Having unlimited power or authority
  S: All-powerful
  A: Weak, Powerless

OMNIPRESENT: Present at all places at all times

ONEROUS: Burdensome
  S: Oppressive
  A: Easy

OPPORTUNE: Suitably said at the right time
  S: Appropriate
  A: Untimely, Unsuitable, Inappropriate

OPULENT: Having much wealth, Rich
  S: Affluence, Wealth
  A: Poverty, Penury, Frugality

ORNITHOLOGY: The branch of zoology dealing with study of birds

OSTENSIBLE: Apparent, Seeming
  S: Apparent, Professed
  A: Improbable, Unlikely, Vague

OSTENTATION: Showy display, Pretentiousness
  S: Pomp
  A: Modesty, Humility

OSTRACIZE: To banish from a group, society, etc.
  S: Expel, Exclude
  A: Welcome

PACIFIST: One opposed to force
  S: Peaceful
  A: Extremist

PALLIATE: Ease pain
  S: Alleviate, Reduce intensity of, Calm
  A: Aggravate, Exacerbate

PANACEA: Cure
  S: Nostrum, Remedy

PANDEMONIUM: Chaos
  S: Confusion
  A: Order

PARITY: Equality
  S: Fair
  A: Unequal

PAROCHIAL: Narrow in outlook
  S: Insular
  A: Broad-minded

PECCADILLO: Slight offence
  S: Trivial
  A: Grave

PEDAGOGY: Art of teaching

PERENNIAL: Long-lasting
  S: Forever
  A: Ephemeral

PERFUNCTORY: Insufficient
  S: Routine
  A: Sincere, Dedicated

PERIPATETIC: Walking about
  A: Stagnant

PERJURY : Making false statement under oath

PERSONABLE: Presentable
  S: Affable
  A: Ugly

PERSPICACIOUS: Plainly expressed
  S: Insightful
  A: Obtuse

PERTINENT: Suitable
  S: Relevant
  A: Irrelevant

PERTURB: Disturb
  A: Soothe

PHILATELIST: Stamp collector

PLACATE: Pacify
  S: Soothe
  A: Antagonize

PLAGIARIZE: Copy

PLATITUDE: Trite remark
  S: Hackneyed
  A: Original

PLAUDITS: Applause

POLARIZE: Split into opposing camps
  S: Divide
  A: Unite

POLEMIC : Full of controversy
  S: Debatable
  A: Acceptable

PRAGMATIC : Practical (as opposed to idealistic), Concerned with the practical worth or impact of something
  S: Realistic
  A: Idealistic

PRECARIOUS : Uncertain
  S: Risky
  A: Safe

PREPOSTEROUS : Absurd, Ridiculous
  S: Silly
  A: Sensible

PRETENTIOUS : Ostentatious, Pompous, Making unjustified claims
  S: Over-ambitious
  A: Genuine

QUAIL: To recoil in fear
  S: Flinch, Recoil

QUAINTNESS: Pleasing, Odd and old-fashioned
  S: Freakish
  A: Modern

QUALM: Uneasiness
  S: Compunction, Scruple, Apprehension
  A: Callous

QUERULOUS: Inclined to find fault
  S: Complaining
  A: Cheerful, Satisfied, Content

QUINTESSENCE: The pure essence or perfect type

QUIP: Give a witty remark
  S: Sally, Retort, Jest
  A: Witty or sarcastic remark

QUIXOTIC: Extravagantly chivalrous or romantic
  S: Idealistic
  A: Practical

RAMIFICATION: A result, Consequence, Repercussion
  S: Branch, Outcome

RAMPANT: Widespread, Raging
  S: Luxuriant
  A: Meagre

RANCOUR: A continuing bitter hate or ill-will
  S: Malice, Enmity, Hatred
  A: Friendship, Love, Respect

RANKLE: To fester
  S: Irritate
  A: Please

RANSACK: To plunder, Pillage
  S: Rummage
  A: Restore, Compensate, Redress

RAPACIOUS: Greedy, Voracious
  S: Grasping, Avaricious, Wolfish
  A: Sparing

RAPPORT: Sympathetic relationship, Harmony
  S: Accord
  A: Hatred, Enmity, Animosity

RAVENOUS: Greedy, Very hungry
  S: Voracious
  A: Assuaged, Full

RECAPITULATE: To repeat
  S: Summarize

RECREANT: Cowardly, Unfaithful, Traitorous
  S: Timid, Mean-spirited
  A: Brave

RECUPERATE: To get well again
  A: Worsen

REFRACTORY: Hard to manage, Obstinate; Hard to melt (metals).
  S: Recalcitrant, Unruly, Headstrong
  A: Docile, Tractable, Amenable

REFULGENT: Shining, Radiant, Glowing
  S: Shining, Brilliant
  A: Dull

REFURBISH: To freshen
  S: Polish

REGRESSION: The act of going back
  S: Reversion, Retrogression
  A: Progress, Advancement

REHABILITATE: To put back to useful life
  S: Restore, Cure
  A: Ruin, Destroy

RENDEZVOUS: A meeting
  S: Appointment

RENEGADE: One who abandons a party, movement, etc. to join the opposition
  S: Apostate, Turncoat
  A: Loyal

REPERCUSSION: After-effect
  S: Effect, Echo

REPLETE: Plentifully supplied
  S: Full, Surfeited, Abundant
  A: Starved, Empty

REPREHEND: To rebuke, Blame or censure
  A: Condone

REPROOF: Blame, Find fault
  S: Rebuke, Censure
  A: Credit, Praise, Commendation

REPUDIATE: To disown, To reject
  S: Discard, Disclaim
  A: Accept, Affirm, Acknowledge

RESILIENCE: Recovering strength, spirits, etc. quickly
  S: Buoyancy, Elasticity.
  A: Susceptibility, Vulnerability

RESPLENDENT: Shining brightly, Dazzling
  S: Brilliant
  A: Dull

RESTIVE: Unruly, Impatient
  S: Restless, Unruly
  A: Quiet, Peaceful, Docile

RESURGENCE: Tending to rise again.
  S: Resilient
  A: Deflated

RETICENT: Silent, Reserved
  S: Taciturn, Laconic
  A: Garrulous, Verbose, Loquacious

RETRACT: Draw back or in (statement, charge, etc.); Move back or inside.
  A: Proceed

RETRENCH: To cut down (especially expenses)
  S: Economize
  A: Lavish

RETRIEVE: To get back
  S: Recover
  A: Retain

REVERIE: Day-dream

REVILE: To use abusive language
  S: Execrate, Rail, Slander
  A: Praise, Laud, Eulogize

RHETORIC: The art of using words effectively especially the art of prose composition

RUBICUND: Reddish
  S: Ruddy
  A: Pale, Pallid

RUDIMENT: A first principle, as of a subject
  S: Fundamentals

RUMINATE: To meditate or reflect
  S: Reflect, Ponder

RUTHLESS: Without pity or compassion
  S: Cruel, Pitiless, Unmerciful
  A: Merciful, Sympathetic

SACROSANCT: Very sacred, Holy
  S: Inviolable
  A: Unholy

SALIENT: Conspicuous, Prominent
  S: Outstanding
  A: Hidden

SALUBRIOUS: Healthy
  S: Wholesome

SANCTIMONIOUS: Pretending to be pious

SANCTUARY: A holy place or a place of refuge or protection

SANGUINE: Cheerful, Optimistic
  S: Enthusiastic
  A: Despairing, Downcast, Pessimistic

SARDONIC: Scornful or bitterly sarcastic
  S: Mocking, Ridiculing
  A: Pleasant

SARTORIAL: Concerned with clothes and tailoring

SAUCY: Rude, Impudent
  S: Insolent
  A: Modest, Humble

SCRUPULOUS: Conscientiously honest and careful of details
  S: Punctilious, Principled
  A: Remiss, Negligent

SEAMY: Unpleasant
  S: Sordid
  A: Pleasant, Decent

SECULAR: Not bound by a monastic vow or religion
  A: Religious, Spiritual

SEDATE: Sober, Serious and unemotional, Calm and composed
  S: Serene
  A: Mercurial, Frivolous

SEDENTARY: Marked by much sitting
  A: Peripatetic

SEDUCE: To tempt into wrong-doing
  S: Allure, Inveigle, Entice
  A: Protect, Guide, Discourage

SEDULOUS: Diligent, Persistent
  S: Attentive, Industrious
  A: Lethargic, Indifferent, Indolent

SEMBLANCE: Outward appearance
  S: Likeness, Form

SHIFTLESS: Incapable, Inefficient
  S: Lazy
  A: Active, Alert

SKINFLINT: Miser
  S: Niggard
  A: Spendthrift

SKITTISH: Lively, Playful
  S: Fidgety, Nervous
  A: Bold, Audacious

SMITHEREENS: Fragments
  S: Pieces
  A: Whole

SMUG: Annoyingly self-satisfied or complacent
  S: Self-satisfied
  A: Persistent

SOLICITUDE: Being solicitous, Care, Concern
  S: Anxiety
  A: Apathy, Indifference

SPORADIC: Happening or appearing in isolated instances
  S: Infrequent, Uncommon, Isolated
  A: Constant, Prevalent, Continual

Verbal Ability / Vocabulary

SPRUCE: Neat and in a smart way
- **S:** Neat
- **A:** Untidy, Slovenly

SPURIOUS: Not genuine, False
- **S:** Counterfeit, Dishonest, Deceptive
- **A:** Genuine, Real, Actual

SQUABBLE: To quarrel noisily over a small matter
- **S:** Wrangle, Dispute

STAID: Sober, Sedate
- **S:** Serious
- **A:** Excited

STERLING: Excellent
- **S:** Genuine, Valuable
- **A:** Spurious, Trivial

STILTED: Artificially formal or dignified
- **S:** Stiff, Unnatural
- **A:** Casual, Informal

STRIDENT: Harsh-sounding, Shrill, Granting
- **A:** Soft

SUCCINCT: Clear and brief, Terse
- **S:** Concise
- **A:** Circumlocutory

SUFFRAGE: The right to vote

SUPERCILIOUS: Disdainful or contemptuous
- **S:** Haughty
- **A:** Kind, Sensitive, Sympathetic

SURFEIT: Too great an amount
- **A:** Meagre, Scanty

SURMISE: To guess
- **S:** Assume
- **A:** Certainty

SURREPTITIOUS: Done, got, acting, etc. in a stealthy way
- **S:** Clandestine
- **A:** Open, Frank

SURROGATE: A substitute or deputy

SURVEILLANCE: Watch kept over a person especially a suspect
- **S:** Supervision, Invigilation

SYLVAN: Rural
- **S:** Rustic
- **A:** Urban

SYMBIOSIS: The living together of two kinds of organisms to their mutual advantage

SYNCHRONISM: To cause to happen at the same time or rate
- **A:** Asynchronous

SYNDROME: A set of symptoms characterizing a disease or condition

TABOO: Any social restriction
- **S:** Forbidden
- **A:** Permit, Allow, Licence

TACITURN: Almost always silent, Not liking to talk
- **S:** Reserved, Reticent, Uncommunicative
- **A:** Talkative, Loquacious

TANTAMOUNT: Equal in value, effect, etc.
- **A:** Unequal

TANTRUM: A violent, wilful outburst or rage, etc.

TARDY: Late, Delayed, Dilatory; Slow moving
- **S:** Procrastinate
- **A:** Prompt, Punctual, Ready

TEDIOUS: Long and dull
- **S:** Slow, Wearisome, Fatiguing
- **A:** Light, Hearty, Cheerful

TEEM: To be prolific, Abound
- **S:** Swarm
- **A:** Paucity

TEETOTALLER: One who practises total abstinence from alcoholic liquor

TEMPESTUOUS: Of or like a tempest, Violent
- **S:** Stormy
- **A:** Sedate, Calm, Peaceful

TENACIOUS: Persistent, Stubborn, One who perseveres
- **S:** Tough, Pertinacious
- **A:** Non-adhesive, Unstable

TENTATIVE: Done as a test, Not final
  A: Established, Certain

TENUOUS: Slender or fine as a fibre
  S: Thin
  A: Strong, Thick

TERMAGANT: A quarrelsome, scolding woman
  S: Shrew

THEATRICAL: Designed for effect, Showy, Unnatural
  S: Dramatic

THESPIAN: Having to do with drama;
      Actor.

THRESHOLD: The beginning point
  S: Beginning, Start
  A: End

TITANIC: Of great size, strength or power
  S: Gigantic, Immense
  A: Tiny, Small

TOPOGRAPHY: Description of surface features of a region on maps and charts

TORPOR: Dullness, Lack of energy
  S: Inactivity
  A: Enthusiasm, Involvement

TRANSIENT: Temporary
  S: Transitory, Brief
  A: Lasting, Permanent, Unending

TRAUMATIC: An emotional shock, often having a lasting psychic effect
  S: Unpleasant, Distressing, Agonizing
  A: Pleasant, Titillating

TREMOR: Trembling
  S: Shaking, Fearful
  A: Brave

TREPIDATION: Trembling movement
  S: Alarm
  A: Composure, Calm

TRIBULATION: Great misery or distress

TUMID: Swollen, Bulging
  S: Distended
  A: Shrunken, Reduced, Concise

TURBID: Muddy, Thick
  S: Muddled
  A: Clear, Transparent, Pure

TURBULENT: Wild or disorderly
  S: Disturbed, Agitated
  A: Calm, Composed, Peaceful

TURGID: Bombastic, Pompous (of language); Swollen, Bloated
  S: High-sounding
  A: Simple, Modest

TUTELAGE: Guardianship, Care, Instruction

UBIQUITOUS: Present everywhere at the same time

ULTERIOR: Lying beyond what is expressed or implied.
  S: Real
  A: Ostensible

ULTIMATUM: A final offer or demand as in negotiations

UMBRAGE: Give or take offence or resentment
  S: Humiliated

UNCTUOUS: Characterized by smooth pretence of fervour or earnestness, Too suave or oily
  S: Flattering
  A: Blunt, Straightforward, Frank

UNEQUIVOCAL: Having one meaning, Clear
  S: Plain
  A: Ambiguous, Confusing, Vague, Abstract

UNHINGED: Mentally unstable
  S: Unsettled
  A: Sane, Rational, Calm

UNILATERAL: Of, occurring on, or affecting one side only
  A: Bilateral

UNISON: Agreement, Harmony
  S: Accord
  A: Discord, Enmity

Verbal Ability / Vocabulary

UNMITIGATED: Absolute
  S: Complete

UNSCRUPULOUS: Not restrained by moral scruples
  S: Unprincipled
  A: Scrupulous, Conscientious

UPBRAID: To rebuke severely, Censure, Scold
  A: Condone, Forgive

UPRISING: Revolt
  S: Insurrection
  A: Submission

UPROAR: Violent disturbance, Tumult
  S: Confusing, Chaos
  A: Peace, Calm, Tranquillity

USURY: Lending money at excessive rate of interest

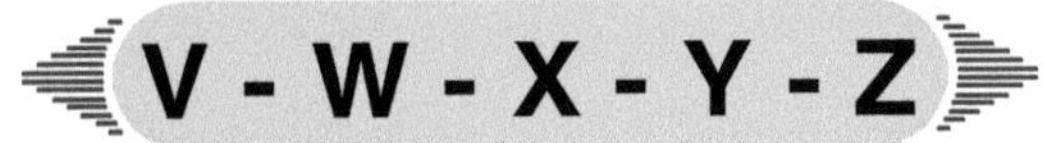

VENAL: Can be bribed
  S: Corrupt
  A: Honest

VENERATE: Respect
  S: Honour
  A: Insult

VERBOSE: Wordy
  S: Elaborate
  A: Precise

VERDANT: Green
  S: Lush
  A: Arid

VERITY: Truthfulness
  A: False

VERTIGINOUS: Dizzying, almost dreamy rise

VERVE: Enthusiasm
  S: Vigour
  A: Languid

VESTIGE: Remains

VIABLE: Conceivable
  S: Practical
  A: Fantastic

VILIFY: Malign
  A : Glorify

VINDICTIVE: Vengeful
  A: Forgiving

VIRULENT: Deadly
  S: Poisonous
  A: Harmless

VOCIFEROUS: Noisy

VORACIOUS: Greedy
  S: Eager
  A: Uninterested

VULPINE: Crafty, Wilful
  S: Wily
  A: Guileless

WASPISH: Bad-tempered, Snappish
  S: Irritable
  A: Affectionate

WAYLAY: To wait for and launch a surprise attack
  S: Accost

WELTER: A confused mixture of things or people

ZANY: A clown or buffoon, Half-witted person
  A: Serious

ZEAL: Intense enthusiasm, Ardour, Fervour
  S: Earnestness
  A: Apathy, Indifference

ZENITH: The highest point
  S: Pinnacle, Summit
  A: Base, Nadir

ZEPHYR: A light breeze

ZEST: Keen enjoyment;
  Stimulating quality.
  S: Gusto
  A: Apathy, Depression, Despondency

Synonyms and Antonyms 2

Exercise – 1

Directions for questions 1 to 5: Select the choice that comes closest in meaning to the word given in the question.

1. renounce
   - (1) accept
   - (2) nullify
   - (3) abdicate
   - (4) mulct

2. abnegation
   - (1) invite
   - (2) deify
   - (3) inaccurate
   - (4) self-denial

3. placate
   - (1) appeal
   - (2) abolish
   - (3) testify
   - (4) soothe

4. abstract
   - (1) calm
   - (2) concrete
   - (3) tangible
   - (4) theoretical

5. retard
   - (1) brake
   - (2) slow down
   - (3) crazy
   - (4) speed up

Directions for questions 6 to 10: Select the choice that comes closest to the opposite in meaning to the word given in the question.

6. routine
   - (1) normal
   - (2) aberration
   - (3) actuate
   - (4) abysmal

7. hedonist
   - (1) cardigan
   - (2) puritan
   - (3) negative
   - (4) spiritual

8. truncate
   - (1) pus
   - (2) break
   - (3) divide
   - (4) join

9. abstruse
   - (1) complex
   - (2) elysian
   - (3) profound
   - (4) lucid

10. accessible
    - (1) free
    - (2) recession
    - (3) approachable
    - (4) unapproachable

Exercise – 2

Directions for questions 11 to 15: Select the choice that comes closest in meaning to the word given in the question.

11. actuary
    - (1) deny
    - (2) disprove
    - (3) approval
    - (4) of statistics

12. unreasonable
    - (1) practical
    - (2) untenable
    - (3) unimpeachable
    - (4) sanity

13. Archipelago
    - (1) arcane
    - (2) archaic
    - (3) peculiar
    - (4) group of islands

14. Armada
    - (1) fleet
    - (2) booty
    - (3) arroyo
    - (4) paltry

15. swollen
    - (1) trivial
    - (2) gully
    - (3) turgid
    - (4) punitive

Directions for questions 16 to 20: Select the choice that comes closest to the opposite in meaning to the word given in the question.

16. balm
    - (1) soothe
    - (2) placate
    - (3) pacify
    - (4) irritant

17. banter
    - (1) joke
    - (2) barrister
    - (3) barricade
    - (4) be serious

18. revel
    - (1) luxuriate
    - (2) enjoy
    - (3) sunshine
    - (4) be infuriated

19. spur
    - (1) hinder
    - (2) obtuse
    - (3) repel
    - (4) bolster

20. cherubic
    - (1) drive
    - (2) bestial
    - (3) avoid
    - (4) mob

Exercise – 3

Directions for questions 21 to 25: Select the choice that comes closest in meaning to the word given in the question.

21. Blarney
    (1) rebuke
    (2) upbraid
    (3) censure
    (4) flattery

22. Diseased
    (1) puritan
    (2) paradigm
    (3) blessed
    (4) blighted

23. Blurt
    (1) loosen
    (2) speak out
    (3) blarney
    (4) mellifluous

24. Support
    (1) lenient
    (2) arrival
    (3) turpitude
    (4) bolster

25. cunning
    (1) astute
    (2) blithe
    (3) stupid
    (4) jiffy

Directions for questions 26 to 30: Select the choice that comes closest to the opposite in meaning to the word given in the question.

26. boorish
    (1) urbane
    (2) rude
    (3) course
    (4) boring

27. porous
    (1) ore
    (2) dull
    (3) boring
    (4) impregnable

28. bravado
    (1) act
    (2) pretend
    (3) fool
    (4) intrepid

29. stoic
    (1) perceived
    (2) bristling
    (3) ageing
    (4) docile

30. brusque
    (1) curt
    (2) rude
    (3) short
    (4) pleasant

Exercise – 4

Directions for questions 31 to 35: Select the choice that comes closest in meaning to the word given in the question.

31. connubial
    (1) connive
    (2) of marriage
    (3) covert
    (4) carnivorous

32. consonance
    (1) punctuate
    (2) harmony
    (3) stillness
    (4) discord

33. dispute
    (1) forfeit
    (2) claim
    (3) complacent
    (4) contend

34. smuggling
    (1) comport
    (2) disband
    (3) contraband
    (4) muzzle

35. riddle
    (1) cooperate
    (2) conundrum
    (3) military
    (4) potential

Directions for questions 36 to 40: Select the choice that comes closest to the opposite in meaning to the word given in the question.

36. comely
    (1) pretty
    (2) unattractive
    (3) lively
    (4) attractive

37. console
    (1) equal
    (2) symmetric
    (3) aggravate
    (4) harmony

38. mandatory
    (1) force
    (2) propel
    (3) drive
    (4) voluntary

39. ruffled
    (1) game
    (2) composed
    (3) patent
    (4) diluted

40. link
    (1) concatenate
    (2) bond
    (3) unite
    (4) separate

Exercise – 5

Directions for questions 41 to 45: Select the choice that comes closest in meaning to the word given in the question.

41. debase
    (1) support
    (2) bolster
    (3) make inferior
    (4) propel

42. behead
    (1) capacity
    (2) roomy
    (3) fragrant
    (4) decapitate

43. downward
    (1) boom
    (2) declivity
    (3) depression
    (4) impetuous

44. embezzle
    (1) falcon
    (2) strange
    (3) expurgate
    (4) mulct

45. corrupt
    (1) abrade
    (2) suave
    (3) polish
    (4) defile

Directions for questions 46 to 50: Select the choice that comes closest to the opposite in meaning to the word given in the question.

46. Defame
    (1) spoil
    (2) ruin
    (3) disrepute
    (4) praise

47. Fatalist
    (1) defeatist
    (2) droop
    (3) persistent
    (4) pessimistic

48. unambiguous
    (1) certain
    (2) clear
    (3) questionable
    (4) definite

49. Deft
    (1) skilled
    (2) dexterous
    (3) slant
    (4) maladroit

50. unhinged
    (1) imbalanced
    (2) ventricle
    (3) insane
    (4) balanced

Exercise – 6

Directions for questions 51 to 55: Select the choice that comes closest in meaning to the word given in the question.

51. inter
    (1) interested
    (2) diverge
    (3) vary
    (4) bury

52. disjointed
    (1) joint
    (2) distress
    (3) discuss
    (4) disconnected

53. martinet
    (1) portly
    (2) stout
    (3) disciplinarian
    (4) loud

54. distil
    (1) stultify
    (2) impasse
    (3) stipulate
    (4) purify

55. green
    (1) don
    (2) verdant
    (3) gripe
    (4) parochial

Directions for questions 56 to 60: Select the choice that comes closest to the opposite in meaning to the word given in the question.

56. don
    (1) adorn
    (2) put on
    (3) doff
    (4) leader

57. dote
    (1) fearless
    (2) intrepid
    (3) timid
    (4) hate

58. dregs
    (1) base
    (2) bottom
    (3) cream
    (4) deep

59. brittle
    (1) shapely
    (2) ploy
    (3) flex
    (4) ductile

60. dutiful
    (1) obedient
    (2) replete
    (3) loyal
    (4) disobedient

Directions for questions 61 to 65: Select the choice that comes closest in meaning to the word given in the question.

61. enumerate
    (1) numerical   (2) list
    (3) ratify   (4) nullify

62. gourmet
    (1) gourmand   (2) palatable
    (3) curator   (4) farthing

63. epistle
    (1) epitaph   (2) numismatist
    (3) letter   (4) stultify

64. libidinous
    (1) quinine   (2) balance
    (3) depart   (4) lusty

65. mislead
    (1) vicarious   (2) apathetic
    (3) vocalize   (4) equivocate

Directions for questions 66 to 70: Select the choice that comes closest to the opposite in meaning to the word given in the question.

66. even-handed
    (1) fair   (2) just
    (3) partial   (4) equitable

67. panegyrize
    (1) praise   (2) encomium
    (3) cordial   (4) criticize

68. excogitate
    (1) ponder   (2) deliberate
    (3) think over   (4) act on impulse

69. heed
    (1) pass   (2) order
    (3) gaffe   (4) overlook

70. exhort
    (1) urge   (2) admonish
    (3) scoff   (4) condone

Directions for questions 71 to 75: Select the choice that comes closest in meaning to the word given in the question.

71. fat
    (1) irrelevant   (2) corpulent
    (3) pleasing   (4) flatterer

72. torrent
    (1) rustic   (2) render
    (3) asunder   (4) flood

73. toxic
    (1) denizen   (2) timorous
    (3) occidental   (4) poisonous

74. sin
    (1) regress   (2) digress
    (3) sanguine   (4) transgress

75. noisome
    (1) ransom   (2) renown
    (3) corporeal   (4) foul

Directions for questions 76 to 80: Select the choice that comes closest to the opposite in meaning to the word given in the question.

76. Turmoil
    (1) disturb   (2) trouble
    (3) peace   (4) chaos

77. wickedness
    (1) turpitude   (2) depraved
    (3) mean   (4) integrity

78. Unaccountable
    (1) mystery   (2) complex
    (3) explicable   (4) difficult

79. Uncouth
    (1) rude   (2) boorish
    (3) crude   (4) refined

80. Unearthly
    (1) weird   (2) eerie
    (3) uncanny   (4) normal

Directions for questions 81 to 85: Select the choice that comes closest in meaning to the word given in the question

81. Vital
    (1) virulent
    (2) placate
    (3) critical
    (4) trivial

82. Vociferous
    (1) embody
    (2) silent
    (3) noisy
    (4) feral

83. Guarantee
    (1) locker
    (2) vapid
    (3) petrify
    (4) vouchsafe

84. Wavy
    (1) airy
    (2) gusto
    (3) yield
    (4) undulating

85. circumspective
    (1) rendition
    (2) arroyo
    (3) special
    (4) wary

Directions for questions 86 to 90: Select the choice that comes closest to the opposite in meaning to the word given in the question.

86. yokel
    (1) bumpkin
    (2) fool
    (3) clumsy
    (4) suave

87. zenith
    (1) apogee
    (2) apex
    (3) climax
    (4) nadir

88. zombie
    (1) dull
    (2) lifeless
    (3) servile
    (4) animated

89. zeal
    (1) energetic
    (2) enthusiastic
    (3) unenthusiastic
    (4) vibrant

90. zany
    (1) crazy
    (2) weird
    (3) sombre
    (4) odd

Directions for questions 91 to 95: Select the choice that comes closest in meaning to the word given in the question.

91. choleric
    (1) stipulated
    (2) demanding
    (3) angry
    (4) fatigued

92. Uncork
    (1) stifle
    (2) release
    (3) suppress
    (4) corrigible

93. Unctuous
    (1) weary
    (2) rectilinear
    (3) oily
    (4) turmoil

94. furtive
    (1) overt
    (2) open-handed
    (3) blunt
    (4) secret

95. novice
    (1) maestro
    (2) coward
    (3) tyro
    (4) underdog

Directions for questions 96 to 100: Select the choice that comes closest to the opposite in meaning to the word given in the question.

96. watertight
    (1) undiluted
    (2) indisputable
    (3) open
    (4) clear

97. prodigal
    (1) wasteful
    (2) careful
    (3) reckless
    (4) extravagant

98. wanton
    (1) lewd
    (2) pervert
    (3) temperate
    (4) licentious

99. wallop
    (1) thrash
    (2) beat
    (3) gulp
    (4) embrace

100. volition
    (1) voluntary
    (2) imposed
    (3) self-determined
    (4) cozy

Sentence Completion **3**

▌ Exercise – I

Directions for questions 1 to 5: Complete the following sentences using the words given in the options:

1. The increasing _______ of oceanic water because of dumping of nuclear waster is posing a serious challenge to the survival of the marine life.
   (1) depletion   (2) degeneration
   (3) density   (4) contamination

2. Macbeth was _______ by his wife to commit the murder of Duncan.
   (1) forced   (2) exuited
   (3) instigated   (4) incited

3. He bought new shoes last month but they are already _______out.
   (1) given   (2) gone
   (3) knocked   (4) worn

4. Make the most of a bad _______.
   (1) bargain   (2) job
   (3) business   (4) work

5. His _______ for his brother's son knew no bounds.
   (1) reverie   (2) melange
   (3) ill-will   (4) malignity

▌ Exercise – 2

Directions for questions 1 to 5: Complete the following sentences using the words given in the options:

1. The lovers were meeting each other secretly but their _______ affair was soon known to everyone.
   (1) clandestine   (2) candid
   (3) unknown   (4) covert

2. Inflation can never be brought under control when prices continue to _______.
   (1) mount   (2) fly
   (3) ascend   (4) soar

3. They were awaiting official _______ of the news they had heard from a friend.
   (1) ratification   (2) Confirmation
   (3) Sanction   (4) recommendation

4. They offered a _______ of incentives to attract qualified people for the post.
   (1) bundle   (2) assurance
   (3) package   (4) gift

5. Those who have _______ the transtition from villages to cities have been able to secure good jobs.
   (1) tried   (2) arranged
   (3) planned   (4) managed.

▌ Exercise – 3

Directions for questions 1 to 5: Complete the following sentences using the words given in the options:

1. Success gives only _______ pleasure.
   (1) mordant   (2) momentary
   (3) monotonous   (4) momentous

2. The striking transport operators have decided to _______ their agitation
   (1) intensify   (2) prolong
   (3) worsen   (4) Aggravate

3. The speaker _______ the scope of his paper on 'work-ethic' at the outset.
   (1) declined   (2) ascribed
   (3) defined   (4) delineated

4. The point you are raising is not _______ to the subject.
   (1) proper   (2) fit
   (3) required   (4) pertinent

5. You cannot devise a method which _______ all possibility of error.
   (1) ignores   (2) avoids
   (3) excludes   (4) includes

▌ Exercise – 4

Directions for questions 1 to 5: Complete the following sentences using the words given in the options:

1. He _______ in wearing the old fashioned coat.
   (1) resists   (2) desists
   (3) persists   (4) insists

2. The _______ of nuclear power feel that it is one of the most dangerous developments in modern civilization.
   (1) activists   (2) antagonists
   (3) victims   (4) opponents

3. The house is in a terrible state; the paint of the doors is _______ badly.
   (1) flaking   (2) nothing
   (3) eroding   (4) decaying

4. A man who is well-bred and honourable invariably shows _______ for the feeling of other people.
   (1) compliance   (2) concern
   (3) consideration   (4) contempt

5. The Board called on a meeting to _______ the financial situation of the company.
   (1) revise   (2) cover
   (3) review   (4) support

Exercise – 5

Directions for questions 1 to 5: Complete the following sentences using the words given in the options:

1. To promote trade, it is necessary for the government to _______ restrictions on exports.
   (1) reduce   (2) relax
   (3) break   (4) modify

2. We had a _______ of warm weather in February.
   (1) phase   (2) length
   (3) spell   (4) time

3. The land-lord has threatened to _______ me, if I do not vacate the house by next month.
   (1) charge   (2) sue
   (3) suspend   (4) accuse

4. The Spanish regarded him as an _______ and called him a villain.
   (1) imposter   (2) apostle
   (3) informer   (4) archer

5. This item will not figure in the _______ for today's meeting.
   (1) list   (2) schedule
   (3) programme   (4) agenda

Exercise – 6

Directions for questions 1 to 5: Complete the following sentences using the words given in the options:

1. If a universal language really existed, people like tourists and businessmen would find it easier to _______ with foreigners.
   (1) transact   (2) communicate
   (3) deal   (4) exchange

2. On account of his humiliating defeat in the recent elections, he appeared generally _______ when I called on him the other day.
   (1) oppressed   (2) repressed
   (3) depressed   (4) suppressed

3. You need _______ shoes for walking in the hills.
   (1) good   (2) comfortable
   (3) satisfactory   (4) sturdy

4. Amongst the two brothers, Sameer being worthier often _______ the young Deepak.
   (1) dominates   (2) eclipses
   (3) subdues   (4) overshadows

5. It was difficult to see through the _______ of the head lights of the cars.
   (1) shine   (2) glare
   (3) dazzle   (4) brilliance

Exercise – 7

Directions for questions 1 to 5: Complete the following sentences using the words given in the options:

1. The teacher ordered Kamal to leave the room and _______ him to return.
   (1) stopped   (2) refused
   (3) forbade   (4) challenged

2. I hope you must have _______ by now that failures are the stepping stones to success.
   (1) known   (2) felt
   (3) decided   (4) realized

3. The tyrant _______ anyone whom he regarded as a rival.
   (1) massacred   (2) killed
   (3) exterminated   (4) slaughtered

4. In a little publicized deal, Pepsi Cola has ______
   the entire soft drink market in Afganisatan.
   (1) conquered   (2) swallowed
   (3) captured   (4) occupied

5. Inspite of some ______, Ashish is a good
   sportsman.
   (1) felonies   (2) mistakes
   (3) offencs   (4) misdemeanours.

Exercise – 8

Directions for questions 1 to 5: Complete the following
sentences using the words given in the options:

1. When the courtier had advanced to the highest
   position attainable, his friends felt jealous about
   his having reached the______.
   (1) vigil   (2) precipice
   (3) threshold   (4) pinnacle

2. The bill in the parliament was ______ by fifty five
   votes.
   (1) accepted   (2) voted
   (3) carried   (4) opposed

3. The principal and staff have made ______ efforts
   to enable the students to attend college on the
   days of the bus strike.
   (1) integrated   (2) deliberate
   (3) concerted   (4) systematic

4. We ______ the family members after expressing
   our grief at the tragedy.
   (1) condoled   (2) satisfied
   (3) mourned   (4) consoled

5. The defending champion ______ to victory in just
   30 minutes.
   (1) led   (2) rushed
   (3) reached   (4) cruised

Exercise – 9

Directions for questions 1 to 5: Complete the following
sentences using the words given in the options:

1. No one likes to be forced into ______ situations.
   (1) humble   (2) insulting
   (3) humiliating   (4) infuriating

2. He admired precision in everything, but it never
   hampered his quick______
   (1) finalisation   (2) dealing
   (3) action   (4) decision

3. He was not willing to accept the ______
   (1) wrong   (2) blame
   (3) fault   (4) sorry

4. The Government's economic policy includes
   certain projects for ______ the living conditions of
   the poor.
   (1) bettering   (2) harmonizing
   (3) manipulating   (4) doing away with

5. The reward is a ______ of her service to mankind.
   (1) momento   (2) memorial
   (3) recognition   (4) witness

Exercise – 10

Directions for questions 1 to 5: Complete the following
sentences using the words given in the options:

1. The little girl ______ for the light switch in the dark.
   (1) groped   (2) grappled
   (3) gripped   (4) groveled

2. The summit meeting provided him the much
   ______ shot in the arm.
   (1) required   (2) desired
   (3) needed   (4) urgent

3. If you drink too much, it will ______ your
   judgement
   (1) obstruct   (2) impede
   (3) impair   (4) hinder

4. The Government should provide attractive tax
   ______ to create the market for quality goods.
   (1) controls
   (2) incentives
   (3) revenues
   (4) structures

5. Each cause conditions a ______ effect and there
   can be no cause without effect.
   (1) specific
   (2) relevant
   (3) requisite
   (4) proper

Exercise – 11

Directions for questions 1 to 5: Complete the following sentences using the words given in the options:

1. The doctor was overcome with _______ when he came to know that the patient had died due to negligence on his part.
   (1) conscience   (2) remorse
   (3) humiliation   (4) emotion

2. Although I have been interested in photography, yet I am only a/an_______
   (1) novice   (2) amateur
   (3) apprentice   (4) unprofessional

3. You will have to face some practical problems while _________ the expenses of the current month.
   (1) prosecuting   (2) projecting
   (3) prescribing   (4) proscribing

4. There are various hobbies for us to _______ in our leisure hours.
   (1) pursue   (2) follow
   (3) absorb   (4) contribute

5. Every Shakespearean here has an integral _______ in his character.
   (1) fault   (2) defeat
   (3) flaw   (4) weakness

Exercise – 12

Directions for questions 1 to 5: Complete the following sentences using the words given in the options:

1. Statistics are _______ as a means of determining public opinion.
   (1) unreliable   (2) dubious
   (3) uncertain   (4) phoney

2. He was able to _______ his small income by working in hotel at night.
   (1) amplify   (2) supplement
   (3) expand   (4) multiply

3. The solution to the problem _______ me.
   (1) outgrew
   (2) outraged
   (3) evaded
   (4) undermined

4. The test _______ no previous knowledge of the subject as any graduate is expected to complete it successfully.
   (1) concerns
   (2) presupposes
   (3) assumes
   (4) necessitates

5. The clever politician _______ his way to the ministerial position in a short time.
   (1) faked   (2) wangled
   (3) scaled   (4) moved

Exercise – 13

Directions for questions 1 to 5: Complete the following sentences using the words given in the options:

1. The rain water that does not flow to the rivers _______ beneath the soil to form underground water.
   (1) flowers   (2) Penetrates
   (3) seeps   (4) percolates

2. The river overflowed its _______ and flooded the area.
   (1) banks   (2) limits
   (3) edges   (4) fronts

3. Questions will be answered by a _______ of experts
   (1) group   (2) staff
   (3) band   (4) Panel

4. Being well qualified, he has good _______ in the profession.
   (1) prospectus   (2) perspectives
   (3) prospects   (4) prospectives

5. The _______ animal was on the look out for food.
   (1) uncivilized   (2) wild
   (3) primitive   (4) savage

Exercise – 14

Directions for questions 1 to 5: Complete the following sentences using the words given in the options:

1. The doctor gave the women a _______ to calm her down.
   (1) tonic   (2) sedative
   (3) antiseptic   (4) antidote

2. He was extremely _______ ; he would believe anything you told him.
   (1) believable   (2) gullible
   (3) affable   (4) reliable

3. Several of our players were injured, so our losing the match was almost _______
   (1) necessary   (2) indispensable
   (3) inevitable   (4) inexcusable

4. The naked human eye cannot _______ minute flaws in complicated mechanisms.
   (1) understand   (2) detect
   (3) comprehend   (4) visualize

5. There could have been a war on it, but in the end reason _______
   (1) persisted   (2) counted
   (3) Prevailed   (4) survived

Exercise – 15

Directions for questions 1 to 5: Complete the following sentences using the words given in the options:

1. The plant has been growing steadily, but of late its growth has_______
   (1) shortened   (2) thwarted
   (3) retarded   (4) hastened

2. Ambition is one of those _______ which is never satisfied.
   (1) needs   (2) ideas
   (3) passions   (4) fancies

3. The prisoner was _______ to answering any of my questions.
   (1) inverse   (2) adverse
   (3) reverse   (4) averse

4. Dying is a very _______ dreary affair.
   (1) boring   (2) dull
   (3) monotonous   (4) drab

5. The new industrial policy is a result of the confidence the government has in the _______ of the Indian industry.
   (1) status
   (2) Profitability
   (3) existence
   (4) maturity

Exercise – 16

Directions for questions 1 to 5: Complete the following sentences using the words given in the options:

1. The senior officials of the Ministry charged the secretary with gross_______of duty and so suspended him.
   (1) disregard
   (2) negligence
   (3) laxity
   (4) dishonesty

2. The resulting of his probing was _______evidence all pointing to a serious treachery.
   (1) incriminating   (2) dangerous
   (3) frivolous   (4) intimidatory

3. His parents did not pay_______attention to his studies.
   (1) suitable   (2) just
   (3) remarkable   (4) proper

4. The top ranking student _______ his success in his studies to his headmaster's guidance.
   (1) accounts   (2) refers
   (3) attributes   (4) claims

5. I do not _______ with the views expressed in your newspaper.
   (1) confirm   (2) coincide
   (3) compromise   (4) concur

Exercise – 17

Directions for questions 1 to 5: Complete the following sentences using the words given in the options:

1. The communalist represents the _______ of everything noble that we have inherited from our culture and history.
   (1) antagonism   (2) immorality
   (3) antidote   (4) antithesis

2. Despite her please, the mistress did not _______ to her request.
   (1) accede   (2) convince
   (3) favour   (4) approve

3. He could not stay here longer because he was not _______ to such environment.
   (1) adept   (2) addicted
   (3) accustomed   (4) conducive

4. He is greatly admired for his _________ behaviour.
(1) decrepit   (2) decorative
(3) decadent   (4) decorous

5. His moral decadence was marked by his _______ from the ways of integrity and honesty.
(1) declivity   (2) departure
(3) obsession   (4) opprobrium

Exercise – 18

Directions for questions 1 to 5: Complete the following sentences using the words given in the options:

1. The government should crush with a heavy hand all the gangs of terrorists and foil their _______design against their integrity of our nation.
(1) foolish   (2) nefarious
(3) ugly   (4) undesirable

2. One_______and you know who among them is the culprit.
(1) gaze   (2) peep
(3) look   (4) sight

3. The speaker_______ the scope of his paper on 'work ethic' at the outset
(1) defined   (2) delineated
(3) ascribed   (4) declined

4. The criminal seems to have acted in _______ with three others.
(1) collision   (2) collusion
(3) cohesion   (4) coalition

5. He _______ a lot over the pros and cons of the issue but could arrive at no fruitful result.
(1) envisioned   (2) contemplated
(3) embodied   (4) envisaged

Exercise – 19

Directions for questions 1 to 5: Complete the following sentences using the words given in the options:

1. If an indelible ink is used, this will not be_______
(1) observed   (2) obligated
(3) obliterated   (4) obviated

2. The custom officers _______ gold worth Rs.1 crore from the smugglers.
(1) snatched   (2) captured
(3) mobbed   (4) confiscated

3. The accused _______ to answer any questions in the absence of his lawyer.
(1) declined   (2) denied
(3) denounced   (4) detested

4. On account of the dearth of grass on the arid plains the cattle became_______
(1) jubiliant   (2) emaciated
(3) Flippant   (4) agitated

5. The new science teacher _______a great respect from his students.
(1) observed   (2) acquired
(3) attained   (4) commanded

Exercise – 20

Directions for questions 1 to 5: Complete the following sentences using the words given in the options:

1. His_______helped him rise so high in life.
(1) cleverness   (2) wisdom
(3) cunningness   (4) genius

2. The sound of the running water of the stream had a pleasantly_______effect on me.
(1) sonorous   (2) amusing
(3) loud   (4) somnolent

3. The speaker painted a _______picture of hunger in parts of India.
(1) poignant   (2) passionate
(3) parsimonious   (4) chimerical.

4. The_______statues resembled ludicrous figures found in ancient monuments.
(1) grotesque   (2) impressive
(3) gregarious   (4) magnificient

5. Some regions of our country still remain _________ to the average man.
(1) impenetrable   (2) impermeable
(3) inaccessible   (4) impossible

Let us learn the literal meanings of the word, analogy, it means :

(a) Partial similarity between two things that are compared.

Example: She drew an analogy between a human heart and a pump.

(b) Process of reasoning based on such similarity.

Example: My theory applies to you and by analogy to others like you.

(c) Way in which words change their form because of their similarity to other words.

Analogy is an interesting variation of the vocabulary question. Bear in mind that questions on analogy are very often set in intelligent tests. Analogy tests your understanding of word meanings as well as your ability to grasp relationships between words and ideas. It judges the ability to think lucidly and to sidestep confusion.

An analogy is the relationship of one word with another. The two words in the question pair bear a certain relation with each other. Your task is to decipher that relationship. For example, in FLOCK: SHEEP, the relation is that a flock comprises of many sheep.

Similarly in MOTHER : DAUGHTER the relation is quite evident that a daughter is the young one of the mother. Four pairs of answer choices will follow the Question Pair. Your task is to select that choice which bears a similar relation to the Question Pair.

For example, choose the answer which represents a similar relationship as in the question.

FLOCK:SHEEP

a.	Herd	:	Men
b.	Bouquet	:	Flowers
c.	Cackle	:	Geese
d.	Book	:	Library

Thus, the right answer is 'c', as both signify a Group and Individual relationship.

The point to be noted here is that option 'e' would have also been right if the order was in the reverse.

Steps to attempt such questions

The following are the two important steps to success in solving analogy questions:

Step one: Determine the relationship between the two words in the Question Pair.

Step two: Find the same relationship among the choices which follows the first two words.

The relationship between words in the Question Pair and the Answer Pair has to be the same, and even the order has to be right.

After you gauge the relation between the words, place the two words in a sentence. Eg., Sheep : Flock.

Many sheep make a flock or flock is a collection of sheep.

Use your knowledge of prefixes and roots to decode the meaning of the word that you are not aware of.

The most important tip to get your analogies right is to have a good vocabulary, so start working on your word power.

The *type of relationship* may vary, so while attempting such questions the first step is to identify the type of relationship, which can be any one of the following :

1. ***Action Object Relationship***

   Example : Shoot is to Gun as Eat is to...........

   | A. Hunger | B. Thirst |
   | C. Dinner | D. Fruit |

Ans. D:

The relationship between the given words is that 'shoot' is the action and 'Gun' is the specified object of action. Similarly 'eat' is the action and 'fruit' is the specified object.

2. ***Association Relationship***

   Example : Glamour is to Stardom as Colour is to........

   | A. Rainbow | B. Shades |
   | C. Art | D. Painting |

Ans. D:

As glamour is associated with stardom so is colour with painting.

3. ***Antonym Relationship***

   Example : INTROVERT : EXTROVERT

   A. ANGLE : TANGENT
   B. EXTREME : INTERIM
   C. AGAINST : FAVOUR
   D. ACTION : LAW

Ans. C:

The related words are opposite in meaning.

4. ***Cause and Effect Relationship***
   Example : INJURY : PAIN
   A. GRADES : MERIT
   B. THUNDER : LIGHTENING
   C. ROTATE : CHURNING
   D. MATTER : LABOUR

Ans. B:

Injury is the cause of pain and so is thunder the cause of lightening.

5. ***Degree Relationship***
   Example : Tepid is to Hot as..... is Wail.
   A. Sob   B. Shout
   C. Smile   D. Calm

Ans. A:

Tepid is less hot and so also the lower degree of wail is sob.

6. ***Grammatical Relationship***
   Example : Clever is to Beautiful as Sour is to.......
   A. Lemon   B. Cunning
   C. Loathing   D. Taste

Ans. B:

The related words are Adjectives.

7. ***Obvious Relationship***
   Example : Mt. EVEREST : NEPAL
   A. MEXICO : SOUTH AMERICA
   B. K2 : CHINA
   C. BIG BEN : RUSSIA
   D. AHMEDABAD : GUJARAT

Ans. D:

Mt. Everest is in Nepal and so Ahmedabad is in Gujarat.

8. ***Part Whole Relationship***
   Example : MAN : MAMMAL
   A. HAIL : SNOW
   B. NATIVE : INHABITANT
   C. OFFSPRING : FAMILY
   D. LIBERTY : LITERATE

Ans. C:

Man is a part of the whole species of mammal so is an offspring of the whole family.

9. ***Purpose Relationship***
   Example : INSTITUTION : EDUCATION
   A. WAR : PEACE
   B. HEALTH : OBESITY
   C. MEDICATION : RECUPERATION
   D. BUILDING : URBANISM

Ans. C:

The purpose of institutions is to impart education and the purpose of medications is quick recuperation (recovery).

10. ***Sequence Relationship***
    Example : .... is to Dusk as Summer is to Monsoon.
    A. Evening   B. Dawn
    C. Night   D. Noon

Ans. A:

Summer is immediately followed by monsoon (rainy season) and evening is immediately followed by dusk.

11. ***Synonym Relationship***
    Example : INDENT : REQUEST
    A. REPLICA : CHEAT   B. DOLE : ALMS
    C. DISMAL : DUNCE   D. EXACT : CHECK

Ans. B: The related words have the same meaning.

12. ***Volume Relationship***
    Example : GALLONS : SWIMMING POOL.
    A. SPECTATORS : AUDITORIUM
    B. CURRENCY : SHARES
    C. DUST : MOUNTAIN
    D. BOOKS : CATALOGUE

Ans. A:

Gallons of water is needed to fill a swimming pool and large number of spectators can be admitted into a auditorium.

Exercise

Analogy Exercise-1

Directions for questions 1 to 50: Select the pair of words which are related in the same way as the words in bold type are related to each other.

1. APPLAUD : APPROVAL
   - (1) crucify : cross
   - (2) sneer : contempt
   - (3) divulge : secret
   - (4) harbour : thought

2. SNIFF : NOSE
   - (1) chorus : singer
   - (2) sneeze : irritation
   - (3) behold : eyes
   - (4) speak : tongue

3. AVIARY : BIRDS
   - (1) scales : reptiles
   - (2) vivipary : mammals
   - (3) binary fission : virus
   - (4) water : amphibians

4. FRATERNITY : MEN
   - (1) convent : nuns
   - (2) reformatory : convicts
   - (3) cathedral : father
   - (4) sorority : women

5. ALLERGIC : ALLERGY
   - (1) microbes : disease
   - (2) carcinogenic : cancer
   - (3) spark : blaze
   - (4) archipelago : islands

6. DILATE : CONTRACT
   - (1) hock : pawn
   - (2) wax : wane
   - (3) contaminate : spread
   - (4) intrude : disturb

7. ANACHRONOUS : TIME
   - (1) Incongruous : place
   - (2) antiquated : old
   - (2) synergy : energy
   - (4) ecosystem : environment

8. OCTOPUS : MOLLUSCA
   - (1) platypus : mammal
   - (2) starfish : cordate
   - (3) fawn : doe
   - (4) regiment : soldier

9. OBSTETRICS : PREGNANCY
   - (1) pediatrics : infants
   - (2) informatics : software
   - (3) aphrodisiac : vitality
   - (4) astronaut : spaceship

10. SURGEON : SCALPEL
    - (1) musician : instrument
    - (2) carpenter : cabinet
    - (3) sculptor : chisel
    - (4) tailor : cloth

11. FELINE : CAT
    - (1) tentacles : hydra
    - (2) boving : donkey
    - (3) equine : horse
    - (4) camouflage : chameleon

12. EMBARRASS : HUMILIATE
    - (1) enquire : ask
    - (2) embezzle : peculate
    - (3) gamble : investment
    - (4) annoy : exasperate

13. SYMPHONY : MUSIC
    - (1) mural : painting
    - (2) ode : prose
    - (3) preface : book
    - (4) editorial : journal

14. SAVAGE : BARBARIC
    - (1) lucid : turbid
    - (2) sallow : yellowish
    - (3) prismatic : colourful
    - (4) venomous : virulent

15. HELMET : HEAD
    - (1) thimble : finger
    - (2) bottle : cap
    - (3) bayonet : rifle
    - (4) ship : mast

16. TOMAHAWK : RED INDIANS
    (1) wheel : Mayans
    (2) chariot : Indus people
    (3) boomerang : Australian aborigines
    (4) rocket : Russians

17. WAIL : DISTRESS
    (1) blush : shame
    (2) manicure : nail
    (3) laugh : joke
    (4) mortgage : possession

18. VACCINATION : DISEASE
    (1) civil servant : furlough
    (2) furnace : heat
    (3) fortification : enemy
    (4) vacation : tourist

19. DIPSOMANIA : ALCOHOL
    (1) acromania : theft
    (2) pyromania : fire
    (3) kleptomania : height
    (4) monomania : multitude

20. PRESCIENCE : PREDICTION
    (1) catcall : derision
    (2) clairvoyant : seance
    (3) hospitality : friend
    (4) telepathy : communication

21. ECSTASY : PLEASURE
    (1) hatred : affection
    (2) joy : grief
    (3) rage : anger
    (4) mumble : speak

22. KNOWLEDGE : IGNORANCE
    (1) cure : health
    (2) conceal : hide
    (3) breath : suffocation
    (4) construction : war

23. BEAR : HIBERNATION
    (1) man : immigration
    (2) bird : migration
    (3) food : adulteration
    (4) frog : aestivation

24. IMPLICATE : INCRIMINATE
    (1) involvement : malpractice
    (2) exonerate : acquit
    (3) embezzlement : charge
    (4) perjury : fraud

25. NECROMANCY : GHOSTS
    (1) romance : stories
    (2) magic : amulets
    (3) alchemy : gold
    (4) sorcery : spirits

26. VERBOSE : WORDS
    (1) drive : roads
    (2) solicitous : concern
    (3) nocturnal : awake
    (4) noxious : salubrious

27. EULOGY : BLAME
    (1) felony : crime
    (2) acquit : convict
    (3) chivalry : naivette
    (4) princely : imperial

28. CANTO : POEM
    (1) lyrics : song
    (2) stanza : play
    (3) chapter : book
    (4) cotton : thread

29. BARK : TREE
    (1) leaves : tree
    (2) bark : dog
    (3) hooves : horses
    (4) scales : fish

30. GLAUCOMA : EYE
    (1) tuberculosis : kidneys
    (2) cirrhosis : liver
    (3) cochlea : ear
    (4) bronchitis : heart

31. SCHIZOPHRENIA : PERSONALITY
    (1) hippomania : hippos
    (2) flaccid : weak
    (3) amnesia : memory
    (4) megalomania : work

32. ARTICULATE : UNDERSTANDABLE
    (1) belligerent : pacify
    (2) garrulous : loquacious
    (3) baroque : modern
    (4) pugnacious : submissive

33. FOX : CUB
    (1) lion : cub
    (2) ox : buffalo
    (3) mare : stallion
    (4) whale : dolphin

Verbal Ability / Vocabulary

34. SELF-DENIAL : ASCETIC
    (1) remission : prodigy
    (2) solitude : hermit
    (3) frugality : spend - thrift
    (4) parochial : catholic

35. KLEPTOMANIA : STEALING
    (1) egomania : oneself
    (2) ergomania : work
    (3) ablutomania : riches
    (4) hedomania : power

36. PRECOCIOUS : RETARDED
    (1) alcazar : palace
    (2) pompous : modesty
    (3) coercion : intimidate
    (4) dotage : senility

37. LEGISLATOR : LAW
    (1) research : student
    (2) management : novice
    (3) sports : youth
    (4) publisher : book

38. MIRTH : LAUGH
    (1) joy : cheer
    (2) creep : crawl
    (3) cacophony : sound
    (4) placate : antagonise

39. LOATHE : TRAITOR
    (1) lathe : iron
    (2) vicarious : actor
    (3) eulogy : hero
    (4) pity : king

40. SUCCESS : ELATION
    (a) gnome : gnarl
    (2) humor : joy
    (3) debacle : dejection
    (4) fear : prejudice

41. APOCRYPHAL : DOUBTFUL
    (1) orthodox : hedonist
    (2) eccentric : odd
    (3) curry : gullible
    (4) maladroit : deceitful

42. TYRO : DEXTEROUS
    (1) neophyte : amateur
    (2) craven : coward

    (3) novice : professional
    (4) yellow : red

43. SEMANTICS : LANGUAGE
    (1) pathology : virus
    (2) semiotics : herbs
    (3) dermatologist : disease
    (4) tautology : tight

44. PHLEGMATIC : PERTURBED
    (1) pithy : verbose
    (2) polygamous : polygymist
    (3) zenith : pinnacle
    (4) quotidian : commonplace

45. MODICUM : ABUNDANCE
    (1) meagre : scarce
    (2) hirsute : hairy
    (3) sham : truth
    (4) pusillanimous : coward

46. WAREHOUSE : STORAGE
    (1) assembly : prayer
    (2) chapel : prayer
    (3) bunker : sleep
    (4) lampoon : ridicule

47. RECLUSE : GREGARIOUS
    (1) coward : yellow
    (2) scholar : erudite
    (3) sycophant : flattery
    (4) ascetic : hedonistic

48. SHELL : NUT
    (1) ribs : lungs
    (2) fruit : flower
    (3) seed : leaves
    (4) bullet : gun

49. BANISH : APOSTATE
    (1) money : pickpocket
    (2) extol : traitor
    (3) welcome : ally
    (4) incarcerate : democrat

50. CORPOREAL : SPIRITUAL
    (1) narcissist : hate
    (2) sergeant : soldier
    (3) chloleric : serene
    (4) commissioner : inspector

Analogy Exercise-2

Directions for questions 1 to 50: Select the pair of words which are related in the same way as the words in bold type are related to each other.

1. CUPIDITY : GENEROSITY
   (1) statistics : number
   (2) diffidence : boldness
   (3) stampede : movement
   (4) splurge : money

2. CUB : BEAR
   (1) piano : orchestra
   (2) puppy : dog
   (3) cat : kitten
   (4) eagle : predator

3. OXYGEN : COMBUSTION
   (1) light : photosynthesis
   (2) iron : rust
   (3) turret : castle
   (4) prologue : play

4. STOIC : PASSION
   (1) expert : skill
   (2) fanatic : devotion
   (3) eunuch : guard
   (4) celibate : coitus

5. DEHUSK : GRAIN
   (1) peel : fruit
   (2) defrost : ice
   (3) deflower : sex
   (4) defoliate : leaf

6. PUNY : MAMMOTH
   (1) large:untidy
   (2) beautiful:small
   (3) stable:unstable
   (4) compact:clumsy

7. RESEARCH PAPER : JOURNAL
   (1) epilogue : prologue
   (2) article : newspaper
   (3) photograph : magazine
   (4) documentary : film

8. RACKET : TENNIS
   (1) pawn : chess   (2) tee : ball
   (3) jockey : horse   (4) club : golf

9. FROG : CROAK
   (1) elephant : trumpet
   (2) lion : roar
   (3) scorpion : dance
   (4) ambrosia : god

10. VIRUS : INFLUENZA
    (1) bacillus : curd
    (2) mosquito : malaria
    (2) marijuana : cannabis
    (4) mercury : marasmus

11. DOVE : PEACE
    (1) white flag : truce
    (2) whisper : prayer
    (3) tear : eyes
    (4) talk : gossip

12. BLOOMERS : DRESS
    (1) guppies : fish
    (2) nicotine : tabacco
    (3) marcel : hairstyle
    (4) silhouette : outline

13. PREFACE : BOOK
    (1) introduction : stranger
    (2) valediction : play
    (3) preamble : constitution
    (4) ragging : freshers

14. PER-SEC : DISTANCE
    (1) pascal : energy
    (2) decibel : sound
    (3) parking : vehicle
    (4) luminosity : light

15. DOCTOR : HOSPITAL
    (1) sports fan : stadium
    (2) cow : farm
    (3) professor : college
    (4) criminal : jail

16. ARGUMENT : DEBATE
    (1) Violence : Peace
    (2) Compete : Contest
    (3) Opponent : Challenge
    (4) Abuse : Scold

17. SPASMODIC : FITFUL
    (1) somnolent : drowsy
    (2) callous : hardy
    (3) sloppy : careless
    (4) callow : immature

18. RUNG : LADDER
     (1) plankton : pond
     (2) axle : wheel
     (3) vertebra : backbone
     (4) chair : theatre

19. TENET : THEOLOGIAN
     (1) predecessor : heir
     (2) hypothesis : researcher
     (3) recluse : rivalry
     (4) arrogance : persecution

20. ALLERGEN : ALLERGY
     (1) microbes : disease
     (2) carcinogenic : cancer
     (3) spark : blaze
     (4) archipelago : islands

21. TEPID : TORRID
     (1) second : minutes
     (2) walk : strut
     (3) yelp : cry
     (4) whisper : shout

22. DALMATIAN : DOG
     (1) oriole : bird
     (2) horse : pony
     (3) shark : great white
     (4) ant : insect

23. BIRD : NEST
     (1) dog : kennel
     (2) squirrel : tree
     (3) beaver : dam
     (4) cat : litter box

24. MALLEABLE : MOULDED
     (1) servile : masterly
     (2) denture : dentist
     (3) knead : dough
     (4) gullible : fooled

25. ROAR : ENGINE
     (1) Whisper : Noise
     (2) Echo : Sound
     (3) Crack : Wall
     (4) Tinkle : Bell

26. PERJURY : OATH
     (1) plagiarism : authority
     (2) embezzlement : trust
     (3) disrespect : age
     (4) testimony : court

27. PRIDE : LIONS
     (1) gaggle : geese
     (2) honour : thieves
     (3) Snarl : wolves
     (4) arrogance : kings

28. DEADBEAT : PAY
     (1) killjoy : lament
     (2) spoilsport : refrain
     (3) daredevil : risk
     (4) diehard : quit

29. MYTH : LEGENDARY
     (1) sermon : lengthy
     (2) anecdote : witty
     (3) fable : didactic
     (4) epic : comic

30. DRUDGERY : IRKSOME
     (1) encumbrance : burdensome
     (2) journey : wearisome
     (3) ambivalence : suspicious
     (4) compliance : forced

31. NAÏVE : INGENUE
     (1) ordinary : genius
     (2) venerable : celebrity
     (3) urbane : sophisticate
     (4) crafty : artisan

32. DWELL : DENIZEN
     (1) shun : outcast
     (2) inherit : heir
     (3) squander : miser
     (4) obey : autocrat

33. HACKNEYED : ORIGINAL
     (1) mature : juvenile
     (2) trite : morbid
     (3) withdrawn : reserved
     (4) evasive : elusive

34. ANNOTATE : TEXT
     (1) enact : law
     (2) prescribe : medication
     (3) caption : photograph
     (4) abridge : novel

35. FOX : CUNNING
     (1) dog : playful
     (2) hyena : amusing
     (3) beaver : industrious
     (4) vixen : cute

36. DESCRY : DISTANT
    (1) mourn : lost
    (2) whisper : muted
    (3) discern : subtle
    (4) destroy : flagrant

37. DETRITUS : GLACIER
    (1) thaw : snowfall
    (2) snow : icecap
    (3) silt : river
    (4) range : mountain

38. IMPROMPTU : REHEARSAL
    (1) practiced : technique
    (2) makeshift : whim
    (3) offhand : premeditation
    (4) glib : fluency

39. DIDACTIC : TEACH
    (1) sophomoric : learn
    (2) satiric : mock
    (3) reticent : complain
    (4) chaotic : rule

40. HERMIT : GREGARIOUS
    (1) miser : penurious
    (2) ascetic : hedonistic
    (3) coward : pusillanimous
    (4) scholar : literate

41. SCALES : JUSTICE
    (1) weights : measures
    (2) laws : courts
    (3) torch : liberty
    (4) laurel : peace

42. GULLIBLE : DUPED
    (1) credible : cheated
    (2) careful : cautioned
    (3) malleable : moulded
    (4) myopic : misled

43. MUSTER : CREW
    (1) convene : committee
    (2) demobilise : troops
    (3) dominate : opposition
    (4) cheer : team

44. AUGER : CARPENTER
    (1) studio : sculptor
    (2) awl : cobbler
    (3) seam : seamstress
    (4) cement : mason

45. SNICKER : DISRESPECT
    (1) whimper : impatience
    (2) chortle : glee
    (3) frown : indifference
    (4) sneer : detachment

46. WOOL : ACRYLIC
    (1) Rayon : Silk
    (2) Winter : Spring
    (3) Cotton : Terylene
    (4) Rubber : Plastic

47. BOUQUET : FLOWER
    (1) Skin : Body
    (2) Chain : Link
    (3) Page : Book
    (4) Product : Factory

48. GERM : DISEASE
    (1) Man : Woman
    (2) War : Destruction
    (3) Doctor : Medicine
    (4) Owner : Shop

49. IGNOMINY : DISLOYALTY
    (1) Fame : Heroism
    (2) Derelict : Fool
    (3) Death : Victory
    (4) Martyr : Man

50. GAZELLE : SWIFT
    (1) Horse : Slow
    (2) Swan : Graceful
    (3) Lion : Roar
    (4) Lamb : Bleat

Verbal Ability / Vocabulary

Critical Reasoning

5

In Critical Reasoning, you are given an argument and you have to answer a question based on it.

Critical Reasoning can be placed more comfortably in the Reading Comprehension family than the Logic family. Yet, it helps to understand key grammatical terms and to have a sound command over vocabulary to avoid misinterpretation. Key words in the argument such as **because**, **for**, and **since** indicate that a statement of evidence is about to follow. Similarly, words such as **therefore**, **hence**, **thus**, **consequently** signal a conclusion point.

Let us take a look at the types of questions which are generally tested.

Conclusion

Let us take a look at the following example.

Students who go on trips to handicraft exhibitions find the concept of craftwork very abstract and confounding. This is because they have not been exposed to the history and evolution of craft forms in their school curriculum.

The conclusion that the author arrives at is:

a. students who have not been exposed to the history of craftwork would not be able to appreciate handicraft items
b. students are no longer interested in craftwork due to their obsession with high-tech gadgets
c. students have no interest in developing a taste for intricacies of art
d. students should be taken for more exhibitions on fine arts

In this question, we have to link related factors to arrive at a conclusion. What is the answer here? (b) and (c) are unlikely answers as we cannot judge likes and dislikes of students based on the information in the passage. (d) appears aimless as the students would be just as blank on craft, no matter how many exhibitions they are taken to. Hence, (a) is the answer as it relates how an ignorance on the history of craftwork leads to a lack of understanding of the work itself.

Assumption

The second type of 'find' question is to look for the assumption.

Whenever I wear my John Bull shirt, people smile at me. So I must wear my John Bull shirt everyday.

The **causal** assumption here is that

a. John Bull shirts are a status symbol of the elite

b. the author is a great fan of John Bull and is flaunting his idol around
c. people like the author because of his John Bull shirt
d. the author has only one shirt in his wardrobe

Let us explore this question and the logic behind it. What do people like? The author or his shirt? Or is it the Pepe jeans that the author normally wears along with the shirt? What if they liked the author's feel-good persona when he wears the John Bull shirt and did not even know whether he was wearing a John Bull shirt, or a John Bear shirt?

What do you think the answer is? (a) talks about a status symbol. So what? (b) has little relevance to the passage. (d) is too pathetic to be a plausible answer. Hence, (c) is the answer. The author assumes that the reason behind the people's admiration is the John Bull shirt.

An assumption is a base for the validity of an argument. If an assumption fails, the whole argument is rendered void.

Strengthen/Weaken the Argument

We'll take an example to test the 'strengthen' variety.

A marketing drive had been undertaken 10 years ago in Connecticut to switch women to smoke cigarettes instead of having tea as a stimulant. The move had failed miserably. Recent efforts, though, have again been made to switch women to adopting a whole range of cigarettes exclusively for women. It is unlikely that this effort is going to reap results.

The above argument would be strengthened if which of the following was true?

a. Women would prefer cigarettes that are sleek in appearance and add to their charisma
b. The previous attempt was made under the same marketing plan and prevalent conditions as the present
c. Women smoking cigarettes is a rare sight lest they be mistaken for loose women
d. A cup of tea is more expensive than a cigarette

In this argument, women's preferences as in (a) would be useless if they do not take to cigarettes at all. (c) talks about a hindering factor, but it fails to explain the technical failure of the marketing plan. Surely, market research would have taken this factor into account. Hence, (b) is the answer that explains the failure of the plan 10 years ago as a precedent for the impending failure.

We will now study an example of the 'weaken' kind. Here goes . . .

The recent success of Avon Products in the Chinese market proves how much influence Avon's CEO, Andrea Jung, can exert over her country of origin. The recent spate of sales has contributed hugely to the sales revenue of the company.

A major flaw that could weaken the above argument is that

   a. Andrea Jung is a shrewd businesswoman
   b. Andrea Jung negotiated well with the Chinese Government and appealed to their nationalistic sense
   c. the passage assumes that Andrea Jung is the only factor that contributed to the corporate's success in China
   d. Avon is the number one cosmetic seller in China

(a) and (d) talks about the existing factors regarding Andrea's personality and Avon's status, these, per se, cannot weaken the argument. They are just the state of affairs. (b) actually strengthens the passage. Hence, it's (c) that is the answer. Is Andrea the only factor? It could just as well be true that the Chinese authorities had just lifted a ban on cosmetic products from China resulting in a sales boom.

Inference

Let's take an example first.

It is possible to induce a measure of compassion in children from elite backgrounds if they are allowed to interact with children from underprivileged backgrounds. This way, they would be able to identify and empathize with deprived children instead of virtually dismissing them as victims of fate.

It can be inferred from the above that

   a. children born into the upper class can identify with children from rural backgrounds
   b. it is impossible to bridge the gap between the rich and the poor
   c. underprivileged children can look forward to better days
   d. children who are born into the upper class routinely despise and abhor street children

Let's study these choices. (a) cannot be true because that is exactly the vision that the author wishes to realize. (b) negates the wishes of the author. (c) would come true if the author's plans are carried out. As of now, it is just wishful thinking, not an inference. The children can see the reality, they do not know how to cope with it. Hence, (d) is the best answer. The words 'routinely despise' are more in agreement with the words in the question 'virtually dismiss them'.

Mimic the Reasoning

Let's check out this example.

Examination toppers do not study for more than 12 hours a day. If you study for more than 12 hours, you are not a topper.

Which of the choices given below has the same style of reasoning adopted in the question?

   a. Olympic athletes practise for more than 10 hr in a day. So they can always win their races.
   b. Cars always take more than 3 min to start. If this starts in less than 3 min, it is not a car.
   c. He takes 8 hr to go through his swimming routine. He is bound to achieve excellent results.
   d. She practises ballet for only 6 hr. But to be world-class, one must practise for 9 hr.

In this question, we have a 'more then ... less than' kind of relation. (a) and (c) do not share this relationship and thus fail. (d) does not employ the relation to qualify the ballet dancer. Hence, (b) is the answer that qualifies the object as 'not a car' because of the 'less than' criterion.

In this type of question, we have to clearly understand the inter-relations, to apply the criteria to all the choices and make a quick match.

Resolve the Paradox

Let us understand this with an example.

In 1985, Panam reported an increase in total number of passengers it carried from the year before, but a decrease in total revenues — even though prices for the tickets on all routes remained unchanged during the two years under consideration.

Which of the following choices best helps to reconcile the apparent paradox in the question?

   a. Passengers travelled shorter (and thus less expensive) distances in 1985, thus increasing total revenue
   b. Passengers travelled longer (and thus less expensive) distances in 1985, thus decreasing total revenue
   c. Passengers travelled shorter (and thus more expensive) distances in 1985, thus decreasing total revenue
   d. Passengers travelled shorter (and thus less expensive) distances in 1985, thus decreasing total revenue

How do you do this one? We are given in the question that the revenues decreased, though the number of passengers increased. This can happen only in case of (d). If the total distance travelled is less, then it has offset the advantage of having a higher number of passengers and thus, the total revenues were hit.

Practice Exercise - Critical Reasoning

Number of questions : 50   **Time :** 40 mins

Direction for questions 1 to 6: Read the argument given in the following questions and mark the appropriate answer.

1. Plato said that art represents 'general truths' about human nature. Our city councilman is arguing in favour of the artistry — a giant mural in front of a jeep dealership, portraying a variety of four-wheel-drive vehicles. He cites Plato's conception of art as his support.

   The passage above raises which of the following questions?
   (1) Can a city councilman understand Plato?
   (2) Which general truths about human nature does a four-wheel-drive mural not represent?
   (3) Could Plato have predicted a modern society filled with sophisticated machines?
   (4) To what extent are four-wheel-drive vehicles representative of a general advance in modern technology?

2. Speaker 1: The holy passion of friendship is so sweet and steady and loyal and enduring a nature that it will last through a whole lifetime.
   Speaker 2: If not asked to lend money.

   The two speakers represent which of the following contrasting attitudes?
   (1) Faith and despair
   (2) Idealism and cynicism
   (3) Idealism
   (4) Socialism and capitalism

3. In 1945, a new industrial code was established to fix a minimum wage of quarter of a pound an hour in the UK. Industrial workers hailed this pronouncement as a blessing.

   What does this statement imply?
   (1) You can fool some of the people some of the time
   (2) Don't count your chicken before they hatch
   (3) Times change
   (4) There's a sucker born every minute

4. Unfortunately, only 12 per cent of the driving public use regular seat belts. Automatic restraints are the answer, and the quicker they are implemented, the sooner highways deaths will be reduced.

   The author's conclusion is based upon which of the following assumptions?
   (1) Only 12 per cent of the driving public care about passengers' lives
   (2) The use of restraints reduces highway deaths
   (3) Regular seat belts are inadequate safety devices
   (4) It is unfortunate that 88 per cent of the driving public does not use regular seat belts

5. In the past, to run for one's country in the Olympics was the ultimate achievement of any athlete. Nowadays an athlete's motives are more and more influenced by financial gain and consequently we do not see our best athletes in the Olympics, which is still only for amateurs.

   Which of the following will most weaken the above conclusion?
   (1) The publicity and fame that can be achieved by competing in the Olympics makes athletes more 'marketable' by agents and potential sponsors, while allowing the athletes to retain their amateur status.
   (2) Winning a race is not as important as participating.
   (3) There is a widely held belief that our best Olympic athletes already receive enough in terms of promotion and sponsorship.
   (4) It has been suggested that professional athletes should be allowed to compete in the games.

6. The function of a food technologist in a large marketing chain of food stores is to ensure that all foodstuffs which are offered for sale in various retail outlets meet certain standard criteria for non-perishability, freshness and fitness for human consumption.

It is the technologist's job to visit the premises of suppliers and food producers (factory or farm), inspect the facilities and report thereon. His responsibility also includes receiving new products from local and foreign suppliers and performing exhaustive quality control testing on them. Finally, he should carry out surprise spot-checks on goods held in the marketing chain's own warehouses and stores.

What conclusion can best be drawn from the preceding paragraph?
(1) A university degree in food technology is a necessary and sufficient condition for becoming a food technologist
(2) Imported products as well as home-produced goods, must be rigorously tested
(3) The food technologist stands between the unhygienic producer and the unsuspecting consumer
(4) Home-produced foodstuffs are safer to eat than goods imported from abroad because they are subject to more regular and closer inspection procedures

Direction for questions 7 and 8: Answer the questions based on the following passage.

The mainstay of our business is credibility. We get that credibility and respect, and the power that goes with it only by being a socially and professionally responsible agent for the public. In some ways we journalists have to have the same attitude to news as an employee of a bank has to money — it is not ours. We are handling it on behalf of other people, so it cannot be converted to our own use. If we do, if is embezzlement.

7. Which of the following criticism would most weaken the comparison between journalists and bank employees?
(1) Different newspapers print different news, just as different banks hold assets from various sources
(2) The heart and soul of the banking business is money, not credibility
(3) A bank teller need not be credible, just responsible
(4) Embezzlement is properly a crime against the bank, not against the depositors

8. The first sentence makes a point with which the following techniques?
(1) Metaphor
(2) Parody
(3) Overstatement
(4) Statistical support

9. The value of a close examination of the circumstances of an aircraft accident lies not only in fixing blame but in learning lessons.

The above statement fits most logically into which of the following types of passages?
(1) A survey of the 'scapegoat phenomenon' in modern society
(2) An argument in favour of including specific details in any academic essay
(3) An argument against the usefulness of the National Transportation Safety Board
(4) A description of the causes of a particular aircraft accident.

10. Consumer are not so easily manipulated as they are often painted. They may know what they want, and what they want may be greatly different from what other people believe they need.

Which of the following statements, if true, most weakens the above argument?
(1) Most people continue to buy the same brand of a product year after year
(2) Companies that advertise the most sell the most products
(3) Store shelves packed with a variety of different brands have the potential to confuse the consumer
(4) Most consumer know which brand they are going to buy before entering a store

11. The daily journey from his home to his office takes John Bond on an average 1 hr and 35 min by car. A friend has told him a different route that is longer in mileage, but will only take an hour and a quarter on average, because it contains stretches of roads where it is possible to drive at higher speeds. John Bond's only consideration apart from the time factor is the cost, and he calculates that his car will consume 10% less gasoline if he takes the suggested new route. John decides to take the new route for the next two weeks as an experiment.

If the above statements were considered, which one of the following may have an effect on the decision John has made?

(1) Major road work is begun on the shorter (in distance) route, which holds up traffic for an extra 10 min. The project will take six months, but after it the improvements will allow the journey to be made in half an hour less than at present.

(2) There is to be a strike at local gas stations and the amount of gasoline drivers may purchase, may be rationed.

(3) John finds a route which is slightly longer than his old route, but shorter than the suggested route.

(4) The old route passes the door of a work colleague who, without a ride, would have to go to work by bus.

12. All elephants are gray. And all mice are gray. Therefore, I conclude that all elephants are gray.

The arguments above is invalid because

(1) the writer bases his argument on another argument that contains circular reasoning

(2) the writer has illogically classified two disparate groups together when there is no relationship between them, except that they share an attribute

(3) the writer has made an analogy between two dissimilar qualities

(4) the writer has used a fallacy which involves an ambiguous description of animals by their colour

Direction for questions 13 and 14: Answer the questions based on the following passage.

The last census showed a sharp rise during the 1970s in the number of Americans living together as unmarried couples, but a more recent increase in the marriage rate in 1981 suggests that matrimony will make a comeback in the 1980s.

13. Which of the following best refutes the argument above?

(1) One of the causes of more marriages is that the large population resulting from the baby boom is now reaching marriageable age

(2) Although information about the 1981 marriage rate is not complete, most analysis consider it to be reliable

(3) Many of those marrying in 1981 were couples who had lived together during the 1970s

(4) The marriage rate increased dramatically in 1971 and fell even more dramatically in following years

14. With which of the following would the author be likely to agree?

(1) Americans should not live together as unmarried couples

(2) Matrimony is preferable to living together

(3) Economic circumstances have made matrimony attractive as a way of paying less income tax

(4) Prevailing attitudes towards marriage tend to persist for more than one year.

15. The shortsightedness of our government and our scientists have virtually nullified all of their great discoveries because of their failure to consider the environmental impact. The situation is far from hopeless, but our government agencies must become better watchdogs.

This argument fails to place any blame on

I. consumers who prefer new technology to clean air.

II. the ability of government to actually police industry.

III. legal loopholes which allow industry abuse of government regulations

(1) I only   (2) II only

(3) III only   (4) I and III

16. Voltaire once said, "Common sense is not so common."
Which of the following most nearly parallels Voltaire's statement?

(1) God must have loved the common man, he certainly made enough of them

(2) The common good is not necessarily best for everyone

(3) Jumbo shrimp may not actually be very big

(4) Good people may not necessarily have good sense

17. There are three main factors that control the risks of becoming dependent on drugs. These factors are the type of drug, the personality of the individual and the adult population and the circumstances in which the drug is taken. Indeed, it could be said that the majority of the adult population have

taken alcohol, very few have become dependent on it. Also, many strong drugs that have been used for medical purposes have not caused the patient to become addicted.

However, it can be demonstrated that people who have taken drugs for fun are more likely to become dependent on the drug. The dependence is not always physiological but may remain psychological, although the effects are still essentially the same. Those at greatest risk appear to be personalities that are psychopathic, immature, or otherwise unstable.

Psychological dependence is very strong with heroin, morphine, cocaine, and amphetamines. Physiological dependence is great with heroin and morphine, but less with amphetamines, barbiturates and alcohol.

Which of the following conclusion can be drawn from the text?
(1) One cannot become addicted to certain drugs if one has a strong personality
(2) Taking drugs for 'kicks' increases the possibility of becoming dependent on drugs
(3) Psychological dependence is the greatest with heroin
(4) Alcohol is a safe drug since very few people become dependent on it

18. Sally overslept. Therefore, she did not eat breakfast. She realized that she was late for school, so she ran as fast as she could and did not see a hole in the ground which was in her path. She tripped and broke her ankle. She was then taken to the hospital and while lying in bed was visited by her friend, who wanted to know why she had got up so late.

Which of the following conclusions can be made from the above passage?
(1) Because Sally did not eat her breakfast, she broke her ankle
(2) Sally's friend visited her in the hospital because she wanted to know why she was late for school
(3) Sally did not notice the hole because she overslept
(4) Sally broken her ankle because she went to bed late the previous night

19. Amit: If an alien species ever visited Earth, it would surely be because they were looking for other intelligent species with whom they could communicate. Since we have not been contacted by aliens, we may conclude that none has ever visited this planet.
Anita: Or, perhaps, they did not think that human beings are intelligent.

How is Anita's response related to Amit's argument?
(1) She misses Amit's point entirely
(2) She attacks Amit personally rather than his reasoning
(3) She points out that Amit made an unwarranted assumption
(4) She ignores the detailed internal development of Amit's logic

20. If quarks are the smallest subatomic particles in the universe, then gluons are needed to hold quarks together. Since gluons are needed to hole quarks together, it follows that quarks are the smallest subatomic particles in the universe.

The logic of the above argument is most nearly paralleled by which of the following?
(1) If this library has a good Spanish literature collection, it will contain a copy of *Les Conquerants* by Marlaux. The collection does contain a copy of *Les Conquerants*. Therefore, the library has a good Spanish literature collection.
(2) If there is a man-in-the-moon, the moon must be made of green cheese for him to eat. There is a man-in-the-moon, so the moon is made of green cheese.
(3) Either helium or hydrogen is the lightest element of the periodic table. Helium is not the lightest element of the periodic table, so hydrogen must be the lightest element of the periodic table.
(4) If Sunita is taller than Ram, and if Ram is taller than Ekta, then if Sunita is taller than Ram, Sunita is also taller than Ekta.

21. In the earliest stages of the common law, a party could have his case heard by a judge only upon the payment of a fee to the court, and then only if his case fit within one of the forms for which there existed a writ. At first the number of such formalized cases of action was very small, but judges invented

new forms which brought more cases and greater revenues.

Which of the following conclusions is most strongly suggested by the paragraph above?
(1) Early judges often decided cases in an arbitrary and haphazard manner
(2) In most early cases, the plaintiff rather than the defendant prevailed
(3) The judiciary at first had greater power than either the legislature or the executive
(4) One of the motivating forces for the early expansion in judicial power was economic considerations

22. A recent survey by the economics department of an French League university revealed that increases in the salaries of preachers are accompanied by increases in the nationwide average of rum consumption. From 1965 to 1970, preachers' salaries increased on the average of 15% and rum sales grew by 14.5%. From 1970 to 1975 average preachers' salaries rose by 17% and rum sales by 17.5%. From 1975 to 1980, rum sales expanded by only 8% and average preachers' salaries also grew by only 8%.

Which of the following is the most likely explanation for the findings cited in the paragraph?
(1) When preachers have more disposable income, they tend to allocate that extra money to alcohol
(2) When preachers are paid more, they preach longer, and longer sermons tend to drive people to drink
(3) Since there were more preachers in the country, there were also more people; and a larger population will consume greater quantities of liquor
(4) The general standard of living increased from 1965 to 1980, which accounts for both the increase in the rum consumption and preachers' average salaries

23. The owners of a local supermarket have decided to make use of three now-redundant checkout counters. They believe that they will attract those customers who lately have been put off by the long checkout lines during the mid-morning and evening rush hours. The owners have concluded that in order to be successful, the increased revenue from added counters will have to be more than the increase in maintenance costs for the added counters.

The underlying goal of the owners can be summarized thus
(1) to improve service to all customers
(2) to attract people who have never been to the store
(3) to make use of the redundant counters
(4) to increase monthly profits

24. In the United States, there is increasing concern over the use of radiation, particularly radiation for medical uses. Mammograms, or breast X-rays, can reveal the early stages of breast cancer, the leading cause of cancer death in American women.

Public awareness of the risk of breast cancer, particularly among those younger than 50, was heightened during the 1970s by the publicity given to the mastectomies of prominent women, including the then First Lady Betty Ford. The establishment in 1973 of a free nationwide screening programme resulted in an unprecedented rush for mammograms.

Within three years, several hundred thousands women had been examined and 1,800 breast cancer cases detected. However, studies showed that mammograms can cause as well as identify cancer, and researchers involved in the studies concluded that the mammography programme produced five cancer cases for every one it detected.

Which one of the following would most strengthen the conclusion drawn by the researchers?
(1) Tests have shown that mammography does not increase the survival rates of women younger than 50
(2) Drug therapy to cure cancers of the breasts were found to be successful
(3) It has been decided that all women over 50 be given a mammogram every three years
(4) The breast has been shown as being extremely sensitive to radiation-induced cancer

25. Two women, one living in Chicago, the other living in Washington City, carried on a lengthy correspondence by mail. The subject of the exchange was a dispute over certain personality traits of Winston Churchill. After some two dozen

letters, the Chicago resident received the following note from her Washington City correspondent: "It seems you were right all along. Yesterday I met some one who actually knew Sir Winston, and he confirmed your opinion."

The two women could have been arguing on the basis of all the following EXCEPT
(1) published biographical information
(2) old news film footage
(3) direct personal acquaintance
(4) assumption

26. The protection of the right of property by the constitution is tenuous at best. It is true that the Fifth Amendment states that the government may not take private property for public use without compensation, but it is the government that defines private property.

Which of the following is most likely the point the author is leading up to?
(1) Individual rights that are protected by the Supreme Court are secure against government encroachment
(2) Private property is neither more nor less than that which the government says is private property
(3) The government has no authority to deprive an individual of liberty
(4) No government that acts arbitrarily can be justified

27. Since all swans I have encountered have been white, it follows that the swans I will see when I visit the Mumbai Zoo will also be white.

Which of the following most closely parallels the reasoning of the preceding argument?
(1) Some birds are incapable of flight: therefore, swans are probably incapable of flight
(2) Every ballet I have attended has failed to interest me: so a theatrical production which fails to interest me must be a ballet
(3) Since all cases of severe depression I have encountered were susceptible to treatment by chlorpromazine, there must be something in the chlorpromazine which adjusts the patient's brain chemistry
(4) Since no medicine I have tried for my allergy has ever helped, this new product probably will not work either

28. EENA: Participation in intramural competitive sports teaches students the importance of teamwork, for no one wants to let his or her teammates down.
MEENA: That is not correct. The real reason students play hard is that such programmes place a premium on winning and no one wants to be a member of a losing team.

Which of the following comments can most reasonably be made about the exchange between Eena and Meena?
(1) If fewer and fewer schools are sponsoring intramural sports programmes now than a decade ago, Eena's position is undermined
(2) If high schools and universities provide financial assistance for the purchase of sports equipment, Meena's assertion about the importance of winning is weakened
(3) If teamwork is essential to success in intramural competitive sports, Eena's position and Meena's position are not necessarily incompatible
(4) Since the argument is one about motivation, it should be possible to resolve the issue by taking a survey of deans at schools which have intramural sports programmes.

29. The cost of housing in many parts of Germany has become so excessive that many young couples, with above-average salaries, can only afford small apartments. Mortgage commitments are so huge that they cannot consider the possibility of starting a family. A new baby would probably mean either the mother or father giving up a well-paid position. The lack of or great cost of child-care facilities precludes the return of both parents to work.

Which of the following adjustments, could practically be made to the situation described above which would allow young couples to improve their housing prospects?
(1) Encourage couples to remain childless
(2) Encourage couples to have one child only
(3) Encourage couples to postpone starting families until at later age than previously acceptable to society
(4) Encourage young couples to move to cheaper areas of Germany.

30. Unless new reserves are found soon, the world's supply of coal is being depleted in such a way that with demand continuing to grow at present rates, reserves will be exhausted by the year 2040.

Which of the following, if true, will most weaken the above argument?
(1) There has been a slowdown in the rate of increase in world demand for coal over the last five years from 10% to 5%
(2) It has been known for many years that there are stocks of coal under Antarctica which have yet to be economically exploited
(3) Oil is being used increasingly in place of coal for many industrial and domestic uses
(4) None of these

31. A cryptographer has intercepted an enemy message that is in code. He knows that the code is a simple substitution of numbers for letters.

Which of the following would be the least helpful in breaking the code?
(1) Knowing the frequency with which the vowels of the language are used
(2) Knowing the frequency with who two vowels appear together in the language
(3) Knowing the frequency with which odd numbers appear relative to even numbers in the message
(4) Knowing the conjugation of the verb to be in the language on which the code is based

32. One way of reducing commuting time for those who work in the cities is to increase the speed at which traffic moves in the heart of the city. This can be accomplished by raising the tolls on the tunnels and bridges connecting the city with other communities. This will discourage auto traffic into the city and will encourage people to use public transportation instead.

Which of the following, if true, would LEAST weaken the above argument?
(1) Nearly all of the traffic in the centre of the city is commercial traffic, which will continue despite toll increases
(2) Some people now driving alone into the city would choose to carpool with each other rather than use the public transportation
(3) Any temporary improvement in traffic flow would be lost because the improvement itself would attract more cars

(4) The numbers of commuters who would be deterred by the toll increases would be insignificant.

33. Statistics published by the Department of Traffic and Highway Safety show that nearly 80% of all traffic fatalities occur at speeds under 35 miles per hour and within 25 miles of home.

Which of the following would be the most reasonable conclusion to draw from these statistics?
(1) A person is less likely to have a fatal accident if he always drives over 35 miles per hour and always at distances greater than 25 miles from his home
(2) There is a direct correlation between distance driven and the likelihood of fatal accident
(3) The greater the likelihood that one is about to be involved in a fatal accident, the more likely it is that he is driving close to home at a speed less than 35 miles per hour
(4) Most driving is done at less than 35 miles per hour and within 25 miles of home

34. A study published by the Department of Education shows that children in the central cities lag far behind students in the suburbs and the rural areas in reading skills. The report blamed this differential on the overcrowding in the classrooms of city schools. I maintain, however, that the real reason that city children are poorer readers than non-city children is that they do not get enough fresh air and sunshine.

Which of the following would LEAST strengthen the author's point in the argument above?
(1) Medical research which shows a correlation between air pollution and learning disabilities.
(2) A report by educational experts demonstrating that there is no relationship between the number of students in a classroom and a student's ability to read.
(3) A notice released by the Department of Education retracting that part of their report which mentions overcrowding as the reason for the differential.
(4) A proposal by the federal government to fund emergency programs to hire more teachers for central city schools in an attempt to reduce overcrowding in the classrooms.

35. In accordance with their powers, many state authorities are introducing fluoridation of drinking water. This follows the conclusion of 8 years of research that the process ensures that children and adults receive the required intake that will strengthen teeth. The maximum level has been set at one part per million. However, there are many who object, claiming that fluoridation removes freedom of choice.

Which of the following will weaken the claim of the proponents of fluoridation?
(1) Fluoridation over a certain prescribed level has been shown to lead to general weakening of teeth
(2) There is no record of the long-term effects of drinking fluoridated water
(3) The people to be affected by fluoridation claim that they have not been given sufficient opportunity to voice their views
(4) Fluoridation is only one part of general dental health

36. Mr and Mrs Smith and their son John want to cross the Dart river. The only way across is with Mr Jones in his rowboat. Mr Jones will not allow anyone to row his boat and will take only one passenger at a time. John is only a little boy, so he cannot be left alone on the river bank.

Which of the following conditions are not part of the successful passage of the Smiths across the river?
(1) Mr Smith crosses the river first
(2) Mr Smith crosses the river last
(3) Mr and Mrs Smith do not cross together
(4) John crosses the river first

37. Some philosophers have argued that there exist certain human or natural rights, which belong to all human beings by virtue of their humanity. But a review of the laws of different societies shows that the rights accorded to a person vary from society to society and even within a society over time. Since there is no right that is universally protected, there are no natural rights.

A defender of the theory that natural rights do exist might respond to this objection by arguing that
(1) some human beings do not have any natural rights
(2) some human rights are natural while others derive from a source such as a constitution
(3) people in one society may have natural rights which people in another society lack
(4) natural rights may exist even though they are not protected by some societies

Direction for questions 38 and 39: Answer the questions based on the following passage.

The single greatest weakness of American parties is their inability to achieve cohesion in the legislature.

Although there is some measure of party unity, it is not uncommon for the majority party to be unable to implement important legislation. The unity is strongest during election campaigns; after the primary elections, the losing candidates all premieres their support to the party nominee. By the time the Congress convenes, the unity has dissipated. This phenomenon is attributable to the fragmented nature of party politics. The national committees are no more than feudal lords who receive nominal fealty from their vassals. A congressman builds his own power upon a local base. Consequently, a congressman is likely to be responsive to local special interest groups. Evidence of this is seen in the differences in voting patterns between the upper and lower houses. In the Senate, where terms are longer, there is more party unity.

38. Which of the following, if true, would most strengthen the author's argument?
(1) On 30 key issues, 18 of the 67 majority party members in the Senate voted against the party leaders
(2) On 30 key issues, 70 of the 305 majority party members in the House voted against the party leaders
(3) On 30 key issues, over half the members of the minority party in both houses voted with the majority party against the leaders of the minority party
(4) Of 30 key legislative proposals introduced by a president whose party controlled a majority in both houses, only four passed both houses

39. Which of the following, if true, would most weaken the author's argument?
(1) Congressmen receive funds from the national party committee
(2) Senators vote against the party leader only two-thirds as often as members of the House
(3) The primary duty of an officeholder is to be responsive to his local constituency rather than party leaders
(4) There is more unity among minority party members than among majority party members

Verbal Ability / Vocabulary

40. SPEAKER: The great majority of people in the United States have access to the best medical care available anywhere in the world.
OBJECTOR: There are thousands of poor in this country who cannot afford to pay to see a doctor.

A possible objection to the speaker's comments would be to point to the existence of
(1) a country which has more medical assistants than the United States
(2) a nation where medical care is provided free of charge by the government
(3) a country in which the people are given better medical care than Americans
(4) government hearings in the United States on the problems poor people have getting medical care

41. Monopoly is characterized by absence of or decline in competition. The ABC company realizes that its operations are in competitive industries.

Which of the following conclusions may be inferred for the above?
(1) ABC's market is not monopolistic
(2) Monopoly is defined as one seller in a market
(3) The ABC company has no domestic competitors
(4) The ABC company is publicly owned

42. Farmers in the south have observed that heavy frost is usually preceded by a full moon. They are convinced that the full moon somehow generates the frost.

Which of the following, if true, would weaken the farmer's conviction?
(1) The temperature must fall below 10 degrees Celsius (50 degrees Fahrenheit) for frost to occur.
(2) Absence of a cloud cover cools the ground which causes frost
(3) Farmers are superstitious
(4) No one has proved that the moon causes frost

43. Some judges have allowed hospitals to disconnect life-support equipment of patients who have no prospects for recovery. But I say that is cold-blooded murder. Either we put a stop to this practice now or we will soon have programmes of euthanasia for the old and infirm as well as others who might be considered a burden. Rather than disconnecting life-support equipment, we should let nature take its course.

Which of the following are valid objections to the above argument?
I. It is internally inconsistent.
II. It employs emotionally charged terms.
III. It presents a false dilemma.
(1) I only   (2) II only
(3) III only   (4) I, II and III

44 PUBLIC ANNOUNCEMENT: When you enrol with Fast Track Career Institute (FTCI), you will have access to our placement counselling service. Last year, 92% of our graduates who asked us to help them find jobs, found them. So go to FTCI for your future!

Which of the following would be appropriate questions to ask in order to determine the value of the preceding claim?
I. How many of your graduates asked FTCI for assistance?
II. How many people graduated from FTCI last year?
III. Did those people who asked for jobs find ones in the areas for which they were trained?
IV. Was FCBI responsible for finding the jobs or did graduates find them independently?
(1) I and II only   (2) I, II and III only
(3) I, II and IV only   (4) I, II, III and IV

45. Why pay outrageously high prices for imported sparkling water when there is now inexpensive water carbonated and bottled here in the India at its source — Gangotri, UP. Neither you nor your guests will taste the difference, but if you would be embarrassed if it were learned that you were serving a domestic sparkling water, then serve Cold Springs Water — but serve it in a leaded crystal decanter.

The advertisement rests on which of the following assumptions?
I. It is difficult if not impossible to distinguish Gangotri water from imported competitors on the basis of taste.
II. Most sparkling waters are not bottled at the source.

III. Some people may purchase an imported sparkling water over a domestic one as a status symbol.
(1) I only   (2) II only
(3) III only   (4) I and III only

46. In our investigation of this murder, we are guided by our previous experience with the Bhopal Killer. You will recall that in that case the victims were also carrying a great deal of money when they were killed, but the money was not taken. As in this case the murder weapon was a pistol. Finally, in that case the murders were also committed between six in the evening and twelve midnight. So we are probably after someone who looks very much like the Bhopal Killer who was finally tried, convicted, and executed: 5' 11" tall, a mustache, short brown hair, walks with a slight limp.

The author makes which of the following assumptions?
I. Crimes similar in detail are likely to be committed by perpetrators who are similar in physical appearance.
II. The Bhopal Killer has apparently escaped from prison and has resumed his criminal activities.
III. The man first convicted as the Bhopal Killer was actually innocent, and the real Bhopal Killer is still loose.
(1) I only
(2) I and II only
(3) II only
(4) I and III only

47. Professor Tembel told his class that the method of student evaluation of teachers is not a valid measure of teaching quality. Students should fill out questionnaires at the end of the semester when courses have been completed.

Which of the following, if true, provides support for Professor Tembel's proposal?
(1) Professor Tembel received low ratings from his students
(2) Students filled out questionnaires after mid-term examination
(3) Students are interested in teacher evaluation
(4) Teachers are not obligated to use the survey results

48. The president lobbied for passage of his new trade bill which would liberalize trade with industrialized countries such as US, members of the European Community and Japan.

Each of the following, if true, could account for the above, EXCEPT
(1) the president is up for reelection and needs to show results
(2) labour unions have petitioned the president to provide more local jobs
(3) the trade agreement could bring a *quid pro quo* on pending negotiations
(4) economists claimed that the passage of the bill would increase the country's trade deficit

49. The main ingredient in this bottle of Dr David's Milk of Magnesia is used by nine out of 10 hospitals across the country as an antacid and laxative.

If this advertising claim is true, which of the following statements must also be true?
I. Nine out of 10 hospitals across the country use Dr David's Milk of Magnesia for some ailments.
II. Only one out of 10 hospitals in the country does not treat acid indigestion and constipation.
III. Only one out of 10 hospitals across the country does not recommend Dr John's Milk of Magnesia for patients who need a milk of magnesia.
(1) I only
(2) II only
(3) I and III
(4) None of the statements is necessarily true

50. Is your company going to continue to discriminate against women in its hiring and promotion policies?

The above question might be considered unfair for which of the following reasons?
I. Its construction seeks a 'yes' or 'no' answer where both might be inappropriate.
II. It is internally inconsistent.
III. It contains a hidden presupposition which the responder might wish to contest.
(1) I only   (2) II only
(3) I and II only (4) I and III only

Verbal Ability / Vocabulary

Answers and Explanations

PART – 1 : QUANTITATIVE ABILITY

1. Number System and Algebra

Exercise – 1

1	3	2	2	3	2	4	1	5	3	6	4	7	1	8	4	9	4	10	4
11	2	12	3	13	4	14	2	15	4	16	4	17	4	18	3	19	3	20	3
21	4	22	2	23	1	24	3	25	1										

Exercise – 2

1	2	2	4	3	2	4	4	5	1	6	4	7	1	8	4	9	4	10	2
11	1	12	1	13	3	14	3	15	1	16	1	17	4	18	2	19	4	20	3
21	2	22	4	23	4	24	3	25	4										

Exercise – 3

1	3	2	2	3	1	4	4	5	1	6	1	7	3	8	1	9	1	10	4
11	2	12	3	13	3	14	3	15	2	16	4	17	3	18	1	19	4	20	2
21	3	22	3	23	2	24	3	25	2										

Exercise – 4

1	1	2	3	3	3	4	3	5	3	6	3	7	1	8	3	9	2	10	3
11	3	12	3	13	2	14	4	15	1	16	2	17	4	18	4	19	4	20	3
21	2	22	2	23	2	24	1	25	3										

2. Ratio, Proportion and Averages

Exercise – 1

1	3	2	4	3	1	4	2	5	4	6	4	7	2	8	3	9	4	10	1
11	4	12	3	13	4	14	4	15	1	16	2	17	2	18	2	19	4	20	1
21	2	22	2	23	3	24	2	25	2										

Exercise – 2

1	4	2	2	3	3	4	1	5	4	6	2	7	3	8	2	9	4	10	3
11	4	12	2	13	4	14	1	15	2	16	4	17	2	18	4	19	3	20	2
21	4	22	4	23	2	24	3	25	4										

Exercise – 3

1	3	2	3	3	4	4	3	5	4	6	2	7	3	8	3	9	3	10	1
11	2	12	2	13	4	14	3	15	4	16	2	17	1	18	3	19	4	20	3

Exercise – 4

1	4	2	2	3	2	4	1	5	1	6	1	7	4	8	1	9	1	10	2
11	4	12	2	13	3	14	2	15	2	16	1	17	3	18	4	19	2	20	3

3. Business Maths

Exercise – 1

1	4	2	1	3	4	4	2	5	3	6	4	7	1	8	4	9	3	10	4
11	2	12	4	13	1	14	2	15	1	16	2	17	2	18	1	19	2	20	3
21	2	22	4	23	1	24	3	25	4										

Exercise – 2

1	3	2	4	3	3	4	3	5	4	6	1	7	4	8	2	9	1	10	4
11	3	12	4	13	4	14	1	15	4	16	4	17	3	18	2	19	1	20	4
21	4	22	4	23	4	24	1	25	2										

Exercise – 3

1	3	2	4	3	4	4	1	5	4	6	3	7	1	8	2	9	4	10	3
11	2	12	1	13	1	14	2	15	3										

Exercise – 4

1	2	2	4	3	1	4	4	5	1	6	2	7	4	8	3	9	1	10	4
11	1	12	4	13	3	14	2	15	3	16	4	17	4	18	4	19	2	20	3

Exercise – 5

1	4	2	1	3	3	4	3	5	1	6	4	7	2	8	2	9	3	10	3
11	2	12	3	13	1	14	2	15	4	16	4	17	1	18	3	19	4	20	2

Exercise – 6

1	4	2	2	3	1	4	2	5	4	6	3	7	2	8	2	9	3	10	3
11	4	12	2	13	4	14	1	15	3										

Exercise – 7

1	1	2	2	3	1	4	3	5	2	6	1	7	2	8	4	9	4	10	2
11	3	12	1	13	1	14	4	15	4	16	4	17	3	18	1	19	4	20	3

4. Time, Work and Distance

Exercise – 1

1	1	2	3	3	2	4	4	5	2	6	4	7	3	8	2	9	1	10	3
11	4	12	4	13	4	14	2	15	4	16	2	17	4	18	2	19	1	20	3
21	4	22	4	23	2	24	1	25	4	26	1	27	1	28	2	29	1	30	2
31	4	32	3	33	1	34	4	35	4	36	3	37	3	38	1	39	2	40	1

Exercise – 2

1	2	2	2	3	2	4	4	5	4	6	4	7	1	8	2	9	3	10	1
11	3	12	2	13	2	14	2	15	1	16	1	17	4	18	2	19	2	20	3
21	2	22	1	23	1	24	4	25	3	26	1	27	1	28	4	29	2	30	2
31	3	32	4	33	4	34	4	35	1	36	3	37	2	38	1	39	3	40	3

Answers and Explanations

5. Geometry

Exercise – 1

1	1	2	3	3	3	4	4	5	4	6	4	7	3	8	4	9	3	10	1
11	2	12	4	13	1	14	2	15	4	16	3	17	2	18	4	19	4	20	3
21	4	22	4	23	2	24	1	25	4										

Exercise – 2

1	4	2	1	3	4	4	2	5	3	6	4	7	4	8	1	9	2	10	4
11	3	12	1	13	3	14	4	15	2	16	3	17	2	18	4	19	4	20	4
21	3	22	1	23	4	24	3	25	2	26	1	27	4	28	2	29	4	30	1
31	4	32	2	33	3	34	3	35	2										

6. Higher Maths

Exercise – 1

1	2	2	4	3	3	4	1	5	4	6	4	7	4	8	1	9	2	10	1
11	1	12	3	13	1	14	2	15	4	16	4	17	2	18	4	19	4	20	3

7. Data Based Reasoning

Exercise – 1

1	1	2	2	3	3	4	4	5	4	6	3	7	1	8	1	9	2	10	2
11	4	12	4	13	3	14	1	15	3	16	2	17	4	18	3	19	3	20	4
21	3	22	3	23	3	24	3	25	3	26	4	27	2	28	2	29	1	30	2
31	1	32	2	33	3	34	4	35	2										

Exercise – 2

1	2	2	1	3	4	4	4	5	3	6	3	7	4	8	3	9	4	10	1
11	3	12	4	13	3	14	4	15	4	16	3	17	1	18	4	19	4	20	4

PART – 2 : REASONING

1. Number Series

1	4	2	4	3	2	4	3	5	4	6	2	7	2	8	4	9	4	10	4
11	4	12	4	13	4	14	3	15	4	16	2	17	1	18	3	19	2	20	3
21	3	22	3	23	1	24	4	25	4	26	1	27	4	28	2	29	4	30	1
31	4	32	2	33	1	34	4	35	4	36	4	37	2	38	2	39	2	40	4
41	3	42	1	43	1	44	4	45	2	46	1	47	4	48	1	49	3	50	4
51	2	52	2	53	4	54	2	55	1	56	1	57	2	58	1	59	3	60	2

1	3	2	3	3	1	4	4	5	2	6	3	7	2	8	3	9	3	10	2
11	3	12	3	13	3	14	3	15	4	16	4	17	3	18	3	19	3	20	4
21	3	22	3	23	4	24	4	25	4	26	2	27	3	28	4	29	1	30	3
31	4	32	2	33	1	34	3	35	4	36	3	37	3	38	3	39	2	40	1
41	2	42	4	43	4	44	1	45	4	46	2	47	4	48	1	49	4	50	4

██ **3. Analogies**

1	3	2	1	3	2	4	4	5	3	6	2	7	2	8	1	9	4	10	1
11	3	12	4	13	2	14	4	15	3	16	2	17	2	18	3	19	2	20	4
21	2	22	1	23	4	24	4	25	1	26	2	27	3	28	3	29	4	30	3
31	4	32	4	33	1	34	4	35	1	36	4	37	4	38	4	39	4	40	1
41	2	42	3	43	1	44	4	45	2	46	3	47	4	48	3	49	4	50	2

██ **4. Odd Man Out**

1	4	2	3	3	2	4	1	5	1	6	2	7	2	8	1	9	4	10	3
11	2	12	2	13	1	14	4	15	3	16	4	17	2	18	4	19	2	20	1
21	1	22	4	23	2	24	4	25	3	26	3	27	2	28	4	29	2	30	1
31	3	32	3	33	1	34	3	35	2	36	3	37	4	38	1	39	1	40	2
41	4	42	3	43	1	44	4	45	2	46	3	47	4	48	2	49	1	50	3
51	2	52	4	53	3	54	4	55	3	56	2	57	3	58	4	59	3	60	1

██ **5. Coding – Decoding**

Type – 1

1	1	2	4	3	3	4	2	5	4	6	3	7	4	8	4	9	1	10	2
11	4	12	4	13	2	14	2	15	1										

Type – 2

1	3	2	4	3	2	4	4	5	4	6	4	7	1	8	3	9	4	10	2

Type – 3

1	3	2	3	3	4	4	3	5	4

Type – 4

1	2	2	4	3	3	4	2	5	4

Type – 5

1	3	2	2	3	1	4	4	5	3

Answers and Explanations

6. Directions

1	2	2	4	3	3	4	4	5	4	6	1	7	3	8	2	9	2	10	1
11	2	12	2	13	1	14	3	15	3	16	4	17	4	18	3	19	3	20	1
21	4	22	1	23	2	24	3	25	3										

7. Blood Relations

1	1	2	4	3	4	4	2	5	4	6	3	7	2	8	2	9	3	10	4
11	2	12	3	13	3	14	4	15	2	16	1	17	3	18	2	19	2	20	4
21	1	22	4	23	3	24	3	25	3	26	3	27	4	28	2	29	4	30	3
31	1	32	3	33	2	34	4	35	2										

8. Analytical Reasoning

1	1	2	4	3	1	4	4	5	4	6	2	7	3	8	4	9	3	10	3
11	2	12	3	13	4	14	4	15	1	16	4	17	4	18	1	19	4	20	4
21	4	22	3	23	2	24	3	25	4	26	4	27	3	28	2	29	4	30	3
31	2	32	2	33	1	34	4	35	2	36	3	37	4	38	1	39	2	40	3
41	1	42	3	43	2	44	4	45	4	46	4	47	3	48	4	49	2	50	4
51	3	52	3	53	3	54	3	55	4	56	3	57	2	58	1	59	2	60	2

9. Calendars

1	2	2	4	3	3	4	3	5	2	6	2	7	4	8	1	9	3	10	4
11	1	12	3	13	3	14	2	15	1										

10. Clocks

1	3	2	4	3	2	4	2	5	2	6	3	7	1	8	1	9	2	10	2
11	3	12	3	13	2	14	3	15	3										

11. True-False Logic

1	2	2	1	3	3	4	1	5	1	6	2	7	3	8	2	9	3	10	1
11	2	12	1	13	2	14	3	15	3	16	3	17	1	18	1	19	3	20	2

12. Cubes

1	3	2	1	3	1	4	1	5	3	6	1	7	3	8	3	9	1	10	3
11	3	12	3	13	3	14	3	15	3	16	3	17	3	18	1	19	2	20	1

13. Venn Diagrams

1	3	2	1	3	1	4	2	5	1	6	4	7	2	8	3	9	1	10	4
11	1	12	2	13	1	14	2	15	4	16	3	17	2	18	3	19	4	20	4
21	1	22	3	23	1	24	4	25	3	26	4	27	4	28	2	29	3	30	2

14. Non-Verbal Reasoning

1	2	2	4	3	3	4	2	5	3	6	2	7	3	8	3	9	4	10	4
11	1	12	1	13	3	14	4	15	3	16	4	17	1	18	2	19	2	20	4
21	4	22	3	23	3	24	3	25	1	26	4	27	3	28	4	29	3	30	2
31	2	32	4	33	4	34	1	35	2	36	4	37	4	38	4	39	4	40	3

15. Logical Deductions & Connectives

1	1	2	3	3	2	4	4	5	1	6	1	7	2	8	2	9	3	10	2
11	1	12	2	13	1	14	4	15	4	16	4	17	4	18	4	19	4	20	4
21	4	22	4	23	4	24	4	25	4	26	4	27	1	28	2	29	2	30	4
31	4	32	4	33	4	34	1	35	2	36	3	37	1	38	3	39	4	40	3

PART – 3 : VERBAL ABILITY / GRAMMAR & RC

2. Prepositions

Exercise

1	1	11	2	21	4	31	2	41	3	51	2	61	3	71	1	81	4	91	2
2	4	12	4	22	3	32	2	42	1	52	3	62	4	72	3	82	3	92	1
3	2	13	2	23	1	33	2	43	1	53	2	63	4	73	2	83	2	93	3
4	3	14	4	24	2	34	2	44	4	54	3	64	3	74	3	84	2	94	2
5	2	15	3	25	3	35	1	45	2	55	2	65	2	75	4	85	2	95	1
6	3	16	4	26	4	36	4	46	1	56	2	66	2	76	2	86	1	96	3
7	4	17	3	27	2	37	1	47	1	57	4	67	1	77	2	87	2	97	2
8	2	18	3	28	2	38	3	48	1	58	4	68	2	78	2	88	2	98	1
9	3	19	4	29	2	39	1	49	2	59	2	69	4	79	3	89	3	99	3
10	4	20	2	30	1	40	2	50	2	60	4	70	3	80	4	90	4	100	3

9. Articles

Grammar Review Exercise – 1

1	2	2	2	3	2	4	1	5	1	6	4	7	1	8	2	9	3	10	3
11	1	12	4	13	3	14	4	15	2	16	4	17	2	18	1	19	3	20	2
21	4	22	4	23	1	24	2	25	3	26	3	27	1	28	2	29	2	30	4
31	1	32	1	33	3	34	4	35	3	36	4	37	3	38	2	39	3	40	3
41	2	42	2	43	1	44	4	45	3	46	1	47	2	48	1	49	2	50	1

Grammar Review Exercise – 2

1	2	2	2	3	3	4	1	5	4	6	1	7	3	8	4	9	3	10	1
11	1	12	3	13	1	14	4	15	2	16	1	17	1	18	4	19	1	20	4
21	1	22	2	23	4	24	1	25	4	26	3	27	3	28	1	29	2	30	2
31	2	32	1	33	2	34	3	35	2	36	1	37	3	38	1	39	2	40	4
41	1	42	4	43	2	44	3	45	2	46	3	47	4	48	2	49	3	50	4

Grammar Review Exercise – 3

1	1	2	3	3	2	4	4	5	2	6	1	7	3	8	2	9	2	10	4
11	1	12	3	13	3	14	3	15	2	16	1	17	4	18	3	19	3	20	1
21	1	22	2	23	4	24	1	25	4	26	2	27	1	28	2	29	3	30	3
31	4	32	1	33	3	34	2	35	4	36	2	37	4	38	2	39	4	40	3
41	4	42	3	43	3	44	4	45	3	46	4	47	3	48	1	49	2	50	3

10. Reading Comprehension

Passages	Questions					
	1	2	3	4	5	6
1	1	3	2	4	4	2
2	4	3	4	4	3	2
3	3	3	3	4	4	1
4	2	4	3	1	4	
5	3	4	4	2	4	

11. Style of RC Passages

Argumentative Style Passages

1	4	2	3	3	1	4	3	5	4	6	3	7	4	8	1	9	3	10	3
11	3	12	1	13	2	14	3	15	4										

Philosophical Style Passages

1	1	2	3	3	4	4	4	5	2	6	2	7	3	8	2	9	4	10	4
11	2	12	3	13	4	14	1	15	2	16	4	17	2	18	1	19	1	20	1

Factual Style Passages

1	2	2	2	3	1	4	3	5	2	6	4	7	3	8	4	9	1	10	3
11	2	12	2	13	4	14	1	15	3										

Analytical Style Passages

1	3	2	4	3	1	4	2	5	4	6	1	7	2	8	1	9	4	10	1
11	2	12	3	13	3	14	2	15	2										

Narrative Style Passages

1	1	2	4	3	3	4	2	5	4	6	2	7	1	8	2	9	4	10	2

PART – 4 : VERBAL ABILITY / VOCABULARY

2. Synonyms and Antonyms

1	3	2	4	3	4	4	4	5	2	6	2	7	4	8	4	9	4	10	4
11	4	12	2	13	4	14	1	15	3	16	4	17	4	18	4	19	1	20	2
21	4	22	4	23	2	24	4	25	1	26	1	27	4	28	4	29	2	30	4
31	2	32	2	33	4	34	3	35	2	36	2	37	3	38	4	39	2	40	4
41	3	42	4	43	2	44	4	45	4	46	4	47	3	48	3	49	4	50	4
51	4	52	4	53	3	54	4	55	2	56	3	57	4	58	3	59	4	60	4
61	2	62	2	63	3	64	4	65	4	66	3	67	4	68	4	69	4	70	4
71	2	72	4	73	4	74	4	75	4	76	3	77	4	78	3	79	4	80	4
81	3	82	3	83	4	84	4	85	4	86	4	87	4	88	4	89	3	90	3
91	3	92	2	93	3	94	4	95	3	96	3	97	2	98	3	99	4	100	2

3. Sentence Completion Practice Sets

Q. No.	Sc 1	Sc 2	Sc 3	Sc 4	Sc 5	Sc 6	Sc 7	Sc 8	Sc 9	Sc 10
1	4	1	2	3	2	2	3	4	3	1
2	4	4	1	3	3	3	4	3	4	3
3	4	2	4	2	2	2	3	3	2	3
4	1	3	4	2	1	4	3	4	1	2
5	4	4	4	4	4	3	4	4	3	1

Q. No.	Sc 11	Sc 12	Sc 13	Sc 14	Sc 15	Sc 16	Sc 17	Sc 18	Sc 19	Sc 20
1	2	1	4	2	3	2	4	2	3	4
2	1	2	1	2	3	1	1	3	4	1
3	2	3	4	3	4	4	3	2	1	1
4	1	3	3	2	2	3	4	2	2	1
5	3	2	2	3	4	4	2	2	4	3

4. Analogies

Exercise – 1

1	2	2	3	3	2	4	4	5	2	6	2	7	1	8	1	9	1	10	3
11	3	12	4	13	1	14	4	15	1	16	3	17	1	18	3	19	2	20	4
21	3	22	3	23	2	24	2	25	4	26	2	27	2	28	3	29	4	30	2
31	3	32	2	33	1	34	2	35	1	36	2	37	4	38	3	39	3	40	3
41	2	42	3	43	1	44	1	45	3	46	2	47	4	48	1	49	3	50	4

Answers and Explanations

Exercise – 2

1	2	2	2	3	1	4	4	5	1	6	3	7	2	8	3	9	1	10	2
11	1	12	3	13	3	14	2	15	3	16	2	17	1	18	3	19	2	20	4
21	4	22	1	23	1	24	4	25	4	26	2	27	1	28	4	29	3	30	1
31	3	32	2	33	1	34	3	35	3	36	3	37	3	38	3	39	2	40	2
41	3	42	3	43	1	44	2	45	2	46	3	47	2	48	2	49	1	50	2

5. Critical Reasoning

1	3	2	2	3	3	4	2	5	1	6	3	7	4	8	1	9	4	10	2
11	3	12	2	13	4	14	4	15	4	16	3	17	2	18	3	19	3	20	1
21	4	22	4	23	4	24	4	25	3	26	2	27	4	28	3	29	3	30	4
31	3	32	2	33	4	34	4	35	2	36	4	37	4	38	4	39	3	40	3
41	1	42	2	43	4	44	4	45	4	46	1	47	2	48	4	49	4	50	4

PART – 1 : QUANTITATIVE ABILITY

I. Number System and Algebra

Exercise – 1

1. 3   LCM × HCF = $N_1 \times N_2$ (Product of numbers)

$$\Rightarrow N_2 = \frac{5200 \times 40}{520} = 400$$

2. 2   Sum of squares of n natural numbers

$$= \frac{n(n+1)(2n+1)}{6} = \frac{10 \times 11 \times 21}{6} = 385$$

3. 2   The sum of first 10 odd numbers = 10^2 = 100

4. 1   HCF of fractions = $\dfrac{\text{HCF of numerators}}{\text{LCM of denominators}}$

$$= \frac{\text{HCF } (3, 12)}{\text{LCM } (5, 13)} = \frac{3}{65}$$

5. 3   According to definition, all numbers in option (3) are irrational.

6. 4   Unit place digit = Unit place digit of (4 × 1 × 9 × 8).
Therefore, unit digit of the number = 8.

7. 1 $(2 + 2 \times 2)^3 = 216,\ [(2+2)^3]^{\frac{1}{2}} = \pm 8$

$2^5 = 32,\ (2 \times 2 - 2)^7 = 128$

8. 4 $(6^5)^{\frac{3}{5}} = 6^3$ = 216 is the smallest.

9. 4 $\because$ The sum of first n even numbers is n (n + 1).
$\therefore$ The sum of first 50 even numbers
= 2 + 4 + 6 + 8 + ... + 100 = 50 × (50 + 1) = 2550.

10. 4   For a number to be divisible by 9, sum of digits has to be divisible by 9.
$\therefore$ a = 7

11. 2 $4056 \div 26$ of $26 - \sqrt[3]{216}$

$$= 4056 \div 676 - (216)^{\frac{1}{3}}$$

$$= 4056 \div 676 - 6 = 6 - 6 = 0$$

12. 3   18.18 ÷ 9 + 2.7 of 3 = 18.18 ÷ 9 + 8.1
= 2.02 + 8.1 = 10.12

13. 4   8127 – 5422 + 1614 – 808 = 9741 – 6230 = 3511

14. 2 $11^2 + 11^4 \div 11^3 - 11 + (0.5)11^2$
= $11^2 + 11 - 11 + 0.5 \times 11^2$
= 121 + 11 – 11 + 0.5 × 121
= 121(1 + 0.5) = 121 × 1.5 = 181.5.

15. 4   Square root of 1296 is 36 not 34.

16. 4   Unit's digit is governed by product of individual unit's digit only. Unit's digit of
(7 × 8 × 7 × 3) is 6.

17. 4 $\because 1 + 2 + 3 + ... + n = \dfrac{n(n+1)}{2}$

$$\therefore 1 + 2 + 3 + ... + 45 = \frac{45 \times 46}{2} = 1035$$

Short cut:
The only option ending with 5 is (4).

18. 3 $\dfrac{451*603}{9}$.

$\because$ Sum of all digits must be divisible by 9,
$\therefore$ * = 8

19. 3   Number formed by last 3 digits must be divisible by 8.
$\therefore$ * = 3

20. 3   Going by options, it should be option (3).

21. 4   1399 × 1399 = $(1400 - 1)^2$
= $(1400)^2 + (1)^2 - 2\,(1400)\,(1)$
= 1960000 + 1 – 2800 = 1957201

22. 2   397 × 397 + 104 × 104 + 2 × 397 × 104
= $(397 + 104)^2 = (501)^2$
= $(500 + 1)^2$
= $(500)^2 + (1)^2 + 2\,(500)\,(1)$
= 250000 + 1 + 1000 = 251001

23. 1   Substitute n = 1, 2

24. 3   LCM of fractions $= \dfrac{\text{LCM of numerators}}{\text{HCF of denominators}}$

$$= \frac{\text{LCM } (1, 1)}{\text{HCF } (4, 8)} = \frac{1}{4}$$

25. 1   Clearly $\dfrac{4}{7} > \dfrac{3}{7}$

Now $\dfrac{4}{7} > \dfrac{2}{5}$ and $\dfrac{4}{7} > \dfrac{4}{9}$

Now we need to compare $\dfrac{4}{7}$ and $\dfrac{7}{13}$

$$\frac{4 \times 13}{7 \times 13} = \frac{52}{91} \text{ and } \frac{7 \times 7}{13 \times 7} = \frac{49}{91}$$

$$\therefore \frac{4}{7} > \frac{7}{13}$$

$\therefore \dfrac{4}{7}$ is the largest.

Exercise – 2

1. 2   Change the fractions into decimals and then check.

2. 4   LCM of 2, 3, 4, 5, 6, 7 = 420
Smallest 4 digit-number divisible by LCM
= 420 × 3 = 1260

Short cut:
1260 is the only option divisible by 3.

3. 2   Difference between divisor and remainder
= 35 − 25 = 45 − 35 = 55 − 45 = 10
LCM of 35, 45, 55 = 5 × 7 × 9 × 11 = 3465
Required number = 3465 − 10 = 3455

Short cut:
3455 is the only option from which when we subtract 35,
we get 3420 which is divisible by 45.

4. 4 $x + y = 2(x − y)$; $xy = 27$.
Only option (4) gives $xy = 27$

5. 1   LCM of 2, 3, 5 = 30
∴ Number of coconuts = 30 + 1 = 31

6. 4   The largest fraction is $\dfrac{5}{6}$.

7. 1   Since 2^7 is 128.
∴ When 128 is divided by 7, it leaves a remainder 2

Alternate Method:
Get a trend

$2^1 \% 7 = 2$, $2^2 \% 7 = 4$, $2^3 \% 7 = 1$, $2^4 \% 7 = 2$

and so on
Where % is modulus operator.

8. 4 $\sqrt{\dfrac{4}{3}} = \sqrt{\dfrac{4}{3}} \times \sqrt{\dfrac{3}{3}} = \dfrac{\sqrt{12}}{\sqrt{9}} = \dfrac{x}{3}$

9. 4   Numbers are 8, 9, 10
∴ Sum = 8 + 9 + 10 = 27

10. 2   Every such number must be divisible by LCM of 4, 5, 6, i.e.,
60.
Such numbers are 240, 300, 360, 420, 480, 540.
There are 6 such numbers.

11. 1   Number should be divisible by 9 and 11 both.

12. 1   Put n as 2, 4, 6, etc.

13. 3 $3 + \dfrac{3}{3 + \dfrac{1 \times 3}{10}} = 3 + \dfrac{3 \times 10}{33} = 3 + \dfrac{10}{11} = \dfrac{43}{11}$

14. 3   Let ten's digit be x. Then, unit's digit = (x + 3)
Sum of the digits = x + (x + 3) = 2x + 3
Number = 10x + (x + 3) = 11x + 3

$\dfrac{11x + 3}{2x + 3} = \dfrac{4}{1} \Rightarrow 11x + 3 = 4(2x + 3) \Rightarrow x = 3$

∴ Required number = (11x + 3) = 36

Alternate Method:
Check the conditions given in the options.

15. 1   Let the numbers be x and 1365 + x.
Then, $1365 + x = 6x + 15 \Rightarrow x = 270$.

16. 1 $\dfrac{A}{2} = \dfrac{B}{3} = \dfrac{C}{4} = x \Rightarrow A = 2x,\ B = 3x$ and $C = 4x$

$\Rightarrow A : B : C = 2 : 3 : 4$

Largest part = $243 \times \dfrac{4}{9} = 108$.

17. 4   Any number which is formed by writing any digit 6 times is
divisible by 1001.
$1001 = 7 \times 11 \times 13$
Hence, (4) is the correct choice.

18. 2   When 99547 is divided by 687, remainder is 619.
∴ Nearest number = 99547 + 68 = 99615

19. 4   99990

20. 3   100011

21. 2   Substitute n = 1.

22. 4 $n = 4 \times Q + 3$ (Q = Quotient)
$2n = 2 \times 4 \times Q + 6$
When 2n is divided by 4, Quotient = 2(Q + 1) and remainder
= 2

23. 4   A number abcabc is obtained when abc is multiplied by
1001, which in turn is a factor of 7, 11 and 13.

24. 3   LCM of 3, 6, 9, 12, 15, 18 is 180.
So, the bells will toll together after every 180 sec,
i.e. 3 min.

In 30 min, they will toll together in $\left(\dfrac{30}{3}\right) + 1 = 11$ times.

25. 4 $n = 5k + 2$

$\Rightarrow n^2 = 25k^2 + 10k + 4$

$\dfrac{n^2}{5} = 5k^2 + 2k + \dfrac{4}{5}$

Hence, the remainder when n^2 is divided by 5 is 4.

Exercise – 3

1. 3   Let the number of boys be x and the number of girls is
(x − 56).
$\Rightarrow x + (x − 56) = 850$
$\Rightarrow 2x = 850 + 56$

$\Rightarrow x = \dfrac{906}{2}$

$\Rightarrow x = 453$

2. 2   Let $\dfrac{1}{x} = a$

∴ The given expression becomes $\dfrac{2a}{5} - \dfrac{5a}{2} = \dfrac{1}{15}$

$\Rightarrow \dfrac{4a - 25a}{10} = \dfrac{1}{15}$

$\Rightarrow 3(4a - 25a) = 2$

$\Rightarrow 12a - 75a = 2$

$\Rightarrow -63a = 2$

$$\Rightarrow a = -\frac{2}{63}$$

$$\therefore x = -\frac{63}{2}$$

3. 1 Let Sachin and Vinod scored x and (x − 15) runs respectively.
According to the given condition:
$\Rightarrow (x - 15) = 245 - x$
$\Rightarrow x + x = 245 + 15$
$\Rightarrow 2x = 260$
$\Rightarrow x = 130$
Vinod scored = 245 − x = 115

4. 4 Let the breath of the rectangle be x m and its length be (x + 7) m.
$\because$ Perimeter of a rectangle = 2 (l + b)
$\Rightarrow 2[x + (x + 7)] = 94$
$\Rightarrow 2(2x + 7) = 94$
$\Rightarrow 2x + 7 = 47$
$\Rightarrow 2x = 40$
$\Rightarrow x = 20$ and x + 7 = 27
$\therefore$ The length of rectangle is 27 m while breadth is 20 m.

5. 1 Let the measure of the small angle be 2x and the measure of the greater angle be 3x.
As they are complementary angles, the sum of their measures will be 90°.
$\Rightarrow 2x + 3x = 90°$
$\Rightarrow 2x = 36°$ and 3x = 54°
The measures of the two angles are 36° and 54°.

6. 1 Let the digit at the unit's place be x and the digit at ten's place be (9 − x).
Hence, the two-digit number is 10(9 − x) + x.
= 90 − 10x + x
= 90 − 9x
Number after interchanging digits
= 10x + (9 − x)
According to the given condition:
$\therefore 90 - 9x + 63 = 10x + 9 - x$
$\Rightarrow 153 - 9x = 9x + 9$
$\Rightarrow 18x = 144$
$\Rightarrow x = 8$

7. 3 $\dfrac{3x+5}{3-2x} = \dfrac{5}{3}$
$\Rightarrow 3(3x + 5) = 5(3 - 2x)$
$\Rightarrow 9x + 15 = 15 - 10x$
$\Rightarrow 19x = 0$
$\Rightarrow x = 0$

8. 1 Let the number be x.
$\Rightarrow 20 - 5x = 3x + 4$
$\Rightarrow 8x = 16 \Rightarrow x = 2$

9. 1 Let the width be x m and length be $\dfrac{5x}{2}$ m.
According to the given condition:
$\Rightarrow 2\left(\dfrac{5x}{2} + x\right) = 70$

$\Rightarrow \dfrac{7x}{2} = 35 \Rightarrow x = \dfrac{35 \times 2}{7} = 10$ m
$\therefore$ Length = $\dfrac{5}{2} \times 10 = 25$ m

10. 4 Let Z has Rs a, Y has Rs. 3a and X has 2(3a) = Rs. 6a
According to the given condition:
$\Rightarrow X + Y + Z = 1000$
$\Rightarrow 6a + 3a + a = 1000$
$\Rightarrow 10a = 1000$
$\Rightarrow a = 100$
$\therefore$ Amount with X = 6 × 100 = 600

11. 2 Let son will be $\dfrac{4}{7}$ of his father's age in x years.
According to the given condition:
$\Rightarrow 9 + x = \dfrac{4}{7}(36 + x)$
$\Rightarrow 7(9+x) = 4(36+x)$
$\Rightarrow 63 + 7x = 144 + 4x$
$\Rightarrow 3x = 81$
$\Rightarrow x = 27$

12. 3 $\quad x - y = 15 \qquad \qquad ...(1)$
and $x = 4y \qquad \qquad ...(2)$
$\Rightarrow x - 4y = 0$
Substract equation (1) from equation (2)
$x - 4y = 0$
$x - y = 15$
$\overline{\quad - 3y = -15\quad}$
$\therefore y = 5$
Putting this value in equation (1)
$x - 5 = 15$
or, x = 20 years

13. 3 Let the second number be x.
$\therefore$ First number is (36 + x).
$\Rightarrow 36 + x = 6x + 1$
$\Rightarrow 5x = 35$
$\Rightarrow x = 7$
Hence, the numbers are 43 and 7.

14. 3 Let the width be x cm and the length is 3x cm.
Now, 2(x + 3x) = 32
4x = 16
x = 4 cm
Hence, length = 12 cm

15. 2 Let son's age be x years and father's age be (x + 20) years.
$\Rightarrow x + 20 + 5 = 3(x+5)$
$\Rightarrow x + 25 = 3x + 15$
$\Rightarrow 2x = 10$
$\Rightarrow x = 5$
$\therefore$ The father's present age is 25 years.

16. 4 Let the digit at tens place be x.
$\therefore$ The number is 10x + 3.
$\Rightarrow x + 3 = \dfrac{1}{7}(10x + 3)$

$\Rightarrow 7(x + 3) = 10x + 3$

$\Rightarrow 7x + 21 = 10x + 3$

$\Rightarrow 3x = 18$

$\Rightarrow x = 6$

$\therefore$ The number is 63.

17. 3 Given

$3x - 2 = 2x + 4$ ... (1)

Putting the value of x in (1)

$$\Rightarrow 3\left(\frac{a+2}{3}\right) - 2 = 2\left(\frac{a+2}{3}\right) + 4$$

$$\Rightarrow a + 2 - 2 = \left(\frac{2a+4}{3}\right) + 4$$

$$\Rightarrow a = \frac{2a+4+12}{3}$$

$\Rightarrow 3a - 2a = 16$

$\Rightarrow a = 16$

18. 1 Let the obtuse angle of the parallelogram be x and its adjacent angle be $(180° - x)$.

$\Rightarrow x = 2(180° - x)$

$\Rightarrow x = 360° - 2x$

$\Rightarrow 3x = 360°$

$\Rightarrow x = 120°$

The four angles are 60°, 60°, 120°, 120°.

19. 4 Let the number be x.

According to the given condition

$\Rightarrow 2x - 16 = 3x - 20$

$\Rightarrow 2x - 3x = -20 + 16$

$\Rightarrow x = 4$

20. 2 Let the smaller integer be x and the greater integer is $(45 - x)$.

$\therefore 45 - x = 2x$

$\therefore 3x = 45$

$\therefore x = 15$

21. 3 Let the three numbers be x, (x + 1) and (x + 2) respectively.

$\Rightarrow x + (x + 1) + (x + 2) = 384$

$\Rightarrow 3x + 3 = 384$

$\Rightarrow 3x = 381$

$$\Rightarrow x = \frac{381}{3}$$

$x = 127$

$\therefore$ The numbers are 127, 128 and 129.

22. 3 Mr. Shah's present age is 5 + 30 = 35 years.

Let after x years, Mr. Shah will become three times as old as his son.

$\Rightarrow 35 + x = 3(5 + x)$

$\Rightarrow 35 + x = 15 + 3x$

$\Rightarrow 2x = 20 \Rightarrow x = 10$

23. 2 Let one integer be x and the other integer be $(62 - x)$.

$\Rightarrow 62 - x - x = 12$

$\Rightarrow 62 - 2x = 12$

$\Rightarrow 2x = 50 \Rightarrow x = 25$

Hence, the numbers are 25 and 37.

24. 3 Let the number be x.

According to the given condition:

$$\Rightarrow x + \frac{x}{2} = 117$$

$\Rightarrow 2x + x = 234$

$\Rightarrow 3x = 234$

$\Rightarrow x = 78$

The required number is 78.

25. 2 Let one integer be x and the other integer be $(25 - x)$.

Now the difference = 5

$\Rightarrow x - (25 - x) = 5$

$\Rightarrow 2x - 25 = 5$

$\Rightarrow 2x = 25 + 5$

$\Rightarrow x = 15$

$\therefore$ Other number = 25 - 15 = 10

$$\therefore \text{Ratio of two number} = \frac{15}{10} = \frac{3}{2}$$

Exercise – 4

1. 1 Let the present age of son be x years.

Then according to the given condition man's age 3x years.

After 14 years, the son becomes (x + 14) years.

After 14 years, the man becomes (3x + 14) years.

Equating the ages we have

Twice son's future age = man's future age.

$\Rightarrow 2(x+14) = 3x + 14$

$\Rightarrow 2x + 28 = 3x + 14$

$\Rightarrow 28 - 14 = 3x - 2x \Rightarrow 14 = x$

Hence, the present ages of the son and the father is 14 years and 42 years

2. 3 Let one part be x and the other part be $(300 - x)$.

It is given that half of one part is 48 less than the other

$$\Rightarrow \frac{1}{2}x = (300 - x) - 48$$

$$\Rightarrow \frac{x}{2} = 300 - x - 48$$

$$\Rightarrow \frac{x}{2} + x = 300 - 48$$

$$\Rightarrow \frac{3x}{2} = 252 \Rightarrow x = \frac{504}{3}$$

$\Rightarrow x = 168$

Hence, one part is 168 and the other part is 300 – 168 = 132.

3. 3 Let the third side be x cm.

According to the given condition:

$\therefore$ Congruent sides = 2x + 2

$\Rightarrow (2x + 2) + (2x + 2) + x = 19$

$\Rightarrow 5x + 4 = 19$

$\Rightarrow 5x = 15$

$\Rightarrow x = 3$

$\Rightarrow$ Length of one of the equal sides

= 2(3) +2 = 8 cm

Answers and Explanations

4. 3   Let Q receives Rs. x from P.

$\Rightarrow 3(P - x) - 120 = Q + x$

$\Rightarrow 3(570 - x) - 120 = 350 + x$

$\Rightarrow 1710 - 3x = 470 + x$

$\Rightarrow 4x = 1240$

$\Rightarrow x = $ Rs. 310

Amount left with P = 570 − 310 = Rs. 260

5. 3   Let the digits in tens and units places be x and y, respectively

$\Rightarrow (10x + y) - (10y + x) = 81$

$\Rightarrow 10x + y - 10y - x = 81$

$\Rightarrow 9x - 9y = 81$

$\Rightarrow x - y = 9$

6. 3   Let the cost of a mango be Rs. x and the cost of an orange be Rs.y

$2x + 5y = 15$ ... (i)

and $4x + 3y = 23$ ... (ii)

Multiplying equation (i) by 2 and subtracting it from (ii), we have

$4x + 3y = 23$ ... (i)

$4x + 10y = 30$ ... (ii)

$\underline{---}$

$- 7y = - 7$

$y = 1$

From (i), $2x + 5 = 15$

$\Rightarrow 2x = 10$

$\Rightarrow x = 5$

∴ Mango costs Rs. 5 and orange cost Re.1

7. 1   Let the numerator be x and the denominator be (11 − x). According to the given condition:

$\Rightarrow \dfrac{x+1}{11-x} = \dfrac{1}{2}$

$\Rightarrow 2(x + 1) = 11 - x$

$\Rightarrow 2x + 2 = 11 - x \Rightarrow 2x + x = 11 - 2 \Rightarrow 3x = 9$

∴ x = 3

∴ Denominator = 11 − 3 = 8

∴ Hence, required fraction is $\dfrac{3}{8}$.

8. 3   Let workman works for x days and remains absent for (30 − x) days.

$\Rightarrow 15x - 3(30 - x) = 360$

$\Rightarrow 18x - 90 = 360$

$\Rightarrow 18x = 450$

∴ x = 25

9. 2   Let the base be x.

The length of each of its congruent side be $\dfrac{23 - x}{2}$.

According to the given condition:

$\Rightarrow \dfrac{23 - x}{2} = 2x - 1$

$\Rightarrow 23 - x = 4x - 2$

$\Rightarrow 5x = 25$

$\Rightarrow x = 5$

and the congruent sides = $\dfrac{23 - 5}{2} = 9$ cm. each

10. 3   Let one number be x and other number be (2490 − x). According to the given condition

$\Rightarrow \dfrac{6.5}{100} x = \dfrac{8.5}{100} (2490 - x)$

$\Rightarrow 6.5x = 8.5 \times 2490 - 8.5x$

$\Rightarrow 15x = 8.5 \times 2490$

$\Rightarrow x = \dfrac{8.5 \times 2490}{15}$

$\Rightarrow x = 8.5 \times 166 = 1411$

11. 3   Let boy hits the "Bull's eye" x times and he missed (50 − x) times.

$\Rightarrow 20(x) - (50 - x)8 = 48$

$\Rightarrow 20x - 400 + 8x = 48$

$\Rightarrow 28x = 448$

$\Rightarrow x = 16$

12. 3   Let son's age be x years and father's age be (25 + x) years. According to the given condition:

$\Rightarrow 25 + x - 5 = 6(x - 5)$

$\Rightarrow x + 20 = 6x - 30$

$\Rightarrow 5x = 50$

$\Rightarrow x = 10$

13. 2   Let the number of days of the tour initially be x.

$\Rightarrow$ Expenses per day = Rs. $\dfrac{3000}{x}$

If the tour is extended by 5 days

New number of days = x + 5

$\Rightarrow$ New expense per day = Rs. $\dfrac{3000}{x + 5}$

Given, old expenses − new expenses = 20

$\Rightarrow \dfrac{3000}{x} - \dfrac{3000}{x + 5} = 20$

$\Rightarrow 150 \left(\dfrac{1}{x} - \dfrac{1}{x + 5} \right) = 1$

$\Rightarrow 150 \times 5 = x^2 + 5x$

$\Rightarrow x^2 + 5x - 750 = 0$

$\Rightarrow (x + 30)(x - 25) = 0$

$\Rightarrow x = 25$ or $x = -30$

∵ $x \neq -30$

$\Rightarrow x = 25$

New number of days = 25 + 5 = 30

14. 4   Let us suppose the three fractions be x, y and z in ascending order.

$\Rightarrow$ Given $x + y + z = \dfrac{59}{24}$ and $\dfrac{z}{x} = \dfrac{7}{6} = y + \dfrac{1}{3}$

$\Rightarrow y = \dfrac{7}{6} - \dfrac{1}{3} = \dfrac{5}{6}$

$\Rightarrow x + \dfrac{5}{6} + \dfrac{7x}{6} = \dfrac{59}{24}$

$\Rightarrow \dfrac{13x}{6} = \dfrac{59}{24} - \dfrac{5}{6}$

$\Rightarrow \dfrac{13x}{6} = \dfrac{59 - 20}{24} = \dfrac{39}{24}$

Answers and Explanations

$$\Rightarrow x = \frac{39}{24} \times \frac{6}{13} = \frac{3}{4}$$

$$\Rightarrow z = \frac{7x}{6} = \frac{7}{6} \times \frac{3}{4} = \frac{7}{8}$$

$$\Rightarrow x, y, z = \frac{3}{4}, \frac{5}{6}, \frac{7}{8}$$

15. 1 Let the present age of A be x and B be y years.

$$\Rightarrow x - 10 = \frac{y-10}{2}$$

$$\Rightarrow 2(x - 10) = y - 10$$
$$\Rightarrow 2x - 20 = y - 10$$
$$\Rightarrow 2x - y = 10 \qquad \ldots (i)$$

According to the second condition

$$\Rightarrow x + 8 = (y + 8)\,\frac{2}{3}$$

$$\Rightarrow 3(x + 8) = 2(y + 8)$$
$$\Rightarrow 3x + 24 = 2y + 16$$
$$\Rightarrow 3x - 2y = -8 \qquad \ldots (ii)$$

Multiplying equation (i) by 2 and subtracting it from (ii), we have

$$3x - 2y = -8 \qquad \ldots (i)$$
$$4x - 2y = 20 \qquad \ldots (ii)$$

$$\underline{\quad - \quad + \quad - \quad}$$

$$\Rightarrow x = 28$$

Putting the value of x in equation (i)
$$\Rightarrow 2(28) - y = 10 \Rightarrow 56 - y = 10$$
$$\therefore y = 46$$

16. 2 Let us assume the number of articles be x.

Price of each article = Rs. $\dfrac{1200}{x}$

If the price per article is increased by Rs. 5.
Number of articles = x – 20

$\therefore$ New price of each article = $\dfrac{1200}{x - 20}$

$$\Rightarrow \frac{1200}{x - 20} - \frac{1200}{x} = 5 \Rightarrow 1200\left(\frac{20}{x(x-20)}\right) = 5$$

$$\Rightarrow 4800 = x(x - 20)$$
$$\Rightarrow x^2 - 20x - 4800 = 0$$
$$\Rightarrow (x - 80)(x + 60) = 0$$
$$x = 80 \text{ and } x \neq -60$$

17. 4 Let the number of eggs purchase be 'x'.

$\because$ C.P. of each egg = $\dfrac{1}{4}$

$\Rightarrow$ C.P. of x eggs = $\dfrac{x}{4}$

Person kept $\dfrac{1}{5}$ th of the eggs and sold the rest.

$\therefore$ Number of eggs sold = $\dfrac{4}{5}x$

S.P. of each egg = $\dfrac{1}{3} \times \dfrac{4}{5}x = \dfrac{4}{15}x$

$\because$ Profit = Re. 1.

$$\Rightarrow \frac{4x}{15} - \frac{x}{4} = 1 \Rightarrow \frac{16x - 15x}{60} = 1$$
or, x = 60

18. 4 20 children $\Leftrightarrow$ 12 adults

$$\therefore \; 5 \text{ children} \Leftrightarrow \frac{12}{20} \times 5 = 3 \text{ adults}$$

$\therefore$ With 15 children, 3 adults are permitted to board the elevator.

19. 4 Let the present ages of the father and son be x years and y years respectively.
2 years ago $\quad : - (x-2) = 3(y-2)^2 \qquad \ldots (i)$
3 years hence $: - (x+3) = 4(y+3) \qquad \ldots (ii)$
From (i) and (ii)
$$\Rightarrow -5 = 3(y-2)^2 - 4(y+3)$$
$$\Rightarrow -5 = 3(y^2 - 4y + 4) - 4y - 12$$
$$\Rightarrow 0 = 3y^2 - 16y + 5 = 3y^2 - 15y - y + 5$$
$$= 3y(y - 5) - 1(y - 5)$$
$$= (3y - 1)(y - 5)$$
$$\therefore \; y = \frac{1}{3} \text{ or } y = 5$$

$y = \dfrac{1}{3}$ rejected as two years ago son's age will be negative.

$$\therefore \; y = 5$$
$$x = 4y + 12 - 3 = 20 + 12 - 3 = 29$$
Father's age = 29 years
Son's age = 5 years

20. 3 Let the number of persons be n.

Then, amount each person receives = $\dfrac{1000}{n}$ paise

$\therefore$ If the number of persons is increased by $\dfrac{1}{4}$ th

$$\Rightarrow \text{New number} = n + \frac{n}{4} = \frac{5n}{4}$$

$\therefore$ Amount, each person will receive = $\dfrac{1000}{\frac{5n}{4}}$

$\therefore$ Amount, each person will receive = $\dfrac{4}{5} \times \dfrac{1000}{n}$

$$\Rightarrow \frac{1000}{n} - \left(\frac{4}{5}\right)\frac{1000}{n} = 5$$

$$\therefore \; \frac{1000}{n} \times \frac{1}{5} = 5$$

$$n = \frac{1000}{25} = 40$$

21. 2 Let Tina's age be x years.
Her sister's age is (x – 3) years.
Her brother is (x + 4) years.
From the condition given in problem -
$$\Rightarrow x + (x - 3) + (x + 4) = 73 \Rightarrow 3x + 1 = 73$$
$$\Rightarrow x = 24. \text{ Tina's age is 24 years}$$

22. 2 Let the cost of ticket be Rs x and reservation charges be Rs. y.

$\therefore$ x + y = 362   ... (i)

and $1\dfrac{1}{2}$x + 2y = 554

$\dfrac{3}{2}$x + 2y = 554   ... (ii)

Multiply equation (i) by 2 and subtract it from

$\dfrac{3}{2}$x + 2y = 554

2 x + 2y = 724
____

$-\dfrac{1}{2}$ x = $-$ 170

x = Rs. 340

$\therefore$ Reservation charges = Rs. 22

23. 2 Let the number of coins of each type be x.

$\therefore$ According to the given condition:

$\Rightarrow$ 50x + 10x + 5x = 13000

$\Rightarrow$ 65x = 13000

$\Rightarrow$ x = $\dfrac{13000}{65}$ = 200

24. 1 Let son's present age be x years.

$\Rightarrow$ 38 $-$ x = x

$\Rightarrow$ 2x = 38

$\Rightarrow$ x = 19

25. 3 Let the number of articles be x.

$\Rightarrow$ C.P. of each article = $\dfrac{50}{5}$ = 10 paise

$\therefore$ C.P. of x articles = 10x paise

$\because$ If the cost was $\dfrac{100}{11}$ paise each.

$\Rightarrow$ C.P. of x articles = $\dfrac{100}{11}$ x

According to the given condition

$\Rightarrow$ 10x $-\dfrac{100x}{11}$ = 50

$\therefore$ x $-\dfrac{10x}{11}$ = 5 $\Rightarrow$ x = 55

▌2. Ratio, Proportion and Averages

Exercise – 1

1. 3 $\dfrac{A}{B} = \dfrac{3}{7}$. Let A = 3x, B = 7x

A + B = 45;   3x + 7x = 45, x = $\dfrac{45}{10}$ = 4.5

B = 7x = 31.5

2. 4 Let the fraction be x/y $\dfrac{x/y}{3/7} = \dfrac{1/27}{1/35}$ or, $\dfrac{7x}{3y} = \dfrac{35}{27}$

$\dfrac{x}{y} = \dfrac{35}{27} \times \dfrac{3}{7} = \dfrac{5}{9}$

3. 1 If a, b and c are in continued proportion, the mean proportional is b.

Therefore, b^2 = ac, b^2 = 8 × 72, b = $\sqrt{576}$ = 24

4. 2 If a, b, c and d are in proportion, $\dfrac{a}{b} = \dfrac{c}{d}$ or $\dfrac{3}{15} = \dfrac{27}{d}$,

or d = 135 is the fourth proportional.

5. 4 Third proportional, c = $\dfrac{b^2}{a}$ = $\dfrac{30 \times 30}{20}$ = 45

6. 4 Let the number added be x. Then,

$\dfrac{4+x}{9+x} = \dfrac{2}{3}$,   12 + 3x = 18 + 2x

x = 6

7. 2 $\dfrac{4^{3.5}}{2^5} = \dfrac{(2^2)^{3.5}}{2^5} = \dfrac{2^7}{2^5} = 2^2 = 4$

$\therefore$ Required ratio = 4 : 1.

8. 3 $\dfrac{x}{y} = \dfrac{2}{7}$ Let x's share = 2a, y's share = 7a

$\dfrac{x's \ share}{x's \ share - y's \ share} = \dfrac{2a}{5a} = \dfrac{2}{5}$

9. 4 $\dfrac{68-x}{49-x} = \dfrac{3}{4}$, $\Rightarrow$ 272 $-$ 4x = 147 $-$ 3x $\Rightarrow$ x = 125

10. 1 $\dfrac{A}{2} = \dfrac{B}{3} = \dfrac{C}{6}$ or   3A = 2B = C

B's part = $\dfrac{B}{\dfrac{2}{3}B + B + 2B} \times 3960$

= $\dfrac{3}{11} \times 3960 = 3 \times 360 = 1080$

11. 4 C's share = 2 B's share

A's share = $\dfrac{2}{3}$ B' share

$\Rightarrow$ required ratio is $\dfrac{\dfrac{2}{3} \ B's \ share}{(2 \ B's \ share - B's \ share)} = \dfrac{2}{3}$

12. 3 Let the number be 5x and 3x, then $\dfrac{5x-9}{3x-9} = \dfrac{23}{12}$

60x $-$ 108 = 69x $-$ 207; 9x = 99, x = 11

The first number is 11 × 5 = 55

13. 4 $4x = 3y = 2z$

$$\Rightarrow \frac{x}{y} = \frac{3}{4} \ \& \ \frac{y}{z} = \frac{2}{3} = \frac{4}{6} \Rightarrow x : y : z = 3 : 4 : 6$$

14. 4   In a ratio A:B, A is called the antecedent and B is called the consequent.
Let antecedent = 4x & consequent be 9x.
$4x = 36 \Rightarrow 9x = 81$.

15. 1 $\dfrac{M}{W} = \dfrac{3}{1}$ in 100 L mixture

Milk = 75 L, Water = 25 L
After adding 200 L of water, water = 225 L and milk = 75 L

Ratio = $\dfrac{75}{225} = 1 : 3$

16. 2   Let $\dfrac{a}{3} = \dfrac{b}{4} = \dfrac{c}{7} = k$

$a = 3k, \ b = 4k, \ c = 7k$

$\dfrac{a + b + c}{c} = \dfrac{3k + 4k + 7k}{7k} = \dfrac{14k}{7k} = 2$

17. 2   **Option a:**
Numbers = 9x, 3x
12x = 84
x = 7; possible.

Option b:
$8x = 84 \Rightarrow$ No whole number x is possible.
Option c and d:
4x = 84
x = 4; Possible.

18. 2   0.35 of x = 0.07 of y

$\therefore \dfrac{x}{y} = \dfrac{0.07}{0.35} = \dfrac{1}{5}$

19. 4   The question uses the same concept as in Q 17.
Number of mugs = 12
The sum of broken and unbroken mugs must be equal to 12.
Sum of ratio = 3, 12, 5, 6, (5 does not divide 12)
$\therefore$ 3 : 2 cannot be the ratio.

20. 1   Let (a + b) = 6k, (b + c) = 7k and (c + a) = 8k
Then, 2(a + b + c)= 21k

$\Rightarrow 2 \times 14 = 21k \Rightarrow k = \dfrac{4}{3}$

$\therefore (a + b) = 6k = 6 \times \dfrac{4}{3} = 8$

$\Rightarrow c = (a + b + c) - (a + b)$
$= 14 - 8 = 6$

21. 2   Let the third proportional be x.
Then, 12 : 30 : : 30 : x $\Leftrightarrow$ 12x = 30 × 30
$\Rightarrow$ x = 75.

Mean proportional between 9 and 25 = $\sqrt{9 \times 25} = 15$
$\therefore$ Required ratio = 75 : 15 = 5 : 1.

22. 2   B's money = $\dfrac{5}{4} \times 800 = 1000$

C's money = $\dfrac{3}{2} \times 1000 = 1500$

Therefore, total amount of money = Rs. 3,300

23. 3   Let the two parts be x, (68 − x)

$$\frac{x}{7} = \frac{1}{10}(68 - x) = \frac{68}{10} - \frac{x}{10}$$

$$\frac{x}{7} + \frac{x}{10} = \frac{68}{10} \text{ or, } \frac{17x}{70} = \frac{68}{10}, \ x = 28$$

24. 2   X's share $\Rightarrow$ 3x + 30
Y's share $\Rightarrow$ 4x + 20
Z's share $\Rightarrow$ 5x + 50
Sum = Rs. 9700
$\Rightarrow$ 12x + 100 = 9700, 12x = 9600, x = 800
Y's share = 4x + 20 = 3200 + 20 = Rs. 3220

25. 2   Ratio of sides = $\dfrac{1}{2} : \dfrac{1}{3} : \dfrac{1}{4} = 6 : 4 : 3$

Largest side = $\left(\dfrac{6}{13} \times 104 \right)$ cm = 48 cm

Exerice – 2

1. 4   Let   B get's   Rs. x
         A get's   Rs. x + 70
         C get's   Rs. x − 80
$\Rightarrow$ x + (x + 70) + (x − 80) = 530
$\Rightarrow$ 3x − 10 = 530, 3x = 540
x = 180

$\dfrac{\text{A's share}}{\text{C's share}} = \dfrac{180 + 70}{180 - 80} = \dfrac{250}{100} = \dfrac{5}{2}$

2. 2 $A = \dfrac{1}{2}B, \ B = 2C$ or $\dfrac{A}{B} = \dfrac{1}{2}, \ \dfrac{B}{C} = \dfrac{2}{1}$
A : B : C = 1 : 2 : 1

Shares of A, B, C are x, 2x, x

$\dfrac{B}{A + B} = \dfrac{2x}{x + 2x} = \dfrac{2x}{3x} = \dfrac{2}{3}$

3. 3   Initially, Number of boys = 250
Number of girls = 250

New Batch: $\dfrac{1}{5} \times 250$ = 50 girls left & 25 boys joined the class.

New ratio = $\dfrac{\text{Boys}}{\text{Girls}} = \dfrac{275}{200} = \dfrac{11}{8}$

4. 1   Let Father's age be 7x, son's age = 2x
After 15 years,

$\dfrac{7x + 15}{2x + 15} = \dfrac{2}{1}, \ $ 7x + 15 = 4x + 30, x = 5

Present age of father = 35
Present age of son = 10
Father's age when son was born = 35 − 10 = 25

5. 4   Let present age of son = x and
present age of father = y
$(y - 4) = 6(x - 4)$ ... (i)
$(y + 12) = 2(x + 12)$ ... (ii)
from (i) and (ii),
$y - 6x + 20 = 0$
$y - 2x - 12 = 0$
$4x = 32$, $x = 8$ years, $y = 28$ years

Ratio of their present ages $= \dfrac{28}{8} = 7 : 2$

6. 2   Let the ages of A and B are 3x years and x years respectively.

Then, $\dfrac{3x + 15}{x + 15} = \dfrac{2}{1} \Rightarrow x = 15$

So, A's age = 3 × 15 = 45 years and B's age = 15 years.

7. 3   In 80 L of mixture,

Milk $= \dfrac{5}{8} \times 80 = 50$ L

Water = (80 − 50) = 30 L.
When we take a 16 L sample of this mixture.

Milk taken out $= \dfrac{5}{8} \times 16 = 10$ L

Water taken out = (16 − 10) = 6 L.
$\Rightarrow$ Milk available = 50 − 10 = 40 L
Water available = 30 − 6 = 24 L.
Now, 16 L of milk is added,
$\Rightarrow$ Milk = 40 L + 16 L = 56 L
Water = 24 L
$\Rightarrow$ Milk : Water = 56 : 24 = 7 : 3.

8. 2   Let copper = 13x
Zinc = 7x
In 500 kg, 13x + 7x = 500

$\Rightarrow x = \dfrac{500}{20} = 25$ kg

Copper = 13 × 25 = 325 kg

9. 4   Simplest form $= \dfrac{2}{7}$

Numerator = 2x
Denominator = 7x
$\Rightarrow 7x - 2x = 40$, $x = 8$

Number $= \dfrac{16}{56}$.

10. 3   For every 100 paise that A gets, B gets 65 paise and C gets 35 paise.

C's share $= 560 = $ Total sum $\times \dfrac{35}{200}$

$\therefore$ Total Sum = Rs. 3,200

11. 4   L : R : O = 5 : 7 : 3
Let Labour cost = 5x, Raw Material cost = 7x
Overheads cost = 3x, Total cost = 15x
Profits = 20% of 15x = 3x

$\dfrac{\text{Raw Material cost}}{\text{Profit}} = \dfrac{7x}{3x} = \dfrac{7}{3}$

12. 2 $\dfrac{B}{G} = \dfrac{7}{5}$

Let number of boys = 7x
Let number of girls = 5x
7x + 5x = 72,   x = 6
Number of boys = 42
Number of girls = 30
12 more girls should be admitted to make the ratio equal.

13. 4   Let A's income = Rs. 3x
B's income = Rs. 2x
A's expenses = Rs. 5y
B's expenses = Rs. 3y
A's savings = 3x − 5y = 3000   ... (i)
B's savings = 2x − 3y = 3000   ... (ii)
Solving (i) and (ii), x = 6000
B's income = 2x = Rs. 12,000

14. 1   Let the number to be added be, x.

Then, $\dfrac{7 + x}{19 + x} = \dfrac{1}{2}$, $x = 5$

15. 2   10% of B $= \dfrac{1}{4} G \Rightarrow \dfrac{10B}{100} = \dfrac{G}{4} \Rightarrow \dfrac{B}{G} = \dfrac{5}{2}$

16. 4 $x \propto \dfrac{1}{y^2} \Rightarrow x = \dfrac{k}{y^2}$

For, y = 2, x = 1

$\Rightarrow 1 = \dfrac{k}{(2)^2}$, $k = 4 \Rightarrow x = \dfrac{4}{y^2}$

For y = 6

$x = \dfrac{4}{6^2} = \dfrac{4}{36} = \dfrac{1}{9}$

17. 2   Required ratio $= \left(\dfrac{2}{3} \times \dfrac{6}{11} \times \dfrac{11}{2} \right) = \dfrac{2}{1} = 2 : 1$

18. 4   Let the original earnings of A and B be Rs. 4x and Rs. 7x.
New earnings of A = 150% of Rs 4x = Rs 6x

New earning of B = 75% of Rs. 7x = Rs.$\dfrac{21}{4}x$

$\therefore$ New ratio $= \dfrac{6x}{\dfrac{21}{4}x} = \dfrac{8}{7}$

This does not give x. So, the given data is inadequate.

19. 3   Total age of 3 boys = (25 × 3) = 75 years
Ratio of their ages = 3 : 5 : 7.

Age of the youngest $= \left(\dfrac{75 \times 3}{15} \right) = 15$ years

20. 2   Let the initial weight be 'w' grams and price be Rs. 'P'.
According to the question

$P \propto w^2$

$\Rightarrow P = kw^2$

Let P' = Price of 2 pieces.

$$P' = k\left(\frac{4}{10}w\right)^2 + k\left(\frac{6}{10}w\right)^2$$

$$\Rightarrow P' = \frac{52kw^2}{100}$$

$$\text{Loss in value } = \left(\frac{P-P'}{P}\right) \times 100$$

$$= \frac{\left(kw^2 - \frac{52kw^2}{100}\right)}{kw^2} \times 100 = 48\%$$

21. 4 Let the number of 50 p, 25 p and 10 p coins be 5x, 9x and 4x respectively.

Then, $\dfrac{5x}{2} + \dfrac{9x}{4} + \dfrac{4x}{10} = 206 \Rightarrow x = 40$

$\therefore$ No. of 50 p = 5x = 5 × 40 = 200.

22. 4
$2x + y = 5z$ ... (1)
$3x - 2y = 4z$ ... (2)
Dividing (1) by (2)

$$\frac{2x+y}{3x-2y} = \frac{5}{4} \Rightarrow y = \frac{x}{2}$$

Putting $y = \dfrac{x}{2}$ in equation (1), we get

$$z = \frac{x}{2} \Rightarrow x : y : z = x : \frac{x}{2} : \frac{x}{2} = 2 : 1 : 1.$$

23. 2 Let the volume of sphere be V and radius be r. According to the question

$V \propto r^3$

$\Rightarrow V = kr^3$

Let, V_T = Volume of recast sphere.
$V_T = k(3)^3 + k(4)^3 + k(5)^3$
$= k \times 216$

$= k(6)^3 \Rightarrow V \propto (6)^3$

$\Rightarrow$ Radius of new sphere = 6 cm.

24. 3 Let C be cost of digging.

$C \propto d$ and $C \propto d^2$

$\Rightarrow C = ad + bd^2$; where a and b are constants.
$10a + (10)^2 b = 2050$ ... (1)
and $15a + (15)^2 b = 4575$ ... (2)
From (1) and (2); a = 5 and b = 20.
$\Rightarrow C = 5d + 20d^2$
For d = 20
$C = 5(20) + 20(20)^2 = $ Rs 8100.

25. 4 Let A be the total amount for b book sold. F be the fixed amount and R be the royalty per book.
$\Rightarrow A = F + bR$
For b = 1000, A = Rs. 30,000 and b = 2000, A = Rs. 50000
$\Rightarrow F + 1000 R = 30,000$ ... (1)
and $F + 2000 R = 50,000$ ... (2)
From (1) and (2)
F = 10,000 and R = 20.
$\Rightarrow$ for b = 5000
A = 10,000 + 20 × 5000 = Rs 1,10,000

$$\Rightarrow \text{Income per book } = \frac{1,10,000}{5,000} = \text{Rs } 22$$

Exercise – 3

1. 3 First nine prime numbers are 2, 3, 5, 7, 11, 13, 17, 19 and 23.

$$\text{Average } = \frac{2+3+5+7+11+13+17+19+23}{9} = 11\frac{1}{9}$$

2. 3
$$\frac{2+7+6+x}{4} = 5 \,(\text{given})$$

$\Rightarrow x = 5$ ... (1)

Also, $\dfrac{18+1+6+x+y}{5} = 10$

$\Rightarrow x + y = 25$
$\Rightarrow y = 25 - x = 25 - 5$ [From (1)]
     = 20

3. 4 Since the number of boys and girls are not known. Hence, average age for the whole class cannot be determined.

4. 3
$$\frac{\text{sum of scores of 10 matches}}{10} = 38.9$$

$\Rightarrow$ Sum of scores of 10 matches = 389   ... (1)

$$\frac{\text{sum of scores of first 6 matches}}{6} = 42$$

$\Rightarrow$ Sum of scores of first 6 matches = 252 ... (2)
Subtracting (2) from (1), we get
Sum of score of last 4 matches
= Sum of score of 10 matches – Sum of score of first 6 matches = 389 – 252 = 137

$$\text{Average of last 4 matches } = \frac{137}{4} = 34.25$$

5. 4 Let the five numbers be a, b, c, d and e.

$$\frac{a+b+c+d+e}{5} = 27$$

$\Rightarrow a + b + c + d + e = 135$ ... (1)
Let e be the excluded number,

Then, $\dfrac{a+b+c+d}{4} = 25$

$\Rightarrow a + b + c + d = 100$ ...(2)
Subtracting (2) from (1), we get
e = 35

6. 2 Let the numbers be $a_1, a_2, a_3, ... a_9$

$$\frac{a_1 + a_2 + a_3 + ... + a_9}{9} = 20$$

$\Rightarrow a_1 + a_2 + a_3 .... + a_9 = 180$ ... (1)

$$\frac{a_1 + a_2 + ... + a_5}{5} = 18$$

$\Rightarrow a_1 + a_2 + a_3 + a_4 + a_5 = 90$ ... (2)

Also, $\dfrac{a_5 + a_6 + ... + a_9}{5} = 23$

$\Rightarrow a_5 + a_6 + ... + a_9 = 115$ ... (3)
Adding (2) and (3), we get
$a_1 + a_2 + ... 2a_5 + a_6 + ... a_9 = 205$ ... (4)
Subtracting (1) from (4), we get
$a_5 = 205 - 180 = 25$

7. 3 Two digit numbers which remained interchanged are 11, 22, 33, ... 99

Average = $\dfrac{11+22+33+.....99}{9}$

$= \dfrac{11}{9}(1+2+3+.....9)$

$= \dfrac{11}{9} \times \dfrac{9 \times 10}{2}\left(\because (1+2+3.....+n) = \dfrac{n(n+1)}{2}\right) = 55$

8. 3 Average weight of 16 boys = 50.25 kg
$\Rightarrow$ Sum of weight of 16 boys = 50.25 × 16 kg
Average weight of 8 boys = 45.15 kg
$\Rightarrow$ Sum of weight of 8 boys = 45.15 × 8 by
Total number of boys = 16 + 8 = 24
Average weight of all the boys

$= \dfrac{50.25 \times 16 + 45.15 \times 8}{24} = \dfrac{50.25 \times 2 + 45.15 \times 1}{3}$

$= 48.55$ kg

9. 3 Let the numbers are a, b, c and d.

$\dfrac{a+b+c+d}{4} = 60$

$\Rightarrow a + b + c + d = 240$ ... (1)

Also, $a = \dfrac{1}{4}(b+c+d)$ ... (2)

From (1) and (2) 5a = 240 $\Rightarrow$ a = 48

10. 1 We know that, if an operation is done to all the numbers, then the average of the numbers changes accordingly.

$\Rightarrow$ Revised average $= \dfrac{7\,(\text{original average}) \times 12 + 6}{15}$

$= \dfrac{84+6}{15} = 6$

11. 2 Average $= \dfrac{a^2 + b^2 + c^2}{3}$

$= \dfrac{(a+b+c)^2 - 2(ab+bc+ca)}{3}$

ab + bc + ca = 0 and a + b + c = 3M

$\Rightarrow$ Average $= \dfrac{(3M)^2 - 2 \times 0}{3} = 3M^2$

12. 2 $\dfrac{x+(x+2)+(x+4)+(x+6)+(x+8)}{5} = 11$

$\Rightarrow$ x = 7
Average of last observations

$= \dfrac{(x+4)+(x+6)+(x+8)}{3} = 13$

13. 4 Let the weight of A, B and C be a kg b kg and c kg respectively.

Then, $\dfrac{a+b+c}{3} = 45$

$\Rightarrow a + b + c = 135$ ... (1)

Also $\dfrac{a+b}{2} = 40$ and $\dfrac{b+c}{2} = 43$

$\Rightarrow$ a + b = 80 and b + c = 86
$\Rightarrow$ a + b + b + c = 166
$\Rightarrow$ a + 2b + c = 166   ... (2)
Subtracting (1) from (2), we get
b = 166 – 135 = 31 kg

14. 3 Total sum of ages of family 3 years ago
= 17 × 5 = 85 years
Total sum of present ages = 85 + 3 × 5 + x
where x is the age of baby

Present Average $= \dfrac{85 + 3 \times 5 + x}{6} = 17$

$\Rightarrow$ x = 102 – 100 = 2 years

15. 4 Let the original average age of 8 men be A and T be the sum of ages of 8 men.

$\Rightarrow A = \dfrac{T}{8}$ ... (1)

and $A + 2 = \dfrac{T - 21 - 23 + x}{8}$ ... (2)

where x is the sum of ages of two new men.
From (1) and (2), we get

$\dfrac{T}{8} + 2 = \dfrac{T}{8} + \dfrac{x}{8} - \dfrac{44}{8}$

$\Rightarrow$ x = 60

Average age of two new men $= \dfrac{x}{2} = \dfrac{60}{2} = 30$ years

16. 2 Let the total number of workers be n
Then, 8000n = 12000 × 7 + 6000 (n – 7)
$\Rightarrow$ n = 21

17. 1 Sum of weights of 24 students = 35 × 24
Let T be the weight of teacher

$\Rightarrow 35 + 0.4 = \dfrac{35 \times 24 + T}{25}$ (new average)

$\Rightarrow$ T = 45 kg

18. 3 Let T be the total marks obtained by all the pupils in the class and n be the number of pupils.
A be the average of marks obtained with wrong entry

$\Rightarrow A = \dfrac{T}{n}$ ... (1)

and $A - \dfrac{1}{2} = \dfrac{T - 83 + 63}{n}$ ... (2)

Subtracting (1) from (2), we get

$-\dfrac{1}{2} = -\dfrac{20}{n} \Rightarrow$ n = 40

19. 4 By the property of averages, if all the numbers contributing to the Average are altered then the Average is also altered by the same proportion.
$\Rightarrow$ If the numbers are increased by 15% then the Average also increases by 15%

20. 3 Let the third number be a
Then, second number = 2a
and first number = 4a

According to the question

$$\frac{\frac{1}{a}+\frac{1}{2a}+\frac{1}{4a}}{3}=\frac{7}{72}$$

$$\Rightarrow \frac{7}{4a}=\frac{7}{24} \Rightarrow 4a = 24$$

$\Rightarrow a = 6, 2a = 12$ and $4a = 24$

$\Rightarrow$ The numbers are 6, 12 and 24

Exercise – 4

1. 4 $\dfrac{C_1}{I_1}=\dfrac{5}{8},\ \dfrac{C_2}{I_2}=\dfrac{5}{3}$

Required ratio $=\dfrac{\text{Copper}}{\text{Iron}}=\dfrac{\frac{5}{13}+\frac{5}{8}}{\frac{8}{13}+\frac{3}{8}}=\dfrac{40+65}{64+39}=\dfrac{105}{103}$

2. 2   Let the required quantity be x kg.

$\therefore$ 20 × 3 + 26x + 30 × 2 = 25 (3 + x + 2) $\Rightarrow$ x = 5

3. 2   Let the amount of second and third quality of sugar in the mixture be 'x' and 'y' kg respectively.

$$\therefore 15\times4+18x+22y = 22\times\frac{100}{110}[4+x+y]$$

$$\Rightarrow y-x = 10$$

4. 1   Mean price of the mixture $= 8\times\dfrac{100}{50}=\text{Rs. }16/\text{kg}$

Let the quantity of second and third variety be 'a' and 'b' kg.

$\therefore$ 15 × 6 + 18a + 20b = 16[6 + a + b] $\Rightarrow a+2b = 3$

a = 1 and b = 1 is the only integral solution.

5. 1   Let the quantity of second and third variety be x and y kg respectively.

$$\therefore 20\times1+30x+24y = 30\times\frac{100}{120}[1+x+y] \Rightarrow 5x-y = 5$$

$\therefore$ For x = 2, y = 5

$\therefore$ option (1) is the right answer.

6. 1   Take 7L of the solution of each mixture,
(LCM of 5 + 2, 6 + 1, 4 + 3)
$\therefore$ net amount of water in the resulting mixture,

$$\frac{5}{7}\times7+\frac{6}{7}\times7+\frac{4}{7}\times7 = 15L$$

The net amount of alcohol is,

$$\frac{2}{7}\times7+\frac{1}{7}\times7+\frac{3}{7}\times7 = 6L$$

Required ratio = 15 : 6 = 5 : 2

7. 4   Let's take
12 L of 5 : 1 sample
24 L of 2 : 1 sample and 36 L of 3 : 1 sample
Amount of milk in the final mixture

$$=\frac{5}{6}\times12+\frac{2}{3}\times24+\frac{3}{4}\times36 = 53\,L$$

Amount of water in the final mixture = 72 – 53 = 19 L

$\Rightarrow$ milk : water = 53 : 19.

8. 1   Using alligation we find the amount of copper (average amount of copper in the final mixture is x)

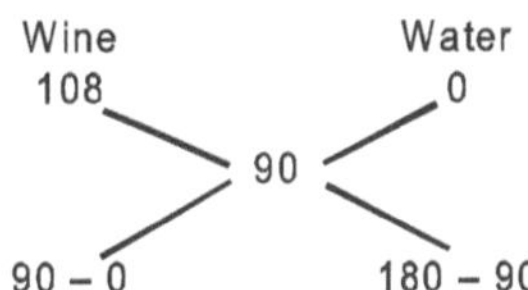

$$\Rightarrow \left(\frac{\frac{7}{10}-x}{x-\frac{2}{5}}\right)=\frac{2}{1} \Rightarrow x = \frac{1}{2}$$

9. 1   Let the amount of sugar at Rs 15 per kg be 2x kgs and at Rs 20 per kg be 3x kgs.

$$\Rightarrow 15\times2x+20\times3x = Z(2x+3x)$$

$$\Rightarrow Z=\frac{15\times2x+20\times3x}{2x+3x}=\frac{90}{5}=\text{Rs 18 per kg.}$$

10. 2   Two lots of whisky having equal quantities are mixed. Let the price of whisky be Rs x per L.

$$\therefore \frac{22-x}{x-18}=\frac{1}{1} \ \therefore\ x = \text{Rs 20 per L}$$

Now this mixture is mixed with water and worth Rs 16 per L.
Hence, the proportion of water to mixture

$$=\frac{20-16}{16-0}=1:4$$

$\therefore$ Quantity of water $=\dfrac{50}{(1+4)}\times1=10$ L.

11. 4   The mean value is Rs 90 per litre and the price of water is Rs 0.

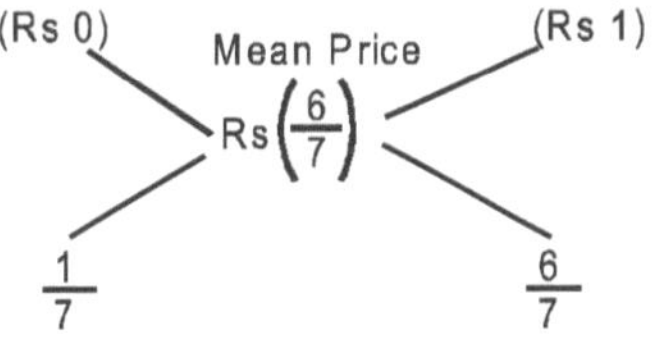

By the Alligation Rule, wine and water are in the ratio of 5 : 1.

$\therefore$ Quantity of wine in the mixture = 5 × 20 = 100 L.

12. 2   Let CP of spirit be Rs 1 per litre.
Then SP of 1 litre of mixture = Rs 1.

Gain $= 16\dfrac{2}{3}\%$

CP of 1 litre of mixture $=\text{Rs}\left(\dfrac{100\times3\times1}{350}\right)=\text{Rs}\left(\dfrac{6}{7}\right)$

CP of 1 litre water (Rs 0)   Mean Price   CP of 1 litre pure spirit (Rs 1)

$$\text{Rs}\left(\frac{6}{7}\right)$$

$$\frac{1}{7} \qquad\qquad \frac{6}{7}$$

$$\Rightarrow \frac{\text{Quantity of water}}{\text{Quantity of spirit}}=\frac{\frac{1}{7}}{\frac{6}{7}}=\frac{1}{6}$$

or Ratio of water : spirit = 1 : 6.

13. 3 The alligation method is applicable on prices, so we should get the average price of mixture.

SP of mixture = Rs 20/litre, Profit = 25%

$\therefore$ Average price $= 20 \times \dfrac{100}{125} =$ Rs 16/litre.

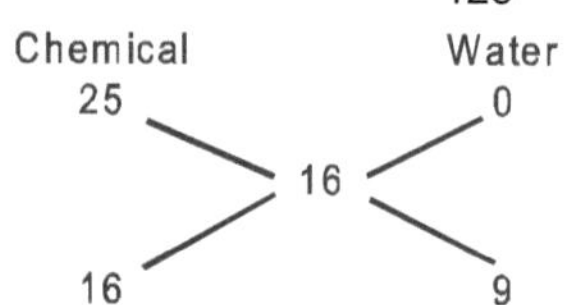

$\therefore$ chemical : water = 16 : 9.

14. 2 Mean value of money per student $= \dfrac{3900}{65} = 60$ p

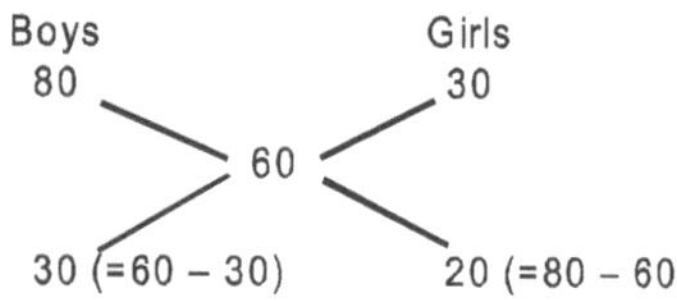

$\therefore$ Boys : Girls = 3:2

$\therefore$ Number of boys $= \dfrac{65}{(3+2)} \times 3 = 39$

15. 2

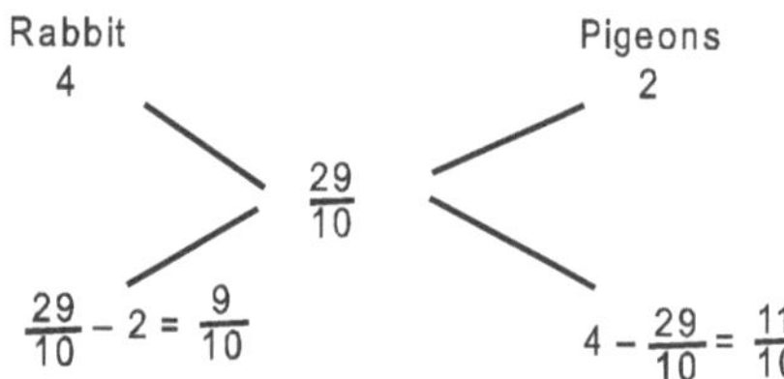

= 4:6 = 2:3

$\therefore$ Quantity sold at 18% profit $= \dfrac{50}{(2+3)} \times 3 = 30$ kg

16. 1 Rule of Alligation is applicable on number of legs per head.

Average number of legs per head $= \dfrac{580}{200} = \dfrac{29}{10}$

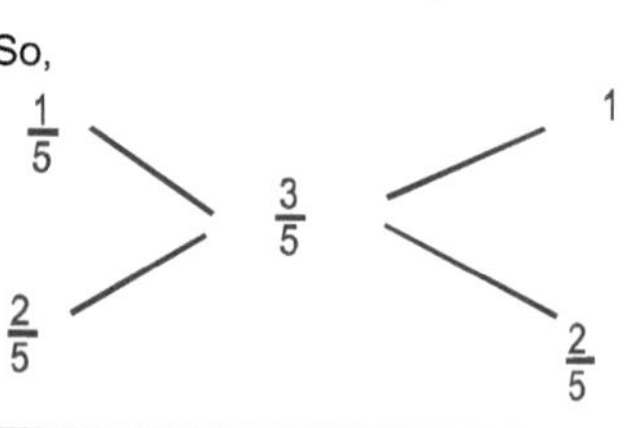

$\therefore$ Rabbits : pigeons = 9:11

$\therefore$ Number of pigeons $= \dfrac{200}{(9+11)} \times 11 = 110$.

17. 3 Fraction of B in original mixture $= \dfrac{1}{5}$

Fraction of B in second mixture = 1

Fraction of B in resulting mixture $= \dfrac{3}{5}$.

So,

Thus, we see that the original mixture and liquid B are mixed in the same ratio. That is, if 10 litres of liquid B is added then after taking out 10 litres of mixture from the jar, there should have been 10 litres of mixture left.

So, the quantity of mixture in the jar = 10 + 10 = 20 litres

and quantity of A in the jar $= \dfrac{20}{5} \times 4 = 16$ litres.

18. 4

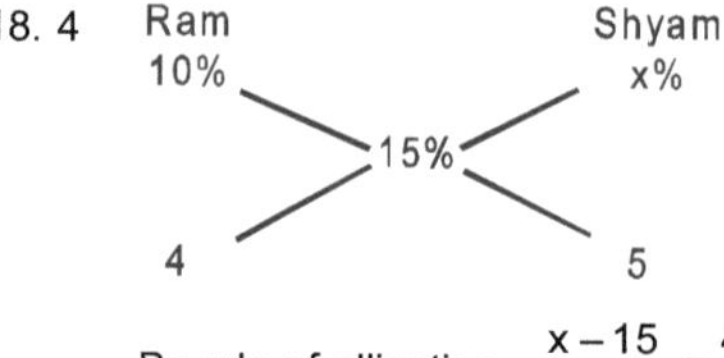

By rule of alligation, $\dfrac{x-15}{15-10} = \dfrac{4}{5}$

$\therefore$ x = 19%

19. 2 We will apply the alligation on price of milk, water and mixture.

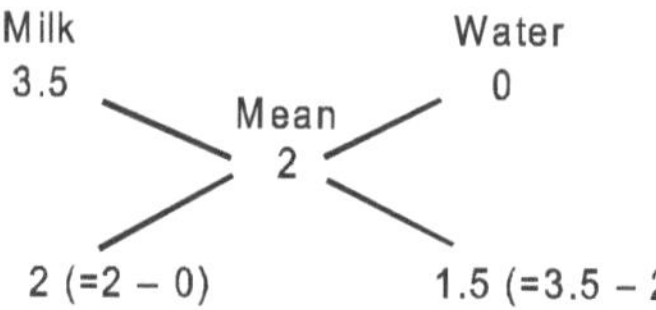

$\therefore$ Ratio of milk and water = 2 : 1.5 = 4 : 3.

$\therefore$ Added water $= \dfrac{40}{4} \times 3 = 30$ litres.

20. 3 Selling price per kg at 10% profit = Rs 7.70.

Selling price per kg at 20% profit = Rs 8.40

Now, the two lots are in ratio = 1:2

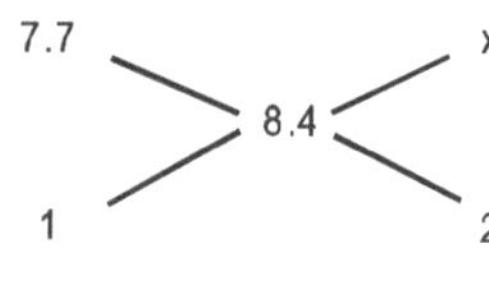

$\Rightarrow \dfrac{8.4 - 7.7}{x - 8.4} = \dfrac{2}{1}$

$\therefore x - 8.4 = \dfrac{0.7}{2} = 0.35$

$\therefore$ x = 8.75

$\therefore$ Selling price per kg of remaining 100 kg = Rs 8.75

3. Business Maths

Exercise – 1

1. 4 $18\dfrac{3}{4}$ % of 2000 $= \dfrac{75}{4} \times \dfrac{2000}{100} = 375$

Alternative Method:

18% of 2000 + $\dfrac{3}{4}$ % of 2000 = 375

2. 1 $\dfrac{26}{48} = \dfrac{13}{24} \times 100 = 54.16\%$

Answers and Explanations

3. 4 $33\frac{1}{3}\%$ of 972 = $\frac{1}{3} \times 972$ = 324

4. 2 $\frac{37}{60} \times 100 = 61.66\%$

5. 3   Percentage increase = $\dfrac{\text{Final Value} - \text{Initial Value}}{\text{Initial Value}} \times 100$

$= \dfrac{7475 - 6500}{6500} = \dfrac{975}{6500} \times 100 = 15\%$

6. 4   90% of 90% of 100 = 90% of 90 = 81

7. 1   1 hour = 60 min

$\therefore \dfrac{50}{60} \times 100 = 83.33\%$

8. 4   A's income = 1.25 of B's income

B's income = $\dfrac{1}{1.25}$ of A's income.

       = 80% of A's income.

9. 3   40% of 200 = 80
He obtained 72, i.e. he failed by 8 marks.

Percentage by which he failed = $\dfrac{8}{200}$ = 4%

10. 4   In 50 L, 35% is water i.e. $\dfrac{35}{100} \times 50$ = 17.5 L.

So, quantity of milk = 50 – 17.5 = 32.5 L.

11. 2   If A is increased by 10%, i.e. A_1 = 1.1A
$\therefore A_1{}^2 = (1.1A)^2 = 1.21A^2$
$\therefore$ A increases by 21%

12. 4   A is $\left(\dfrac{15}{9}\right) \times 100\%$ of $\left(\dfrac{9A}{15}\right)$ i.e. 166%

13. 1   Length becomes 0.9L
Breadth become 0.9B
Area = 0.9L × 0.9B = 0.81LB
$\therefore$ Area decreases by 19%

14. 2   30% of 55% of 100 = 30% of 55 = 16.5

15. 1 $66\frac{1}{6}\%$, $\dfrac{3}{5}$ = 60%;

$0.65 = 65\%$, $\dfrac{16}{25}$ = 64%

16. 2   After 20% increase,
Men = 2500 × 1.2 = 3000
After 20% decrease
Women = 2500 × 0.8 = 2000
So, women as a percentage of men

$= \dfrac{2000}{3000}$ = 66.66%

17. 2   Let the original fraction = $\dfrac{x}{y}$

$\therefore \dfrac{x + 25\% \text{ of } x}{y - 20\% \text{ of } y} = \dfrac{5}{4}$, $\dfrac{1.25x}{0.8y} = \dfrac{5}{4} \Rightarrow \dfrac{x}{y} = \dfrac{4}{5}$

18. 1   In 1 kg pack, ghee is 10%, i.e. 100 g
So, in 2 kg, ghee will be 200 g

19. 2   Let original salary = Rs. 100
Now final salary = 150% of (50% of 100)

$= \left(\dfrac{150}{100} \times \dfrac{50}{100} \times 100\right) =$ Rs. 75
Decrease = 25%

20. 3   20% increase for 2 consecutive years

$= 20 + 20 + \dfrac{400}{100} \{a + b + \dfrac{ab}{100}\} = 44\%$

New population after 2 years = 2500 × 1.44 = 3600.

Short cut:
Population after 2 years = $2500(1.2)^2$

21. 2   Let 37% of x = 990.86. Then,

$\dfrac{37}{100} \times x = 990.86$

or, x = $\dfrac{990.86 \times 100}{37} = \dfrac{99086}{37}$ = 2678.

Now, 19% of 2678 = $\dfrac{19}{100} \times 2678$ = 508.82

or, 500 approx.

Alternative Method:
Since 37% of a number = 990.86 then, 18.5% of a number

$= \dfrac{990.86}{2} = 495.43$

Hence, 19% of a number would be near to 500, only one
option (2) is close.

22. 4   Loss percentage = $\dfrac{4}{20} = \dfrac{1}{5}$ = 20%

23. 1   If X = 120% of Y, then Y = $\dfrac{100}{120}$ of X = 83.33% of X.

24. 3   Price of rice after 15% increase = 1.15 × 15
                           = Rs. 17.25
After 30 paise reduction, price = Rs 16.95

Net increase = $\dfrac{16.95 - 15}{15} \times 100$ = 13%

Alternative Method:
Since 30 paise is equivalent to 2% of Rs. 15.
Hence, net increase would be close to (15–2) = 13%

25. 4   Let the number be n, then
20% of n – 16% of n = 16
0.2n – 0.16n = 16 or 0.04n = 16
$\Rightarrow$ n = 400

Exercise – 2

1. 3 Since sales = Quantity × Price [or S = Q × P]

$$1.28\ S = Q \times 0.8\ P \text{ or } Q = \frac{1.28\ S}{0.8\ P} = 1.6\frac{S}{P}$$

Hence, no. of units sold increased by 60%.

2. 4 If a number is N, then (43 – 28)% of N = 75
15% of N = 75. Hence, 30% of N = 150.

3. 3 A student failed by 15%, i.e. he has got only 30%.
So, 30% of total marks = 138

$$\therefore \text{ Total marks} = \frac{1380}{3} = 460$$

4. 3 Error $37\frac{1}{2} = \left(37\frac{1}{2}^\circ - 36^\circ\right) = 1\frac{1}{2}^\circ$

$$\therefore \text{ Percentage error} = \left(\frac{3}{2} \times \frac{2}{75} \times 100\right) = 4\%$$

5. 4 M + 60 = 50% of K.
Clearly, M cannot be determined.

6. 1 Let A's salary = x. Then, B's = (2000 – x)

5% of A = 15% of B, i.e. $\frac{5}{100}x = \frac{15}{100}(2000 - x)$

or x = 1500

7. 4 $A = \frac{90}{100}\ B, \quad B = \frac{125}{100}\ C \quad \text{and} \quad C = \frac{80}{100}\ D$

$B = \frac{10}{9}\ A, \quad C = \frac{4}{5}\ B \quad \text{and} \quad D = \frac{5}{4}\ C$

$B = \frac{10}{9} \times 360 = 400, \quad C = \frac{4}{5} \times 400 = 320 \quad \text{and}$

$D = \frac{5}{4} \times 320 = 400$

Percentage of D = $\left(\frac{400}{500} \times 100\right)\% = 80\%$

8. 2 Let the total number of students be x.
Number passed in one or both is given by

$n(A \cup B) = n(A) + n(B) - n(A \cap B)$

= 80% of x + 85% of x – 75% of x

$= \left(\frac{80}{100}x + \frac{85}{100}x - \frac{75}{100}x\right) = \frac{90}{100}x = \frac{9x}{10}$

Failed in both = $\left(x - \frac{9x}{100}\right) = \frac{x}{10}$

$\frac{x}{10} = 40$ or x = 400

9. 1 p = 6q. So, q is less than p by 5q.
Note that q has been compared with p.
Required percentage

$= \left(\frac{5q}{p} \times 100\right)\% = \left(\frac{5q}{6q} \times 100\right)\% = 83\frac{1}{3}\%$

10. 4 Let the valid votes be x.
Then, 52% of x – 48% of x = 98 $\Rightarrow$ 4% of x = 98.

$\therefore \frac{4}{100}x = 98$ or x = 98 × 25 = 2450.

$\therefore$ Total votes polled = (2450 + 68) = 2518.

11. 3 Let original consumption be 1 unit costing Rs. 100.
New cost = Rs. 125.

New consumption = $\left(\frac{1}{125} \times 100\right) = \frac{4}{5}$ unit

$\dfrac{\text{Reduction in consumption}}{\text{Original consumption}} = \dfrac{\left(1 - \frac{4}{5}\right)}{1} = \frac{1}{5}$, i.e. 1 : 5

12. 4 Net growth on 1000 = (32 – 11) = 21

Net growth on 100 = $\left(\frac{21}{1000} \times 100\right) = 2.1\%$

13. 4 Let length = l and breadth = b
Area = l × b, if new dimensions of breadth = b_1, then

$A \Rightarrow l \times b = 1.6 l \times b_1$ or $b_1 = \frac{b}{1.6}$

or, b_1 = 0.625b
Hence, breadth would decrease by b – 0.625 b
= 0.375b or 37.5%

14. 1 In a class of 300 students,
Boys = 200, Girls = 100
50% Boys = 100, 48% Girls = 48
Total students who appeared = 148.
152 did not appear.

15. 4 20% solution of sugar means $\frac{1}{5}$th of sugar

In 5 L of solution, 1 L is sugar and 4 L is water.
After adding 1 L of water,

Percentage of sugar = $\frac{1}{6}$ = 16.67%

16. 4 Suppose he had Rs. 100. He invested Rs. 40 in shares. Out of remaining Rs. 60, he invested Rs. 12 in property. Out of the remaining Rs. 48, he lost Rs. 12 at a casino. He was left with Rs. 36, i.e. 36%.

17. 3 Let the winner get 'x' votes.

$\therefore$ The loser got (x – 60) or $\frac{2}{3}$x votes.

$\therefore \frac{2x}{3} = (x - 60)$

$\therefore$ x = 180, i.e. the winner got 180 votes and the loser got 120 votes.

18. 2 180 + 120 = 300

19. 1 $\frac{180}{300} = \frac{6}{10} = \frac{3}{5} = 60\%$

20. 4 If S.P. = 121, P = 10%

C.P. = $\frac{121 \times 100}{110}$ = Rs. 110

If S.P. is reduced by Rs. 11
New S.P. = 121 – 11 = Rs. 110
Hence, no profit no loss.

21. 4 Let the original price be Rs. x.

Then increased price = Rs. $\left(\dfrac{130}{100}\right)x$

$\therefore \dfrac{7.80}{x} - \dfrac{7.80}{\left(\dfrac{130}{100}\right)x} = 3$

$\Rightarrow x = $ Rs. 0.6

Increased price = $\dfrac{130}{100}x = $ Rs. 0.78

So, present price per dozen = Rs. 12 × 0.78
= Rs. 9.36.

22. 4 30% on petrol = Rs. 300.
Hence, total sum = Rs. 1,000

$\dfrac{1}{4}$th of the remaining 70% = $\dfrac{1}{4}$th of 700 = Rs. 175

23. 4 x% of a = y% of b $\Rightarrow \dfrac{x}{100}a = \dfrac{y}{100}b$

$\Rightarrow b = \left(\dfrac{x}{100} \times \dfrac{100}{y}\right)a = \left(\dfrac{x}{y}\right)a$

z% of b = $\left(z\% \text{ of } \dfrac{x}{y}\right)a = \left(\dfrac{xz}{y \times 100}\right)a$

$= \left(\dfrac{xz}{y}\right)\%$ of a

24. 1 Let original consumption = 100 units and original price
= Rs. 100/unit
Original expenditure = Rs. (100 × 100) = Rs. 10,000
New expenditure = Rs. (120 × 75) = Rs. 9,000

Decrease in expenditure = $\left(\dfrac{1000}{10000} \times 100\right)\% = 10\%$

25. 2 Basic rate = Rs. $\dfrac{20}{40}$ per hr = 50p per hr

Overtime rate = 1.25 × 50p = 62.5p per hr.

= Rs. $\dfrac{5}{8}$ per hr.

Let overtime hour = x

Then, $\dfrac{5}{8}x = 5 \Rightarrow x = \dfrac{5 \times 8}{5} = 8$ hr

So, he worked for (40 + 8) hr = 48 hr

Exercise – 3

1. 3 3 Balls = 2 Pads, 3 Pads = 2 Gloves
3 Gloves = 2 Bats, Bat = Rs. 54

Glove = $\dfrac{2}{3}$ × 54 = Rs. 36

Pad = $\dfrac{2}{3}$ × 36 = Rs. 24

Ball = $\dfrac{2}{3}$ × 24 = Rs. 16

2. 4 Nothing is said about the number of books.

3. 4 C.P. of 20 articles = S.P. of 15 articles
S.P. of 15 = C.P. of 15 + C.P. of 5
S.P. = C.P. + Profit

$\therefore$ Profit = $\dfrac{5}{15}$ × 100 = 33.33%

4. 1 Let C.P. = x, Then,

S.P. = $\dfrac{4x}{3}$ Gain = $\left(\dfrac{4x}{3} - x\right) = \dfrac{x}{3}$

$\therefore$ Gain percentage = $\left(\dfrac{x}{3} \times \dfrac{1}{x} \times 100\right) = 33\dfrac{1}{3}\%$

5. 4 Gain percentage = $\dfrac{100}{900} \times 100 = 11.11\%$

6. 3 If he uses a weight of x gm, then profit percentage

$= \dfrac{1000 - x}{x} \times 100$, which is equal to $6\dfrac{18}{47}\%$

Therefore, x = 940 gm

7. 1 S.P.$_1$ = S.P.$_2$ = Rs. 4,000
Gain$_1$ = 25%, Loss$_2$ = ?

C.P.$_1$ = $4000 \times \dfrac{100}{125}$ = Rs. 3,200

$\therefore$ C.P.$_2$ = Rs. (8000 – 3200) = Rs. 4,800
($\because$ Total S.P. = Total C.P.)

Therefore, loss percentage = $\dfrac{800}{4800} \times 100 = 16.66\%$

8. 2 When S.P. of two articles is same; one is sold at a loss of
x% and other at a gain of x% then there, is always an

overall loss, given by $\dfrac{x^2}{100}\%$ and the absolute loss

$\dfrac{2x^2}{100^2 - x^2} \times$ S.P. $= \dfrac{2 \times 20 \times 20 \times 12000}{10000 - 400} = $ Rs. 1000

9. 4 30%, 20%, 10% successive discounts.

(Considering 1 and 2) :

Discount = $- 30 - 20 + \dfrac{600}{100} = -44\%$

Considering (1 and 2) and 3 :

Discount = $-44 - 10 + \dfrac{440}{100} = -49.6\%$

Alternative Method:
0.7 × 0.8 × 0.9 = 0.504 = 50.4%.
Therefore, 100 – 50.4 = 49.6%

10. 3 36% and 4% successive discounts equal to

$$-36 - 4 + \frac{144}{100} = -38.56\%$$

Difference = 40 − 38.56 = 1.44%
∴ 1.44% of 500 = Rs. 7.2

11. 2 $M.P. = C.P. \dfrac{(100 + \text{Profit percentage})}{(100 - \text{Discount percentage})}$

$M.P. = C.P. \times \dfrac{133}{95} = 1.4 \; C.P.$

∴ 40% above the C.P.

12. 1 Net discount = $-20 - 10 + \dfrac{200}{100} = 28\%$

$S.P. = M.P. \dfrac{(100 - \text{Discount}\%)}{100}$

$108 = M.P. \times \dfrac{72}{100}$, M.P. = Rs. 150

13. 1 If C.P. of tea is Re. 1 per gram, then he is receiving Rs. 1,000 for something which is worth Rs. 900.
But he gives a discount of 10% on Rs. 1000, i.e. sells at Rs. 900.

14. 2 S.P. of 16 books = C.P. of 12 books
S.P. of 16 = C.P. of 16 − C.P. of 4

Loss = $\dfrac{4}{16} \times 100 = 25\%$

15. 3 Loss = S.P. of 4 apples on selling 36 apples
∴ S.P. of 40 = C.P. of 36 = C.P. of 40 − C.P. of 4

Loss = $\dfrac{4}{40} \times 100 = 10\%$

Exercise – 4

1. 2 $P = \dfrac{1}{4}$ of C.P., S.P. = 375

Profit = S.P. − C.P.

$\dfrac{1}{4} \; C.P. = 375 - C.P.$ or, $375 = \left(1 + \dfrac{1}{4}\right) C.P.$

$C.P. = 375 \times \dfrac{4}{5} = Rs. 300$

2. 4 C.P. of one banana of first quality = Re. $\dfrac{1}{3}$

C.P. of one banana of second quality = Re. $\dfrac{1}{2}$

Average C.P. = $\dfrac{\dfrac{1}{3} + \dfrac{1}{2}}{2} = \dfrac{5}{12}$, P = 20%

$S.P. = C.P. \dfrac{(100 + \text{Gain percentage})}{100}$

$S.P. = \dfrac{5}{12} \times \dfrac{120}{100} = Rs. \dfrac{1}{2}$ per banana

Price per dozen = $\dfrac{1}{2} \times 12 = Rs. 6$

3. 1 C.P. of 1 dozen oranges of first quality = Rs. 5
C.P. of 1 dozen oranges of second quality = Rs. 2

Average C.P. = $\dfrac{5 + 2}{2} = Rs. 3.5$ per dozen

S.P. = Rs. 5.50
Profit per dozen = Rs. 2
Total profit = Rs. 50

∴ Number of dozens = $\dfrac{50}{2} = 25$

4. 4 C.P. of first = Rs. 18 per kilogram
C.P. of second = Rs. 20 per kilogram
Suppose he mixes 5 kg of first and 3 kg of second
Total C.P. = 18 × 5 + 20 × 3 = 90 + 60 = Rs. 150
Total S.P. = 21 × 8 = Rs. 168

$Profit = \dfrac{18}{150} \times 100 = 18 \times \dfrac{2}{3} = 12\%$

5. 1 Number of toffees = $\dfrac{1}{\left(\dfrac{1}{20}\right)\left(\dfrac{1.2}{0.96}\right)} = 16$

6. 2 Let C.P. = 100. Therefore, S.P. = 110
If S.P. = 220, profit percentage = 120%

7. 4 Let C.P. for A = Rs. x
Total C.P. after repairs = Rs. (x + 110)
B's C.P. = (x + 110) × 1.2
C's C.P. = (x + 110) × 1.2 × 0.9
C's S.P. = (x + 110) × 1.2 × 0.9 × 1.1 = Rs. 1,188

∴ $x + 110 = \dfrac{1188 \times 1000}{12 \times 9 \times 11}$

x + 110 = 1000
x = Rs. 890

8. 3 Let C.P. per kilogram = Re. 1
So, total C.P. of 24 kg = Rs. 24
Let him sell x kg apple at 20% gain and
(24 − x) kg at 5% loss.

$S.P._1 = \dfrac{120x}{100} = 1.2x$ … (i)

$S.P._2 = 0.95(24 - x) = 22.8 - 0.95x$ … (ii)
Overall profit = 10% on Rs. 24 = Rs. 2.4
But total S.P. − total C.P. = Rs. 2.4
[1.2x + 22.8 − 0.95x] − 24 = 2.4
Solving for x , x = Rs. 14.4
∴ Amount sold at loss is 24 − x = 9.6 kg

9. 1 C.P. = 40% of S.P. = 0.4 S.P.

$S.P. = \dfrac{10}{4} \; C.P. \times 100 = 250 \; C.P. = 250\%$

10. 4 Profit and loss are calculated on the cost price.
∴ Difference in percentages = 5 − (− 2.5) = 7.5%

7.5% of C.P. = Rs. 6

$$C.P. = \frac{6 \times 100}{7.5} = Rs.\ 80$$

11. 1 $C.P. = \dfrac{355 + 425}{2} = 390$

12. 4   Let C.P. = Rs. x
Profit = S.P. – C.P. = (900 – x)
Loss = C.P. – S.P. = (x – 450)
∴ 900 – x = 2 (x – 450)
900 – x = 2x – 900, or 1800 = 3x, x = Rs. 600 = C.P.
Now, to make a profit of 25%,

$$S.P. = 600 \times \frac{125}{100} = Rs.\ 750$$

13. 3   Let M.P. = Rs. 100 = S.P. (Initially)
After a discount of 10%, S.P. would be Rs. 90.
But, the shopkeeper wants to maintain the current price,
i.e., S.P. = Rs. 100
when S.P. = Rs. 90, M.P. = Rs. 100

∴ When S.P. = Rs. 100, M.P. = Rs. $100 \times \dfrac{100}{90}$

= Rs. 111.11 or 11.11% increase

14. 2   C.P. per kg = $\dfrac{492}{78}$ = Rs. 6.3.

For an overall gain of 25%, the S.P. of 78 kg

$$= 492 \times \frac{1.25}{100} = Rs.\ 615$$

By selling 40%, i.e. 31.2 kg at a loss of 20%

$$S.P._1 = 31.2 \times \left(\frac{492}{78}\right) \times \frac{80}{100} = Rs.\ 157.44$$

Now, the remaining, i.e. 78 – 31.2
= 46.8 kg wheat is to be sold for Rs. 615 – 157.44
= Rs. 457.56

$$S.P._2 = \frac{457.56}{46.8} = Rs.\ 9.77 \text{ per kg}$$

$$Markup = \frac{9.77 - 6.3}{6.3} = 55\%$$

15. 3   Let C.P. per L milk = Rs. x
For 25 L, C.P. = Rs. 25x, S.P. = Rs. 1,250,
Profit = Rs. 5x = S.P. – C.P.
Or, 5x = 1250 – 25x or, x = Rs. 41.66/L.

$$Profit\ percentage = \frac{50 - 41.66}{41.66} \times 100 = 20\%$$

Alternative Method:
S.P. of 25 L – C.P. of 25 L = C.P. of 5 L
⇒ S.P. of 25 L = C.P. of 30 L

$$\frac{S.P.}{C.P.} = \frac{30}{25} \Rightarrow 1.2$$

Hence, profit percentage = 20%

16. 4   Let S.P. of 1 kg rice = Rs. x
S.P. of 100 kg rice = Rs. 100 x
C.P. of 100 kg rice = Rs. 1,100

∴ Loss = Rs. 20x = C.P. – S.P. = 1100 – 100x

Or, x = $\dfrac{1100}{120}$ = Rs. 9.16

17. 4   Total C.P. = 35 × 9.5 + 30 × 10.5
= 332.5 + 315 = Rs. 647.5 (For 65 kg rice)

$$S.P. = C.P.\ \frac{(100 + Gain\ percentage)}{100}$$

$$S.P. = \frac{647.5}{65} \times \frac{135}{100} = Rs.\ 13.5$$

18. 4   Let the original price be Rs. 100.
The C.P. = Rs. 80
S.P. = 140% of 80 = Rs. 112.

∴ Required percentage = $\dfrac{(112 - 100)}{100} \times 100 = 12\%$

19. 2   Let the C.P. be x and S.P. be y. According to the question.

$$\frac{(1.1y - 0.9x)}{0.9x} \times 100 = 2 \times \frac{(y - x)}{x} \times 100 \Rightarrow y = \frac{9}{7}x$$

$$\Rightarrow Profit\ \% = \frac{(y - x)}{x} \times 100 = \frac{\left(\frac{9}{7}x - x\right)}{x} \times 100 = 28.56\%$$

20. 3   Let the C.P. of 1 mango = Rs. 1
Total C.P. = 20
Total profit = 5

So profit is $\dfrac{5}{20} \times 100 = 25\%$

Exercise – 5

1. 4   A's share = $P \times \dfrac{x}{x + y + z} = 3610 \times \dfrac{2000}{4750} = Rs.\ 1,520$

Where P = Profit and x, y and z are respective shares of A, B and C.

2. 1   A's effective investment = 16000 × 6 = Rs. 96,000
B's effective investment = 12000 × 8 = Rs. 96,000
C's effective investment = 1000 × 12 = Rs. 12,000
Profit sharing ratio = 96 : 96 : 12 or 8 : 8 : 1

3. 3   Ratio of their profits = Ratio of their investments
= 4000 × 12 : 8000 × 9 : 12000 × 2
48 : 72 : 24
2 : 3 : 1

Bs' share = $\dfrac{3}{6} \times 5200 = 2600$

4. 3   Let A's, B's and C's investments be 8x, 7x, 5x
A's effective investment = (8x) × 5 + (4x) × 7
                 = 40x + 28x = 68 x
B's effective investment = 7x × 12 = 84x
C's effective investment = 5x × 12 = 60x

B's share = $\dfrac{84}{212} \times 26500 = 10,500$

5. 1 Arun : Kamal : Vinay = $(8000 \times 6) : (4000 \times 8) : (8000 \times 8)$
$= 3 : 2 : 4$

$\therefore$ Kamal's share $= \left(\dfrac{2}{9} \times 4005\right) = $ Rs 890

6. 4 A : B : C = $(50000 \times 1 + 70000 \times 2) : (70000 \times 2 + 50000 \times 1)$
$: (60000 \times 3)$
$= (1,90,000) : (1,90,000) : (1,80,000)$
$= 19 : 19 : 18$

7. 2 Hire charges of A : B : C = $7 : 8 : 9$

$\Rightarrow$ Charges paid by B $= \dfrac{8}{(7+8+9)} \times 480 = $ Rs 160

8. 2 Initial share of A : B : C $= \dfrac{1}{2} : \dfrac{1}{3} : \dfrac{1}{4} = 6 : 4 : 3$

After 2 months, share of A : B : C = $3 : 4 : 3$
$\Rightarrow$ Ratio of share if A, B and C for the year
$= (6 \times 2 + 3 \times 10) : (4 \times 12) : (3 \times 12)$
$= 42 : 48 : 36 = 7 : 8 : 6$

$\Rightarrow$ B's share in profit $= \dfrac{8}{(7+8+6)} \times 378$

$= 8 \times 18 = $ Rs 144

9. 3 Let B's investment is for x months.
Now A's share : B's share = 1 : 1
$\Rightarrow (21000 \times 12) : (36,000 \times x) = 1 : 1$
$\Rightarrow 21000 \times 12 = 36000 \times x$
$\Rightarrow x = 7$
$\Rightarrow$ B invested for 7 months
Hence, B joined after 5 months.

10. 3 Let B's money be used for 'x' months
Investment ratio of A and B = Profit ratio of A and B.

$\Rightarrow \dfrac{1}{4} \times 15 : \dfrac{3}{4} \times x = \dfrac{1}{3} : \dfrac{2}{3} \Rightarrow 15 : 3x = 1 : 2$

$\Rightarrow x = 10$ months.

11. 2 A's share of available profit $= \dfrac{3}{(3+2)}$ of available profit

$\Rightarrow \dfrac{3}{5}$ of available profit = Rs. 855

$\Rightarrow$ Available profit $= \dfrac{855 \times 5}{3} = $ Rs 1425

Now, available profit = 95% of total profit

$\Rightarrow$ Total profit $= 1425 \times \dfrac{100}{95} = $ Rs 1,500

12. 3 Investment ratio of A and C = 2 : 1
Investment ratio of A and B = 3 : 2
$\Rightarrow$ A : B : C = 6 : 4 : 3

$\Rightarrow$ B's share $= \dfrac{4}{13} \times 1,57,300 = $ Rs 48,400

13. 1 Arun's share : Sanjay's share : : $(1,00,000 \times 6 + 75,000 \times 6)$
$: (1,50,000 \times 4 + 2,50,000 \times 4)$
$= 21 : 32$

14. 2 Let the profit be P.
According to the question
20% of $(P - 10,000) = 10,000$

$\Rightarrow \dfrac{(P - 10000)}{5} = 10000$

$\Rightarrow$ P = Rs 60,000

15. 4 We know that
$P_x : P_y : P_z = at_x : bt_y : ct_z$
Where, P_x, P_y and P_z are the profits,
a, b, c are investments and t_x, t_y and t_z are the time periods
respectively for which investments have been made.
$\Rightarrow 3 \times tx : 5 \times ty : 8 \times tz = 24 : 35 : 56$

$\Rightarrow tx : ty : tz = \dfrac{24}{3} : \dfrac{35}{5} : \dfrac{56}{8} = 8 : 7 : 7$

16. 4 Time period for investments for A, B and C are 12 months,
$(12 - x)$ and $(12 - x)$ months respectively.
$\Rightarrow$ Profit of A : B : C
$= 50,000 \times 12 : 60000 \times (12 - x) : 70000 \times (12 - x)$
$\Rightarrow 20 : 18 : 21 = 60 : 6\,(12 - x) : 7\,(12 - x)$

$\Rightarrow \dfrac{20}{18} = \dfrac{60}{6\,(12 - x)}$

$\Rightarrow 12 - x = 9$
$\Rightarrow x = 3$ months

17. 1 Profit of A : B = $93,000 : 1,02,000 = 31 : 34$
Salary of A in the year = Rs. $500 \times 12 = $ Rs. 6,000.
$\Rightarrow$ Profit available for distribution = Rs. $(45000 - 6000)$
= Rs. 39,000

$\Rightarrow$ Share of A $= \dfrac{31}{(31 + 34)} \times 39,000 = 18,600$

$\Rightarrow$ and share of B $= \dfrac{31}{(31 + 34)} \times 39,000 = 20,400$

Earning of A = Rs. $(18,600 + 6,000) = $ Rs. 24,600
and earnings of B = Rs 20,4000.
Difference in earnings of A and B
= Rs. $(24600 - 20400) = $ Rs 4200

18. 3 Let the capitals of Rohan, Mohan and Sohan be
Rs x, Rs y and Rs z respectively
$\Rightarrow 3x = 2y = 4z$

$\Rightarrow x : y : z = \dfrac{1}{3} : \dfrac{1}{2} : \dfrac{1}{4} = 4 : 6 : 3$

$\Rightarrow$ Rohan's Share $= \dfrac{4}{(4 + 6 + 3)} \times 52000 = $ Rs 16,000

19. 4 Let C joined after x months. The time period for the investment
of C is $(12 - x)$ months.
$\Rightarrow$ Ratio of profit of A, B and C = $20000 \times 12 : 30000 \times$
$12 : 40000 \times (12 - x)$
$= 24 : x : 4(12 - x)$

$\Rightarrow$ C's share $= \dfrac{4\,(12 - x)}{(24 + 36 + 4\,(12 - x))} = \dfrac{4,000}{14,000}$

$\Rightarrow 14(12 - x) = 60 + 4\,(12 - x)$
$\Rightarrow 10(12 - x) = 60$
$\Rightarrow 12 - x = 6$
$\Rightarrow x = 6$ months.
Hence, C joined after 6 months.

Answers and Explanations

20. 2 Share of Arun : Keshav : Jiten
$= 1640 \times x : 3280 \times 12 : 1230 \times 2x$
$= 4 : 24 : 6$

$$\Rightarrow \frac{1640x}{3280 \times 12} = \frac{4}{24}$$

$\Rightarrow x = 4$ months

Exercise – 6

1. 4 Interest $= \dfrac{3500 \times 5 \times 5}{100}$ = Rs. 875

Amount = P + I = 3500 + 875 = Rs. 4375

2. 2 $2P = \dfrac{P \times 20 \times t}{100}$, t = 10 years

3. 1 $C.I. = P\left[1 + \dfrac{r}{100}\right]^{3} - P$

$= 1000 \, [1.1]^3 - 1000 = 1331 - 1000 = $ Rs. 331

4. 2 $C.I. = 1010 = P\left(1 + \dfrac{2}{100}\right)^{2} - P$

$1010 = P[(1.02)^2 - 1] = 0.0404 \, P$
Or, P = Rs. 25,000

5. 4 Nothing is said about C.I. or S.I.

6. 3 $T = \dfrac{9 \times 100 \times 4}{36 \times 25} = 4$ years

7. 2 $\dfrac{400 \times 8 \times 5}{100}$ = Rs. 160

8. 2 $r = \dfrac{9 \times 100}{1 \times 50} = 18\%$

9. 3 $\dfrac{500 \times R_1 \times 2}{100} - \dfrac{500 \times R_2 \times 2}{100} = 2.50$
or $1000 \, (R_1 - R_2) = 250$

$R_1 - R_2 = \dfrac{250}{1000} = \dfrac{1}{4} = 0.25\%$

10. 3 C.I. for 3 years $= 700\left[1 + \dfrac{10}{100}\right]^{3} - 700 = 231.7$

S.I. for 3 years $= \dfrac{700 \times 10 \times 3}{100} = 210$

$\therefore C.I._3 - S.I._3 = $ Rs. 21.7

11. 4 $S.I. = \dfrac{P}{4}$

$\therefore \dfrac{P}{4} = \dfrac{P \times r \times t}{100}$

Also r = t, $\therefore r^2 = \dfrac{100}{4}$, $r = \dfrac{10}{2} = 5\%$

12. 2 $154 = \dfrac{P \times 5 \times 2}{100}$ or P = Rs. 1,540

13. 4 $\dfrac{1500}{1 + \dfrac{6.25 \times 4}{100}} = $ Rs. 1200

14. 1 After 8 month worth of Rs. 400 @ 15% would be

$\left(400 + \dfrac{2}{3} \times 15 \times \dfrac{400}{100}\right) = $ Rs. 440 , but he sold at Rs. 460, i.e. a profit of Rs. 20 on Rs. 440.

Hence, gain percentage $= \dfrac{20}{440} \times 100 = 4.54\%$

15. 3 (I) $S.I. = \dfrac{5000 \times 3 \times 11}{100} = $ Rs. 1,650

(II) $C.I. = 5000\left(1 + \dfrac{10}{100}\right)^{3} - 5000 = $ Rs. 1,655

Short cut:
Effective rate at S.I. and C.I. = 33 % and 33.1% respectively.

Exercise – 7

1. 1 Let the sum be Rs. x and original rate be R%.
Then,

$$\frac{x \times (R + 3) \times 2}{100} - \frac{x \times R \times 2}{100} = 72$$

or 2Rx + 6x – 2Rx = 7200 or x = Rs. 1200

Alternative Method:
If principal in P, the difference of Rs. 72 is equivalent to 3% for 2 years, i.e. (3% × 2)P = 72

$= \dfrac{72}{6} \times 100 = $ Rs. 1200

2. 2 Let sum = x. Then, S.I. = x

Rate $= \left(\dfrac{100 \times x}{x \times 8}\right)\% = 12\dfrac{1}{2}\%$

3. 1 $\left(\dfrac{2000 \times 8 \times 1}{100}\right) + \left(4000 \times \dfrac{15}{2} \times \dfrac{1}{100}\right) + \left(1400 \times \dfrac{17}{2} \times \dfrac{1}{100}\right)$

$+ \, 2600 \times R \times \dfrac{1}{100} = \dfrac{8.13}{100} \times 10000$

Or, 160 + 300 + 119 + 26R = 813 or R = 9%

4. 3 Let the sum be x. Then,

$C.\,I. = x\left(1 + \dfrac{5}{100}\right)^{2} - x = \left(\dfrac{441x}{400} - x\right) = \dfrac{41x}{400}$

$S.\,I. = \dfrac{x \times 10 \times 1}{100} = \dfrac{x}{10}$

$(C.I.) - (S.I.) = \dfrac{41x}{400} - \dfrac{x}{10} = \dfrac{x}{400}$

$\therefore \dfrac{x}{400} = 25$ or x = 10000

5. 2   C.I. = Rs. $\left[800\times\left(1+\dfrac{10}{100}\right)^2 - 800\right]$ = Rs. 168

S.I. = Rs. $\left(\dfrac{800\times10\times2}{100}\right)$ = Rs. 160

Gain = (C. I.) – (S.I.) = Rs. (168 – 160) = Rs. 8

6. 1   Interest on Rs. 4,624 for 1 year = 4913 – 4624 = 289

$\therefore$ Rate = $\dfrac{289}{4624} = \dfrac{25}{4}$ %

Now, if principal amount is x

$x\left(1+\dfrac{25}{4\ \times\ 100}\right)^2 = 4624$ or $x\times\dfrac{17}{16}\times\dfrac{17}{16} = 4624$

$\therefore x = \left(4624\times\dfrac{16}{17}\times\dfrac{16}{17}\right)$ = Rs. 4,096

7. 2 $12000\times\left(1+\dfrac{R}{100}\right)^5 = 24000 \Rightarrow \left(1+\dfrac{R}{100}\right)^5 = 2$

$\therefore \left[\left(1+\dfrac{R}{100}\right)^5\right]^4 = 2^4 = 16$ or $\left(1+\dfrac{R}{100}\right)^{20} = 16$

Or, $P\left(1+\dfrac{R}{100}\right)^{20} = 16P$

Or, $12000\left(1+\dfrac{R}{100}\right)^{20} = 16\times12000 = 192000$

8. 4 $P\left(1+\dfrac{20}{100}\right)^n > 2P \Rightarrow (1.2)^n > 2$

Here, pick up the value of n and check the condition, it follows for n = 4.

9. 4   Increase percentage = $\left(\dfrac{1}{8}\times100\right)\% = 12\dfrac{1}{2}\%$

Higher after 2 years = $\left[64\times\left(1+\dfrac{25}{2\times100}\right)^2\right]$ cm

= $\left(64\times\dfrac{9}{8}\times\dfrac{9}{8}\right)$ cm = 81 cm

10. 2 $1200\times\left(1+\dfrac{R}{100}\right)^2 = 1348.32$

or $\left(1+\dfrac{R}{100}\right)^2 = \dfrac{134832}{12000} = \dfrac{11236}{10000}$

$\therefore \left(1+\dfrac{R}{100}\right)^2 = \left(\dfrac{106}{100}\right)^2$ or $1+\dfrac{R}{100}$ or $R = 6\%$

11. 3   Interest on Rs. 800 for 1 year = Rs. (840 – 800)

= Rs. 40

$\therefore$ Rate = $\left(\dfrac{100\times40}{800\times1}\right)\% = 5\%$

12. 1 $\dfrac{9}{25}\times P = \dfrac{P\times R^2}{100}$, $R^2 = \dfrac{9\times100}{25}$

So, R = 6% and time durations = R = 6 years.

13. 1   S.I. For 1st year = $\dfrac{360}{3} = 120$ = C.I. for 1st year

C.I. for 2 years = 270 $\Rightarrow$ 120 + C.I. for 2nd year
C.I. for 2nd year 270 – 120 = 150
Difference between CI and SI in 2nd year
= 150 – 120 = 30.

Hence, rate of interest = $\dfrac{30}{120}\times100 = 25\%$

14. 4 $\dfrac{400\times3\times r}{100} + \dfrac{600\times3\times r}{100} = 90$

30 r = 90; r = 3%

15. 4   C.I. = 203 = $P\left(1+\dfrac{3}{100}\right)^2 - P$

203 = P[(1.03)^2 – 1]

or P = $\dfrac{203}{0.069}$ = Rs. 3,333

S.I. = $\dfrac{P\times R\times T}{100} = \dfrac{3333\times3\times2}{100} \approx$ Rs. 200

Short cut:
S.I. must be less than C.I.

16. 4   Let the sum at 5% be Rs. x. Then,

$\dfrac{x\times5\times3}{100} + \dfrac{(1550 - x)\times8\times3}{100} = 300$ or x = 800

$\dfrac{\text{Money at 5\%}}{\text{Money at 8\%}} = \dfrac{800}{(1550 - 800)} = \dfrac{800}{750} = \dfrac{16}{15}$

17. 3   Let total capital be x, then,

$\left(\dfrac{x}{3}\times\dfrac{7}{100}\times1\right) + \left(\dfrac{x}{4}\times\dfrac{8}{100}\times1\right) + \left(\dfrac{5x}{12}\times\dfrac{10}{100}\times1\right) = 561$

Or, $\dfrac{7x}{300} + \dfrac{x}{50} + \dfrac{x}{24} = 561$

Or, x = $\left(\dfrac{561\times600}{51}\right)$ = Rs. 6600

18. 1   Let these parts be x, y and z.
Assume x be the largest and z be the smallest part.
Hence, by the simple interest formula, (1.04)x
= (1.08)y = (1.12)z and x + y + z = 2189
Solving the above equation, z = Rs. 703

Answers and Explanations

19. 4 $\text{Sum} = \text{Rs.} \left(\dfrac{100 \times 1200}{3 \times 5} \right) = \text{Rs. } 8,000$

$$\text{Amount} = \text{Rs.} \left[8000 \times \left(1 + \dfrac{5}{100} \right)^3 \right]$$

$$= \text{Rs.} \left(8000 \times \dfrac{21}{20} \times \dfrac{21}{20} \times \dfrac{21}{20} \right) = \text{Rs. } 9,261$$

$\therefore$ C.I. = Rs. (9261 – 8000) = Rs. 1,261

20. 3   Number of days in (March + April + May)

$= 23 + 30 + 21 = 74 \text{ days} = \dfrac{74}{365} \text{ year}$

$= \dfrac{1}{5} \text{ years (approx.)}$

$\therefore$ Interest $= \text{Rs.} \left(1820 \times \dfrac{1}{5} \times \dfrac{7.5}{100} \right) = \text{Rs. } 27.30$

4. Time, Work and Distance

Exercise – 1

1. 1   A takes $7 \times 9 = 63$ hr,

$\therefore$ In 1 hr A does $= \dfrac{1}{63}$ of work

B takes $6 \times 7 = 42$ hr,

$\therefore$ In 1 hr B does $= \dfrac{1}{42}$ of work

$A + B \text{ in 1 hr} = \dfrac{1}{63} + \dfrac{1}{42}$

$A + B \text{ in } \dfrac{42}{5} \text{ hr} = \left(\dfrac{1}{63} + \dfrac{1}{42} \right) \times \dfrac{42}{5}$

$= \dfrac{105}{2646} \times \dfrac{42}{5} = \dfrac{4410}{13230} = 0.33$

$\therefore$ Number of days $= \dfrac{1}{0.33} = 3$.

2. 3   A's work in 1 day $= \dfrac{1}{80}$,

$\therefore$ 10 days' work $= \dfrac{10}{80} = \dfrac{1}{8}$

Part of work to be done by B $= \left(1 - \dfrac{1}{8} \right) = \dfrac{7}{8}$

$42x = \dfrac{7}{8}$, $x = \dfrac{7}{42 \times 8} = \dfrac{7}{336}$

Number of days required by B $= \dfrac{336}{7} = 48$ days

Work done by (A + B) together $= \dfrac{1}{80} + \dfrac{1}{48} = \dfrac{128}{80 \times 48}$

$\therefore$ Number of days $= \dfrac{80 \times 48}{128} = 30$.

3. 2   B's work lasts for 23 days,

$\therefore$ Work done in 23 days by B $= \dfrac{23}{40}$

Remaining work $= \left(1 - \dfrac{23}{40} \right) = \dfrac{17}{40}$

Work done by (A + B) together in 1 day $= \left(\dfrac{1}{45} + \dfrac{1}{40} \right)$ part of work.

Number of days required to finish $\dfrac{17}{40}$ of work.

$= \dfrac{17}{40} \times \dfrac{(40 \times 45)}{(45 + 40)} = \dfrac{17 \times 40 \times 45}{40 \times 85} = 9$.

4. 4   A's 10 days' work $= \dfrac{1}{25} \times 10 = \dfrac{2}{5}$

Remaining work $= \dfrac{3}{5}$

$\left(\dfrac{1}{25} + \dfrac{1}{20} \right)$ work is done by (A + B) in 1 day

$\dfrac{3}{5}$ work is done by them in $= \dfrac{100}{9} \times \dfrac{3}{5} = 6.66$ days

Number of days $= 10 + 6.66 = 16.66$.

5. 2   A + B = 72 days, B + C = 120 days,
A + C = 90 days.
Assume units of work = 360 = [(LCM (72, 120, 90)]

$\therefore$ A + B units of work in 1 day $= \dfrac{360}{72} = 5$.

B + C units of work in 1 day $= \dfrac{360}{120} = 3$.

A + C units of work in 1 day $= \dfrac{360}{90} = 4$.

$\therefore$ 2(A + B + C) units in 1 day = 5 + 3 + 4 = 12.

A + B + C units in 1 day $= \dfrac{12}{2} = 6$

$\therefore$ A units in 1 day = 6 – 3 = 3

A will finish 360 units in $\dfrac{360}{3} = 120$ days.

6. 4   Assume units of work = LCM of (12, 16) = 48.

A + B in 1 day $= \dfrac{48}{12} = 4$ units.

B + C in 1 day $= \dfrac{48}{16} = 3$ units.

A + B worked for 5 days = 4 × 5 = 20 units done.
B + C worked for 7 days = 3 × 7 = 21 units done.
Work remains = 48 – (20 + 21) = 7
C finishes the rest 7 units in 7 days.

$\therefore$ Units of work done by C in 1 day $= \dfrac{7}{7} = 1$

$\therefore$ Number of days required for C to do the whole work $= \dfrac{48}{1}$

= 48 days.

7. 3 Total work = 12 × 8 = 96.
12 men finish 6 days of work = 12 × 6 = 72
∴ Work left = 96 – 72 = 24
Now, number of men = 12 + 4 = 16

∴ Time taken = $\dfrac{24}{16}$ = $1\dfrac{1}{2}$ = 1.5 days.

8. 2 10 men completes the job in 20 days.
∴ 5 men will complete the job in 40 days.
20 women completes the job in 15 days.
∴ 10 women will complete the job in 30 days.

∴ 5 men + 10 women will complete the job in $\dfrac{1}{\left(\dfrac{1}{40}+\dfrac{1}{30}\right)}$ days

= $\dfrac{1200}{70}$ days = $17\dfrac{1}{7}$ days.

9. 1 Assume units of work done = 24 = [LCM (12, 8)]

Units of work done by R in a day = $\dfrac{24}{8}$ = 3

Units of work done by S in a day = $\dfrac{24}{12}$ = 2

2 days' units of work done = 5
8 days' units of work done = 20
9 days' units of work done = 23
(as on the 9th day it is R's turn)
On 10th day work to be done = 24 – 23
= 1 unit which will be done by S.

∴ Time required by S = $\dfrac{1}{2}$ day

∴ Total time = $9\dfrac{1}{2}$ days.

10. 3 Units of work done = 220 = LCM (11, 20, 55).
Unit work in a day by A, B, C = 20, 11, 4.
1st day = (A + B) = 31, 2nd day = 24.
∴ Work done in 2 days = 55 units.
⇒ In 8 days work completed = 220 units.

11. 4 A in 1 hr = 2000
B in 1 hr = 1333.33
(A + B) in 2 hr = 3333.33
(A + B) in 4 hr = 6666.66
in 5th hr work to be done = 8000 – 6666.66
= 1333.33.

Number of hours required by A = $\dfrac{1333.33}{2000}$ = 0.66

Total number of hours = 4.66

12. 4 A : B = 1 : 2
C : (A + B) = 1.5 : 3
If C does 1.5 units of work per day,
A does 1 and B does 2.
Total units done by C = 40 × 1.5 = 60
A + B + C units = 4.5

Number of days by (A + B + C) = $\dfrac{60}{4.5}$ = 13.33.

13. 4 Let the work was completed in x days.
⇒ B worked for x days and A worked for (x – 5) days.
(Part of work done by A) + (Part of work done by B)

= $\left(\dfrac{x-5}{10}\right)+\left(\dfrac{x}{20}\right)=1$

⇒ x = 10 days.

14. 2 Work done by 24 men in 16 days
= Work done by 32 women in 24 days.
⇒ 24 × 16m = 32 × 24w
⇒ m = 2w
Now, work done by (16 men + 16 women) in 12 days is equivalent to (16 men + 8 men) in 12 days = 24 men in 12 days.
Total work = 24 × 16m
Work completed = 24 × 12m
Work left = 24 ×16m – 24 × 12m = 24m × 4
Therefore, number of men required to complete 24 × 4m

work in 2 days = $\dfrac{24\times4}{2}=48$ men

⇒ Extra men required = 48 – 24 = 24 men.

15. 4 25 men and 15 women can complete, a piece of work in 12 days.

∴ work done by them in 8 days = $\dfrac{8}{12}=\dfrac{2}{3}$.

Remaining work is completed by 25 men in 6 days.
∴ Time taken by 25 men to complete the whole work

= $\dfrac{3\times6}{1}=18$ days

From the question,
Time taken by 15 women to complete the whole work

= $\dfrac{36}{3-2}=36$ days

∴ Time taken by 1 woman = 15 × 36 = 540 days.

16. 2 One man alone finishes the work in 100 days.
∴ 10 men finish the work in 10 days.
From the question,

15 women finish in one day, $\dfrac{1}{5}-\dfrac{1}{10}=\dfrac{1}{10}$ work

∴ 15 women finish the whole work in 10 days.
∴ 1 woman finishes the whole work in 15 × 10 = 150 days.

17. 4 Part of work completed by (A + B) in 3 days

= $\dfrac{3}{12}+\dfrac{3}{8}=\dfrac{15}{24}$

Part of work left for C = $1-\dfrac{15}{24}=\dfrac{9}{24}$

Time taken by C to complete the whole job = $\dfrac{4}{5}\left(\dfrac{12\times8}{12+8}\right)$

= $\dfrac{96}{25}$ days

Time taken by C to complete $\dfrac{9}{24}$ of job

= $\dfrac{9}{24}\times\dfrac{96}{25}=1.44$ days

18. 2 $12M \times 18 = 12W \times 18 \times \dfrac{4}{3}$ $\therefore W = \dfrac{3}{4}M$

$10M + 8W = 10M + 8 \times \dfrac{3}{4}M = 16M$

$\therefore$ 16 men can complete the same work in

$\dfrac{12 \times 18}{16} = \dfrac{27}{2} = 13\dfrac{1}{2}$ days

19. 1   Let the number of days in which work finishes = x days.
$\Rightarrow$ B worked for x days and A worked for (x − 5) days.

$\Rightarrow \dfrac{x-5}{10} + \dfrac{x}{15} = 1$

$\therefore$ x = 9 days.

20. 3   Suppose B takes x days to do the work

$\therefore$ A takes $\left(2 \times \dfrac{3}{4}x\right)$ ie $\dfrac{3x}{2}$ days to do it.

Now, (A + B)'s 1 day's work $= \dfrac{1}{18}$.

$\therefore \therefore \dfrac{1}{x} + \dfrac{2}{3x} = \dfrac{1}{18}$ or x = 30.

21. 4   Ram mows the whole lawn in x hours.

$\therefore$ Ram mows, in 2 hours, $\dfrac{2}{x}$ of the lawn.

$\therefore$ Unmowed part $= 1 - \dfrac{2}{x} = \dfrac{x-2}{x}$.

22. 4   Factory A turns out $\dfrac{x}{2}$ cars in one hour. Factory B turns out $\dfrac{y}{2}$ cars in one hour.

In one hour both the factories A and B can turn out $\left(\dfrac{x}{2} + \dfrac{y}{2}\right)$ cars.

$\therefore$ in 8 hours both factories turn our $8\left(\dfrac{x}{2} + \dfrac{y}{2}\right)$ cars i.e. 4(x + y) cars.

23. 2   Ramesh alone finished $\dfrac{1}{2}$ of the work in 10 days.

Remaining $\dfrac{1}{2}$ of the job was finished by Ramesh and Dinesh together in 2 days.
Therefore, they both together can finish the complete job in 4 days.

Hence, Dinesh can complete the job in $\dfrac{20 \times 4}{20 - 4} = 5$ days.

24. 1   A's 1 day's work $= \dfrac{1}{12}$

B's day's work $= \dfrac{1}{12} + 60\%$ of $\dfrac{1}{12} = \dfrac{2}{15}$.

$\therefore$ B can do the work in $\dfrac{15}{2}$ ie $7\dfrac{1}{2}$ days

25. 4   12 men can complete $\dfrac{1}{3}$ of the work in 3 days and the remaining $\dfrac{2}{3}$ of the work in 6 days.

1 man can complete $\dfrac{2}{3}$ of the work in (12 × 6) = 72 days.

$\therefore$ 12 − 2 + 6 = 16 men can complete $\dfrac{2}{3}$ of the work in

$\dfrac{72}{16} = 4\dfrac{1}{2}$ days.

26. 1   Let A finish the work in x days
$\therefore$ B will finish the work in 4x days
$\Rightarrow$ 4x − x = 45 days
$\Rightarrow$ x = 15 days and 4x = 60 days
So, number of days both A and B will take to finish the work

$= \dfrac{15 \times 60}{75} = 12$ days

27. 1   Ratio of work of A : B in same time = 1 : 2
(as B is 100% more efficient)
A can finish a work in 12 days
$\therefore$ Units of work = 12 × 1 = 12

$\therefore$ B can finish the work in $\dfrac{12}{2}$ days = 6 days.

28. 2   Work done A : B = 2 : 1
Assume that A + B units of work done in 1 day = 3
$\therefore$ A + B units of work done in 14 days = 14 × 3 = 42

$\therefore$ A finishes the work in $= \dfrac{42}{2} = 21$ days.

29. 1   Assume unit of work = 18.
Father in 1 hr = (6 + 3) × 2 = 18 units
$\therefore$ Time taken = 1 hr.

30. 2   A's 1 day's work $= \dfrac{1}{6}$

B's 1 day's work $= \dfrac{1}{5}$

$\therefore$ ratio of ther wages $= \dfrac{1}{6} : \dfrac{1}{5} = 5 : 6$

$\therefore$ B's share $= \dfrac{220}{5+6} \times 6 = Rs\ 120.$

31. 4   The boy can do the work in $\dfrac{10 \times 6}{10 - 6} = 15$ days
Man's share : Boy's share = 15 : 10 = 3 : 2

Man's share $= \dfrac{50}{5} \times 3 = Rs\ 30$

Boy's share $= \dfrac{50}{5} \times 2 = Rs\ 20.$

32. 3 (3m + 4b) in 1 day earn Rs $\dfrac{756}{7}$ = Rs 108 ... (1)

(11m + 13b) in 1 day earn Rs $\dfrac{308}{8}$ = Rs 376 ... (2)

From (1) and (2), we get
m = 20 and b = 12
∴ 7m + 9b earn Rs (7 × 20 + 9 × 12) = Rs 248 in 1 day
∴ 7m + 9b earn Rs 2480 in 10 days.

33. 1 Daily earning of A + B + C

$= \dfrac{Rs\,1350}{9}$ = Rs 150 ... (1)

Daily earning of A + C $= \dfrac{Rs\,470}{5}$ = Rs 94 ... (2)

Daily earning of B + C $= \dfrac{Rs\,760}{10}$ = Rs 76 ... (3)

By, [Eq. (2) + Eq. (3) – Eq. (1)], we get the daily earning of
C = Rs. 20.

34. 4 Units to fill up = LCM (20, 15, 12) = 60.
Units filled up by A, B, C in 1 min = 3, 4, 5

Time taken by A + B + C to fill up = $\dfrac{60}{12}$ = 5 min.

35. 4 Capacity in units = LCM (9 ,10) = 90.

Fill in units = 10 per hour ... $\left(\dfrac{90}{9}\right)$

Fill out units = 9 per hour ... $\left(\dfrac{90}{10}\right)$

∴ Resultant outflow = 10 – 9 = 1 unit per hr.
Total outflow = 90 units.

∴ Time taken to empty the full cistern is $\dfrac{90}{1}$ = 90 hr.

36. 3 Say, capacity in units = LCM (10, 12, 20) = 60.

Rate of A, B, C per hour = $\dfrac{60}{10}, \dfrac{60}{12}, \dfrac{60}{20}$ = 6, 5 and 3

∴ A + B = 11 units, C = 3 units
∴ Per hour intake = 11 – 3 = 8 units

Time to fill up = $\dfrac{60}{8}$ = 7.5 hr.

37. 3 Pipes A + B are there,

∴ $\dfrac{1}{A} + \dfrac{1}{B} = \dfrac{1}{12}$, say A takes x hours to fill, then B will take
x – 10 hours to fill the tank.

$\dfrac{1}{x} + \dfrac{1}{x-10} = \dfrac{1}{12} \;\Rightarrow\; \dfrac{x-10+x}{x(x-10)}$

$= \dfrac{1}{12} \;\Rightarrow\; \dfrac{2x-10}{x(x-10)} = \dfrac{1}{12}$

24x – 120 = x² – 10x
x² – 34x + 120 = 0
x² – 30x – 4x + 120 = 0
x(x – 30) – 4 (x – 30) = 0

(x – 4) (x – 30) = 0   x = 4, 30
∴ 30 hours (∵ x cannot be 4)

38. 1 Say, capacity of tank = LCM (12, 15) = 60 units

1 min total intake in units = $\dfrac{60}{12} + \dfrac{60}{15}$ = 9

3 min total intake in units = 9 × 3 = 27
Units to be filled = 60 – 27 = 33

Time taken by B = $\dfrac{33}{4}$ = 8.25 (8 min 15 s)

39. 2 Say capacity of tank = 12 units

A can fill = $\dfrac{12}{6}$ = 2 units/hour

B can fill = $\dfrac{12}{4}$ = 3 units/hour

A + B alternate in 2 hr = 2 + 3 = 5 units
A + B alternate in 4 hr = 5 × 2 = 10 units
In 5th hr – A is opened .
∴ A fills the remaining 2 units.
∴ Total hours = 5.

40. 1 4 L per minutes = 240 l per hour.
Let's assume that capacity of tank
= LCM (6, 8) = 24 units.

When inlet is also opened, net outflow = $\dfrac{24}{8}$ = 3 units per
hour.
∴ 4 – 3 = 1 unit per hour of water contributed by pipe. ∴ 1
unit = 240 L
24 units = 24 × 240 = 5760 L.

Exercise – 2

1. 2 Distance to be covered = 100 m.
Speed of the person = 36 km/hr = 10 m/s.

Therefore, time taken = $\dfrac{100\ m}{10\ m/s}$ = 10 s.

2. 2 (a) Distance = Speed × Time = 48 × 10 = 480 km
(b) To cover the same distance in 8 hr.

Speed = $\dfrac{d}{t} = \dfrac{480}{8}$ = 60 km/hr

∴ Speed must be increased by 60 – 48 = 12 km/hr

3. 2 Total time = 60 + 24 = $\dfrac{84}{60}$ hr

at 4 km/hr $t_1 = \dfrac{2/3d}{4} = \dfrac{1}{6}d$ hr

at 5 km/hr $t_2 = \dfrac{1/3d}{5} = \dfrac{1}{15}d$ hr

Total time = $\dfrac{d}{6} + \dfrac{d}{15} = \dfrac{84}{60}$ or d = 6 km.

Answers and Explanations

4. 4   Let the distance travelled by the man be x km.

Therefore, time taken at a speed of 10 km/hr = $\dfrac{x}{10}$ hr.

Time taken at a speed of 20 km/hr = $\dfrac{x}{20}$ hr.

Hence, $\dfrac{x}{10} - \dfrac{x}{20} = \dfrac{45}{60}$

Solving, we get x = 15 km.
Therefore,

$\dfrac{x}{25} - \dfrac{x}{40} = \dfrac{15}{25} - \dfrac{15}{40} = 0.225 \text{ hr} = 13.5 \text{ min}$

5. 4   Average speed = $\dfrac{2 \times 75 \times 50}{[75 + 50]} = 60 \text{ km/hr}$

6. 4   Average speed = $\dfrac{2xy}{x+y} = \dfrac{2 \times 24 \times 36}{24 + 36}$

$= \dfrac{144}{5} = 28.8$ km/hr

7. 1   Average speed = $\dfrac{\text{Total distance}}{\text{Total time}}$

$= \dfrac{2500 + 1200 + 500}{\dfrac{2500}{500} + \dfrac{1200}{400} + \dfrac{500}{250}} = \dfrac{4200}{10} = 420$ km/hr.

8. 2   d = s × t

$\dfrac{1}{2}$ journey $(= 40 \text{ km})$ in $\dfrac{3}{5}$ of time $(= 6 \text{hr})$

Total distance = 80 km.
Total time = 10 hr
$80 = 40 + S_2 \times 4$
$S_2 = 10$ km/hr.

9. 3   **Method 1:**
Let the total distance between A and B be x.
Since B had to travel 145 km to reach A, this means they
met at a distance of 145 km from A.
Hence, distance between the meeting place and B
= (x – 145) km.
Ratio of speed = Ratios of distance
25 : 49 : : 145 : (x – 145).
Therefore, x = 429.2 km.

Method 2:

$x = \left\{ \dfrac{(49 + 25)}{25} \right\} \times 145 = 429.2$ km

10. 1   The following question can be illustrated with the help of the
diagram given below.

7 a.m.   A   B   8 a.m.
20 km ph →   ← 25 km ph

P   Q

←————— 110 —————→

Since A and B are starting at different times, we cannot
apply the concept of relative speed directly.

Their starting times have to be made the same, i.e. when B
started, A has already travelled for 1 hr.
∴ Distance travelled by A is 20 km.
The remaining distance to be covered is 110 – 20 = 90 km.
According to the concept of relative speed when two objects
are moving in opposite directions, the relative speed is given
as the summation of their individual speeds.

$\therefore S_R = \dfrac{\text{Distance between two objects}}{\text{Time}}$

$\therefore 25 + 20 = \dfrac{90}{\text{Time}} \quad \therefore 45 = \dfrac{90}{\text{Time}}$

∴ Time = 2 hr from 8 a.m., i.e. 10 a.m.

11. 3   Let his usual time be t hours and his usual speed be s km/hr.

Distance, $d = st = \dfrac{3}{4} s \times (t + 2.5)$

or 4t = 3t + 7.5   t = 7.5 hr.

12. 2   Let his normal speed be s km/hr.
Let his normal time be t hours

$d = st \implies 4 \left(t - \dfrac{1}{6} \right) = 3 \left(t + \dfrac{1}{6} \right)$

$4t - \dfrac{4}{6} = 3t + \dfrac{3}{6}, \ t = \dfrac{7}{6}$ hr

Distance $= 4 \times \left(\dfrac{7}{6} - \dfrac{1}{6} \right) = 4$ km.

Short cut:
Let the distance from the boy's house to school be d km.

So, $\dfrac{d}{3} - \dfrac{d}{4} = \dfrac{20}{60}$

(∵ The differential of the times is 20 min)

$\therefore \dfrac{d}{12} = \dfrac{1}{3}$.

So d = 4 km.

13. 2   A takes a lead of (3.5 km/hr) (2.5 hr) = 8.75 km over B.
Hence, when B starts he has to travel a relative distance of
8.75 km and at a relative speed of (4.5–3.5) km/hr
= 1 km/hr, which means B will take 8.75 hr to catch up and
then overtake A.

14. 2   The thief travels for 2 hr (7.00 p.m. to 9.00 p.m.) and takes a
lead of (4.5 km/hr)(2hr) = 9 km.
The policeman is required to cover up a distance of 9
km at a relative speed of 1.5 km/hr. Therefore, the policeman
will take 6 hr after 9 p.m. to catch up with the thief, i.e at 3
a.m.

15. 1   Let the required distance be x km.

Then time taken during the first journey = $\dfrac{x}{3}$ hr and   time

taken during the second journey = $\dfrac{x}{2}$ hr

$\therefore \dfrac{x}{3} + \dfrac{x}{2} = 5 \implies \dfrac{2x + 3x}{6} = 5$

∴ x = 6
∴ required distance = 6 km

16. 1 When B meets A at R, B has walked the distance PQ + QR and A the distance PR. That is, both of them have together walked twice the distance from P to Q, i.e., 42 km.
Now, the rates of A and B are 3 : 4 and they have walked 42 km.

Hence the distance PR travelled by A = $\frac{3}{7}$ of 42 km = 18 km

17. 4 Due to stoppage, it covers 9 km less.

Time taken to cover 9 km = $\left(\frac{9}{54} \times 60\right)$ min = 10 min.

18. 2 Total relative distance travelled by the car
= [40 + 60] m = 100 m.

The relative speed = $\frac{100 \text{ m}}{20 \text{ sec}} = 5 \text{ m/s}$.

The relative speed is also equal to (30 – v) km/hr

= $(30 - v) \times \left(\frac{5}{18}\right)$ m/s, where 'v' is the speed of the bus.

Therefore, $(30 - v) \times \frac{5}{18} = 5$ or, v = 12 km/hr.

19. 2 Speed of first train = $\frac{200}{10}$ m/s = 20 m/s.

Speed of second train = $\frac{200}{15}$ m/s = $\frac{40}{3}$ m/s.

Relative speed of the two trains (when they move in

opposite directions) = $20 + \frac{40}{3} = \frac{100}{3}$

Time taken by the two trains to completely pass each other

= $\frac{200 + 200}{100/3}$ = 12 s

20. 3 Let x be the distance between A and B.
The train which leaves A travels a total distance of
x + (x – 200) = 2x – 200.
The train which leaves B travels a total distance of
x + 200.
The ratio of distances travelled by the trains = Ratio of the speeds.
Therefore, (2x – 200) : (x + 200) : : 40 : 60
Or x = 250 km.

21. 2 Let speed of A = 3x km/hr
Let speed of B = 4x km/hr

Time taken by A = $t_B + \frac{1}{2}$ hr

Time taken by B = t_B hr
d $\Rightarrow$ s × t $\Rightarrow$

$3x \times \left(t_B + \frac{1}{2}\right) = 4x \times t_B$

or $3 t_B + \frac{3}{2} = 4 t_B$

or $t_B = \frac{3}{2}$, $t_A = \frac{1}{2} + \frac{3}{2} = 2$ hr

22. 1 Length of the bridge = 1 km
Length of the train = 0.5 km

Time to clear the bridge = 2 min = $\frac{2}{60}$ hr

Speed = $\frac{1 + 0.5}{2/60} = \frac{1.5}{2} \times 60 = 45$ km/hr

23. 1 Length of the faster train

= $(36 + 45) \times \frac{5}{18} \times 8$ m = $81 \times \frac{5}{18} \times 8 = 180$ m.

24. 4 Length of train = 110 m.
Since the train and the man are moving in the same direction, the relative speed of train with respect to the man = (58 – 4)

$\times \frac{5}{18} = 54 \times \frac{5}{18}$ m/s = 15 m/s

Time = $\frac{110}{15} = 7.33$ s.

25. 3 Let the speed of boat be x km/hr.
Let the speed of stream be y km/hr.

Speed upstream = $\frac{13}{5} = x - y$ ... (i)

Speed downstream = $\frac{28}{5} = x + y$ ... (ii)

Solving for (y) $\Rightarrow$ y = 1.5 km/hr

26. 1 Speed of stream = 1 km/hr
Let the speed of boat in still water = x km/hr
Total time = 12 hr

$12 = \frac{35}{x-1} + \frac{35}{x+1} = 35\left[\frac{1}{x-1} + \frac{1}{x+1}\right] = 35\left[\frac{2x}{x^2-1}\right]$

$12x^2 - 70x - 12 = 0$

$x = \frac{70 \pm \sqrt{4900 + 576}}{24} = \frac{70 \pm \sqrt{5476}}{24} = \frac{70 \pm 74}{24}$

$x = \frac{144}{24} = 6$ km/hr, $-\frac{1}{6}$ km/hr

(Negative value is neglected.)

27. 1 Speed downstream = v + u (where, v = Speed of the boat in still water, and u = Speed of the stream).
Speed upstream = v – u.
Distance downstream = Distance upstream
(v + u) 45 = (v – u)75   or, u : v = 1 : 4.

28. 4 Normal day it travels a distance = 25 (50 + u)

On that particular day it completes $\frac{1}{2}$ the journey in same time (12.5 hr).

But in half time due to engine problem it takes $2\frac{1}{2}$ hr extra.

So it take 15 hr to complete the remaining half journey.

So, $15(40 + u) = \frac{1}{2} \times 25(50 + u)$

$30(40 + u) = 25 \times 50 + 25$ u
$30u - 25u = 1250 - 1200$; 5 u = 50; u = 10 km/hr

Answers and Explanations

29. 2 When Pawan runs 100 m then Arun runs 96 m and Rahul runs 98 m.

⇒ When Rahul runs 100 m, then Arun will run

$$= \frac{100}{98} \times 96 = 97.96 \text{m}$$

⇒ In a 100 m runs, Rahul will best Arun by
100 – 97.96 = 2.04 m.

30. 2 A's speed : B's speed 2 : 1
We may say that A gains 2 – 1 = 1 m in a race of 2 metres.

Therefore, he will cover 60 m in a race of $\frac{2}{1} \times 60$ = 120m

31. 3 Krishna : Arjun : Virat = 200 : 200 – 31 : 200 – 18
= 200 : 169 :182

$$\therefore \frac{\text{Virat}}{\text{Arjun}} = \frac{182}{169} = \frac{182\left(\frac{350}{182}\right)}{169\left(\frac{350}{182}\right)} = \frac{350}{325}$$

∴ Virat beats Arjun by 350 – 325 = 25 m

32. 4 To reach the winning post A covers 500 – 140 = 360 m.

$$\therefore \text{B covers } 360\left(\frac{4}{3}\right) = 480 \text{ m when A reaches the winning}$$

post.
So, A reaches the winning post while B remain 20 m behind.
∴ A wins by 20m.

33. 4 Ratio of speed of Bhim and Arjun = 7 : 4.
(Since the ratio of the times = 4 : 7)
If the length of circular track = 28 m, the speeds of Bhim and Arjun are 7 and 4 m/min.
The time when they are together the first time will be when Bhim (the faster one) has taken one round more than Arjun (the slower one).
Therefore, if time when they meet is 't', then

$$7t - 4t = 28, \text{ which means } t = \frac{28}{3} \text{ min.}$$

34. 4 Ratio of speed of Bhim and Arjun = 7 : 4.
(Since the ratio of the times = 4 : 7)
They will meet at the starting place the first time at a t i m e which is the LCM of the times each one of them takes to reach the starting place.
Therefore, LCM of 4 and 7 is 28 min.

35. 1 Ratio of distances = Ratio of speeds = 20 : 23 :27.

36. 3 Relative speed of the two hands = $5\frac{1}{2}^{\circ}$ per min.

⇒ In 1 min, minute hand covers $5\frac{1}{2}^{\circ}$

At 1 am, the angle between hur and minute hand = 30°

Time required to cover 30° = $\dfrac{30}{5\frac{1}{2}}$

$$= \frac{60}{11} = 5\frac{5}{11} \text{min}$$

So, the hour hand and the minute hand will be together at 1 hour and $5\frac{5}{11}$ mins

37. 2 As A starts puffing, the length of burnt cigarette in one cycle

is $\left(\text{A} \xrightarrow[\text{gap}]{} \text{B} \xrightarrow[\text{gap}]{} \right)$

= 2 × 3 + 3 + 3 × 3 + 3 = 6 + 3 + 9 + 3 = 21 mm.

As there are three such cycles $\left(\because \frac{63}{21} = 3 \right)$,

time taken in one cycle = 2 + 3 + 3 + 3 = 11s.
So total time = 3 × 11 = 33 s.

38. 1 The rate of burning of first candle = 1 cm/hr.
The rate of burning of second candle = 1.5 cm/hr.
They will be of the same length when the longer candle melts by a relative length of (10 – 8) = 2 cm.
Therefore, time after which they will be of the same

length = $\dfrac{2 \text{ cm}}{[1.5 \text{ cm/hr} - 1 \text{ cm/hr}]}$ = 4 hr.

After 4 hr, the candle of length 8 cm is now 8 – 4 = 4 cm long which would be of the same length as the length of the other candle.

39. 3 3t = 6
Hence, t = 2
Distance travelled by bus is equal to area under the curve,

i.e. $\dfrac{1}{2} \times Vm_1 \times 2 + Vm_1 \times 2 + \dfrac{1}{2} \times Vm_1 \times 2$

= $4V_{m1}$ [V_{m1} = Bus (maximum speed)]
Distance travelled by jeep.

$$\frac{1}{2} V_{m2} \times 2 + Vm_2 \times 2 + \frac{1}{2} \times V_{m2} \times 2$$

= $4V_{m2}$ [V_{m2} = geeps maximum speed]
So $4Vm_1 + 4Vm_2 = 280$
$Vm_1 + Vm_2 = 70$
$Vm_1 - Vm_2 = 10$
$Vm_1 = 40$ km/hr
$Vm_2 = 30$ km/hr

40. 3 Average speed by bus

$$= \frac{\text{Distance travelled by bus}}{\text{Time taken by bus}}$$

$$= \frac{4Vm_1}{6}$$

$$= \frac{2}{3} \times 40 = \frac{80}{3} \text{ km/hr}$$

Average speed by jeep

$$= \frac{\text{Distance travelled by Jeep}}{\text{Time taken by jeep}}$$

$$= \frac{4Vm_2}{6} = \frac{2}{3} \times 30 = 20 \text{ km/hr}$$

Exercise –1

1. 1

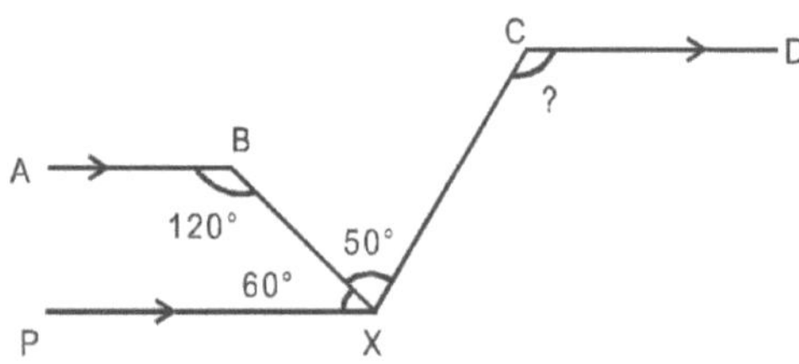

Draw PX parallel to AB.

∴ ∠PXB = 60 as sum of interior ∠S = 180°

∠PXC = 110
∠PXC = 110 and ∠PXC = ∠XCD
(As PX || CD and these angles are vertically opposite angle)
∴ ∠PXC = ∠XCD = 110

2. 3

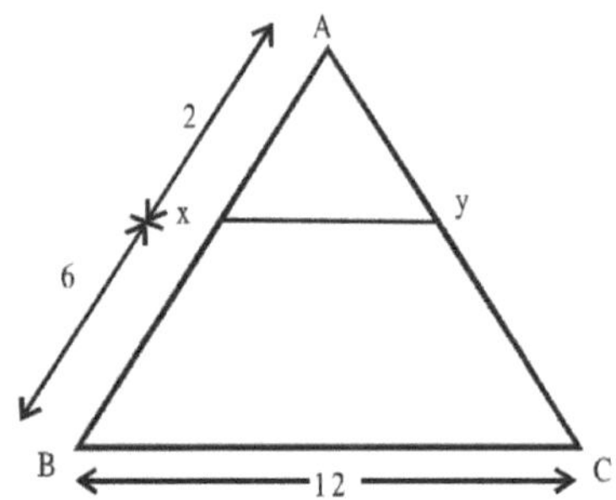

XY || BC
∴ ΔAXY and ΔABC are similar
Applying properties of similar Δ's

$$\frac{AX}{AB} = \frac{XY}{BC}$$

AB = AX + XB
   = 2 + 6 = 8

$$\frac{2}{8} = \frac{XY}{12}$$

$$XY = \frac{24}{8} = 3$$

3. 3

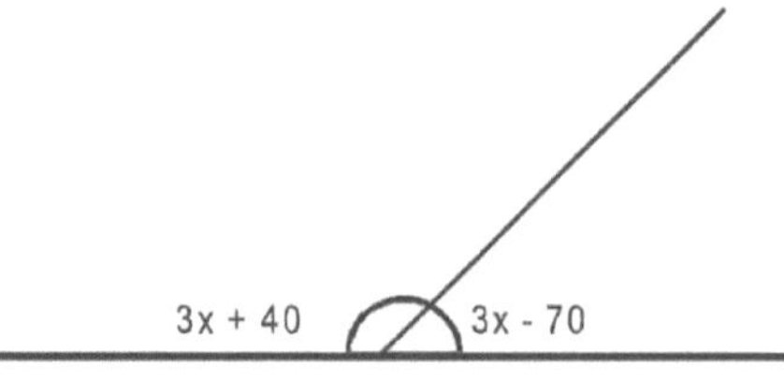

3x + 40 + 3x − 70 = 180°
6x = 210°
x = 35°

4. 4   Let A be the angle.

So $A = \frac{1}{4}(180° - A)$

4A = 180° − A
5A = 180°
A = 36°

5. 4

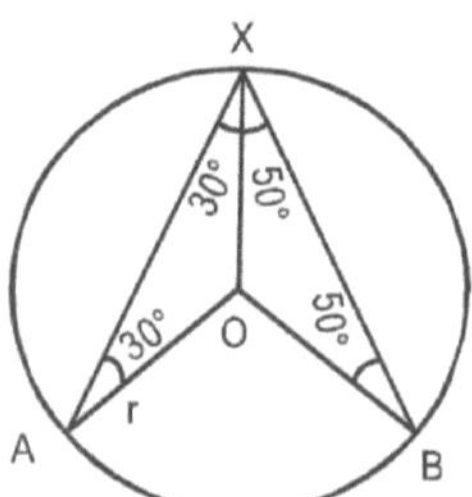

OA = OB = OX   (radius of circle)
∴ ΔXOA is isosceles triangle

∴ ∠AXO = ∠OAX = 30° and ∠OBX = ∠OXB = 50°
∴ ∠AXB = 80° and ∠AOB = 2 ∠AXB
   = 2 × 80° = 160°

6. 4

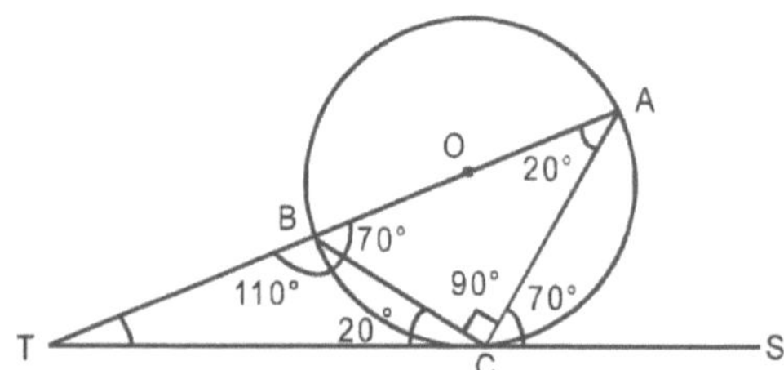

∠ACS = ∠ABC   (By alternate segment theorem)
and ∠BCA = 90° (The angle that diameter makes
        with circumference = 90°)
∠TBC = 180 − ∠CBA = 180 − 70 = 110°
∠BCT = 180 − ∠BCA − ∠ACS
    = 180° − 90° − 70° = 20°
∴ ∠BTC = 180 − ∠TBC − ∠BCT
    = 180° − 110° − 20° = 50°

7. 3

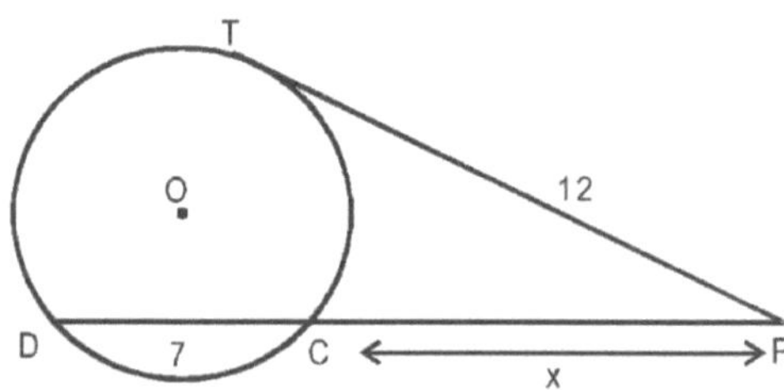

PC × PD = PT²
x × (x + 7) = 12²
x² + 7x − 144 = 0
(x + 16) (x − 9) = 0
x = 9

8. 4   Let ∠B and ∠C be 3x and 4x
Then 3x + 4x = 140
x = 20° (Sum of opposite interior angle is equal to exterior angle)
∴ ∠B = 3x = 3 × 20 = 60°
and ∠C = 4x = 4 × 20 = 80°

Answers and Explanations

9. 3

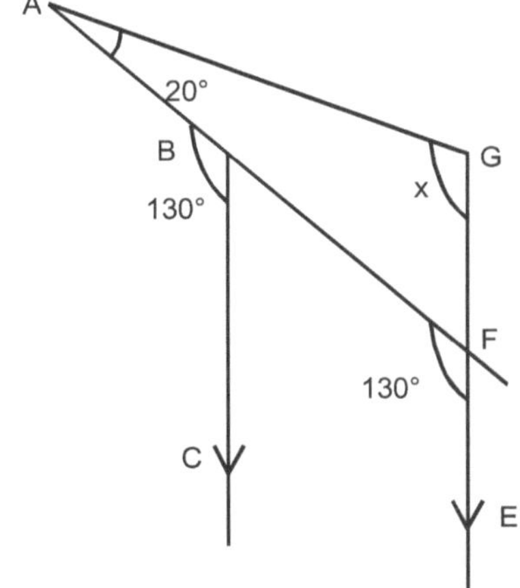

CB || EG

∴ ∠ABC = ∠BFE = 130

∴ ∠BFG = 180 – 130 = 50°

x = 180° – 20° – 50° = 110°

10. 1

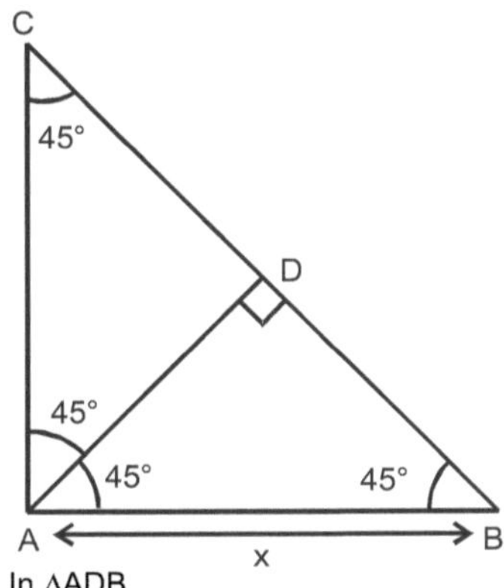

In ΔADB

$$\cos 45 = \frac{AD}{AB}$$

AD = x cos 45

$$AD = \frac{x}{\sqrt{2}}$$

11. 2

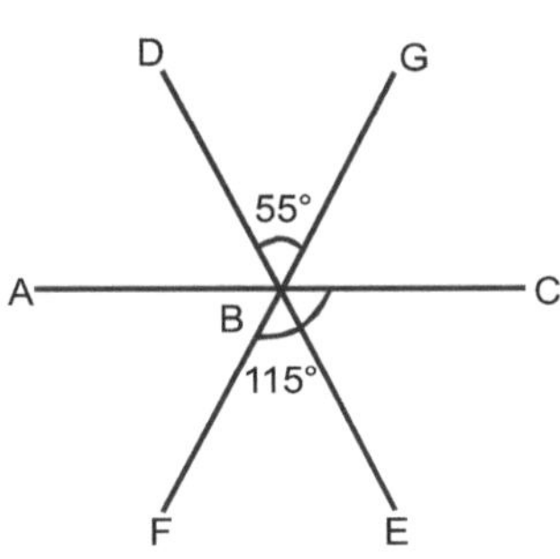

Since ∠DBG + ∠GBE = 180°

∠GBE = 180° − ∠DBG = 180° − 55° = 125°

12. 4

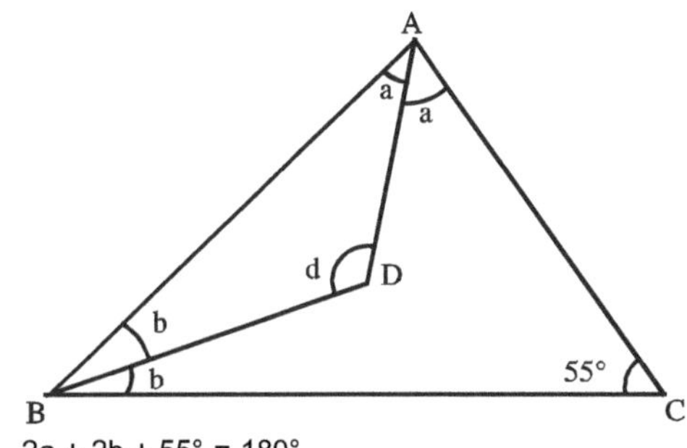

2a + 2b + 55° = 180°

(Sum of all the angles of triangle = 180°)

∴ a + b = 62.5°

∠d = 180 – (a + b) = 180 – 62.5

∠d = 117.5°

13. 1

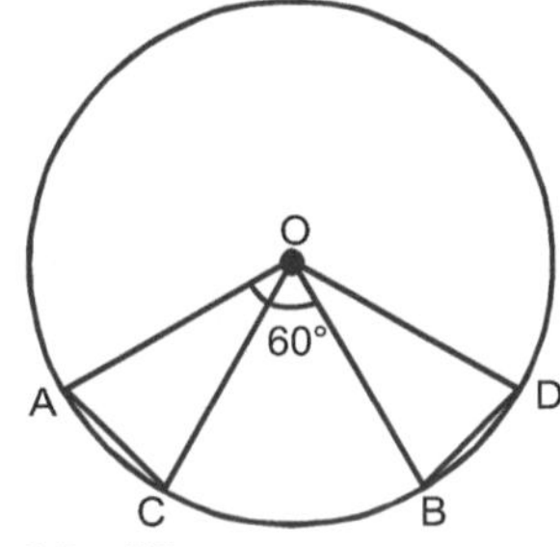

AC = BD

Equal chords makes equal angle with the centre.

∠AOB = 60

∠BOC = 15

∴ ∠AOC = 45°

∠AOC = ∠BOD = 45°

14. 2

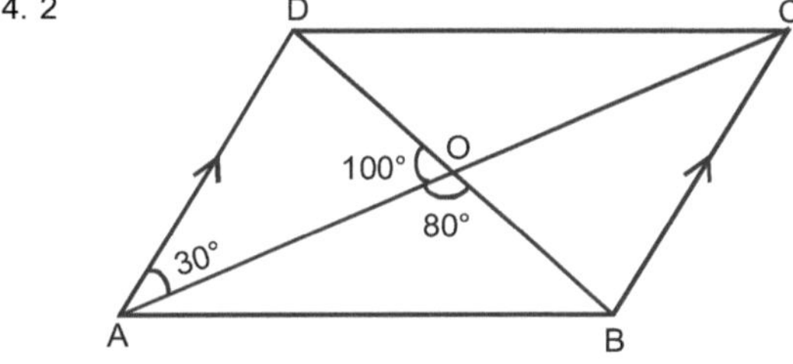

∠AOB + ∠DOA = 180

∠DOA = 180 – 80 = 100°

∠ADO = 180 – ∠DAO – ∠DOA

∠ADO = 180 – 30 – 100 = 50°

∠ADO = ∠DBC   (As AD || BC and DC || AB)

∴ ∠DBC = 50°

15. 4

$$\frac{\text{Area of } \Delta\,ABC}{\text{Area of } \Delta\,DEF} = \frac{\text{Square of side}}{\text{Square of side}} = \frac{AB^2}{DE^2}$$

(When two triangles ABC and DEF are similar)

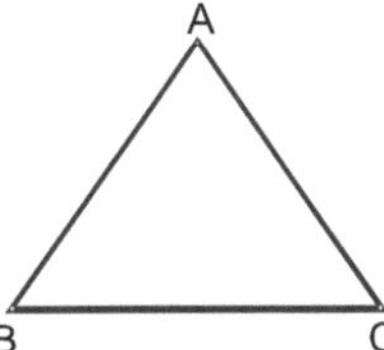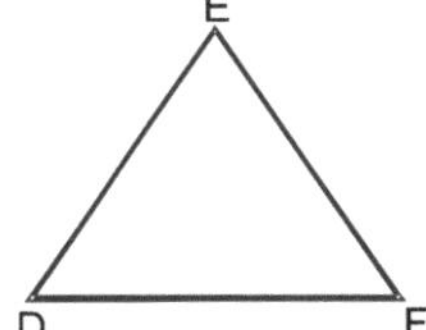

$$\frac{AB^2}{DE^2} = \frac{64}{49}$$

$$\frac{49}{DE^2} = \frac{64}{49}$$

$$DE = \sqrt{\frac{49 \times 49}{64}}$$

$$DE = \frac{49}{8}$$

16. 3

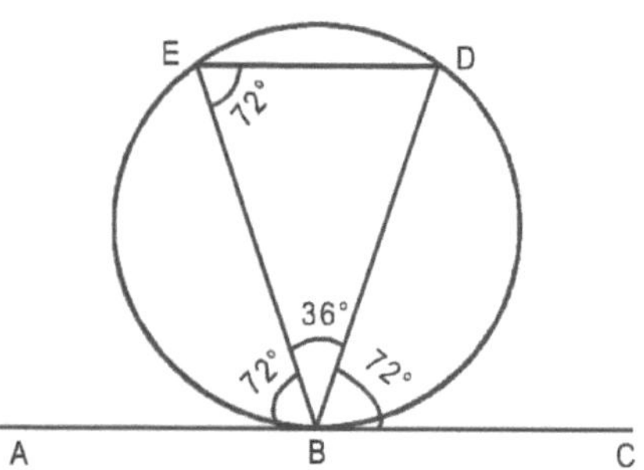

$\angle CBD = \angle BED$
(By alternate segment theorem)
$\angle EBA = 180 - \angle CBD - \angle DBE$
$= 180 - 36 - 72 = 72$
$\angle BDE = 180 - \angle EBD - \angle DEB$
$= 180 - 36 - 72$
$= \angle BDE = 72°$

17. 2

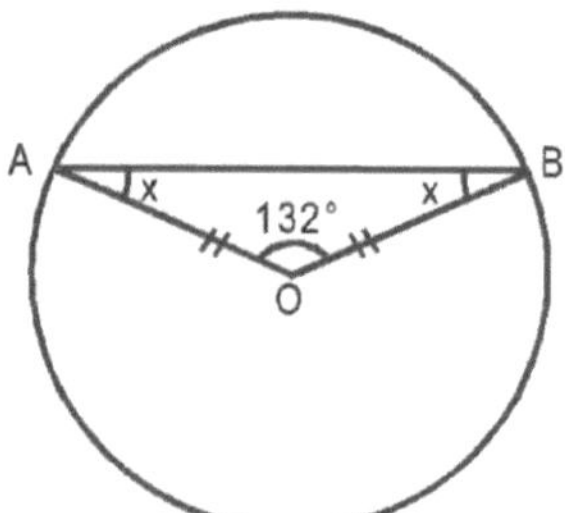

OA = OB = radius = 8
($\therefore$ AOB becomes isosceles triangle)
$\angle OAB + \angle ABO + \angle AOB = 180°$
(as $\angle OAB = \angle ABO$)
$x° + x° + 132 = 180$
$2x° = 48°$
$x = 24°$

18. 4

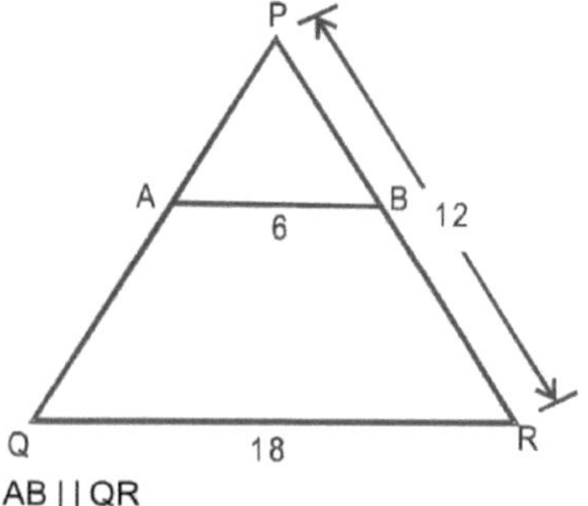

AB || QR

$\therefore$ $\triangle$APB and $\triangle$QPR are similar triangles

$$\therefore \quad \frac{AB}{QR} = \frac{PB}{PR}$$

$$\frac{6}{18} = \frac{PB}{12}$$

$$PB = \frac{12 \times 6}{18} = 4$$

19. 4

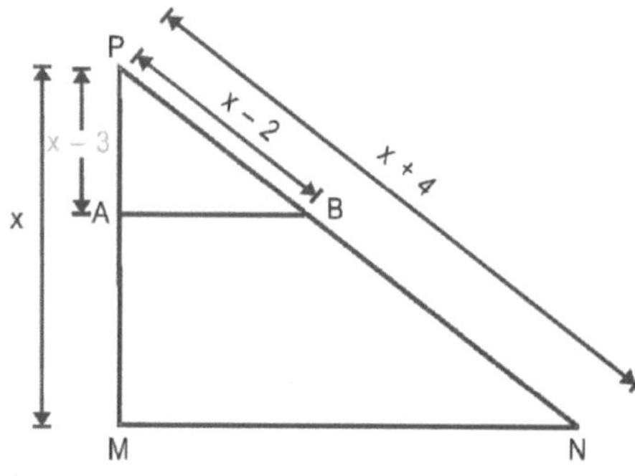

As AB || MN
$\therefore$ $\triangle$APB and $\triangle$MPN are similar

$$\therefore \quad \frac{PM}{PA} = \frac{PN}{PB} \Rightarrow \frac{x}{x-3} = \frac{x+4}{x-2}$$

$x(x - 2) = (x - 3)(x + 4)$
$x^2 - 2x = x^2 + 4x - 3x - 12$
$x = 4$

Alternative method
Since PA $\Rightarrow$ x − 3 > 0 and x > 3 only on option says
x > 3, i.e. (4).

20. 3

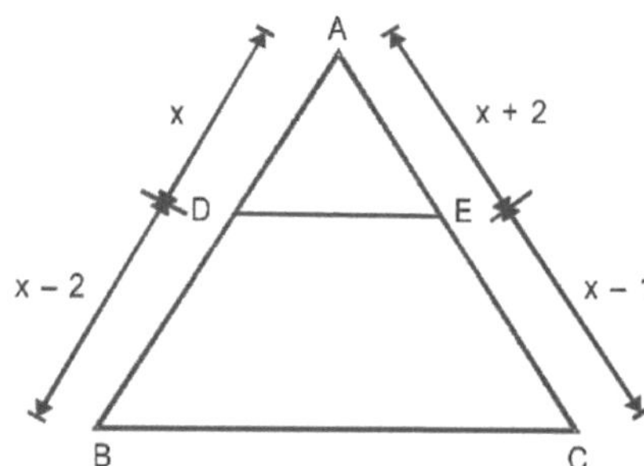

DE || BC

$\triangle$ADE and $\triangle$ABC are similar $\dfrac{AD}{AB} = \dfrac{AE}{AC}$

$$\frac{AD}{AD + DB} = \frac{AE}{AE + EC}$$

$$\frac{x}{x + x - 2} = \frac{x+2}{x+2+x-1} \Rightarrow \frac{x}{2x-2} = \frac{x+2}{2x+1}$$

$(2x + 1)x = (2x - 2)(x + 2)$
$2x^2 + x = 2x^2 + 4x - 2x - 4$
$x - 4x + 2x + 4 = 0$
$-x + 4 = 0 \Rightarrow x = 4$

Answers and Explanations

21. 4

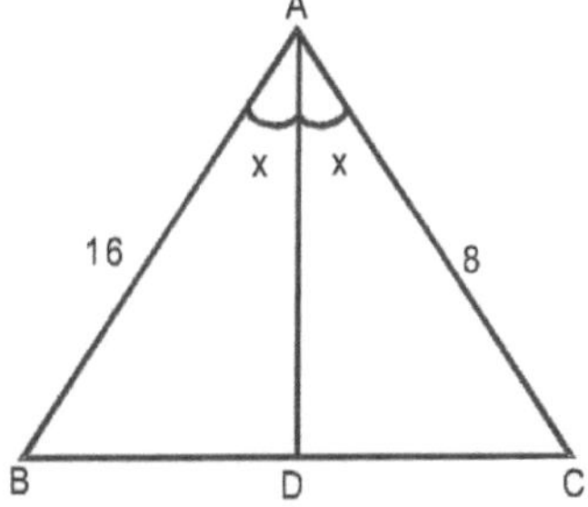

AD is the bisector
$\therefore \angle BAD = \angle DAC = x°$

$$\frac{AB}{AC} = \frac{BD}{DC} \quad \text{(Internal angle bisector theorem)}$$

$$\frac{16}{8} = \frac{BD}{DC} = \frac{2}{1}$$

22. 4

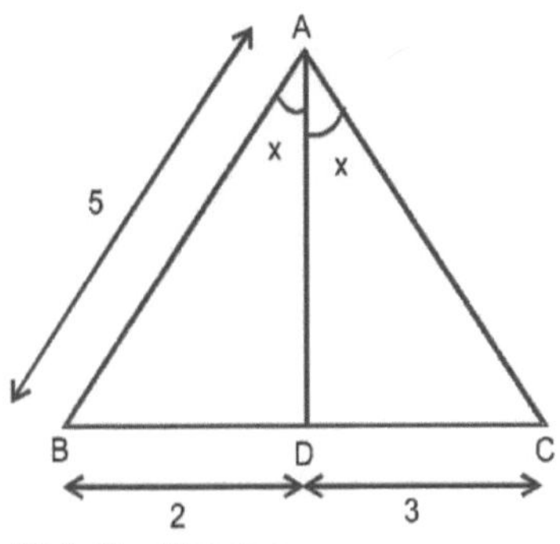

AD is the bisector
$\therefore \angle BAD = \angle CAD = x$

$$\frac{AB}{AC} = \frac{BD}{DC} \quad \text{(Internal angle bisector theorem)}$$

$$\frac{5}{AC} = \frac{2}{3}$$

$$AC = \frac{15}{2} = 7.5$$

23. 2   We know exterior angle = sum of interior angles opposite angles
$\therefore \angle ECD = \angle CAB + \angle ABC = 45° + 50°$
and $\angle BED = \angle ECD + \angle EDC = 95° + 25° = 120°$

24. 1

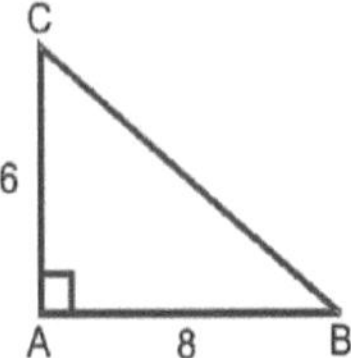

In $\triangle ABC$ which is a right angle triangle.

$$BC = \sqrt{6^2 + 8^2} = 10$$

Hence perimeter = 6 + 8 + 10 = 24 cm

25. 4   In an equilateral triangle, the circumcentre, orthocentre, and incentre is coincident.

Exercise – 2

1. 4 $a^2 + a^2 = d^2$

$d = a\sqrt{2}$

$d = 60$

$$a = \frac{60}{\sqrt{2}}$$

Area of square is = $a \times a = \dfrac{60 \times 60}{2} = 1800$ m^2

2. 1   Let the side of square be a
$\therefore$ Perimeter of square = $4a = 8x + 40$

$$a = \frac{8x + 40}{4} = 2x + 10$$

Diagonal $d = a\sqrt{2} = \sqrt{2}\ (2x + 10)$

3. 4   Area of triangle = 32 cm^2.
Base = b = 8 cm.

Area = $\dfrac{1}{2}$ base $\times$ height = $\dfrac{1}{2} \times 8 \times h = 32$

h = 8 cm.

4. 2

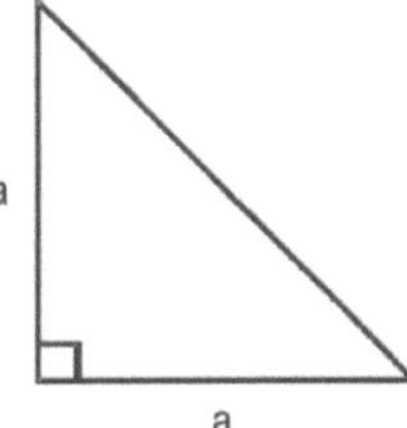

Area of isosceles triangle = $\dfrac{1}{2} \times a \times a = 800$

$a^2 = 1600$
a = 40 cm.

Hypotenuse = $\sqrt{a^2 + a^2} = a\sqrt{2} = 40\sqrt{2}$ cm

5. 3   Let the side of triangles be, a, b and c
So a = 6 cm, b = 7 cm and c = 11 cm

$$S = \text{semi-perimeter} = \frac{a+b+c}{2} = 12$$

Area of triangle = $\sqrt{s(s-a)\ (s-b)\ (s-c)}$

$$= \sqrt{12(12-6)\ (12-7)\ (12-11)} = \sqrt{12 \times 6 \times 5 \times 1}$$

$$= \sqrt{3 \times 4 \times 3 \times 2 \times 5} = 3 \times 2\sqrt{10} = 6\sqrt{10} \text{ cm}^2$$

6. 4   Area of equivalent triangle = $\dfrac{\sqrt{3}}{4}$ (side)^2

$$= \frac{\sqrt{3}}{4}(4a)^2 = 4\sqrt{3}\ a^2$$

Also area of equilateral triangle = $\dfrac{1}{2} \times$ base $\times$ height

$$\Rightarrow \frac{1}{2} \times 4a \times \text{height} = 4\sqrt{3}\ a^2$$

Height = $\dfrac{4\sqrt{3}a^2 \times 2}{4a}$

Height = $2\sqrt{3}\,a$

7. 4

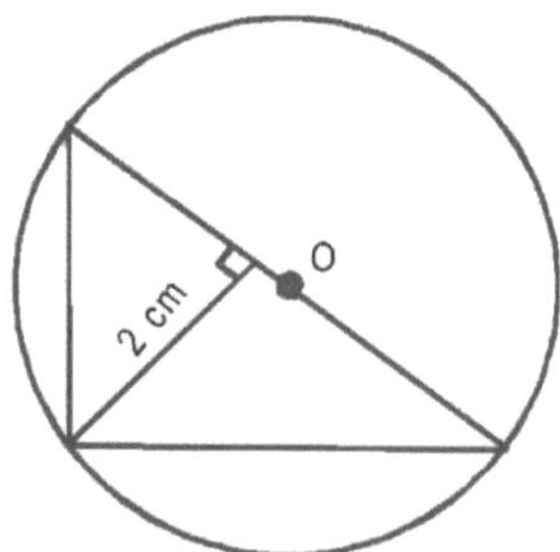

Hypotenuse of right-angled triangle = 2 radius of circle
= 2 × 3 = 6 cm
Altitude = 2 cm

Area = $\dfrac{1}{2}$ × base × height = $\dfrac{1}{2} \times 6 \times 2 = 6\ cm^2$

8. 1 Area of a rhombus = $\dfrac{1}{2}$ (Product of two diagonals).

$\dfrac{1}{2}$ × 10 × 8 = 40 sq. cm

9. 2 Radius of circle = 14
Angle of sector = 18°

Length of one of sector = $\dfrac{\theta}{360} \times 2\pi r$

$= \dfrac{18}{360} \times 2 \times \dfrac{22}{7} \times 14 = 4.4$

Area of sector = $\dfrac{\theta}{360} \times \pi r^2$

$= \dfrac{18}{360} \times \dfrac{22}{7} \times 14 \times 14 = 308 = 30.8$

10. 4 Surface area of cube = 6 × (side)^2
6 × (side)^2 = 150
(side)^2 = 25
⇒ side = 5

11. 3 Let length of side of square = a
and diagonal = d

∴ $d^2 = a^2 + a^2$; $d = a\sqrt{2}$

Sum of lengths of two diagonals = $2a\sqrt{2}$

∴ $2a\sqrt{2} = 196$; $a = \dfrac{98}{\sqrt{2}}$

Perimeter of square = 4a = $\dfrac{4 \times 98}{\sqrt{2}} = 196\sqrt{2}$ cm

12. 1 Cost of 100 sq. m = 80 paise = 0.8 R

Cost of 1 sq. m = Rs. $\dfrac{0.8}{100} = \dfrac{80}{10000}$

Area of square ground = $\dfrac{\text{Total Cost}}{\text{Cost per m}^2}$ t

$= \dfrac{28.8}{80} \times 10000 = 3600\ m^2$

Side of square = $\sqrt{\text{Area of sq.}} = \sqrt{3600} = 60$ m
Perimeter of square = 4 × side = 4 × 60 = 240 m
Cost of fencing = Rs. 0.6 × 240 = Rs. 144

13. 3 Area of square a^2 = 2.56.
a = 1.6 (side of a square)
∴ length of side of chess board = 1.6 × 8 = 12.8 cm

14. 4 Length of rectangular lawn = 80 m.
Its width = 40 m
Area of lawn = 80 × 40 = 3200 sq. m
Length of lawn including footpath = 80 + 3(2) = 86 m
Breadth of lawn including footpath = 40 + 3(2) = 46 m
Area of lawn including footpath = 86 × 46 = 3956 m^2
Area of path = Area of lawn including footpath − Area of lawn
= 86 × 46 − 3200 = 3956 − 3200 = 756 m^2.

15. 2 Let the sides of the triangle be
a = 6x, b = 8x, c = 10x,
Perimeter of triangle = 6x + 8x + 10x = 24x = 240 m
x = 10
Hence a = 60, b = 80 and c = 100

$s = \dfrac{a+b+c}{2} = \dfrac{240}{2} = 120$

Area = $\sqrt{s(s-a)\ (s-b)\ (s-c)}$

$= \sqrt{120\ (120-60)\ (120-80)\ (120-100)}$

$= \sqrt{120 \times 60 \times 40 \times 20} = 2400\ m^2$

Alternative method:
Since sides are in the ratio of 6 : 8 : 10 which is in the form
of pythagoras triplet. Hence this is a right angled triangle.

Area = $\dfrac{1}{2} \times 60 \times 80 = 2400\ m^2$

16. 3 Radius of circle is 28 cm
∴ Length of wire = Circumference of circle, i.e. $2\pi r$.

$\dfrac{2 \times 22 \times 28}{7} = 176$ cm

The circle is bent to form a square, so 176 cm is perimeter of square.
So if side of square is l
Then perimeter of square = 4l
4l = 176
l = 44 cm

17. 2

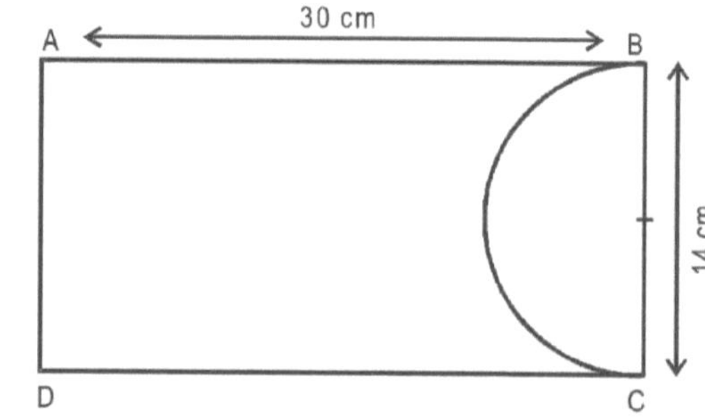

Answers and Explanations

Area of remaining position
= Area of rectangle – Area of semicircle

$$= 30 \times 14 - \frac{\pi}{2} \times 7 \times 7 = 420 - 77 = 343$$

18. 4

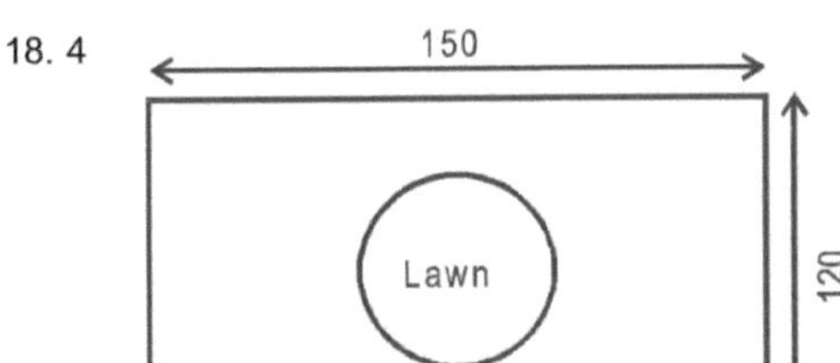

Area of park excluding lawn
= Area of rectangle – Area of lawn

$$5500 = 120 \times 150 - \frac{22}{7} r^2$$

$$\Rightarrow r = \sqrt{3977.27} = 63.06$$

19. 4

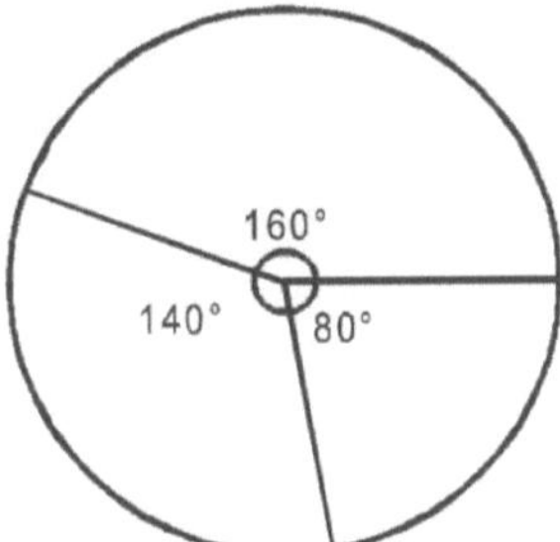

Since 160 + 140 + 80 = 380 which is greater than 360°. Hence data inconsistent.

20. 4 The longest pole will be the diagonal of the room

Diagonal = $\sqrt{l^2 + b^2 + h^2} = \sqrt{20^2 + 10^2 + 5^2} = \sqrt{525}$

21. 3 Diagonal = $8\sqrt{3}$ cm

$\sqrt{3} \times \text{side} = \text{Diagonal} = 8\sqrt{3}$

side = 8 cm

$\therefore$ Volume of cube = $(8)^3 = 512$ cm^3

22. 1 Let 'R' be the radius of the sphere, then

Volume of sphere = $\frac{4}{3} \pi r^3$

and total surface area = $4\pi r^2$

$$\Rightarrow \frac{\frac{4}{3} \pi r^3}{4\pi r^2} = 5$$

$$\Rightarrow r = 3 \times 5 = 15 \text{ cm}$$

23. 4 Let 'r' and 'h' be the radius and height of cylinder

Original volume of cylinder = $\pi r^2 h$

Increased height = $h + \frac{200}{100} h = 3h$

Increased radius = $r + \frac{200}{100} r = 3r$

Changed volume = $\pi (3r)^2 \times 3h = 27 \times$ original volume

24. 3 Volume of metal sphere is equal to volume of wire formed. Let 'L' be the length of wire, then

$$\frac{4}{3} \pi \times 10^3 = \pi \times (0.1)^2 \times L$$

$$L = \frac{\frac{4}{3} \pi \times 1000}{\pi \times .01} = \frac{4}{3} \times 100000 = 133333.33 \text{ cm}$$

$$= 1333.33 \text{ m}$$

25. 2 Let the amount of water that has fallen be up to height 'h', then

150 × 25 × h = 2250

$$h = \frac{90}{150} = 0.6 \text{ m} = 60 \text{ cm}$$

26. 1 Surface area of cube = 6 × (side)^2
6 × (side)^2 = 216
(side)^2 = 36
$\Rightarrow$ side = 6
Volume of cube = (side)^3 = 6^3 = 216 m^3

27. 4 Perimeter of circular wire = Perimeter of square

$$2 \times \frac{22}{7} \times 28 = 4 \times (\text{side})^2$$

side = 44 cm

$$\frac{\text{Area of circle}}{\text{Area of square}} = \frac{\frac{22}{7} \times 28 \times 28}{44 \times 44} = \frac{14}{11}$$

28. 2 The biggest possible circle will have the breadth of rectangle as its diameter.

$$\text{Radius of circle} = \frac{\text{diameter}}{2} = \frac{8}{2} = 4 \text{ cm}$$

Area of circle = $\pi \times (4)^2 = 16\pi$

29. 4 Let 'l' and 'b' be original length and width of the rectangle, then
area = l × b

Increased length = $\frac{160}{100} l = \frac{8}{5} l$

New area = $\frac{8}{5} l \times b = \frac{8}{5} l \times b$

$$\frac{\text{New area of rectangle}}{\text{Initial area of rectangle}} = \frac{\frac{8}{5} l \times b}{lb} = \frac{8}{5} = 8 : 5$$

30. 1 If length and breadth of rectangle increased by a metres and b metres respectively, then percentage increase in area

$$= a + b + \frac{a \times b}{100} = 10 + 20 + \frac{10 \times 20}{100} = 32$$

31. 4 If radius and height of cylinder changes by a metres and b metres, respectively, then the change in base area

$$= a + b + \frac{ab}{100} = 10 + 10 + \frac{100}{100} = 21$$

and then, change in volume is $21 + 20 + \frac{20 \times 21}{100} = 45.2$

32. 2 If side of cube is x, then radius of the sphere which will fit

exactly inside the cube is $\dfrac{x}{2}$

$\therefore$ ratio of their volumes

$$= x^3 \; : \; \frac{4}{3}\pi\left(\frac{x}{2}\right)^3 = 1 : \frac{4\pi}{24} = 1 : \frac{\pi}{6} = 6 : \pi$$

33. 3 Check the option, only option (3) satisfy.

34. 3 Let r_1, r_2 and h_1, h_2 be radius and height of the two cones.

$$\therefore \; \frac{r_1}{r_2} = \frac{2}{3} \Rightarrow r_1 = \frac{2}{3}r_2$$

$$\frac{\pi}{3}r_1^2 h_1 = \frac{\pi}{3}r_2^2 h_2$$

$$\Rightarrow \left(\frac{2}{3}r_2\right)^2 \times h_1 = r_2^2 h_2 \Rightarrow \frac{h_1}{h_2} = \frac{9}{4}$$

35. 2

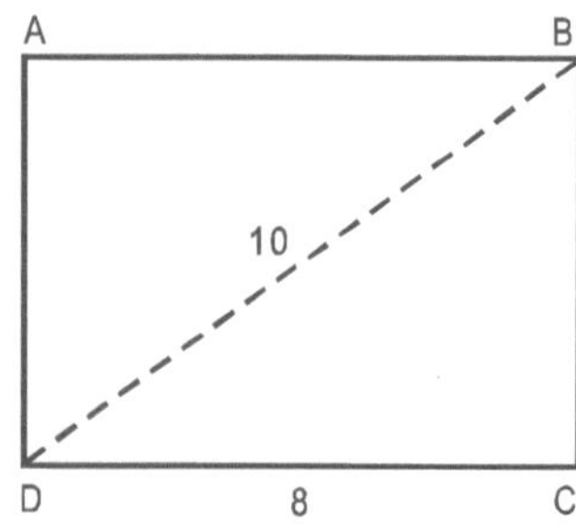

$$BC^2 = BD^2 - DC^2 = 100 - 64 = 36$$

$$\Rightarrow BC = \sqrt{36} = 6$$

Area = 6 × 8 = 48 cm²

6. Higher Maths

Exercise –1

1. 2 $\quad {}^8P_6 = \dfrac{8!}{(8-6)!}$

$\qquad\quad = \dfrac{8!}{2!} = 20160$

2. 4 $\quad {}^8C_6 = {}^8C_2 = \dfrac{8 \times 7}{1 \times 2} = 28$

3. 3 Since there are 5 letters in the word

So the total number of rearrangement is 5! – 1! or ${}^5P_5 - 1$ that is 119.

4. 1 In the word AMERICA there are 7 letters and the letter 'A' is coming twice.
So the total number of rearrangement

$$= \frac{7!}{2!} = \frac{7 \times 6 \times 5 \times 4 \times 3 \times 2 \times 1}{2 \times 1} - 1 = 2519$$

5. 4 In the word CALCUTTA, there are 8 letters
Letter C is coming twice
Letter A is coming twice
Letter T is coming twice
So the total number of rearrangements

$$= \frac{8!}{2! \times 2! \times 2!} - 1 = 5039$$

6. 4 If any one of the consonant start, next 5 letters can be

arranged in $\dfrac{5!}{2} = 60$ ways. And the first consonants itself

can be selected in 4 ways. Hence total number of arrangements = 4 × 60 = 240

7. 4 Letter a can be placed in all 4 positions.
Similarly b can be placed in all 4 positions.
Similarly c can be placed in all 4 positions.
Similarly d can be placed in all 4 positions.
So the total number of arrangement is
4 × 4 × 4 × 4 = 256

8. 1 Thousand's place can be filled only with two digits 4 or 5
Hundred's place can be filled in 3 ways.
Ten's place can be filled in 2 ways.
Unit's place can be filled in 1 way.
So total number of number formed = 2 × 3 × 2 × 1 = 12

9. 2 Thousands place can be filled in two ways.
Hundred's place can be filled with any of the 4 digits.
Ten's place can be filled with any of the 4 digits.
Unit's place can be filled with any of the 4 digits.
So the total numbers formed = 2 × 4 × 4 × 4 = 128.

10. 1 P (If Red ball in first attempt) $= \dfrac{4}{10} = \dfrac{2}{5}$

Here probability will remain same for the next two attempt.

$$\therefore \text{Probability} = \frac{2}{5} \times \frac{2}{5} \times \frac{2}{5} = \frac{8}{125}$$

11. 1 P(white ball) $= \dfrac{6}{10} = \dfrac{3}{5}$ and P(Red ball) $= \dfrac{2}{5}$

Hence probability of 2 white and 1 Red ball is $\dfrac{3}{5} \times \dfrac{3}{5} \times \dfrac{2}{5} = \dfrac{18}{125}$

This will be multiplied by 3 as red ball can be attain in any of

the attempt, i.e. $3 \times \dfrac{18}{125} = \dfrac{54}{125}$

12. 3 The following combinations are possible. First white, second red, third red, or first red, second white, third red or first red, second red, third white
So the probability

$$= \left(\frac{6}{10} \times \frac{4}{9} \times \frac{3}{8}\right) + \left(\frac{4}{10} \times \frac{6}{9} \times \frac{3}{8}\right) + \left(\frac{4}{10} \times \frac{3}{9} \times \frac{6}{8}\right) = 0.3$$

13. 1 Probability that A will pass in exam $= \dfrac{1}{3}$

$\therefore$ Probability that A will fail in exam $= \dfrac{2}{3}$

Probability that B will pass in exam = $\dfrac{1}{2}$

Probability that B will fail in exam = $\dfrac{1}{2}$

Probability that both will pass in the exam
= Probability that A will pass and probability that B will pass

$= \dfrac{1}{3} \times \dfrac{1}{2} = \dfrac{1}{6}$

14. 2 Probability that only one person will pass
So the possibility can be either A pass and B fails or A fails and B pass i.e (A pass and B fail) or (A fail and B pass)

$= \dfrac{1}{3} \times \dfrac{1}{2} + \dfrac{2}{3} \times \dfrac{1}{2} = \dfrac{1}{6} + \dfrac{1}{3} = \dfrac{1}{2}$

15. 4 Probability that at least one person, will pass, so the possibilities can be (A pass and B fails), or (A fails and B pass) or (Both A and B pass)

i.e. $= \dfrac{1}{3} \times \dfrac{1}{2} + \dfrac{2}{3} \times \dfrac{1}{2} + \dfrac{1}{3} \times \dfrac{1}{2} = \dfrac{1}{6} + \dfrac{1}{3} + \dfrac{1}{6} = \dfrac{2}{3}$

Alternate method:
1 – (None of them pass) i.e. (A fails and B fails)

$= 1 - \dfrac{2}{3} \times \dfrac{1}{2} = \dfrac{2}{3}$

16. 4 The probability that no one will pass

i.e., both A and B fails $= \dfrac{2}{3} \times \dfrac{1}{2} = \dfrac{1}{3}$

17. 2 There are 13 spades

Two spades out of 13 spades can be taken out in $^{13}C_2$ ways

Total number of sample spaces = $^{52}C_2$

Required probability = $\dfrac{^{13}C_2}{^{52}C_2}$

18. 4 There are 4 kings

Two kings out 4 kings can be drawn in $^4C_2$ ways.

Required probability = $\dfrac{^4C_2}{^{52}C_2}$

19. 4 There are 13 spades and 13 hearts. One spade and one heart can be taken out in $^{13}C_1 \times {}^{13}C_1$ ways.

Required probability = $\dfrac{^{13}C_1 \times {}^{13}C_1}{^{52}C_2}$

20. 3 There are 4 kings. One king can be taken out in $^4C_1$ ways. Now out of remaining 48 cards, any one card can be taken out in $^{48}C_1$ ways.

$\therefore$ Required probability = $\dfrac{^4C_1 \times {}^{48}C_1}{^{52}C_2}$

7. Data Based Reasoning

Exercise – 1

1. 1 Degrees for Hindi and Maths = 90 + 70 = 160
Degrees for English and Social Science = 65 + 55 = 120

Difference: 40° i.e. $\dfrac{40}{360} \times \dfrac{540}{1} = 60$.

2. 2 $\dfrac{22.2}{100} \times 360^\circ = 79.9^\circ \approx 80^\circ$

Therefore, he scored 22.2% marks in Science.

3. 3 Marks in Hindi = $\dfrac{70}{360} \times 540 = 105$.

4. 4 Total degrees for E + S + S.S
Science = 55 + 65 + 80 = 200°

Therefore, percentage = $\dfrac{200}{360} \times 100$ = 55.5.

5. 4 Marks in Mathematics = $\dfrac{90}{360} \times 100 = 25\%$.

6. 3 $\dfrac{\text{Personal service earning}}{\text{Transportation earning}} = \dfrac{25 \times 2}{40} = 5 : 4$.

7. 1 $\dfrac{\text{Avg. wage of commerce}}{\text{Avg. wage of transport}} = \dfrac{\frac{2}{115}}{\frac{1}{40}} = \dfrac{80}{115} = \dfrac{16}{23}$.

8. 1 Assume that 360° = 360 units.

$\therefore$ Total no. of wage-earners = $\dfrac{110}{100} \times 360 = 396$.

or wage-earners in commerce = $\dfrac{115}{100} \times 115 = 132$.

Unit of commerce in degrees = $\dfrac{132}{396} \times 360^\circ = 120^\circ$.

9. 2 Manufacturing percentage = $\dfrac{85}{360} \times 100 = 23.6$

For questions 10 to 14:

Year	Revenue (Rs.)	Cost (Rs.)	Profit (Rs.)
1997	10000	8000	2000
1998	12000	10000	2000
1999	15000	12000	3000
2000	18000	14400	3600

10. 2   **11. 4**   **12. 4**   **13. 3**   **14. 1**

15. 3 Wheat $= \dfrac{(131-100)}{100} \times 100 = 31\%$

Rice $= \dfrac{(107-91)}{91} \times 100 = 17.58\%$

Sugar cane $= \dfrac{(25-15)}{15} \times 100 = 66.66\%$

Pulses $= \dfrac{(88-71)}{71} \times 100 = 23.94\%$

16. 2 $\left(\dfrac{75}{383}\right) \times 100 = 19.58\%$

17. 4 We can take total production , because the number of years is same in both cases.

$\dfrac{476-79}{79} \times 100 = 502$

18. 3 $\dfrac{131-100}{100} \times \dfrac{1}{3} = \dfrac{31}{100} = 10.33\%$

19. 3 Average growth is 10.3.
Hence, the actual value of wheat in 2001 is
131 + 10.3 = 141.3 MT

20. 4 0.28x = 196, x = 700
0.33x = 0.33 ×700 = Rs. 231 crore

21. 3 Sales of Coke in 1998 = Rs. 154 crore.
and Sales in 1999 = Rs. 208 crore.

Therefore % increase $= \dfrac{(208-154)}{154} \times 100 = 35.$

22. 3 Pepsi in 1998 = 0.33 x 550 = 181.5
Pepsi in 1999 = 0.29 x 650 = 188.5

Percentage growth $= \left(\dfrac{188.5-181.5}{181.5}\right) \times 100 = 3.8$

23. 3 0.3 × 550 = 165.

24. 3 Pepsi in 1998 = 600 x 0.33 = 198
Coke in 1999 = 650 x 0.32 = 208
So difference = 208 – 198 = 10

For questions 25 to 29:
The following table summarizes the given information:

	AAA Ltd	BB Ltd	CC Ltd	DDD Ltd
Sales	100,000 (given)	150,000 (profits are 25% of sales)	125,000 (costs + profits)	300,000 (given, sales are double that of BB Ltd)
Costs	62,500 (sales – profits)	112,500 (sales – profit)	100,000 (given)	250,000 (double the sales of CCC Ltd)

	AAA Ltd	BB Ltd	CC Ltd	DDD Ltd
Profits	37,500 (3/2 of CC's profits)	37,500 (given)	25,000 (25% on cost)	50,000 (sales – costs)
Assets	–	50,000 (since asset turnover ratio is given as 3)	–	100,000 (based on given ratio)
Asset turnover ratio	–	3 (given)	–	3 (given)

25. 3   **26. 4**   **27. 2**   **28. 2**

29. 1 Profit as a percentage of sales for:
AAA = 37.5%
BB = 25%
CC = 20%
DDD = 16.66%

30. 2 Urban population for MP, Punjab & Kerala = 1075053
Number of urban towns in MP, Punjab & Kerala = 13047
Average population/urban town = 82.4.

31. 1 Average population per urban town for Rajasthan

$= \dfrac{259980}{3089} = 84.16$

Average population per rural town for Rajasthan

$= \dfrac{122550}{64437} = 1.90$

Difference in average population = 82.26

32. 2 Population (approximate) per urban town for:

Maharashtra $= \dfrac{1224}{15.5} = 79$

Goa $= \dfrac{173}{2.07} = 83.6$

Haryana $= \dfrac{241.6}{3.1} = 7.8$

Gujarat $= \dfrac{707.1}{10.9} = 65$

Hence, it is the highest for Goa.

33. 3 Population (approximate) per rural town for:

Maharashtra $= \dfrac{355.9}{68} = 5.2$

Goa $= \dfrac{19.9}{5.3} = 3.75$

Haryana $= \dfrac{105.6}{79.9} = 1.3$

Gujarat $= \dfrac{276.9}{94.9} = 2.9$

Hence, it is minimum for Haryana.

Answers and Explanations

34. 4   No data is available for literacy rates of the states.

35. 2   Population per urban town for:

$$UP = \frac{797.1}{9.8} = 81.34$$

$$TN = \frac{938.9}{13.8} = 68$$

Hence, population per urban town of UP exceeds that of TN

by $= \frac{(81.34 - 68)}{68} = 19.6\%$.

Exercise – 2

1. 2   Statement I gives us an inequality which is not enough to answer the question. Statement II indicates that g is greater than h because irrespective of the sign of the integer, the integer whose cube is greater will obviously be the greater one. Therefore, statement II alone is enough.

2. 1   Statement I alone can answer the question. From statement II we cannot infer the speed of Raju.

3. 4   L.C.M. of 51 is possible by 17, 3 or 1, 51 or 3, 51 or 17, 51. Neither statement I nor statement II is enough to answer the question.

4. 4   Both taken together are not sufficient as the actual scores of either team at any point of time during or at the end of the game cannot be determined.

5. 3   Statement I is very tempting as 4 = 4 x 1, but both these numbers can be negative also, hence statement I is not sufficient. Statement II says that both A and B are positive. So, both the statements taken together solves the problem.

6. 3   Statements I and II together indicate that the number of people attending both meetings = 85 – (35 + 47) = 3
∴ Number of people attending meeting x = 38, number of people attending meeting y = 50.

7. 4   Data is not sufficient to answer the question, since total number of men and total number of women are unknown.

8. 3   With the help of statement I, we can find how many days C takes. Similarly, with the help of statement II, we can find out how many days B takes. So, with this information we can find how many days A takes.

9. 4   Statement I: Let N and M be two numbers. Then,
N = (Divisor)x + 11 and M = (Divisor)y + 21
From these two equations, we cannot find the divisor.
Statement II: Divisor > 2
Using both the statements together, we cannot answer the question.

10. 1   From statement I we have the number in the form of 5x + 3. So, its square is $25x^2 + 30x + 9$. Except 9, first two terms are divisible by 5. So, remainder is 4. Statement II cannot answer the question.

11. 3   Statement I indicates that the numbers are of the form 9x, 9y where x, y are co-primes. Statement II indicates that 9x + 9y = 153. Solving, we get the two numbers.

12. 4   Considering both the statements carefully, it is not possible to prove congruency of the two triangles, as even though both are right-angled and have the same perimeter, their corresponding sides might measure differently and they might still add up to the same perimeter.

13. 3   From statement I or II alone we cannot answer the question. Combining both statements, let
Case I: This year is a leap year, then today is Monday.
Case II: This year is a non-leap year, then today is Sunday.
From both cases, we get today is not Friday.

14. 4   From both the statements, we cannot answer the question. Since both the normal speed and the distance are not known, we cannot find the answer.

15. 4   From statement I, we get the profit of P and Q in the 2nd year. But we cannot get the investment of P and Q in the 1st year. So, from statement I alone we cannot answer the question. Statement II does not give any information about first year's investment. So, from statement II alone we cannot answer the question.
Using both statements together, we cannot answer the question.
Hence, the correct answer is (4).

16. 3   From statements I and II, we get two 25-paise coins, one 10-paise coin.

17. 1   From statement I, we have $\left(1 - \dfrac{8}{C}\right)^2 = \dfrac{9}{9 + 16}$.

So, we get C = 20 L. Hence, statement I is sufficient to answer the question. Statement II by itself is not enough.

18. 4   We have no information regarding which side is the hypotenuse. So, the area cannot be determined.

19. 4   There are two unknowns, C.P. of each book and the number of books. So, net C.P. of each book cannot be determined.

20. 4   From both statements the method of calculating interest i.e. C.I. or S.I. is not known. So, we cannot answer the question. Hence, the correct answer is (4).

PART – 2 : REASONING

I. Number Series

1. 4 The series is squares of even numbers starting from 2 and hence, $8^2 = 64$.

2. 4 The series is squares of 2, 5, 8, 11, 14 and hence, next number is $17^2 = 289$.

3. 2 The series is cubes of 0, 1, 2, 3, 4 and hence, next number is $5^3 = 125$.

4. 3 These are cubes of 2, 3, 5, 7 i.e., prime numbers and the next cube is $11^3 = 1331$.

5. 4 Numbers at the even positions are the squares of numbers at the odd positions. Hence is, $6^2 = 36$.

6. 2 The given series is a prime number series.
Hence, the next prime number after 11 is 13.

7. 2 In this series, all the terms differ by a difference of 2. Hence, the next number is 19.

8. 4 The series from the first term onwards is +3, +5, +7 and then +9. Hence, the answer is 26. OR
$1^2 + 1 = 2$, $2^2 + 1 = 5$, $3^2 + 1 = 10$, $4^2 + 1 = 17$.
Hence next term is $5^2 + 1 = 26$.

9. 4 The difference in the successive terms of the series is +1, +3, +5, +7 and hence, now it is 21 + 9 = 30.

10. 4 The difference in the successive terms of the series is +4, +6, +8, +10. The next term is 30 + 12 = 42. Also, each term follows the pattern $(n^2 + n)$ i.e., $1^2 + 1 = 2$, $2^2 + 2 = 6$, $3^2 + 3 = 12$, $4^2 + 4 = 20$, $5^2 + 5 = 30$, hence the next number will be $6^2 + 6 = 42$.

11. 4 The difference in the terms of the series starting from the first term is +10, +20, +40, +80 and now 155 + 160 = 315.

12. 4 The difference in the terms of the series starting from the first term is +3, +5, +7 and finally it is +9.

13. 4 The difference in the terms of the series starting from the first term is +4, +8, +16 and finally it is +32.

14. 3 The pattern of the series is 9 + 2 = 11, 11 + 4 = 15, 15 + 8 = 23 and finally, it is 23 + 16 = 39.

15. 4 The terms of the series differ by +4, +6, +8, +10, +12 and +14.

16. 2 All the terms differ by 9. Hence, the required number is 54.

17. 1 The difference in the terms of the series starting from the first term is +0, +2, +4, +6 and + 8. Hence, the required number is 14.

18. 3 The difference between any two consecutive numbers is a square.

$$1, \; 2, \; 6, \; 15, \; 31, \; 56, \; 93, \; \boxed{141}$$
$$1 \quad 4 \quad 9 \quad 16 \quad 25 \quad 36 \quad \boxed{49}$$
$$9 \quad 9 \quad 9 \quad 9 \quad 9 \quad 9 \quad 8$$
$$1^2 \quad 2^2 \quad 3^2 \quad 4^2 \quad 5^2 \quad 6^2 \quad \boxed{7^2}$$

19. 2 The difference between the two consecutive terms is following a pattern +1, +2 and +4. Hence, the required number is 18 + 4 = 22.

20. 3 Add and multiply 3 alternately.

21. 3 Subtract 5 to get the next number.

22. 3 The difference in the terms of the series starting from the first term is +6, +8, +10, +12 and +14.

23. 1 Deduct 3, 4, 5, 6 successively.

24. 4 The difference between consecutive numbers is increasing by 4, 6, 8, 10, 12, 14, 16, etc.

25. 4 The difference goes on becoming three times.

26. 1 The pattern of the series is 3 + 12 = 15, 15 + 20 = 35, so now it is 35 + 28 = 63, then 63 + 36 = 99. So, the difference itself differs by +8.

27. 4 The pattern of the series is 4 + 6 = 10, 10 + 12 = 22, 22 + 24 = 46 and hence, now it is 46 + 48 = 94.

28. 2 The pattern of the series is 84 – 20 = 64, 64 – 18 = 46, 46 – 16 = 30 and hence, now it is 30 – 14 = 16.
The difference goes on doubling itself.

29. 4 Add 5, 7, 9, 11 and in the same sequence 47 + 13 = 60.

30. 1 The difference between consecutive numbers is increasing by 4.

31. 4 In this series, from the first term onwards add 2 then add 4 alternately.
So, the next number in the series is 19 + 2 = 23.

32. 2 The difference in the successive terms of the series is increasing by 4. That is, 5 + 9 =14, then 14 + 13 = 27, then 27 + 17 = 44, and 44 + 21 = 65. The difference is increasing by 4. Hence, the next difference will be 25 and 65 + 25 = 90.

33. 1
$$0, \; 5, \; 2 \; 2, \; 5 \; 7, \; 116, \; \boxed{205}$$
$$5 \quad 17 \quad 35 \quad 59 \quad \boxed{89}$$
$$12 \quad 18 \quad 24 \quad \boxed{30}$$

34. 4 The series is 7 + (17 × 1) = 24. Then, 24 + 51 (17 × 3) = 75, 75 + 153 (51 × 3) = 228.
So, now it is 228 + (153 × 3) = 687. OR
7 × 3 + 3 = 24, 24 × 3 + 3 = 75, 75 × 3 + 3 = 228. Hence next number is 228 × 3 + 3 = 687.

35. 4 This is an alternate series arrangement. The odd terms in the series form an even number series. The even terms in the series differ by +4.

Answers and Explanations

36. 4 This is an alternate series arrangement. The odd terms is a series of squares of numbers 1, 3, 5 and 7. The even terms is a series of cubes of numbers 2, 4, 6 and 8. Hence, the answer is 49, 512.

37. 2 This is an alternate series arrangement. The odd terms and even terms differ by 3.

38. 2 This is an alternate series arrangement. The odd terms differ by +3, +5, +7 and even terms differ by +4, +6.

39. 2 The difference between 1st and 2nd numbers is 1, between 2nd and 3rd is 2, and then alternates.

40. 4 Jump 1 alternate no. in ascending order.

41. 3 1st, 3rd, 5th numbers are increasing by 1, and 2nd, 4th, 6th numbers are decreasing by 1.

42. 1 It is a mixture of two series.
4, 12, 36, 108 and 4, 16, 36 and 64
x3 x3 x3 2^2 4^2 6^2 8^2

43. 1 This is an alternate series.
18, 21, 24, 27, 30, 33

44. 4 There are two series, which alternate. The even terms differ by 4, 6, 8, and so on. The odd terms differ by 6, 12, 24 and hence, it is 48 added to 46 which gives 94.

45. 2 This is an alternate series arrangement. The odd terms differ by 11. The common difference between each set of alternate numbers is 11.
So, the answer is 41 + 11 = 52.

46. 1 An alternate series arrangement. The odd terms differ by 9 and hence the next number is 25 + 9 = 34.

47. 4 This is an alternate series arrangement. The odd terms is an even number series. The even terms is a double series, that is 2 × 2 = 4, 4 × 2 = 8 and 8 × 2 = 16.

48. 1 This is a double alternate series.
2, –, –, 7, –, –, 12, –, –, 17, –, –, 22
+5   +5   +5   +5

49. 3 This is a double alternate series.
12, –, –, 13, –, –, 14, –, –, 15, –, –, 16.

50. 4 The series is made up of two different series of alternate terms. The difference between the terms increases by 1. Hence, 5 + 4 = 9, 9 + 5 = 14, 14 + 6 = 20, 20 + 7 = 27 and 27 + 8 = 35.

51. 2 This is a double alternate series.
3, –, –, 5, –, –, 8, –, –, 12, –, –, 17

52. 2 The series is alternate term ×2, +3.
E.g. 1 × 2 = 2, 2 + 3 = 5, 5 × 2 = 10, 10 + 3 = 13, 13 × 2 = 26.

53. 4 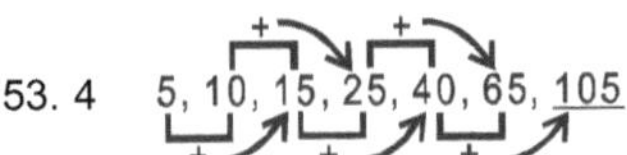

54. 2 In this series, every number is the sum of the previous two numbers, as in the previous question.

55. 1 The pattern of the series is 3 × 3 = 9, 9 × 4 = 36, 36 × 5 = 180 and finally 180 × 6 = 1080.

56. 1 The series is 17 × 1^2 = 17, 17 × 2^2 = 68, 68 × 3^2 = 612. Hence, 612 × 4^2 = 9792.

57. 2 In every triplet, third number is thrice the second and second number is twice the first number. So the series goes as × 2, × 3, × $\frac{1}{2}$, × 2, × 3, × $\frac{1}{2}$, and so on.

58. 1 Even-positioned numbers are half of odd-positioned numbers.

59. 3 Add and multiply 3 alternately.

60. 2 This series is based on previous term – 3, × 2, and so on.

2. Letter Series

1. 3 Leave out one letter starting from the letter A, i.e. drop the letters B, D, F, H and J. So, the answer is K.

2. 3 From right to left starting with O, leave out one letter in-between to establish the series given in the question.

3. 1 From left to right, starting with the letter Z, drop one, two, three, four and five letters to get the last letter as F in the series.

4. 4 The pattern of the series is A + 7 = H, H + 6 = N, N + 5 = S, then S + 4 = W and finally W + 3 = Z.

5. 2 The pattern of the series is C + 3 = F, F + 5 = K, K + 7 = R and finally R + 9 = A.

6. 3 Starting from the letter X, the subsequent letters in the series differ by + 3.

7. 2 Starting from the letter T, the subsequent letters are obtained by leaving out one letter and three letters alternately, or by following + 2, + 4 pattern alternately.

8. 3 The pattern of the series is Z – 2 = X, X – 3 = U. Then, again U – 2 = S, S – 3 = P. So, now it is P – 2 = N.

9. 3 Starting from the letter Q, the subsequent letters are obtained by leaving out two letters and one letter alternately, or by following + 3, + 2 pattern alternately.

10. 2 Starting from the letter H, the subsequent letters are obtained by leaving out three letters in-between or by following +4 pattern.

11. 3 The first letter of each pair is found as A + 1 = B; B + 2 = D; D + 3 = G; hence G + 4 = K. The second letter is the corresponding letter from the other end, and for K it is P.

12. 3 The first letter and the second letter of all the terms in the series with respect to the subsequent terms differ by 11. Within the terms itself, the letters differ by 6.

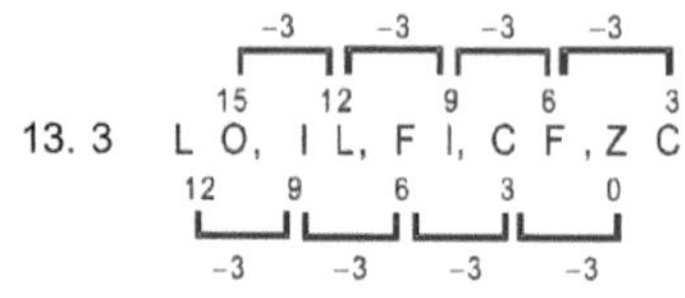

13. 3 L O, I L, F I, C F, Z C

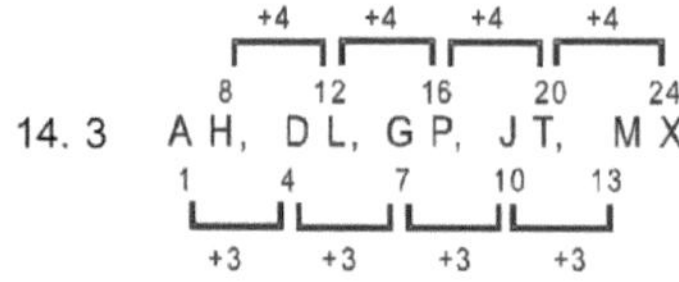

14. 3 A H, D L, G P, J T, M X

15. 4 In each pair of the series, the letters differ by 5, that is AF, EJ, IN, OT. So, the only answer option that matches is UZ wherein the letters differ by 5.

16. 4 The first group is TYU, i.e. T + 5 = Y and Y – 4 = U.
Similarly, N + 5 = S and S – 4 = O. Hence, the answer is BGC.

17. 3 The first letters of all the groups in the series are Z, Y, X, W and V. The second letters of all the terms in the series are S, T, U, V and W. The third letters of all the groups in the series are D, C, B, A and Z. So, the answer is V W Z.

18. 3 The first, second and third letters of every term differ by 4. So, the answer is SYH.

19. 3 The first letters of each group, the second letters and the third letters differ by 8.

20. 4 By observation, the answer is (d) because the three letters in every group form a series of + 2.

21. 3 The first letter of every group in the series differs by 4. The second letter of the groups exhibits the pattern as follows:
M – 4 = I, I – 3 = F, F – 2 = D and hence, now it is D – 1 = C. The third letter of the groups differs by – 2. Hence, the final answer is HCD.

22. 3 The first, second and the third letters of all the groups in the series differ by +2. Hence, N + 2 = P, K + 2 = M and P + 2 = R.

23. 4 Take the first group YAL.
Pattern: Y – 5 = T, A + 2 = C and L + 4 = P.
Similarly, J – 5 = E, G + 2 = I and X + 4 = B to give the final answer EIB.

24. 4 The groups are LRX, DJP, VBH and NTZ.
The pattern is as follows:

First letter: L – 8 = D, D – 8 = V, V – 8 = N and N – 8 = F.

Second letter: R – 8 = J, J – 8 = B, B – 8 = T.
Hence, T – 8 = L.

Third letter also behaves similar to second letter. Hence, final answer is FLR.

25. 4 The first, second and third letters of each group differ by +1. Hence, answer is EXP.

26. 2

```
    1    2     3     4    5
   A Z, B Y, C X, D W, E V
   26   25    24   23   22
```
This is a series of corresponding letters from the two ends.

27. 3

```
9→(+2)→11←(3)→14←(+4)→18←(+5)→23
I R,   K P, N M,  R I,  W D
18→(–2)→16←(–3)→13←(–4)→9←(–5)→4
```
Also, each pair consists of corresponding letters from the two ends of the alphabet.

28. 4

```
   1    2     3    4    5
  A N, B O, C P, D Q, E R
  14   15   16   19   18
```
Also, each pair consists of corresponding letters in the two halves of the alphabet.

29. 1

```
20 →(+2)→  22 →(+3)→ 25 →(+4)–3  →(+5)   – 8
T      G,     V      I,    Y    L, C    P,    H      U
       7 →(+2)→  9 →(+3)→12 ←(–4)→16→(–5)→ –21
```

30. 3

```
     +2        +2       +2
   1        3       5      7      9
  Z A N,  X C P,  V E R,  T G T,  R I V
  26  14  24  16  22  18  20  20  18  22
```
Also, in each group, the first letter is the corresponding letter from the other end and the third letter is corres in the other half with respect to the second letter.

31. 4

```
  1       5       9       15       21
 N A Z,  R E V,  V I R,  B O L,  H U F
 14  26  18  22  22  18  2  12   8   6
```
The middle letter in each group is a vowel – A, E, I, O – next vowel is U. On left side of the vowel (first letter in each group) is its corres letter in the other half. On right side of the vowel (third letter in each group) is its corres letter from the other end.

32. 2

```
        +2      +2      +2      +2
     14     16     18     20     22
   M N A, O P C, Q R E, S T G, U V I
   13  1 15  3 17  5 19  7 21  9
        +2      +2      +2      +2
        +2      +2      +2      +2
```
Also, let us consider the middle term in each group. To the left of it is the corresponding letter from the other end and to the right of it is the corresponding letter in the other half of the alphabet.

33. 1

```
   21(+3) 24   5(+4)   15(+5) 20   1(+6) 7   9(+7) 17
  F  U  X,  V  E  I,  L  O  T,  Z  A  G,  R  I  P
  6       22      12      26      18
```
The middle letter in each group is a vowel. Starting from U, talking the cyclicity, we get the alternate vowel as the middle term in each group.

U → E → O → A → I ......

The first term in each group is the corresponding letter from the other end for the vowel (the second term). The last term in each group is +3, +4, +5, +6, +7, +8 of the vowel, as in alphabet.

34. 3 A E I O, U E O A, I A O E, U O I E, A A A A
In the first group, the vowels are written in continuous order. In the second group, the vowels are written alternately,

starting from U, → U → E → O → A

In the third group, two vowels are skipped to get the third vowel, starting from I.

Answers and Explanations

$$\text{①} \cancel{\text{Ø}} \cancel{\text{Ϟ}} \text{Ⓐ} \cancel{\text{Ɛ}} \cancel{\text{Ϟ}} \text{Ⓞ} \cancel{\text{Ϟ}} \cancel{\text{Ϟ}} \text{Ⓔ}$$

In the fourth group, three vowels are skipped to get the fourth vowel, starting from U.

$$\text{Ⓤ} \cancel{\text{Ϟ}} \cancel{\text{Ɛ}} \cancel{\text{Ϟ}} \text{Ⓞ} \cancel{\text{Ϟ}} \cancel{\text{Ϟ}} \cancel{\text{Ɛ}} \text{①} \cancel{\text{Ø}} \cancel{\text{Ϟ}} \cancel{\text{Ϟ}} \text{Ⓔ}$$

Thus, in the fifth group (the answer group), four vowels are skipped, starting from A, which gets back A.

35. 4

$$\underset{1}{A}^{+2}\underset{3}{C}^{+4}\underset{7}{G}^{(+6)},\ \underset{13}{M}^{+2}\underset{15}{O}^{+4}\underset{19}{S}^{(+6)},\ \underset{25}{Y}^{+2}\underset{1}{A}^{+4}\underset{5}{E}^{(+6)},\ \underset{11}{K}^{+2}\underset{13}{M}^{+4}\underset{17}{Q}^{(+6)},\ \underset{\underline{23}}{W}^{+2}\underset{\underline{25}}{Y}^{+4}\underset{\underline{3}}{C}$$

36. 3

$$\underset{1}{A}\ \overset{26}{Z},\ \underset{2}{B}\ \overset{15}{O},\ \underset{4}{D}\ \overset{23}{W},\ \underset{8}{H}\ \overset{21}{U},\ \underset{16}{P}\ \overset{3}{C}$$
(×2, ×2, ×2, ×2)

AZ and DW are the corresponding letters from the two ends. BO and HU are the corresponding letters in the two halves and the answer PC follows alternatively.

37. 3

$$\underset{16}{P}\ K^{11(-5)}\ \underset{6\ \ 10}{F,\ J}\ Q^{17(-4)}\ \underset{13\ \ 18}{M,\ R}\ I^{-9(-3)}\ \underset{6\ \ 12}{F,\ L}\ O^{15(-2)}\ \underset{13}{M}$$
(+4, +5, +6)

In each group, first two letters are corresponding letters from two ends. The third letter is second letter −5, −4, −3, −2 and the first letter in the next group is +4, +5, +6 of the last letter in the previous group.

38. 3 a b c | c b a | a b c | c b a

After filling in the letters in choice (c), we observe that 'abc' and 'cba' are occuring alternatively.

39. 2

I	II	III
a b c b a	b c d c b	c d e d c

After filling in the letters in choice (b), we observe that group-I has 'abc' followed with first two letter reversed i.e. ba. This is followed by an increase in letter value in group-II, i.e. now group-II starts with 'bcd' and ends in 'cb'. Similarly in group-III, it proceeds to 'cde' followed with 'dc'.

40. 1 a b b a | a b a b | a b b a | a b a b

After filling in choice (a), we observe that 'abba' and 'abab' occur alternately.

41. 2 Alternate letters form a reverse series of consecutive letters: hij, xyz.

42. 4 Skip 3 letters to obtain the next letter.

43. 4 a + 1 = b, b + 2 = d, d + 3 = g, g + 4 = k, k + 5 = p, p + 6 = v

44. 1 There are two series being formed. A forward series of abcdefghi and a reverse series of zyxwvutsr.

45. 4 The series is formed by every alternate term. The first is the series of vowels aeiou, and the second is zyxw.

46. 2 Every letter is followed by the square of the numerical position it holds in the English alphabet. For example, f is followed by 6^2.

47. 4 Two alternate series a, e, i, o, u
w, _, _, _, _, _, q, _, _, _, _, _, l, _, _, _, h, _, _, e

48. 1 a + 5 = f, f + 5 = k ...

49. 4 These letters are the series of consecutive consonants.

50. 4 t, u, _, w, _, _, z, _, _, _, d, _, _, _, _, i, _, _, _, _, _, o

1. 3 The logic is 2n : 3n. Here n = 11 in the second case

2. 1 Logic is $\dfrac{3}{2}n - 1$

∴ 16 will be $16 \times \dfrac{3}{2} - 1 = 23$

3. 2 The logic is $n^3 : (n+1)^3 :: (n+2)^3 : (n+3)^3$.

4. 4 The logic is $\dfrac{1}{n} : \dfrac{1}{2n}$

5. 3 The logic is n : n / 100

6. 2 The logic is $n : n^2 - 1$

7. 2 $n \rightarrow 4n + \dfrac{n}{2}$

for $12 \rightarrow 12 \times 4 + \dfrac{12}{2}$

∴ for 8, it is $8 \times 4 + \dfrac{8}{2} = 36$

8. 1 The logic is n : 4n

9. 4 m × n
∴ 44 = 4 × 4 = 16

10. 1 The logic is 25 × 4 − 1 : 25 × 3 + 1 : : 25 ×1 − 1 : 25 × 0 + 1

11. 3 The logic is n : 3n + 2

12. 4 The logic is n : n + 221

13. 2 The logic is ab : ba

14. 4 Logic is the number is form n(n + 1)
30 = 5 × 6, 45 = 6 × 7, 56 = 7 × 8
∴ next number will be 8 × 9 = 72

15. 3 The logic is 3 digit sum

16. 2 The logic is n : 9n

17. 2 The series is form $2^2 + 2$, $3^2 + 3$, $4^2 + 4$
∴ Last one will be $5^2 + 5 = 30$.

18. 3 The logic is $n : \dfrac{(n)^2}{2}$

19. 2 The logic is n : 2n

20. 4 The logic is $n : \dfrac{n}{7}$

21. 2 The logic is $n : n^3 + 3$

22. 1 The logic is remove the middle digit and reverse the remaining digits.

23. 4   m × n
since 36 is 3 × 6
∴ 72 = 7 × 2 = 14

24. 4   Sum of digits
162 becomes 1 + 6 + 2 = 9
∴ 310 will becomes 3 + 1 + 0 = 4

25. 1   n → n + 4
Since 13 → 17
∴ 15 → 19

26. 2   The logic is $n : \sqrt{n}$

27. 3   The logic is 3n : 3(n + 1)

28. 3   The logic is n : 2n + 1

29. 4   The logic is n : 9n

30. 3   Square each digit
∴ 201 = 401

31. 4   The logic is ab : aob

32. 4   Logic is $n^2 × 2$
∴ 8 becomes $8^2 × 2 = 128$

33. 1   Logic is 2(n + m)
94 becomes 2(9 + 4) = 26
∴ 62 = 2(6 + 2) = 16

34. 4   For 12 : 18,
Square ten's digit and cube unit's digit
$1^2 = 1$; $2^3 = 8$
∴ for 32 : ?, $(3)^2 (2)^3 = 98$

35. 1   Double the number and reverse it
14 × 2 = 28,
∴ 82 is the answer.

36. 4   A : E : : I : _____
1   5   9
(a) A, E and I are vowels. The next vowel after A is E. Similarly, the next vowel after I is O.
(b) The place value of A is 1 and of E is 5. 1 + 4 = 5. Similarly, considering the place value of I, which is 9, we get 9 + 5 = 14, which is N.
(c) (A) 1 × 5 = 5 (E). Similarly. (I) 9 × 5 = 45, and 45 – 26 = 19, which is S.
Hence, all the above follow.

37. 4   G : T : : L : _____
7   20   12
(a) G and T are corresponding letters in the two halves of the alphabet, as the difference in their place values is 13. Similarly (L) 12 + 13 = 25 (Y).
(b) G and T are corresponding letters from the two ends of the alphabet, as the sum of their place values is 27. Similarly 27 – 12 (L) = 15 (O).
(c) Considering the place values, 7 × 3 – 1 = 20. Similarly, 12 × 3 – 1 = 35, and 35 – 26 = 9, which is I.
Hence, all the above follow.

38. 4   B : D : : C : _____
2   4   3

(a) Taking the place values, (B) 2 × 2 = 4 (D). Similarly, (C) 3 × 2 = 6 (F).
(b) (B) $2^2 = 4$ (D). Similarly, (C) $3^2 = 9$ (I).
(c) (B) 2 + 2 = 4 (D). Similarly, (C) 3 + 2 = 5 (E).
Hence, all the above follow.

39. 4   I : R : : P : _____
(a) I and R are corresponding from two ends (9 + 18 = 27). Similarly, 27 – 16 (P) = 11 (K).
(c) (I) 9 × 2 = 18 (R). Similarly, (P) 16 × 2 = 32, and 32 – 26 = 6 (F). Hence, both (a) and (c) follow.

40. 1   17   10   23
I Q : R J : : L W : _____
9   18   12
From the two ends of the alphabet, I corresponds to R and Q corresponds to J. Similarly, L corresponds to O and W corresponds to D.

41. 2   H   K : S   V : : _____ : Q   T
8   11   19   22   17   20
        +3   +3   +3
H and S are corresponding from two ends. Similarly, corresponding letter from the other end for Q is J. (H) 8 + 3 = 11 (K). Similarly, (J) 10 + 3 = 13 (M).

42. 3   F   J : I   M : : P   T : S   W
6   9   16   19
          +3   +3

43. 1   F   L   Y , Similarly, R   I   G
6   12   25   18   9   20
+1 +2 +3   +1 +2 +3
7   14   2   19   11   23
G   N   B   S   K   W

44. 4   P   A   I   R , Similarly, G   R   O   W
16   27(26 + 1) 9   18   7   18   15   23
–2   –3   –4   –5   –2   –3   –4   –5
14   24   5   13   5   15   11   18
N   X   E   M   E   O   K   R

45. 2   B   E   A   R , Similarly, K   I   L   L
2   5   1   18   11   9   12   12
+2 –3 +5 –7   +2 –3 +5 –7
4   2   6   11   13   6   17   5
D   B   F   K   M   F   Q   E

46. 3   A   J   M   E   R , Similarly,
10   13   18
+2   –3   +4
12   10   22
E   L   J   V

Next vowel

Answers and Explanations

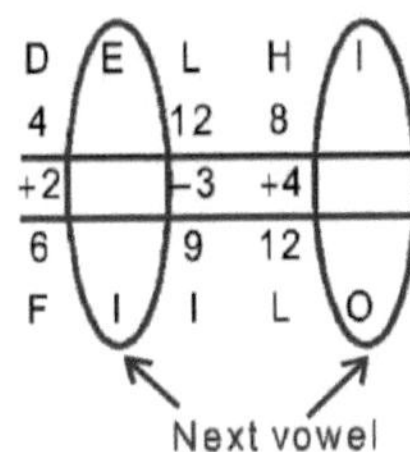

47. 4 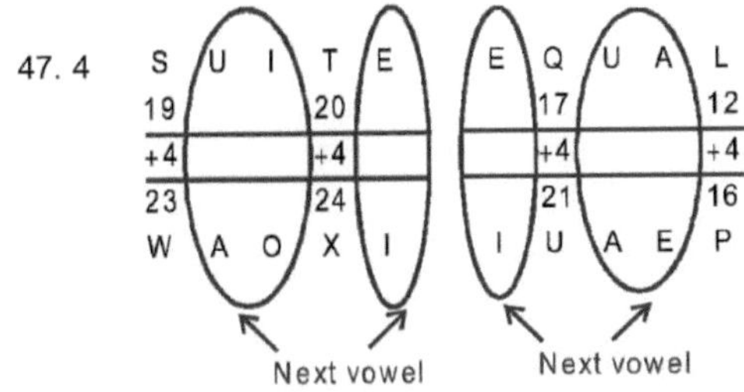

48. 3

$$\begin{array}{ccccccc} & 3 & & 6 & & & 17 \\ \text{P} & \text{C} & \text{X} & : & \text{S} & \text{F} & \text{U} & :: & \underline{\quad\quad} & : & \text{D} & \text{Q} & \text{J} \\ 16 & 24 & 19 & & 21 & & & & & & 4 & & 10 \end{array}$$

On LHS, for letter C, P and X are the corresponding letters in the other half and from the other end of the alphabet, respectively. (C) 3 + 3 = 6 (F). Similarly, (Q) 17 − 3 = 14 (N). Applying the same analogy, corresponding letter in the other half and from the other end for N will be A and M, respectively.

49. 4

$$\begin{array}{cccc} \text{C} & \text{A} & \text{B} \text{, Similarly,} & \text{D} & \text{I} & \text{P} \\ 3 & 1 & 2 & 4 & 9 & 16 \\ \times 2 & \times 3 & \times 4 & \times 2 & \times 3 & \times 4 \\ 6 & 3 & 8 & 8 & 27 & 64 = 12 \\ \text{F} & \text{C} & \text{H} & \text{H} & \text{A} & \text{L} \end{array}$$

50. 2

$$\begin{array}{c}\quad\text{P}\qquad\quad\text{I}\qquad\quad\text{N}\\ -1\quad +1\;|\;-1\quad +1\;|\;-1\quad +1\text{, Similarly,}\\ \text{O}\qquad\text{Q}\;|\;\text{H}\qquad\text{J}\;|\;\text{M}\qquad\text{O}\end{array}$$

$$\begin{array}{c}\quad\text{D}\qquad\quad\text{U}\qquad\quad\text{B}\\ -1\quad +1\;|\;-1\quad +1\;|\;-1\quad +1\\ \text{C}\qquad\text{E}\;|\;\text{T}\qquad\text{V}\;|\;\text{A}\qquad\text{C}\end{array}$$

4. Odd Man Out

1. 4   The other three form a group of 2-digit nos.

2. 3   The other three form a group of even nos.

3. 2   41, 43 & 47 are primes; 45 is not.

4. 1   Except 256, the other three are divisible by 9.

5. 1 $25 = 5^2$, $125 = 5^3$ and $625 = 5^4$, 1225 cannot be expressed as a power of 5.

6. 2   Except 33, the other three are divisible by 7.

7. 2   Except 55 (5 × 11), the other three are multiples of consecutive primes (15 = 3 × 5, 35 = 5 × 7, 77 = 7 × 11)

8. 1   Except 8, the other three are squares.

9. 4   Except 324, the other three are cubes.

10. 3   Except 125, the other three are squares as well as cubes.

11. 2   Except 729, the other three are cubes of prime nos.

12. 2   Except 1089, the other three are squares of prime nos.

13. 1   Except 1561, the other three are squares.

14. 4   Except 38, the other three follow $(n^2 + 1)$ pattern.

15. 3   Except 38, the other three follow $(n^2 - 2)$ pattern.

16. 4   Except 205, the other three follow $\left(n^2 + \dfrac{n}{2}\right)$ pattern.

17. 2   Except 1423, the other three follow $\left(n^2 - \dfrac{n}{2}\right)$ pattern.

18. 4   Except 274, the other three follow $(n^2 + n)$ pattern.

19. 2   Except 125, the other three follow $(n^3 + 1)$ pattern.

20. 1   Except 730, the other three follow $(n^3 - 1)$ pattern.

21. 1   Except 520, the other three follow $\left(n^3 + \dfrac{n}{2}\right)$ pattern.

22. 4   Except 60, the other three follow $\left(n^3 - \dfrac{n}{2}\right)$ pattern.

23. 2   Except 4114, the other three follow $(n^3 + n)$ pattern.

24. 4   Except 350, the other three follow $(n^3 - n)$ pattern.

25. 3   Except 30, the other three follow $(n^3 - 3n)$ pattern.

26. 3   Except 74, the other three follow $(n^3 + 3n)$ pattern.

27. 2   Except 350, the other three follow $(n^3 + n^2)$ pattern.

28. 4   Except 1220, the other three follow $(n^3 - n^2)$ pattern.

29. 2   Except in 2468, the digits in the other three numbers are consecutive natural numbers.

30. 1   Except 2456, the other three follow the pattern: 1st digit + 2 = 2nd digit; 2nd digit + 2 = 3rd digit; 3rd digit + 1 = 4th digit.

31. 3   Except 5476, the other three are odd nos.

32. 3   Except 553, the other three are based on the following logic: (2nd digit) × (3rd digit) = 1st digit.

33. 1   Except in 10, the other three nos. have a digit followed by it's cube.

34. 3   Except 72, which is 8 × $\boxed{9}$, the other three are 8 multiplied with an even no. 8 × $\boxed{2}$ = 16; 8 × $\boxed{4}$ = 32; 8 × $\boxed{6}$ = 48.

35. 2 Except in 324, the other three nos. are formed with the same digits – 1, 6 and 9; even though each of the four choices is a square.

36. 3 Except D, the other three are vowels.

37. 4 Except O, the other three are in the first half of the alphabet.

38. 1 Except M, the other three belong to the second half of the alphabet.

39. 1 Except A, the other three are consonants.

40. 2 The place values of letters are P = 16, Y = 25, I = 9, each of which is a perfect square; whereas E = 5 is not a perfect square.

41. 4 Except UE, the other three choices consist of the corresponding letters from the two ends of the alphabet.

42. 3 Except JQ, the other three choices consist of the corresponding letters in the two halves of the alphabet.

43. 1 Except in KPC, the 1st and 3rd letter in each of the groups for the 2nd letter is corresponding letter, in the other half and corresponding letter from the other end of the alphabet respectively.

44. 4 Except in RTWI, the logic followed amongst the letters in each group is 1st letter +2 = 2nd letter; 2nd letter + 5 = 3rd letter; The fourth letter is a vowel in each case, and is the corresponding letter from the other end of the alphabet, for the first letter.

45. 2 Except in LMQV, in each of the groups, starting from the 1st letter, subtract 2, 3 and 5 in the place values to get the next letter in the group, from left to right.

46. 3 Except SIP, the other three words create the same sound. Alternatively, each of the other three choices has the vowel A in the middle, unlike in SIP.

47. 4 Reverse the order of the letters in each group, we get BRINJAL, POTATO and TOMATO, which are vegetables, and GUAVA is not (it is a fruit).

48. 2 Except Infosys, each company has its headquarters abroad.

49. 1 Except Car, each of the other three is an electrical appliance / runs on electricity.

50. 3 Except Wolf, the other three belong to the cat family of animals.

51. 2 Ostrich is a flightless bird, whereas the other three can fly.

52. 4 'Sister' is a gender specific relation, whereas the other three relations gender is neuter.

53. 3 Except Flute, the other three musical instruments have strings.

54. 4 Except Spain, the other three countries lie in the continent of Asia.

55. 3 Except Badminton, the other sport are played outdoors.

56. 2 Lake is a water body surrounded by land, whereas Bay, Sea and Ocean are water bodies surrounding land.

57. 3 Except 4:16, the other three are based on the pattern n: n^3.

58. 4 The digits on the LHS are multiplied to get the number on the RHS. Eg. $1 \times 2 \times 3 = 6$; $2 \times 3 \times 4 = 24$; $3 \times 4 \times 5 = 60$; $4 \times 5 \times 6 \neq 110$.

59. 3 $16 : 16 = 4^2 : 2^4$; $25 : 32 = 5^2 : 2^5$; $49 : 128 = 7^2 : 2^7$. The choices follow the pattern $(a)^x : (x)^a$, whereas $36 : 32 = 6^2 : 2^5$, does not follow this pattern.

60. 1 Reverse the nos. on the RHS to get the following: 31 : 961; 17 : 289; 25 : 625, which follows the pattern $n : n^2$, 12 : 144 does not follow this.

5. Coding – Decoding

Type – 1

1. 1 The first letter has next letter as its code and all the other letters have preceding letters as their code.

2. 4 In word COBRA, the third letter has come to first position and second letter stays in the same position making it 'BO'. Letter C has gone to third position and along with A, you get the word BOCAR. Use the same logic to get the answer as (4).

3. 3 Reverse the word and use the preceding letters as the codes.

4. 2 The word GOOD is coded as follows:
G + 1 = H, O + 2 = Q, O + 3 = R and D + 4 = H. Use the same logic to get the answer as (2).

5. 4 In the main word CONSULTS, the first and second letters interchange their positions, then third and fourth letters interchange their positions, then fifth and sixth and finally seventh and eight letters interchange their positions to get the coded word. Use the same logic to get the answer as (4).

6. 3 The first, third, fifth and seventh letters have preceding two letters (leave one letter in-between), as their codes, the remaining ones have next two letters (leave out one letter in-between) as their codes.

7. 4 The code for SOCIAL is obtained by leaving out zero, one, two, three, four and five letters starting from left to right on the forward direction of English alphabet. Similarly, DIMPLE ≡ EKPTQK.

8. 4 The code of JAPAN is obtained by leaving out zero, one, two, three and four letters when you move from left to right in the forward direction of the English alphabet. Similarly, CASTLE ≡ DCVXQK.

9. 1 The code for TRAIN is obtained by leaving out one letter in-between in the reverse direction of the English alphabet. So SCOOTER ≡ QAMMRCP.

10. 2 The code of RADIO is obtained by leaving out one letter in-between in the reverse direction of the English alphabet. So,

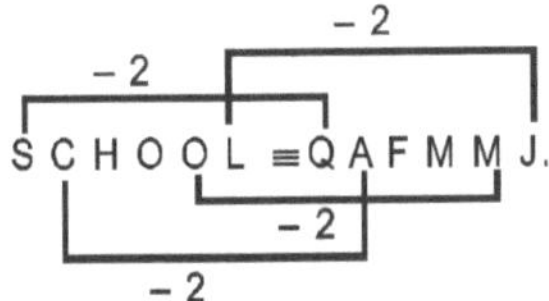

11. 4 The code for PEARL is obtained by leaving out two letters in-between in the reverse direction of the English alphabet. So

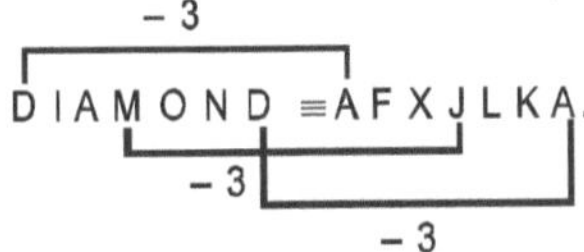

12. 4 Each letter of the word MENTAL is coded by taking its preceding letter and the next letter. That is 'M' is coded as L and N, 'E' as D and F and so on.
Similarly, TEST ≡ SUDFRTSU.

13. 2 Preceding and succeeding letters and coded alternately starting with the preceding letter.

14. 2 In this pattern of coding, only letters at the odd-numbered places are taken as code.

15. 1 In this pattern of coding there is a succeeding positional increase in the letter and its coding.

Type – 2

1. 3 Given: S = 19, T = 20, A = 1, R = 18
∴ STAR = 1920118

2. 4 From the two words we get,
B = 2, O = 1, X = 3, T = 7, I = 0, E = 4 and R = 9
Hence, BOXER = 21349

3. 2 Using the numbers as codes we get the word as PICTURE.

4. 4 Each letter is replaced by its number in the reverse alphabetical series.

5. 4 From the codes we get,
T = 8, R = 6, P = 2, A = 4, O = 1
Hence, 246618 = PARROT

6. 4 Clearly from the codes we get
1 = O, 3 = F, 5 = E, 2 = R, 7 = I and 9 = C.
Hence, 1337952 = OFFICER.

7. 1 It is clear from the codes that 1 = B, 2 = O, 3 = K,
6 = T, 7 = M and 9 = A.
Hence, the number 126627 = BOTTOM

8. 3 Add up the relative positions of letters in the English alphabet, that is B = 2, O = 15 and K = 11.
Hence, BOOK = 43. Accordingly PEN = 16 + 5 + 14 = 35.

9. 4 The logic is similar to question number 21.
Hence, POWER = 16 + 15 + 23 + 5 + 18 = 77.

10. 2 Here, M = 13, A = 1 and N = 14. Hence, MAN = 28.
Hence, CHILD = 3 + 8 + 9 + 12 + 4 = 36

Type – 3

1. 3 The colour of blood is 'red'. But, 'red' is called 'white'.

2. 3 The colour of sky is 'blue'. But, 'blue' would be called 'rain' in that language.

3. 4 Lizard is a living creature which 'crawl' and those which 'crawl' are called as 'flying'.

4. 3 A 'bag' is used to carry the 'books' and in this language 'bag' is called 'book'.

5. 4 A person writes with a 'pencil' and a 'pencil' is called 'paper'.

Type – 4

1. 2 Comparing the first two sentences, extracting the common word we get 'mot' = is. From the second and third sentences, we get 'baj' as dancing. Hence, 'min' stands for good.

2. 4 From the first two sentences and extracting the common word, we get 'pul' = 'food'. From, the second and third sentences, we get 'sop' = 'good'. Hence, 'tir' = 'is'.

3. 3 By comparing the first and the third sentences and extracting the common word we get 'fin' = 'fruit'. From second and third sentences on a similar comparison we get, 'sig' = 'rose'. Hence, 'and' = 'lon'.

4. 2 Comparing the first and second sentences and extracting the common word we get 'nop' = 'is'. Similarly, comparing first and third sentences, we get 'pul' = 'good'. Hence, 'ta' = 'fruit'.

5. 4 Comparing all the sentences we do not get a common code for 'Eternal'. Hence, answer cannot be determined.

Type – 5

1. 3 From the first and last statements, '4' = 'is'. Hence, answer is (3).

2. 2 From first and second statements, we get '3' = 'hot'. From second and third statements, we get '5' = 'day'. Hence, '6' = 'very'.

3. 1 Comparing all the statements and extracting the common digit, we get '2' = 'good', '5' = 'are'.
Hence, '6' = 'you'.

4. 4 Extracting the common digit from all the statements, we get '3' = 'toy', '4' = 'bring'. Hence, '8' = 'good'. Hence, answer can be found out, but it is not given in the answer choices. Hence (4).

5. 3 Extracting the common digit from all the statements, we get '8' = 'apple', '5' = 'green', '6' = 'bring'. Hence, 'me' = '7'.

1. 2

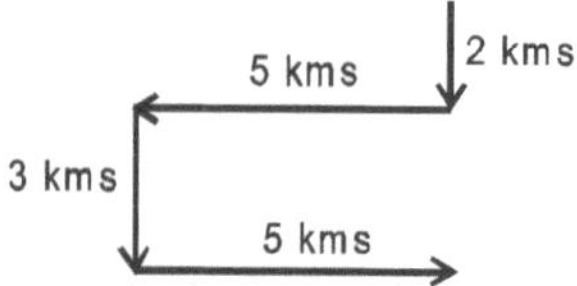

Hence, direction from the starting point is South.

2. 4

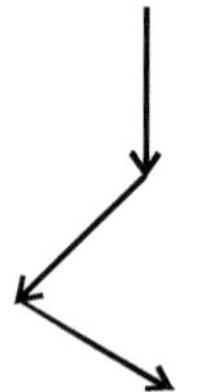

Hence, direction in which he is walking is South-east.

3. 3

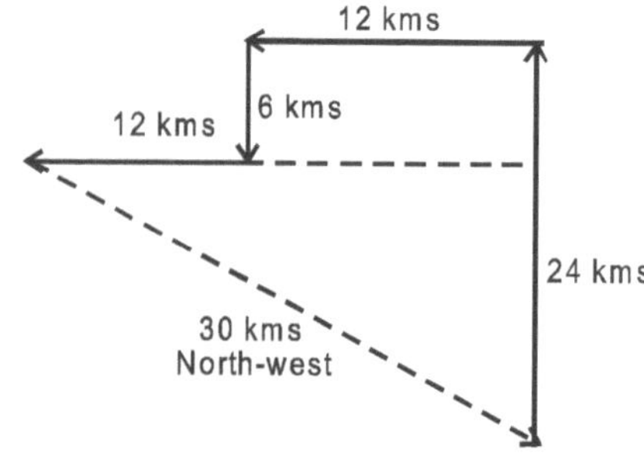

Hence, he is 30 kms South-west.

4. 4 The movement is:

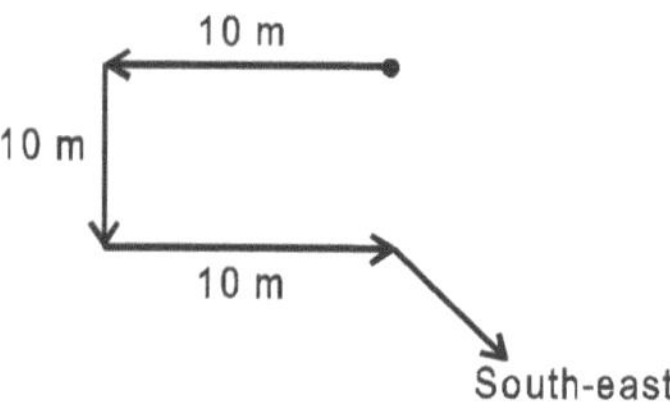

5. 4

```
    M              M
K  L     or        N

   N            K  L
```

So, city 'K' is either North-west or South-west of city 'N'.

6. 1

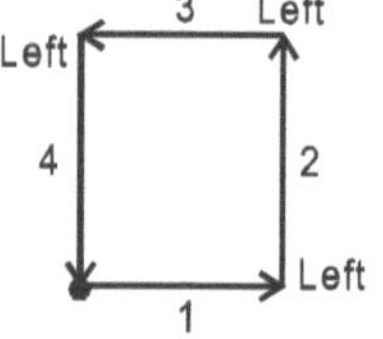

7. 3

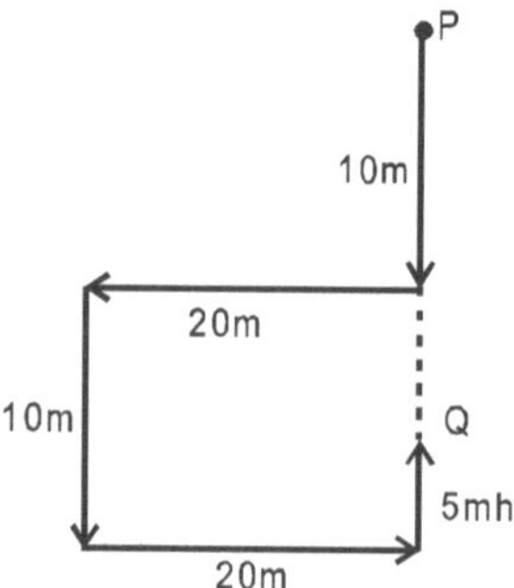

8. 2 Since number of left turns is equal to the number of right turns, he will be facing north.

9. 2 180° CW + 135° ACW = 180 – 135 = 45° CW
So, he will be facing south-east direction.

10. 1

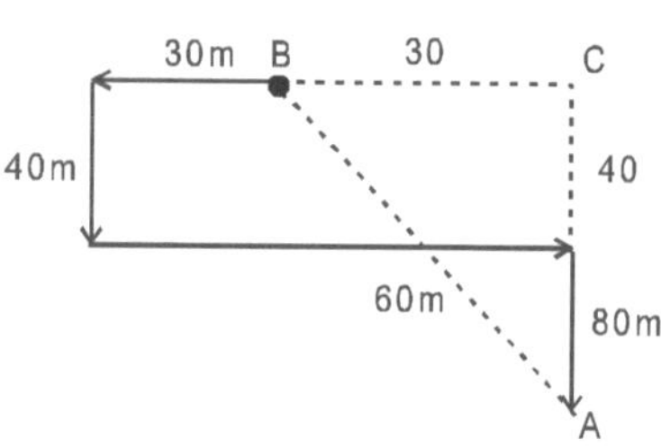

$AB^2 = BC^2 + AC^2 = (30)^2 + (120)^2 = 15300$

So, $AC = 10\sqrt{153}$ m.

11. 2

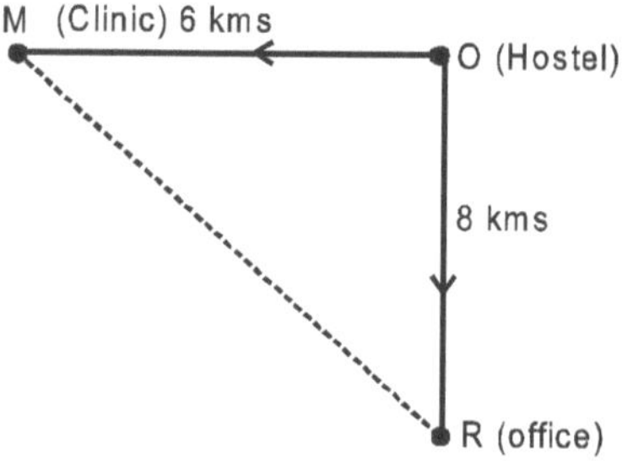

Shortest distance = $RM = \sqrt{8^2 + 6^2}$

$= \sqrt{100} = 10$ kms

12. 2 It was evening and the shadow of the man fell to the elephant's right.
This means that the Sun was towards the elephant's i.e., in West. So, the elephant was facing North.

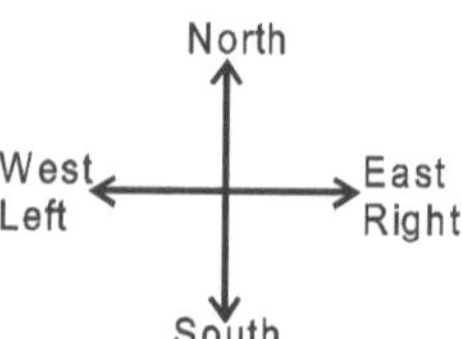

13. 1 It was evening, (Sun in West) and Suraj's shadow fell to his right. So, Suraj was facing North. Hence, Dhiraj was facing South.

Answers and Explanations

14. 3 It was morning and the shadow of the man coming towards Rajeev from the opposite direction fell to Rajeev's left.
This means Sum was towards Rajeev's Right.
So, Rajeev was walking towards the North.
He takes right turn ahead. This means, now he is walking towards East.

15. 3 Clock is placed, in such a way that the minute-hand point towards the North at 3 a.m.

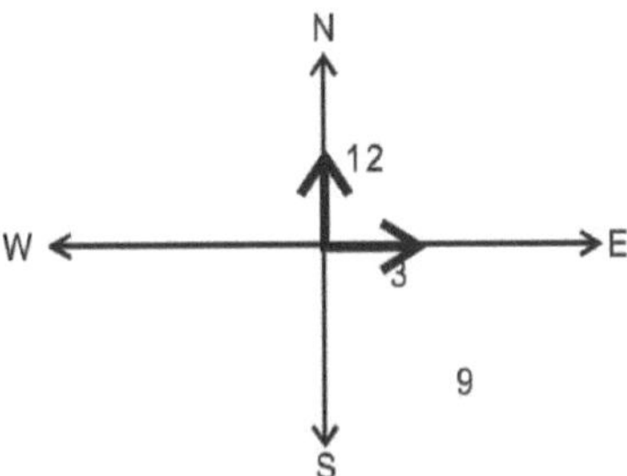

Hence, at 6 p.m. the hour-hand will points towards South.

16. 4 At a 5:45, minute-hand points towards the North-West.

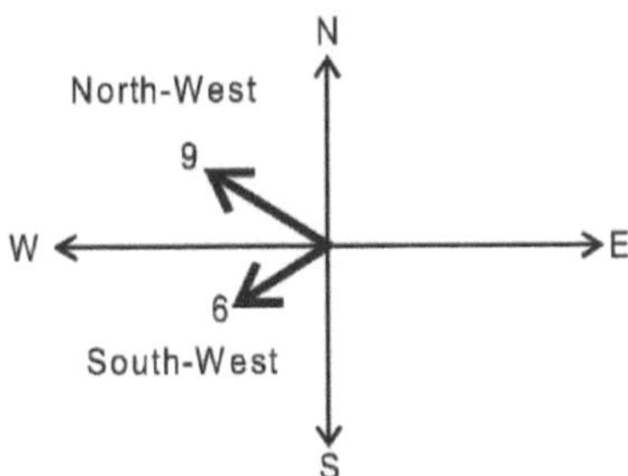

Hence, the hour-hand will points towards South-West.

17. 4

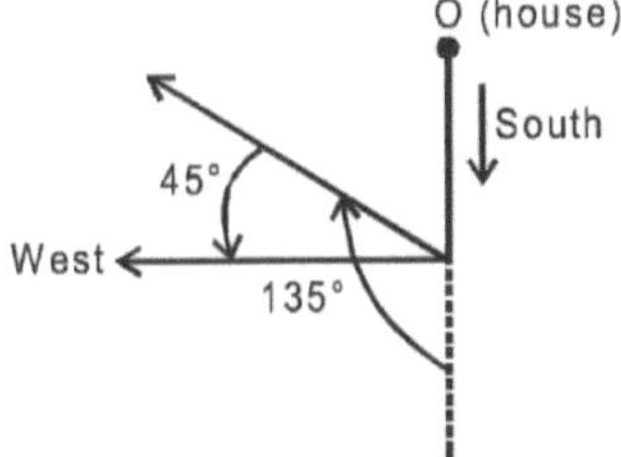

She is finally facing West.

18. 3 The logic is, after every four right turns, Ajay will be facing the same direction and as 128 is a multiple of 4, therefore he will be facing south. Therefore, choice (3) is the correct answer.

19. 3

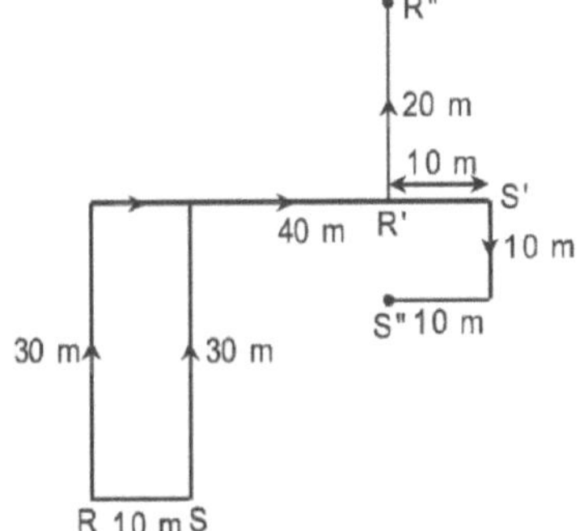

Here R and S are Radha's and Sita's starting position but R" and S" are their final positions.
R"S" = R"R' + R'S" = R"R' + S'S"   R'S" = S'S")
= 20 + 10 = 30 m

20. 1 Following diagram will help in arriving at the answer

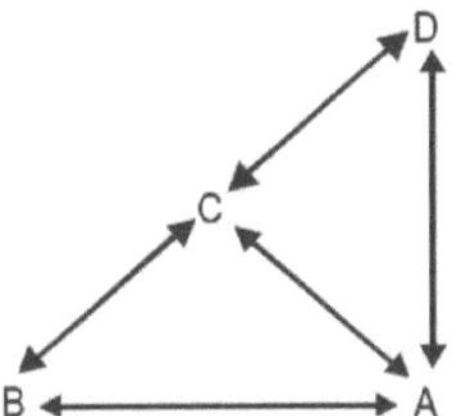

21. 4 The location of the towns from west to east is in the following order:
Bopri - Kakran - Akram - Takhoda - Paranda

For questions 22 to 25:
From the given data.

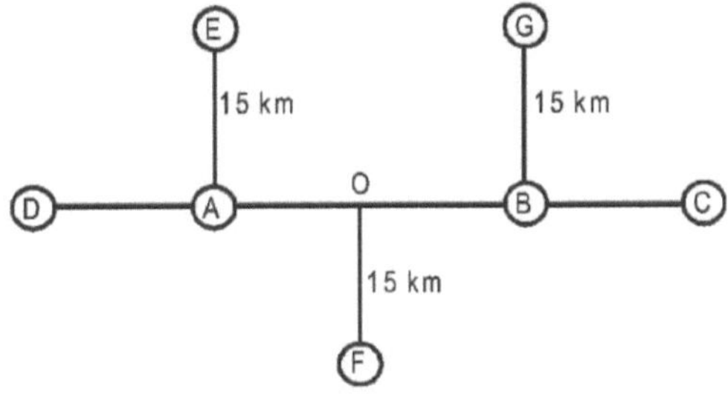

22. 1 City which is situated on the extreme West is 'D'.

23. 2 Position of 'G' with respect to 'D' is North-East.

24. 3
$$AE = 15 \text{ km} \left.\right\} \text{given}$$
$$AD = 15 \text{ km}$$

Shortest distance between 'E' and 'D'

$$= ED = \sqrt{15^2 + 15^2} = \sqrt{225 \times 2} = 15\sqrt{2} \text{ km} \cdot$$

25. 3 Pointer which is showing North is now showing East.
That means, compass will now becomes as shown below,

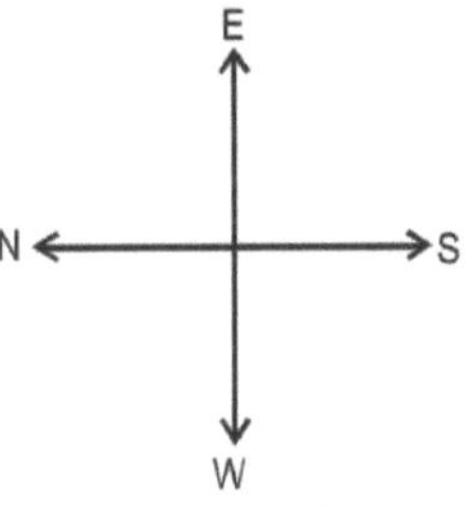

Now, position of 'F' with respect to 'D' is South-West.

7. Blood Relations

1. 1 Son of Sunil's son is Sunil's grandson. Since Akshay is his brother, even he should be Sunil's grandson.

2. 4 Since A is the mother of B who has two more siblings, it can be said that A has three children.

3. 4   Since T is R's father's nephew, he should be R's cousin. Since U is also R's cousin, T and U should be siblings. So, if not brother, U should be the sister of T.

4. 2   Himani's nephew is Ashish's wife's brother. Hence, Ashish's wife should be niece of Himani or Himani should be Ashish's wife's aunt.

5. 4   The son of one's grandmother should be one's father or uncle. Hence, the man being pointed at should be her brother or cousin. Conversely, she should either be his sister or his cousin.

6. 3   'Father of the brother of my father' is also the father of my father and hence is my (woman's) grandfather.

7. 2   Mother's husband is father. Now, the lady is sister of the girl's father or the girl is the daughter of the lady's brother, so the girl is lady's niece.

8. 2   Clearly, maternal grandfather of the children of my husband's sister is my father-in-law.

9. 3   'Daughter of the wife of my brother' is also the daughter of my brother. Now, brother of the daughter of my brother is also the son of my brother, i.e. my nephew.

10. 4   Daughter of a woman's father-in-law is also the sister of woman's husband or brother-in-law. So, the man in photograph is either husband or brother-in-law of girl's mother. So, the girl is either niece or daughter of the man in photograph.

11. 2   'Father-in-law of my mother' is also my grandfather. The only son of the girl's grandfather could only be the girl's father. So the man is the father of the girl.

12. 3   A + B = A is the daughter of B.
B × C = B is the brother of C. Thus, A is the niece of C.

13. 3   A + B = A is the daughter of B.
B – C = B is the husband of C.
Thus, C is the mother of A.

14. 4   A × B = A is the brother of B.
B + C = B is the daughter of C. Thus, A is the son of C.

15. 2   Exploring option (2):
P × D = P is the brother of D.
D + Q = D is the father of Q.
Hence, P is the uncle of Q.

16. 1   Statement III can be dispensed with.

17. 3   It is quite clear that the three of them are siblings. Hence, A is the brother of C.

18. 2

19. 2   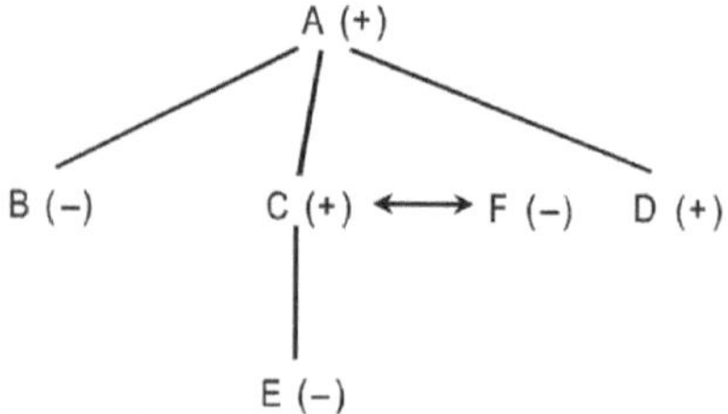

Note: Since E is the niece of B and D. F is the wife of C and mother of E.

20. 4   Cannot be determined

21. 1   Given that U is Q's son, Q is R's sister and R who is unmarried is T's son. We have the following family tree using these statements.
Also given that V is the grand daughter of P. So, V is female. Since we have two married couples in the family, the married members have to be T, Q, S and P. U, V and R are unmarried. As the family consists of three generations, P has to be T's spouse but P's sex cannot be determined. So, V is Q's daughter and S is Q's husband. The complete family tree is as follows:

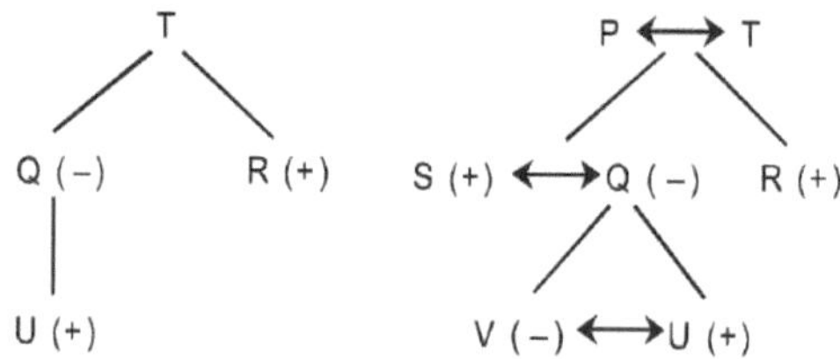

Since P's sex cannot be determined, P's relation with U cannot be determined exactly. Also, S is V's father.

For questions 22 to 26:
From the given data, we get the following tree diagram.

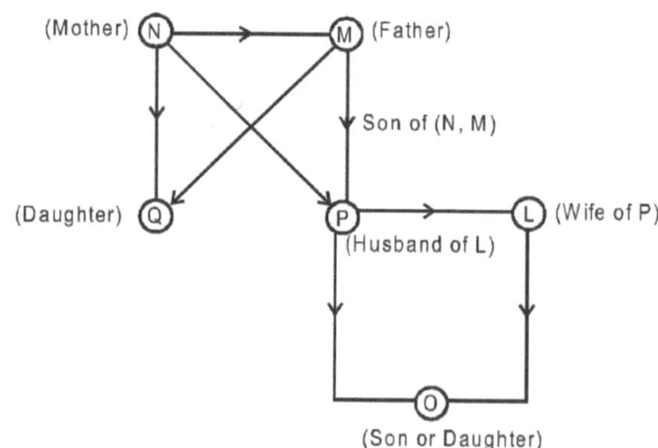

22. 4   Gender of 'O' is not mentioned.

23. 3   As gender of 'O' is not mentioned, 'O' can be Q's either 'nephew' or 'niece'.

24. 3   The son of the father of L is L's brother, who is the maternal uncle of O.

25. 3   'Q' is the sister of L's husband.

26. 3   N is the grandmother of O.

Answers and Explanations

From the given data, we get the following tree diagram.

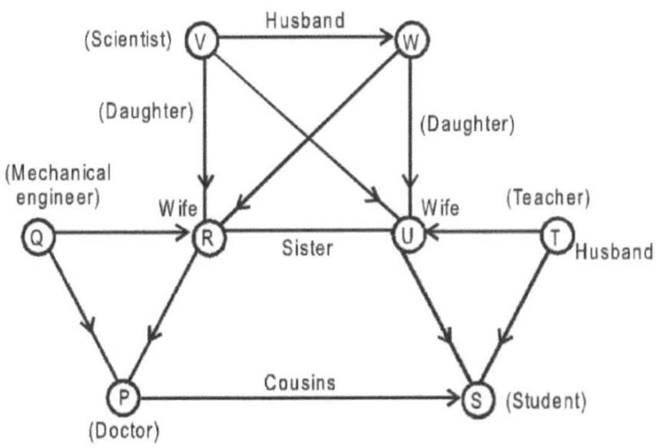

27. 4   As gender of S is not mentioned, S can be either nephew or niece of the Computer Engineer.

28. 2   The Scientist 'V' is the grand father of S.

29. 4   As gender of S is not mentioned the number of female members in the family is either '3' or '4'.

30. 3   T is the brother-in-law of R.

For questions 31 to 35:
From the given data, we get following tree diagram.

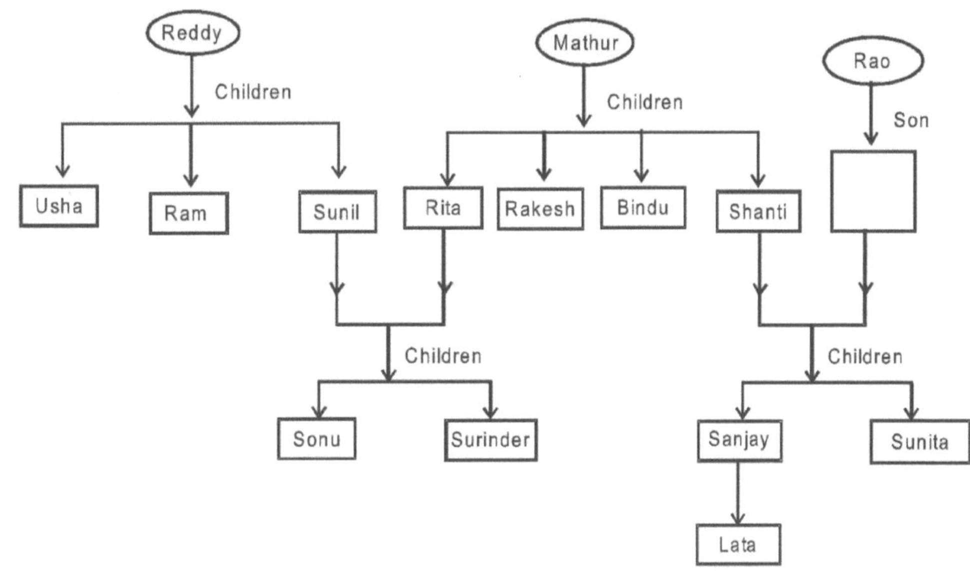

31. 1   Lata is the grand-daughter of Mr. Rao's Son.

32. 3   Sonu is the grandson of Mr. Reddy.

33. 2   Mrs. Mathur is the mother-in-law of Sunil.

34. 4   Sunil is brother-in-law of Rakesh.

35. 2   Mr. Rao is the great grandfather of Lata.

▮ 8. Analytical Reasoning

For questions 1 to 5:
From (i) and (ii):

$$\overline{1}\ \overline{2}\ \overline{3}\ \overline{4}\ \overline{5}\ \uparrow \text{North}$$

From (iii):
Alok   Jayesh

From (iv): (a)   <u>Bhagat</u>   <u>Pramod</u>   <u>Sobodh</u> OR
     (b)   <u>Soubodh</u> <u>Pramod</u> <u>Bhagat</u>

From (v): (a)   <u>Jayesh</u>   <u>Subodh</u>   <u>Pramod</u> OR
    (b)   <u>Pramod</u>   <u>Subodh</u>   <u>Jayesh</u>

Let us start with the arrangement obtained from condition (iii).
Alok   Jayesh
Hence, (v)(a) can't be possible.
From the above reasoning, we get the following final arrangement.
    <u>Alok</u>   <u>Jayesh</u>   <u>Subodh</u>   <u>Pramod</u>   <u>Bhagat</u>

1. 1   Alok is at the extreme left end.

2. 4   Subodh is in the middle.

3. 1   All statements are necessary.

4. 4   Bhagat stands between Alok and Pramod.

5. 4   As Sukhdev stands at the extreme right end, he has only one neighbour, Bhagat.

$\overline{1}\ \overline{2}\ \overline{3}\ \overline{4}\ \overline{5}\ \overline{6}\ \overline{7}\ \overline{8}\ \overline{9}\ \overline{10}\ \overline{11}$ ↑

From (ii):

$$\underline{C}\ \_\ \underline{D}\ \underline{F}$$

From (iii): $\dfrac{\underline{E}}{1}\ \_\ \dfrac{\underline{A}}{3}$ (1 2 3)

From (iv) and (v): (a) $\underline{A}\ \underline{J}\ \underline{B}\ \underline{I}\ \underline{G}$ OR

(b) $\underline{B}\ \underline{J}\ \underline{A}\ \underline{I}\ \underline{G}$

Let us start with the arrangement obtained from condition (iii).

$$\dfrac{\underline{E}}{1}\ \_\ \dfrac{\underline{A}}{3}\quad(1\ 2\ 3)$$

Hence, (v) (b) can't be possible.

From (iii), (iv) and (v) (a), we get the following arrangement.

$$\underline{E}\ \_\ \underline{A}\ \underline{J}\ \underline{B}\ \underline{I}\ \underline{G}$$
$$1\ 2\ 3\ 4\ 5\ 6\ 7$$

Now, from (i), we get that C will occupy seat 8.

Hence, we will get the following arrangement.

$$\underline{E}\ \underline{H/K}\ \underline{A}\ \underline{J}\ \underline{B}\ \underline{I}\ \underline{G}\ \underline{C}\ \underline{K/H}\ \underline{D}\ \underline{F}$$
$$1\ \ \ 2\ \ \ 3\ \ 4\ \ 5\ \ 6\ \ 7\ \ 8\ \ \ 9\ \ \ 10\ 11$$

So, H can occupy either seat 2 or seat 9.

Also, K can occupy seat 2 or seat 9.

6. 2   I is sitting in the middle of the row.

7. 3   The group of friends sitting to the right of G could be CHDF.

8. 4   None is superfluous.

9. 3   B is sitting between J and I.

10. 3   The new arrangement is

$$\underline{D}\ \underline{F}\ \underline{H}\ \underline{J}\ \underline{C}\ \underline{J}\ \underline{G}\ \underline{B}\ \underline{A}\ \underline{E}\ \underline{K}↑$$

So, D and K are sitting at two ends.

For questions 11 to 15:

S sits 3 places to the right of T and Q, 2 places to the right of T. Fix up these positions first.

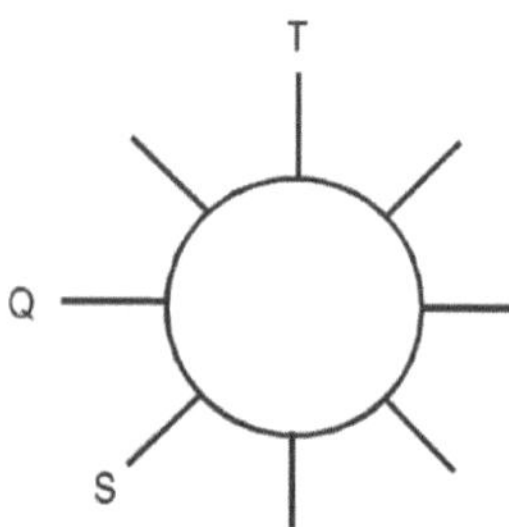

Now, if R has to sit between L and S, it has to be to the right of S else Q will clash with R. We can also get the position of M relative to R. However, the positions of N and P cannot be determined for sure.

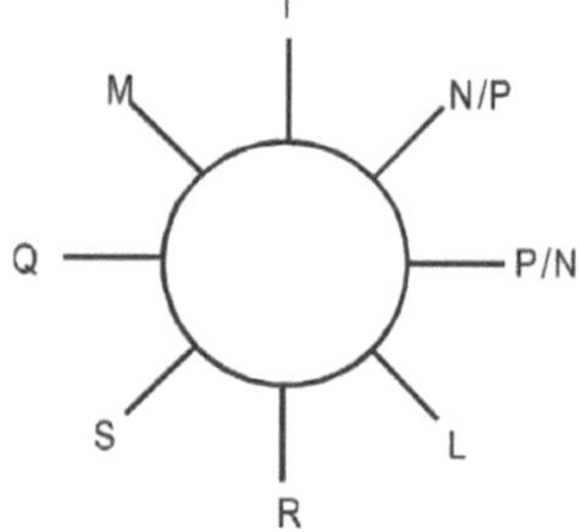

11. 2   L sits opposite M.

12. 3   S is sitting between R and Q.

13. 4   Either N or P sits opposite S.

14. 4   S is Q's neighbour.

15. 1   R is to the left of L.

16. 4   There are two arrangements possible.

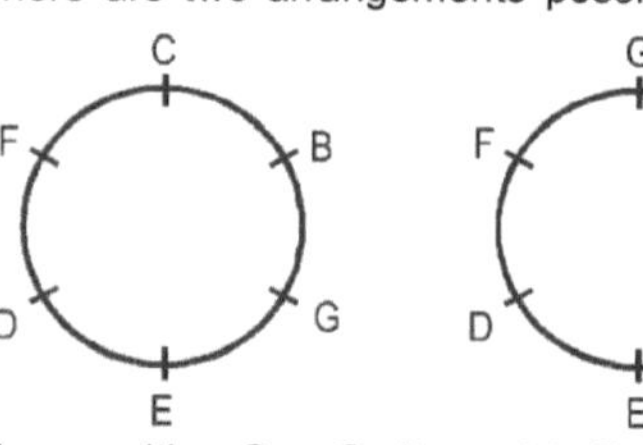

Hence, either C or G sits next to E.

17. 4

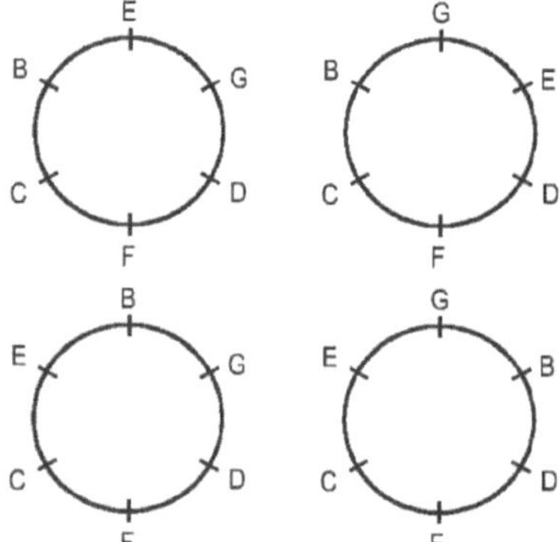

Hence, C and G sit next to E.

18. 1

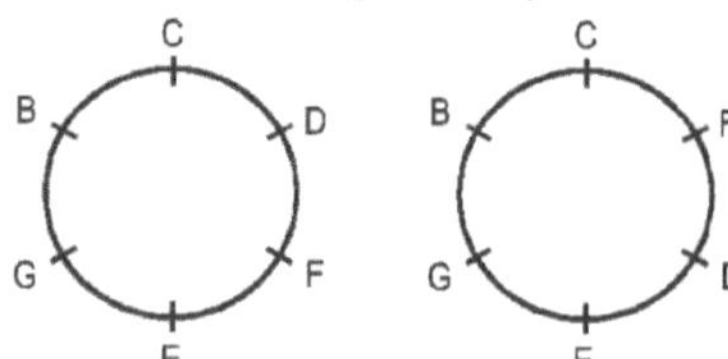

B sits opposite F.

19. 4   There are 4 arrangements possible.

20. 4   There are 2 arrangements possible.

In both the arrangements position of G is between B and E only.

Answers and Explanations

For questions 21 to 25:
Start by fixing the position of one of the persons. The best statement to start with is (iii), since the two opposite positions are fixed simultaneously and the remaining positions can be derived relative to these positions.
There are two possible arrangements.

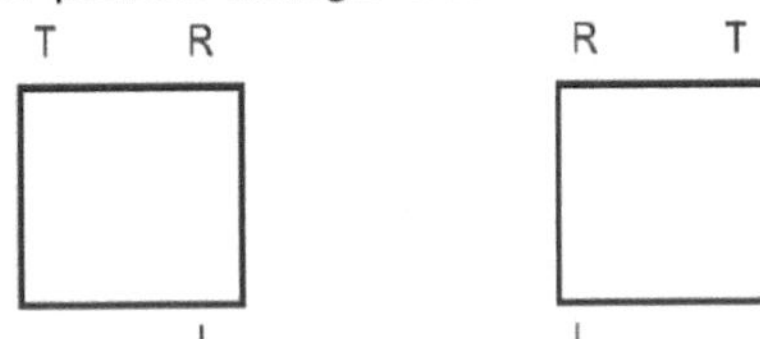

Using statement (ii), we get

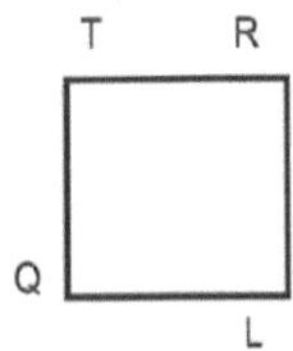 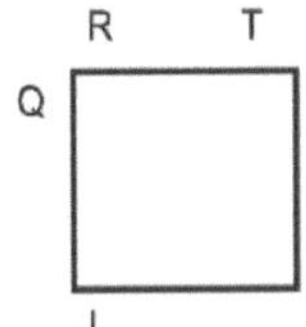

Using statement (i), we get

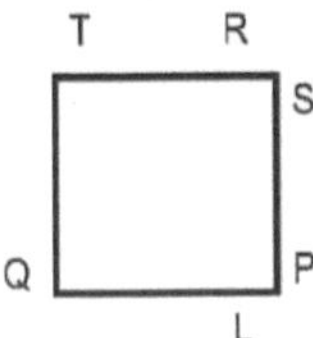 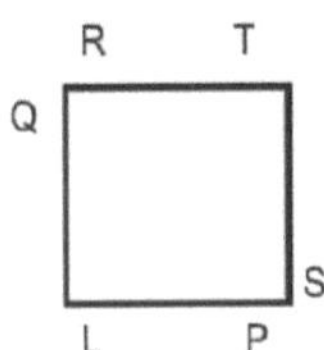

Now, according to statement (iv) M sits 2 places to the left of R which is not possible in arrangement 1 as P is already present there. So, only arrangement 2 is possible. The final arrangement is as follows:

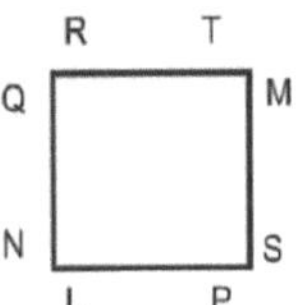

21. 4   T sits opposite P.

22. 3   T sits two places to the right of S.

23. 2   L is sitting between N and P.

24. 3   P is L's neighbour.

25. 4   M sits opposite Q.

For questions 26 to 30:
C is the last book. The combinations B-D and A-E in that order have to compulsorily exist. Now, the order will have to start with B-D, since A cannot be started with (from (ii)).

1	2	3	4	5	6
B	D				C

If the fourth hour is the break, then the combination A-E cannot be fitted without a break in-between.

1	2	3	4	5	6
B	D		X		C

Again, if the fifth hour is the break, we will have the following sequence.

1	2	3	4	5	6
B	D	A	E	X	C

However, this is not possible since A cannot follow D immediately. Hence, the break has to be in the third hour and the arrangement is as follows:

1	2	3	4	5	6
B	D	X	A	E	C

26. 4   3rd hour is the break.

27. 3   B is the first book to be proofread.

28. 2   A is to be proofread immediately after the breakfast.

29. 4   None of these.

30. 3   C is to be proofread immediately after E.

For questions 31 to 35:
From (i), we see that the holiday has to be between Monday and Friday (both days included). Biology has to be done on Thursday. Since Physics cannot immediately precede Biology and also cannot start the series, it cannot be scheduled on either Wednesday or Sunday. Also, Physics has to be done two days before Astronomy. So, Physics cannot be done on Tuesday, else Astronomy would clash with Biology. Therefore, Physics has to be scheduled for Sunday and thus, Astronomy on Wednesday.

Algebra has to be immediately before Geometry. The only space available for this combination is Friday-Saturday. That leaves Chemistry. Since Sunday cannot be free, the holiday has to be on Tuesday and Chemistry on Sunday. Therefore, we get the following as the final table.

Sunday	Monday	Tuesday	Wednesday	Thursday	Friday	Saturday
Chemistry	Physics	X	Astronomy	Biology	Algebra	Geometry

31. 2   Chemistry will start the series of lectures.

32. 2   Tuesday is the holiday.

33. 1   Physics lecture is on Monday.

34. 4   Geometry lecture is on Saturday.

35. 2   Biology is scheduled 3 days after Physics.

For questions 36 to 40:
1 – C   –   S. Sciences x Chemistry ... from (iii)
2 – E   –   Female, Zoology ... from (iv)
3 – G   –   Female, Physics ... from (iv)
4 – A   –   Maths, not married to Physics teacher ... from (v)
5 – B   –   Does teach Chemistry or Commerce ... from (vi)
6 – F   –   Male, unmarried ... from (vii)
7 – D   –   Male ... from (vii)
8 – 3 females and 4 males, 2 married couples ... from (ii)

'F' is unmarried, therefore, 'C' is married to 'D' ... (using 8)
And given that 'C' is married to Chemistry teacher, therefore,
    D is male (using vii) and teaches Chemistry
    C is female   ... [using (iii) and (vii)]
    B is male   ... (using 8)
    F teaches Commerce   ... [using (vi)]

Therefore, the final table would look like as shown below.

Teachers	Sex	Subjects	Married to
A	Male	Maths	E – Zoology
B	Male	–	Unmarried
C	Female	S.Sciences	D – Chemistry
D	Male	Chemistry	C – S.Sciences
E	Female	Zoology	A – Maths
F	Male	Commerce	Unmarried
G	Female	Physics	Unmarried

The correct choices are:

36. 3   F teaches commerce.

37. 4   Can't be determined.

38. 1   DC and AE are the two pairs of couples.

39. 2   A's wife teaches Zoology.

40. 3   A and D are married males.

For questions 41 to 45:
Fill up all the absolute data given. You will get the following table:

	Caps	Snacks
Amit	Blue	
Bharati	Yellow	
Cheryl		Sandwich
Deepak		
Eric		Pizza

Now from (i), red cap and pastries have to be a combination. This cannot fit in anywhere but for Deepak it fits, since parts of the other combinations have filled. That leaves us with two colours of caps – green and white and two snacks – ice-cream and burgers. For caps, Eric does not wear green cap; hence out of the colours left, he has to wear the white cap. Again, Amit does not eat ice-cream, therefore, he has to eat burgers. So, we get the following table.

	Caps	Snacks
Amit	Blue	Burgers
Bharati	Yellow	Ice-cream
Cheryl	Green	Sandwich
Deepak	Red	Pastries
Eric	White	Pizza

41. 1   Amit is eating burgers.

42. 3   Cheryl is wearing the green cap.

43. 2   Bharati is eating the ice-cream.

44. 4   Eric is wearing the white cap.

45. 4   'Bharati + Burger' is not the right combination.

46. 4   Ranking of Karan is not defined, as R and K > V > S > A consequently either Ramesh or Karan is tallest.

47. 3   There is a comparison in height and weight of persons. Arranging the given information in decreasing order, we get
Weight : D > B > A > C
Height : C > B > D > A
D and C are the heaviest and the tallest, respectively.

48. 4   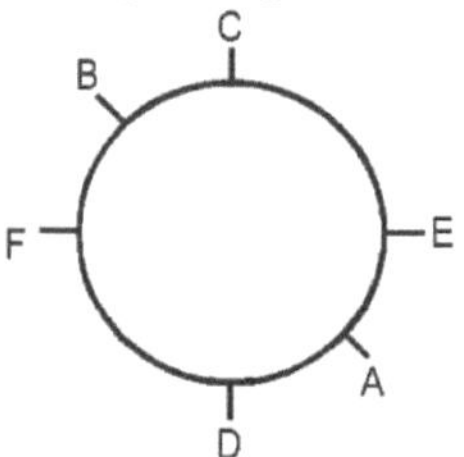

Total no. of students in the class
$\Rightarrow 5 + 6 + 6 + 7 \Rightarrow 24$

49. 2   As P gets the first rank in IInd game, he has to get Ist and IIIrd ranks in the other two games. As R gets the Ist rank in the second game, he has to get IInd and IIIrd ranks in the other two games.
From above statements, P gets IIIrd rank in game II and Ist in game III.

Game	Rank		
	Ist	IInd	IIIrd
I	Q	R	P
II	P	Q	R
III	R	P	Q

So, Q got the IIIrd rank in game III.

50. 4   By arranging the given information, we will get the following seating arrangement.
B M V K R Q
So, V is sitting between M and K.

51. 3   Seating arrangement:

Clearly, D is sitting between A and F.

52. 3   Books are kept from top to bottom in the following sequence.
Physics
Maths
Civics
English
History
Computer
Hence, the Computer book is at the bottom of the pile.

53. 3   Order in which a musician had sung four classical Raagas is as follows:
(1) Kedar
(2) Bhairavi
(3) Durbari
(4) Todi
So, Durbari was sung immediately after Bhairavi.

54. 3   Given:
(i) Ram and Shyam cannot be in the same team.
(ii) Raju and Amit must be selected together.
(iii) Rohit and Dinesh can't be in the same team.
As at least one of Ram and Shyam must be rejected and at least one of Rohit and Dinesh must be rejected, both Raju and Amit must be selected.
So, Amit must be in the team.

55. 4   Given:
A and B cannot be together.
A and D cannot be together.
B and C must be together.
Hence, the correct team is B, C and F.

Answers and Explanations

56. 3   S, U and N are the third, sixth and ninth letters of the word RESTAURANT. SUN is the only meaningful word.

57. 2   When the first and the seventh, the second and the eighth, and so on ... letters are interchanged, the new word is ONSHIPRELATI.
Now, the third letter from the right, if the second half of this word is reversed, [ONSHIPITALER] will be L.

58. 1   Clearly, such a letter-pair is N and S. In the word NECESSARY, there are four letters between them: E, C, E and S. In the alphabet too, N and S have four letters between them: O, P Q and R.

59. 2   Numbers satisfying the given condition are underlined in the given series:
1 3 <u>4 6</u> 7 5 4 6 9 8 <u>3 5 6</u> 9 1 7 3 <u>6 5 8</u> 5 6
There are four such numbers.

60. 2   The A's that satisfy the given condition are underlined in the sequence.
A M B <u>Z A B</u> M N A B <u>Z A B</u> A Z B A M Z B A B <u>Z A B</u>
There are three such A's.

9. Calendars

1. 2   Total number of odd days = 1600 years have 0 odd day + 300 years have 1 odd day + 49 years (12 leap + 37 ordinary) have 5 odd days + 26 days of Jan have 5 odd days = 0 + 1 + 5 + 5 = 4 odd days
So, the day was Thursday.

2. 4   1600 years have 0 odd day
200 years have 2 × 5 = 10, i.e., 3 odd days.
68 years contain 17 leap years and 51 ordinary years.
That is, 17 × 2 + 51 = 85 days, i.e., 1 odd day.
In 1869, upto 2nd Oct., total number of odd days = 31(Jan.) + 28(Feb.) + 31(Mar.) + 30(Apr.) + 31(May) + 30(Jun.) + 31(Jul.) + 31(Aug.) + 30(Sep.) + 2(Oct.) = 275 days = 2 odd days.
∴ Total odd days = 0 + 3 + 1 + 2 = 6 odd days.
∴ The day was Saturday.

3. 3   15 Aug., 1947 = (1600 + 300 + 46) years + 1 Jan. to 15 Aug. of 1947
= (1600 + 300 + 46) years + 365 - 16
Aug. to 31 Dec 1947
= (1600 + 300 + 46) years + (365 - 138) days
Number of odd days = 0 + 1 + 1 (from 11 leap years and 35 ordinary years) + 3 = 5 odd days.
∴ The day was Friday.

4. 3   83 years contain 20 leap years and 63 ordinary years and therefore (40 + 0) odd days
i.e., 5 odd days.
∴ 1983 years contain (0 + 1 + 5) i.e., 6 odd days.
Number of days from Jan., 1984 to 31st Oct., 1984.
= (31 + 29 + 31 + 30 + 31 + 30 + 31 + 31 + 30 + 31)
= 305 days = 4 odd days.
∴ Total number of odd days = 6 + 4 = 10 i.e., 3 odd days.
So, 31st Oct., 1984 was Wednesday.

5. 2   20th June, 1837 means "1836 complete years + first 5 months of the year 1837 + 20 days of June"

1600 years give   no odd day
200 years give   3 odd days
36 years give   3 odd days.
[36 years contain 9 leap years and 27 ordinary years. Therefore, (27 + 18 =) 45 odd days = 3 odd days.]
∴ 1836 years give (0 + 3 + 3) = 6 odd days
Now, from first January to 20th, June, we have,
        Jan. Feb. Mar. Apr.   May Jun.
odd days: 3 + 0 + 3 + 2 + 3 + 6
= 17 i.e., 3 odd days.
∴ Total number of odd days = (6 + 3) = 9 odd days i.e., 2 odd days.
This means that the 20th June fell on the 2nd day commencing from Monday. Therefore the required day was Tuesday.

6. 2   Counting the number of days after 23rd April, 1984 we have:
April   may June July August
days: 7 + 31 + 30 + 31 + 15 = 114 days
Number of odd days in 114 days
$$= \frac{114}{7} = 16 \text{ weeks } +2 \text{ odd days}$$
2nd day after Monday is Wednesday.

7. 4   It is given that 3rd March, 1984 was a Sunday So, 3rd March, 1987, was three days after Sunday, i.e., on Wednesday.
Number of days from 3rd March, 1987 to 13th July, 1987:
March April May   June July
Days: 28 + 30 + 31 + 30 + 13 = 132
$$= \frac{132}{7} = 6 \text{ odd days}$$
6th day after Wednesday is Tuesday.

8. 1   It is given that 10th April, 1883 was a Wednesday.
Number of days from 10th April, 1883 to 23rd August 1883.
          April May June July August
Days: 20 + 31 + 30 + 31 + 23   = 135
Number of odd days in 135 days = $\frac{135}{7}$ = 2 odd days.

2 days after Wednesday is Friday.
Number of odd days from 23rd August 1879 to 23rd August 1883 are five. So, 23rd August, 1879 is five days back to Friday is Sunday.

9. 3   First we look for the leap years during this period.
1997, 1998, 1999 are not leap years.
1998 and 1999 together have net 2 odd days.
Number of days remaining in 1997 = 365 − 16 = 349 days
= 49 weeks 6 odd days.
∴ Total number of odd days = 2 + 6 + 4 = 12 days
= 7 days (1 week) + 5 odd days
Hence, January 4, 2000 will be 5 days beyond Thursday i.e., it was Tuesday.

10. 4   Year 2000 is a leap year.
Therefore, March 5, 2000 will be two days beyond Friday, i.e., on Sunday.

11. 1   Counting the number of days after 3rd November, 1987 we have :
         Nov. Dec. Jan. Feb. Mar.   Apr.
Days: 27 + 31 + 31 + 29 + 31 + 4
= 153 days, containing 6 odd days.
i.e., (7 − 6) = 1 day beyond the day on 4th April, 1988.
So, the day was Tuesday.

12. 3 We go on counting the odd days from 1991 onwards till the sum is divisible by 7. The number of such days are 14 upto the year 2032.

So, the calendar for 1991 will be repeated in the year 2002.

13. 3 The year 2004 is a leap year and a leap year repeats itself after 28 years 2004 + 28 = 2032

So, 2032 will have the same calendar as that of 2004.

14. 2 As the given year starts and ends with Monday means the next year will start with Tuesday. Hence, the given year is a non-leap year.

There will be 53 Mondays in the year.

15. 1 1st April, 2012:

2000 + 11 + Number of days from 1st January 2012 to 1st April, 2012.

Number of odd days in 2000 years = 0

Number of odd days in 11 years = 13

$$\begin{array}{ccccccc} & \text{January} & \text{February} & \text{March} & \text{April} \\ \text{Odd days:} & 3 & + & 1 & + & 3 & + & 1 & = 8 \end{array}$$

Total number of odd days = 8 + 13 + 0 = 21

= 0 odd days.

Hence, 1st April, 2012 is a Sunday.

1st, 8th, 15th, 22nd and 29th of April, 2012 are Sunday's.

10. Clocks

1. 3 Angle traced by hour-hand in 12 hrs. = 360°

Angle traced by hour-hand in 5 hrs 10 min. i.e. $\dfrac{31}{6}$ hrs.

$$= \left(\dfrac{360}{12} \times \dfrac{31}{6}\right)^\circ = 155^\circ$$

2. 4 Angle traced by hour-hand in 6 hours

$$= \left(\dfrac{360}{12} \times 6\right)^\circ = 180^\circ$$

3. 2 When the two hands of the clock coincide, then the angle between them is 0°.

$$\boxed{\theta = \dfrac{11}{2}m - 30h}$$

Here, $\theta = 0^\circ$ and h = 9

$$\theta = \dfrac{11}{2}m - 30 \times 9$$

$$\therefore m = \dfrac{270 \times 2}{11}\text{min.} = 49\dfrac{1}{11}\text{min.}$$

Therefore, the hands of the clock are together at 9 hrs. $49\dfrac{1}{11}$min.

4. 2 The angle between the two hands of a clock at 8:30 is

$$\theta = \dfrac{11}{2}m - 30h.$$

Here, m = 30 and h = 8

$$\therefore \theta = \dfrac{11}{2} \times 30 - 30 \times 8 \Rightarrow \text{Here, } \dfrac{11}{2}m < 30h$$

$$\therefore \theta = 30h - \dfrac{11}{2}m \Rightarrow = 30 \times 8 - \dfrac{11}{2} \times 30$$

$$\boxed{\theta = 75^\circ}$$

5. 2 At 5 o'clock, the minute-hand and the hour-hand are 25 min. spaces apart.

Case (i) : Minute-hand is 3 min. spaces behind the hour-hand.

In this case, the minute-hand has to gain (25–3) = 22 min. spaces.

Now, 55 min. are gained in 60 min.

$$\therefore 22 \text{ min. are gained in } \left(\dfrac{60}{55} \times 22\right)\text{min} = 24\text{min.}$$

$\therefore$ The hands will be 3 min. apart at 24 min. past 5.

Case (ii) : Minute-hand is 3 min. spaces ahead of the hour-hand.

In this case, the minute-hand has to gain (25 + 3) = 28 min. spaces

Now, 55 min. are gained in 60 min.

$$28 \text{ min. are gained in } \left(\dfrac{60}{55} \times 28\right) = 30\dfrac{6}{11}\text{min.}$$

$\therefore$ The hands will be 3 minutes apart at

$30\dfrac{6}{11}$min. past 5.

6. 3 The hands of a clock coincide 11 times in every 12 hours (Since between 11 and 1, they coincide only once, i.e. at 12 O'clock).

$\therefore$ The hands of a clock coincide 22 times in a day.

7. 1 In a correct clock, the minute-hand gains 55 minute spaces over the hour-hand in every 60 minutes. To be together again, the minute-hand must gain 60 minutes over the hour-hand.

55 min. spaces are gained in 60 min.

$$\therefore 60 \text{ min. spaces are gained in } \dfrac{60}{55} \times 60 \text{ min.}$$

$$= 65\dfrac{5}{11}\text{min.}$$

But they are together at an interval of 64 minutes.

$\therefore$ Gain in every 64 minutes.

$$= \left(65\dfrac{5}{11} - 64\right)\text{min.} = 1\dfrac{5}{11}\text{min.}$$

Gain in a day.

$$= \dfrac{16}{11} \times \dfrac{24 \times 60}{64} = \dfrac{360}{11} = 32\dfrac{8}{11}\text{min.}$$

8. 1 In a correct clock, the hands of a clock coincide every

$65\dfrac{5}{11}$ minutes, hence clock loses time.

$$\text{Loss in 67 minutes} = \left(67 - 65\dfrac{5}{11}\right)$$

$$= 2\dfrac{6}{11}\text{minutes} = \dfrac{28}{11}\text{minutes}$$

Loss in one day (24 hours)

$$= \dfrac{28}{11} \times \dfrac{60}{68} \times 24 = 53\dfrac{169}{187}\text{minutes}$$

Answers and Explanations

9. 2   Time from 12 p.m. on Monday to 2 p.m. on the following Monday = 7 days 2 hours = 170 hours

$\therefore$ The watch gains $\left(2 + 4\dfrac{4}{5}\right)$ min. or $\dfrac{34}{5}$ min. in 170 hrs.

Now, $\dfrac{34}{5}$ min. are gained in 170 hrs.

$\therefore$ 2 min. are gained in $\left(170 \times \dfrac{5}{34} \times 2\right)$ hrs = 50 hrs.

$\therefore$ Watch is correct 2 days 2 hrs. after 12 p.m. on Monday i.e., it will be correct at 2 p.m. on Wednesday.

10. 2   Time from 7 a.m. to 4.15 p.m. = 9 hrs 15 min. = $\dfrac{37}{4}$ hrs.

3 min. 5 sec. of this clock = 3 min. of the correct clock.

$\Rightarrow \dfrac{37}{720}$ hrs. of this clock = $\dfrac{1}{20}$ hrs. of the correct clock

$\Rightarrow \dfrac{37}{4}$ hrs. of this clock = $\left(\dfrac{1}{20} \times \dfrac{720}{37} \times \dfrac{37}{4}\right)$ hrs. of the correct clock = 9 hrs. of the correct clock.

$\therefore$ The correct time is 9 hrs. after 7 a.m. i.e. 4 p.m.

11. 3   Total time in hours from Sunday at 4 p.m. to the following Sunday at 8 a.m. = 6 × 24 + 16 = 160 hrs.

Thus, the watch gain $\left(6 + 10\dfrac{2}{3}\right) = 16\dfrac{2}{3}$ min. in 160 hrs.

$\dfrac{50}{3}$ min. are gained in 160 hrs.

$\therefore$ 6 min. are gained in

$= 160 \times \dfrac{3}{50} \times 6 = \dfrac{288}{5}$ hrs. $= 57\dfrac{3}{5}$ hrs.

The watch was correct on Wednesday at 1.36 a.m.

12. 3   Total number of hours from Monday at 8 a.m. to following Wednesday at 6 p.m. 24 × 2 + 10 = 58 hrs.
24 hrs. 10 min. of this clock are same as 24 hrs. of a correct clock.

$\dfrac{145}{6}$ hrs. of the incorrect clock = 24 hrs. of the correct clock

$\therefore$ 58 hrs. of the incorrect clock = $\left(\dfrac{24 \times 6}{145} \times 58\right)$ hrs. of the correct clock.

$= 57\dfrac{2}{3}$ hrs. of the correct clock.

$\therefore$ The correct time on the following Wednesday will be 5 : 36 p.m.

13. 2   Total number of hours from 5 a.m. on first day to 10 p.m. on 4th day is 89 hrs.
23 hrs. 44 min. of this clock are same as 24 hrs. of a correct clock.

$\dfrac{356}{15}$ hrs. of this clock = 24 hrs. of correct clock

$\therefore$ 89 hrs. of this $= \left(\dfrac{24 \times 15}{356} \times 89\right)$ hrs. of correct clock.

= 90 hrs. of correct clock.

$\therefore$ The correct time is 11 p.m.

14. 3   Difference in minute between the two clocks in one hour = 1 minute.
Number of hours = 11 hours.
In 11 hours, one of the clock gains 22 minutes and shows the time as 9:22 p.m. The other clock which gains 1 minute per hour shows the time as 9:11 p.m.

15. 3   The time shown by the clock when seen in the mirror = 12 hrs. – 6 hrs. 45 min. = 5 hrs. 15 min.

▋ 11. True-False Logic

For questions 1 to 4:
It is given that, among three persons exactly one is truth-teller, one is liar and one is alternator.
Let us assume that Ajay is the truth-teller.

	Statements		Profession
	I	II	
Ajay	T	T	Engineer
Vijay	T	F	Scientist
Mahesh	F	F	Doctor

So, from the above table,

1. 2   Vijay is the scientist.

2. 1   Ajay is the truth-teller.

3. 3   Mahesh is the liar.

4. 1   Ajay is the Engineer.

For questions 5 to 7:
It is given that each among Krishna, Dinesh and Anuj is an alternator.
Let us assume that Krishna's first statement be true and second statement be false.

	Statements		Subject
	I	II	
Krishna	T	F	Biology
Dinesh	F	F	Chemistry
Anuj			Maths

Here Dinesh is not an alternator.
As it violates the conditions, lets us assume that Krishna's first statements is false and second statement is true.

	Statements		Subject
	I	II	
Krishna	F	T	Maths
Dinesh	T	F	Biology
Anuj	F	T	Chemistry

5. 1   Anuj is the Chemistry professor.

6. 2   Dinesh is the Biology professor.

7. 3   Krishna is the Maths professor.

For questions 8 to 11:

It is given that the among three friends two are alternators and one is the truth-teller.

Let us assume that, Sania is the truth-teller.

	Statements		Colour
	I	II	
Sania	T	T	Blue
Megha	F	F	Red
Manasi			Green

Megha cannot be the liar. It violates the given conditions.

Let us assume that Megha is the truth-teller.

	Statements		Colour
	I	II	
Sania	F	F	Red
Megha	T	T	Green
Manasi			Blue

Sania can't be the liar.

Finally, we assume that the Manasi is the truth-teller. As Manasis both the statements are not certain, we will assume that Sania's first statement is true and second is false.

	Statements		Colour
	I	II	
Sania	T	F	Blue
Megha	T	F	Green
Manasi	T	T	Red

8. 2   Manasi is the truth-teller.

9. 3   Manasi likes red colour.

10. 1   Sania likes blue colour.

11. 2   Megha likes green colour.

For questions 12 to 15:

Let us assume that Ram is the truth-teller.

	Statements			Game
	I	II	III	
Ram	T	T	T	Chess
Sachin	F	F	T	Carrom
Rahul	T	T	F	Cricket

It violates the given conditions.

Let us assume that Sachin is the truth-teller.

	Statements			
	I	II	III	Game
Ram	F	T	F	Carrom
Sachin	T	T	T	Chess
Rahul	F	F	F	Cricket

12. 1   Rahul is the liar.

13. 2   Sachin is the truth-teller.

14. 3   Sachin plays chess.

15. 3   Rahul plays Cricket.

16. 3   Let us assume that Raj is the truth-teller.

	Statement
Raj	T
Nilesh	T

Hence, both are truth-tellers.

Let us assume that Raj is a liar.

	Statement
Raj	F
Nilesh	F

Hence, both are liars.

17. 1   Let us assume that Krishna is the truth-letter. We will get the following table.

	Statement
Krishna	T
Ravi	T
Ajay	F

As it is given that, exactly one person among the three person is the truth-teller, Krishna can't be the truth-teller. Now let us assume that Ravi is the truth-teller, we will get the following table.

	Statement
Krishna	T
Ravi	T
Ajay	F

Hence, Ravi can't be Truth-teller. Let us assume that the Ajay is the truth-teller we will get the following table.

	Statement
Krishna	F
Ravi	F
Ajay	T

Hence, Ajay could be the truth-teller.

18. 1   Let us assume that Amit is the truth-teller.

	Statements	
	I	II
Amit	T	T
Mohit	F	F
Manish	F	F

So, Amit is the truth-teller.

19. 3   It is given that exactly one person among the three person is the truth-teller, one is liar and one is the alternator.

Let us assume that Amit is the truth-teller.

	Statements	
	I	II
Amit	T	T
Raja	F	F
Albert	T	F

As, Amit is the truth-teller, Raja is the singer.

20. 2   Let us assume that P is the truth-teller.

	Statements	
	I	II
P	T	T
Q	T	F
R	F	F

As P is the truth-teller, Q is the thief.

Answers and Explanations

12. Cubes

1. 3   As, $n = \dfrac{6}{3} + 1 = 3$

Maximum number of cubes $= n^3 = 3^3 = 27$.

2. 1   Here number of cuts is not a multiple of 3.

$$1 + 1 + 2 \quad \Rightarrow 4$$

$$\begin{array}{ccc} 1 & 1 & 2 \\ +1 & +1 & +1 \\ \hline 2\times & 2\times & 3 \end{array}$$

So, maximum number of cubes $= 2 \times 2 \times 3 = 12$.

3. 1   Here, number of cuts is not a multiple of 3.

$$5 + 6 + 6 \Rightarrow 17$$

$$\begin{array}{ccc} 5 & 6 & 6 \\ +1 & +1 & +1 \\ \hline 6\times & 7\times & 7 \end{array}$$

So, maximum number of cubes $= 6 \times 7 \times 7 = 294$.

4. 1   As, $n = \dfrac{27}{3} + 1 = 9 + 1 = 10$

$\therefore$ Maximum number of cubes $= 10^3 = 1000$.

5. 3 $100 \Rightarrow 5 \times 5 \times 4$

$$\begin{array}{ccc} 5 & 5 & 4 \\ -1 & -1 & -1 \\ \hline 4 & +4 & +3 \Rightarrow 11 \end{array}$$

So, least number of cuts required to cut a cube into hundred identical pieces is 11.

6. 1 $48 \Rightarrow 4 \times 4 \times 3$

$$\begin{array}{ccc} 4 & 4 & 3 \\ -1 & -1 & -1 \\ \hline 3 & +3 & +2 \Rightarrow 8 \end{array}$$

So, least number of cuts required to cut a cube into 48 identical pieces is 8.

7. 3 $64 \Rightarrow 4 \times 4 \times 4$

So, to cover this cube completely we require a $6 \times 6 \times 6$ cube.

Hence, additional cubes required are $= 6^3 - 4^3 = 152$.

8. 3   Eight cuts on one face will give 9 identical cubes. Now, the two cuts can be along the other two perpendicular directions.

So, maximum number of identical pieces $= 8 \times 2 \times 2$

$$= 32 \text{ pieces.}$$

For questions 9 to 12:
Total number of cubes = 216
$216 \Rightarrow 6 \times 6 \times 6 \therefore n = 6$
[Only visible faces can be painted.]
Number of cubes having three visible faces = 8 cubes.
Number of cubes having only two visible faces $= 12 \, (n - 2)$
$$= 12 \, (6 - 2) = 48.$$
Number of cubes having only one visible faces $= (n - 2)^2 \times 6$
$$= (6 - 2)^2 \times 6 = 96.$$
Number of cubes having no visible faces
$$= (n - 2)^3 = (6 - 2)^3 = 64.$$

9. 1   64 cubes have no face painted at all.

10. 3   96 cubes have only one face painted.

11. 3   48 cubes have only two faces painted.

12. 3   8 cubes have three faces painted.

For questions 13 to 16:
Total number of cubes = 64
$64 \Rightarrow 4 \times 4 \times 4$
Only visible faces can be painted.
Number of cubes having three visible faces = 8.
Number of cubes having only two visible faces = 12 (n − 2).
Number of cubes having only one visible face $= 6 \times (n - 2)^2$
$$= 6 \times 2^2 = 24.$$
Number of cubes invisible $= (n - 2)^3 = (4 - 2)^3 = 8$.

13. 3   8 cubes have no face painted at all.

14. 3   24 cubes have only one face painted.

15. 3   24 cubes have only two faces painted.

16. 3   8 cubes have three faces painted.

For questions 17 to 20:
It is given that there are six cubes which have exactly one face painted.
$\therefore 6 \times (n - 2)^2 = 6 \therefore (n - 2)^2 = 1 \therefore n = 3$

17. 3   Maximum number of cubes $= n^3 = 3^3 = 27$.

18. 1   Number of smaller cubes which have exactly two faces painted $= 12(n - 2) = 12 \times 1 = 12$

19. 2   Number of smaller cubes which have three faces painted = 8.

20. 1   Number of smaller cubes which have no face painted at all $= (n - 2)^3 = (3 - 2)^3 = 1$

13. Venn Diagram

For questions 1 to 4:
From the given data, we can draw the following Venn Diagram.

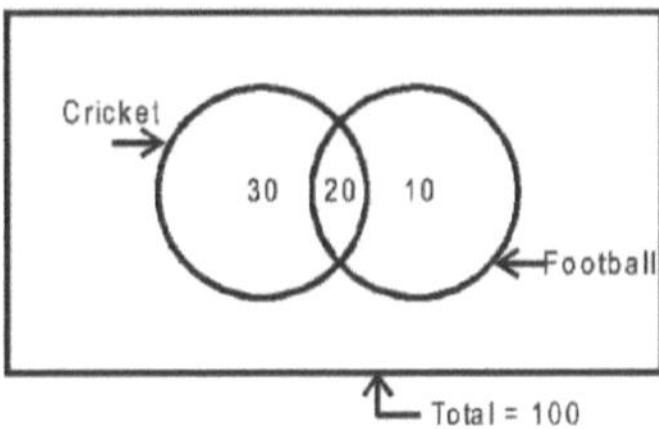

1. 3   30 students like only Cricket.

2. 1   10 students like only Football.

3. 1 $(100 - (30 + 20 + 10)) = 40$.
So, 40 students do not like either Cricket or Football.

4. 2 $(30 + 20 + 10) = 60$ students like either Football or Cricket.

For questions 5 to 8:
Total workers = 120

40% of $120 = \dfrac{40}{100} \times 120 = 48$.

10% of $120 = \dfrac{10}{100} \times 120 = 12$

20% of $120 = \dfrac{20}{100} \times 120 = 24$

Finally, we can draw the following Venn diagram.

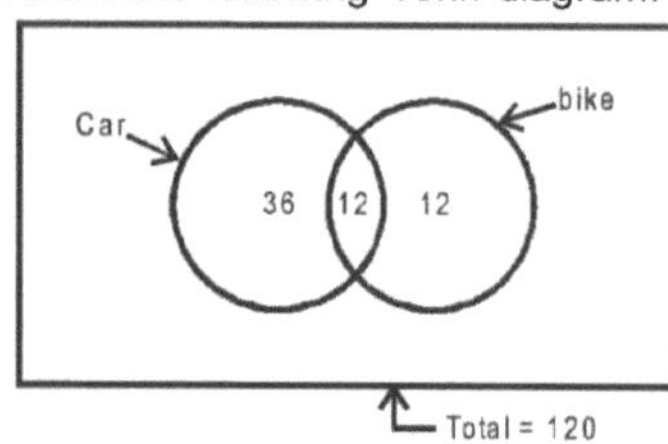

5. 1   36 workers own only car.

6. 4   12 workers own only bike.

7. 2   (36 + 12 + 12) = 60 workers own either a bike or a car.

8. 3   (120 − 60) = 60 workers own neither a bike nor a car.

For questions 9 to 12:
From the given data we can draw the following Venn diagram.

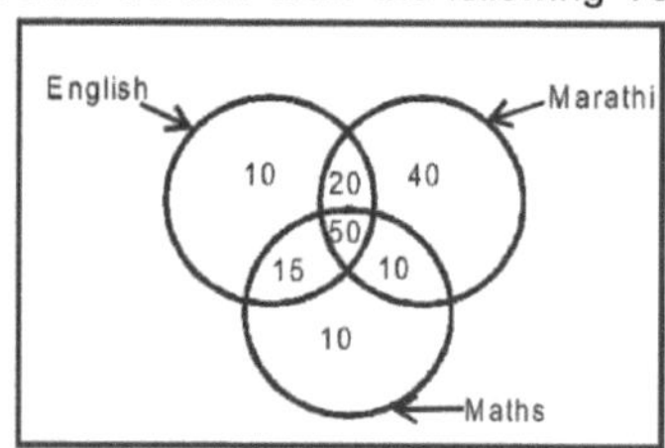

9. 1   10 students passed only in Maths.

10. 4   40 students passed only in Marathi.

11. 1   20 students passed both in Marathi and English but not in Maths.

12. 2   15 students passed only in Maths and English but not in Marathi.

For questions 13 to 16:
From the given information we can draw the following Venn diagram.

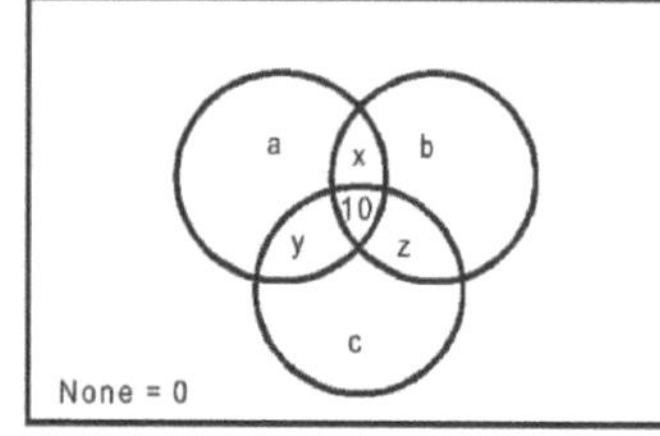

From the given data:
$a + b + c = 50$
$x + y + z = 25$

13. 1   Total students in the class = (a + b + c) + (x + y + z) + 10
= 50 + 25 + 10 = 85.

14. 2   Number of students who play at least two games
= (x + y + z) + 10
= 25 + 10 = 35

15. 4   Number of students who play cricket cannot be determined.

16. 3   25 students play exactly two games.
85 students play atleast one game.

$\therefore$ Percentage $= \dfrac{25}{85} \times 100 = 30\%$

For questions 17 to 20:
From the given information we can draw the following Venn diagram.

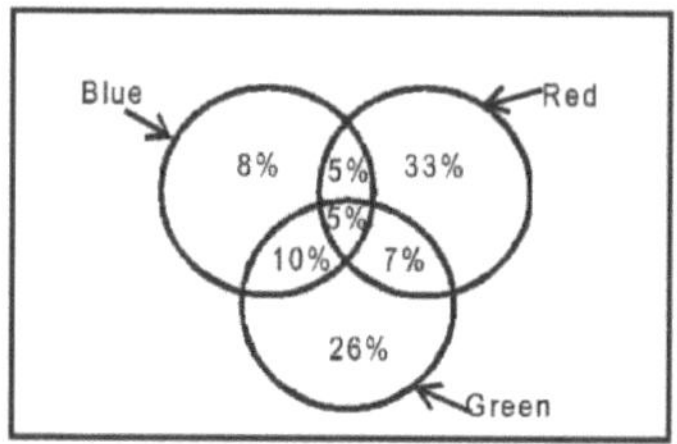

17. 2   Percentage of members who like atleast one colour
= (8 + 33 + 26 + 5 + 10 + 7 + 5)% = 94%
$\therefore$ 6% of the members do not like any of the three colours.
But it is given that,

Total members $\times \dfrac{6}{100} = 12$

$\therefore$ Total members = 200
200 members are there in the club.

18. 3   (5% + 7% + 10%) = 22% of 200
= 44 members like exactly two colours.

19. 4   (8% + 23% + 26%) = 67% of 200
= 134 members like exactly one colour.

20. 4   8% of 200 = 16 members like only blue.
33% of 200 = 66 members like only red.

$\therefore$ Percentage $= \dfrac{16}{66} \times 100 = 25\%$

For questions 21 to 24:
Out of four cars, people owning exactly two cars is possible for 6 different combinations.
They are:
Mercedez − Scorpio, Scorpio − Maruti,
Maruti − Innova, Innova − Mercedez,
Innova − Scorpio, Mercedez − Maruti
$\therefore$ Number of people having exactly two cars= 6 × 30 = 180.
40 people have all the four cars.   ...(Given)

To find number of people owning only one car, we have to subtract (30 × 30 + 40) from the given number of people owning a particular car.

[We will substract (3 × 30), because people owning two cars are 30 in number and for each car, there will be three ways of pairing with other cars.]
[We will substract 40 because, it is given that the number of people having all the four cars are 40.]

Answers and Explanations

So,
Number of people owning only Innova = 230 − 3 × 30 − 40 = 70
Number of people owning only Scorpio = 150 − 3 × 30 + 40 = 20
Number of people owning only Maruti = 175 − 3 × 30 + 40 = 45
Number of people owning only Mercedez
= 145 − 3 × 30 − 40 = 15

Total number of people owning exactly one car
= 70 + 20 +45 + 15 = 150

Total number of people owning atleast one car
= 150 + 180 + 40 = 370
400 is 74% of the total number of people.

∴ Total number of people $= \dfrac{370}{0.74} = 500$

Number of people do not have 500 − 370 = 130
From the above, we can draw the following Venn diagram.

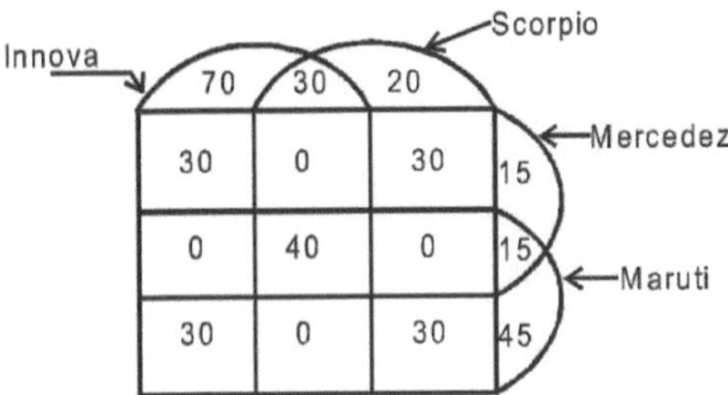

21. 1   180 people own exactly two cars.

22. 3   150 people own exactly one car.

23. 1   130 people do not own even one car.

24. 4   Percentage $= \dfrac{40}{370} \times 100 = 10.8\%$

For questions 25 to 28 :
From the given information, we can draw the following Venn diagram.

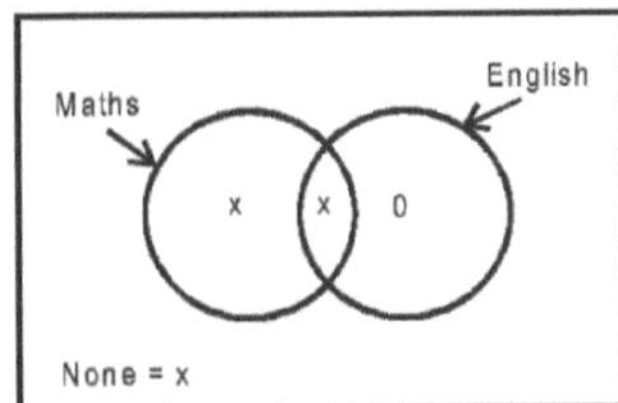

Total Student = 72
Maths : English = 6 : 3 = 2 : 1
Maths : Both Maths and English :
None = 12 : 6 : 6 = 2 : 1 : 1 = 2x : x : x
∴ x + x + x = 72
∴ x = 24

25. 3   24 students like only Maths.

26. 4   None like only English.

27. 4   24 students like both Maths and English.

28. 2   Percentage $= \dfrac{24}{72} \times 100 \approx 33\%$

For questions 29 and 30 :

29. 3   From the given data, we can draw the following Venn diagram.

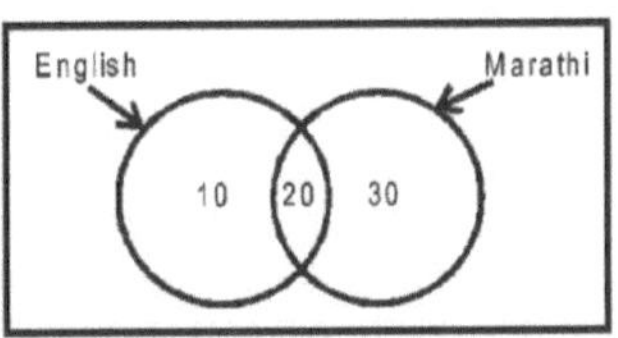

So, 10 students take only English.

30. 2   From the given information we can draw the following Venn diagram.

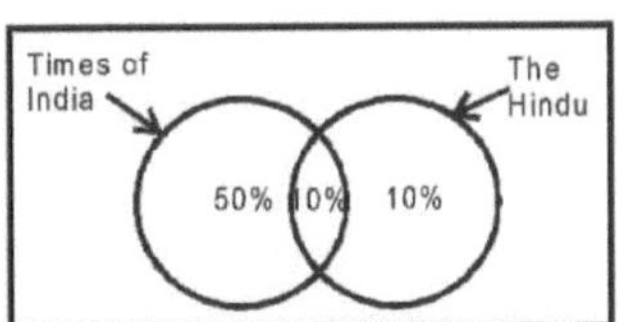

60% people read only one newspaper.
∴ 60% of 100 = 60

14. Non-Verbal Reasoning

1. 2   The shading moves in a particular order (anticlockwise). The lower object gets replaced by a new one after every step separated by 10 letters. A similar arrowhead occurs in the upper part of the figure in every third step.

2. 4   For the left figure, it follows the successive water image series. For the right figure, a similar figure repeats in every third step and each time a figure reappears, the left part remains the same while the half arrow in the right part gets rotated through 90°.

3. 3   From the first figure to the second, third to the fourth and fifth to the sixth, the arrow gets rotated through 90° ACW and moves to the adjacent side CW. In each of these pairs of figures, the other object rotates through 90° CW and alternately forms mirror and water images.

4. 2   In each step, every object moves two steps in anticlockwise directions; the last object (in anticlockwise direction) is lost and a new object appears in front of those already present.

5. 3   The objects in the upper row move clockwise by 3 steps. The objects the lower row move clockwise by 2 steps. In object at extreme right in last row move clockwise by 5 steps. In each step, the object that reaches extreme left position in top row gets replaced.

6. 2   The objects move in the following order: The top right object is new every time, the middle left object disappears and the movement is 1− 6 − 3 − 2 − 5 − 1 i.e. object at positon 1 moves to position 6, object at position 6 moves to position 3, object at position 3 moves to position 2, object at position 2 moves to position 5 and object at position 5 moves to postion 1.

7. 3   The objects move in the following order: A new object appears at the top right corner. The centre figure disappears. The movement is 1 − 7 − 8 − 2 − 9 − 4 − 6 − 5 − 3 − 1.

8. 3 The figure rotates through 90° CW in one step and 45° ACW in the next step. In each step, the black and the white portions interchange positions. Also, the arrowheads get inverted in each step and an extra arrowhead is added in every second step.

9. 4 The L-shaped object rotates through 90° ACW and moves CW one and a half sides along the boundary of the square. The circle gets black and white alternately and moves one and a half sides ACW along the boundary of the square. The figure at the centre gets black and white in successive steps and is replaced by a figure with one side more in every second step.

10. 4 The figure rotates CW through 45°, 45°, 90°, 90°, 135°, 135°. Each time a new half petal is added — first at the beginning and then at the end of the existing petals.

11. 1 The four corner figures move clockwise, the $ - O pair interchanges, every object of the middle column moves down, and there is a growth on the L figure.

12. 1 The number of lines increases. The number of new dots = the number of new lines.

13. 3 The arc revolves from one corner to the other in CW direction. The dot moves randomly. Number of '+' increases by one. Number of arrows increases by two and one successively.

14. 4 The lolly pop rotates through 45° and 90° alternately in CW direction, while the angle rotates through 90° CW.

15. 3 The curve moves one place at a time in ACW direction. Alternate figures have single and double lines. The doublelines immediately precede the curve, while the single line immediately follows the curve.

16. 4 The numbers on each face successively increase by 1.

17. 1 The rightmost two objects move one place in CW direction and come to the bottommost position. The topmost positions get new objects.

18. 2 The outer shade moves through 30° ACW, while the inner shade moves through 90° CW.

19. 2 Each of the arrow rotates through 45° ACW, while the curve successively moves in CW direction.

20. 4 Each object moves one place along the diagonal. The square rotates through 45°, the rectangle by 90° and the triangle by 180°.

21. 4 The single at the bottom rotate CW through 45°. The line in figure 4 should have been vertically inclined towards North-West.

22. 3 In every figure three arcs open towards the central figure and two away from it. While in figure 3, four arcs open towards central figure and one away from it.

23. 3 Minute hand minus the hour hand equals to the second hand 10 − 2 = 8; 12 − 3 = 9; 2 − 5 = − 3. But − 3 is not represented by the figure.

24. 3 The object N has given a water image in figure 3.

25. 1 Number of free short lines = number of sides of the polygon.

26. 4 The dot moves to successive peaks. When the number at the bottom is even, the arrow points clockwise, while, when the number is odd, the arrow points anticlockwise.

27. 3 In all other figures, the number of enclosed space is three, while in figure 3, it is four.

28. 4 Quadrants 1 and 2 are mirror images of each other. Quadrant 4 is a water image of quadrant 2. While quadrant 3 is obtained by rotating quadrant 4 by 90° CW.

29. 3 By rotating the figure, you can get every other figure, but you will never get figure 3.

30. 2 In every other figure, the top and the bottom rows have two arcs pointing in one direction and one in opposite direction. In figure 2, the bottom row has all the three arcs pointing in one direction.

31. 2 The arrow moves successively from one vertex to another in anticlockwise direction. Whenever the dot is at the top, we have a normal 'T'. While when the dot is at the bottom, we have an inverted 'T'. This does not happen in figure 2.

32. 4 In all other figures, there is a mathematical operator outside the quadrilateral. In figure 4, there is letter 'Q'.

33. 4 In every figure, three arrows are pointing towards top, two arrows are pointing towards bottom, two are pointing towards right and one towards the left. The central object is rotating through 90° CW in successive figures. In figure 4, there are three arrows pointing towards bottom and one towards right.

34. 1 Figure 1 is different from others. In all the other figures, one end is a straight-line and the other is a curve, while in figure 1 both the ends are curves.

35. 2 The main object can be rotated to get all the other figures except 2. You will never get figure 2 unless you take a mirror image of the object.

36. 4 In no other figure you will find enclosed spaces.

37. 4 Each type of element always occurs in pairs which is not the same as given in option (4).

38. 4 Every figure has some curves and lines. In every figure a curve intersects with a line. In figure 4, two lines intersect.

39. 4 Only figure 4 has a closed object.

40. 3 The number of arrowheads increases by one in successive figures. Alternate figures have a '+' and 'x'. The half-shaded circle is moving through 90° CW direction. Among two central arrows, one remains stationary, while the other one rotates through 45° in ACW direction. The 'P' rotates through 90° in CW direction in successive figures. The last movement happens wrongly in figure 3.

Answers and Explanations

15. Logical Deductions and Connectives

1. 1 The middle term 'icecreams' is distributed.
As, All + All = All/some, hence, "All cakes are toffees" or "some toffees are cakes". Only conclusion (I) follows.

2. 3 The middle term 'pencils' is distributed.
As, All + All = All/Some hence, "All pens are erasers" or "some erasers are pen".
Both conclusion (I) and (II) follow.

3. 2 The middle term 'bottles' is distributed. But both 'cans' and 'tanks' or not distributed.
Hence, we can conclude 'Some cans are tanks' or 'some tanks are cans'.
Conclusion (I) can't follow, as 'tanks' is distributed in the conclusion which is not possible as 'tanks' is not distributed in the premise. Hence, only conclusion (II) can be drawn.

4. 4 The middle term 'gold' is distributed in the first statement (premise).
But, we know that All + Some = Some, whereas both the conclusions are universal statements (All). Hence, none of the conclusion follows.

5. 1 The middle term 'fools' is distributed in the first statement.
As, All + Some = Some, hence
'Some wise are men' or 'some men are wise'.
Hence, only conclusion (I) follows.

6. 1 The middle term 'professor' is distributed in the second statement
As, All + No = No/Some not, hence 'No teacher is Principal' or 'No Principal is teacher' or 'Some teacher are not Principal' or 'Some Principal are not teacher'.
Hence, only conclusion (I) follows.

7. 2 The middles term 'animal' is distributed in second statement. Only conclusion (II) i.e. 'cows are not herbivorous' or 'All cows are not herbivorous'.

8. 2 The middle term 'heros' is distributed in both the statements, so a conclusion can be drawn. The conclusion will be a negation as statement (II) is in negation. Also 'popular' should not be distributed in the conclusion as 'popular' is not distributed in the premise.
Hence, only conclusion (II) i.e. 'Some popular are not kind' follows.

9. 3 The middle term 'bags' is distributed in the second statement.
As, All + No = No
Hence, conclusion 'No coats are toys' can be drawn which is further equivalent to 'No toys are coats.' Conclusion (I) and (II) both can be drawn.

10. 2 The middle term 'brave' is distributed in second statement.
As, some + Not = Some Not
Hence, 'Some men are not warriors' is the drawn conclusion.

Note: Conclusion 'Some warriors are not men' can not be drawn as 'men' is not distributed in premise and therefore it cannot be distributed in conclusion.

11. 1 The middle terms 'locks' is distributed in the first statement.
As, some + Not = Some Not
Hence, the conclusion 'Some spoons are not keys' can be drawn.

12. 2 The middle term 'cows' is distributed is statement (II).
As, All + Some not = Some not
Hence, conclusion (II) 'Some horses are not dogs' can be drawn.

13. 1 The middle term 'rocks' is distributed in Statement (II). As, All + Some + Some not = Some not.
Hence, conclusion (I) i.e., 'Some clips are not stones.' can be drawn.

14. 4 The middle term 'girls' is not distributed in either of the statements.
More over, Some + Some = No conclusion
Hence, no conclusion follows.

15. 4 The middle term 'helpful' is not distributed in either of the statements. Moreover,
Some + Some = No conclusion (as per rule [6])
Hence, no conclusion can be drawn.

16. 4 Although, the middle term 'scooters' is distributed in statement (II) but still no conclusion can be drawn as Some + Some Not = No conclusion.

17. 4 Some + Some Not = No conclusion
Hence, no conclusion can be drawn despite middle term 'intelligent' being distributed in the first statement.

18. 4 Some Not + Some Not = No conclusion
Remember Rule [5] and Rule [6] of "Rules for deductions"

19. 4 No + Some Not = No conclusion
As per Rule [5] of "Rules for deductions" two negative statements cannot yield a conclusion.

20. 4 No + No = No conclusion
As per Rule [5] of "Rules for deductions" no conclusion can be drawn.

21. 4 The middle terms 'pages' is not distributed in either of the statements. Hence, as per Rule [2], no conclusion can be drawn.

22. 4 The middle terms 'oranges' is not distributed in either of the statements. Hence, as per Rule [2], no conclusion can be drawn.

23. 4 The middle term 'knights' is not distributed in either of the statements.
Hence, no conclusion can be drawn.

24. 4 The middle term 'murderer' is not distributed in either of the statements.
Hence, no conclusion can be drawn.

25. 4 The middle term 'thieves' is not distributed is either of the statements.
Hence, no conclusion can be drawn.

26. 4 If $\boxed{\text{it rains}}$, then $\boxed{\text{I'll wear a raincoat}}$

For statement "If p, then q",

the implications are $p \Rightarrow q$ and $\sim q \Rightarrow \sim p$.

$\therefore$ Both (2) and (3) logically follow.

27. 1 If $\boxed{\text{gold is silver}}$, then $\boxed{\text{copper is bronze}}$.

For statement "If p, then q" the implications are $p \Rightarrow q$ and $\sim q \Rightarrow \sim p$.

Hence, by implication $\sim q \Rightarrow \sim p$, statement (1) follows.

28. 2 $\boxed{\text{The ground is wet}}$, if $\boxed{\text{the water is in abundance}}$.

For statement "q, if p" implications are $p \Rightarrow q$ and $\sim q \Rightarrow \sim p$.

Hence, by implication $\sim q \Rightarrow \sim p$ statement (2) follows.

29. 2 Whenever $\boxed{\text{Rahul is hungry}}$, $\boxed{\text{Rahul eats}}$.

For statement "Whenever p, q" the implications are $p \Rightarrow q$ and $\sim q \Rightarrow \sim p$.

Hence, by implication $\sim q \Rightarrow \sim p$, statement (2) follows.

30. 4 $\boxed{\text{The minister is elected}}$, whenever $\boxed{\text{he wins the elections}}$.

For statement "q, whenever p" the implications are $p \Rightarrow q$ and $\sim q \Rightarrow \sim p$.

Hence, by implication $p \Rightarrow q$, statement (4) follows.

31. 4 Either $\boxed{\text{the pen is heavy}}$ or $\boxed{\text{the pencil is light}}$.

For statement "Either p or q" the implications are $\sim p \Rightarrow q$ and $\sim q \Rightarrow p$.

Hence, both the statement (1) and (2) are the logical conclusions.

32. 4 Either $\boxed{\text{the tank in empty}}$ or $\boxed{\text{the plug is short}}$.

For statement "Either p or q" the implication are $\sim p \Rightarrow q$ and $\sim q \Rightarrow p$.

But none of such statements is present in the answer options.

33. 4 Unless $\boxed{\text{Dhoni is the captain}}$, $\boxed{\text{India will lose all its matches}}$.

For statement "Unless p, q", the implications are $\sim p \Rightarrow q$ and $\sim q \Rightarrow p$.

Both the statement (1) and (2) can be derived.

34. 1 Unless $\boxed{\text{the tea is hot}}$, $\boxed{\text{Rohan will eat cake}}$.

For statement "Unless p, q" the implications are $\sim p \Rightarrow q$ and $\sim q \Rightarrow p$.

Hence by the implication $\sim p \Rightarrow q$, statement (1) follows.

35. 2 $\boxed{\text{Sonu will play cricket}}$, unless $\boxed{\text{Sonu will play cricket}}$,

For statement "q, unless p", the implications are $\sim p \Rightarrow q$ and $\sim q \Rightarrow p$.

Hence by implication $\sim p \Rightarrow q$, statement (2) follows.

36. 3 $\boxed{\text{He drinks the}}$, only if $\boxed{\text{she drinks coffee}}$.

For statement "q, only if p," the implications are $q \Rightarrow p$ and $\sim p \Rightarrow \sim q$.

Hence, but he the statements (1) and (2) follows.

37. 1 Only if $\boxed{\text{he wins the race}}$, $\boxed{\text{he will win a a gold medal}}$.

For statement "Only if p, q", the implications are $q \Rightarrow p$ and $\sim p \Rightarrow q$.

Hence, by the implication $\sim p \Rightarrow \sim q$, statement (1) follows.

38. 3 Only if $\boxed{\text{Suni's parents are with him}}$, $\boxed{\text{he will go to circus}}$.

For statement "Only if p, q", the implications are $q \Rightarrow p$ and $\sim p \Rightarrow \sim q$.

Hence by the implication $q \Rightarrow p$ statement (3) follows.

39. 4 $\boxed{\text{Amit dances}}$, if and only if $\boxed{\text{Rahul sings}}$.

For statement "p, if and only if q" the implications are $p \Rightarrow q, q \Rightarrow p, \sim p \Rightarrow \sim q$ and $\sim q \Rightarrow \sim p$.

Hence, by the implication $q \Rightarrow p$, statement (1) follows, by $p \Rightarrow q$, statement (2) follows and by $\sim p \Rightarrow \sim q$, statement (3) follows.

40. 3 $\boxed{\text{Ajay is honest}}$, if and only if $\boxed{\text{Raja is dishonest}}$.

For statement "p, if and only if q" the implications are $p \Rightarrow q, q \Rightarrow p, \sim p \Rightarrow \sim q$ and $\sim q \Rightarrow \sim p$.

Hence, by implication $q \Rightarrow p$, statement (3) follows.

9. Articles

Grammar Review Exercise – 1

1. 2 Usual collocation.

2. 2 Usual collocation.

3. 2 'Watching a film' is the correct phrase.

4. 1 Conditonal involving present tense in the main clause.

5. 1 They is plural, so plural verb and simple present tense.

6. 4 Conditional statement so singular verb 'leaves'.

7. 1 Simple present singular verb.

8. 2 Present participle making has to be used.

9. 3 Gerund 'working' should be used.

10. 3 'Since' indicates that it is present perfect tense.

11. 1 'So far' indicates past tense.

12. 4 'Yet' indicates present perfect tense.

13. 3 'Since' indicates present perfect tense.

14. 4 'Since yesterday' indicates present perfect continuous tense.

15. 2 Point of time in the past.

16. 4 'to' +gerund should be used.

17. 2 Conditional statement, so simple present.

18. 1 A gerund is required with 'to'.

19. 3 Main clause present tense only can be followed by present in subordinate clause.

20. 2 Universal truth so simple present

21. 4 'Since' indicates the use of present perfect continuous tense.

22. 4 Indicates an event that should have happened.

23. 1 Improbable, imaginary (wish) uses 'were'.

24. 2 Reported speech - 'will' changes to 'would'.

25. 3 Past continuous is most appropriate here for reported speech.

26. 3 Reported speech, so past continuous.

27. 1 Since the action has to take place, so future tense is used.

28. 2 Conditional statement, so simple present tense is used.

29. 2 Present tense or future tense in main clause is followed by any tense not so for past tense.

30. 4 Conditional statement, so simple present tense is used.

31. 1 Improbable conditional statement as in last question.

32. 1 Improbable conditional.

33. 3 Past for past is past perfect.

34. 4 In reported speech, simple past changes to past perfect.

35. 3 Unfulfilled conditional

36. 4 Imaginary conditional

37. 3 Probable conditional

38. 2 'Did not meet'.

39. 3 has + 3rd form of the verb (gone)

40. 3 bare infinitive

41. 2 'Used to' takes simple present tense.

42. 2 Conditional in future tense take present tense

43. 1 Conditional in present/future tense. Refer to previous question.

44. 4 Conditional in present/future tense.

45. 3 Noun / gerend / noun clause is required as object.

46. 1 Past tense is required.

47. 2 'lest' takes future tense.

48. 1 Noun/gerund as object of enjoys

49. 2 Indicates point of time.

50. 1 Imaginary conditional.

Grammar Review Exercise – 2

1. 2 'Knock out' is the correct answer . It means to cause someone to become unconscious.

2. 2 'Made out' means to claim or pretend something.

3. 3 The correct answer is (3). 'Come around' means to regain consciousness.

4. 1 'Pull out of' something means to stop taking part in something.

5. 4 The correct answer is (4).'Keep in' someone means not to let someone go anywhere.

6. 1 'Hinge on' means to depend on something so (1) is the answer.

7. 3   'Put up' means to provide money to pay for something so option (3) is the answer.

8. 4   'Dish out ' means to distribute something.

9 .3   'Put up' means to provide accommodation temporarily.

10. 1   To 'smash up' means to damage something badly so that it is in pieces,so option (1) is the answer.

11. 1   In the question statement , 'hasn't' refers to the subject 'science teacher' so it takes a singular form. In the answer, 'you' becomes the subject and hence it takes the phrasal verb 'haven't'.

12. 3   'The perfume odour' becomes the subject when the sentence is converted to passive voice. Similarly, the verb 'spreads' changes to 'is spread' in the passive voice as the verb has to be used in simple present tense only.

13. 1   The object 'me' changes to the subject 'I'. Similarly, only option (1) is in simple past tense as given in the question statement. Hence, answer is (1).

14. 4   The last sentence is in present tense and correctly changes the object 'me' to subject 'I' and vice versa.

15. 2   Only option (2) is in the simple past tense as the question statement.

16. 1   Option (1) is the correct answer as it rightly uses 'the next day' in indirect form for the word 'tomorrow' used in direct speech.

17. 1   Only option (1) changes 'will' to 'would'.

18. 4   Option (4) is correct since the verb 'may' in direct speech appropriately changes to 'might' in indirect speech.

19. 1   Option (1) correctly uses the past perfect form of the verb as given in the question statement.

20. 4   Since option (4) rightly uses the simple past form of the verb given in the question statement, it has to be the most appropriate answer.

21. 1   '1' is the right answer since it uses the past tense as used in indirect speech.

22. 2   '2' is the right option since it is in indirect speech.

23. 4   '4' is the right option since it uses the past tense as used in indirect speech.

24. 1   '1' is the right option.

25. 4   '4' is the right option.

26. 3   Since the 'event' that is being talked about is a particular event, 'the' is used.

27. 3   Since the statement is talking about a particular process 'absorption', 'the' is used.

28. 1   Since the verb 'stare' refers to a particular 'menu', so definite article 'the' is used.

29. 2   'Liver' is the main subject which is being talked about. 'Weight' is talked about only in the latter part of the sentence and since it is a common noun, the article being used is 'a' .

30. 2   Since the 'piece of wood' is not particular, so 'a' is used.

31. 2   'It was an unusually difficult answer'. Here, the indefinite article 'an' should be used before the word beginning with the vowel 'u'.

32. 1   'World peace is a very commonly debated topic'. Here, the indefinite article 'a' should be used.

33. 2   'An exaggerated statement is called a hyperbole.' Here, the indefinite article 'an' should be used before the word beginning with the vowel 'e'.

34. 3   'One who gives directions from behind the scene is a prompter.'
Here, the definite article 'the' should be used because the sentence refers to a specific job description.

35. 2   'An assistant came up to me and asked me if I needed assistance.' Here, the indefinite article 'an' should be used with the vowel 'a'. It also suggests that any assistant approached him.

36. 1   The present perfect continuous tense has been used correctly in the given sentence. Option (2) uses past tense that changes the meaning of the given sentence. Option (3) contains an incorrect verb 'have' and (4) refers to the future tense. So, option (1) is correct.

37. 3   In the given sentence the simple present form 'When you receive' should be used. 'When' expresses a particular time so simple present should be used. Option (1) uses past perfect, (2) uses the future continuous tense and (4) uses the past tense and distorts the sentence. So, option (3) is correct.

38. 1   The past continuous is used to indicate an action which was interrupted. Option (2) uses the past perfect which is incorrect. Option (3) changes the meaning of the given sentence. Option (4) uses the past perfect continuous. So, option (1) is correct.

39. 2   The sentence is in past continuous tense so it should be 'was talking'. So, option (2) is correct.

40. 4   Here the sentence expresses a plan that is to be followed in the future. So, 'I am not going to do' should be used here.

41. 1	42. 4	43. 2	44. 3	45. 2
46. 3	47. 4	48. 2	49. 3	50. 4

Grammar Review Exercise – 3

1. 1	2. 3	3. 2	4. 4	5. 2

6. 1   Since the sentence is talking about a specific car, the definite article 'the' is used.

7. 3   The correct article to be used here is 'a' because the word 'European' does not have the vowel sound of 'e'. Rather it begins with the consonant sound of the letter 'u'.

Answers and Explanations

8. 2   Sine the sentence is talking about a particular board of directors, the definite article 'the' has to be used in the sentence.

9. 2   The correct article to be used here is 'an' as the word 'audacious' has been used after the blank.

10. 4   The sentence does not require any specific article.

11. 1   The subject 'Jack' changes to the object form in the passive voice and the present perfect form of the verb is also maintained in the passive voice. Hence, (1) is the correct answer.

12. 3   The answer option correctly places the subject "The Chopras' in the object form and also maintains the present continuous form of the verb.

13. 3   Option (3) appropriately places 'this bill' as the subject and also uses the correct form of the verb.

14. 3   This option correctly makes 'the final decision' its subject and so this is the correct answer.

15. 2   This option makes "The entire show' its subject and uses 'we' in the objective form i.e. 'us'.

16. 1   '1' is the correct option because the sentence is in active voice in which the 'Board of Trustees had approved..' Other options are factually and grammatically incorrect.

17. 4   '4' is the correct option because it is in active voice and uses the simple past tense as given in the original sentence.

18. 3   '3' is the correct option because it is the only option that is in active voice.

19. 3   '3' is the option because it is in active voice whereas other options are in passive voice.

20. 1   '1' is the correct option because it gives the active voice for the original statement.

21. 1   '1' is the right answer since it uses the past tense as used in indirect speech.

22. 2   '2' is the right option since it is in indirect speech.

23. 4   '4' is the right option since it uses the past tense as used in indirect speech.

24. 1   '1' is the right option.

25. 4   '4' is the right option.

26. 2   '2' is the correct option because it is written within quotation marks and the present tense is used appropriately. 'a' is inappropriate because in that case 'I' seems to be unaware that his help maybe required whereas the given sentence reveals that help is needed but whether 'I' decides to help him or not that is the real question.

27. 1   '1' is the correct option because the wording is appropriate. Options '3' and '4' have a harsh tone because 'Churchill' is given within inverted commas and hence inappropriate.

28. 2   '2' is the right option.

29. 3   '3' is the correct option because it uses the present tense and the quotation marks appropriately.

30. 3   '3' is the correct option.

31. 4   The correct phrasal verb is 'to get through to' which means to make someone understand something.

32. 1   The correct phrasal verb is 'muddled through' which means to succeed in doing something although in not a very good manner.

33. 3   The correct phrasal verb that is suitable for the given sentence is 'pin down' which means to force someone to give prcise information or firm opinion on something.

34. 2   The correct phrasal verb to be used here is 'keep off' which means to stay away from.

35. 4   The correct phrasal verb to be used here is 'impressed on' which means to give emphasis on something.

36. 2	37. 4	38. 2	39. 4	40. 3
41. 4	42. 3	43. 3	44. 4	45. 3
46. 4	47. 3	48. 1	49. 2	50. 3

10. Reading Comprehension

Passage – 1

1. 1   Refer to 2nd para 1st line.

2. 3   Refer 4th para 1st line.

3. 2   Refer 4th para 2nd line.

4. 4   Refer 4th para last line

5. 4   1, 2, 3 are mentioned in the passage the passage is discussed about Kerouac and its his writings.

6. 2

Passage – 2

1. 4   Refer to the 1st line of passage

2. 3   Except Elvis Presley all are mentioned in 1st para, 3rd line.

3. 4   Refer 1st para 4th and 5th lines.

4. 4   Refer 1st para 1st line

5. 3   3rd para 2nd line.

6. 2   Refer 2nd para.

Passage – 3

1. 3   Refer 1st para 3rd line

2. 3   Except (3), monotremes share all other qualities with mammals.

3. 3   Refer 3rd para 2 and 3 lines.

4. 4   Refer 1st para last line

5. 4

6. 1   Last para 3rd line.

Passage – 4

1. 2   Refer 1st para 1st line

2. 4   Refer 1st para 3rd line

3. 3   Refer 1st para 8th line

4. 1   Refer 2nd para 4th and 5th line

5. 4   Refer 2nd para 6th to 8th line

Passage – 5

1. 3   1st para 3rd lines

2. 4   2nd para last 2 lines

3. 4   2nd para 3rd and 4th lines.

4. 2   2nd para 4th and 5th lines.

5. 4   There is no information available to explain it fully.

▌ I I. Style of RC Passages

Argumentative Style Passages

Passage – 1

1. 4   Second line of the first paragraph clearly indicates (4).

2. 3   First line of the second paragraph imply (3).

3. 1   Last paragraph clearly implies (1).

4. 3   Refer to first line of the 4th paragraph.

5. 4   Refer to the last line of 4th paragraph.

Passage – 2

6. 3   Refer to the 2nd line of the 1st paragraph.

7. 4   Refer to the first line of the last paragraph. The meaning implied is in (4).

8. 1   The second line of the second paragraph tells that Zimbabwe is more interested in diamond mines than restoring peace in Congo.

9. 3   The opening statement of the passage introduces that there have been 'Violent' conflicts' in African continent.

10. 3   Read the last line of the last paragraph. It clearly indicates that use of tanks and infantry has been useless.

Passage – 3

11. 3   The author is fighting for animal rights in general and says that they have equal rights as humans.

12. 1   The first sentence of the last paragraph mentions "Homo sapiens'.

13. 2   The first line of the passage says that such societies believed that 'animals deserve protection when human interests are not at stake'. This means that humans' and animals' interests are should be different.

14. 3   The first line of second paragraph says that 'non human animals should not be held criminally responsible for what they do'. This means that the author disagrees with (2).

15. 4   Refer to second line of the last paragraph.

Philosophical Style Passages

Passage – 1

1. 1   Refer to the 4th line, 3rd paragraph of the passage. Similar hint is also given in the 1st line of the last paragraph of the passage.

2. 3   'Abasement' means the act of being low or lowering one's reputation. Hence, option (3).

3. 4   Refer to the second last line, 3rd paragraph of the passage.

4. 4   Refer to 1st line, 4th paragraph of the passage.

5. 2   Refer to the 2nd and 3rd lines of the first paragraph of the passage.

Passage – 2

6. 2   Refer to the 3rd line, 1st paragraph of the passage.

7. 3   According to the passage, 'indiscreet' means lacking prudence, judgement and introspection.
Hence, option (3).

8. 2   The first line of the passage refutes the idea presented in (2). It says "A virtue such as honesty is not just a tendency to do what is honest...",

9. 4   Refer to the second last line of the first paragraph. All except (4) are mentioned.

10. 4   The last line of the first paragraph and the first line of the second paragraph imply (4). The rest of the options are not true.

Passage – 3

11. 2   Refer to the first line of the second paragraph.

12. 3   Refer to second last line of the passage. Faith is metaphysical and not science.

Answers and Explanations

13. 4 The first line of the passage says that popper holds that "orthodoxy is the death of knowledge". This makes (4) correct.

14. 1 Third line of the second paragraph gives the definition of falsification. It says that science means guesses followed by criticism. If these guesses (hypotheses) match (clash) with observation, they are counted as scientific.

15. 2 Refer to the last line of the first passage. It clearly indicates that "homage of reason" would be approved by God than "blind folded fear". This is restated in (2).

Passage – 4

16. 4 The passage is about virtue lying between vices - so option (4) is most appropriate.

17. 2 The first two lines of the second paragraph hold the answer.

18. 1 First line of the second paragraph mentions Aristotle wrote the book dealing with the theory of the mean.

19. 1 Aristotle feels that virtues should be in the "right amount". This is mentioned in the third paragraph. So only option (1) is the correct.

20. 1 The first line of the fourth paragraph clearly mentions that mean does not mean "a mathematical middle".

Factual Style Passages

Passage – 1

1. 2 The passage mentions that earthquakes release stress as mentioned in the 2nd line of the first paragraph of the passage.

2. 2 Earthquakes don't last for more than a minute.

3. 1 It acts like the crust.

4. 3 Tectonics works on the movement of the continent as stated in the 1st line of the last paragraph of the passage.

5. 2 Refer to the 3rd line, last paragraph of the passage.

Passage – 2

6. 4 Education is the highest realization of one's capability as stated in the 2nd line of the first paragraph of the passage.

7. 3 A person with specialized knowledge and degrees.

8. 4 The lack of a multi-dimensional approach leads into a lack of awareness regarding other fields.

9. 1 The lines "we learn those things quickly and easily to which we are exposed early and frequently" supports option (1).

10. 3 Refer to the 3rd line, last paragraph of the passage.

Passage – 3

11. 2 Culture and technology are the saviors.

12. 2 Manmade skills aided survival.

13. 4 Culture has helped population growth.

14. 1 The rapid growth of culture deterred natural selection.

15. 3 The lines "culture provided the necessary warmth during winter times" makes option (3) correct.

Analytical Style Passages

Passage – 1

1. 3 The 1st line clearly mentions that incubation causes the author to show lifelong sympathy for children and animals.

2. 4 'Baa Baa, Black Sheep' is Kipling's autobiographical story.

3. 1 While Saki's father was away to India, he and his siblings were deprived of love and affection.

4. 2 "Abandoned to the care of cold and neurotic aunts", these lines from the passage substantiate option (2).

5. 4 The passage very clearly mentions the "cresting" of the suffrage movement.

Passage – 2

6. 1 Mirrors are made of highly polished metal or of glass with a coating of metal on the back.

7. 2 The passage talks about mirrors being able to reflect back incident light.

8. 1 Mirrors help scientist in exploring questions concerning perception and cognition.

9. 4 The passage talks about healing post- stroke paralysis.

10. 1 The brain changes two-dimensional images, reconstructing them into three- dimensional images.

Passage – 3

11. 2 The dream of a snake forming a ring helped Kekulé to deduce that benzene's structure formed a ring.

12. 3 The realization led to an improved understanding of organic chemistry.

13. 3 The passages mentions that once we sleep the brain starts handling the day's inputs.

14. 2 As discussed in the passage, the technique is a familiar condition faced by many.

15. 2   Slumber helps us to arrive at the right answers because it helps in unraveling what we have learnt.

Narrative Style Passages

Passage – 1

1. 1   The passage mentions that the speaker was in a state of despair.

2. 4   The passage describes the refuge provider as an old man.

3. 3   Option (3) is correct.

4. 2   In the passage, the daughter sees slavery coming to an end if the Free states came to know about the sinful activities.

5. 4   The passage ends on a note of yearning making option (4) correct.

Passage – 2

6. 2   From the lines "in hopes that one day I will find the life that was destined for me", it can be inferred that there is unhappiness in life.

7. 1   The author states that the pursuit of love is not his objective because he has experienced true love.

8. 2   The passage discusses the incompleteness of true love without happiness.

9. 4   The speaker states that he possesses everything except for true happiness.

10. 2   Admitting the problem is discussed as the first step towards resolving the problem.

PART – 4 : VERBAL ABILITY / VOCABULARY

5. Critical Reasoning

Practice Exercise – Critical Reasoning

1. 3   We have to check how applicable Plato's comment is in the present context.

2. 2   The first speaker has a rosy outlook and the second is quite a cynic.

3. 3   The sentence is about preventing exploitation of labour and so (3) is the best answer.

4. 2   The author attributes restraint directly to effectiveness in preventing highway deaths.

5. 1   (1) weakens the conclusion by stating that the financial motives are best realised through the Olympic route.

6. 3   Considering the extent of the technologist's duties, he is probably the only saviour of the consumer.

7. 4   The definition of embezzlement is attacked, and so the premise of 'on behalf of other people' does not hold good.

8. 1   'Metaphor' means to have an image of credibility as the mainstay.

9. 4   We learn lessons first of all by determining what went wrong, how it went wrong, when it started going wrong, where and so on ... to prevent future accidents.

10. 2   If advertisements have such a profound effect on buyer behaviour, then consumers can be easily led.

11. 3   This new route falls pat in-between the old route and the suggested route in terms of distance. So it's worth considering.

12. 2   There can be no possible relation between elephants and mice to justify any conclusion.

13. 4   The best rebut to the argument can come by stating that the 1970 figures were themselves not representative of the true picture of the number of marriages versus the number of unmarried couples.

14. 4   The author definitely takes a large period of 10 years to study changing trends.

15. 4   The argument does not blame the ignorant consumer or the manipulative industrialists.

16. 3   The word here need not necessarily be taken in the literal sense — 'common' being 'rare' and 'jumbo' being 'diminutive'.

17. 2   People who try drugs just for the heck of it are likely to experiment again and again.

18. 3   The story starts with 'Sally overslept' and ends with 'tripped in hole'.

19. 3   Amit assumes that earthlings are intelligent enough to warrant extra-terrestrial interest.

20. 1   This is an example of circular reasoning, if X, then Y. Y, so X.

21. 4   Money was an incentive for innovative solutions to attract more consumers.

22. 4   The increase in rum sales and the increase in preachers' wages can both be attributed to rising living standards.

23. 4   The owners want to make sure that the new move will contribute to the profits as well.

24. 4   If the breast has been shown to be sensitive to radiation-induced cancer, then the researchers' concern is valid.

25. 3   The direct personal acquaintance was not there, it entered towards the end of the correspondence.

26. 2   The government has the final say in both the definition and use of private property.

Answers and Explanations

27. 4 This is a case of generalizing a phenomenon from specific instances.

28. 3 There is nothing intrinsically different in Eena's and Meena's arguments.

29. 3 (3) is the best answer from the humanitarian point of view.

30. 4 (2) is an unexplored option in the literal sense, we do not know how far (1) and (3) helps to relieve the tension.

31. 3 The numbers are to be deciphered, so we cannot assume anything about them unless we work on the letters.

32. 2 (1), (3), and (4) are all deterring factors, whereas (2) indirectly helps to reduce cars on the road.

33. 4 The safest and most reasonable conclusion would be (4) since 80% of traffic fatalities occur at the general speed of under 35 miles per hour and within 25 miles.

34. 4 (4) attributes the poor performance of the central city schoolchildren to overcrowding in classrooms and not on the lack of fresh air.

35. 2 If it's too early to predict the long-term results of fluoridation, then the proponents' claim is questionable.

36. 4 John can never cross the river first because, then Mr Jones will have to leave him behind alone on the river bank when he comes back to the Smiths.

37. 4 A natural right can be violated in lawless societies but the rights nonetheless do exist.

38. 4 (4) is the most telling illustration of a majority party being crippled by polarity.

39. 3 If the officeholder is being pulled from both ends by his constituency and his party leader, then the shift is more towards the local constituency.

40. 3 Since the speaker is focusing on the superior facilities of medical attention in the United States, an objection would be to question the validity of this observation. The other choices are specific and touches only specific aspects of the problem.

41. 1 If ABC's market is not characterized by competition, then the market is not monopolistic.

42. 2 (2) attributes the presence of the frost to factors other than the full moon, i.e. the absence of the cloud cover.

43. 4 If nature should take its own course, medical sciences can have little say anyway. The term 'burden' stays undefined. The 'to do' or 'not to do' factor provides no solution either through euthanasia or natural causes.

44. 4 If there were just a handful of graduates in FTCI, the statistics offer little support. 'Jobs' is too vague a term. Then so is 'help'.

45. 4 The difference between Gangotri water and imported water is not conspicuous. But cold springs does get sold to status conscious Indian families. The technical aspect of bottling is not important here.

46. 1 (II) and (III) touch the frontier of credibility. (I) is a valid answer as similar crimes are attributed to similar criminals.

47. 2 If students filled up the questionnaire after a particularly horrendous mid-term examination, the ratings are likely to be biased.

48. 4 The new trade bill can decrease the country's trade deficit.

49. 4 All choices are tinted with doubtful terms 'for some ailments', 'does not treat', 'does not recommend'.

50. 4 If the response is 'no', then the respondent is confessing to gender discrimination in the past. A 'yes' reply would be unimaginable. Also before replying, the responder may question the assumptions.

COMPANY SPECIFIC MOCKS

MOCK -1

(HCL - I)

1. In a cycle race there are 5 persons named as J, K, L, M, N participated for 5 positions so that in how many number of ways can M make always before N?
   - (a) 50
   - (b) 60
   - (c) 70
   - (d) 80

2. There are 1000 junior and 800 senior students in a class. And there are 60 sibling pairs where each pair has 1 junior and 1 senior. 1 student is chosen from senior and 1 from junior randomly. What is the probability that the two selected students are from a sibling pair?
   - (a) 5620/800000
   - (b) 7140/800000
   - (c) 6140/800000
   - (d) 6240/800000

3. Aman started a business investing Rs. 70,000. Ram joined him after six months with an amount of Rs.1,05,000 and Sam joined them with Rs. 1.4 lakhs after another six months. The amount of profit earned should be distributed in what ratio among Aman, Rakhi and Sagar respectively, 3 years after Aman started the business?
   - (a) 7 : 6 : 10
   - (b) 12 : 15 : 16
   - (c) 42 : 45 : 46
   - (d) Cannot be determined

4. A bottle contains 3/4 of milk and the rest water. How much of the mixture must be taken away and replaced by equal quantity of water so that the mixture has half milk and half water?
   - (a) 0.25
   - (b) 331.2%
   - (c) 0.45
   - (d) 0.5

5. Two goods train each 500 m long, are running in opposite directions on parallel tracks. Their speeds are 45 km/hr and 30 km/hr respectively. Find the time taken by the slower train to pass the driver of the faster one.
   - (a) 12 sec
   - (b) 24 sec
   - (c) 48 sec
   - (d) 60 sec

6. When a local train travels at a speed of 60kmph, it reaches the destination on time. When the same train travels at speed of 50 kmph, it reaches its destination 15mnts late. What is the length of journey?
   - (a) 75 kms
   - (b) 50 kms
   - (c) 60 kms
   - (d) 85 kms

7. If the simple interest on a sum at 4% per annum for 2 years is Rs. 80, then the compound interest on the same sum for the same period is :
   - (a) Rs. 86.80
   - (b) Rs. 86.10
   - (c) Rs. 88.65
   - (d) Rs. 81.60

8. Find the value of p which satisfies the relation $\log_2(p-1) + 2 = \log_2(3p+1))$
   - (a) 1
   - (b) 3
   - (c) 5
   - (d) 7

9. If the selling price of a watch is halved, the profit becomes quartered. Find the profit percentage of the watch?
   - (a) 50%
   - (b) 0.6667
   - (c) 1
   - (d) 2

10. Find the greatest number that divides 125, 218, 280 and 342 so as to leave the same remainder in each case.
    - (a) 37
    - (b) 35
    - (c) 33
    - (d) 31.0

11. A basket contains 3 blue, 5 black and 3 red balls. If 3 balls are drawn at random what is the probability that all are black?
    - (a) 2/33
    - (b) 1/33
    - (c) 3/11
    - (d) 8/33

12. There are 3 main steps of completion of a project- Development, Review and Roll out. After development, there are 4 people who can independently work and lead the process to the process to the next step i.e. Review. Further ahead, there are 5 people who can work independently and lead to the next step i.e. Roll-out. In how many ways can a project manager complete the project?
    - (a) 20
    - (b) 9
    - (c) 15
    - (d) 25

13. A and B are places that are 200 kms apart. A train starts from A at the speed of 20 km/hr and another train starts from B at the same time at the speed of 30 km/hr, towards each other. At what distance from A will these two trains meet and how much time will the trains take to reach the meeting point ?
    - (a) 120 km, 4 hrs
    - (b) 80 km, 4 hrs
    - (c) 120 km, 8 hrs
    - (d) 80 km, 6 hrs

14. If I walk at 4km/h, I miss the bus by 10 min. If I walk at 5 km/h, I reach 5 min. before the arrival of the bus. How far I walk to reach the bus stand?
    (a) 5 km   (b) 15 km
    (c) 10 km   (d) 55 km

15. Nitish sold his watch and sun glasses at a loss of 4% and gain of 4% respectively for 2600 to Kamal. Kamal sold the same sun glasses and watch at a loss of 4% and gain of 4% respectively for 2700. The price of watch and sun glasses to Nitish were.
    (a) Rs.1960, Rs.700   (b) Rs.2000, Rs.1000
    (c) Rs.1500, Rs.700   (d) Rs.800, Rs.2000

LOGICAL REASONING

16. What is the 8th term in the series 1,4, 9, 25, 35, 63, . . .
    (a) 262   (b) 272
    (c) 282   (d) 292

17. USA + USSR = PEACE ; P + E + A + C + E = ?
    (a) 10   (b) 20
    (c) 30   (d) 40

18. GOOD is coded as 164 then BAD coded as 21.if ugly coded as 260 then JUMP?
    (a) 240   (b) 250
    (c) 255   (d) 260

19. Find the 8th term in series?
    2, 2, 12, 12, 30, 30, – – – – –
    (a) 46   (b) 56
    (c) 86   (d) 96

20. **Statements :**
    All alphabets are numbers, some alphabets are digits
    Conclusions :
    I.   At least some digits are numbers
    II. No digit is a number
    (a) Either conclusion I or II follows
    (b) Neither conclusion I nor II follows
    (c) Only conclusion II follows
    (d) Only conclusion I follow

21. **Statements :**
    Some wins are losses, All trophies are losses.
    Conclusions :
    I.   All trophies are wins
    II. All losses are trophies
    (a) Either conclusion I or II follows
    (b) Both conclusions I and II follow
    (c) Only conclusion II follows
    (d) Neither conclusion I nor II follows

Directions for the question 22 to 24 : Read the information given below and answer the question that follows.

A, B, C, D, E, F and G are standing in a straight line facing north with equal distance between them, not necessary in the same order. Each one is pursuing a different profession – actor, reporter, doctor, engineer, lawyer, teacher and painter not necessary in the same order. G is fifth to the left of C. The reporter is third to the right of G. F is fifth to the right of A. E is second to the left of B. The engineer is second to the left of D. There are only three people between the engineer and the painter. The doctor is to the immediate left of the engineer. The lawyer is to the immediate right of the teacher.

22. Who amongst the following is the actor?
    (a) E   (b) F
    (c) C   (d) B

23. What is D's position with respect to the painter?
    (a) Third to the left   (b) Second to the left
    (c) Fourth to the right (d) Third to the right

24. Who among the following are standing at the extremes?
    (a) A and F   (b) A and C
    (c) G and F   (d) A and B

Directions for the question 25 : Solve the following question and mark the best possible option.

In a certain code,

'very large risk associated' is written as 'nu ta ro gi'

'risk is very low' is written as ' gi se nu mi'

'is that also associated' is written as 'ta mi po fu'

'inherent risk also damaging' is written as 'fu nu di yu'

(All the codes are two letter codes only.

25. What does the code 'di' stand for?
    (a) Either 'damaging' or 'inherent'
    (b) Inherent
    (c) Also
    (d) low

Directions for the question 26 : Solve the following question and mark the best possible option.

Point A is 14m north of point B

Point C is 11m east of point B

Point D is 5m north of point C

Point E is 7m west of point D

Point F is 6m north of point E

Point G is 4m west of point F

26. How far is F from point A ?

    (a) 5m   (b) 5.67m

    (c) 6m   (d) 3m

Directions for the questions 27 : The question below consists of a question and two statements numbered I and II given below it. You have to decide whether the data provided in the statements are sufficient to answer the question. Read both the statements and mark.

27. How many students are there in the class?

    I. There are more than 20 but less than 27 students in the class.

    II. There are more than 24 but less than 31 students in the class. the number of students in the class can be divided into groups such that each group contains 5 students.

    (a) The data in both the Statements I and II together are necessary to answer the question.

    (b) The data neither in Statement I nor in Statement II are sufficient to answer the question

    (c) The data either in Statement I alone or in Statement II alone are sufficient to answer the question

    (d) The data in Statement I alone are sufficient to answer the question, while the data in Statement II alone are not sufficient to answer the question

28. Oceans is to deserts and waves is to

    (a) Dust   (b) Sand Dunes

    (c) Ripples   (d) Sea

29. Bacteria : Decomposition ::

    (a) oxygen : treatment

    (b) yeast : fermentation

    (c) volcano : eruption

    (d) antibiotic : injection

30. Fruits : Apple :: Monuments :

    (a) Tajmahal   (b) Students

    (c) Knowledge   (d) History

VERBAL ABILITY

Directions for questions 31-33 : A word has been written in four different ways out of which only one is correctly spelt. Choose the correctly spelt word.

31. 1. scriptare   2. skripture

    3. scripture   4. Scripcher

    (a) 1   (b) 2

    (c) 3   (d) 4

32. 1. tariff   2. tarriff

    3. tarif   4. Tarrif

    (a) 1   (b) 2

    (c) 3   (d) 4

33. 1. commitee   2. committe

    3. comittee   4. Committee

    (a) 1   (b) 2

    (c) 3   (d) 4

Directions for questions 34-35 : Fill in the blanks.

34. We have to _______ in our young men and women a sense of discipline, which is a _______ for "progress and happiness"

    (a) generate, concomitant

    (b) instill, need

    (c) produce, necessity

    (d) inculcate, pre-requisite

35. At a function to inaugurate the world-class terminal of Thiruvananthapuram International Airport, the Prime Minister said the Centre's policy on airport _______ was to stay ahead of demand and to _______ the maximum share of traffic in the region.

    (a) sector, ensure   (b) regions, witness

    (c) building, garnish   (d) infrastructure, garner

Directions for questions 36 to 37 : Choose the word which is opposite in meaning of the given word.

36. Modesty

    (a) Honesty   (b) Vanity

    (c) Originality   (d) Variety

37. Spite

    (a) Spleen   (b) Venom

    (c) Spirit   (d) Affection

Directions for questions 38-40 : Answer the questions that follow the passage.

Nepal has promised India that it would end discrimination against car imports from the country and allow imports on the basis of selfcertification by Indian Government authorized manufacturers. India, too, has removed special additional duty of 4% on all imports from Nepal that enjoy zero basic customs duty under the Indo-Nepal treaty of trade following requests from the Nepalese government that its exports were losing competitiveness in the Indian market. The assurances on the long standing grouses were given by Commerce Secretaries from both countries in a meeting in New Delhi on Tuesday. India had complained to Nepal that it permitted all countries, other than India, to sell vehicles through self certified 'type approvals' or TAs, which was a confirmation of procedure commitment given by the manufacturer. "The Nepalese side said that if the Government of India authorizes any manufacturer for giving self certified TAs, the Government of Nepal will recognize the same," according to the minutes of the meeting. To help Nepal export products to India, the country has done away with special additional duty of 4% on import of all products that are imported duty free under the Indo-Nepal trade treaty. The SAD was imposed in 2006. Nepal's export to India is just $500 million, against India's exports of $2.2 billion. India has, however, turned down Nepal's request of waiving excise on propane and butane imported by Nepalese companies from third countries, which are mixed in India and exported to Nepal. India said that such mixing was considered production activity which is subject to excise. India also asked Nepal to restore margin of preference on import duty for Indian goods which was brought down from 20% in 2001-02, to 5% in 2006-07. Margin of preference is the difference in import duty levied on the preferred country as opposed to other countries. Under the South Asia Free Trade Agreement, of which both India and Nepal are signatories, Nepal gives margin of preference of 25% on applicable goods. Nepal said that it would favourably consider the request in its forthcoming budget session.

38. Choose the statement that is "true" as per the passage

(a) Indo-Nepal treaty of trade is the only trade agreement under which the two countries can do export-import business.

(b) Presently India is not exporting cars to Nepal.

(c) Nepal has decided to stop importing cars from India.

(d) The Commerce Secretaries of India and Nepal had met recently to discuss bi-lateral trade issues.

39. What has been the primary bone of contention from a Nepalese perspective, in respect of its trade ties with India?

(a) India has been discriminating against Nepal in the matter of car exports.

(b) Excise duty is being levied on butane and propane being exported to Nepal by India.

(c) India had been levying a special additional duty on exports from Nepal into India.

(d) India has been demanding restoration of margin of preference on import duty for Indian goods.

40. It is evident from the passage that

(a) India and Nepal have political differences.

(b) India and Nepal are at loggerheads on trade issues.

(c) India and Nepal do not have much cross-border trade.

(d) Governments of India and Nepal are making higher level efforts to resolve trade issues, on give-and-take basis.

Direction for Questions 41 – 45 : Each question has a set of four jumbled sentences which when properly arranged form a coherent paragraph. Each sentence is labelled with a letter. Choose the most logical order of sentences from among the four given choices.

41. A. What were the 'boundary conditions' at the beginning of universe?

B. Science seems to have uncovered a set of laws that within the limits set by the uncertainty principle, tell us how the universe will develop with time, if we know its state at any one time.

C. But how did he choose the initial stage or configuration of the universe?

D. God may have originally decreed these laws, but it appears that he has since left the universe to evolve according to them and does not now intervene in it.

(a) BCAD   (b) ACDB

(c) BACD   (d) BDCA

42. A. So for a sufficiently large number of matter particles, gravitational forces can dominate over all other forces.

B. This does not matter too much, because gravity is such a weak force that its effects can usually be neglected when we are dealing with elementary particles or atoms.

C. Grand unified theories do not include the force of gravity.

D. However, the fact that it is both long range and always attractive means that its effects all add up.

(a) CABD   (b) CBDA

(c) CADB   (d) ABDC

43. A. Some people attribute my success to marketing gimmicks, but the truth is that I did not use the same program to solve the problems of these three very different companies.

B. To do this, I learned to rely more on the frontline people, who deal with the customers, and less on my own edicts.

C. Vingresor, Linjeflug, and SAS were three big Scandinavian Companies, all connected with the travel industry, that I helped lead out of difficult times.

D. Rather, I succeeded because I reoriented each company toward the needs of the market it serves.

(a) ADCB (b) CADB

(c) CABD (d) ABDC

44. A. KLM airlines in Holland has a problem with the population of its home base.

B. By running flights to lesser known cities in Germany and England, KLM pulled passengers away from their own national airlines, and at one time KLM was flying more Germans across the Atlantic than Lufthansa, the country's nation airline

C. So KLM developed the successful concept of 'feeder' airlines.

D. It was very small compared to that of other airlines crossing the Atlantic (USA, UK, Germany, France etc.,

(a) ABCD (b) ADCB

(c) ABDC (d) BADC

45. A. In rejecting the functionalism in positivist organization theory, either wholly or partially, there is often a move towards a political model of organization theory.

B. Thus, the analysis would shift to the power resources possessed by different groups in the organization and the way they use these resources in actual power plays to shape the organizational structure.

C. At the extreme, in one set of writing, the growth of administrators in the organization is held to be completely unrelated to the work to be done and to be caused totally by the political pursuit of self-interest.

D. The political model holds that individual interests are pursued in organizational life through the exercise of power and influence.

(a) ADBC (b) CBAD

(c) DBCA (d) ABDC

TECHNICAL ABILITY

46. What will be the output of the program ?

```
#include<stdio.h>
int main()
{
enum days {MON=-1, TUE, WED=6, THU, FRI, SAT};
printf("%d, %d, %d, %d, %d, %d\n", MON, TUE, WED, THU, FRI, SAT);
return 0;
}
```

(a) -1, 0, 1, 2, 3, 4 (b) -1, 2, 6, 3, 4, 5

(c) -1, 0, 6, 7, 8, 9 (d) None of these

47. What do the following declaration signify?

```
int *ptr[30];
```

(a) ptr is a pointer to an array of 30 integer pointers.

(b) ptr is a array of 30 pointers to integers.

(c) ptr is a array of 30 integer pointers.

(d) ptr is a array 30 pointers.

48. Is the following code legal?

```
void main()
{
typedef struct a aType;
aType someVariable;
struct a
{
int x;
aType *b;
};
}
```

(a) Yes (b) No

(c) Compile time Error (d) Cannot be determined

49. What will be the output of the program?

```
#include<stdio.h>
typedef void v;
typedef int i;
int main()
{
v fun(i, i);
fun(2, 3.;
return 0;
}
v fun(i a, i b)
{
i s=2;
float i;
printf("%d,", sizeof(i));
printf(" %d", a*b*s);
}
```

(a) 2, 8 (b) 4, 8

(c) 2, 4 (d) 4, 12

50. What will be the output of the program?

```
#include<stdio.h>
int main()
{
const int x=5;
const int *ptrx;
ptrx = &x;
*ptrx = 10;
printf("%d\n", x);
return 0;
}
```

(a) 5.0   (b) 10.0

(c) Error   (d) Garbage value

51. The maximum combined length of the command-line arguments including the spaces between adjacent arguments is

(a) 128 characters

(b) 256 characters

(c) 67 characters

(d) It may vary from one operating system to another

52. What will be the output of the program (myprog.c) given below if it is executed from the command line?

```
cmd> myprog one two three
/* myprog.c */
#include<stdio.h>
#include<stdlib.h>
int main(int argc, char **argv)
{
printf("%s\n", *++argv);
return 0;
}
```

(a) myprog   (b) One

(c) Two   (d) three

53. What will be the output of the program

```
#include<stdio.h>
void fun(int);
int main(int argc)
{
printf("%d\n", argc);
fun(argc);
return 0;
}
void fun(int i)
```

```
{
if(i!=4)
main(++i);
}
```

(a) 1 2 3   (b) 1 2 3 4

(c) 2 3 4   (d) 1.0

54. Which of the following function is correct that finds the length of a string?

```
A.  int xstrlen(char s)
    {
    int length=0;
    while(*s!='\0')
    length++;
    s++;
    return (length);
    }

B.  int xstrlen(char *s)
    {
    int length=0;
    while(*s!='\0')
    length++;
    return (length);
    }

C.  int xstrlen(char *s)
    {
    int length=0;
    while(*s!='\0')
    s++;
    return (length);
    }
```

(a) A   (b) B

(c) C   (d) D

55. Which of the following function is more appropriate for reading in a multi-word string?

(a) printf();   (b) scanf();

(c) gets();   (d) puts();

56. What is the notation for following functions?

```
1.  int f(int a, float b.
    {
    /* Some code */
    }

2.  int f(a, b)
    int a; float b;
    {
    /* Some code */
    }
```

(a) 1. KR Notation
    2. ANSI Notation
(b) 1. Pre ANSI C Notation
    2. KR Notation
(c) 1. ANSI Notation
    2. KR Notation
(d) 1. ANSI Notation
    2. Pre ANSI Notation

57. Which bitwise operator is suitable for turning on a particular bit in a number?

(a) && operator   (b) & operator

(c) || operator   (d) | operator

58. #include <stdio.h>

```
int fun(int n)
{
if (n == 4)
return n;
else return 2*fun(n+1);
}
int main()
{
printf("%d ", fun(2));
return 0;
}
```

(a) 4.0

(b) 8.0

(c) 16.0

(d) Runtime Error

59. Find the output.

```
main()
{
char a[4]="HELL";
printf("%s",a);
}
```

(a) HELL%@!~@!@???@~~!

(b) HELL%@!

(c) HELL@!

(d) HELL %@!@??

60. Drawbacks of file processing system

(a) Data redundancy

(b) Limited data sharing

(c) lack of security

(d) all of the above

ANSWERS

1. (b)	**2.** (b)	**3.** (b)	**4.** (b)	**5.** (b)	**6.** (a)	**7.** (d)	**8.** (c)	**9.** (d)	**10.** (d)
11. (a)	**12.** (a)	**13.** (b)	**14.** (a)	**15.** (a)	**16.** (a)	**17.** (a)	**18.** (a)	**19.** (b)	**20.** (d)
21. (c)	**22.** (c)	**23.** (b)	**24.** (b)	**25.** (a)	**26.** (a)	**27.** (a)	**28.** (b)	**29.** (b)	**30.** (a)
31. (c)	**32.** (a)	**33.** (d)	**34.** (d)	**35.** (d)	**36.** (b)	**37.** (d)	**38.** (d)	**39.** (c)	**40.** (d)
41. (d)	**42.** (b)	**43.** (b)	**44.** (c)	**45.** (a)	**46.** (d)	**47.** (b)	**48.** (a)	**49.** (d)	**50.** (c)
51. (d)	**52.** (b)	**53.** (b)	**54.** (a)	**55.** (c)	**56.** (c)	**57.** (d)	**58.** (c)	**59.** (a)	**60.** (d)

EXPLANATIONS

1. Say M came first.

The remaining 4 positions can be filled in

$4! = 24$ ways.

Now M came in second.

N can finish the race in 3rd, 4th or 5th position.

So total ways are $3 \times 3! = 18$.

M came in third.

N can finish the race in 2 positions. $2 \times 3! = 12$.

M came in second.

N can finish in only one way. $1 \times 3! = 6$

Total ways are $24 + 18 + 12 + 6 = 60$.

2. Junior student = 1000

Senior student = 800

60 sibling pair = $2 \times 60 = 120$ students

Probability that 1 student chosen from senior = 800

Probability that 1 student chosen from junior = 1000

Therefore, number of ways in which 1 student chosen from senior and 1 student chosen from junior = $800 \times 1000 = 800000$

Number of ways in which two selected students are from a sibling pair = $^{120}C_2 = 7140$

Required probability, 7140/800000.

3. Aman : Rakhi : Sagar = $(70,000 \times 36)$:

$(1,05,000 \times 30) : (1,40,000 \times 24) = 12 : 15 : 16$.

4. Let the total quantity of mixture = 1 liter.

Now supposing x liters of mixture is withdrawn which contains 3/4x milk and rest water.

So, according to the question $3/4 - 3/4x = 1/2$.

Solving x = 1/3 which means 1/3 of mixture is to be withdrawn to serve the purpose.

So, answer is 33.33%.

5. Relative speed = $(45 + 30)$ km/hr

$= (75 \times 5/18)$ m/sec

$= (125 / 6)$m / sec

We have to find the time taken by the slower train to pass the DRIVER of the faster train and not the complete train.

So, distance covered = Length of the slower train.

Therefore, Distance covered = 500 m.

Required time = $(500 \times 6 / 125) = 24$ sec

6. Distance is constant.

So let time taken be t when it travels with 60kmph.

Let time be t' when it travels with 50kmph

$d = st$

Therefore

$st = s't'$

$60 \times t = 50 \times (t + 15/60$ (in hrs)

On solving

$t = 5/4$ hrs

$d = 60 \times 5/4 = 75$km

7. Let take x as principal

$SI = (PNR/100)$

$80 = (x \times 2 \times 4/100)$

$80 \times 100/4 \times 2 = x$

$1000 = x =$ principal

Hence, Amount

$= [1000(1 + 4/100]^2$

$= 1000 \times 26/25 \times 26/25$

$= 1081.6$

CI = $(1081.6 - 1000. =$ Rs. 81.6.

8. $\log_2(p - 1) + 2 = \log_2(3p + 1)$

$\log_2(p - 1) + \log_2 2^2 = \log_2(3p + 1.$ $(\because \log_2 2^2 = 2)$

$\log_2 2^2 (p - 1) = \log_2 (3p + 1)$ $(\because \log a + \log b = \log ab)$

$4p - 4 = 3p + 1$

$P = 5$

9. $1/4(SP - CP) = (SP/2 - CP)$

$CP/SP = 1/3$

$P\% = 2 \times 100/1 = 200\%$

10. $218 - 125 = 93, 280 - 218 = 62,$

$280 - 125 = 155, 324 - 218 = 124,$

$342 - 125 = 217, 342 - 125 = 217$

H.C.F of 93, 155, 217, 62, 124, 217 is 31.

11. Ways of selecting 3 black balls out of $5 - \,^5C_3$

Total ways of selecting 3 balls = $^{11}C_3$

Thus required probability = $^5C_3 / \,^{11}C_3$

$= 10/165 = 2/33$

12. $^4C_1 \times \,^5C_1 = 4 \times 5 = 20$ (Combinations)

13. Required time = $200/(20 + 30) = 4$ hrs

Distance from A at which they will meet

$= 4 \times 20 = 80$ km.

14. Let d be the distance & t be the time diff. between departure time of the bus and the time he leaves.

$d/4 = t + 1/6$

$d/5 = t - 1/12$

subtracting to eliminate "t",

$d/20 = 3/12$

$d = 5$ km

15. Let the CP of watch be Rs. x and sun glasses be Rs. y.

$2600 = 96x/100 + 104y/100$

$2700 = 104x/100 + 96y/100$

On solving,

$y = 700$

$x = 1960$

16. 1, 4, 9, 18, 35, 68, . . .

The pattern is

$1 = 2^1 - 1$

$4 = 2^2 + 0$

$9 = 2^3 + 1$

$18 = 2^4 + 2$

$35 = 2^5 + 3$

$68 = 2^6 + 4$

So 8th term is $2^8 + 6 = 262$

17. 3 Digit number + 4 digit number = 5 digit number.

So P is 1 and U is 9, E is 0.

Now S repeated three times, A repeated 2 times. Just give values for S.

We can easily get the following table.

USA = 932 and USSR = 9338

PEACE = 10270

$P + E + A + C + E = 1 + 0 + 2 + 7 + 0 = 10$

18. Coding = Sum of position of alphabets × Number of letters in the given word

$GOOD = (7 + 15 + 15 + 4) \times 4 = 164$

$BAD = (2 + 1 + 4) \times 3 = 21$

$UGLY = (21 + 7 + 12 + 25) \times 4 = 260$

So, $JUMP = (10 + 21 + 13 + 16) \times 4 = 240$

19. $1^1 + 1 = 2$

$2^2 - 2 = 2$

$3^2 + 3 = 12$

$4^2 - 4 = 12$

$5^2 + 5 = 30$

$6^2 - 6 = 30$

So 7th term = $7^2 + 7 = 56$ and 8th term

$= 8^2 - 8 = 56$

Answer is 56

20. From the given statements, we get the following relation :

Therefore,

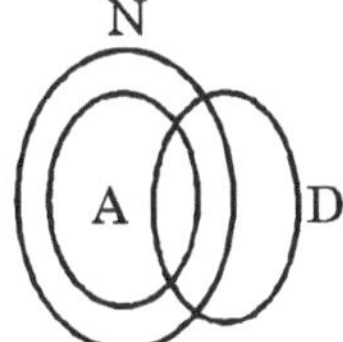

Conclusion I : At least some digits are numbers is true

Conclusion II : No digit is a number is not true

So the correct option is (d).

21. From the given statements, we get the following relation :

Therefore,

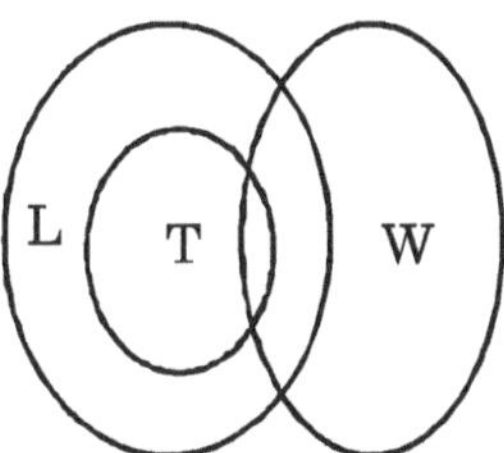

Conclusion I : All trophies are wins is not true.

Conclusion II : All losses are trophies is also not true. Some losses are trophies

So the correct option is (e).

22. From the given information, we have the following arrangement :

C is the actor.

Hence option (c).

23. D's position with respect to the painter is second to the left.

Hence option (e).

24. A and C are standing at the extremes.

Hence option (e).

25. 'very large risk associated' is written as 'nu ta ro gi'-(1.

'risk is very low' is written as ' gi se nu mi-----(2.

'is that also associated' is written as 'ta mi po fu'----(3.

'inherent risk also damaging' is written as 'fu nu di yu'---(4.

From statements 1 and 3, we have 'associated' as the common word and the common code is 'ta'

From statements 3 and 4, we have 'also' as the common word and the common code is 'fu'

From statements 2 and 4, we have 'risk' as the common word and the common code is 'nu'

From statements 2 and 3, we have 'is' as the common word and the common code is 'mi'

From statements 1 and 2, we can conclude that the code of 'very' is 'gi'

Therefore, from statement 1, the code of 'large' will be 'ro'

Similarly, from statement 2, the code of 'low' is 'se' and from statement 3, the code of 'that' is 'po'

Word	Code
very	gi
risk	nu
is	mi
also	fu
low	se
large	ro
that	po
associated	ta
inherient	di/yu
damaging	di/yu

'di' can either be 'damaging' or 'inherent'.

Hence option (a).

26. The distance between F and A i.e

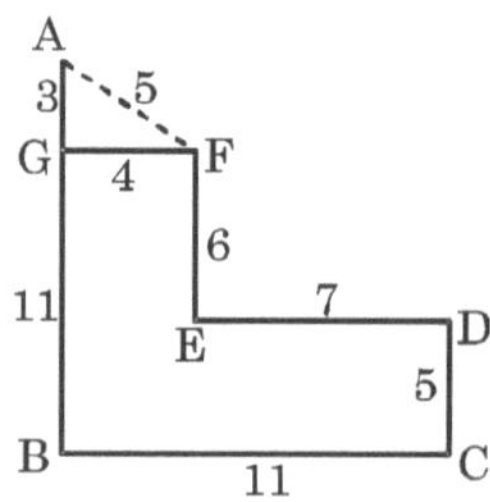

$$FA = \sqrt{AG^2 + GF^2}. = \sqrt{(3^2 + 4^2)}. = \sqrt{25} = 5m.$$

27. From statement I, the no of students can be 21, 22, 23, 24, 25 or 26. So no certain answer is obtained.

From statement II, the no of students can be either 25 or 30. So again no unique answer is obtained.

On combining the statements, we get 25 as the unique answer.

Therefore, the data in both the Statements I and II together are necessary to answer the question. Hence option A.

28. Sand Dunes

29. yeast : fermentation

30. Tajmahal

MOCK -2

(HCL - II)

1. A got 36% of the marks in an exam and 20 marks more than the pass mark. B got 30% of the marks which is 10 marks less than the pass mark. Find the pass mark as a percentage of total marks?

a) 31   b) 32

c) 33   d) 34

2. Before 3 years the average age of a five member family was 17 years. A baby having been born and the average of family is now 17 years. The present age of the baby is

a) 3 years   b) 2 years

c) 1 year   d) None

3. A shopkeeper offers three successive discounts of 10%, 20% and 30% to a customer. If the marked price of the item is Rs.10,000, what is the price the customer has to pay the shopkeeper?

a) Rs. 4000   b) Rs. 5040

c) Rs. 9940   d) Rs. 8465.0

4. A bus for Delhi leaves every thirty minutes from a bus stand. An enquiry clerk told a passenger that the bus had already left ten minutes ago and the next bus will leave at 9.35 a.m. At what time did the enquiry clerk give this information to the passenger?

a) 9.10 am   b) 8.55 am

c) 9.08 am   d) 9.15 am

5. A school has gathered 80% of the required donation from 60% of the donors who gave an average of 500 per head. How much, on average, should the remaining donors contribute so that the school receives exactly the money it requires?

a) Rs.150   b) Rs.170

c) Rs.180   d) Rs.187.5

6. Working alone, A can complete a task in 100 minutes. B can complete the same task in two hours. They work together for 30 minutes when C, a new employee, joins and begins helping. They finish the task 20 minutes later. How long would it take C to complete the task alone?

a) 5 hours

b) 4 hours

c) 3 hours

d) 6 hours

7. Akhil, Bhanu and Chandu can do a piece of work in 24, 30 and 40 days respectively. They start the work together and work for 5 days after which Akhil quits the job and Bhanu develops a fever which reduces his efficiency by a half. How many more days will be required to complete the work?

a) 20 days   b) 14 days

c) 12 days   d) 16 days

8. An item is bought for Rs.350 and sold to a middleman at a 20% profit who sells it to the final customer at a 20% profit. Find the profit made by the middleman.

a) Rs.70   b) Rs.78

c) Rs.84   d) Rs.90

9. A solid cylinder has total surface area of 462 sq.cm. Curved surface area is 1/3 rd of its total surface area. The volume of the cylinder is

a) 530 cm^3 b) 536 cm^3

c) 539 cm^3 d) 545 cm^3

10. A car covers 1/5 of the distance from A to B at the speed of 8 km/hr, 1/10 of the distance at 25 km per hour and the remaining at the speed of 20 km per hour. Find the average speed of the whole journey.

a) 12.625 km/hr   b) 13.625 km/hr

c) 14.625 km/hr   d) 15.625 km/hr

11. If $a^4 + a^2b^2 + b^4 = 8$ and $a^2 + ab + b^2 = 4$ then the value of ab is

a) -1 b) 0

c) 2   d) 1

12. A car travels a distance AB with an average speed of 40 km/hr. At what speed must it return (i.e. travel from B to A) so that the average speed for the entire journey is 80 km/hr?

a) 100 km/hr   b) 120 km/hr

c) 110 km/hr   d) Not possible

13. Pressure varies inversely with volume while temperature varies directly with volume. When Volume = 50 m^3, Temperature = 25 K and Pressure = 1 atmosphere. If the volume is increased to 300 m^3 and the pressure remains unchanged, then the temperature will be

a) 100 K   b) 50 K

c) 125 K   d) 150 K

14. If $a + b + c = 0$, then the value of $[a^2 + b^2 + c^2]/[a^2 - bc]$ is

a) 2
b) 3
c) 0
d) 1

15. Two trains of lengths 200 m and 250 m are travelling in opposite directions. They cross each other completely in 20 seconds. If they were travelling in same direction, the time taken by the faster train to cross the slower train would be 50 seconds.

Find the ratio of the speed of the faster train to that of the slower train?

a) 43 : 11
b) 21 : 9
c) 23 : 7
d) 35 : 11

LOGICAL REASONING

Directions for questions 16 to 18 : In each question, there is a premise followed by two statements labeled I & II. Study the statements and mark your answer choice as per the instructions given below.(Note that a conclusion can follow from even either of the statements given in the premise.)

Mark your answer as :

(1) If only conclusion I follows.

(2) If only conclusion II follows.

(3) If both conclusions I & II follow.

(4) If neither conclusion I nor conclusion II follow

16. Statements :

All tiger are wild.

All wild are ferocious.

Conclusions :

I. Some tigers are ferocious.

II. Some wild are ferocious.

17. Statements :

Some teachers are followers

Some followers are famous

Conclusions :

I. Some teachers are famous.

II. Some followers are teachers

18. Statements :

Some dedicated souls are angels.

All social workers are angels.

Conclusions :

I. Some dedicated souls are social workers.

II. Some social workers are dedicated souls.

19. Thermometer : Temperature :: Seismograph : ?

a) Current
b) Humidity
c) Earthquakes
d) Speed

20. ABCD : WXYZ :: EFGH : ?

a) STUV
b) VUTS
c) STVW
d) HIJK

Directions for questions 21 to 24 : Read the following information carefully to answer the questions given below:

 (i) P + Q means P is father of Q

(ii) P – Q means means P is wife of Q

(iii) P × Q means P is brother of Q

(iv) P ÷ Q means P is daughter of Q

21. If A ÷ C + D + B, which of the following is true?

a) A is the daughter of B
b) B is the aunt of A
c) A is the aunt of B
d) A is the mother of B

22. If A – C + B and A ÷ D, which of the following is true?

a) D is the grandfather of B
b) B is the grandson of D
c) D is the grandmother of B
d) Cannot be determined

23. If D + A × C ÷ B, how is B related to D?

a) Husband
b) Daughter
c) Son
d) Wife

24. If A × C – B, which of the following is true?

a) A is the brother in law of B
b) A is the brother of B
c) A is the father of B
d) A is the uncle of B

25. Which letter will be midway between 8th letter from the left and 16th letter from the left in the English alphabet?

a) B
b) L
c) M
d) K

Directions for questions 26-27: Each question is followed by two statements, (I) and (II).

Mark your answer as:

(1) If the question can be answered by using statement (I) alone but not by using statement (II) alone.

(2) If the question can be answered by using statement (II) alone but not by using statement (I) alone.

(3) If the question can be answered by using both the statements together but not by either of the statements alone.

(4) If the question cannot be answered even by using both the statements together.

26. Is X a prime number, given that X is a positive integer?

(I) $X^4 > 3000$

(II) $X^4 < 10,000$

27. Who has secured the maximum marks among six friends – A, B, C, D, E and F?

(I) B scored less than A and F but not less than C, D and E.

(II) F scored more than B but not as much as A.

VERBAL ABILITY

28.

125	192	56
25	?	28
5	12	14
1	3	7

a) 64.0   b) 56.0

c) 48.0   d) 40.0

29.

9	13	12
19	10	5
8	?	11

a) 9.0   b) 15.0

c) 13.0   d) 11.0

30. How many letters in the following series are immediately preceded by B but not immediately followed by D?

R S P Q B A H M A C F B A D N O P B A C D

a) 4.0   b) 3.0

c) 2.0   d) 1.0

In the following the questions choose the word which best expresses the meaning of the given word.

31. BARE

a) Uncovered   b) Covered

c) Clear   d) Neat

32. PIOUS

a) Pure   b) Clean

c) Pretentious   d) Devout

In the following questions choose the word which is the exact OPPOSITE of the given words.

33. FLORID

a) Weak   b) Pale

c) Monotonus   d) Ugly

34. PERSPICUITY

a) Vagueness   b) Dullness

c) Unfairness   d) Unwillingness

Directions for Questions (35-36) : In the following questions a part of the sentence is BOLD. Below are given alternatives to the bold part at

35. Obviously he isn't **cut up** to be a good teacher.

a) cut out   b) cut in

c) cut for   d) No improvement

36. The weak man is a slave to his **sensuous** pleasures.

a) sensory   b) sensual

c) secondary   d) No improvement

Directions for questions (37-38) : In the following questions, find out which part of a sentence which has an error. Choose your answer as (d) if the sentence has No Error.

37. He who has suffered most (a)/for the cause, (b)/let him speak, (c)/No error (d)

38. After knowing truth, (a)/they took the right decision (b)/in the matter (c)/No error (d)

Directions for Questions (39-42) : Read the passage carefully and choose the best answer to each question out of the four alternatives.

Simple definition of Online Shopping or Shopping on the Web is enabling you to buy and sell through your computer online using Web or Internet **environment**. One reason people like without a salesperson because you can browse inside the shop for number of hours at your leisure time without a salesperson **peering** over the shoulder and making unwanted recommendations. As a customer, we may find this approach convenient and less time consuming, but how does this affect the economy as a whole? Is it safe to pay credit card online? Is buying and selling products over the internet considered as a risky business for merchants? Is the Web going to replace old-fashioned stores? **Is virtual shopping** really is better than the real thing? Cyberspace is a vast territory where computers meet and exchange information. In this 21st century, cyberspace has already to your computer will look you into wealth of goods and services.

In your home, **modern** box attached to your computer will look you into wealth of goods and services. Not only does it allow you to talk to your friends on the other side of the world, but also allows you to watch a movie, buy airline tickets, pay **bills** and even get cash, people in developed countries like U.S. and Canada have already started using Online Shopping as a routine mode of their purchasing goods and services. Internet shoppers still believe that there is no secure and convenient way of paying on the Internet. Consumers are concerned with two main security fears. They are worried that their credit card information is jeopardizing while travelling over the net. They also express concern over data privacy whereby the vendors and blanking institutions can tamper with the data and easily record their purchasing habits. These fears over privacy and security have kept E-Commerce from taking off.

39. What does the passage imply by the word 'Virtual shopping'?

a) shopping widely   b) shopping spree

c) literal shopping   d) net shopping

40. Why is it risky to pay online?

a) It reveals the identity of the buyer

b) It intrudes upon the privacy of the buyer

c) The buyer is apprehensive of his credit card details going over the net

d) The merchants may record the buyer's purchasing habits.

41. Which of the following statement is/are TRUE _______?

(A) Cyberspace has opened an immense wealth of services but has affected the economy too.

(B) Data privacy is no longer a thing of the past.

(C) People in developing countries use online shopping as a routine mode

a) Only a   b) Only b and c

c) a, b and c   d) Only c

42. What is the authors view regarding shopping on the web?

a) shopping on the net makes the buyers wary of financial transactions.

b) shopping in the stores is on obsolete idea.

c) Net shopping has affected our economy on the whole

d) Payment by credit card easily outnumbers cash transactions.

Directions for Questions (43-45) : Four alternatives are given for the Idiom/Phrase bold in the sentence. Choose the alternative which best expresses the meaning of the Idiom/Phrase and mark it in the Answer Sheet.

43. Your remarks during the discussion **added fuel to the fire.**

a) got others angry

b) ignited the fireplace

c) worsened matters

d) created warmth all around

44. Why do you **fight shy** of me?

a) fight with   b) avoid

c) embarrass   d) shout at

45. They have **latched on to** tourism as a way of boosting the local ecomony

a) promoted   b) discovered

c) exposed   d) explored

TECHNICAL ABILITY

46. Which of the following about the following two declaration is true?

(i) int *F()

(ii) int (*F)()

a) Both are identical

b) The first is a correct declaration and the second is wrong

c) The first declaraion is a function returning a pointer to an integer and the second is a pointer to function returning int

d) Both are different ways of declare in pointer to a function

47. What are the values printed by the following program?

```
#define dprint(expr) printf(#expr "=%d ",expr)
main()
{
int x = 7;
int y = 3;
dprintf(x/y);
}
```

a) #2 = 2   b) expr = 2

c) x/y = 2   d) none

48. When an array is passed as parameter to a function, which of the following statement is correct?

a) The function can change values in the original array

b) In C parameters are passed by value. The function cannot change the original value in the array

c) It results in compilation error when the function tries to access the elements in the array

d) Results in a run time error when the function tries to access the elements in the array

49. The type of the controlling expression of a switch statement cannot be of the type

a) int   b) char

c) short   d) float

50. What is the value of the expression $(3\wedge6) + (a\wedge a)$?

a) 3.0   b) 5.0

c) 6.0   d) a + 18

51. What is the value assigned to the variable X if b is 7 ?

X = b > 8 ? b << 3 : b > 4 ? b >> 1 : b;

a) 7.0   b) 28.0

c) 3.0   d) 14

52. Which is the output produced by the following program.

```
main()
{
int n = 2;
printf("%d %d ", ++n, n*n);
}
```

a) 3,6   b) 3,4

c) 2,4   d) cannot determined

53. How many stacks are needed to implement a queue. Consider the situation where no other data structure like arrays, linked list is available to you.

a) 1.0   b) 2.0

c) 3.0   d) 4.0

54. A priority queue can efficiently implemented using which of the following data structures? Assume that the number of insert and peek (operation to see the current highest priority item) and extraction (remove the highest priority item) operations are almost same.

a) Array

b) Linked List

c) Heap Data Structures like Binary Heap, Fibonacci Heap

d) None of the above

55. Suppose a circular queue of capacity $(n - 1)$ elements is implemented with an array of n elements. Assume that the insertion and deletion operation are carried out using REAR and FRONT as array index variables, respectively. Initially, REAR = FRONT = 0. The conditions to detect queue full and queue empty are

a) Full : (REAR+1) mod n == FRONT, empty: REAR == FRONT

b) Full : (REAR+1) mod n == FRONT, empty: (FRONT+1) mod n == REAR

c) Full : REAR == FRONT, empty: (REAR+1) mod n == FRONT

d) Full : (FRONT+1) mod n == REAR, empty: REAR == FRONT

56. A Priority-Queue is implemented as a Max-Heap. Initially, it has 5 elements. The level-order traversal of the heap is given below :

10, 8, 5, 3, 2

Two new elements "1" and "7" are inserted in the heap in that order. The level-order traversal of the heap after the insertion of the elements is :

a) 10, 8, 7, 5, 3, 2, 1   b) 10, 8, 7, 2, 3, 1, 5

c) 10, 8, 7, 1, 2, 3, 5   d) 10, 8, 7, 3, 2, 1, 5

57. How many different insertion sequences of the key values using the same hash function and linear probing will result in the hash table shown above?

a) 10.0

b) 20.0

c) 30.0

d) 40.0

58. Given a hash table T with 25 slots that stores 2000 elements, the load factor α for T is ______

a) 80.0   b) 0.0125

c) 8000.0   d) 1.25

59. What is the worst case time complexity for search, insert and delete operations in a general Binary Search Tree?

a) O(n) for all

b) O(Logn) for all

c) O(Logn) for search and insert, and O(n) for delete

d) O(Logn) for search, and O(n) for insert and delete

60. Which of the following traversal outputs the data in sorted order in a BST?

a) Preorder   b) Inorder

c) Postorder   d) Level order

ANSWERS

1. (b)	**2.** (b)	**3.** (b)	**4** (d)	**5.** (d)	**6.** (b)	**7.** (c)	**8.** (c)	**9** (c)	**10.** (d)
11. (d)	**12.** (d)	**13.** (d)	**14.** (a)	**15.** (b)	**16.** (a)	**17.** (d)	**18.** (d)	**19.** (c)	**20.** (a)
21. (c)	**22.** (d)	**23.** (d)	**24.** (a)	**25.** (b)	**26.** (b)	**27.** (c)	**28.** (c)	**29.** (b)	**30.** (c)
31. (a)	**32.** (d)	**33.** (b)	**34.** (a)	**35.** (a)	**36.** (b)	**37.** (c)	**38.** (a)	**39.** (d)	**40.** (c)
41. (a)	**42.** (c)	**43.** (c)	**44.** (b)	**45.** (a)	**46.** (c)	**47.** (c)	**48.** (a)	**49.** (d)	**50.** (b)
51. (c)	**52.** (b)	**53.** (b)	**54.** (c)	**55.** (a)	**56.** (d)	**57.** (c)	**58.** (a)	**59.** (a)	**60.** (b)

EXPLANATIONS

1. Let x be the total marks.

$36x / 100 = PM + 20$

$30x / 100 = PM - 10$

Solving the two we get, $x = 500$

Passmark = 160

Passmark as a % of total marks = 32

2. Average height of 10 students = 105 cm

Total height of 10 students

$= 105 \times 10 = 1050$ cm

Average height of 20 new students

$= 120 \times 20 = 2400$ cm

Total height of the class = 3450 / 30 = 115 cm

3. $10,000 \times 0.9 \times 0.8 \times 0.7 = 5,040$

4. As the next bus is at 9.35 am the last bus must have left at 9.05 am

Therefore, the enquiry clerk gave this information at 9.15 am

5. Let total number of donors = 100

60 of them contributed Rs 500 each.

Total contribution obtained = $60 \times 500 = 30000$

Now 30000 = 80 % of required donation.

So required donation = 37500

Remaining 7500 has to be collected form 40 donors.

Each donor on an average contributes = 187.5

6. Work done in 30 minutes

$= 30(1 / 100 + 1 / 120)$

$= 11 / 20$.

Work left $= 9 / 20$

$= 20(1 / 100 + 1 / 120 + 1 / x)$.

$X = 240$ minutes = 4 hours

7. Total work = 120 units i.e. LCM of 24, 30 and 40.

Thus, work done by A, B and C in one day will be

5, 4 and 3 units respectively.

5 days work = $12 \times 5 = 60$ units.

Work left = $120 - 60 = 60$ units.

Required time = $60/(2 + 3) = 12$ days.

8. Cost price = 350, Profit = 70

Cost price for middleman = 420

Profit = 20% = Rs 84

9. Total surface area of cylinder = $2\pi r^2 + 2\pi rh$

$462 = 2\pi r^2 + 2\pi rh$ ... (1)

Area of curved surfaces = $2\pi rh = 1/3 \times 462$

$= 154 = 2\pi r^2 + 154 = 462$

$2\pi r^2 = 462 - 154 = 308$

$2 \times 22 / 7 \times r^2 = 308$

$r^2 = 308 \times 7 / 2 \times 22$

$r = 7$ m

$2\pi rh = 154$

$2 \times 22/7 \times 7 \times h = 154$

$H = 7 /2$ cm

Volume of cylinder = $\pi r^2 h$

$= 22 / 7 \times 7 \times 7 \times 7 / 2$

$= 539$ cm

10. Total time = $1 / (5 \times 8) + 1 / (10 \times 25)$

$+ (1 - 1/5 - 1/10) / 20$

$= 1 / 40 + 1 / 250 + [(10 - 2 - 1 / 10) / 20)$

$= 1/ 40 + 1 /250 + 7 / 200$

$= 64 / 1000 = 8/125$ hr

Hence, average speed = 125 / 8 = 15.625 km/hr

11. $a^4 + a^2b^2 + b^4 = 8 = (a^2 + ab + b^2)(a^2 - ab + b^2)$

$8 = 4(a^2 - ab + b^2$

$a^2 - ab + b^2 = 2$ ... (1)

$a^2 + ab + b^2 = 4$ ...(2)

By equation (ii) – (i)

$a^2 + ab + b^2 - a^2 + ab - b^2 = 4 - 2$

$2ab = 2$ or $ab = 1$

12. $D/40 + D/x = 2D/80$

$D/x = 0$

Not Possible

13. $T \infty V$

$T/V = \text{Const}$

$25 / 50 = T / 300$

$T = 150$

14. $a + b + c = 0, b + c = -a$

On squaring, $(b + c)^2 = a^2$

$b^2 + c^2 + 2abc = a^2, a^2 + b^2 + c^2 + 2bc = 2a^2$

$a^2 + b^2 + c^2 = 2a^2 - 2bc = 2(a^2 - bc)$

$= 2(a^2 - bc)/(a^2 - bc) = 2$

15. $L1 + L2 / S1 + S2 = 20$

$L1 + L2 / S1 - S2 = 50$

$S1 + S2 = 22.5$

$S1 - S2 = 9.0$

$S1 = 15.5$

$S2 = 6.75$

$S1 : S2 = 21 : 9$

16. Some tigers are ferocious.

17. If neither conclusion I nor conclusion I follow.

18. Some dedicated souls are social workers.

Some social workers are dedicated souls.

19. EarthQuakes

20. STUV

21. A is the aunt of B

22. Cannot be determined

23. Wife

24. A is the brother in law of B

25. Here, m = 8 and n = 16

then middle letter = 8 +16/2 = 24/2

= 12th letter from left in the alphabet

= L

26. If the question can be answered by using statement (II) alone but not by using statement (I) alone.

27. If the question can be answered by using both the statements together but not by either of the statements alone.

28. 48 = 12(4) COLUMN 2

29. The sum of all numbers each row is = 34

Then the missing number

= 8 + 11 + x = 34

19 + x = 34

X = 15

30. R S P Q B A H M A C F B A D N O P B A C D

Only the two times A fulfill the given condition and those A have been marked with the correct sign (ü). Those not fulfilling the condition have been marked with the cross sign (×). \ Required answer is 2.

MOCK -3

(HP - I)

QUANTITATIVE ABILITY

1. A certain party consists of four different group of people 30 students, 35 politicians, 20 actors and 27 leaders. On a particular function day, the total cost spent on party members was Rs.9000. It was found that 6 students spent as much as 7 politicians, 15 politicians spent as much as 12 actors and 10 actors spent as much as 9 leaders. How much did students spend?

(a) 2245   (b) 2285

(c) 2290   (d) 2291

2. A group of 5 pair of friends went for movie; each pair contains a male and a female. in how many different ways can they be arranged to sit on chairs in theatre which kept in straight line such that each male and female should sit alternatively.

(a) 24800   (b) 28800

(c) 24400   (d) 26600

3. Two cyclist,20 miles apart,start at the same instant and ride towards each other along a straight road at a speed of 10 miles per hour. at the same instant a fly on the forehead ofone of the riders starts to fly at 15 mile per hour toward the other rider, alights on his forehead, and the immediately flies back to the first rider. the fly travels back and forth over the continously decreasing distance between the two riders until the two riders meet. how far has the fly flown when all its journeys are added together.

(a) 15 km   (b) 10 km

(c) 12 km   (d) 20 km

4. In a chess competition involving some men and women, every player needs to play exactly one game with every other player. It was found that in 45 games, both the players were women and in 190 games, both players were men. What is the number of games in which one person was a man and other person was a woman?

(a) 40   (b) 200

(c) 180   (d) 120

5. In a 500 m race, the ratio of the speeds of two contestants A and B is 3 : 4. A has a start of 140 m. Then, A wins by:

(a) 60 m   (b) 20 m

(c) 40 m   (d) 10 m

6. Arun bought a computer with 15% discount on the labelled price. He sold the computer for Rs. 2880 with 20% profit on the labelled price. At what price did he buy the computer?

(a) Rs. 3000   (b) Rs. 2080

(c) Rs. 2040   (d) Rs. 2000

7. John bought 20 kg of wheat at the rate of Rs.8.50 per kg and 35 kg at the rate of Rs.8.75 per kg. He mixed the two. Approximately at what price per kg should he sell the mixture to make 40% profit at the cost price?

(a) Rs. 12   (b) Rs. 8

(c) Rs. 16   (d) Rs. 20

8. There are 4 oranges, 5 apples and 6 mangoes in a basket. In how many ways can a person make a selection of fruits among the fruits in the basket?

(a) 210   (b) 209

(c) 256   (d) 220

9. A family consists of two grandparents, two parents and three grandchildren. The average age of the grandparents is 67 years, that of the parents is 35 years and that of the grandchildren is 6 years. The average age of the family is

(a) 246/7 years   (b) 222/7 years

(c) 225/7 years   (d) 242/7 years

10. The batting average for 40 innings of a cricket player is 50 runs. His highest score exceeds his lowest score by 172 runs.

If these two innings are excluded, the average of the remaining 38 innings is 48 runs. Find out the highest score of the player.

(a) 150

(b) 174

(c) 180

(d) 166

11. In a locality, there are ten houses in a row. On a particular night a thief planned to steal from three houses of the locality. In how many ways can he plan such that no two of them are next to each other?

(a) 23

(b) 24

(c) 64

(d) 56

12. Two cyclists are moving towards each other at 10 miles/hour. They are now 50 miles apart. At this instance a fly starts from one cyclist and move towards other and moves to and fro till the two cyclist meet each other. If the fly is moving at 15 miles/hour, what is the total distance covered by the fly?

(a) 37.5 miles   (b) 38.5 miles

(c) 40 miles   (d) 32 miles

VERBAL ABILITY

Directions for the Question 13-17 : Answer the questions that follow each passage.

Recent technological advances in manned and unmanned undersea vehicles, along with breakthroughts in satellite technology and computer equipment, have overcome some of the limitations of diverse and diving equipments for scientists doing research on the great oceans of the world. Without a vehicle, divers often became sluggish, and their mental concentration was severely limited. Because undersea pressure affects their speech organs, communication among divers has always been difficult or impossible. But today, most oceanographers avoid the use of vulnerable human divers, preferring to reduce the risk to human life and make direct observations by means of instruments that are lowered into the ocean, from samples taken from the water, or from photographs made by orbiting satellites. Direct observations of the ocean floor can be made not only by divers but also by deep diving submarines in the water and even by the technology of sophisticated aerial photography from vantage points above the surface of the water. Some submarines can dive to depths of more than seven miles and cruise at dephs of

13. How is a radio-equipped buoy operated?

(a) By operators inside the vehicle in the part underwater

(b) By operators outside the vehicle on a ship

(c) By operators outside the vehicle on a diving platform

(d) By operators outside the vehicle in a laboratory on shore

14. The word cruise in the given paragraph could best be replaced by

(a) Travel at a constant speed

(b) Function without problems

(c) Stay in communication

(d) Remain still

15. Which of the following are NOT shown in satellite photograph?

(a) The temperature of the ocean's surface

(b) Cloud formations over the ocean

(c) A model of the ocean's movements

(d) The location of sea ice

16. Undersea vehicles

(a) Are too small for a man to fit inside

(b) Are very slow to respond

(c) Have the same limitations that divers have

(d) Make direct observations of the ocean floor

17. With what topic is the passage primarily concerned?

(a) Technological advances in oceanography

(b) Communication among divers

(c) Direct observation of the ocean floor

(d) Undersea vehicles

Directions for the question 18-19 : Fill in the blanks using the appropriate options.

18. The argument that the need for a looser fiscal policy to _______ demand outweighs the need to _______ budget deficits is persuasive.

(a) assess, minimize   (b) stimulate, control

(c) outstrip, eliminate   (d) restrain, conceal

19. This simplified _______ to the decision-making process is a must read for anyone _______ important real estate, personal, or professional decisions.

(a) primer, maximizing   (b) introduction, under

(c) tract, enacting   (d) guide, facing

Directions for the question 20 : Sentences are given with blanks to be filled in with an appropriate word.

Choose the correct word out of the four.

20. He is the friend .... I trust most.

(a) who   (b) whom

(c) which   (d) him

TECHNICAL ABILITY

21. Memory is allocated from _______ for each and every malloc function call

(a) Stack

(b) Heap

(c) Static memory area

(d) Cache

22. Every time the function containing it is called.

(a) When it is globally declared

(b) Only when declared within a function.

(c) Only the first time the function containing it is called

(d) Only the first time the function containing it is called

23. What would be the output of following code?

```
#include
int main(int argc,char **argv)
{
int iVar = 0, iCnt, aiArr[] = {56,23,4,89,-200,34};
for(iCnt = 1; iCnt <6; iCnt++)
{ if(aiArr[iCnt] < aiArr[iVar])
iVar = iCnt;
}
printf("%d",iVar);
return 0;
}
```

(a) 4.0

(b) 89.0

(c) 3.0

(d) -200.0

24. Under which of the following Big O notation it is suggested to review design of algorithm?

(a) $O(n^2)$

(b) $O(nlogn)$

(c) $O(n)$

(d) $O(2^n)$

25. Which of the following is true about linked lists?

(a) It can be considered as series of nodes

(b) Each node has a single pointer to the next node

(c) In the last node there is a null pointer

(d) All of these

26.
```
#include
main()
{
int a = 6,y = 3,z;
float t = 4.55;
z = a/y+t+a/y-t+a-2*t;
printf("%d",z);
}
```

(a) 3.0

(b) 3.00000

(c) 3.55

(d) None

27. Which of the following statements are correct ?

1. A string is a collection of characters terminated by.

2. The format specifier %s is used to print a string.

3. The length of the string can be obtained by strlen().

4. The pointer CANNOT work on string.

(a) A, B

(b) A, B, C

(c) B, D

(d) C, D

28. What is the similarity between a structure, union and enumeration?

(a) All of them let you define new values

(b) All of them let you define new data types

(c) All of them let you define new pointers

(d) All of them let you define new structures

29. What will be the output of the program ?

```
#include<stdio.h>
int main()
{
enum days {MON=-1, TUE, WED = 6, THU, FRI, SAT};
printf("%d, %d, %d, %d, %d, %d ", MON, TUE, WED, THU, FRI, SAT);
return 0;
}
```

(a) -1, 0, 1, 2, 3, 4

(b) -1, 2, 6, 3, 4, 5

(c) -1, 0, 6, 2, 3, 4

(d) -1, 0, 6, 7, 8, 9

30. In which stage the following code
```
#include<stdio.h>
```
gets replaced by the contents of the file stdio.h

(a) During editing

(b) During linking

(c) During execution

(d) During preprocessing

31. Main ()
```
{
Static char a[3][4]={"abcd","mnop" ,"fghi"}
Putchar(**(a);
}
```

(a) will not compile successfully

(b) prints a

(c) prints m

(d) prints garbage

32. What is the output of the following problem?
```
#define INC(X) X++
main()
{
int X = 4;
printf("%d",INC(X++));
}
```

(a) 4.0

(b) 5.0

(c) 6.0

(d) compilation error

33. What is the value assigned to the variable X if b is 7? X = b > 8? b <<3 : b > 4? b >> 1 : b;

(a) 7.0   (b) 28.0

(c) 3.0   (d) 14.0

34. Which is the output produced by the following program

```
main()
{
int n = 2;
printf("%d %d \n", ++n, n*n);
}
```

(a) 3, 6   (b) 3, 4

(c) 2, 4   (d) cannot determined

35. char 1 byte , short of 2 bytes , integer of 4 byte,

```
struct
{
char a;
char b;
int a[2];
short d;
int e;
char i;
} name;
sizeof(name)
```

(a) 16.0   (b) 18.0

(c) 20.0   (d) 19.0

36. What is the output of this C code?

```
#include <stdio.h>
struct student
{
char a[5];
};
void main()
{
struct student s[] = {"hi", "hey"};
printf("%c", s[0].a[1]); }
```

(a) h   (b) I

(c) e   (d) y

37. What is the output of this C code?

```
#include <stdio.h>
void main()
{
static int x;
if (x++ < 2)
main();
}
```

(a) Infinite calls to main

(b) Run time error

(c) Varies

(d) main is called twice

38. Which of the following is not possible?

(a) A structure variable pointing to itself

(b) A structure variable pointing to another structure variable of same type

(c) 2 different type of structure variable pointing at each other.

(d) None of these

39. Property of external variable to be accessed by any source file is called by C90 standard as

(a) external linkage   (b) external scope

(c) global scope   (d) global linkage

40.
```
#include <stdio.h> int main()
{
char chr;
chr = 128;
printf("%d \n", chr);
return 0;
}
```

(a) 128.0

(b) −128.0

(c) Depends on the compiler

(d) None of the mentioned

41. What is the output of this C code?

```
#include <stdio.h>
int main()
{
char *p[1] = {"hello"};
printf("%s", (p)[0]);
return 0;
}
```

(a) Compile time error

(b) Undefined behavior

(c) hello

(d) None of the mentioned

42. What is the output of this C code?

```
#include <stdio.h>
int main()
{
int a = 10;
if (a == a--)
printf("TRUE 1 \t");
```

```
a = 10;
if (a == – – a)
printf("TRUE 2\t");
}
```

(a) TRUE 1 (b) TRUE 2
(c) TRUE 1 TRUE 2 (d) No output

43. The scope of an automatic variable is:
   (a) the block it appears
   (b) Within the blocks of the block it appears
   (c) Until the end of program
   (d) Both (a) and (b)

44. Default storage class if not any is specified for a local variable, is auto
   (a) True
   (b) False
   (c) Depends on the standard
   (d) None of the mentioned

45. Functional Dependencies are the types of constraints that are based on______
   (a) Key (b) Key revisited
   (c) Superset key (d) None of these

46. Empdt1 (empcode, name, street, city, state, pincode). For any pincode, there is only one city and state. Also, for given street, city and state, there is just one pincode. In normalization terms, empdt1 is a relation in
   (a) 1 NF only
   (b) 2 NF and hence also in 1 NF
   (c) 3NF and hence also in 2NF and 1NF
   (d) BCNF and hence also in 3NF, 2NF and 1NF

47. A ______ file system is software that enables multiple computers to share file storage while maintaining consistent space allocation and file content.
   (a) Storage (b) Tertiary
   (c) Secondary (d) Cluster

48. Which of the following is used to get back all the transactions back after rollback ?
   (a) Commit (b) Rollback
   (c) Flashback (d) Redo

49. The CREATE TRIGGER statement is used to create the trigger. THE _____ clause specifies the table name on which the trigger is to be attached. The ______ specifies that this is an AFTER INSERT trigger.
   (a) for insert, on (b) On, for insert
   (c) For, insert (d) Both a and c

50. The deadlock state can be changed back to stable state by using ______ statement.
   (a) Commit (b) Rollback
   (c) Savepoint (d) Deadlock

51. A system is in a ______ state if there exists a set of transactions such that every transaction in the set is waiting for another transaction in the set.
   (a) Idle (b) Waiting
   (c) Deadlock (d) Ready

52. For which one of the following reasons does Internet Protocol (IP)use the timeto- live (TTL) field in the IP datagram header
   (a) Ensure packets reach destination within that time
   (b) Discard packets that reach later than that time
   (c) Prevent packets from looping indefinitely
   (d) Limit the time for which a packet gets queued in intermediate routers.

53. A process executes the code
   fork(); fork(); fork();
   The total number of child processes created is
   (a) 3.0 (b) 4.0
   (c) 7.0 (d) 8.0

54. Which of the following is true about virtual functions in C++.
   (a) Virtual functions are functions that can be overridden in derived class with the same signature.
   (b) Virtual functions enable run-time polymorphism in a inheritance hierarchy.
   (c) If a function is 'virtual' in the base class, the most-derived class's implementation of the function is called according to the actual type of the object referred to, regardless of the declared type of the pointer or reference. In non-virtual functions, the functions are called according to the type of reference or pointer.
   (d) All of the above

55. Which of the following is true about pure virtual functions?
   (1) Their implementation is not provided in a class where they are declared.
   (2) If a class has a pure virtual function, then the class becomes abstract class and an instance of this class cannot be created.
   (a) Both 1 and 2 (b) Only 1
   (c) Only 2 (d) Neither 1 nor 2

ANSWERS

1. (d)	**2.** (b)	**3.** (a)	**4.** (b)	**5.** (b)	**6.** (c)	**7.** (a)	**8.** (b)	**9.** (b)	**10.** (b)
11. (d)	**12.** (a)	**13.** (d)	**14.** (a)	**15.** (c)	**16.** (d)	**17.** (a)	**18.** (b)	**19.** (d)	**20.** (b)
21. (b)	**22.** (d)	**23.** (a)	**24.** (d)	**25.** (d)	**26.** (d)	**27.** (b)	**28.** (b)	**29.** (d)	**30.** (d)
31. (b)	**32.** (d)	**33.** (c)	**34.** (b)	**35.** (a)	**36.** (b)	**37.** (d)	**38.** (d)	**39.** (a)	**40.** (b)
41. (c)	**42.** (c)	**43.** (d)	**44.** (a)	**45.** (a)	**46.** (b)	**47.** (d)	**48.** (c)	**49.** (b)	**50.** (b)
51. (c)	**52.** (c)	**53.** (c)	**54.** (d)	**55.** (c)					

EXPLANATIONS

1. Let the amout spent for all students, politicians, actors and leaders be S, P, A and L respectively.

Given that, 6 students spent as much as 7 politicians.

So, Amount spent per student × 6 = Amout spent per politician × 7

Or (Total amount spent on students/Total Students) × 6 = (Total amount spent on politicians / Total politicians) × 7

Or, $(S/30) \times 6 = (P/35) \times 7$

$\Rightarrow S/5 = P/5$

$\Rightarrow S = P$ ...(i)

15 politicians spent as much as 12 actors :

Therefore, $(P/35) \times 15 = (A/20) \times 12$

$\Rightarrow 3P/7 = 3A/5$

$\Rightarrow 5P = 7P$

$\Rightarrow 5S = 7A$ (since S = P)

$\Rightarrow A = 5S/7$ ...(ii)

And 10 actors spent as much as 9 leaders :

Therefore, $(A/20) \times 10 = (L/27) \times 9$

$\Rightarrow 3A = 2L$

$\Rightarrow A = 2L/3$

$\Rightarrow 5S/7 = 2L/3$ (since A = 5S/7)

$\Rightarrow L = 15S/14$ ...(iii)

The total amount spent for the party is Rs. 9000

i.e., S + P + A + L = 9000

from eqn. (i), eq. (ii) and eq. (iii), we have

$\Rightarrow S + S + 5S/7 + 15S/14 = 9000$

$\Rightarrow 53S/14 = 9000$

$\Rightarrow S = 9000 * 14/53$

$\Rightarrow S = 2290.90 \sim 2291$.

Hence, the answer is Rs. 2291

2. M1F1M2F2M3F3M4F4M5F5 = 5! × 5!

OR

F1M1F2M2F3M3F4M4F5M5 = 5! × 5!

= 2 × 5! × 5!

= 28800

3. The fly take off toward the opposite cyclist, but at the same time the cyclist is coming toward the fly.

This means we have 15t + 10t = 20.

25t = 20

t = 4/5 hrs or 48 minutes the fly has flown and the cyclist has pedaled.

In this time the fly flew 12 km and each cyclist traveled 8 km. 15(4/5) = 12.

Since the cylists are pedaling 10 kph toward each other, in 1 hour they will meet.

But as the fly heads back to the other cyclist, the cyclist is heading toward him at 10 km/hr.

There is 4 km left to cover as the fly heads back to the cyclist it started out on.

In 12 minutes the fly covers 15(1/5) = 3 km

Thus, the fly covers 12 + 3 = 15 km altogether.

4. Let total number of women = w

total number of men = m

Number of games in which both players were women = 45

$\Rightarrow {}^{w}C_2 = 45$

$\Rightarrow w(w - 1) / 2 = 45$

$\Rightarrow w(w - 1) = 90$

$\Rightarrow w = 10$

Number of games in which both players were men = 190

$\Rightarrow {}^{m}C_2 = 190$

$\Rightarrow$ m(m – 1) / 2 = 190

$\Rightarrow$ m(m – 1) = 380

$\Rightarrow$ m = 20

We have got that

Total number of women = 10

Total number of men = 20

Required number of games in which one person was a man and other person was a woman

$= {}^{20}C_1 \times {}^{10}C_1 = 20 \times 10$

$= 200$

5. To reach the winning point, A will have to cover a distance of 500 – 140 = 360 metre

ratio of the speeds of two contestants A and B is 3 : 4

i.e., when A covers 3 metre, B covers 4 metre.

$\Rightarrow$ When A covers 360 metre,

B covers 4 / 3 $\times$ 360 = 480 metre.

Remaining distance B have to cover

$= 500 - 480 = 20$ metre

$\Rightarrow$ A wins by 20 metre

6. Selling price = 2880

Labelled price = 2880 $\times$ 100/120 = 2400

Price at which he bought the computer

$= 2400 - (2400 \times 15/100) = 2040$

7. Total CP = 20 $\times$ 8.5 + 35 $\times$ 8.75

$= 170 + 306.25 = 476.25$

Profit = 40%

SP = (100 + Profit%) / 100 $\times$ CP

$= (100 + 40) / 100 \times 476.25$

$= 140 / 100 \times 476.25$

$= 140/4 \times 19.05 = 35 \times 19.05$

Total quantity = 20 + 35 = 55 kg

SP per kg = 35 $\times$ 19.05 / 55 = 7 $\times$ 19.05 / 11

$= 7 \times 19 / 11 \approx 133 / 11 \approx 12$

8. Whenever it is not explicitly mentioned that fruits are distinct, we take them as identical. (Persons/men/women are normally considered as distinct.)

00 or more oranges can be selected from 4 identical oranges in (4 + 1) = 5 ways.

00 or more apples can be selected from 5 identical apples in (5 + 1) = 6 ways.

00 or more mangoes can be selected from 6 identical mangoes in (6 + 1) = 7 ways.

Total number of ways = 5 $\times$ 6 $\times$ 7 = 210

But in these 210210 selections, there is one selection where count of each fruit is 00 (i.e., no fruit is selected). Hence we need to reduce this selection.

Therefore, required number of ways

$= 210 - 1 = 209$

9. Total age of the grandparents = 67 $\times$ 2

Total age of the parents = 35 $\times$ 2

Total age of the grandchildren = 6 $\times$ 3

Average age of the family

$= [(67 \times 2) + (35 \times 2) + (6 \times 3)] / 7$

$= [134 + 70 + 18] / 7 = 222 / 7$

10. Total runs scored by the player in 40 innings
$= 40 \times 50$

Total runs scored by the player in 38 innings after excluding two innings = 38 $\times$ 48

Sum of the scores of the excluded innings

$= 40 \times 50 - 38 \times 48 = 2000 - 1824 = 176$

Given that the scores of the excluded innings differ by 172.

Hence let's take the highest score as x + 172 and lowest score as x

Now x + 172 + x = 176

$\Rightarrow$ 2x = 4

$\Rightarrow$ x = 2

Highest score = x + 172 = 2 + 172 = 174

11. Initially, let's remove the 3 houses where the thief planned to steal from. Then we are left with 10 – 3 = 7 houses as numbered below.

* 1 * 2 * 3 * 4 * 5 * 6 * 7 *

Now there are 8 positions as marked as * above to place the 3 houses (from where the thief steals) such that no two such houses are next to each other. This can be done in ${}^8C_3$ ways.

Hence, required number of ways

$= {}^8C_3 = 8 \times 7 = 56.$

12. time taken by cyclists to meet
$= 50/20 = 2.5$ hrs

distance covered by fly during 2.5 hrs
$= 15 \times 2.5 = 37.5$ miles

■■

MOCK -4

(HP - II)

QUANTITATIVE ABILITY

1. In measuring the sides of a rectangle, one side is taken 5% in excess and the other 4% in deficit. Find the error percent in the area, calculate from measurements.

(a) 0.7%   (b) 0.8%

(c) 0.9%   (d) 0.3%

2. Jack takes 20 minutes to jog around the race course one time, and 25 minutes to jog around a second time. What is his average speed in miles per hour for the whole jog if the course is 3 miles long?

(a) 6   (b) 8

(c) 9   (d) 10

3. A train overtakes two girls who are walking in the opposite direction in which the train is going at the rate of 3 km/h and 6km/h and passes them completely in 36 seconds and 30 seconds respectively. The length of the train is:

(a) 120 m   (b) 150 m

(c) 125 m   (d) None of these

4. If Rs.10 be allowed as true discount on a bill of Rs.110 at the end of a certain time , then the discount allowed on the same sum due at the end of double the time is

(a) 18.20   (b) 18.33

(c) 18   (d) 18.3

5. A man in a train notices that he can count 41 telephone posts in one minute. If they are known to be 50 metres apart, then at what speed is the train travelling?

(a) 60 km/hr   (b) 100 km/hr

(c) 110 km/hr   (d) 120km/hr

6. Nine different letters of alphabet are given, words with 5 letters are formed from these given letters. Then, how many such words can be formed which have at least one letter repeated ?

(a) 43929.0   (b) 59049.0

(c) 15120.0   (d) 0.0

7. A town having teenagers (boys & girls) of 5000 requires 150 litre of water per head. It has a tank measuring 20 m × 15 m × 5 m. The water of this tank will sufficient for ____ days.

(a) 8.0   (b) 6.0

(c) 4.0   (d) 2.0

8. The Manager of a company accepts only one employees leave request for a particular day. If five employees namely Roshan, Mahesh, Sripad, Laxmipriya and Shreyan applied for the leave on the occasion of Diwali. What is the probability that Laxmi priya's leave request will be approved?

(a) 1.0   (b) 1/5

(c) 5.0   (d) 4/5

9. The compound interest earned by Sunil on a certain amount at the end of two years at the rate of 8% p.a. was Rs. 2828.80. Find the total amount tAhat Sunil got back at the end of two years in the form of principal plus interest earned?

(a) 11828.80   (b) 19828.8

(c) 9828.8   (d) 19328.8

10. If two dice are thrown together, the probability of getting an even number on one die and an odd number on the other is ?

(a) 1   (b) ½

(c) 0   (d) 3/5

11. P and Q can complete a job in 24 days working together. P alone can complete it in 32 days. Both of them worked together for 8 days and then P left. The number of days Q will take to complete the remaining work is ?

(a) 56 days   (b) 54 days

(c) 60 days   (d) 64 days

12. To fill 8 vacancies there are 15 candidates of which 5 are from ST. If 3 of the vacancies are reserved for ST candidates while the rest are open to all, Find the number of ways in which the selection can be done ?

(a) 7920.0   (b) 74841.0

(c) 14874.0   (d) 10213.0

VERBAL ABILITY

13. Rearrange these parts which are labeled P, Q, R and S to produce the correct sentence.

It has been established that

P : Einstein was

Q : although a great scientist

R : weak in arithmetic

S : right from his school days

The Proper sequence should be:

(a) SRPQ   (b) QPRS

(c) QPSR   (d) RQPS

14. The first and sixth sentences are given in the beginning. The middle four sentences in each have been removed and jumbled up. These are labeled as P, Q, R and S. Find out the proper order for the four sentences.

S1 : I keep on flapping my big ears all day.

P : They also fear that I will flip them all away.

Q : But children wonder why I flap them so.

R : I flap them so to make sure they are safely there on either side of my head.

S : But I know what I am doing.

S6 : Am I not a smart, intelligent elephant?

The Proper sequence should be :

(a) SRQP   (b) QPSR

(c) QPRS   (d) PSRQ

15. The weather outside was extremely pleasant and hence we decided to ______

(a) utilise our time in watching the television

(b) refrain from going out for a morning walk

(c) enjoy a morning ride in the open

(d) employ this rare opportunity for writing letters

16. He has no money now ______

(a) although he was very poor once

(b) as he has given up all his wealth

(c) because he was very rich once

(d) because he was very greedy about wealth

Directions for (17 - 18) : Each of the following questions consists of a word in capital letters, followed by four words or groups of words.

Select the word or group of words that is most similar in meaning (Synonym) to the word in capital letters.

17. FINESSE

(a) Skill   (b) Softness

(c) Charm   (d) Gist

18. IMPROMPTU

(a) Offhand   (b) Unimportant

(c) Unreal   (d) Effective

Directions for (19 – 20) : In the following questions choose the word which is the exact OPPOSITE of the given words.

19. HAPLESS

(a) Cheerful   (b) Consistent

(c) Fortunate   (d) Shapely

20. ANNOY

(a) Praise   (b) Rejoice

(c) Please   (d) Reward

TECHNICAL ABILITY

21. Assume that size of an integer is 32 bit. What is the output of following program?

```c
#include<stdio.h>
struct st
{
int x;
static int y;
};
int main()
{
printf("%d", sizeof(struct st));
return 0;
}
```

(a) 4.0   (b) 8.0

(c) Compiler Error   (d) Runtime Error

22.

```c
#include<stdio.h>
struct st
{
int x;
struct st next;
};
int main()
{
struct st temp;
temp.x = 10;
temp.next = temp;
printf("%d", temp.next.x);
return 0;
}
```

(a) Compiler Error   (b) 10.0

(c) Runtime Error   (d) Garbage Value

23. What is the output of the following program?

```cpp
#include<iostream>
using namespace std;
class Base {
public:
void f() {
cout<<"Base \n";
}
};
class Derived:public Base {
public:
void f() {
```

```
cout<<"Derived\n";
}
};
main() {
Base *p = new Derived();
p->f();
}
```

(a) Base   (b) Derived

(c) Compile error (d) None of the above

24. In the given below code, what will be return by the function get ()?

```
#include<stdio.h>
int get();
int main()
{
const int x = get();
printf("%d", x);
return 0;
}
int get()
{
return 40;
}
```

(a) 40.0   (b) 20.0

(c) 0.0   (d) Error

25. What is the output of the following program?

```
#include<iostream>
using namespace std;
main () {
int i = 13, j = 60;
i^ = j;
j^ = i;
i^ = j;
cout< }
```

(a) 73 73   (b) 60 13

(c) 13 60   (d) 60 60

26. Pick the correct statement for const and volatile.

(a) const is the opposite of volatile and vice versa.

(b) const and volatile can't be used for struct and union.

(c) const and volatile can't be used for enum.

(d) const and volatile are independent i.e. it's possible that a variable is defined as both const and volatile.

27.
```
#include <iostream>
using namespace std;
class Player
{
private:
int id;
static int next_id;
public:
int getID() { return id; }
Player(){ id = next_id++; }
};
int Player::next_id = 1;
int main ()
{
Player p1;
Player p2;
Player p3;
cout << p1.getID () << " ";
cout << p2.getID () << " ";
cout << p3.getID ();
return 0;
}
```

(a) Compiler Error (b) 1 2 3

(c) 1 1 1   (d) 3 3 3

28. Predict the output of below program :

```
#include <stdio.h>
int main()
{
int arr[5];
// Assume base address of arr is 2000 and size of integer is 32 bit
printf("%u %u", arr + 1, &arr + 1);
return 0;
}
```

(a) 2004 2020

(b) 2004 2004

(c) 2004 Garbage value

(d) The program fails to compile because Address-of operator cannot be used with array name

29. In the worst case, the number of comparisons needed to search a singly linked list of length n for a given element is

(a) log 2 n   (b) n/2

(c) log 2 n – 1   (d) n

30. Suppose each set is represented as a linked list with elements in arbitrary order. Which of the operations among union, intersection, membership, cardinality will be the slowest?

(a) union only

(b) intersection, membership

(c) membership, cardinality

(d) union, intersection

31. Output of following program?

```c
# include <stdio.h>
void fun(int *ptr)
{
*ptr = 30;
}
int main()
{
int y = 20;
fun(&y);
printf("%d", y);
return 0;
}
```

(a) 20.0

(b) 30.0

(c) Compiler Error

(d) Runtime Error

32.
```c
#include <stdio.h>
#if X == 3
#define Y 3
#else
#define Y 5
#endif
int main()
{
printf("%d", Y);
return 0;
}
```

What is the output of the above program?

(a) 3.0

(b) 5.0

(c) 3 or 5 depending on value of X

(d) Compile time error

33. Which of the following operations is not O(1) for an array of sorted data. You may assume that array elements are distinct.

(a) Find the ith largest element

(b) Delete an element

(c) Find the ith smallest element

(d) All of the above

34.
```c
#include<stdio.h>
int main()
{
typedef int *i;
int j = 10;
i *a = &j;
printf("%d", **a);
return 0;
}
```

(a) Compiler Error

(b) Garbage Value

(c) 10.0

(d) 0.0

35. A program P reads in 500 integers in the range [0..100] exe presenting the scores of 500 students. It then prints the frequency of each score above 50. What would be the best way for P to store the frequencies?

(a) An array of 50 numbers

(b) An array of 100 numbers

(c) An array of 500 numbers

(d) A dynamically allocated array of 550 numbers

36. How many different insertion sequences of the key values using the same hash function and linear probing will result in the hash table shown above?

(a) 10.0

(b) 20.0

(c) 30.0

(d) 40.0

37. How many stacks are needed to implement a queue. Consider the situation where no other data structure like arrays, linked list is available to you.

(a) 1.0

(b) 2.0

(c) 3.0

(d) 4.0

38. What is the value of the expression $(3^{\wedge}6) + (a^{\wedge}(a)$?

(a) 3.0

(b) 5.0

(c) 6.0

(d) a+18

39. Which of the following traversal outputs the data in sorted order in a BST?

(a) Preorder

(b) Inorder

(c) Postorder

(d) Level order

40. The type of the controlling expression of a switch statement cannot be of the type

(a) int

(b) char

(c) short

(d) float

41. A company needs to develop digital signal processing software for one of its newest inventions. The software is expected to have 40000 lines of code. The company needs to determine the effort in person-months needed to develop this software using the basic COCOMO model. The multiplicative factor for this model is given as 2.8 for the software development on embedded systems, while the exponentiation factor is given as 1.20. What is the estimated effort in person-months?

(a) 234.25 (b) 932.5

(c) 287.8 (d) 122.4

42. Which one of the following is NOT desired in a good Software Requirement Specifications (SRS) document?

(a) Functional Requirements

(b) Non-Functional Requirements

(c) Goals of Implementation

(d) Algorithms for Software Implementation

43. Which of the following page replacement algorithms suffers from Belady's anomaly?

(a) FIFO

(b) LRU

(c) Optimal Page Replacement

(d) Both LRU and FIFO

44. What is the swap space in the disk used for?

(a) Saving temporary html pages

(b) Saving process data

(c) Storing the super-block

(d) Storing device drivers

45. Increasing the RAM of a computer typically improves performance because:

(a) Virtual memory increases

(b) Larger RAMs are faster

(c) Fewer page faults occur

(d) Fewer segmentation faults occur

46. Which of the following scenarios may lead to an irrecoverable error in a database system?

(a) A transaction writes a data item after it is read by an uncommitted transaction

(b) A transaction reads a data item after it is read by an uncommitted transaction

(c) A transaction reads a data item after it is written by a committed transaction

(d) A transaction reads a data item after it is written by an uncommitted transaction

47. Consider the following transaction involving two bank accounts x and y.

read(x); x := x – 50; write(x); read(y); y := y + 50; write(y)

The constraint that the sum of the accounts x and y should remain constant is that of

(a) Atomicity (b) Consistency

(c) Isolation (d) Durability

48. #include <stdio.h>

```
int main()
{
int a[5] = {1,2,3,4,5};
int *ptr = (int*)(&a+1);
printf("%d %d", *(a+1), *(ptr-1));
return 0;
}
```

(a) 2 5

(b) Garbage Value

(c) Compiler Error

(d) Segmentation Fault

49. Page fault occurs when

(a) When a requested page is in memory

(b) When a requested page is not in memory

(c) When a page is corrupted

(d) When an exception is thrown

50. Thrashing occurs when

(a) When a page fault occurs

(b) Processes on system frequently access pages not memory

(c) Processes on system are in running state

(d) Processes on system are in waiting state

51. Drawbacks of file processing system

(a) Data redundancy

(b) Limited data sharing

(c) lack of security

(d) all of the above

52. Which bitwise operator is suitable for turning on a particular bit in a number?

(a) && operator (b) & operator

(c) || operator (d) | operator

53. What will be the output of the program?

```
#include<stdio.h>
typedef void v;
typedef int i;
int main()
```

```
{
v fun(i, i);
fun(2, 3);
return 0;
}
v fun(i a, i b)
{
i s=2;
float i;
printf("%d,", sizeof(i));
printf(" %d", a*b*s);
}
```

(a) 2, 8   (b) 4, 8
(c) 2, 4   (d) 4, 12

54. What will be the output of the program?
```
#include<stdio.h>
int main()
{
const int x=5;
const int *ptrx;
ptrx = &x;
*ptrx = 10;
printf("%d\n", x);
return 0;
}
```
(a) 5.0   (b) 10.0
(c) Error   (d) Garbage value

55. What will be the output of the program
```
#include<stdio.h>
void fun(int);
int main(int arg (c)
{
printf("%d\n", argc);
fun(argc);
return 0;
}
void fun(int i
{
if(i!=4)
main(++i);
}
```
(a) 1 2 3   (b) 1 2 3 4
(c) 2 3 4   (a) 1.0

ANSWERS

1. (b)	**2.** (b)	**3.** (b)	**4.** (b)	**5.** (d)	**6.** (a)	**7.** (d)	**8.** (b)	**9.** (b)	**10.** (b)
11. (d)	**12.** (a)	**13.** (b)	**14.** (b)	**15.** (c)	**16.** (b)	**17.** (a)	**18.** (a)	**19.** (c)	**20.** (c)
21. (c)	**22.** (a)	**23.** (a)	**24.** (a)	**25.** (b)	**26.** (d)	**27.** (b)	**28.** (a)	**29.** (d)	**30.** (d)
31. (b)	**32.** (b)	**33.** (b)	**34.** (a)	**35.** (a)	**36.** (c)	**37.** (b)	**38.** (b)	**39.** (b)	**40.** (d)
41. (c)	**42.** (c)	**43.** (d)	**44.** (a)	**45.** (a)	**46.** (d)	**47.** (b)	**48.** (a)	**49.** (b)	**50.** (b)
51. (d)	**52.** (d)	**53.** (d)	**54.** (c)	**55.** (b)					

EXPLANATIONS

1. Let x and y be the sides of the rectangle then
   correct area = 105x/100 × 96y/100
   = 504 xy/500 – xy = 4 xy / 500
   Error % = 4xy / 500 × 1 / xy × 100
   = 4 / 5
   = 0.8 %

2. Average speed = total distance / total time
   Total distance covered = 6 miles;
   total time = 45 minutes = 0.75 hours
   Average speed = 6/ 0.75 = 8 miles/hour

3. Let the length of the train be x meter, and let the speed of train be y km/h, then
   x = (y + 3) × 5/18 × 36   ...(1)
   x = (y + 6) × 5/18 × 30   ...(2)
   and from eq (1) and (2), we get
   (y + 3) × 36 = (y + 6) × 30
   y = 12 km/h
   x = (y + 3) × 5 / 18 × 36
   x = 150 m

4. Present worth = Amount – True Discount
   = 110 – 10 = Rs.100
   SI on Rs.100 for a certain time = Rs.10
   SI on Rs.100 for doube the time = Rs.20
   TrueDiscount on Rs.120 = 120 – 100 = Rs.20
   TrueDiscount on Rs.110 = Rs.18.33

5. Number of gaps between 41 poles = 40
   So total distance between 41 poles = 40 × 50
   = 2000 meter = 2 km
   In 1 minute train is moving 2 km/minute.
   Speed in hour = 2 × 60 = 120 km/hour

6. Number of words with 5 letters from given 9 alphabets formed = 9^5
   Number of words with 5 letters from given 9 alphabets formed such that no letter is repeated is = $^9P_5$
   Number of words can be formed which have at least one letter repeated = $9^5 - {}^9P_5$
   = 59049 – 15120
   = 43929

7. Total water reqduired = 5000 × 150 liter
   = 750,000 litres = 750 cu.m.
   Volume of tank = 20 × 15 × 5 = 1500 cu.m.
   Number of days required =1500/750 = 2 days.

8. Number of applicants = 5
   On a day, only 1 leave is approved.
   Now favourable events = 1 of 5 applicants is approved
   Probability that Laxmi priya's leave is granted = 1/5.

9. Let the sum be Rs. P
   $P\{(1 + 8 / 100)^2 - 1\} = 2828.80$
   It is in the form of
   P(8/100)(2 + 8/100) = 2828.80
   P = 2828.80 / (0.08)(2.08)
   = 1360/0.08 = 17000
   Principal + Interest = Rs. 19828.80

10. The number of exhaustive outcomes is 36.
    Let E be the event of getting an even number on one die and an odd number on the other.
    Let the event of getting either both even or both odd then = 18/36 = 1/2
    P(E) = 1 – 1/2 = 1/2.

11. (P + Q)'s 1 day work = 1/24
    P's 1 day work = 1/32
    ⇒ Q's 1 day work = 1/24 – 1/32 = 1/96
    Work done by (P + Q) in 8 days = 8/24 = 1/3
    Remainining work = 1 – 1/3 = 2/3
    Time taken by Q to complete the remaining work = 2/3 × 96 = 64 days.

12. ST candidates vacancies can be filled by $^5C_3$ ways = 10
    Remaining vacancies are 5 that are to be filled by 12
    ⇒ $^{12}C_5$ = (12 × 11 × 10 × 9 × 8)/(5 × 4 × 3 × 2 × 1)
    = 792
    Total number of filling the vacancies
    = 10 × 792 = 7920

MOCK - 5

(IBM-I)

1. What are the total number of divisors of 600 (including 1 and 600)?

(a) 24   (b) 40

(c) 16   (d) 20

2. What is the sum of the squares of the first 20 natural numbers (1 to 20)?

(a) 2870   (b) 2000

(c) 5650   (d) 44100

3. For two sets A and B, let ADB denote the set of elements which belong to A or B but not both. If $P = \{1, 2, 3, 4\}$, $Q = \{2, 3, 5, 6,\}$, $R = \{1, 3, 7, 8, 9\}$, $S = \{2, 4, 9, 10\}$, then the number of elements in (PDQ)D(RDS) is

(a) 7   (b) 8

(c) 9   (d) 6

4.
$$\frac{1}{\log_2 100} - \frac{1}{\log_4 100} + \frac{1}{\log_5 100} - \frac{1}{\log_{10} 100}$$
$$+ \frac{1}{\log_{20} 100} - \frac{1}{\log_{25} 100} + \frac{1}{\log_{50} 100} = ?$$

(a) 0   (b) 10

(c) −4   (d) $\dfrac{1}{2}$

5. A call center agent has a list of 305 phone numbers of people in alphabetic order of names (but she does not have any of the names). She needs to quickly contact Deepak Sharma to convey a message to him. If each call takes 2 minutes to complete, and every call is answered, what is the minimum amount of time in which she can guarantee to deliver the message to Mr Sharma.

(a) 18 minutes   (b) 610 minutes

(c) 206 minutes   (d) 34 minutes

6. The times taken by a phone operator to complete 5 calls are 2, 9, 3, 1, 5 minutes respectively. What is the average time per call?

(a) 4 minutes   (b) 7 minutes

(c) 1 minutes   (d) 5 minutes

7. The times taken by a phone operator to complete a call are 2, 9, 3, 1, 5 minutes respectively. What is the median time per call?

(a) 5 minutes   (b) 7 minutes

(c) 1 minutes   (d) 4 minutes

8. Eric throws two dice, and his score is the sum of the values shown. Sandra throws one die, and her score is the square of the value shown. What is the probability that Sandra's score will be strictly higher than Eric's score?

(a) 137/216   (b) 17/36

(c) 173/216   (d) 5/6

9. What is the largest integer that divides all three numbers 23400, 272304, 205248 without leaving a remainder?

(a) 48.0   (b) 24.0

(c) 96   (d) 72

10. Of the 38 people in my office, 10 like to drink chocolate, 15 are cricket fans, and 20 neither like chocolate nor like cricket.

How many people like both cricket and chocolate?

(a) 7.0   (b) 10.0

(c) 15   (d) 18

11. If $f(x) = 2x + 2$ what is $f(f(3))$?

(a) 18   (b) 8

(c) 64   (d) 16

12. If $f(x) = 7x + 12$, what is $f - 1(x)$ (the inverse function)?

(a) $(x - 12)/7$ (b) $7x + 12$

(c) $1/(7x + 12)$ (d) No inverse exists

13. In a tournament, there are 43 junior level and 51 senior level participants. Each pair of juniors play one match. Each pair of seniors play one match. There is no junior versus senior match. The number of girl versus girl matches in junior level is 153, while the number of boy versus boy matches in senior level is 276. The number of matches a boy plays against a girl is

(a) 1098   (b) 1697

(c) 1121   (d) 2158

14. What is the maximum value of $x^3y^3 + 3xy$ when $x + y = 8$?

(a) 4144   (b) 256

(c) 8192   (d) 102

15. How many two-digit numbers, with a non-zero digit in the units place, are there which are more than thrice the number formed by interchanging the positions of its digits?

(1) 7   (2) 6

(3) 5   (4) 8

16. There are equal number of boys and girls in a class. If 12 girls are moved out, twice the boys as girls remain. What was the total number of students in the class?

(a) 32 (b) 48

(c) 42 (d) 38

17. a bb ccc dddd eeeee ....What is the 120th letter?

(a) p (b) r

(c) m (d) o

18. There are 120 male and 100 female in a society. Out of 25% male and 20% female are rural. 20% of male and 25% of female rural people passed in the exam. What % of rural students have passed the exam?

(a) 16% (b) 12%

(c) 0.22 (d) 18%

LOGICAL REASONING

19. Look at this series : 2, 1, (1/2), (1/4), ... What number should come next?

(a) (1/3) (b) (1/8)

(c) (2/8) (d) (1/16)

20. Look at this series: 7, 10, 8, 11, 9, 12, ... What number should come next?

(a) 7 (b) 10

(c) 12 (d) 13

21. Look at this series: 36, 34, 30, 28, 24, ... What number should come next?

(a) 20 (b) 22

(c) 23 (d) 26

22. Look at this series: 22, 21, 23, 22, 24, 23, ... What number should come next?

(a) 22 (b) 24

(c) 25 (d) 26

23. Look at this series: 53, 53, 40, 40, 27, 27, ... What number should come next?

(a) 12 (b) 14

(c) 27 (d) 53

24. Look at this series: 21, 9, 21, 11, 21, 13, 21, ... What number should come next?

(a) 14

(b) 15

(c) 21

(d) 23

25. Look at this series: 58, 52, 46, 40, 34, ... What number should come next?

(a) 26 (b) 28

(c) 30 (d) 32

26. Look at this series: 3, 4, 7, 8, 11, 12, ... What number should come next?

(a) 7 (b) 10

(c) 14 (d) 15

27. Look at this series: 8, 22, 8, 28, 8, ... What number should come next?

(a) 9 (b) 29

(c) 32 (d) 34

28. Look at this series: 31, 29, 24, 22, 17, ... What number should come next?

(a) 15 (b) 14

(c) 13 (d) 12

29. Look at this series : 1.5, 2.3, 3.1, 3.9, ... What number should come next?

(a) 4.2 (b) 4.4

(c) 4.7 (d) 5.1

30. Look at this series : 14, 28, 20, 40, 32, 64, ... What number should come next?

(a) 52 (b) 56

(c) 96 (d) 128

31. Look at this series: 2, 4, 6, 8, 10, ... What number should come next?

(a) 11 (b) 12

(c) 13 (d) 14

32. Look at this series : 201, 202, 204, 207, ... What number should come next?

(a) 205 (b) 208

(c) 210 (d) 211

33. Look at this series: 544, 509, 474, 439, ... What number should come next?

(a) 404 (b) 414

(c) 420 (d) 445

34. Look at this series: 80, 10, 70, 15, 60, ... What number should come next?

(a) 20 (b) 25

(c) 30 (d) 50

35. Look at this series: 2, 6, 18, 54, ... What number should come next?

(a) 108 (b) 148

(c) 162 (d) 216

36. Look at this series: 5.2, 4.8, 4.4, 4, ... What number should come next?

(a) 3.0 (b) 3.3

(c) 3.5 (d) 3.6

VERBAL ABILITY

Direction: Find the correctly spelt words.

37. (solve as per the direction given above)

(a) Efficient (b) Treatmeant

(c) Beterment (d) Employd

38. (solve as per the direction given above)

(a) Foreign

(b) Foreine

(c) Fariegn

(d) Forein

39. (solve as per the direction given above)

(a) Ommineous

(b) Omineous

(c) Ominous

(d) Omenous

40. (solve as per the direction given above)

(a) Pessenger   (b) Passenger

(c) Pasanger   (d) Pesanger

41. (solve as per the direction given above)

(a) Benefitted   (b) Benifited

(c) Benefited   (d) Benefeted

Direction : Rearrange the following five sentences in proper sequence so as to for a meaningful paragraph, then answer the questions given below them.

1. After Examining him, the doctor smiled at him mischievously and took out a syringe.

2. Thinking that he was really sick, his father summoned the family doctor.

3. That day, Mintu wanted to take a day off from school

4. Immediately, Mintu jumped up from his bed and swore the he was fine

Therefor; he pretended to be sick and remained in bed.

42. Which sentence should come **third** in the paragraph?

(a) 1   (b) 2

(c) 3   (d) 4

43. Which sentence should come **last** in the paragraph?

(a) 1   (b) 2

(c) 3   (d) 4

44. Which sentence should come **fourth** in the paragraph?

(a) 1   (b) 2

(c) 3   (d) 4

45. Which sentence should come **second** in the paragraph?

(a) 1   (b) 2

(c) 3   (d) 4

46. Which sentence should come **first** in the paragraph?

(a) 1   (b) 2

(c) 3   (d) 4

Directions: In questions given below out of four alternatives, choose the one which can be substituted for the given word/sentence.

47. Extreme old age when a man behaves like a fool

(a) Imbecility   (b) Senility

(c) Dotage   (d) Superannuation

48. That which cannot be corrected

(a) Unintelligible   (b) Indelible

(c) Illegible   (d) Incorrigible

49. The study of ancient societies

(a) Anthropology   (b) Archaeology

(c) History   (d) Ethnology

50. A person of good understanding knowledge and reasoning power

(a) Expert   (b) Intellectual

(c) Snob   (d) Literate

51. A person who insists on something

(a) Disciplinarian   (b) Stickler

(c) Instantaneous   (d) Boaster

52. State in which the few govern the many

(a) Monarchy   (b) Oligarchy

(c) Plutocracy   (d) Autocracy

Directions: Which of phrases given below each sentence should replace the phrase printed in **bold** type to make the grammatically correct? If the sentence is correct as it is, mark 'E' as the answer.

53. The small child does whatever his father **was done**.

(a) has done   (b) did

(c) does   (d) had done

54. You need not come unless you want to.

(a) You don't need to come unless you want to

(b) You come only when you want to

(c) You come unless you don't want to

(d) You needn't come until you don't want to

55. There are not many men who are so famous that they are frequently referred to by their **short names** only

(a) initials

(b) signatures

(c) pictures

(d) middle names

56. The man **to who I sold** my house was a cheat.

(a) to whom I sell   (b) to who I sell

(c) who was sold to   (d) to whom I sold

57. They **were all shocked at** his failure in the competition.

(a) were shocked at all
(b) had all shocked at
(c) had all shocked by
(d) No correction required

58. I need not offer any explanation regarding this incident - my behaviour **is speaking itself**.

(a) will speak to itself
(b) speaks for itself
(c) has been speaking
(d) speaks about itself

ANSWERS

1. (a)   **2.** (a)   **3.** (a)   **4.** (d)   **5.** (a)   **6.** (a)   **7.** (a)   **8.** (a)   **9.** (b)   **10.** (a)

11. (a)   **12.** (a)   **13.** (a)   **14.** (a)   **15.** (b)   **16.** (b)   **17.** (d)   **18.** (c)   **19.** (b)   **20.** (b)

21. (b)   **22.** (c)   **23.** (b)   **24.** (b)   **25.** (b)   **26.** (d)   **27.** (d)   **28.** (a)   **29.** (c)   **30.** (b)

31. (b)   **32.** (d)   **33.** (a)   **34.** (a)   **35.** (c)   **36.** (d)   **37.** (a)   **38.** (a)   **39.** (c)   **40.** (b)

41. (c)   **42.** (b)   **43.** (d)   **44.** (a)   **45.** (d)   **46.** (c)   **47.** (c)   **48.** (d)   **49.** (b)   **50.** (b)

51. (b)   **52.** (b)   **53.** (c)   **54.** (a)   **55.** (a)   **56.** (a)   **57.** (d)   **58.** (b)

EXPLANATIONS

1. If $N = ap \times bq \times cr .... N = ap \times bq \times cr....$

then the number of factors of

$$N = (p + 1)(q + 1)(r + 1) ....$$

$$600 = 2^3 \times 3^1 \times 5^2$$

So, number of factors of $600 = (3 + 1)(1 + 1)(2 + 1)$
$$= 24$$

2. Using formula $n(n + 1)(2n + 1)/6$, we get the required sum as $20 \times 21 \times 41/6 = 2870$.

3. $(P \Delta Q) = (1, 4, 5, 6)$ and $(R \Delta S) = (1, 2, 3, 4, 7, 8, 10)$

$\Rightarrow (P \Delta Q)\Delta(R \Delta S) = (2, 3, 5, 6, 7, 8, 10)$

4. The given expression can be written as:

$$\frac{1}{\log 100} \times (\log 2 - \log 4 + \log 5 - \log 10 + \log 20 - \log 25 + \log 50)$$

$$= \frac{1}{\log 100} \times (\log 2 \times 5 \times 20 \times 50 - \log 4 \times 10 \times 25)$$

$$= \frac{1}{2} \times \frac{1}{\log 10} \times \log \frac{10000}{1000} = \frac{1}{2}.$$

9. Find GCD

13. Let the number of girls in junior section be g, thus
$$^9C_2 = 153$$

$$\Rightarrow \frac{g(g-1)}{2} = 153$$

$$\Rightarrow g = 18$$

Therefore, number of girls in junior section = 18 and that of boys = 25

Again, let the number of boys in senior section be b

$$\Rightarrow \frac{b(b-1)}{2} = 276$$

$$\Rightarrow b = 24$$

Therefore, number of boys in senior section = 24 and that of girls = 26

Hence, the number of matches played between boys and girls = 25 × 18 + 24 × 27 = 1098.

14. Substitute x = 4 and y = 4

15. Given that: 10a + b > 3(10b + a)

$$\Rightarrow 7a > 29b$$

For b = 1 we get a = 5, 6, 7, 8 and 9

For b = 2 we get a = 9

Hence, required answer will be 6.

17. Number of letters in each term are in AP.

1, 2, 3, ...

So $n(n + 1)/2 \leq 120$

For $n = 15$, we get LHS = 120.

So 15th letter in the alphabet is o.

So 15th term contains 15 o's.

18.

	Male	Female	
	120	100	
Rural	30	20	= 50
Passed	6	5	= 11

From the above data,

Rural male = 25% of (120) = 30,

Rural female = 20% of (100) = 20.

Passed students from rural: male = 20% of (30) = 6, female = 25% of (20) = 5

Required percentage = $11/50 \times 100 = 22\%$

19. This is a simple division series; each number is one-half of the previous number.

In other terms to say, the number is divided by 2 successively to get the next result.

$4/2 = 2$

$2/2 = 1$

$1/2 = 1/2$

$(1/2)/2 = 1/4$

$(1/4)/2 = 1/8$ and so on.

20. This is a simple alternating addition and subtraction series. In the first pattern, 3 is added; in the second, 2 is subtracted.

21. This is an alternating number subtraction series. First, 2 is subtracted, then 4, then 2, and so on.

22. In this simple alternating subtraction and addition series; 1 is subtracted, then 2 is added, and so on.

23. In this series, each number is repeated, then 13 is subtracted to arrive at the next number.

24. In this alternating repetition series, the random number 21 is interpolated every other number into an otherwise simple addition series that increases by 2, beginning with the number 9.

25. This is a simple subtraction series. Each number is 6 less than the previous number.

26. This alternating addition series begins with 3; then 1 is added to give 4; then 3 is added to give 7; then 1 is added, and so on.

27. This is a simple addition series with a random number, 8, interpolated as every other number. In the series, 6 is added to each number except 8, to arrive at the next number.

28. This is a simple alternating subtraction series, which subtracts 2, then 5.

29. In this simple addition series, each number increases by 0.8.

30. This is an alternating multiplication and subtracting series: First, multiply by 2 and then subtract 8.

31. This is a simple addition series. Each number increases by 2.

32. In this addition series, 1 is added to the first number; 2 is added to the second number; 3 is added to the third number; 4 is added to the fourth number; and go on.

33. This is a simple subtraction series. Each number is 35 less than the previous number.

34. This is an alternating addition and subtraction series. In the first pattern, 10 is subtracted from each number to arrive at the next. In the second, 5 is added to each number to arrive at the next

35. This is a simple multiplication series. Each number is 3 times more than the previous number.

36. In this simple subtraction series, each number decreases by 0.4.

MOCK-6

(IBM-II)

1. In particular language if A = 0, B = 1, C = 2,....., Y = 24, Z = 25 then what is the value of ONE + ONE (in the form of alphabets only)
   (a) BDAI
   (b) ABDI
   (c) DABI
   (d) CIDAA

2. Find the number of perfect squares in the given series 2013, 2020, 2027,..............., 2300
   (Hint $44^2 = 1936$)
   (a) 1
   (b) 2
   (c) 3
   (d) Can't be determined

3. What is in the 200th position of 1234 12344 123444 1234444....?
   (a) 56
   (b) 4
   (c) 19
   (d) 13

4. 2345 23455 234555 234555 .... what was last 2 numbers at 200th digit?
   (a) 25
   (b) 40
   (c) 55
   (d) 13

5. Each of 74 students in a class studies at least one of the three subjects H, E and P. Ten students study all three subjects, while twenty study H and E, but not P. Every student who studies P also studies H or E or both. If the number of students studying H equals that studying E, then the number of students studying H is
   (a) 52
   (b) 89
   (c) 53
   (d) 51

6. How many numbers with two or more digits can be formed with the digits 1,2,3,4,5,6,7,8,9, so that in every such number, each digit is used at most once and the digits appear in the ascending order?
   (a) 502
   (b) 504
   (c) 499
   (d) 601

7. Let x, y, z be three positive real numbers in a geometric progression such that x < y < z. If 5x, 16y, and 12z are in an arithmetic progression then the common ratio of the geometric progression is
   (a) $\dfrac{5}{2}$
   (b) $\dfrac{3}{6}$
   (c) $\dfrac{3}{2}$
   (d) $\dfrac{1}{6}$

8. 1/7 th of the tank contains fuel. If 22 litres of fuel is poured into the tank the indicator rests at 1/5th mark. What is the quantity of the tank?
   (a) 565
   (b) 425
   (c) 285
   (d) 130

9. What is the probability of getting sum 3 or 4 when 2 dice are rolled?
   (a) 5/26
   (b) 5/36
   (c) 15/369
   (d) 15/363

10. The inner diameter of a well is 18 meters. If the well is 28 metres deep then what is its volume?
    (a) 7218 cu m
    (b) 7282 cu m
    (c) 7128 cu m
    (d) 7028 cu

11. Ayesha's father was 38 years of age when she was born while her mother was 36 years old when her brother four years younger to her was born. What is the difference between the ages of her parents?
    (a) 2 years
    (b) 4 years
    (c) 6 years
    (d) 8 years

12. A person's present age is two-fifth of the age of his mother. After 8 years, he will be one-half of the age of his mother.
    How old is the mother at present?
    (a) 32 years
    (b) 36 years
    (c) 40 years
    (d) 48 years

13. A milk vendor has 2 cans of milk. The first contains 25% water and the rest milk. The second contains 50% water. How much milk should he mix from each of the containers so as to get 12 litres of milk such that the ratio of water to milk is 3 : 5?
    (a) 4 litres, 8 litres
    (b) 6 litres, 6 litres
    (c) 5 litres, 7 litres
    (d) 7 litres, 5 litres

14. In what ratio must a grocer mix two varieties of pulses costing Rs. 15 and Rs. 20 per kg respectively so as to get a mixture worth Rs. 16.50 kg?
    (a) 3 : 7
    (b) 5 : 7
    (c) 7 : 3
    (d) 7 : 5

15. One pipe can fill a tank three times as fast as another pipe. If together the two pipes can fill the tank in 36 minutes, then the slower pipe alone will be able to fill the tank in :
    (a) 81 min.
    (b) 108 min.
    (c) 144 min.
    (d) 192 min.

16. A large tanker can be filled by two pipes A and B in 60 minutes and 40 minutes respectively. How many minutes will it take to fill the tanker from empty state if B is used for half the time and A and B fill it together for the other half?

(a) 15 min

(b) 20 min

(c) 27.5 min

(d) 30 min

17. In covering a distance of 30 km, Abhay takes 2 hours more than Sameer. If Abhay doubles his speed, then he would take 1 hour less than Sameer. Abhay's speed is :

(a) 5 kmph   (b) 6 kmph

(c) 6.25 kmph   (d) 7.5 kmph

18. Robert is travelling on his cycle and has calculated to reach point A at 2 P.M. if he travels at 10 kmph, he will reach there at 12 noon if he travels at 15 kmph. At what speed must he travel to reach A at 1 P.M.?

(a) 8 kmph   (b) 11 kmph

(c) 12 kmph   (d) 14 kmph

LOGICAL REASONING

19. 4, 3, 4, 9, 32 ......

(a) 125.0   (b) 135.0

(c) 145.0   (d) 155.0

20. 16 (81) 25   49 (169) 36   64 (?) 4

(a) 121.0   (b) 84.0

(c) 81.0   (d) 100

21. 1.5, 3, 5.5, 9, 13.5, 19, ...

(a) 81.0   (b) 15.5

(c) 21.5   (d) 25.5

22. Which term of the series 5, 8, 11, 14, ... is 320?

(a) 104th   (b) 105th

(c) 106th   (d) 64th

23. In the series 5, 10, 20, 40,....what will be the 10th term?

(a) 1280.0   (b) 2560.0

(c) 1820.0   (d) 2650.0

24. Pointing to Manju, Raju said, "The son of her only brother is the brother of my wife". How is Manju related to Raju?

(a) Mother's sister

(b) Grandmother

(c) Mother-in-law

(d) Sister of father-in-law

25. Introducing a man to her husband, a woman said, "His brother's father is the only son of my grandfather." How is the woman related to this man?

(a) Mother   (b) Aunt

(c) Sister   (d) Daughter

26. How is Radha's mother's mother's daughter-in-law's daughter related to Radha?

(a) Sister   (b) Mother

(c) Cousin   (d) Aunt

27. A is the husband of B. E is the daughter of C. A is the father of C. How is B related to E?

(a) Mother   (b) Grandmother

(c) Aunt   (d) Cousin

28. Mr.Ramu's mother's father-in-law's only son's only daughter's son is Chetan. How is Ramu related to Chetan?

(a) Uncle   (b) Nephew

(c) Niece   (d) Father

Directions (Q. 29- 33) : There are five friends Sachin, Kunal, Mohit, Anuj and Rohan. Sachin ia shorter than Kunal but taller than Rohan. Mohit is tallest. Anuj is a little shorter than Kunal and little taller than Sachin.

29. Who is the shortest?

(a) Rohan   (b) Sachin

(c) Anuj   (d) Kunal

30. If they stand in the order of their heights, who will be in the middle?

(a) Kunal   (b) Rohan

(c) Sachin   (d) Anuj

31. If they stand in the order of increasing heights, who will be the second?

(a) Anuj   (b) Sachin

(c) Rohan   (d) Kunal

32. Who is the second tallest?

(a) Sachin   (b) Kunal

(c) Anuj   (d) Rohan

33. Who is taller than Anuj but shorter than Mohit?

(a) Kunal   (b) Rohan

(c) Sachin   (d) Data Inadequate

Directions (34 to 36) : Read the following information carefully and answer the questions that follow.

  I. P, Q, R, S, T and U are six students procuring their Master's degree in six different subjects- English, History, Philosophy, Physics, Statistics and Mathematics.

II. Two of them stay in hostel; two stay as paying guest (PG) and the remaining two stay at their home.

III. R does not stay as PG and studies Philosophy.

IV. The students studying Statistics and History do not stay as PG.

V. T studies Mathematics and S studies Physics.

VI. U and S stay in hostel. T stays as PG and Q stays at home.

34. Who studies English?

    (a) R   (b) P

    (c) T   (d) U

35. Which of the following combinations of subjects and place of stay is not correct?

    (a) English-Hostel   (b) Mathematics-PG

    (c) Philosophy-Home   (d) Physics-Hostel

36. Which of the following pairs of students stay one each at hostel and at home?

    (a) QR   (b) SR

    (c) US   (d) Data inadequate

VERBAL ABILITY

Directions (Q. 37-41): In each of the following sentences there are two blank spaces. Below each five pairs of words have been denoted by letters (A), (B), (C) and (D). Find out which pair of words can be filled up in the blanks in the sentence in the same sequence to make the sentence meaningfully complete.

37. A committee has been .... to .... the transformation of the city into an International finance centre.

    (a) constituted, convert

    (b) appointed, oversee

    (c) converged, evaluate

    (d) inducted, change

38. Keeping in mind the .... to develop the sector the government has .... solicited foreign investment.

    (a) importance, never (b) proposal, forcibly

    (c) objective, wanted (d) need, actively

39. In his speech he vowed to .... the four billion unbanked individuals across the world into the .... of financial inclusion.

    (a) represent, sphere

    (b) target, area

    (c) bring, realm

    (d) engage, achievement

40. Although he puts in .... of overtime and takes few holidays, he .... cannot support his family.

    (a) sufficient, however

    (b) lot, besides

    (c) much, thus

    (d) plenty, still

41. They have been .... on incentives to .... these practices are implemented nat grass root level.

    (a) relying, ensure

    (b) improving, secure

    (c) advocating, confirm

    (d) debating, necessitate

Directions (Q. 42-55) : In the following passage there are blanks, each of which has been numbered. These numbers are printed below the passage and against each, five words are suggested, one of which fits the blank appropriately. Find out the appropriate word in each case.

He was a charismatic leader, an entrepreneur and highly effective manager all rolled into one. As a leader, he ...(42)... the company's growth plan in a dedicated manner and he never ...(43)... focus. The cement industry in those days was doing badly ...(44)... to everyone's expectations he sanctioned an additional plant in ...(45)... time. He was ...(46)... that since the cement industry was cyclic in nature, by the time the plant was ...(47)... the market would have improved. It did happen and the decision brought rich ...(48)... when the plant was commissioned. Not only was he a great entrepreneur but he also ...(49)... all this senior people to be 'practicing entrepreneurs'. I have a seen similar example at the Asian Institute of Management, which allows its professors to ...(50)... their own business. This made their lectures more practical and less theoretical. It is the ...(51)... of the Institute's success.

42. (a) achieved   (b) implemented

    (c) visualized   (d) persevered

43. (a) moved   (b) shifts

    (c) missed   (d) changes

44. (a) Contrary   (b) Opposite

    (c) Yet   (d) Obedient

45. (a) any   (b) mean

    (c) short   (d) no

46. (a) known   (b) calculating

    (c) certain   (d) dreamt

47. (a) operational   (b) install

    (c) use   (d) produced

48. (a) supply   (b) diversity
(c) rewards   (d) pay

49. (a) thought   (b) tried
(c) wished   (d) encourage

50. (a) expand   (b) function
(c) chose   (d) run

51. (a) responsibility   (b) secret
(c) guarantee   (d) prize

52. Which happened first?
    (a) An earthquake damaged the Coliseum.
    (b) The Coliseum was struck by lightning.
    (c) The Coliseum appeared on the back of a coin.
    (d) The Coliseum was used as a castle.

53. When did the Roman finish building the Coliseum?
    (a) The year 70   (b) The year 523
    (c) The year 80   (d) The year 240

54. What caused the fire that damaged the upper levels of the Coliseum?
    (a) A bolt of lightning
    (b) Rowdy people who came to watch the events
    (c) An attacking army
    (d) An angry mob

55. For which purpose was the Coliseum not used?
    (a) People fought other people in it.
    (b) It was a private castle.
    (c) People fought animals in it.
    (d) It was a meeting place for the government.

56. Which caused the most damage to the Coliseum?
    (a) Fires   (b) Earthquakes
    (c) Wars   (d) Hurricanes

Read the passage and answer below questions (57-58) :

The Coliseum is an ancient stadium in the center of Rome. It is the largest of its Kind. It is very old. They started building it in the year 70. It took ten years to build. It is still around today. The Coliseum has been used in many ways. In ancient Rome, men fought each other in it. They fought against lions, tigers, and bears. Oh my! It was dreadful. But most of the people loved t. As many as 80,000 Romans would pack inside to watch. These gruesome events went on until 523. The Coliseum has been damaged many times over the years. It was struck by lightning in the year 217. This started a fire. Much of the Coliseum is made of stone. But the fire damaged the upper levels. They were made of wood. This damage took many years to repair. It was not finished until the year 240. The worst damage happened in 1349. A mighty earthquake shook Rome and the Coliseum. The south side of the building collapsed. Pieces of the arena were all over the ground. Many people took the fallen stones. Others took stones from the seating areas. They used them to repaid houses and churches. The Romans of those days were not connected to the Coliseum. It had last been used as castle. Before that it was graveyard. It has been hundreds of years since the games. The damage to the Coliseum was never repaired. Its good thing the outer wall of it still stands strong. Today the Coliseum is one of Rome's most popular attractions. People from all over the world come to Italy to see it. It has even appeared on the back of a coin. I guess that makes it a symbol that many people want too.

57. What did the people do with the stones that they took from the Coliseum?
    (a) They repaired buildings.
    (b) They sold them.
    (c) They used them as weapons.
    (d) They used them as tombstones.

58. Which best defines the word gruesome as it is used in the second paragraph?
    (a) Exciting   (b) Funny
    (c) Horrifying   (d) Boring

ANSWERS

1. (a)	**2.** (a)	**3.** (b)	**4.** (a)	**5.** (a)	**6.** (a)	**7.** (a)	**8.** (c)	**9.** (b)	**10.** (c)
11. (c)	**12.** (c)	**13.** (b)	**14.** (c)	**15.** (c)	**16.** (d)	**17.** (a)	**18.** (c)	**19.** (d)	**20.** (d)
21. (d)	**22.** (c)	**23.** (b)	**24.** (d)	**25.** (c)	**26.** (c)	**27.** (b)	**28.** (a)	**29.** (a)	**30.** (d)
31. (b)	**32.** (b)	**33.** (a)	**34.** (b)	**35.** (a)	**36.** (b)	**37.** (b)	**38.** (d)	**39.** (b)	**40.** (d)
41. (a)	**42.** (b)	**43.** (c)	**44.** (a)	**45.** (d)	**46.** (b)	**47.** (a)	**48.** (c)	**49.** (c)	**50.** (d)
51. (b)	**52.** (b)	**53.** (c)	**54.** (a)	**55.** (d)	**56.** (b)	**57.** (a)	**58.** (a)		

EXPLANATIONS

1. This problem is based on Base 26 rather than regular base 10 (decimal system) that we normally use. In base 10 there are 10 digits 0 to 9 exist. In base 26 there are 26 digits 0 to 25 exist. To convert any number into base 26, we have to divide the number with 26 and find the remainder. (Study this Base system chapter).

Here, ONE + ONE =

E has value of 4. So E + E = 8 which is equal to I.

Now N + N = 13 + 13 = 26.

But in base 26, there is no 26.

So $(26)10 = (10)26(26)10 = (10)26$

$$
\begin{array}{r|l}
26 & 26 \\
\hline
26 & 1 \quad - 0 \uparrow \\
\hline
& 0 \quad - 1
\end{array}
$$

So we put 0 and 1 carry over. But 0 in this system is A.

Now O + O + 1 = 14 + 14 + 1 = 29

$$
\begin{array}{r|l}
26 & 26 \\
\hline
26 & 1 \quad - 0 \uparrow \\
\hline
& 0 \quad - 1
\end{array}
$$

Therefore, $(29)10 = (13)26(29)10 = (13)26$

But 1 = B and 3 = D in that system.

So ONE + ONE = BDAI

2. The given series is an AP with common difference of 7.

So the terms in the above series are in the form of 2013 + 7k.

We have to find the perfect squares in this format in the given series.

Given that $44^2 = 1936$.

Shortcut : To find the next perfect square, add 45th odd number to 44^2.

So $45^2 = 1936 + (2 \times 45 - 1) = 2025$

$46^2 = 2025 + (2 \times 46 - 1) = 2116$

$47^2 = 2116 + (2 \times 47 - 1) = 2209$

Now subtract 2013 from the above numbers and divide by 7.

Only 2209 is in the format of 2013 + 7k.

Hence, only one number satisfies.

3. The given series is 1234, 12344, 123444, 1234444, ...

So the number of digits in each term are 4, 5, 6, ... or (3 + 1), (3 + 2), (3 + 3), ...upto n terms $= 3n + \dfrac{n(n+1)}{2}3n + \dfrac{n(n+1)}{2}$

So $3n + \dfrac{n(n+1)}{2} \le 2003n + \dfrac{n(n+1)}{2} \le 200$

For n = 16, We get 184 in the left hand side. So after 16 terms the number of digits equal to 184. And 16 them contains 16 + 3 = 19 digits.

Now 17 term contains 20 digits and 123444 ...... 4 ...... 17 times123444 ...... 4 ...... 17 times.

So last digit is 4 and last two digits are 44.

4. Proceed as above.

The last two digits in the 200th place is 55.

5. 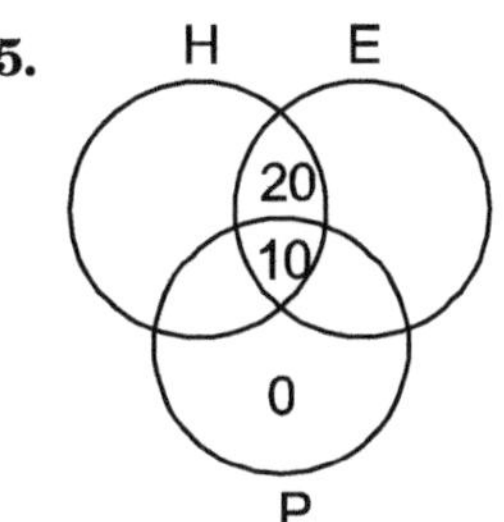

Number of students studying H equals that studying E = z + 30

As total number of students = 74

$\therefore$ z + z + 30 = 74

2z + 30 = 74

2z = 44

z = 22

So, the number of students studying H is z + 30 = 22 + 30 = 52.

6. Digits available = 1, 2, 3, 4, 5, 6, 7, 8, 9

The numbers will be $^9C_2 + ^9C_3 + \dots\dots ^9C_9$.

$$= 2^9 - {}^9C_0 - {}^9C_1.$$

$$= 512 - 1 - 9 = 502.$$

7. x, y and z are in G.P.

$\therefore$ $y^2 = xz$

$$x = \frac{y^2}{z}.$$

5x, 16y and 12z are in A.P.

32y = 12z + 5x

$$32y = 12z + \frac{5y^2}{z} \left[\because x = \frac{y^2}{z} \right]$$

$$32yz = 12z^2 + 5y^2.$$

$$12z^2 - 32yz + 5y^2 = 0$$

Divide by y^2

$$12\left(\frac{z}{y}\right)^2 32\left(\frac{z}{y}\right) + 5 = 0$$

On solving this quadratic equation, we get

$$\frac{z}{y} = \frac{1}{6} \text{ or } \frac{5}{2}$$

But as $z > y$, therefore $\dfrac{z}{y} = \dfrac{5}{2}$ is the only possible value, which is the common ratio of G.P.

8. Let the tank capacity = vv liters.

Given, v7 + 22 = v5v7 + 22 = v5

v5 – v7 = 22

$\Rightarrow$ v = 385v5 – v7 = 22

$\Rightarrow$ v = 385

9. Required number of ways = (2, 1), (1, 2), (1, 3), (3, 1), (2, 2) = 5

Total ways = 62 = 3662 = 36

Probability = 536536

10. A = Knight, B = Spy, C = Knave

Let us say A is Knight and speaks truth.

So C is Knave and B is spy.

So C's statement is false and B's statement is true.

This case is possible.

Let us say B is Knight.

This is not possible as A also becomes Knight as B speaks truth.

Let us say C is Knight.

This is clearly contradicted by C's statement itself.

11. Mother's age when Ayesha's brother was born

= 36 years.

Father's age when Ayesha's brother was born

$$= (38 + 4) \text{ years}$$
$$= 42 \text{ years.}$$

$\therefore$ Required difference = (42 – 36) years

$$= 6 \text{ years.}$$

12. Let the mother's present age be x years.

Then, the person's present age = $\left(\dfrac{2}{5}x\right)$ years.

$\therefore$ $\left(\dfrac{2}{5}x + 8\right) = \dfrac{1}{2}(x + 8)$

$\Rightarrow$ 2(2x + 40) = 5(x + 8)

$\Rightarrow$ x = 40

Let the cost of 1 litre milk be Re. 1

Milk in 1 litre mix. in 1st can = $\dfrac{3}{4}$ litre,

C.P. of 1 litre mix. in 1st can Re. $\dfrac{3}{4}$

Milk in 1 litre mix. in 2nd can = $\dfrac{1}{2}$ litre,

C.P. of 1 litre mix. in 2nd can Re. $\dfrac{1}{2}$

Milk in 1 litre of final mix. = $\dfrac{5}{8}$ litre,

Mean price = Re. $\dfrac{5}{8}$

By the rule of alligation, we have :

C.P. of 1 litre mixture in 1st can	C.P. of 1 litre mixture in 2nd can
3/4	1/2
	Mean price
	5/8
1/8	1/8

$\therefore$ Ratio of two mixtures = $\dfrac{1}{8} : \dfrac{1}{8} = 1 : 1$

So, quantity of mixture taken from each can = (1/2 × 12) = 6 litres

13. By the rule of alligation :

Cost of 1 kg pulses of 1st kind	Cost of 1 kg pulses of 2nd kind
Rs. 15	Rs. 20
	Mean price
	Rs. 16.50
3.50	1.50

$\therefore$ Required rate = 3.50 : 1.50

$$= 7 : 3.$$

14. Let the slower pipe alone fill the tank in x minutes.

Then, faster pipe will fill it in $\dfrac{x}{3}$ minutes.

$\therefore$ $\dfrac{1}{x} + \dfrac{3}{x} = \dfrac{1}{36}$

$\Rightarrow$ $\dfrac{4}{x} = \dfrac{1}{36}$

$\Rightarrow$ x = 144 min.

15. Part filled by (A + B) in 1 minute

$$= \left(\frac{1}{60} + \frac{1}{40}\right) = \frac{1}{24}$$

Suppose the tank is filled in x minutes.

Then, $\dfrac{x}{2}\left(\dfrac{1}{24}+\dfrac{1}{40}\right)=1$

$\Rightarrow \dfrac{x}{2}\times\dfrac{1}{15}=1$

$\Rightarrow x=30$ mi

16. Let Abhay's speed be x km/hr.

Then, $\dfrac{30}{x}-\dfrac{30}{2x}=3$

$\Rightarrow 6x=30$

$\Rightarrow x=5$ km/hr

Let the distance travelled by x km.

Then, $\dfrac{x}{10}-\dfrac{x}{15}=2$

$\Rightarrow 3x-2x=60$

$\Rightarrow x=60$ km.

Time taken to travel 60 km at 10 km/hr

$=\left(\dfrac{60}{10}\right)_{hrs}=6$ hrs.

17. So, Robert started 6 hours before 2 P.M. i.e., at 8 A.M.

$\therefore$ Required speed $=\left(\dfrac{60}{5}\right)_{kmph}=12$ kmph.

19. The numbers are $(x*1)-1$; $(x2)-2$; $(x3)-3$....
Hence the series would be $(32*5)-5=155$

20. The pattern is 8^2 (?) 2^2; $?=8+2=10^2=100$

21. The pattern is get by adding 1.5, 2.5, 3.5 .....
Then, $19+6.5=25.5$

22. Clearly, $5+3=8$, $8+3=11$, $11+3=14$,....
So this is an A.P series in which a = 5, d = 3.
Let the number of the terms be n
Then, $320=5+(n-1)*3$;
$\qquad 3n=318$; $n=106$

23. This is an G.P series in which a = 5; r = 2
10th term $=ar^{(n-1)}=5*2^{(10-1)}=5*2^9=2560$

24. Brother of Raju's wife – Raju's brother-in-law;
Son of Manju's brother is the brother-in-law of Raju.
So Manju's brother is Raju's father-in-law
ie, Manju is the sister of Raju's father-in-law.

25. Only son of her grandfather – her father; man's brother's father- man's father.
So, man's father is her father ie, She is the man's sister.

26. Mother's mother- grandmother; grandmother's daughter-in- law's daughter- grandmother's son's daughter-Radha's cousin.

27. Couples A-B; A is the father of C; C's daughter is E.
So, E's grandmother is B.

28. Mr. Ramu's mother's father-in-law's only son is Ramu's father. Ramu's father's only daughter is Ramu's sister.
Ramu's sister's son is Chetan. Hence, Ramu is uncle of Chetan.

29. Let us denote the five boys by the first letter of their names,namely S, K, M, A and R.
Then , R < S < K < M and S < A < K.
R < S < A < K < M
Rohan is shortest.

30. R < S < A < K < M
Anuj is in the middle.

31. R < S < A < K < M.
In the order of increasing heights i,e shortest to tallest, Sachin is second.

32. R < S < A < K < M
Kunal is second tallest.

33. R < S < A < K < M.
Kunal is taller than Anuj but shorter than Mohit

34. P studies English.

35. Clearly the incorrect combination is English-Hostel

36. S stays in hostel and R stays at home.

MOCK-7
(INFOSYS-I)

QUANTITATIVE APTITUDE

1. There are 3 friends namely A, B and C. There is a cake on a table at night. At 1 o'clock A wake up take over $1/3^{rd}$ of the cake, then at 2 o'clock B wake up take over $1/3^{rd}$ of the remaining cake and then again 3 o'clock C takes $1/3^{rd}$ from remaining cake without knowing to each other.Then,at morning they divided among themselves as each having 16 pieces each. How many pieces were there on the table initially?

   (a) 162   (b) 108

   (c) 54   (d) 182

2. The last 2 digits in the expansion of 15^{2018} will be

   (a) 15   (b) 35

   (c) 75   (d) 25

3. The sum of series represented as $1/(1 \times 5) + 1/(5 \times 9) + 1/(9 \times 13) + \ldots\ldots + 1/(221 \times 225)$ is

   (a) 28/221   (b) 56/221

   (c) 56/225   (d) none of these

4. A, B and C inherited few gold coins. If they share those coins in the ratio $1 : 5 : 8$, then 1 coin remain left out. But, if they share the coins in the ratio $1 : 3 : 7$, then no coin is left. Comparing both the cases, what is the, minimum possible difference in number of coins that C can get?

   (a) 7   (b) 6

   (c) 11   (d) 8

5. Seven digits in this subtraction problem are 0,1,2,3,4,5 and 6. What digit is by each other mention value of B,F,E,G ?

   DADCB
   EBEG
   ____
   BFEG
   ____

   (a) 1,2,3,4   (b) 6,4,5,3

   (c) 1,3,5,6   (d) 3,6,0,2

6. A five-digit number is formed using digits 1, 3, 5, 7 and 9 without repeating anyone them. What is the sum of all such possible numbers?

   (a) 6660000

   (b) 6666600

   (c) 6666000

   (d) 6600000

7. 20 litre mixture of milk and water contains milk and water in the ratio 3 : 2. 10 litres of the mixture is removed and replaced with pure milk and the operation is repeated once more. At the end of the two removal and replacement, what is the ratio of milk and water in the resultant mixture?

   (a) 17 : 3   (b) 9 : 1

   (c) 3 : 17   (d) 5 : 3

8. Each interior angle of regular polygon is greater than 120° than each exterior angle. How many sides are there in a polygon?

   (a) 6   (b) 8

   (c) 12   (d) 7

9. Find next number in the series: 10, 14, 28, 52, 134, ?

   (a) 304   (b) 303

   (c) 335   (d) 402

10. A and B take part in a gunshot. A can strike with an accuracy of 0.4. B can strike the task with an accuracy of 0.6. A has the first shot, post which they strike alternately. What is the probability that A wins the gunshot?

    (a) 10/19   (b) 1/15

    (c) 2/13   (d) 3/11

LOGICAL REASONING

11. Snehal correctly remembers that Kiran's birthday was after Tuesday but before Friday. Rajan correctly remembers that Kiran's birthday was after Wednesday but before Sunday, on which day of the week does Kiran's birthday definitely fall?

    (a) Monday   (b) Thursday

    (c) Saturday   (d) Cannot be determined

12. Pointing to boy Uma said, "He is the son of my mother-in-law's only child".

    How is the boy related to Uma?

    (a) Grandson   (b) Son

    (c) Nephew   (d) Data inadequate

13. If '+' means '×', '×' means '÷', '÷' means '−' and '−' means '+'; then what is the value of $285 \times 19 - 25 + 4 \div 60 = ?$

    (a) 160   (b) 120

    (c) 80   (d) None of these

14. If in the number 5608391467, the position of the first and the sixth digits are interchanged, the second and seventh digits are interchanged and so on up to the fifth and the tenth digits. Then which will be the fourth digit from the left end after interchange?

    (a) 1   (b) 6

    (c) 8   (d) 3

Directions for questions 15 to 17 : Study the following information carefully and answer the questions given below :

A, B, C, D, E, F, G, H and J are sitting around a circle facing the center. C is third to the left of A. E is fourth to the right of A. D is fourth to the left of J who is second to the right of A. F is third to the right of B. G is not an immediate neighbour of A

15. What is H's position with respect to E ?

    (a) Third to the left

    (b) Fourth to the left

    (c) Fifth to the right

    (d) Fifth to the left

16. Who is third to the right of G ?

    (a) B   (b) D

    (c) A   (d) None of these

17. Who is fifth to the right of E ?

    (a) F   (b) C

    (c) H   (d) A

Directions for questions 18 to 20 : In each of the questions given below, there are three statements followed by two conclusions numbered I and II. You have to take the given statements to be true even if they seem to be at variance with commonly known facts. Read all the conclusions and then decide which of the given conclusions logically follow(s) from the given statements disregarding commonly known facts.

Mark :

a. if only conclusion I follows

b. if only conclusion II follows

c. if neither conclusion I nor II follows

d. if both conclusions I and II follow

18. **Statements :**

    All jugs are plates.

    All plates are cups.

    All cups are bottles.

    Conclusions :

    I. Some bottles are jugs.

    II. All plates are bottles.

    (a) a   (b) b

    (c) c   (d) d

19. **Statements :**

    All pigeons are trees.

    Some trees are channels.

    All channels are baskets.

    Conclusions :

    I. Some baskets are trees.

    II. Some channels are pigeons.

    (a) a   (b) b

    (c) c   (d) d

20. **Statements :**

    Some chains are trucks.

    No truck is a car.

    All cars are trains.

    Conclusions :

    I. Some trains are trucks.

    II. Some cars are chains.

    (a) a   (b) b

    (c) c   (d) d

Directions (Q. 21 to 25) : Study the following information carefully to answer these questions.

Strength (number of students) of seven Institutes over the years

	A	B	C	D	E	F
2002	750	640	680	780	740	620
2003	700	600	720	800	720	580
2004	800	620	730	820	760	640
2005	820	660	670	760	750	560
2006	740	760	690	790	780	650
2007	720	740	700	810	730	630
2008	780	700	660	840	720	660

21. Strength of Institute F in 2004 is what percent of the total strength of that Institute for all seven years together?

    (rounded off to two digits after decimal).

    (a) 14.28   (b) 14.98

    (c) 12.9   (d) 14.75

22. What is the difference between the total number of students in 2006 for all the Institutes together and total number of students in 2008 for all the Institutes together?

    (a) 50   (b) 70

    (c) 10   (d) 30

23. What is the ratio between total strength of Institutes A, B and C together in 2003 and the total strength of Institutes E, F and G together in 2005 respectively?

    (a) 103 : 101   (b) 101 : 103

    (c) 51 : 53   (d) None of these

24. If in 2002, the overall percentage of students passed from all the Institutes is 70%. Total how many students passed in 2002 from all the Institutes together?

    (a) 3402   (b) 3420

    (c) 3422   (d) None of these

25. If from Institute B, overall 60% students passed for all the given years, approximately what is the average number of students passed?

    (a) 430   (b) 425

    (c) 390   (d) 405

VERBAL ABILITY

Directions for questions 26 to 33 : In each of the following questions, sentences are given with blanks to be filled in with an appropriate word. Four alternatives are suggested for each question. Choose the correct alternative out of the four.

26. The foreigners were stubbornly reluctant ______ accept our ways.

    (a) to   (b) through

    (c) in   (d) at

27. Does she ______ coffee?

    (a) likes   (b) like

    (c) liked   (d) liking

28. He ______ in Japan since he left school.

    (a) will be living   (b) has been living

    (c) have been living   (d) lived

29. Rather than considering if their research is right or wrong, the scientists are increasingly adopting a completely ______ attitude.

    (a) amoral   (b) immoral

    (c) flimsy   (d) filthy

30. She saw no reason to ______ the committee of what had happened.

    (a) apprise   (b) check

    (c) enquire   (d) appraise

31. The earthquake warnings and the fragility of our houses made us certain that a disaster was ______.

    (a) catastrophic   (b) imminent

    (c) available   (d) distant

32. The Supreme Court has mandated the river-linking project, and the administration now has to plan to ______ the detailed strategies that would help share water resources across the country.

    (a) strive   (b) execute

    (c) maneuver   (d) program

33. It will perhaps be unfair to judge Ms. Patel against her predecessor given his larger-than-life image, but the new Chief Minister will find that such comparisons are ______.

    (a) improvident   (b) improbable

    (c) inevitable   (d) inadunate

Directions for questions 34 to 49 : In each question, a part of the sentence is underlined. Below are given alternatives to the underlined part which may improve the sentence. Choose the correct alternative. In case no improvement is needed, your answer is d.

34. I am afraid you two are <u>at cross purpose</u>.

    (a) at cross-purposes

    (b) are in cross-purposes

    (c) are at a cross-purpose

    (d) No improvement

35. Take care <u>that you are not to be cheated</u>.

    (a) that you will not be cheated

    (b) you will not be cheated

    (c) that you are not cheated

    (d) No improvement

36. Can you tell me <u>where has he gone</u>?

    (a) where has gone he

    (b) where gone has he

    (c) where he has gone

    (d) No improvement

37. <u>No sooner I heard the shot when</u> I rushed to the spot.

    (a) No sooner I heard the shot than

    (b) No sooner did I hear the shot when

    (c) No sooner did I hear the shot than

    (d) No improvement

38. The authors plan to <u>follow with</u> studies of infants and perhaps other animal species.

    (a) follow to with   (b) follow up with

    (c) follow in with   (d) No improvement

39. The examination will soon be <u>upon</u> us.

    (a) in   (b) over

    (c) through   (d) No improvement

40. You are <u>in with</u> the right team.

    (a) in to   (b) in under

    (c) in for   (d) No improvement

41. Many of his suggestions <u>have been incorporated to</u> the training module.

    (a) have been incorporated in

    (b) have been incorporated at

    (c) have been incorporated with

    (d) No improvement

42. She's a good wife, <u>for</u> all her nagging.

    (a) to   (b) by

    (c) in   (d) No improvement

43. For the purpose you need a nominee who will <u>vouch for</u> you.

    (a) vouch with   (b) vouch to

    (c) vouch against   (d) No improvement

44. The bright lights and quiet surroundings were conducive about a relaxed discussion.

    (a) conducive under   (b) conducive to

    (c) conducive over   (d) No improvement

45. She is already <u>acquainted about</u> the latest developments of the situation.

    (a) acquainted on   (b) acquainted in

    (c) acquainted with   (d) No improvement

46. An executive cannot answer questions for the employee but can <u>confer about</u> the employee and address the meeting.

    (a) confer with   (b) confer to

    (c) confer on   (d) No improvement

47. Pakistan is <u>conflicting</u> to discussing Afghanistan with India, fearing that would legitimise India's interests in that country.

    (a) deniable   (b) segregative

    (c) averse   (d) No improvement

48. The President deliberately <u>arranged</u> the rules to allow rich men to fund his craving for power.

    (a) flouted   (b) postulated

    (c) tempered   (d) No improvement

49. The Prime Minister laid a <u>writhe</u> at the India Gate in New Delhi.

    (a) wrath   (b) wreath

    (c) wreathe   (d) No improvement

Directions for questions 50 to 54 : Read the passage carefully and answer the questions that follow.

Ever since Woolf's recuperation by feminists in the 1970s, critics have attempted to overcome the powerful stereotype of her as a fragile genius, unconnected with the world. This view, so dominant in Recollections of Virginia Woolf by Her Contemporaries, and more recently in the book and movie The Hours, has been difficult to dislodge. Fortunately, these three books confirm Woolf's deep engagement with the social and political world of her times. Moreover, Black and Cuddy-Keane concentrate on Woolf as a professional writer, as someone who had to meet deadlines, work with editors, and persuade readers. Cuddy-Keane examines how Woolf responded to specific political events, while Black integrates Woolf's lifelong feminism with her anti-war arguments. Humm concentrates on Woolf and her sister, Vanessa Bell, as amateur photographers, showing how their fascination with contemporary visual technologies affected their work. All three would agree that this quintessential modernist appeals to a post-modern sensibility in her insistent creation of multiple layers and points of view. Like Woolf, all are very aware of their own critical biases.

These authors acknowledge a characteristic that either endears or annoys readers : Woolf's repeated use of ironic fantasy, or what Black calls her "dense, whimsical, and semi-academic style". Each effectively defends Woolf's idiosyncratic (characteristic) style for its effective balancing of different arguments and positions. To paraphrase Woolf, they see her as one of the few English writers writing for grown-up people. Black notes how Woolf insisted that readers undertake an imaginative engagement with her argument because of her use of provocative asides, digressions from the subject at hand, and a discordant combination of anger and humor. Cuddy-Keane concludes that Woolf's elliptical style encouraged her readers to think for themselves. Humm compliments Woolf's sophisticated use of "photographic tropes of illumination and reflection", which draw attention to the elusive, evanescent nature of reality. These critics each provide such good close readings of Woolf's essays that I wish they had considered more fully the stylistic relationship between her nonfiction and fiction. Woolf's unique critical voice combines fact and fiction in psychologically and politically unsettling ways that are well worth exploring.

50. In the first paragraph, the author gives examples of critics Black, Cuddy-Keane and Humm in order to

    (a) acclaim Woolf for her sheer genius.

    (b) present different types of viewpoints on Woolf's works.

    (c) bust popular perception that her works were dissociated from the world.

    (d) prove the fact that having critical biases is natural.

51. According to the author, which of the following was amiss in Black, Cuddy-Keane and Humm's reading of Woolf's works?

    (a) They thought that Woolf's writings were not for children.

    (b) They did not fully explore the stylistic relation between her fictions and non-fictions.

    (c) They believed her elusiveness made her texts complex.

    (d) They believed her works were very engaging.

52. What is common among Cuddy-Kean, Black and Humm?

    (a) They are oblivious of their critical biases.

    (b) They underlined the recurrent use of ironic fantacy in her works.

    (c) They criticized Woolf's idiosyncratic style.

    (d) They regarded Woolf's work as one suitable for mature readers.

53. Which of the following techniques are not used by Woolf to engage readers?

    (a) Creation of suspense

    (b) Use of provocative asides

    (c) Diversion from subject in focus

    (d) Use of anger and humour together

54. What triggered a change in attitude towards Woolf's works?

    (a) Acclamation by renowned critics

    (b) Works of art that dislodged the popular negativity towards her works

    (c) Support from feminists in the 1970s

    (d) None of the above

Directions for questions 55 to 59 : Read the passage carefully and answer the questions that follow.

Ask those who've entered the thick of middle age what they think about their mental capacities and you're likely to hear a slew of complaints — their brains don't work as quickly as they used to, they're distractable and unfocused, and they can never remember anyone's name. While some of these complaints reflect real declines in brain function in our middle years, the deficiencies of a middle-aged brain have been overstated by anecdotal evidence and even by some scientific studies. Contrary to its reputation as a slower, duller version of a youthful brain, it seems that the middle-aged mind not only maintains many of the abilities of youth but actually acquires some new ones. The adult brain seems to be capable of rewiring itself well into middle age, incorporating decades of experiences and behaviors. Research suggests, for example, the middle-aged mind is calmer, less neurotic and better able to sort through social situations. Some middle agers even have improved cognitive abilities.

"There is an enduring potential for plasticity, reorganization and preservation of capacities," says cognitive neuroscientist Patricia Reuter- Lorenz, PhD, of the University of Michigan in Ann Arbor. Researchers now have an unprecedented wealth of data on the aging brain from the Seattle Longitudinal Study, which has tracked the cognitive abilities of thousands of adults over the past 50 years. These results show that middle-aged adults perform better on four out of six cognitive tests than those same individuals did as young adults, says study leader Sherry Willis, PhD, of the University of Washington in Seattle.

While memorization skills and perceptual speed both start to decline in middle age, verbal abilities, spatial reasoning, simple math abilities and abstract reasoning skills all improve in middle age. Cognitive skills in the aging brain have also been studied extensively in pilots and air-traffic controllers. Again, older pilots show declines in processing speed and memory capacity, but their overall performance seems to remain intact. In a study published in 2007, researchers tested pilots age 40 to 69 as they performed on flight simulators. Older pilots took longer to learn to use the simulators but did a better job than their younger colleagues at achieving their objective: avoiding collisions.

55. According to the passage, the following conclusion(s) can be drawn :

    (a) While it is true that some skills undergo a decline, the overall ability of the brain is enhanced.

    (b) Scientific studies and observation of some people have wrongly captured the shortcomings of middle aged brain.

    (c) Both (a) and (b)

    (d) Neither (a) nor (b)

56. Which of the following inferences cannot be drawn from the passage?

    (a) After a certain age group, cognitive abilities of people are reduced.

    (b) Only some of the skills of the human brain are affected in middle age.

    (c) Memorization skills of young people are better than those of middle aged people.

    (d) Human brain can be molded and re wired at any age.

57. What was the objective of the pilots in the study conducted for them?

 (a) They had to memorize the air path in their travels.

 (b) They needed to calculate their spatial position based on the co-ordinates provided by air traffic control.

 (c) They were required to prevent any collision in their course of flight.

 (d) They needed to learn how to use simulators.

58. According to the passage, which of the following is a valid conclusion?

 (a) After reaching a certain age, the human mind becomes stagnant and loses its ability to assimilate things.

 (b) Human brain acts on the basis of the information and experiences acquired by an individual during the youth.

 (c) In middle age, people tend to lose their memory and reasoning skills.

 (d) Middle aged people are clear in their thinking and have a better understanding of social norms.

59. Why do middle aged people complain about their brains?

 (a) They are envious of the mental abilities of the younger generation.

 (b) Their ability to focus and remember names of other people has declined.

 (c) They are being unreasonably petulant for the loss of their skills.

 (d) They think that there is a gradual loss of sympathy towards them.

Directions for questions 60 to 61 : In each of the following questions, read the given argument and answer the question that follows it.

60. The International Monetary Fund, which has 2,370 employees, most based in Washington, has repositioned itself periodically since its creation after World War II. Its initial focus was to oversee the exchange rate system established under the Bretton Woods agreements. That role ended in the 1970s. In the 1980s, it emerged as the manager of the Latin American debt crisis. In the 1990s, it stepped in to deal with the Mexican and East Asian financial crises.

The information above most strongly supports which one of the following?

 (a) The International Monetary Fund has been ineffective in most of its dealings.

 (b) Changing roles too often has earned a bad name for the International Monetary Fund.

 (c) The International Monetary Fund has been receptive to the changes in economic environment of the world and adapted itself accordingly.

 (d) The IMF is a panacea of all the problems that ail the world economy.

61. The dusty stacks of the nation's great university and research libraries are full of orphans — books that the author and publisher have essentially abandoned. They are out of print, and while they remain under copyright, the rights holders are unknown or cannot be found. Now millions of orphan books may get a new legal guardian. Google has been scanning the pages of those books and others as part of its plan to bring a digital library and bookstore, unprecedented in scope, to computer screens across the United States.

Which one of the following can be inferred from the information given above?

 (a) The long forgotten owners of the books may start laying claims to their work.

 (b) Readers will have access to the hitherto unknown and forgotten works which may not have seen the light of the day otherwise

 (c) Copyrights may become a bone of contention between writers and Google.

 (d) The step taken by Google would be appreciated by every Tom, Dick and Harry.

For questions 62 and 63 : In a study of the most and the least safe places to cycle in Britain, it shows that where there are more riders on the roads there is generally a lower accident rate, while in areas less popular for bikes, cycling can be notably more risky. Contradicting the notion that a mass of inexperienced riders taking to the streets causes injuries and deaths, the research by the Cyclists Touring Club (CTC), the UK's main cycling organization, rates local authority areas in England on a scale of A to E according to how safe they are. The trend is clear, with areas popular for cyclists tending to be safer on average, with the differences sometimes significant. Top of the list is traditionally bike-friendly York, where around one in eight commuters cycle to work and 0.1% are badly hurt in accidents each year. Not far down the road, Calderdale, West Yorkshire, a district centred around Halifax, is at the other end of the scale. Here, fewer than 1 in 120 commuters use bikes, and those that do face a danger level 15 times higher than in York.

62. Which of the following statements best resolves the paradox in the above paragraph?

(a) Areas less popular for bikes tend to be a high speed zone for other vehicles.

(b) The more the number of cyclists on the road, the more careful the drivers of other vehicles are.

(c) Many of the accidents to cyclists are caused by other cyclists.

(d) Areas less popular for bikers have very few policemen.

63. The conclusion " If you decide to cycle in Britain, you had better cycle with a couple of other cyclists ratherthan cycling alone" is

(a) completely valid

(b) completely invalid

(c) probably true

(d) vague

64. A vote on support for the legislation was on an initial agenda for Tuesday's meeting, and many council members and residents arrived expecting a vote. But by meeting day, the agenda had been reprinted without the vote. Ms. Bland rushed through a perfunctory agenda, then gaveled the meeting to a close before another member could introduce a motion to vote on the bill. Ms. Bland exited the room without explanation, leaving colleagues speechless and residents in attendance furious.Reasonable people can disagree on whether the stadium is a good idea. But there's no excuse for Ms.Bland snuffing out a debate about its merits.

The statements above, if true, most strongly support which one of the following?

(a) Ms. Bland had some reasons of her own that compelled her to shy away from the issue at hand.

(b) Ms. Bland did not believe in the process of voting on an unimportant issue.

(c) Ms. Bland had misgivings about the idea of a stadium in the midst of the town.

(d) Ms. Bland was averse to dragging the matter further by conducting another round of vote.

65. Consumers are using their mobile phones to download tens of millions of games, songs, ring tones and video programs.

And they shell out money for these items, even as they resist paying for similar digital goodies online using their computers. It is a curious equation : pay for stuff on a tiny, low-resolution screen while getting some of the very same games and video free on a fancy widescreen monitor.If all of the statements in the passage are true, each of the following must also be true EXCEPT:

(a) Mobile phones are a status symbol for today's consumers.

(b) The companies producing mobile content are thriving.

(c) The users enjoy the availability of music download at their fingertips.

(d) Stuff on computer seems to be easily available so why pay money.

ANSWERS

1. (a)	**2.** (d)	**3.** (c)	**4.** (a)	**5.** (b)	**6.** (b)	**7.** (b)	**8.** (c)	**9.** (a)	**10.** (a)
11. (b)	**12.** (b)	**13.** (d)	**14.** (b)	**15.** (a)	**16.** (d)	**17.** (d)	**18.** (d)	**19.** (a)	**20.** (c)
21. (d)	**22.** (c)	**23.** (b)	**24.** (a)	**25.** (d)	**26.** (d)	**27.** (c)	**28.** (a)	**29.** (d)	**30.** (c)
31. (c)	**32.** (b)	**33.** (c)	**34.** (d)	**35.** (b)	**36.** (c)	**37.** (b)	**38.** (d)	**39.** (a)	**40.** (b)
41. (a)	**42.** (b)	**43.** (d)	**44.** (b)	**45.** (c)	**46.** (b)	**47.** (a)	**48.** (a)	**49.** (b)	**50.** (c)
51. (a)	**52.** (d)	**53.** (b)	**54.** (b)	**55.** (c)	**56.** (a)	**57.** (c)	**58.** (d)	**59.** (b)	**60.** (c)
61. (b)	**62.** (b)	**63.** (d)	**64.** (a)	**65.** (a)					

EXPLANATIONS

1. Best way is to go through the options and get $16 \times 3 = 48$ at the end.

2. $15^{odd} = 75$ (will be last 2 numbers)

   $15^{even} = 25$ (will be last 2 numbers)

3. $1/4 \times [(5 - 1)/1 \times 5 + (9 - 5)/5 \times 9 + \ldots\ldots (225 - 221)/(221 \times 225)$

   $= 1/4 \times [(1 - 1/5)+(1/5 - 1/9)+\ldots\ldots(1/221 - 1/225)]$

   $= 1/4 \times (1 - 1/225)$

   $= 1/4 \times (224/225) = 56/225$

4. Suppose in the 1st case number of coins possessed by A, B and C are x, 5x, 8x repectively.

   So, total number of coins = (14x + 1).

   Similarly, in the second case, Number of coins possessed by A,B and C are y, 3y and 7y respectively.

   So, total number of coins = 11y.

   Therefore, the total number of coins is a multiple of 11, but 1 more than a multiple of 14. '99' is the minimum possible number conforming to these conditions.

   So, in 1st case C would have got, $98 \times 8/14 = 56$ coins $99 \times 7/11 = 63$ coins.

   Hence, difference is 7.

5. A = 2; B = 6; C = 0; D = 1; E = 5; F = 4; G = 3

6. The sum of all the numbers formed by the digits $a_1, a_2, a_3, \ldots\ldots\ldots an$, without repetition of the digits is given by :

   $(n - 1)!(a_1 + a_2 + a_3 + \ldots\ldots a_n) (10^n - 1)/9$

   Hence, the sum of the given numbers

   $= 4!(1 + 3 + 5 + 7 + 9) \times 11111 = 6666600.$

7. We are essentially replacing water in the mixture with pure milk.

   Let WO be the amount of water in the mixture originally = 8 litres.

   Let WR be the amount of water in the mixture after the replacements have taken place.

   WR/WO = (1-R/M)N, where R is the amount of the mixture replaced by milk in each of the steps, M is the total volume of the mixture and N is the number of times the cycle is repeated.

   Hence, $(1 - 10/20)^2 = 1/4 \times$ WR/WO = 1/4

   $\qquad$ WR = WO/4 = 8/4 = 2L

8. Let an exterior angle be A°. Then each interior angle will be 120 + A°.

   We know that in any regular polygon, the sum of an exterior and interior angle is always = 180°.

   Therefore, $A + 120 + A = 180 \Rightarrow A = 30°$.

   No. of sides of a polygon = 360/each exterior angle = 360/30 = 12 sides

9. $10 \times 3 - 2 = 28$

   $14 \times 4 - 4 = 52$

   $28 \times 5 - 6 = 134$

   $52 \times 6 - 8 = 304$

10. A and B take part in a gunshot A can strike with an accuracy of 0.4.

    B can strike the task with an accuracy of 0.6.

    First B(win)

    A(miss)

    P(a in 1 sty shot) = 0.4

    P(A in 3 rd shot) = $0.6 \times 0.4 \times 0.4$

    P(A in 5 th shot) = $0.6 \times 0.4 \times 0.6 \times 0.4 \times 0.4$

    $0.4 + 0.6 \times 0.4 \times 0.4 + 0.6 \times 0.4 \times 0.6 \times 0.4 \times 0.4$

    $+ \ldots\ldots 0.4 + 0.4(0.6 \times 0.4) + 0.4(0.6 \times 0.4) 2 + \ldots.$

    $a/1 - r = 0.4/1 - 0.24 = 10/19$

11. According to Sneha, Kiran's birthday may be on Wednesday or Thursday. According to Rajan, Kiran's birthday may be on Thursday, Friday or Saturday Common Day Thursday.

12. Mother in-law's is child is father of the pointing boy.

    So, he must be son.

13. $285 \times 19 - 25 + 4 \div 60$

    $= 285 \div 19 + 25 \times 4 - 60$

    $= 15 + 100 - 60 = 55$

14. 5 6 0 8 3 9 1 4 6 7

    9 1 4 6 7 5 6 0 8 3

    (after interchange according to question)

15. 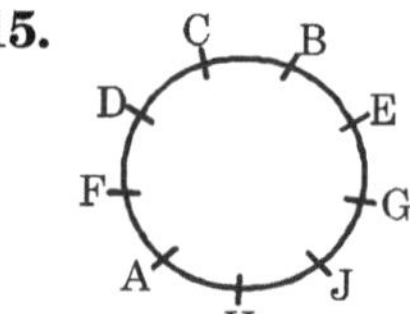

16.

17. 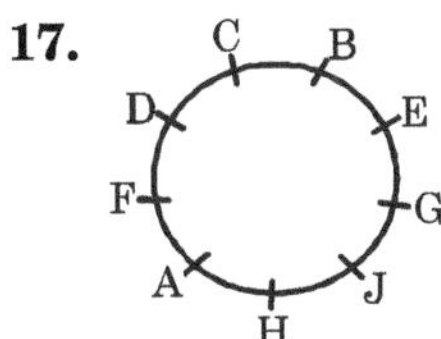

18. s-1 : All jugs are plates.

s-2 : All plates are cups.

s-3 : All cups are bottles.

To obtain conclusion 1 : Some bottles are jugs.

Join 2 + 3 and then it will be like All plates are bottles.+ s − 1 = conclusion-1

To obtain conclusion 2 : All plates are bottles

Join 2 + 3 = conclusion 2 is obtained.

19. s-1 : All pigeons are trees.

s-2 : Some trees are channels.

s-3 : All channels are baskets

To obtain conclusion 1 : Some baskets are trees.

Join 2 + 3 = conclusion1

To obtain conclusion 2 : Some channels are pigeons.

Join 1 + 2 = conclusion

20. s-1 : Some chains are trucks.

s-2 : No truck is a car.

s-3 : All cars are trains

To obtain conclusion 1 or 2 :

Some trains are trucks or Some cars are chains

Combining of any 2 of above statement will never conclusion-1

21. Required percentage

640/4340 *100 = 14.75%

22. Difference = 40 − 60 + 30 + 50 − 60 + 10 + 60 = 10

23. The ratio = 2020 : 2060 = 101 : 103

24. Total students = 4860

70% of 4860 = 3402

25. Required Averege 4720*60/100*1/7 = 405

26. The word 'reluctant' is usually followed by the preposition 'to'.

27. The auxiliary verb 'does' is followed by the first form of the verb without 's' or 'es'.

28. The action (He is living in Japan) in the sentence began in the past (when he left school) and is still continuing in the present (He still lives in Japan).

So, the sentence should be in present perfect continuous tense.

29. 'Amoral' means lacking a moral sense; unconcerned with the rightness or wrongness of something.

30. 'Apprise' means inform or tell (someone).

31. 'Imminent' means about to happen.

32. The correct answer is option b, 'execute' because the other options would not logically fit in the sentence. It is clear that a verb will fit in the given blank. 'Strive' is to try, 'maneuver' is to move skillfully and 'program' is to make something or someone behave in a particular manner.

33. The sentence suggests that there should be no comparison and the blank is the adjective describing these comparisons. 'Improvident' means thoughtless and 'inadunate' means not united. Both these options do not fit into the given blank. 'Improbable' means unlikely. This seems to go against the meaning of the sentence because the conjunction 'but' suggests something contradictory to the unfair comparison. With the same logic, option c is the correct answer.

34. The phrase 'at cross purposes' means misunderstanding or having different aims from one another.

35. Sentence warning somebody to 'take care' should be in simple present tense.

For example : Take care to not miss the deadline.

36. The question in the sentence is "Can you tell me?" and not "Where has he gone?".

Therefore, the verb will follow the noun. Another similar example would be – He asked me how I was.

37. The correct structure is 'No sooner...than.'

38. Option d is incorrect since one cannot follow with 'studies' because then it would mean in the company or presence of study, which is logically incorrect.

39. 'Upon someone' means that something will happen or arrive very soon. Hence, option d is the correct answer. Options a and c are incorrect usages in the given context. 'In' means within and 'through' means from one end or side of something to the other. 'Over' as a preposition means in or at a position above or higher than something or somebody. Thus, b would render incorrect meaning to the sentence.

40. Option d is the correct answer because 'in with' means in league or association with. For example, "He is in with the wrong crowd". Options a and c would make the sentence meaningless. 'In to' means in order to, or inside (something) to (do something). 'In for' means acknowledge to do something. 'Under' as a preposition is used to denote in a lower position or place than something or somebody.

Thus, option b is an incorrect usage in the given context.

41. The sentence means that the suggestions have been included as part of the training module and 'incorporated in' means that something is being included in or within something. Thus, option a is the most suitable answer in the given context. The preposition 'at' is used to indicate a place where someone is or a person or thing towards which an action is aimed. In the given context, 'at' is incorrect and so it doesn't go with the word 'incorporated'. 'To' is incorrect because it means in the direction of something. 'With' is inept because it means in the company or presence of somebody or something.

42. In the given context, 'for' is used to denote despite; notwithstanding. It is implied that she is a good wife despite her nagging behaviour. The correct sentence is: She's a good wife, for all her nagging. Hence, option d is correct. All other options are incorrect because they render the sentence meaningless.

43. 'Vouch for' is the correct phrase because it is used to say that you believe that somebody will behave well and that you will be responsible for their actions. Hence, option d is the correct answer. All other options are incorrect because they do not go with the word 'vouch'.

44. 'Conducive to something' means making it easy, possible or likely for something to happen. All other options are incorrect because they do not go with the word 'conducive'. Hence, option b is the correct answer.

45. The word 'acquaint' is generally followed by the preposition 'with'. 'Acquaint somebody or yourself with something' means to make somebody/ yourself familiar with or aware of something. Hence, option c is the correct answer. Other options are incorrect because they do not go with the word 'acquaint'.

46. 'Confer with' is the correct usage as it means to discuss something with somebody, in order to exchange opinions or get advice. 'Confer on' means to grant something. 'Confer to' and 'confer about' are incorrect usages in the given context. Hence, option a is the correct answer.

47. 'Averse to something / to doing something' means not liking something or wanting to do something or opposed to doing something. In the given sentence, Pakistan is not willing to discuss Afghanistan with India, hence, option c, 'averse', is the correct answer. 'Deniable' refers to something that can be denied. 'Segregative' is the adjective form of the word 'segregate', which means to separate groups of people because of their particular race, religion, etc.

Options a, b and d are incorrect since none of these can come before 'to' to make the given sentence meaningful.

48. 'Flouted the rules' is the correct usage. 'Flout' means to show lack of respect for something (such as a rule) by openly disobeying it. Hence, option a is the correct answer. 'Postulate' means to suggest something in order to start a discussion. 'Tempered' means bringing to desired hardness or strength by heating and cooling or to make something less severe.

49. 'Wreath' means an arrangement of flowers and leaves, especially in the shape of a circle, placed on graves, etc. as a sign of respect for somebody who has died. Hence, option b is the correct answer. 'Wrath' means extreme anger. 'Wreath' means to surround or cover something. 'Writhe' is to twist or move your body often because you are in great pain.

50. The first paragraph states that Woolf was stigmatized to be a fragile "genius, unconnected with the world" but now critics, like some books, "confirm Woolf's deep engagement in the social and political world of her times". Then the author gives examples of critics Black, Cuddy-Keane and Humm who prove that Woolf's world was not unconnected to the world, opposed to the stereotype attached to her. Hence, option c is the correct answer. All other options are incorrect because of the same reason.

51. Refer to the following lines from the second paragraph,

"These critics each provide such good close readings of Woolf's essays, that I wish they had considered more fully the stylistic relationship between her nonfiction and fiction. Hence, option b is the correct answer. All other options are incorrect because they are not backed by any evidence from the passage.

52. The passage states that the three critics acknowledged "Woolf's repeated use of ironic fantasy, or what Black calls her "dense, whimsical, and semiacademic style". Hence, option b is the correct answer. Option a is negated by the last line of the first paragraph, "Like Woolf, all (the critics) are very aware of their own critical biases". Option c is incorrect because the passage states that the critics defended Woolf's idiosyncratic style. Option d is incorrect because the passage states that Woolf wrote for grown-up people, which could only mean adults. Also, the passage does not talk about 'suitability'.

53. Refer to the following lines from the second paragraph, "Black notes how Woolf insisted that readers undertake an imaginative engagement with her argument because of her use of provocative asides, digressions from the subject at hand, and a discordant combination of anger and humor". Thus, all other options except option a are the techniques used by Woolf.

54. Refer to the first line of the paragraph, "Ever since Woolf's recuperation by feminists in the 1970s, critics have attempted to overcome the powerful stereotype of her as a fragile genius, unconnected with the world. From this, we can infer option c and hence, it is the correct answer.

55. Option a is correct because the passage clearly states that some skills of the human brain undergo a decline in middle age but the overall ability is enhanced.The author further supports this statement with the help of a research conducted on pilots. Option b is also correct because in the first paragraph of the passage, it is mentioned that anecdotal evidence and scientific studies have overestimated the deficiencies of a middle aged brain.

56. Option a is the best option because it clearly contradicts the main point of the passage. Option b can be ruled out because it is given in the passage that some abilities of brain indeed undergo a decline. Option c can also be ruled out because the passage finds mention of the fact that memorization skills of middle aged people become weak. Hence, it can be inferred that young people have better memorization skills.Option d can again be inferred from the main idea of the passage.

57. It is clearly mentioned in the passage that the main objective of the pilots was to avoid collision.

58. (d) is the correct option because in the first paragraph, it is mentioned that middle aged people are less confused and are able to sort through social situations in a better manner. Option a is incorrect as it is in sharp contradiction to what the passage is trying to convey. Option b can also be ruled out because it states something that is beyond the context of the passage or its primary idea.

Option c can be negated because while it is mentioned that there is a decline in the memorization abilities of middle aged people, it can not be concluded that they lose their memory altogether.

59. The opening line of the passage states that middle aged people complain about their brain due to their inability to focus and remembering the names of other people.

60. (c) is correct because it reaffirms the fact that IMF has changed its role according to the changing requirements of the world economy.

Options a, b, and d are not supported by the information given in the passage. Option e is too vague.

61. a, c, d and e all talk of future possibilities that cannot be inferred from the passage. Option b is an obvious inference from the argument as Google's act of restoring long forgotten books will ensure that these books are available for reading by a much wider audience. Thus, option b is the correct answer.

62. We do not know whether areas that are less popular for bikes are high speed zones for other vehicles.Thus, option a is negated. Option c can be negated because we do not know what is the proportion of accidents caused to cyclists by other cyclists to the total number of cyclists accidents. Options d and e are beyond the scope of the passage. Only option b gives the best rationale for resolving the apparent paradox in the situation.

63. The paragraph talks about how zones more popular for cyclists are also more safe. The issue is not whether one should travel alone or with a couple of cyclists.Thus the conclusion is rather vague and option d is the correct answer.

64. a is the correct answer as the given information suggests that Ms. Bland withdrew without any reason. Other options indicate towards various reasons. None of them are validated by the given information.

65. b, c, d and e can all be inferred to be true in context of the given extract. Option a however is not implied by the extract and is thus the correct answer.

MOCK-8

(INFOSYS-II)

QUANTITATIVE APTITUDE

1. What is sum of alphabets of JUNE, where NOON + MOON + SOON = JUNE where each alphabets takes distinct values from 0 to 9?

  (a) 21   (b) 20

  (c) 23   (d) 24

2. A and B are planning to go shopping at the mall. They plan to meet at the mall between 12.00 noon and 1.00 pm. The one who arrives first agrees to wait 15 minutes for the other to arrive. After 15 minutes, that person will leave and continue shopping. What is the probability that they will meet if each of the girls arrives at any time between 12.00 noon and 1.00pm?

  (a) $\dfrac{2}{13}$ (b) $\dfrac{7}{16}$

  (c) $\dfrac{3}{19}$ (d) $\dfrac{2}{17}$

3. In how many ways can a group of 5 men and 2 women be made out of a total of 7 men and 3 women?

  (a) 63   (b) 90

  (c) 126   (d) 45

4. Mr. Paul gave 40% of the money he had, to his wife. He also gave 20% of the remaining amount to each of his three sons. Half of the amount now left was spent on miscellaneous items and the remaining amount of Rs. 12,000 was deposited in the bank. How much money did Mr. Paul have initially?

  (a) 100000   (b) 99000

  (c) 110000   (d) 115000

5. When the price of the product was decreased by 10%, the number sold increased by 30%. What was the effect on the total revenue?

  (a) 17%   (b) 19%

  (c) 23%   (d) 31%

6. A takes twice as much time as B or thrice as much time to finish a piece of work. Working together, they can finish the work in 2 days. B can do the work alone in:

  (a) 4 hrs   (b) 6 hrs

  (c) 8 hrs   (d) 12 hrs

7. What should come in place of question mark (?) in each of the following number series (?) 27, 57, ?, 705, 3531

  (a) 171   (b) 175

  (c) 178   (d) 169

8. There are 864 bananas packed in dozens in 9 boxes. Each box has the same number of bananas. How many dozens of bananas are packed in each box?

  (a) 12   (b) 9

  (c) 8   (d) 6

9. $10^{25} - 7$ is divisible by

  (a) 2   (b) 3

  (c) 9   (d) both a and b

10. Rs. 5625 is to be divided among A, B and C so that A may receive $\dfrac{1}{2}$ as much as B and C together receive and B receives $\dfrac{1}{4}$ of what A and C together receive. The share of A is more than that of B by

  (a) Rs. 750   (b) Rs. 1000.0

  (c) Rs. 870   (d) Rs. 890

LOGICAL REASONING

11. How many three letter meaningful words can be formed from the word TEAR beginning with 'A' and without repeating any letter within that word?

  (a) One   (b) Three

  (c) Five   (d) Two

12. If the letters of the word ARROGANCE are interchanged, first and fifth, second and sixth, third and seventh, fourth and eighth and the position of the ninth remains unchanged then what will the new arrangement of letters be?

  (a) GANACRROE   (b) GANCRAROE

  (c) GNACORRAE   (d) GANCARROE

13. In a certain code language 'do re me' means 'he is late', 'fa me la' means 'she is early' and 'so ti do' means 'he leaves soon'. Which word in that language means 'late'?

  (a) la   (b) do

  (c) me   (d) None of these

Directions for question 14 to 18: Study the following in formation carefully and answer the questions that follow. Following are the conditions for selecting Manager in an organization: The candidate must:

(i) be a Civil Engineer and should have obtained at least 65 percent marks in Engineering.

(ii) be at least 25 years and not more than 35 years old as on 16.01.2012.

(iii) have secured at least 50 percent marks in the written examination.

(iv) have secured at least 55 percent marks in the selection interview.

(v) have post-qualification work experience of at least 4 years in chemical or civil sector.

In the case of a candidate who satisfies all the conditions EXCEPT –

a. (i), but has secured at least 65 percent marks in M. Tech (Civil), the case is to be referred to the DGM.

b. (ii), but has post-qualification experience of at least five years as Deputy Manager (in infrastructure sector), the case is to be referred to the GM. In each question below, details of candidates are given. You have to take one of the following courses of action base on the information provided and the condition and sub-condition given above and mark the number of that course of action as your answer. You are not to assume anything other than the information provided for each candidate. All these cases are given to you as on 16.01.2012.

Mark

a. if the candidate is not to be selected.

b. if the candidate is to be selected.

c. if the case is to be referred to DGM

d. if the case is to be referred to GM.

14. Aakash was born on 23rd October 1986. He was a brilliant student and completed Bachelor of Technology (civil) with 74 percent marks. He was keen to work and joined a big civil sector company since the year 2007. He has scored 60 percent marks in the interview and 50 percent marks in the written examination.

(a) a

(b) b

(c) c

(d) d

15. Supriya Boparai was born on 19th August 1982. She has secured 55 percent marks in the interview. She completed her B. Tech in Civil Engineering from a reputed institute with 67.56 percent marks. She joined a civil sector firm in 2006. She obtained 49.9 percent marks in the written examination.

(a) a   (b) b

(c) c   (d) d

16. Tanvi Jain has secured 55 percent marks in the written examination. She completed her B.Tech in Civil Engineering from a reputed institute with 72.57 percent marks. She obtained 55 percent marks in the interview. She has been working in the chemical sector since 2006. She was born on 17th August 1987.

(a) a   (b) b

(c) c   (d) d

17. Vikram was born on 6th April 1979. He has secured 55 percent marks in B.Tech (civil). He completed his M.Tech (civil) with 71 percent marks. He is working in a chemical sector firm since the year 2001. He has obtained 45 percent marks in written examination and 55 percent marks in the selection interview.

(a) a   (b) b

(c) c   (d) d

18. Sunil Kumar was born on 22nd June 1979. He has secured 65 percent marks in B.Tech (civil). He is working in a civil sector company since 2006. He has obtained 65 percent marks in both written examination and selection interview.

(a) a   (b) b

(c) c   (d) d

Directions for questions 19 to 22: Each of the questions below consists of a question and two statement, numbered I and II given below it. You have to decide whether the data provided in the statements are sufficient to answer the question. Read both the statements and give the answer.

a. If the data in only statement I alone or in only statement II alone is sufficient to answer the question.

b. If the data in either statement I or in statement II are sufficient to answer the question.

c. If the data in both the statements I and II together are not sufficient to answer the question.

d. If the data in both the statements I and II together are necessary to answer the question.

19. In a six storey building (consisting of floors numbered 1, 2, 3, 4, 5 and 6. The ground floor is numbered 1, the floor above it is numbered 2 and so on) the third floor is unoccupied. The building houses different people viz. P, Q, R, S and T, each living on a different floor. On which of the floors does T live?

    I.   S lives between the floors on which R and T live.

    II. There are two floors between T's floor and Q's floor.

    (a) a   (b) b

    (c) c   (d) d

20. How is 'see' written in the code language?

    I.   'hope to seen you' is written as '3692' 'do you see that' is written as '1973'.

    II. 'to pray and hope' is written as '0286' and 'hope I do well' is written as '5467'.

    (a) a   (b) b

    (c) c   (d) d

21. Among five friends A, B, C, D and E sitting at a circular table and facing the centre, who is sitting to the immediate left of A?

    I.   A is sitting third to the right of B. D is not an immediate neighbour of B.

    II. B is an immediate neighbour of C.

    (a) a   (b) b

    (c) c   (d) d

22. Among P, Q, R, S and T, which bag is the lightest?

    I.   P is heavier than Q. R is as heavy as Q. T is lighter than R.

    II. S is lighter than Q but heavier than T.

    (a) a

    (b) b

    (c) c

    (d) d

Directions for questions 23 to 25: In each of the questions below, three statements are followed by two conclusions numbered I and II. You have to take the given statements to be true even if they seem to be at variance with commonly known facts and then decide which of the given conclusion(s) logically follow(s) from the given statements.

    Give answer :

    a. if only conclusion I follows

    b. if only conclusion II follows

    c. if neither conclusion I nor II follows

    d. if both conclusions I and II follow

23. Statements:

    Some Inbox are Outbox

    All Outbox are Documents

    No Document is a Paper

    Conclusions:

    I.   Some Inbox are Paper

    II. Some Documents are Inbox

    (a) a   (b) b

    (c) c   (d) d

24. Statements:

    No Glass is a Computer

    Some Glasses are Facts

    All Computer are Given

    Conclusions:

    I.   Some Facts are Given

    II. All Computer are Facts

    (a) a   (b) b

    (c) c   (d) d

25. Statements:

    All Gangs are New

    Some New are Old

    All Old are Young

    Conclusions:

    I.   Some New are Young

    II. Some Gangs are Young

    (a) a   (b) b

    (c) c   (d) d

VERBAL ABILITY

Directions for questions 26 to 34: In questions given below, a part of the sentence is underlined part which may improve the sentence. Choose the correct alternative. In case no improvement is needed, option d. is the answer.

26. Practically <u>every part</u> of the banana tree is used by man.

    (a) each part   (b) any part

    (c) most part   (d) No improvement

27. My <u>opinion</u> for the film is that it will bag the national ward.

    (a) opinion to   (b) opinion about

    (c) opinion on   (d) No improvement

28. Whenever my students come across new words, I ask them <u>to look for them</u> in the dictionary.

    (a) to look it up   (b) to look them up

    (c) to look at them   (d) No improvement

29. Realising is the significance of technical education for developing country, the government <u>laid aside</u> a large sum on it during the last plan-period.

(a) laid up   (b) set aside

(c) laid out   (d) No improvement

30. If you are not clear about the meaning of a word, it is wise to <u>look to</u> a dictionary.

(a) look for   (b) look at

(c) loop up   (d) No improvement

31. You are warned <u>against committing</u> the same mistake again.

(a) to commit   (b) for committing

(c) against to commit   (d) No improvement

32. No sooner <u>he had returned home then</u> his mother felt happy.

(a) had he returned home when

(b) he had returned home than

(c) did he return home than

(d) No improvement

33. He should move on to the next point, and not <u>harp one sting only</u>.

(a) harp on string only

(b) harp only one string

(c) harp upon one string only

(d) No improvement

34. Either <u>he or I am going</u>.

(a) he or I are going   (b) he is going or I am

(c) I or he is going   (d) No improvement

Directions for questions 35 to 39: In each of the following questions, fill in the blanks with the most appropriate word to make the sentence grammatically correct.

35. When post offices try to improve their service, they sometimes send an electronic probe _____ the mail.

(a) at   (b) on

(c) over   (d) through

36. What's left over in the core, the radioactive material, will continue to give _____ heat for a long time.

(a) about   (b) in

(c) off   (d) by

37. It is dangerous to run _____ the road.

(a) in   (b) across

(c) with   (d) through

38. The kids paid eight hundred dollars each for the five days, _____ travel or lodging.

(a) amount   (b) off

(c) in   (d) sans

39. Early whales plied the shallows but still hauled themselves _____ the shore, probably to rest and to give birth.

(a) onto   (b) into

(c) by   (d) in

Directions for questions 40 to 44: Each of the following questions contains a small paragraph followed by question on it. Read each paragraph carefully and answer the question that follow.

40. The cost of housing in many urban parts of India has become so excessive that many young couples, with above-average salaries, can only afford small apartments. EMI and rent commitments are so huge that they cannot consider the possibility of starting a family since a new baby would probably mean either the mother or father giving up a well-paid position, something they can ill afford. The lack of or great cost of child care facilities further necessitate the return of both parents to work.

Which of the following adjustments could practically be made to the situation described above which would allow young couples to improve their housing prospects?

(a) Encourage couples to have only one child.

(b) Encourage couples to remain childless.

(c) Encourage young couples to move to cheaper areas for living.

(d) None of these is likely to have an impact on the current situation.

41. We live by the mantra of instant gratification. As a result, when something is not happening, rather than leaving it alone for a while, we are liable to go at it with hammer and tongs in a bid to make it happen. When it still refuses to happen, we reach a point where we simply want to be done with it. We end up settling for an end product that is vastly inferior to how we first envisioned it. As I mentioned before, sometimes contractual and commercial obligations are responsible for such a turn of events. That, however, does not apply to first-time novelists who rarely, if ever, write with a book contract in hand. Edison once said: Many of life's failures are people who did not realize how close they were to success when they gave up. We would all do well to remember those words, before settling for mediocrity.

The author is likely to not agree with which of the following?

(a) Patience is an important virtue.

(b) "When things go wrong as they sometimes will, rest if you must but don't you quit."

(c) "Better is the enemy of good."

(d) "Use what talent you possess: the woods would be very silent if no birds sang except those that sang best."

42. It is a matter of common experience that things get more disordered and chaotic with time. This observation can be elevated to the status of a law, the so-called Second Law of Thermodynamics. This says that the total amount of disorder, or entropy, in the universe, always increases with time. However, the Law refers only to the total amount of disorder. The order in one body can increase, provided that the amount of disorder in its surroundings increases by a greater amount. This is what happens in a living being. One can define Life to be an ordered system that can sustain itself against the tendency to disorder, and can reproduce itself.

Which of the following statements is true according to the passage?

(a) The laws of science can be extended to life.

(b) Every system is bound to get more chaotic with time.

(c) Increase in order in one entity occurs simultaneously with increase in disorder in some other entity.

(d) Reproduction is also an example of increasing entropy.

43. Do not imagine, comrades, that leadership is a pleasure. On the contrary, it is a deep and heavy responsibility. No one believes more firmly than Comrade Napoleon that all animals are equal. He would be only too happy to let you make your decisions for yourselves. But sometimes you might make the wrong decisions, comrades, and then where should we be? The tone of the author in the entire passage is

(a) Narrative   (b) Sarcastic

(c) Didactic   (d) Caviling

44. The skipper, an admirable seaman but nothing more, favored us with very little of his society, except at his table, and the young woman, Miss Janette Harford, and I became very well acquainted. We were, in truth, nearly always together, and being of an introspective turn of mind I often endeavored to analyze and define the novel feeling with which she inspired me-a secret, subtle, but powerful attraction which constantly impelled me to seek her, but the attempt was hopeless. I could only be sure that at least it was not love. The author of the passage is likely to agree with which of the following statements?

(a) He was infatuated with Miss Harford.

(b) He and Miss Harford were drawn together because of loneliness.

(c) He and Miss Harford were drawn together because of the attitude of the skipper.

(d) He could not give name to his feelings for Miss Harford.

45. Four alternative summaries are given below. Choose the option that best captures the essence of the text.

You seemed at first to take no notice of your school-fellows, or rather to set yourself against them because they were strangers to you. They knew as little of you as you did of them, this would have been the reason for their keeping aloof from you as well, which you would have felt as a hardship. Learn never to conceive a prejudice against another because you know nothing of them. It is bad reasoning and makes enemies of half the world. Do not think ill of them till they behave ill to you, and then strive to avoid the faults which you see in them. This will disarm their hostility sooner than pique or resentment or complaint.

(a) You encountered hardship amongst your school-fellows because you did not know them well. You should learn to not make enemies because of your prejudices irrespective of their behaviour towards you.

(b) The discomfort you felt with your school-fellows was because both sides knew little of each other. Avoid prejudice and negative thoughts till you encounter bad behaviour from other, and then win them over by shunning the faults you have observed.

(c) The discomfort you felt with your school-fellows was because both sides knew little of each other. You should not complain unless you find others prejudiced against you and have attempted to carefully analyze the faults you have observed in them.

(d) You encountered hardship amongst your school-fellows because you did not know them well. You should learn to not make enemies because of your prejudices unless they behave badly with you.

Directions for questions 46 to 57: Each passage in this section is followed by a group of questions to be answered on the basis of what is stated or implied in the passage. For some questions, more than one of the choices conceivably answer the question. However, you have to choose the best answer, that is, the response that most accurately and completely answers the question.

Passage-1

The story is told of how Harun Al Raschid, the caliph of Baghdad, would disguise himself as a beggar in order to discover what his subjects were thinking. This story is a famous image of despotism, a system of order created by conquest, resting on fear, and issuing in caprice. In a despotic system of government, the ultimate principle of order issues from the inclinations of the despot himself. Yet, despotism is not a system in which justice is entirely meaningless: it has generally prevailed in highly traditional societies where custom is king and the prevailing terms of justice are accepted as part of the natural order of things. Each person fits into a divinely recognized scheme. Dynasties rise and fall according to what the Chinese used to call 'the mandate of heaven', but life for the peasant changes little. Everything depends on the wisdom of the ruler. In the eleventh century BC, the Israelites, having trouble with the Philistines, went to the prophet Samuel who ruled them and asked to have a king who would both judge them and lead them in battle. Samuel warned against this move, advising that such a king would seize their property and enslave their energies. But they insisted that they wanted to be like other nations, and a king they must have. 'King' in this Middle Eastern context meant a ruler who would deal despotically with them, a governor quite different from the constitutional rulers of Europe. 'Despotism' is a catch-all category containing large variations. In one form or another, non-European civilizations have almost invariably been ruled despotically. The Western imagination, however, has generally been repelled by despots – cruel pharaohs, deranged Roman emperors like Caligula and Nero, exotic and remote emperors in India or China. In Europe, the desire for despotic power must disguise itself. Europeans have sometimes been beguiled by a despotism that comes concealed in the seductive form of an ideal – as it did in the cases of Hitler and Stalin. This fact may remind us that the possibility of despotism is remote neither in space nor in time. Many countries are still ruled in this manner, and it can threaten pain or death at any moment, it is like living in a madhouse. Today we define despotism (along with dictatorship and totalitarianism) as a form of government. This would have horrified the classical Greeks, whose very identity (and sense of superiority to other peoples) was based on distinguishing themselves from the despotism endured by their eastern neighbours. What this contrast reveals is that politics is so central to our civilization that its meaning changes with every change of culture and circumstance. For this reason, our first move in trying to understand politics must be to free ourselves from the unreflective beliefs of the present.

46. Which of the following is true as per the passage?

(a) Europeans have never been ruled by despotic leaders.

(b) Despotism and justice are mutually exclusive terms.

(c) Westerners, just like the non-European civilizations, despise the idea of despotism.

(d) Greeks were averse to the idea of a despotic ruler.

47. Which of the following is not a feature of the despotic rule/ruler as per the passage?

(a) it prevailed usually in traditional societies.

(b) Conquest was a common way of acquiring power.

(c) Natural order of things determined the terms of justice.

(d) Despotic rule was prevalent in Asia.

48. Which of the following is the author likely to disagree with?

(a) Politics is a dynamic field.

(b) Europeans used the term 'king' to mean 'a constitutional leader'.

(c) Traditionally, despotism was not considered a form of government.

(d) 'King' in the Middle-East meant a despotic ruler.

49. Which of the following can be inferred from the passage above?

   (a) Greece has never faced despotism.

   (b) Despotism was much more common in Asia than in Europe.

   (c) The author does not disapprove of despotic rule.

   (d) In despotism, laws are based on the judgments of the King as well as those of his subjects.

50. The author alludes to Indian, Chinese and Roman rulers in order to talk about:

   (a) despotic rulers who disguised themselves in beguiling forms.

   (b) rulers whom their European counterparts aspired to emulate.

   (c) rulers whom their western counterparts despised.

   (d) totalitarian leaders.

51. Which of the following is the closest in meaning to the word 'caprice' as used in the passage?

   (a) Whim   (b) Detail

   (c) Malice   (d) Distress

Directions for questions 52 to 57 : Each passage in this section is followed by a group of questions to be answered on the basis of what is stated or implied in the passage. For some questions, more than one of the choices conceivably answers the question. However, you have to choose the best answer, that is, the response that most accurately and completely answers the question.

Passage-2

War kills people and destroys property, and rationalists blame it on the passions. Why in that case is the history of a rational species so dismal a tale? Part of the explanation is necessity. Since defeat in war, especially in the pre-modern era, could mean extinction as a people, and since there were always some states that were, or might become, expansionist, warriors were everywhere needed for protection. These warriors had an ethic of honour. Valour in battle was glorious and sacrifice would win, as it seemed, undying glory. In the millennium between the end of Rome in the west and the beginning of the modern world, these aristocratic protectors were to become the problem rather than the solution to the desire for peace. The death and destruction resulting from their feuding was brought to an end by the ascendancy of absolute monarchs, who then themselves became the source of the problem.

War was now the pastime of kings, cannons, ran the motto, are the arguments of princes. By marriage and diplomacy, but above all by war, a state could grow to be a power. Over several centuries, the mosaic of small dominions inherited from the Middle Ages was consolidated by these means into the relatively simple political map of the Europe we know today. War, as Clausewitz put it, is the continuation of policy – that is, politics – by other means. Rulers attack for advantage, and defend to protect the national interest. As in chess, one side or the other must win, and even stalemate is merely a precarious equilibrium. To lose this international game may be a desperate thing, as the Poles discovered when the feebleness of their government left them to the partitioning mercies of the Russians, Prussians, and Austrians, and as many states discovered when overrun by Nazi Germany after 1939. The best explanation of political conflict was given by Thomas Hobbes in Leviathan. Hobbes called any situation in which men do not acknowledge a common superior a 'state of nature' and his thesis was that a state of nature is always a state of war, in which the life of man would be 'nasty, poor, solitary, brutish and short'. As he put it in the famous thirteenth chapter: 'men have no pleasure, but on the contrary a great deal of grief, in keeping company, where there is no power able to over-awe them all.' Hobbes suggested three basic reasons for this. We have already mentioned two of them: the scarcity of the things men value (such as well-watered land), and the human passion for glory. The third was something Hobbes called 'diffidence' or mistrust of others. The very fear of the future aggression of others might well lead to a policy of pre-emptive strikes, which have a terrifying logic: Alpha fears that Beta will attack, and decides to strike first, but Beta already fears this, and wants to get in even earlier, fearing which Alpha . . . and so on.

52. As per the passage, states in the pre-modern era went in for war to:

   (a) vent their expansionist desire.

   (b) protect its people from expansionist states.

   (c) glorify one's state by exhibiting valour.

   (d) extend the ethics of honour.

53. Which of the following is true as per the passage?

   (a) As per Thomas Hobbes, a state in its natural form will always be at war.

(b) A situation, in which a people lack trust in others, will always result in war.

(c) Diplomacy, marriage and war were the only ways in which a state could attain power.

(d) Thomas Hobbes justifies his theory by citing the example of the Nazis.

54. Which of the following sums up Thomas Hobbes' explanation of political conflict?

(a) Until men live without a common power to keep them all in awe, they are in that condition which is called war.

(b) People subjugated by a superior power, lead a miserable life.

(c) Conflict is an essential outcome of mistrust.

(d) The lack of acknowledgement of a common superior leads to a 'state of nature' which translates into a 'state of war'.

55. Which of the following words is the closest in meaning to the word 'mosaic' as used in the passage above?

(a) Amalgamation   (b) Collection

(c) Rulers   (d) Entities

56. The phrase in the first line of the passage, "The rationalists blame the war on passions" implies that:

(a) passion is the most common cause of war.

(b) only rationalists fight wars.

(c) the rationalists are right in judging the cause of the war.

(d) a certain section of the society views that war results when human emotions break open the floodgates of tolerance.

57. Which of the following is said about the Poles in the passage above?

(a) The Poles were decimated by Nazi Germany after 1939.

(b) The Poles did not anticipate a German attack.

(c) A weak government was the sole reason for the affliction of the Poles.

(d) The Poles predicament fell into Clausewitz's theory on war.

Directions for questions 58 to 65: Which of the phrases given below should replace the part of the sentence marked in bold to make it grammatically correct? If the sentence is correct as it is, mark option d. as the answer.

58. **Beside** of its small size, a luggage lock can be a big help in providing you peace of mind when you travel.

(a) Besides   (b) In spite

(c) Just   (d) No correction required

59. To **who** should I write?

(a) whom   (b) whoever

(c) how   (d) No correction required

60. Let us **have done** with name-calling.

(a) has done   (b) were doing

(c) had do   (d) No correction required

61. They used to be **foes** but now they are sworn enemies.

(a) friends   (b) antagonist

(c) together   (d) No correction required

62. There are not many men who are so famous that they are frequently referred to by their **short names** only

(a) initials

(b) signatures

(c) picture

(d) No correction required

63. The man **to who I sold** my house was a cheat.

(a) to whom I sell

(b) to who I sell

(c) to whom I sold

(d) No correction required

64. I need not offer any explanation regarding this incident - my behaviour **is speaking itself**.

(a) will speak to itself   (b) speaks for itself

(c) has been speaking   (d) No correction required

65. He is too important **for tolerating** any delay.

(a) to tolerate   (b) to tolerating

(c) at tolerating   (d) No correction required

ANSWERS

1. (b)	**2.** (b)	**3.** (a)	**4.** (a)	**5.** (a)	**6.** (b)	**7.** (b)	**8.** (c)	**9.** (b)	**10.** (a)
11. (b)	**12.** (d)	**13.** (d)	**14.** (b)	**15.** (a)	**16.** (a)	**17.** (a)	**18.** (b)	**19.** (d)	**20.** (c)
21. (a)	**22.** (d)	**23.** (b)	**24.** (c)	**25.** (a)	**26.** (d)	**27.** (b)	**28.** (b)	**29.** (b)	**30.** (c)
31. (d)	**32.** (c)	**33.** (c)	**34.** (d)	**35.** (d)	**36.** (c)	**37.** (b)	**38.** (d)	**39.** (a)	**40.** (c)
41. (c)	**42.** (c)	**43.** (c)	**44.** (d)	**45.** (b)	**46.** (d)	**47.** (c)	**48.** (b)	**49.** (b)	**50.** (c)
51. (a)	**52.** (b)	**53.** (a)	**54.** (d)	**55.** (b)	**56.** (d)	**57.** (d)	**58.** (b)	**59.** (a)	**60.** (d)
61. (a)	**62.** (a)	**63.** (c)	**64.** (b)	**65.** (a)					

EXPLANATIONS

1. N-2, O-0, U-3, E-6, M-1, S-5, J-9

2. As each girl can come within a timespan of 60 minutes, let the time when A comes can be represented as 60, minutes along X axis and B comes can be represented as 60 minutes along Y axis. When both come at same time x = y

   OR

   If A comes before B $y - x = 15$

   OR

   If B comes before A $x - y = 15$

   The overall outlook of the graph looks like a square of each axis 60(Minutes)

   Therefore probability of they meet each other

   = required area in which they meet/total area

   $$= 15 \times 15 \times \frac{7}{60} \times 60 = \frac{7}{16}$$

3. Required number of ways

   $$= {}^7C_5 \times {}^3C_2 = {}^7C_2 \times {}^3C_1 = \left(\frac{(7 \times 6)}{2 \times 1}\right) \times 3 = 63$$

4. Consider the initial amount with Mr.Paul be Rs. x

   Mr.Paul gave 40% of the money he had, to his wife.

   i.e., remaining $(100 - 40)\%$ of x

   He also gave 20% of the remaining amount to each of his three sons

   i.e., remaining $(100 - (3 \times 20))\%$ of x

   Half of the amount now left was spent on miscellaneous items and the remaining amount of Rs.12,000 i.e., $\frac{1}{2}$ [(100 − 60)% of x (100 − 40)% of x] = Rs.12000

   Convert percentage into fractions

   $$\left(\frac{1}{2}\right) \times \left(\frac{40}{100}\right) \times \left(\frac{60}{100}\right) \times x = 12000$$

   $$x = \frac{(12000 \times 2 \times 100)}{(60 \times 40)} = 100000$$

   $$= \text{Rs. } 100000$$

5. Consider the price of the product be Rs.100

   consider the original sale be 100 pieces

   then, total revenue = Rs.(100 * 100) = Rs.10000

   if the price of product was decreased by 10% and number of pieces be increased by 30%

   then, new total revenue = Rs. (90 × 130) = Rs.11700

   increase in revenue = $\left(\left(\frac{11700}{10000}\right) \times 100\right)\% = 17\%$

6. suppose, A, B and C take x, $\frac{x}{2}$ and $\frac{x}{3}$ hrs respectively to finish the work then,

   $$\left(\frac{1}{x}\right) + \left(\frac{2}{x}\right) + \left(\frac{3}{x}\right) = \frac{1}{2}$$

   i.e. $\dfrac{6}{x} = \dfrac{1}{2}$

   $x = 12$ hrs, B = $\dfrac{x}{2} = \dfrac{12}{2} = 6$ hrs

7. The series is moving as:

   $57 = 27 \times 2 + 3$

   $175 = 57 \times 3 + 4$

   $705 = 175 \times 4 + 5$

   $3531 = 705 \times 5 + 6$

   Thus $= 705 \times 5 + 6$

   Thus, the term replacing (?) would be 175.

8. Number of dozens of bananas in each box

   $$\frac{864}{12 \times 9} = 8$$

9. To find the number of factors of a given number, express the number as a product of powers of prime numbers.

   $1025 - 7 = (1025 - 1) - 6$

   The number $1025 - 1 = 99.....9$ (25 digits) is divisible by 3.

   Therefore, $(1025 - 1) - 6 = $ (24 nines and unit digit is 3) 99.......93.

   This number is divisible by 3 (from amongst the given choices).

10. A+ B +C = 5625

    $$B = \frac{1}{4}(A + C) \Rightarrow A + C = 4B$$

    $4B + B = 5625$

    $B = 1125$

    Also A = $\frac{1}{2}$ (B + C) $\Rightarrow$ B + C = 2A

A + C = 4B = 4 × 1125 = 4500

Also B = 2A – C

2A – C = 1125

Now solving A + C = 4500 and 2A – C = 1125

Then A = 1875 and C = 2625

A – B = 1875 – 1125 = Rs. 750

11. Required words are-Art, Ate and Are.

12. A R R O G A N C E

1 2 3 4 5 6 7 8 9

G A N C A R R O E

13. do re me = he is late   ...(1)

fa me la = she is early   ...(2)

so ti do = he leaves soon   ...(3)

From (1) and (2),

me = is

and from (1) and (3),

do = he

∴ 'late' = re.

14. The candidate (Aakash fulfills all the above mentioned criteria and should be selected.

15. The candidate (Supriya Bopari) does not fulfill the above mentioned criteria, as she did not secure 50% marks in the written examination. Hence, the candidate should not be selected.

16. The candidate (Tanvi Jain) does not fulfill the above mentioned criteria, as she is not 25 years old and should not be selected.

17. The candidate (Vikram) does not fulfill the above mentioned criteria, as he did not secure 50% marks in the written examination. Hence, the candidate should not be selected.

18. The candidate (Sunil Kumar) fulfills all the above mentioned criteria and should be selected.

19. From statement I and II: The arrangement can be shown as:

6 R

5 S

4 T

3 Unoccupied

2 P

1 Q

Hence, T lives on floor numbered 4.

20. From statement I:

Code for 'you seen' will be '39'.

From statement II:

Code for 'hope' will be '6'.

Hence, the data in both statement I and II are not sufficient to answer the question.

21. From statement I:

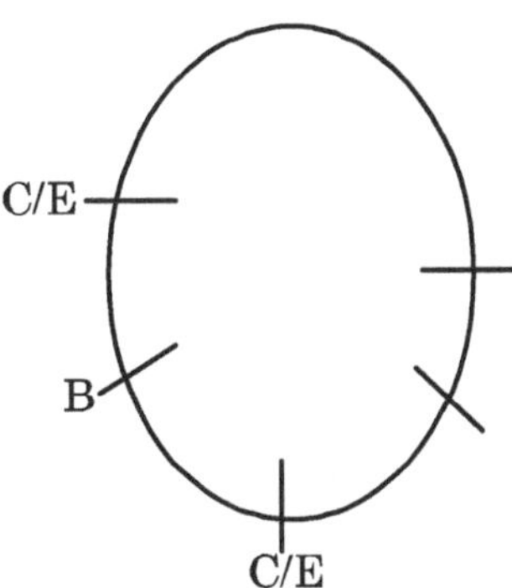

D is sitting to the immediate left of A.

Hence, data in statement I alone are sufficient to answer the question.

22. From statement I: P > Q = R > T

From statement II: Q > S > T

From statement I and II: P > Q = R > S > T

Hence , T is the lightest among the five bags.

23. st-1: Some Inbox are Outbox

st-2: All Outbox are Documents

st-3: No Document is a Paper

To obtain conclusion 1- Some Inbox are Paper

Join 1 + 2 = Some inbox are Documents, then it with 3 = some inbox are not paper.

To obtain conclusion 2 – Some Documents are Inbox

Join 1 + 2 = conclusion 2 follows

24. st-1: No Glass is a Computer

st-2: Some Glasses are Facts

st-3: All Computer are Given

To obtain conclusion 1 – Some Facts are Given

Join 1 + 2 = Some facts are not computer.

Then with joining with 3 = some facts are not given.

To obtain conclusion 2 – All Computer are Facts

Joining 1 + 2 = some facts are not computer.

25. st-1: All Gangs are New

st-2: Some New are Old

st-3: All Old are Young

To obtain conclusion 1 – Some New are Young

Join 1 + 2 = Some New are Young

To obtain conclusion 2 – Some Gangs are Young

Join 1 + 2 = Some gangs are old.

Then, join with 3 = Some gangs are Young.

35. 'Through' means by means of. Hence, option (d) is the correct answer. 'At' is used to suggest where something/somebody is. 'On' means in or into a position covering, touching or forming a part of the surface. 'Over' means from one side to another. Options (a), (b) and (c) will render the meaning of the sentence incorrect.

36. The sentence means that the radioactive material will emit heat for a long time. 'Off' is used to indicate separation, distance or removal. Hence, option (c) is the correct answer. 'About' is used to indicate the subject of something said or written or the object of a thought, feeling, or action. 'In' means inside something. 'By' means close to or next to something.

37. 'Across' means from one side to the other side of something. Hence, option (b) is the correct answer. 'Run with the road' suggests that the road is also running literally. 'Run in' or 'run through' the road are grammatically incorrect in this context.

38. So, option (d), 'sans' which means 'without' is the correct answer. The sentence means that each kid paid money for five days, which did not include travel or lodging. All other options are logically incorrect in this context.

39. The sentence means that the early whales lying on the shore pushed themselves on its surface to rest and to give birth. 'Onto' is used with verbs to express movement on or to a particular place or position. Hence, option (a) is the correct answer. 'Into', 'by' and 'in' will therefore not fit into the given context.

40. The passage talks about high housing cost, so the problem can be rectified if they move to cheaper areas. Option (b) is impractical in the given situation. Also, having one child cannot help in improving housing prospects for young couples.

41. "Best is the enemy of good" means that insisting on perfection often results in no improvement at all. This is completely opposite to what the author says in the passage (don't settle for anything less than your best). The author also advocates patience and hence would agree with option (a) Similarly, he would agree with option (b) where it is being said that we should not quit if we are unable to achieve something. Option (d) states that people should use their talent to the maximum potential. The author agrees with this statement. Option (d) also states that even if relative to the others your talent is less, you

should still use it. The passage doesn't say anything about this and hence it cannot be concluded whether the author agrees with the second part of the statement. Hence, option (c) is correct.

42. Refer to the line – 'The order in one body can increase, provided that the amount of disorder in its surroundings increases by a greater amount'. This means that if there is order in one entity, there has to be an increased disorder in another. Hence, option (c) is true as per the passage. The author talks only about the Second Law of Thermodynamics and so we cannot say that laws of science can be extended to life. This makes option a. incorrect. Option (b) is the opposite of what the author says in the passage. Option (d) has not been stated in the passage.

43. By looking at the passage we can say that the speaker is conveying information and instruction on leadership and decision making to the comrades. The author is neither narrating an incident nor has he used sarcasm in the text. Also, no objections have been raised about any issues in the passage (Caviling). Hence, the correct option is (c) i.e. *Didactic*.

44. The last few lines of the passage state that the author hopelessly tried to analyze and define the feelings he had for Miss Harford. He had no name for these feelings. All he knew was that he did not feel love for her. Hence, option (d) is the correct answer. Options (b) and (c) cannot be inferred from the passage. Also, the author states that he was inspired by Miss Harford but does not go on to mention that he was infatuated by her. Hence, option (a) is untrue.

45. Option (b) covers the major points of the given paragraph. The discomfort you felt with your schoolfellows was because both sides knew little of each other. Avoid prejudice and negative thoughts till you encounter ill behaviour from others and eventually win then over (disarm their hostility) by shunning or avoiding the faults that you observe in them.

46. Refer to the lines, "Today we define despotism...by their eastern neighbours." Hence, option (d) is true. Refer to the line, "In Europe, the desire... neither in space nor in time." Hence, option (a) is incorrect. Refer to the line, "Yet despotism is not a system in which justice is entirely meaningless." Hence, option (b) is incorrect. Refer to the lines, "'Despotism' is a catch-all category...however, has generally been repelled by despots..." Hence, option (c) is also incorrect.

47. Refer to the line, "...it has generally prevailed in highly traditional societies..." This proves option a. as a feature of despotic rule. Refer to the line, "This story is a famous image of despotism, a system of order created by...order of things." Hence, option b. is also a feature. Option d. is clearly stated in the passage. Option c. is not a feature because the passage states that the prevailing terms of justice, under despotism, is "accepted" as part of the natural order of things. It doesn't mean that natural order of things determined the terms of justice. Hence, option c. is the correct answer.

48. Refer to the lines, "'King' in this Middle Eastern context meant a ruler... a governor quite different from the constitutional rulers of Europe." Hence, we cannot infer option b. and it is therefore the correct answer. Refer to the lines, "...politics is so central to our civilization that its meaning changes with every change of culture and circumstance." This proves that politics is a dynamic field. Hence, option a. is incorrect because the author agrees with it. Refer to the lines, "Today we define despotism (along with dictatorship and totalitarianism) as a form of government." This implies that previously, despotism was not considered a form of government. Hence, we can infer option c.. Option d. is a fact given in the passage and hence true.

49. The passage talks about classical Greeks, but not about Greeks thereafter. Thus, option a. cannot be inferred. Option c. can be negated since the author compares a despotic society to a madhouse. The passage clearly states that King was the ultimate authority in a despotic rule. Hence, option d. can be negated. The passage only talks of the Israelites in the eleventh century BC, and not thereafter. Refer to the line, "In one form or another...ruled despotically." From this we can infer that option b. is the correct answer.

50. Consider the following line from the passage, "The western imagination...in India or China". This clearly indicates that the aforementioned Asian rulers were despised by western rulers. Thus, option c. is correct. Option (a) is incorrect because Chinese, Roman and Indian rulers did not disguise themselves in 'beguiling forms'. Option b. is incorrect because European rulers did not want to emulate Indian, Chinese and Roman rulers. Option (d) is incorrect because the said rulers are despots not totalitarian or anarchical rulers.

51. The statement "This story...is issuing in caprice" suggests that despotism is subject to the unpredictable or whimsical behaviour of the despot. Therefore, the word 'caprice' as used in the passage means 'a tendency to change your mind suddenly or behave unexpectedly'. Thus, 'whim', which means 'a sudden wish to do or have something, especially something unusual or unnecessary' 'is synonymous with 'caprice'. Thus, option a. is correct. The word 'malice' means 'a feeling of hatred for somebody that causes a desire to harm them'. The word 'distress' means 'a feeling of great worry or unhappiness, great suffering'.

52. Refer to the lines, "Part of the explanation is...would win, as it seemed, undying glory", which argue that states went in for war to protect their people from other states who had expansionist intentions. Hence the prime reason is mentioned in option (b) Option a. is incorrect because the passage does not state the presence of any 'desire' in rulers that needed to be vented. Options c. and d. are incorrect because 'ethics of honour' and 'valour in war' were glorified in order to realize the prime goal, i.e. of protection.

53. Refer to the lines, "Hobbes called any situation...an would be 'nasty, poor, solitary, brutish and short." Hence, option a. is correct. Refer to the line, "The very fear of the future...might well lead to pre-emptive strikes..." It states that a situation in which mistrust is prevalent 'might' end up in a war but war is not its definite end result. Thus, option b. is incorrect. Diplomacy, marriage and war were three reasons to go to war, but we do not know if they were the 'only' reasons. Thus, option c. is incorrect. Clausewitz cited the example of the Nazis to justify his theory not Hobbes, and Hobbes cited 'diffidence' as a reason for war. Thus, option d. is incorrect.

54. Refer to the lines, "...'men have no pleasure, but on the contrary... where there is no power able to overawe them all'. " Also, "Hobbes called any situation in which men do not..............would be 'nasty, poor, solitary, brutish and short'." Option a. is incorrect because such a condition is called a 'state of nature' and not war. From the lines quoted above, it can be inferred that option b. is completely opposite to what Hobbes argues. Hence, it is incorrect. Refer to the lines, "The third was something Hobbes called 'diffidence'...which have a terrifying logic." Hobbes says that conflict 'might' be a result, and he does not say that it is a 'definite' result. Hence, option c. is incorrect. Option d. clearly explains Hobbes' theory and therefore, is the correct answer.

55. The statement "Over several centuries, the mosaic of small dominions…" refers to a collection of pieces of land inherited by rulers in the middle ages which when put together form a simple political map of Europe today. Therefore, the word 'mosaic' as used in the passage means 'something made of different things that together form a pattern'. Thus, option b. i.e. 'collection' is the correct answer. The word 'amalgamation' means 'a consolidation or merger, as of several corporations'. The word 'entities' means 'things that exists separately from other things and has its own identity'.

56. The given phrase implies that the rationalist section of the society blames 'human passions' for the wars that happen. Option d. correctly states the meaning of the aforementioned phrase and thus, is the answer. It also proves all the other options incorrect.

57. The author does not mention the names of countries overrun by Nazi Germany after 1939. So, option a. is incorrect. There is no evidence supporting option b., and thus it is incorrect as well. The passage gives no information to suggest that its weak government was the 'sole' reason for Poland's affliction. Thus, option c. is incorrect as well. In the phrase "To lose this international game", 'this international game' refers to Clauswitz theory of politics. Clauswitz states that countries conquer territories for their advantage and then go about protecting the conquered lands in national interest, just as Poland was overpowered by a number of countries, which after conquering, afflicted the Poles to maintain their rule. Therefore, option d. is correct as the passage clearly mentions the Poles' condition as an example of Clausewitz's theory.

MOCK-9

(WIPRO - I)

1. The causes of productivity loss are to be written around a circle in the annual report. In how many ways can an analyst write them around the circle, if the number of causes are 5?

  (a) 5!   (b) 4!

  (c) $^5P_5$ (d) $^5C_2$

2. In designing a new keyboard, sample keyboards are prepared by rearranging the alphabet keys. What is the possible number of keyboards formed?

  (a) 26!   (b) $^{26}C_1$

  (c) $^{26}P_1$ (d) 26.0

3. Rahul can finish one-fifth of his homework in one hour. Neha can finish three-seventh of her homework in one hour thirty minutes and Riya can finish three fourth of her homework in three hours thirty minutes. If all of them start their homework at 12.00 p.m. and can go to play as soon as they all finish their homework, when can they start to play, if they take a break at 3.30 p.m. for thirty minutes?

  (a) 5.00 pm   (b) 5.30 pm

  (c) 4.40 pm   (d) 6.30 pm

4. A large rubber cushion can be filled with air pump in 10 minutes, another pump can fill the same cushion in 12 minutes. If both the pumps operate together, how long will it take to fill the cushion?

  (a) $5\dfrac{5}{11}$ mins   (b) $6\dfrac{6}{11}$ mins

  (c) 6 mins   (d) 5 mins

5. Riya sold her car for Rs. 50,000 less than what she bought it for and lost 8%. At what price should she have sold the car, if she wanted to gain as much as she lost in the first transaction?

  (a) Rs. 6.25L   (b) Rs. 6.50L

  (c) Rs. 6.375L   (d) Rs. 6.75L

6. A man deposits Rs. 5,000 in his bank account for 5 years to earn an interest of 12%. What amount will he get after 5 years?

  (a) 2000   (b) 3000

  (c) 5300   (d) 8000

7. 3 empty CDs and 2 pen drives cost Rs. 790. 2 empty CDs and 3 pen drive cost Rs. 1110. what is the cost of one pen drive?

  (a) 30   (b) 300

  (c) 25   (d) 350

8. What is the value of 6^{-2}?

  (a) 36   (b) −36

  (c) $\dfrac{1}{36}$ (d) $-\dfrac{1}{36}$

9. Two trains starting at the same time from two stations 200 km apart, and going in opposite directions cross each other at a distance of 110 km from one of the stations. What is the ratio of their speeds?

  (a) 9 : 20   (b) 11 : 9

  (c) 11 : 20   (d) 11 : 6

10. The number of six digit even number that can be made from the number 214635 are?

  (a) 18   (b) 72

  (c) 120   (d) 360

11. A runs $\dfrac{5}{3}$ times as fast as B. If A gives B a start of 80m. How far must the winning post be so that A and B might reach it at the same time?

  (a) 300 m   (b) 200 m

  (c) 160 m   (d) 270 m

12. In a race of 600m. A can beat B by 60m and in a race of 500m. B can beat C by 50m. By how many m will A beat C in a race of 400m?

  (a) 72 m   (b) 74 m

  (c) 78 m   (d) 76 m

13. Three numbers are in the ratio 3 : 4 : 5 and their L.C.M is 2400. Their H.C.F is ?

  (a) 10.0   (b) 30.0

  (c) 40.0   (d) 20 m

14. A boat can travel with a speed of 13 km/hr in still water. If the speed of the stream is 4 km/hr, find the time taken by the boat to go 68km downstream ?

  (a) 4 hours

  (b) 2 hours

  (c) 3 hours

  (d) 5 hours

15. Present ages of Sameer and Anand are in the ratio 5 : 4 respectively. Three years hence, the ratio of their ages will become 11 : 9 respectively. What is Anand's present age in years?

(a) 24.0   (b) 40.0

(c) 10.0   (d) 27.0

16. What is the LCM of 3, 2.7 and 0.09?

(a) 0.27   (b) 2.7

(c) 27   (d) 2700

17. A is $2\frac{1}{3}$ times as fast as B. If A gives B a start of 80 m, how long should the race course be so that both of them reach at the same time?

(a) 170 metre   (b) 150 metre

(c) 140 metre   (d) 160 metre

18. A can run 224 metre in 28 seconds and B in 32 seconds. By what distance A beat B?

(a) 36 metre   (b) 24 metre

(c) 32 metre   (d) 28 metre

LOGICAL REASONING

Directions for Q19 to Q21: From the given choices select the odd one out

19. (a) FHKO

(b) CEHL

(c) ZBEJ

(d) XZCG

20. (a) PRS   (b) TVX

(c) FIK   (d) LME

21. (a) AE6   (b) DE9

(c) HN14   (d) KP18

Directions for Q22 to Q24: Select the right option from the given alternatives.

22. Building : Bricks : : Flower :?

(a) Seed

(b) Fruit

(c) Honey

(d) Petals

23. ADWZ : FIBE : : KNPM :?

(a) PSUT

(b) PSUR

(c) PSER

(d) PVUR

24. 985 : 874 : : 763 :?

(a) 641   (b) 542

(c) 722   (d) 652

25. A player "X" stands 50 yards away from "Y" in the West. He moves 10 yards straight towards South and then turns Eastward going up to 50 yards, while Y also comes down Southward and meets X at the same point. How far is Y from his original position (in yards)?

(a) 50.0   (b) 40.0

(c) 20.0   (d) 10.0

26. Radha is facing South. She turns 1350 in the anticlockwise direction and then 450 in the clockwise direction. Which direction is she facing now?

(a) West   (b) North

(c) South   (d) East

27. A man runs 4 km towards North, then 20 km towards East. Then he runs 4 km towards South. How far is he from his initial position?

(a) 4 km   (b) 20 km

(c) 24 km   (d) 16 km

28. Aaron was riding his bike. He rode 50 metres South and took a left turn to ride another 70 metres. After that he took another left turn and rode 50 metres again and finally he took a right turn to ride 60 metres more. How far and in which direction is he from the starting point?

(a) 120 metres, West   (b) 110 metres, East

(c) 110 metres, West   (d) 130 metres, East

29. A is B's sister. C is B's mother. D is C's father. E is D's mother. Then, how is A related to D?

(a) grandfather   (b) Granddaughter

(c) Niece   (d) Sister

30. 2, 3, 6, 18, 108, ...

(a) 54   (b) 1002

(c) 216   (d) 1944

31. In a certain code JOHN is written as LSNV. How is MARK written in that code?

(a) OEYS

(b) OEXS

(c) OEXT

(d) OEYT

32. If Neena says, "Anita's father Raman is the only son of my father-in-law Mahipal", then how is Bindu, who is the sister of Anita, related to Mahipal ?

(a) Niece   (b) Daughter

(c) Wife   (d) Daughter-in-low

33. How many points will be on the face opposite to in face which contains 2 points?

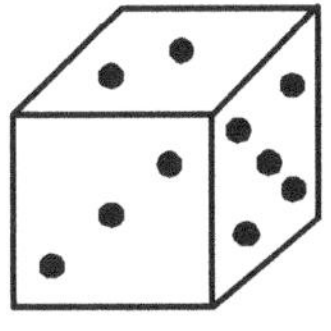
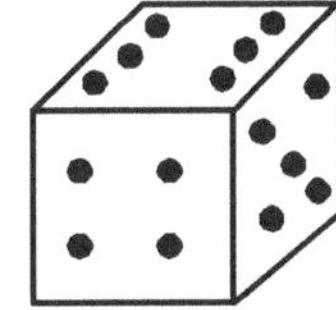

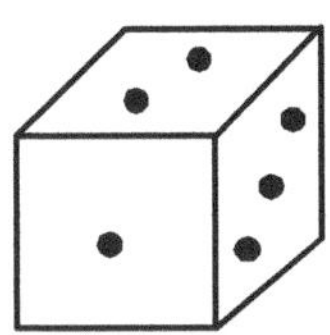
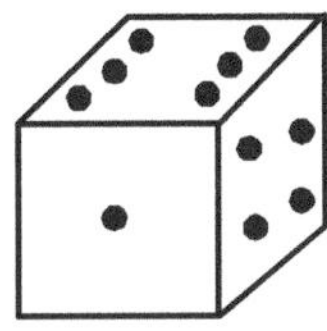

(a) 1   (b) 5
(c) 4   (d) 6

34. From the four positions of a dice given below, find the color which is opposite to yellow?

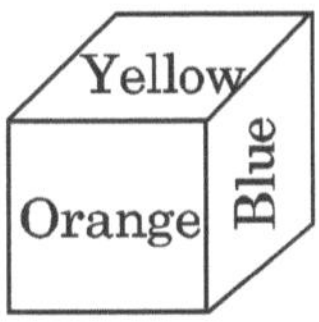

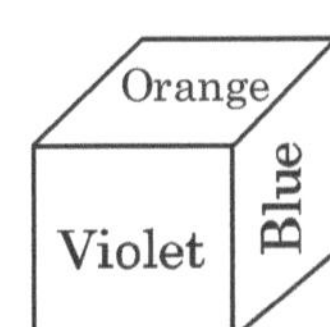

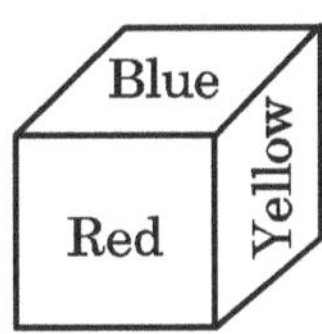

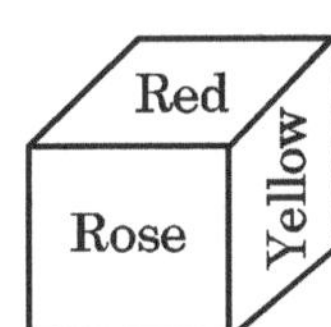

(a) Violet   (b) Red
(c) Rose   (d) Blue

VERBAL REASONING

Directions for 35 to 37: Select the word or phrase which best expresses the meaning of the given word.

35. CONTAGIOUS
   (a) Communicable
   (b) Harmful
   (c) Preventive
   (d) Survival

36. UNILATERAL
   (a) Sloping
   (b) One-sided
   (c) Parabola
   (d) Innumerable

37. VANISH
   (a) Evacuate   (b) Decrease
   (c) Disappear   (d) Harm

Directions for 38 to 40: Select the option that is most nearly opposite to the given word

38. HUMOROUS
   (a) Entertaining   (b) Witty
   (c) Comical   (d) Depressing

39. FIGURATIVE
   (a) Symbolic   (b) Illustrative
   (c) Literal   (d) Pictoral

40. PRANKISH
   (a) Whimsical   (b) Machiavellian
   (c) Impish   (d) Serious

Direction for Q. 41 :- Select the word or phrase which best expresses the meaning of the word typed in bold.

41. We didn't believe in his statement, but **subsequent** events proved that he was right
   (a) later   (b) many
   (c) few   (d) earlier

Directions for 42 to 44: In the question, a part of the sentence is italicised. Alternatives to the italicised part are given which may improve the construction of the sentence. Select the correct alternative.

42. After Michael typed the letter, *he gave it to Jane to sign*.
   (a) he was giving it to jane to sign
   (b) he gives it to jane to sign
   (c) he had been giving it to jane to sign
   (d) No change

43. We will not go to work, *if it shall snow tomorrow*.
   (a) it would snow tomorrow
   (b) it will snow tomorrow
   (c) it snows tomorrow
   (d) it can snow tomorrow

44. There must be a reason why Tom & Jerry cartoons play western *classical music riffs in their background score*
   (a) classical, musical riff as their background score.
   (b) classical, music riffs as their background scores
   (c) classical, music riffs as there background score.
   (d) classical, music riffs in their background scores.

Direction for Q. 45:- Read the sentence to find out whether is any grammatical error in it. The error, if any, will be in one part of the sentence. The letter of that part is the answer. Ignore the error of punctuation, if any.

45. (A) His low marks in English/ (B) suggested that he did/ (C) not know nothing/ (D) about the language./ (E) No error.

(a) A   (b) B

(c) C   (d) D

46. Find grammatical error.

(A) Big brands like Sony, Samsung and

(B) Nokia have been launched many phones having latest

(C) features like facebook application, orkut tool and much more.

(a) (A)   (b) (B)

(c) (C)   (d) No error

47. Choose the alternative part to the quotation part She "HAS LIVED" in Chennai she was eight years

(a) Lived   (b) Has been Living

(c) Had Stayed   (d) is living

Direction for Questions 48 to 51:

Passage

The Kingdom of Spain was created in 1492 with the unification of the Kingdom of Castile and the Kingdom of Aragon. For the next three centuries Spain was the most important colonial power in the world. It was the most powerful state in Europe and the foremost global power during the 16th century and the greater part of the 17th century. Spain established a vast empire in the Americas, stretching from California to Patagonia, and colonies in the western Pacific.

Spain's European wars, however, led to economic damage, and the latter part of the 17th century saw a gradual decline of power under an increasingly neglectful and inept Habsburg regime. The decline culminated in the War of the Spanish Succession, where Spain's decline from the position of a leading Western power, to that of a secondary one, was confirmed, although it remained the leading colonial power.

The eighteenth century saw a new dynasty, the Bourbons, which directed considerable effort towards the institutional renewal of the state, with some success, peaking in a successful involvement in the American War of Independence.

The end of the eighteenth and the start of the nineteenth centuries saw turmoil unleashed throughout Europe by the French Revolutionary and Napoleonic Wars, which finally led to a French occupation of much of the continent, including Spain. This triggered a successful but devastating war of independence that shattered the country and created an opening for what would ultimately be the successful independence of Spain's mainland American colonies.

Following a period of growing political instability in the early twentieth century, in 1936 Spain was plunged into a bloody civil war. The war ended in a nationalist dictatorship, led by Francisco Franco which controlled the Spanish government until 1975.

48. What was the result of Napoleanic wars?

(a) A small part of the continent was occupied by French people

(b) Spain was occupied by the French

(c) War of independence was unable to yield any positive result

(d) American colonies were destroyed after the war

49. What is the meaning of the term 'culminated'?

(a) Follow a particular path

(b) Guide or transform

(c) Reach the highest point

(d) Introduce on a grand scale

50. What is the summary of the passage?

(a) The rise and fall of a national empire

(b) The downfall of successive regimes in Spain

(c) The history of Spain

(d) Spain in eighteenth century

51. What occurred in the later part of 17th century?

(a) War of succession confirmed the leading position of Spain

(b) Spain was no longer regarded as the ruling colonial power

(c) A vast empire was established in Europe

(d) Power steadily declined under Habsburg regime

52. These clothes are very nice, but the are terribly __________

(a) ugly   (b) overpriced

(c) desired   (d) adorable

53. Today _________ the inaugural day of the pub, the drinks were served free of cost.

(a) was

(b) been

(c) is

(d) being

54. Given below are six sentence. The first and the sixth sentence are given in the beginning. The middle four labelled - P, Q, R and S are jumbled up. Select the proper order for the four sentences.

S1: Ms. Parasuram started a petrol pump in Madras.

P: A total of twelve girls now work at the pump.

Q: She advertised in newspapers for women staff

R: They operate in two shifts.

S: The response was good.

S6: Thus she has shown the way for many others.

(a) PQSR   (b) SQPR

(c) QSPR   (d) PQRS

55. In India, women _________ only three percent of senior management

(a) contain

(b) contains

(c) involve

(d) comprises

56. The roads to hills _________ closed because of landslides.

(a) was

(b) is

(c) were

(d) be

ANSWERS

1. (b)	**2.** (a)	**3.** (b)	**4.** (a)	**5.** (d)	**6.** (d)	**7.** (d)	**8.** (c)	**9.** (b)	**10.** (d)
11. (b)	**12.** (d)	**13.** (c)	**14.** (a)	**15.** (a)	**16.** (c)	**17.** (c)	**18.** (d)	**19.** (c)	**20.** (d)
21. (d)	**22.** (d)	**23.** (b)	**24.** (d)	**25.** (d)	**26.** (d)	**27.** (b)	**28.** (d)	**29.** (b)	**30.** (d)
31. (b)	**32.** (a)	**33.** (d)	**34.** (a)	**35.** (a)	**36.** (b)	**37.** (c)	**38.** (d)	**39.** (c)	**40.** (d)
41. (a)	**42.** (b)	**43.** (a)	**44.** (d)	**45.** (c)	**46.** (b)	**47.** (c)	**48.** (b)	**49.** (b)	**50.** (c)
51. (d)	**52.** (b)	**53.** (a)	**54.** (c)	**55.** (d)	**56.** (c)				

EXPLANATIONS

1. In circular arrangement, no of ways is $(n-1)!$

$n = 5$

so $(n-1)! = 4! = 24$

2. 26!

3. Let the work be 1

Then Rahul do $\dfrac{1}{5}$ work in 60 min

So Rahul do 1 work in 300 min

Then Neha do $\dfrac{3}{7}$ work in 90 min

So Neha do 1 work in 210 min

Then Riya do $\dfrac{3}{4}$ work in 210 min

So Riya do 1 work in 280 min

By 300 min i.e 5 hour all will complete their work so

12-1, 1-2, 2-3, 3-3 : 30 , 4-4 : 30, 4 : 30-5 : 30

By 5 : 30 they all go to play

4. Simple formula :

$$\frac{p \times q}{p+q} \Rightarrow \frac{10 \times 12}{10+12}$$

Therefore ans is $\dfrac{55}{11}$

5. 8% of CP = 50,000

Thus, 108% of CP =

$$\frac{(50,000 \times 108)}{8} = 675000$$

6. S.I = $\dfrac{pnr}{100}$

$p = 5000; n = 5; r = 12$

Thus, S.I = 3000

and amount after 5 yrs = principle + S.I

= Rs. 8000.

7. Two equations can be formed here....

$3x + 2y = 790$

$2x + 3y = 1110$

Now solve the equations simultaneously..

You will get the answer 350

8. $6^{-2} = \dfrac{1}{36}$

9. We know total distance is 200 Km

If both trains crossed each other at a distance of 110 km then one train covered 110 km and other 90 km [110 + 90 = 200 km] So ratio of their speed = 110 : 90 = 11 : 9

10. 360

for 6 digit even number...

in unit place always 2, 4, 6 will come.. rest of place we can fill any given number, so solution will be - $5 \times 4 \times 3 \times 2 \times 1 \times 3 = 360$.

11. 200 m

Ratio of the speeds of A and B = 5 : 3

Thus, in a race of 5 m, A gains 2 m over B

2 m are gained by A in a race of 5 m.

$80 \text{ m} = \dfrac{5}{2} \times 80 = 200 \text{ m}$

12. Let's assume A finishes the 600 m race in 60 sec,

then $\dfrac{600}{60} = 10$ m/sec is his speed

B traveled (600 − 60 = 540 m in 60 sec, therefore

$\dfrac{540}{60} = 9$ m/sec is B's speed

$\dfrac{500}{9} = 55.56$ sec is B's time to finish a 500 m race

C traveled 500 − 50 = 450 m in 55.56 sec, therefore

$\dfrac{450}{55.56} = 8.1$ m/sec is C's speed

$\dfrac{400}{10} = 40$ sec for A to run a 400 m race

C will travel 8.1 × 40 = 324 m in 40 sec

C will be 400 − 324 = 76 m

13. Let the numbers be 3x, 4x and 5x.

Then, their L.C.M. = 60x.

So, 60x = 2400 or x = 40.

The numbers are (3 × 40), (4 × 40) and (5 × 40).

Hence, required H.C.F. = 40.

14. Speed downstream = (13 + 4) km/hr

$\qquad\qquad\qquad\quad$ = 17 km/hr.

Time taken to travel 68 km downstream

$= \dfrac{68}{17}$ hrs = 4 hrs.

15. Let the present ages of Sameer and Anand be 5x years and 4x years respectively.

Then, $\dfrac{(5x+3)}{(4x+3)} = \dfrac{11}{9}$

45x − 44x = 33 − 27

x = 6.

Anand's present age = 4x = 24 years

16. L.C.M. of 3, 2.7, 0.9 = LCM of (3,27,9)/HCF of

(1,10, 100) = $\dfrac{27}{1}$ = 27.

17. Speed of A : Speed of B = $\dfrac{7}{3}$: 1 = 7 : 3

It means, in a race of 7 m, A gains (7 − 3) = 4 metre

If A needs to gain 80 metre, race should be of 74 × 80 = 140 metre

18. Clearly, A beats B by 4 seconds

Now find out how much B will run in these 4 seconds

Speed of B = Distance

Time taken by B = 22432 = 284 = 7 m/s

Distance covered by B in 4 seconds

= Speed × time = 7 × 4 = 28 metre

i.e., A beat B by 28 metre

22. Building - made up of bricks

Flower - made up of petals

30. d   2 × 3 = 6

3 × 6 = 18

6 × 18 = 108

18 × 108 = 1944

therefore next no. is 1944

32. Only son of Neena's father-in-law Mahipal - Neena's husband.

So, Raman is Neena's husband and Anita and Bindu are his daughters.

Thus, Bindu is the grand daughter of Mahipal.

34. The colours adjacent to yellow are orange, blue, red and rose. Hence violet will be opposite to yellow.

40. Prank means childish behaviour, to put pranks on others. So opposite to this is serious. Machiavellian means cunning, and impish means lack of seriousness.

■■

MOCK-10
(WIPRO II)

1. Martha was supposed to multiply the number of cans and sold with the price , one can to ascertain the amount earned by her. Instead of taking 41 as the number of cans, she wrote 14 by mistake. As a result, the product went down by 135. What is the other multiplier?

   (a) 5   (b) 7

   (c) 9   (d) 12

2. What is the number that should be subtracted from 682 to make it a perfect square?

   (a) 2   (b) 4

   (c) 6   (d) 8

3. What number should be divided by $(0.81)^{\frac{1}{2}}$ to give the result as 81?

   (a) 9   (b) 81

   (c) 72.9   (d) 0.9

4. A seller buys 10 phone chargers for Rs. 800 and sells them at the rate of Rs. I00 per charger. His gain percent is

   (a) 25   (b) 20

   (c) 30   (d) 15

5. A store has a banner of 25% off on MRP of all branded items. Sheetal goes into the store and buys a belt worth Rs. 75, a shirt of Rs. l,999 and a shawl of Rs. 2,900. How much amount will she have to pay?

   (a) Rs. 1243.50   (b) Rs. 1240

   (c) Rs. 3,700   (d) Rs. 3,730.50

6. A man sells 45 lemons for Rs. 40 with 20% loss. How many lemons should he sell for Rs. 24 to gain 20% profit?

   (a) 15   (b) 18

   (c) 12   (d) 16

7. In an annual sale, there was a flat discount of 40% on all items. Komal bought a pair of jeans for Rs. 480. What is the labeled price of the pair of jeans?

   (a) Rs. 799   (b) Rs. 899

   (c) Rs. 699   (d) Rs. 720

8. The population of a town increases every year by 4%. If its present population is 50,000, then after 2 years it will be

   (a) 53900   (b) 54000

   (c) 54080   (d) 54900

9. A street seller bought maize corns for Rs. 20 per kg. In one kg, there are approximately 5 heads of corn. He sells roasted corns for RS. 8 per piece. How many corns will he have to sell in order to earn a profit of Rs. 200 in a day?

   (a) 60   (b) 50

   (c) 40   (d) 80

10. Express 0.824 as a fraction of the smallest form.

    (a) $\dfrac{103}{125}$ (b) $\dfrac{4}{25}$

    (c) $\dfrac{102}{125}$ (d) $\dfrac{17}{20}$

11. Recycling 900 kg of paper saves 17 trees . How many trees are saved when 1200 kg of paper are recycled?

    (a) 19   (b) 25

    (c) 20   (d) 22

12. How many different four letter words can be formed (the words need not to be meaningful) using the letters of the word PACIFIC such that the first letter is p and the last letter is F?

    (a) 8   (b) 3

    (c) 6   (d) $\dfrac{7!}{5!}$

13. Mauli purchased a designer saree from Mumbai at $\dfrac{8}{9}$th of its MRP. When she came back to Delhi, her neighbour coaxed mauli to sell the saree to her. She was even ready to pay 9% more than its MRP. What would Mauli's gain percentage be, if she decides to sell the saree to her neighbour?

    (a) 0.1559

    (b) 0.1661

    (c) 0.2036

    (d) 0.2265

14. A goods carriage of length 2km, headed to Srinagar from Punjab was running at a speed of 30 km/hr. It crosses a tunnel which is 58 km long with that speed. Find the time taken by the goods carriage to cross the tunnel?

(a) 4 hours   (b) 3 hours

(c) 2 hours   (d) 1 hours

15. A lucky draw is organized as part of the first anniversary celebration of new Age Company. There are 25 chits in a bowl one for each employee and the chits are marked from 1 – 25. Sarika and Rajesh have chits marked with numbers that are multiples of 3 or 7. They want to know if there are chances of them being awarded the trip to Goa which is the first prize of the lucky draw. When one chit is drawn at random, what is the probability that the chit has a number which is a multiple of 3 or 7?

(a) $\dfrac{3}{25}$ (b) $\dfrac{2}{11}$

(c) $\dfrac{11}{25}$ (d) $\dfrac{10}{25}$

16. What is the loss percentage incurred by a company when it buys an asset for Rs. 1,50,000 and sells it for Rs. 75,500?

(a) 0.4967   (b) 0.4934

(c) 0.9868   (d) 0.9834

17. If Ruparno is expected to spend Rs. 2,300 on electricity bill in the first 3 months of the year, what amount can he be expected to spend on electricity bill for the rest of the year?

(a) Rs. 5,400   (b) Rs. 5,700

(c) Rs. 6,200   (d) Rs. 6,900

18. Out of every 100 people in police department, 10 are women. Out of every 100 people in military forces, 3 are women. In a batch of 180 police personnel and 200 army personnel, how many of them would be women?

(a) 24   (b) 30

(c) 18   (d) 6

LOGICAL REASONING

19. These questions consists of a problem statement followed by two statements I & II. Find out if the information given in the statement(s) is sufficient to answer the question.

Problem statement: Are Seetha & Geetha siblings?

Statements:

I) Both Seetha & Geetha's husband are brothers.

II) Mr Kumar is the maternal grandfather of Seetha & Geetha

Choices:

(a) Statement I alone is sufficient

(b) Statement II alone is sufficient

(c) Both statements put together are sufficient

(d) Both statements put together are not sufficient

20. These questions consists of a problem statement followed by two statements I & II. Find out if the information given in the statement(s) is sufficient to answer the question.

Problem statement: What is the time shown by the clock?

Statements:

(I) Between 3 o'clock & 4 o'clock, hands of the clock make an angle of 90 degree with each other.

(II) The minute hand of the clock is at 12 o'clock position

Choices:

(a) Statement I alone is sufficient

(b) Statement II alone is sufficient

(c) Both statements put together are sufficient

(d) Both statements put together are not sufficient

21. Find the value of ? in the analogy below.

13 : 170 : : 17 : ?

(a) 130.0   (b) 210.0

(c) 290.0   (d) None of the above

22. In a certain code language if COMPLETE is coded as DQPTQKAM, then in the same language VISION is coded as __________.

(a) WKVMTM   (b) WKVMTT

(c) WKVTMT   (d) WKVMTT

23. In a certain code language BRAVE is coded as 53, MIGHTY is coded as 88, then how is CORRECT coded in the same language?

(a) 98.0   (b) 95.0

(c) 85.0   (d) 89.0

24. Complete the analogy in the question below.

(a) Question: MADAM : MADAM : : MASTER __________

(b) MASTER

(c) RETSA

(d) ASRETM

25. Study the coding pattern in the following statements & answer the questions that follow

STATEMENT	CODE
WORK IS WORSHIP	JIN KIN MIN
ALMIGHTY IS GREAT	DIN HIN MIN
WORSHIP THE ALMIGHTY	KIN HIN FIN

How is "GREAT" coded in this system of coding?

(a) FIN (b) KIN

(c) DIN (d) MIN

26. Pointing to the photograph of a woman in his room, Amar tells his friend," I am her brother's Sister's son. How is the woman in the photograph related to Amar?

(a) Aunt (b) Paternal Aunt

(c) Maternal Aunt (d) Cannot be determined

27. Rahul starts from home to take part in the youth club get together. He travels towards west for some time, takes a left turn, travels in this direction for some time & takes a right turn again to reach the youth club premises. In which direction is Rahul' residence with respect to the youth club premises?

(a) South - West (b) South - East

(c) North - East (d) South

28. A person was walking inside a park & observing everything around him (right from the flower pots kept at the entrance to the park, the water fountains, games made available for children to play etc.) He wished to track his own shadow, but all his attempts were in vain. Based on this information can you find out the most probable time when the person spent his leisure time inside the park?

(a) 7:00 hrs to 8:00 hrs

(b) 12:00 hrs to 13:00 hrs

(c) 14:30 hrs to 18:15 hrs

(d) 10:00 to 11:00 hrs

29. The question below contains some statements followed by some conclusions. Decide which of the given conclusions logically follows from the given statements, disregarding commonly known facts.

Statements:

Some pens are pencils

Some pencils are books

No book is readable.

Conclusions:

(I) some pens are not pencils.

(II) Some that are readable are not books.

(III) Some pens are books.

(a) Only (I) & (II) follow

(b) Only (II) follows

(c) All follow

(d) None of these

30. The question below contain some statements followed by some conclusions. Decide which of the given conclusions logically follows from the given statements, disregarding commonly known facts.

Statements:

All audits are time bound.

All time bound are result oriented.

All result oriented have tangible benefits.

Conclusions:

(I) All audits have tangible benefits.

(II) Some result oriented has tangible benefits.

(III) Some that are time bound are audits.

(a) Only (I) follows

(b) Only (II) follows

(c) Only (I) & (III) follow

(d) All follow

31. What can be inferred from the following conversation taking place between two students X & Y who attended a class in the past one hour?

X: Right from the beginning of the class, the flow of the topic was good, easily understandable with excellent illustrative examples.

Y: I think out of 500 students, who registered for this course, about 90 % would have attended this class.

(a) Students are very committed towards the subject taught by that particular professor.

(b) The professor in charge is a strict disciplinarian.

(c) The professor in the context as above is very popular among students.

(d) The students do not like the professor.

32. The train departed from the terminus at its usual time, but reached its destination half an hour late. On all days the train is overcrowded, as it operates during peak hour. The journey was quite smooth without any untoward incident. The most probable reason for the delay of half an hour could be,

(a) Passengers could not board the train due to overcrowding, due to which frequent chain pulling was resorted to.

(b) The signaling system could have malfunctioned in certain portions of the journey causing the delay.

(c) The train could not be hauled by the locomotive comfortably

(d) There was an accident in the route

33. Which number in the following numbers does not fit into the string below?

17, 34, 53, 76, 104, 136, 173

(a) 136   (b) 76

(c) 104   (d) 34

34. When a clock shows 3 pm on the dial, its hour hand is pointing towards the south. In which direction will the minute hand point to when the time is 6:15 pm?

(a) South - East

(b) South

(c) West

(d) North - West

VERBAL ABILITY

35. In this question, a part of the sentence is italicized. Alternatives to the italicized parts are given which may improve the construction of the sentence. Select the correct alternative.

Peter *had told* me that he hasn't done it yet.

(a) tells

(b) told

(c) was telling

(d) No Correction required

36. Select the correct option that fills the blank to make the sentence meaningfully complete.

The machine is difficult to build ______ easy to maintain.

(a) and   (b) but

(c) if   (d) so

37. Which of the following explains the meaning of the proverb "A stitch in time saves nine"?

(a) Time waits for none

(b) It is better to have timely action for something

(c) Something is better than nothing

(d) Prevention is better than cure

38. Select the correct option that fills the blank to make the sentence meaningfully complete.

The ______ of the Minister's statement cannot be verified by people who have no access to official records.

(a) verbosity   (b) ambiguity

(c) veracity   (d) plurality

39. In this question, a part of the sentence is italicized. Alternatives to the italicized parts are given which may improve the construction of the sentence. Select the correct alternative.

The end of the examinations is (a/an) *opportunity* for celebrating.

(a) chance

(b) moment

(c) occasion

(d) No Correction required

40. Select the word or phrase which best expresses the meaning of the given word.

(a) Close   (b) Bluff

(c) Inform   (d) Threaten

41. Select the word or phrase which best expresses the meaning of the given word.

MENDACIOUS

(a) Confident   (b) FALSE

(c) Encouraging   (d) Frustrating

42. Select the option that is most nearly opposite in meaning to the given word.

STRINGENT

(a) Lenient   (b) Popular

(c) General   (d) Vehement

43. Select the option that is most nearly opposite in meaning to the given word.

GULLIBLE

(a) Fickle   (b) Naive

(c) Incredulous   (d) Glutton

44. In this question, six sentences are given to form a meaningful paragraph. The first and the sixth are given in the beginning. The middle four sentences have been removed and jumbled up. These are labelled P, Q, R and S. Select the proper order for the four sentences.

S1: Due to sudden sprain Nirmal fell down.

S6: He had to lie down hopelessly, till he saw a flash light

P: Nirmal was shocked when he realised that the leg had lost sensation.

Q: When he tried to get up, he felt his leg was very heavy.

R: It was an odd night time and hence nobody heard his voice.

S: Nervous with this realisation, he called out for help.

(a) PQSR (b) QSPR

(c) QPSR (d) SPQR

45. Among the many groups of students in American colleges, Asian students _________

(a) are often written about in magazines like News Week

(b) are most successful academically

(c) have proved that they are as good as the whites

(d) have only a minority status like the blacks

46. The student of Asian origin in America include_______.

(a) a fair number from India

(b) a small group from India

(c) persons from India who are very proud

(d) Indians who are the most hard working of all

47. In general, the talented young Indians studying in America _______

(a) have a reputation for being hard working

(b) have the opportunity to contribute to India's development

(c) can solve the brain drain problem because of recent changes in policy

(d) will not return to pursue their careers in India

48. There is talk now of the 'brain bank'. This idea _______

(a) is a solution to the brain drain problem

(b) is a new problem caused partly by the brain drain

(c) is a new way of looking at the role of qualified Indians living abroad

(d) is based on a plan to utilize foreign exchange remittances to stimulate research and development

Select the correct answer option based on the passage.

At this stage of civilisation, when many nations are brought in to close and vital contact for good and evil, it is essential, as never before, that their gross ignorance of one another should be diminished, that they should begin to understand a little of one another's historical experience and resulting mentality. It is the fault of the English to expect the people of other countries to react as they do, to political and international situations. Our genuine goodwill and good intentions are often brought to nothing, because we expect other people to be like us. This would be corrected if we knew the history, not necessarily in detail but in broad outlines, of the social and political conditions which have given to each nation its present character.

49. According to the author his countrymen should _________

(a) read the story of other nations

(b) have a better understanding of other nations

(c) not react to other actions

(d) have vital contacts with other nations

Select the correct answer option based on the passage.

Courage is not only the basis of virtue; it is its expression. Faith, hope, charity and all the rest don't become virtues until it takes courage to exercise them. There are roughly two types of courage. The first, an emotional state which urges a man to risk injury or death, is physical courage. The second, reasoning attitude which enables him to take his career coolly. His whole future or his judgment of what he thinks either right or worthwhile, is moral courage. I have known many men, who had marked physical courage, but lacked moral courage. Some of them were in high places, but they failed to be great in themselves because they lacked moral courage. On the other hand I have seen men who undoubtedly possessed moral courage but were very cautious about taking physical risks. But I have never met a man with moral courage who couldn't, when it was really necessary, face a situation boldly.

50. According to the passage, a man of courage is _________

(a) curious (b) intelligent

(c) cunning (d) careful

Select the correct answer option based on the passage.

Many sociologists have argued that there is functional relationship between education and economic system. They point to the fact that mass formal education began in industrial society. They note that the expansion of the economies of industrial societies is accompanied by a corresponding expansion of their educational systems. They explain this correspondence in terms of the needs of industry for skilled and trained manpower, needs which are met by the educational system. Thus, the provision of mass elementary education in Britain in 1870 can be seen as a response to the needs of industry for a literate and numerate workforce at a time when industrial processes were becoming more complex and the demand for technical skills was steadily growing.

51. In the given passage the author argues that

(a) Industrial society gave rise to vocational education

(b) Industrial society changed the pattern of education

(c) Formal education can be traced to industrial society

(d) Industrial society is responsible for expansion of education at mass level

52. There is talk now of the 'brain bank'. This idea ______

(a) is a solution to the brain drain problem

(b) is a new problem caused partly by the brain drain

(c) is a new way of looking at the role of qualified Indians living abroad

(d) is based on a plan to utilize foreign exchange remittances to stimulate research and development

53. The brain bank has limitations like all banks in the sense that ______

(a) a bank's services go mainly to those near it

(b) small neighbourhood banks are not visible in this age of multinationals

(c) only what is deposited can be withdrawn and utilized

(d) no one can be forced to put his assets in a bank

54. I want ramesh and she to be the captain for the rest of the year.

(a) her to be the captains for the rest of the year.

(b) she to be the captain for the rest of the year.

(c) her as the captains for the rest of the year.

(d) she both be captains for the rest of the year.

55. Conceited(Meaning)

(a) Arrogant (b) False

(c) Deceive (d) Misconception

56. Find out any grammatical error or not?

(a) (A) Yauhan do not understand
(B) the importance of money as
(C) he never had to earn himself

(b) A

(c) B

(d) C

ANSWERS

1. (a)	**2.** (c)	**3.** (c)	**4.** (a)	**5.** (d)	**6.** (b)	**7.** (a)	**8.** (c)	**9.** (b)	**10.** (a)
11. (d)	**12.** (d)	**13.** (d)	**14.** (c)	**15.** (d)	**16.** (b)	**17.** (d)	**18.** (a)	**19.** (d)	**20.** (c)
21. (c)	**22.** (b)	**23.** (d)	**24.** (d)	**25.** (c)	**26.** (d)	**27.** (c)	**28.** (b)	**29.** (b)	**30.** (d)
31. (c)	**32.** (b)	**33.** (c)	**34.** (d)	**35.** (a)	**36.** (b)	**37.** (b)	**38.** (c)	**39.** (b)	**40.** (d)
41. (b)	**42.** (a)	**43.** (c)	**44.** (c)	**45.** (c)	**46.** (a)	**47.** (d)	**48.** (c)	**49.** (b)	**50.** (d)
51. (c)	**52.** (c)	**53.** (a)	**54.** (c)	**55.** (a)	**56.** (a)				

EXPLANATIONS

1. $41x = 14c + 135$

ie $= x = 5$

2. $682 = 26^2 + 6 = 676 + 6$

4. Cost price $= \dfrac{800}{10} = 80$

Selling price $= 100$; gain $= 20$

Gain percent $= \dfrac{20}{80} * 100 = 25\%$

5. The discount is 25% so she has to pay 75% of the total bill.

Total $= (75 + 1999 + 2900) = 4974$

Now, $\dfrac{75}{100} \times 4974 = $ Rs. 3730.50

6. Cost price of 45 lemons $= 50$

Selling price of 45 lemons to gain 20% profit = Rs.60

Number of lemons he should sell for Rs. 24 to gain 20% profit = 18

7. discount $=40\%$

ie $100 - 40 = 60$

for 1% $\dfrac{480}{60} = 80$

for 100% $= 8 \times 100 = 800$

(i.e) Rs. 799 approx.

8. Here we can use the compound interest based formula,

Population after n years $= P \times \left[1 + \left(\dfrac{r}{100}\right)\right]^n$

Population after 2 years $= 50{,}000 \times \left[1 + \left(\dfrac{4}{100}\right)\right]^2$

Population after 2 years $= 54{,}080$

9. In one kg there are 5 heads of corn so one kg maize corns is 20 Rs.

Cost price of 1 head corn is $\dfrac{20}{5}$ that is Rs. 4

Selling price of 1 corn is Rs. 8

In one day we should get profit Rs. 200.

Let x be no. of maize corn should be sold to get 200 Rs as profit..

We know that profit = SP – CP.

So, $8x - 4x = 200$ or $x = 50$.

11. 900 kg papers = 17 trees; 1200 kg papers = ? ; The trees to find is = X

$X = 1200 \times \dfrac{17}{900} = \dfrac{68}{3} = 22$

12. PACIFIC

Total number of letters n = 7

R = 2

$Npr = \dfrac{n!}{(n!-1)!}$

$= \dfrac{7!}{(7-2)!} = \dfrac{7!}{5!}$

13. assume that MRP rate $= 100$

cost prize $= \dfrac{800}{9}$

selling prize $= \left(\dfrac{100 \times 9}{100}\right) + 100 = 109$

$sp = \left(\dfrac{100 + gain\%}{100}\right) cp$

$109 = \left(\dfrac{(100 + gain\%)}{100}\right) \dfrac{800}{9}$

By solving above equation we get gain $= \dfrac{181}{8} = 22.65\%$

14. In this we have to add the distances. The goods carriage 2 km and to cross tunnel distance 58 km. time = ? Speed = 30 km/hr

$Time = \dfrac{distance}{speed}$

$= \dfrac{(2 + 56)}{30}$

$Time = \dfrac{60}{30} = 2 \text{ hours}$

15. Number of chits $= 25$

Sarika and Ragesh chits are multiples of 3 and 7

3 multiples up to 25 = 8

7 multiples up to 25 = 2

Total multiples = 8 + 2 = 10

$$= \frac{\text{total multiples}}{\text{total no of chits}} = \frac{10}{25}$$

16. loss = cost prize – selling prize

$= 1,50,000 - 75000$

$= 74,500$

$$\text{Loss\%} \left(\frac{\text{loss}}{\text{cp}}\right) \times 100 = \left(\frac{74000}{150000}\right) \times 100 = 49.34\%$$

17. $6,900 = (2,300 \times 3)$

18. $18 + 6 = 24$

35. The second clause "he hasn't done" is in present tense. So, 'tells' is the only correct choice.

36. The sentence shows contrast. So, 'but' is the right choice

37. "A stitch in time saves nine" means "It is better to deal with something immediately."

38. 'veracity or truthfulness' of the statement needs to be verified. So, the correct choice is (C).

39. The end of examinations is a point of time. So, 'moment' is the correct choice. This is neither a chance nor an occasion.

40. 'Intimidate' means 'threaten'.

41. 'Mendacious' means 'not telling the truth'. So, 'false' is the appropriate choice.

42. 'Stringent' means 'very strict'. So, 'Lenient' is the appropriate opposite word for this.

43. 'Gullible' means 'believing others easily'. So, 'incredulous' is the appropriate opposite word

44. Sentence S follows P. Sentence Q comes after the first sentence S1. Hence the correct answer is (C).

49. The third line of the passage explains this.

50. The passage describes a man of courage as 'careful'. 'Cunning' & 'curious' are inappropriate. As per the passage, 'intelligent' is not a better choice.

51. The second sentence of the passage explains this.

Printed by Libri Plureos GmbH in Hamburg,
Germany